DISCARD

Educators' handbook on
effective testing

Educators' Handbook on Effective Testing

Books of Related Interest

Handbook on Effective Instructional Strategies: Evidence for Decision-Making
Myles I. Friedman and Steven P. Fisher

Ensuring Student Success: A Handbook of Evidence-Based Strategies
Myles I. Friedman

Educators' Handbook on Effective Testing

Myles I. Friedman, Charles W. Hatch,
Jacqueline E. Jacobs, Aileen C. Lau-Dickinson,
Amanda B. Nickerson, and Katherine C. Schnepel

Foreword by Lawrence W. Lezotte

EDIE

THE INSTITUTE FOR EVIDENCE-BASED
DECISION-MAKING IN EDUCATION, INC.

Library of Congress Control Number: 2002113689
ISBN: 0-9666588-2-5

First published in 2003

The Institute for Evidence-Based Decision-Making in Education, Inc. (EDIE)
A South Carolina non-profit corporation
P.O. Box 122, Columbia, SC 29202

Printed in the United States of America

The paper used in this book complies with the
Permanent Paper Standard issued by the National
Information Standards Organization (Z39.48–1984).

10   9   8   7   6   5   4   3   2   1

Copyright Acknowledgments

Brief Table of Contents

Detailed Table of Contents

Foreword

The standards, assessment, and accountability movement of the last 10 years continues to intensify with no end in sight. No educator is immune from the effects of this powerful force. The 2002 federal law, No Child Left Behind, represents the capstone of the standards, assessment, and accountability movement in that it covers virtually all school-age children, requires expanded assessment, and incorporates severe sanctions when a school or district fails to meet the "adequate yearly progress" requirements. Clearly, this new law—and each state's variation of it—signals that a new day has dawned for American educators!

The response of educators who work on or near the "shop floor" of K–12 education—namely, classroom teachers and building-level administrators—has been mixed. For some, these new policies are seen as simply one more reason to do the right thing for students and the larger community. Perhaps the more prevalent view is that higher standards, more assessment, and increased accountability simply mean more *work*. From a worst-case perspective, these educators see too many standards to be taught in the time available, testing that is simply an intrusion on and diversion from student learning, and an accountability system that ascribes too much responsibility and offers educators too little authority when it comes to student learning.

While most educators fall somewhere between the two positions described above, virtually all educators would benefit from more knowledge and better tools that could be used to respond to the standards, assessment, and accountability movement. What knowledge and tools would teachers and building administrators see as adding value to the teaching/learning process?

For more than 20 years I have been a passionate evangelist of the "Learning for All" mission. Because of my long history with this mission, I have had to constantly confront issues of accountability and testing. As a result, I have formed several conclusions that may help teachers come to terms with their new realities.

First, assessment may be seen as an intrusion on and diversion from *teaching*, but there is no way that monitoring and assessment can be seen as a diversion from *learn-

ing. Once teachers and administrators accept and embrace the notion that they are no longer in the "teaching business" but in the "learning business," they will quickly recognize that learning can be significantly enhanced by careful monitoring and assessment.

Second, the primary beneficiaries of any testing that occurs in school should be the students and the teachers who teach them. The reason that many educators see assessment as a distraction from teaching and learning is that they see no benefit to the students or themselves as teachers. For much of the current mandated testing in our schools, this criticism is probably valid.

Third, to be seen as adding value to the learning mission, testing and other assessments must satisfy several criteria. If the assessment is being used for accountability purposes, there must be a tight alignment between the intended, taught, and assessed curriculum. For assessment results to add value to the learning mission, they must provide relatively immediate results so that teacher decision-making can be informed. Furthermore, the feedback that comes from testing must be precise and detailed enough to provide guidance to teachers, parents, and the students themselves.

New work generally requires new tools or new applications of existing tools. The new work brought on by the standards, assessment, and accountability movement requires the efficient and effective use of testing as a way to enhance learning. This will require a new mind-set. Without it, we will not come close to achieving the lofty goals that have been set before our nation's schools. But to change the prevailing mental model of assessment, educators need training and technical assistance of the type provided by this handbook.

The *Educators' Handbook on Effective Testing* is a rich resource for helping busy teachers and administrators make better decisions—decisions that will truly enhance and advance the "Learning for All" mission. It provides valuable technical knowledge about the psychometric aspects of tests and testing, knowledge that most teachers do not get in the typical teacher training program. It reviews many different tools that can be used to assess prerequisites, monitor achievement, predict success, and evaluate programs, to mention a few.

The *Educators' Handbook on Effective Testing* should be used as a focus for staff development for all educators who care about "Learning for All."

Lawrence W. Lezotte, Ph.D.
Educational Consultant and Commentator,
Effective Schools Products
Former Chair, Department of Educational Administration,
Michigan State University

Acknowledgments

Many people have contributed to this book. We are indebted to Drs. Lorin Anderson, Arthur Stellar, Joseph Rudnicki, Harold Duran, Lawrence Lezotte, Jeanne R. Miyasaka, Joseph Ryan, Walter Procko, Marvin Efron, John King, Tom Surratt, and Arnold Fege for critiquing a pre-publication rendition of the book and contributing greatly to its improvement. We want to thank John Donohue, Betty Friedman, and Phil Logan for preparing the book for publication, and Martin Greenberg for his marketing guidance. We are also grateful to the Melrene Fund and First Citizens Bank for their financial support and to Robin Campbell for her help.

User's Guide

THE PURPOSE OF THE HANDBOOK

The purpose of the handbook is to improve educators' ability to understand testing, interpret test results, and defend their selection, construction, and use of tests. In our litigious society, educators may be required to defend their use of tests before grievance committees or courts of law. Militant students more frequently than ever protest low scores that are given to them and they, their parents, and lawyers contest them. Most educators do not receive sufficient training in tests and measurements to feel confident to defend themselves, and often engage psychometricians as test experts to advise and defend them. However, many psychometricians are not experts in the field of education and may not be able to offer the best defense. They communicate in psychometric terms and cite statistics that judges, jurors, and lawyers, as well as educators, have difficulty understanding. Furthermore, defending conclusions drawn from test results requires more than defending the test itself. Conclusions drawn from test results are affected by many additional factors, as you will see.

The handbook makes it quite possible for educators to learn how to defend the tests they use without becoming psychometricians. Since they are often required to defend the test scores and grades they assign, it behooves them to be able to meet the challenge.

Although reports are available on most published tests, there is no one compilation of test reports published solely to meet the needs of educators at all levels of education. The Buros Institute of Mental Measurements (2001) claims that their *Mental Measurements* yearbooks are "an indispensable reference for professionals in education, psychology, business, health care, counseling, research, social science, law, and many other areas." However, their yearbooks are not tailored to the needs of educators, and their reviews are best understood by test specialists who are well versed in psychometric terminology and statistics. This handbook is written expressly for educators, and only tests used by educators are analyzed in the handbook. Other books that provide information on tests are not sufficiently germane and comprehensive to cover the test and testing information educators need to select and use tests. *Tests: A Comprehensive Reference for Assessments in Psychology, Education and Business* (Sweetland & Keyser, 1991) provides descriptive information about tests such as title, author, publisher, price, and age range of the appropriate populations. However, it does not include evaluations of the tests listed. The ERIC Clearinghouse on Assessment and Evaluation has a web site that can be used to locate and obtain descriptions of tests used in education (www.ericae.net/testcol.htm). It also provides evaluations of the tests described. *Test Critiques*, volumes 1–10 (Keyser & Sweetland, 1984–1994) contains evaluations of tests, some of which are used by educators. However, the critiques do not focus on the needs of educators. *A Consumer's Guide to Tests in Print* (Hammill, Brown, & Bryant, 1992) also evaluates tests, but only individually administered standardized, norm-referenced tests for grades K–12. Equally valuable to educators is information on criterion-referenced tests they use to determine the extent to which learning objectives are achieved. Textbooks that include critical reviews of tests tend to be limited in scope. Many are in the field of special education—for example, *Assessment* (Salvia & Ysseldyke, 2001), *Assessing Students with Special Needs* (McLoughlin & Lewis, 2001), and *A Guide to 75 Tests for Special Education* (Compton, 1984). Of course, many professional journals, such as the *Journal of Psychoeducational Assessments*, review tests, but that is not their focus.

Guidelines are also provided to help educators construct and defend their own achievement tests.

THE NEED FOR THE HANDBOOK

Tests and testing are affecting educators more than ever before. Accountability legislation and tests profoundly impact the lives of all public school educators. Those educators whose students repeatedly fail accountability tests often receive sanctions and can be discharged. Many complain that they are being coerced to "teach to the test." Schools in which a sizable number of students repeatedly fail to meet accountability standards can be restaffed or closed. The fate of educators is becoming more and more dependent on test results.

Educators can't afford to be naïve about tests that affect their lives and the lives of their students. The handbook is designed to provide in clear language a practical analysis of published tests used in schools. In reading the analyses of the tests educators can become familiar with the appropriate uses of the tests as well as their strengths and weaknesses, which will enable them to make informed decisions.

In general, tests are instruments that facilitate descriptions of characteristics. For example, the Stanford-Binet test facilitates the description of the characteristic "intelligence." Types of tests used in education include interview schedules, questionnaires, interest inventories, aptitude tests, academic achievement tests, attitude tests, rating scales, tally sheets, flow charts, checklists, time-motion logs, projective techniques, vision tests, hearing tests, sociometric devices, and personality tests. Educators use academic achievement tests much more often than any other type of test. Typically, most other types of tests are used by school psychologists, school counselors, school nurses, and others from the helping professions that serve schools.

CONTENTS OF THE HANDBOOK

The handbook contains (1) reviews of tests used routinely to make educational decisions and to assess skills taught by educators; (2) an index of test titles; (3) an index of acronyms, since many tests are known by their acronyms more than by their titles; (4) an index of characteristics to refer educators to tests that assess characteristics of interest to them; (5) a test classification index, which identifies the primary purpose of each test (for example, reading); (6) an index of test authors and (7) an index of reference authors for educators interested in knowing about tests developed by particular authors; (8) a directory of educational test publishers that provides complete contact information; (9) guidelines for defending tests and testing; (10) explanations and definitions of key testing terms; and (11) analyses of current testing issues and problems, such as accountability testing, assessing student academic potential, and teacher-made tests.

MAKING THE HANDBOOK USEFUL FOR EDUCATORS

Our main objective is to make the handbook as useful to educators as possible. To accomplish this:

1. All test reviews are keyed to the decisions that educators routinely make.
2. Each test review is written in plain English and provides the information educators need to decide whether to select a test. Educators do not need others to select tests for them. They need test reviews they can understand, reviews that enable them to make their own data-based choices.
3. All test reviewers are educators who have expertise in testing. The reviewers know both psychometrics and the educational decisions tests are used to make.

Keying Test Reviews to Educational Decision-Making

Five types of decisions were identified that educators routinely use test results to make: admission decisions, placement decisions, instructional prescription decisions, achievement certification decisions, and referral decisions. Accordingly, test reviews are grouped together in the Table of Contents and in the text of the handbook under the following functional headings: "Admission Testing and Decision-Making," "Placement Testing and Decision-Making," "Instructional Prescription Testing and Decision-Making," "Achievement Certification Testing and Decision-Making," and "Referral Testing and Decision-Making."

Admission Testing and Decision-Making

In general, admission testing is done to determine how capable candidates for admission are of meeting the demands of some entry-level position. Three types of admission tests are reviewed.

1. Early childhood school admission tests are used to determine the extent to which young children are ready to begin school. These tests assess children's readiness in a number of different areas including social, self-help, language, coordination, and cognitive readiness. The Mullen Scales of Early Learning is an example of an early childhood school admission test that is reviewed in the handbook.

2. College admission tests are used to determine whether college applicants meet admission standards. Examples of college admission tests reviewed in the handbook are the Scholastic Assessment Test (SAT), which is used for admission to undergraduate school, and the Graduate Record Exam (GRE), which is used to determine graduate-level admission.

3. There are tests to determine admission to the teaching profession. These tests are used by state departments of education to determine whether candidates meet state requirements for certification and licensure. For example, the PRAXIS tests are used to determine whether candidates meet licensure requirements for teachers. Other tests are used to determine whether candidates to become school principals and superintendents meet licensure requirements.

Placement Testing and Decision-Making

Once students are admitted to school, educators use tests to place them in instructional programs based on their abilities. For example, intelligence tests are used to help educators determine the placement of students in instructional programs for the "gifted" and for the "educable mentally retarded." Laws enacted to benefit students with disabilities govern the testing and placement of the latter students.

Instructional Prescription Testing and Decision-Making

Once students are placed in and begin instructional programs, instructional prescription tests are used to maximize their chances for success. An instructional prescription test is used to make one of two decisions:

1. Students have *not* mastered the skills as yet and need corrective instruction to achieve mastery. Effective instructional prescription tests pinpoint deficiencies in subskills needed to master the skill being taught so that the deficiencies can be corrected through instruction.

2. Students have mastered the skills taught and are ready to progress to the next learning task.

Achievement Certification Testing and Decision-Making

After educators complete an instructional program, they use achievement certification tests to certify that the learning objectives of the instructional program have been achieved and the students are ready to be advanced to the next instructional program, the next grade level, or to graduate from school. Achievement certification tests assess level of achievement in the subject areas covered by the test. Most allow students' performance to be compared to other students who have taken the test. Multiple-skill achievement certification tests such as the Stanford Achievement Tests allow profiles to be derived showing variations in level of achievement in the different skill areas covered by the test. Typically, achievement certification tests do not probe each skill area in sufficient depth and breadth to enable subskill deficiencies to be pinpointed.

Referral Testing and Decision-Making

When students fail to learn from the instruction they receive, they are given tests to identify possible underlying causes. For example, the Snellen Eye Chart is used to identify impaired vision. Although most educators are not qualified to make diagnoses based on test results, they can use test results to determine whether a referral is warranted. This section of the book reviews tests used to make (1) visual impairment referrals, (2) hearing impairment referrals, (3) problem behavior referrals, (4) psychomotor impairment referrals, and (5) adaptive deficiency referrals. Also covered in this section are tests such as the Strong Interest Inventory, which is used to help students identify and pursue their educational and vocational interests. School regulations usually indicate to whom referrals are to be made.

A sixth section, "Criteria for Evaluating Educational Practice and Decision-Making," was added to the handbook because of its relevance to educational testing and decision-making.

Criteria for Evaluating Educational Practices and Decision-Making

Evaluation is a prominent and important aspect of educational testing and decision-making. Educational personnel, programs, and student achievement are routinely evaluated, and the consequences for failing accountability evaluations can be harsh. Evaluation merits attention in any account or handbook on educational testing. However, we found evaluation too complex and variable a topic to deal with in its entirety in a section of the handbook. Books are written to describe evaluation systems. There is an almost endless variety of evaluation instruments available, many of which have not been assessed for technical adequacy. After due deliberation, we decided to limit the scope of this section to criteria used to conduct educational evaluations because of their paramount significance. If the criteria of desirable performance used in an evaluation are not valid, the evaluation cannot be valid. If the criteria are valid, any number of scale formats can be appended to the criteria to assess conformity to the criteria—for instance, a Likert scale.

Although focusing on criteria limited the scope of this section, there is no shortage of criteria that can be reported. Many criteria are derived by professional education organizations to define good practice in their field. For instance, the National Council of Teachers of English and the International Reading Association developed criteria for evaluating English language arts curricula. In contrast, other criteria are derived from research. Criteria specifying effective classroom discipline practices have been derived from research. The application of these classroom practices has been shown to reduce classroom disruptions (Friedman, 2000). The review of evaluation criteria derived through committee work and/or research is very revealing and enlightening. Never before have these criteria been summarized side by side.

The handbook is divided into six parts corresponding to the six designations above: Part I, "Admission Testing and Decision-Making"; Part II, "Placement Testing and Decision-Making"; Part III, "Instructional Prescription Testing and Decision-Making"; Part IV, "Achievement Certification Testing and Decision-Making"; Part V, "Referral Testing and Decision-Making"; and Part VI, "Criteria for Evaluating Educational Practice and Decision-Making."

Benefiting from the Introductions to Parts of the Handbook

A very useful feature of the handbook is the introduction to each of the six parts. Each of the six parts covers a different testing/decision-making area. Each introduction provides an up-to-date orientation to the testing and decision-making issues relevant to the area. The introduction to Part I discusses issues relevant to admissions testing and decision-making; the introduction to Part II discusses issues relevant to placement testing and decision-making; the introduction to Part III discusses issues relevant to instructional prescription testing and decision-making; and so on. Educators interested in selecting a test in a particular part of the handbook can benefit from reading the introduction to that part. It will prepare them to make a more well-informed test selection.

Designing Test Reviews for Educators

Test reviews are designed to provide information about tests that educators need to evaluate before making a selection. Most test reviews focus on the technical adequacy of tests and use psychometric terminology to evaluate them. Our test reviews focus on using tests to help educators make educational decisions. Technical adequacy is evaluated in easy-to-understand language, and feasibility issues are addressed as well. Sometimes, because of price, testing time, and other practical considerations, it is not feasible to use a test, regardless of how technically adequate a test may be. Special features of tests are also discussed so that they may be considered before selecting tests—for example, aids provided to help in the scoring of tests and the interpretation of test results. Excerpts from other reviews of the test are included so that diversity of opinion can be considered before selecting tests. In addition, contact information is provided to make it easy to order or obtain more information about tests from publishers.

Below is an annotated outline explaining the standard format used to review all tests in the handbook.

Test Review Format

Name of the Test (followed by its acronym in parentheses)

Name of the Test Reviewer

Usefulness of the Test for Educators

Test Author's Purpose: A summary of the author's stated purposes of the test is presented.

Decision-Making Applications: Although each test is used primarily to make either admission, placement, instructional prescription, achievement certification, or referral decisions and is classified accordingly, it may be used to make other decisions as well. The test reviewer comments on the appropriate uses of tests for decision-making, which do not always agree with the author's statement of the purposes of a test.

Relevant Population: Attributes of the population to whom the test is to be administered are described.

Characteristics Described: Each of the characteristics assessed by the test is identified, elaborated, and explained. Methods and test items used are often provided to clarify the assessment of characteristics.

Test Scores Obtained: All scores derived for a test are specified and explained as need be, including total score/subtest score relationships (i.e., when more than one score is derived).

Technical Adequacy: The technical adequacy of tests is determined by assessing the validity, reliability, and objectivity of tests, as will be elaborated later in the User's Guide.

Validity Confirmation: Summary of confirming evidence.

Reliability Confirmation: Summary of confirming evidence.

Objectivity Confirmation: Summary of confirming evidence.

Evidence provided by the authors to confirm the validity, reliability, and objectivity of their tests is summarized. Comments about the evidence provided are offered as warranted. Plain English is used instead of technical terminology whenever possible.

Statistical Confirmation: References to where statistical evidence can be obtained on validity, reliability, objectivity, and norms are provided.

Special Features: Special features of tests that can facilitate and affect their selection and use are described.

Acronyms: Acronyms used to identify most tests are specified. Acronyms for tests change over the years with the development of test revisions.

Levels of the Test: Different levels of a test may be constructed, usually to accommodate differences in age and grade levels.

Number of Test Forms: Equivalent forms of a test may be developed so that a test (in different forms) may be administered to students over time to assess changes in the students.

Norm-Referenced? Yes or No. If applicable, traits of the norm population are discussed so that educators can determine whether a test is appropriate for their students.

Criterion-Referenced? Yes or No. If applicable, instructional and curriculum objectives assessed by the test are discussed so that educators can determine whether a test assesses the objectives their students are assigned to pursue.

Other Features: For example, practice tests and scoring assistance may be provided by the test publisher.

Feasibility Considerations: In addition to other factors, feasibility considerations such as time, money, and the personal capabilities of the test administrator need to be taken into account when selecting a test.

Testing Time: Time available for testing is always a consideration in selecting tests.

For Testing Groups? Individuals? Tests designated to be administered to individuals only are often appropriate but are most often more costly in time and money than group tests.

Test Administration and Scoring: Amount of training required to be able to administer, score, and interpret test results is always a consideration in selecting tests. Extended training, certification, or licensing is required to qualify for the administration of some tests.

Test Materials and Approximate Costs: The cost of test materials is usually a consideration in the selection of tests. Costs of tests very widely from less than $30 to over $600 for complete testing kits.

Adequacy of Test Manuals: Companion test manuals should be appraised before selecting a test. Some manuals are clearly and simply written and comprehensively cover important details about the test. Manuals should present needed information for determining the technical adequacy of tests as well as using the test. Training may not be required to administer, score, and interpret a test if instructions are sufficiently simple, clear, and detailed.

Excerpts from Other Test Reviews: This feature is unique. It enables educators to compare and contrast opinions of test experts when considering the selection of a test.

Ordering Information: Obtaining additional information about the test or ordering it is made as simple as possible.

Publisher: The street address, phone number, fax number, e-mail address, and web site designation are reported as available.

Author(s): Names of the authors are provided.

Publication Date: Dates of publication of forms of tests are provided.

Cautions and Comments: Here the test reviewer highlights key features, appropriate applications, and limitations of the tests.

References: References are given for all citations.

More will be said about the use of information in the test reviews to decision-making later in the User's Guide.

Qualifications of Test Reviewers

Test reviewers were selected with great care. Having expertise in psychometrics was necessary but not sufficient to be selected. Test reviewers also needed to be familiar with education both as a field of study and as a profession, to have an earned Ph.D., and to have expertise in reviewing the particular type of tests they were assigned to review: admission, placement, instructional prescription, achievement certification, referral, or evaluation instruments.

The primary reviewer of admissions tests is a consultant to state departments of education on certification tests educators must pass to be admitted to the education profession. For example, many states require applicants for teacher certification to pass PRAXIS tests. He also offers workshops to prepare applicants for teacher certification to pass the PRAXIS tests and college applicants and aspirants to pass tests such as the SAT and American College Testing Assessment (ACT) tests. He is also familiar with the early childhood tests used to determine the extent to which young children are ready to be admitted to school for the first time. He has an earned Ph.D. in Educational Research and Measurement.

The primary reviewer of placement tests has an earned doctorate in Special Education with a specialization in assessment testing. She is very familiar with all of the federal disability laws that must be heeded when placing disabled students in programs. When appropriate she refers to laws in her reviews. She has been involved in placement decisions affecting a great many students and knows the protocol for making placements.

The primary reviewer of instructional prescription tests has an earned Ph.D. in Educational Research and Measurement with a concentration in instruction. She is experienced in evaluating instructional programs and classroom instruction, and has expertise in diagnosing academic inadequacies and prescribing corrective instruction to remediate them. She is very familiar with tests used to diagnose inadequate mastery of subskills needed to perform major skills taught in school, such as reading.

The primary reviewer of achievement certification tests has an earned doctorate in Educational Psychology with an emphasis on research and measurement. He has constructed achievement tests and served as a consultant to the federal government, state departments of education, and schools on the assessment of student achievement. He also established a master's and doctoral program in Research and Measurement.

The primary reviewer of referral tests has an earned Ph.D. in School Psychology and teaches school psychology at a university. School psychologists are usually more involved in referral decisions than other school employees. They not only have expertise in academic testing, they also are experienced with tests that diagnose underlying causes of academic failure, such as tests that identify behavior, psychomotor, adaptation, hearing, and vision problems. The school psychologist who reviewed the referral tests in the handbook is experienced in evaluating causes of failure to learn and in making referrals to alleviate the causes. She has conducted needs assessments and worked with school teams to make referral decisions.

The primary reviewer of criteria for evaluating educational practices has an earned doctorate in Special Education and Higher Education Administration and has taught evaluation and measurement courses in special education. Her current position as Associate Professor, Department of Educational Leadership and Policies, and prior position as a school principal provide her with the experience required to understand the educational practices that are and need to be evaluated, as well as criteria used to evaluate the practices.

All of the reviewers are authors of the handbook. More detail on their background and personal achievements can be obtained in the "About the Authors of the Handbook" chapter.

Criteria for Including Tests in the Handbook

Since the handbook is written for educators, an attempt was made to include only reviews of tests relevant to the decisions educators make. As discussed previously, these are admissions tests, placement tests, instructional prescription tests, achievement certification tests, and referral tests. In addition, only tests that meet minimum validity, reliability, and objectivity criteria are included. Educators' time is precious. They should not need to consider useless tests when attempting to select a test for their purpose. However, an attempt is made to be liberal in establishing minimum criteria and to make exceptions when it is thought that a test may still be useful for a particular purpose. When exceptions are allowed explanations are given and test limitations are acknowledged. Buros' *Mental Measurements* yearbooks attempt to assess all mental tests in print, many of which are not relevant to the decisions educators make, and many are reviewed that provide little or no evidence of validity and/or reliability. *A Consumer's Guide to Tests in Print* (Hammill et al., 1992) does use criteria for assessing tests, but only assesses tests that are individually administered, standardized, norm-referenced tests. Moreover, many, if not most, of the tests assessed in the guide are rated as "not recommended," and criterion-referenced tests so important to the work of educators are not included in the guide.

Minimum Validity Criteria

Tests will be included in the handbook if some evidence of validity is provided for the tests. Test validation involves amassing research evidence confirming the validity of a test. Confirmation is a matter of judgment. It is difficult to say when sufficient evidence has been amassed to declare in any absolute terms that a test is valid. Moreover, there is always variation in research results from one validation study to another, and research studies are very expensive and time consuming to conduct. Large corporations that produce tests sold in great volume can best afford research to confirm the validity of their tests. Educators and other individuals that produce tests cannot afford to amass as much validation evidence. From our perspective, if evidence of validity is provided a test should not be excluded from the handbook. An analysis of test validity confirmation will be presented later in this chapter.

Minimum Reliability Criteria

Establishing minimum reliability criteria for including tests in the handbook is both simple and difficult. The choice is simple because test reliability is usually expressed simply as a reliability correlation coefficient; the choice is difficult because test experts do not agree on minimum reliability criteria. Following is a brief historical account to show the variation of their positions.

1927   Kelley, a pioneer in psychometrics, recommended a minimum reliability coefficient of .50 for tests used to assess group achievement, .90 for tests used to assess differences in group achievement, and .94 for tests used to assess individual achievement. Many of his successors regarded his distinctions as extreme.

1978   Nunnally considered .90 as a minimal standard for tests used to assess individual performance.

1988   Sattler recommended that .80 be the minimum for tests used to assess individual performance. Aiken (1988) recommended .85 for this purpose.

2001   Salvia and Ysseldyke recommend as minimum standards .60 for tests used to assess group performance, .80 for tests used as screening tests for individuals, and .90 for tests used to make definitive decisions for individuals, such as placement decisions.

Since it is our purpose to cull out tests that are not sufficiently reliable for the purposes of educators, it was decided to include in the handbook tests with a reliability coefficient of .60 or higher for tests as a whole. The correlation coefficient would need to be significant at the .05 level of probability.

Minimum Objectivity Criteria

To meet minimum objectivity requirements, a test must provide a key or criteria for obtaining test results. When keys or criteria are provided, it is likely that there will be more consistency in the test results obtained by different test scorers or interpreters. In selecting a test it is well to keep in mind that a scoring key is more appropriate in subject areas where there is less ambiguity in designating a correct answer, such as math. Also, when complex scoring criteria are provided, it might be necessary to train scorers to use the criteria appropriately and to certify their competency before allowing them to score test responses. Of course, there are tests (such as questionnaires) that do not require scoring keys or criteria to obtain objectivity. Scorers and interpreters of test taker responses who can read the language should have little difficulty agreeing on what they read. However, there might be disagreement on the meaning of what was said.

A test must meet minimum validity criteria, minimum reliability criteria, and minimum objectivity criteria to be included in the handbook, unless an exception is made. When exceptions are made, explanations will be given. The establishment of criteria is always somewhat arbitrary. Admittedly, the minimum criteria for including a test in the handbook are too, but necessarily so, because the handbook was conceived from its inception to include only tests that meet minimum standards of adequacy so that they may not be considered useless. To avail yourself of a much larger selection of published tests consult Buros' *Mental Measurements* yearbooks, with the understanding that the test reviews are not written expressly for educators and may not include all the information you need on tests.

Some tests can be used to make more than one type of decision. For example, the same test may be used to make placement and referral decisions for students with learning difficulties. However, most often a test is better suited for one type of decision than another. It is also important to note that disability legislation requires more than one type of test to be used to make certain diagnoses, such as mental retardation. Although each test will be reviewed in one decision-making category, test reviews will describe other decisions for which a test may be used. Ultimately, the readers need to decide whether a test is suitable for their purpose.

Many published tests are not constructed to make the previously mentioned decisions educators routinely make. A great number of tests are constructed primarily for use by psychologists and other clinicians who frequently do not use them for educational purposes. When they do use their tests to test students, it is most often to identify and treat underlying causes of student failure, such as psychological disorders. It is also the case that tests constructed for the use of psychologists and other clinicians are categorized to help them make clinical decisions, different from the decisions educators routinely make. Their tests are listed under categories such as Adaptive Behavior, Personality, Intelligence, Aptitude, Perceptual Functioning, Adjustment, Motor Abilities, Anxiety, Social Relations, Conduct Disorders, Attention, Autonomy, Affect, or Language and Auditory Processing Disorders.

In contrast to other professionals who serve the needs of our youth, *the primary goal and dedication of educators is to produce academic achievement through instruction*—despite the disabling conditions that may severely limit the learning potential of some students. It is time for more tests to be constructed specifically to help educators make the routine decisions they need to make.

Education is a multi-billion-dollar industry, and outsiders who have specialized expertise to offer relentlessly attempt to get a piece of the pie. In many cases educators appreciate the services and products they provide but do not understand enough about the technical aspects of their work to evaluate it. Under these conditions educators become vulnerable and subject to their influence. Because testing plays such a large role in education and most educators lack expertise in psychometrics, they have been insidiously and inadvertently influenced by the tests psychometricians construct for education. In some instances the influence has become so pronounced that it affects the way education operates—"the tail is wagging the dog." For instance, states adopt published standardized, nationally normed achievement test batteries that are administered to most public school students in the states and sometimes are used to determine whether legislated accountability standards have been met. Since there are dire consequences for educators whose students fail the tests and for the students as well, teachers gravitate toward teaching to the tests, in which case the tests are to a great extent dictating the states' curriculum, whatever the specified curriculum may be. As you will see, the ill-advised use of published tests can have many undesirable effects on education.

We cannot stop policymakers, interest groups, or the public from imposing their views on education. Education is everyone's business. And we cannot stop entrepreneurs from selling their services and products to educators. But we need not allow them to dictate educational practice.

Focus and Limitations of the Handbook

Although the pre-service course of study of most school administrators and teachers does not prepare them to be test experts, they should not need to be experts to select a test to meet their needs or to understand the merits of the tests imposed upon them that affect their work and careers. Psychometrics requires the study of test construction technology and statistics; this handbook does not. Whereas Buros' *Mental Measurements* yearbooks attempt to review all published mental tests, this handbook contains only reviews of tests that meet minimum standards of accuracy and are relevant to educational decision-making, including tests used to make admission, placement, instructional prescription, achievement certification, and referral decisions.

Tests used by school and other psychologists to diagnose self and social insufficiency or psychological and social disorders that require clinical therapy are not included in the handbook. Only tests that educators can use to help them determine whether or not to refer students to clinicians for further diagnosis are included under "referral tests."

Using the Indexes

Indexes are organized to help you find the tests and information you need as easily as possible.

Index of Test Titles

If you know the title of a specific test you are interested in, you can find the page number of the review of the test in this index.

Index of Test Acronyms

If you know a test by acronym rather than by title, you can find the page number of the test review in this index.

Characteristics Index

If you are interested in observing or describing a particular characteristic, you are likely to find the various tests that describe the characteristic in this index.

Test Classification Index

If you are interested in tests that assess a particular type of skill or attribute, such as reading, you can look up the skill or attribute in this index to find tests that assess it.

Test Classification Categories

Achievement

Adaptive behavior

College readiness and admission

Early childhood readiness and admission

Educator certification

Hearing

Intelligence, ability, aptitude

Language

Mathematics

Motor coordination

Problem behavior

Reading

Vision

Vocational

Writing

Index of Test Authors

If you are interested in tests developed by particular authors, you can find them in this index.

Index of Reference Authors

If you are interested in the citations of a particular test expert or educator referenced in the handbook, you can find the page numbers of the citations in this index.

Directory of Educational Test Publishers

If you are interested in knowing about a test publisher and means of contacting the publisher, you can find the information in this index.

Glossary

The glossary provides handy definitions of key terms used in the handbook. As much as we attempt to provide definitions in easy-to-understand language, some definitions may not be fully understood without an introductory knowledge of tests and measurements.

DEFENDING YOUR TESTING

To defend your testing decisions (for example, a grade assigned to a student), it is necessary to defend (1) the test itself, (2) that the test was appropriate for your purpose, (3) the test administration conditions, (4) the conclusions drawn from the test results, and (5) the selection of the test.

Defending Tests

To defend the test itself, educators must defend the validity, reliability, and objectivity of the test.

Tests are tools and people have thought of validity, reliability, and objectivity in referring to the tools they invented, built, and used for a long time. Tools are built for particular purposes. When a tool is used for its intended purpose, we consider it to be a valid use of the tool. Pliers and screwdrivers have different valid uses, and we do not try to use pliers to insert a screw because it won't work. We also think of tools as reliable. When they do the job they were intended to do consistently, we consider the tool to be reliable. Manufacturers of tools provide objective standards for using their tools. The instructions they provide facilitate objectivity or consistency in the way different people use the tools.

Most educators have a good idea of what test validity, reliability, and objectivity mean in the context of their schoolwork. They know that tests they administer to students must validly assess student achievement of school learning objectives. They know that they must reliably test student achievement of learning objectives. That is, they know that they need to repeatedly observe students' performance before deciding whether or not students have achieved an objective. And they know what objectivity means. They construct objective tests, such as multiple-choice and true-false tests, to ensure that they and others who score the tests will obtain similar results. However, many things they are taught when they study tests and measurement in courses do not jive with their practical understanding of validity, reliability, and objectivity. Many psychometric interpretations of these terms often expressed statistically are not clearly understood by educators. And educators who do fathom psychometric interpretations often find them inconsistent with the use of the terms in educational practice.

Following is an attempt to define validity, reliability, and objectivity in an educational context. The definitions are not inconsistent with some psychometric definitions of the terms, allowing that psychometricians disagree on their interpretations of validity, reliability, and objectivity and the means of assessing them, as you will see shortly.

What Is Test Validity?

In judging the validity of a test, it is well to remember that the authors of the test constructed it to describe characteristics in a particular population. In our context the characteristics pertain to some aspect of schooling, such academic achievement. The population usually of concern is some group of students. However, descriptions of a test relevant to schooling might be the administrative ability (characteristic) of principals (population).

Thus, a test is valid to the extent that it facilitates the description of the characteristics in the population it was constructed to describe.

This definition acknowledges that test authors invest a great deal of time and effort constructing their tests for the purpose of describing particular characteristics in a particular population, which are specified in the test manual they prepare. Validation entails confirming that tests describe the characteristics in the populations the authors constructed the tests to describe. Some test experts suggest that a test might have other valid uses, but searching for them would seem to be a monumental waste of time.

What Is Test Reliability?

A test is reliable to the extent that there is consistency in the results of repeated administrations of the test to the same individuals or population. Since a test is constructed to describe the characteristics of a particular population and is validated on that population, it is expected to yield consistent results when repeatedly administered to members of the population. Repeatedly administering a test to members of the same population over a short span of time and demonstrating that there is consistency in the results obtained establishes test reliability.

What Is Test Objectivity?

A third factor assessed to establish the adequacy of a test is objectivity. *A test is objective to the extent that different interpreters of the same test results are consistent in their interpretations*. Objectivity is facilitated when keys or criteria are stipulated for deriving test results because they enhance agreement in the interpretations of different interpreters.

An attempt was made to define validity, reliability, and objectivity as discrete factors. They need to be discrete, because if they are not it is difficult to determine the contribution of each factor to the adequacy of tests. These discrete factors complement each other. If any of the three factors is not taken into account the assessment of test adequacy is incomplete.

The following simplified example helps to clarify the meaning of validity, reliability, and objectivity, their relationship, and complementary functions in the context of education. Suppose teachers want to construct a test to describe the handwriting ability of 9-year-old students. They prepare instructions that tell students to write the first line of "The Star-Spangled Banner" in longhand or cursive, as well as criteria for rating students' handwriting as acceptable or unacceptable. To assess the validity of the test the teachers would administer it to students and rate test results according to instructions. If the teachers were able to clearly distinguish acceptable from unacceptable handwriting samples, evidence of test validity would have been obtained. The test when applied actually rates the handwriting of 9-year-olds as it was constructed to do. Obtaining additional writing samples from the same students and rating them would assess reliability. To the extent that ratings of each student's samples are consistent, evidence of the reliability of the test has been obtained. Objectivity would be assessed by training other handwriting teachers to use the rating criteria and then having them rate the same handwriting samples. If their ratings are consistent, evidence of objectivity has been obtained. Having obtained sufficient evidence of validity, reliability, and objectivity, the adequacy of the test has been established.

Definitions are building blocks that form the foundation of logical discourses. The preceding definitions of validity, reliability, and objectivity serve as underpinnings for ensuing discussions of test adequacy and are in keeping with common understanding of these terms. However, there is considerable controversy among test experts on the conceptualization of validity, reliability, and objectivity and methods of assessing them.

Those who have had an introduction to tests and measurement terms may want to consider the following controversies among test experts. Three types of validity are usually distinguished in chapters, books, and courses that teach tests and measurement: (1) construct validity, (2) content validity, and (3) criterion-related validity. However, Anastasi (1988), a respected test expert, disagrees: "Content, criterion-related, and construct validation do not correspond to distinct or logically coordinate categories. On the contrary, construct validity is a comprehensive concept, which includes the other types" (pp. 152–153). Fitzpatrick (1983) and Messick (1989) agree. In addition, test experts disagree on the interpretation of internal consistency in testing. For some test experts internal consistency is indicative of test reliability. Internal consistency is a standard label used to denote a type of reliability. For others internal consistency is indicative of test validity. Internal consistency of test items can be indicative of content validity. Internal consistency of test responses can be indicative of construct validity. Are not validity and reliability supposed to be discrete factors? Experts also differ on their views of reliability and objectivity. Some consider objectivity to be a type of test reliability, often called "inter-rater reliability." Others do not conceive of objectivity as an inherent attribute of tests. They consider objectivity to be a requirement of science for making accurate observations, whether or not a test is used to make the observations. There is also a controversy on test validity. Some consider test validity to be an inherent attribute of tests and define validity accordingly. Our previously stated definition serves as an example. Another example of such a definition is: A test is valid when it measures the qualities or attributes it is designed to measure. Anastasi (1988) evidently agrees in stating that validity should be built into a test from the outset (p. 158). Others consider validity to be a property of test-based inferences and not a property of the test itself. For example, test validity may be defined as the extent to which inferences made on the basis of test results are reasonable and appropriate. The latter type of definition will not do for our purposes. A main purpose of this handbook is to help educators select accurate tests. Inferences made from test results are affected by many factors other than the test itself. Inaccurate inferences can be caused by the faulty reasoning of the person making the inferences, the inappropriate use of statistical formulas in deriving test results, poor testing conditions, and many other factors that can and do affect test result interpretation, in addition to the test. How can test validity be based entirely on test result inferences when there are so many factors other than tests themselves that can affect test results, and so many additional factors that affect test result inferences?

It appears that with the passage of time, definitions of validity, reliability, and objectivity and the techniques for assessing them proliferate, making it more difficult to understand and apply the terms.

If test and testing terminology cannot be interpreted and applied by educators to educational practice, it is of no use to education. To improve educational testing, it is time to try to improve the conceptualization of test and testing terminology. For what it's worth, the following logic was used to conceptualize the terms in the handbook.

1. Purpose: Tests are instruments constructed to facilitate the description of phenomena.

2. To improve description, tests must be constructed to facilitate the description of particular characteristics in a population. For this reason, test developers must construct test instructions and items that facilitate the description of characteristics in the population they want to describe.

3. Once a test is constructed, its technical adequacy can be determined by assessing the validity, reliability, and objectivity of the test.

4. Validity: To assess the validity of a test, one attempts to determine the extent to which it facilitates the description of the characteristics in the population it was constructed to describe. The more the research evidence one amasses demonstrates that a test facilitates the description of the characteristics in the

population it was constructed to describe, the more the validity of the test has been confirmed.

5. Reliability: To assess the reliability of tests, one repeatedly administers the tests to the same population over a short period of time and checks the results for consistency. The more consistent the results, the more the reliability of the tests has been confirmed.

6. Objectivity: To assess the objectivity of tests, one has different interpreters interpret the same test results. The more consistency there is among their interpretations, the more the objectivity of the tests has been confirmed.

7. After the validity, reliability, and objectivity of tests have been assessed, the combined results are considered to assess the overall adequacy of the tests.

Although, as previously noted, some consider objectivity to be a type of reliability (inter-rater reliability), objectivity and reliability are entirely different sources or causes of inconsistency that are remedied in entirely different ways. Reliability pertains to the consistency of test results obtained from repeated administrations of the same test to the same population over time. In contrast, objectivity pertains to a different factor: consistency in different people's interpretation of the same observed event.

Many educators have difficulty relating psychometricians' discussions of reliability and objectivity to educational practice as they know it. When educators study the fundamentals of test and measurement in introductory educational research and test and measurement textbooks, validity and reliability are usually listed in the table of contents and discussed under major headings in the text. Objectivity is not presented as a major concept, but rather relegated to one of several aspects of reliability, that is, inter-rater reliability. In discussions of inter-rater reliability the term "objectivity" may never be used. Although psychometricians may not consider objectivity to be a preeminent testing concept, it has become very important to educators. The objectivity of the tests they construct is challenged by irate students, their parents, and lawyers. School administrators are stressing the importance of using and constructing objective tests that can be defended. What's more, the Individuals with Disabilities Education Act (IDEA) mandates that Individual Education Plans (IEPs) contain "appropriate objective criteria . . . for determining whether the short-term instructional objectives are being achieved" (34 CFR 300.46 (a) (5)). So from an educator's perspective, objectivity is much more than one aspect of reliability masked as inter-rater reliability.

Establishing the Validity, Reliability, and Objectivity of Tests

In the following discussion of methods of establishing the validity, reliability, and objectivity of tests, common terminology understandable to educators will be used whenever possible instead of previously discussed psychometric terms that test specialists argue about. Sometimes test concepts will be clarified by using operational definitions, that is, by specifying in plain English the procedures that are to be used when applying the concept.

Establishing the Validity of Tests

Tests must be constructed to be valid, and then afterwards test responses are studied for further validation. Thus, validity can be established first by inspecting the test instructions and items that were constructed to determine whether the items actually test the characteristics they were constructed to test, and second by determining the extent to which test responses actually describe the characteristics in the population intended by the authors. For instance, the validity of a spelling achievement test can be established by determining the extent to which (1) the items of the test require students to spell and (2) by determining whether responses to the test items indicate spelling achievement. In this vein, two types of validation will be discussed: *test item validity* and *test response validity*.

Comparing test items for congruence with the characteristics in the population the items were constructed to describe can assess test item validation. The greater the number of test items that are *judged* to elicit descriptions of the characteristic, the greater the test item validation. Judgment is one way of establishing validity and has been used for a long time (to establish face, content, and sometimes construct validity of tests).

Making judgments necessary to assess test item validity is not possible if test items are not constructed to overtly test for the characteristics in the population specified. If there is a covert relationship between test items and the characteristics being assessed, test item validity judgments cannot be made. In achievement tests and most other tests educators use routinely, test items are constructed to be overtly related to the characteristics to be tested. Such is also the case in vision, hearing, and some aptitude tests, such as musical aptitude tests. On the other hand, in projective tests, such as the Rorschach Test and some interest inventories, the relationship between test items and the characteristics being assessed is covert—but these tests are used primarily by psychologists and other clinicians.

Test response validity is established by administering the test to members of the defined population and demonstrating that their responses actually do describe the characteristics in the population the test was constructed to describe.

Establishing the validity of academic achievement tests is of utmost importance to educators. The population usually of interest is some student body. The characteristic of interest is the achievement of particular learning objectives. The following example illustrates how test item and test response validity can be established for a math achievement test. Suppose an achievement test is constructed to describe the extent to which fifth grade students have learned to add fractions, the learning objective. Test item validity would be established by developing test items pertaining to the addition of fractions with like denominators, such as 1/2 + 1/2, unlike denominators such as 1/2 + 3/4, and complex fractions such as 1 1/4 + 5 3/4. Then agreement among qualified judges is obtained indicating that the test items adequately cover the subject of adding fractions. Test items are refined as needed until agreement among judges is obtained.

Test response validity could be established by demonstrating that the more students have been taught about adding fractions, the higher their score will be on the test. Students prior to instruction would be hypothesized to score lower than students who have partially been taught to add fractions, and students who have completed instruction would score the highest. The more research studies demonstrate that test scores of fifth graders are positively correlated with knowledge of adding fractions, the greater the confirmation of test response validity. That is, the evidence would confirm that test responses indicate the extent to which fifth graders have learned to add fractions, the learning objective.

Test response validation procedures would vary depending on the purpose for which a test is constructed. Tests other than academic achievement tests are constructed for different purposes and would, therefore, be validated somewhat differently. Some tests are constructed for the purpose of predicting particular outcomes, in which case test response validation would need to show that test responses can actually be used to predict the outcome. Aptitude tests are implicitly, if not explicitly, constructed to predict particular outcomes. For instance, those who score high on a musical aptitude test are predicted to be more successful in a musical career than those who score low on the test. Intelligence tests are often categorized as aptitude tests. Those scoring high on intelligence tests are predicted to be more successful at tasks that require mental ability, such as academic tasks, problem solving, and attainment of high-paying or status positions. It might also be predicted that thieves who score high on an intelligence test would be arrested less frequently than thieves who score low on the test. Vocational interest inventories are also validated by confirming the prediction that those whose test scores are high in a particular vocational area are more likely to succeed in the vocation than those who score low in the vocational area.

It should be pointed out that the purpose of academic achievement tests is to assess achievement of learning objectives that result from past instruction and learning. Achievement tests do not need to predict future achievement or any other future event to be valid. To be valid, achievement tests only need to describe the extent to which learning objectives have been achieved, as explained previously. However, achievement test results can also be used for other purposes—for instance, to predict future achievement. In this case achievement tests are functioning as aptitude tests as well as achievement tests. Multiple uses of tests will be considered further when assessing student academic potential is discussed.

Predictive validation takes a great deal of time, work, and money. Confirming the prediction that people who score high on a test will succeed in a particular way sometime in the future requires longitudinal research. Repeated observations need to be made of their status over an extended period of time. To save time and money, concurrent validation has been used as a shortcut. Rather than waiting perhaps many years to complete a predictive validation study, a concurrent validation study can be completed instead in short order. For instance, rather than waiting decades to see if students who score high on an intelligence test attain higher-paying or status jobs than students who score low on the test, a concurrent validation study is often done instead. Two groups of workers are given intelligence tests: a group of blue-collar employees who hold low-status/low-paying jobs and a group of executives holding high-paying/high-status jobs. If the executives score significantly higher on the intelligence test than the blue-collar workers, concurrent validation has been attained. Such a concurrent validation study requires only one testing of two groups at about the same time, so both time and money are saved.

Concurrent validation of tests is also obtained by showing that scores on a new test (for example a newly constructed intelligence test) correlate highly with a well-respected test of the same ilk, such as the Stanford-Binet Intelligence Test. Both tests can be given to the same group over a short span of time to determine whether there is a high correlation between the test scores of the two. It would be even more economical if the new test were given to people who have already taken the Binet. In this case only one testing session would be needed.

Establishing the Reliability and Objectivity of Tests

Correlation coefficients are often used to establish the reliability and objectivity of tests. Correlation coefficients are statistical expressions of similarity. They are obtained by using a statistical correlation formula to detect similarities in data. Correlation coefficients are not easy to interpret for those who have not had experience drawing conclusions from them. However, a percentage can be derived by squaring a correlation coefficient, and most people have experience interpreting percentages. For example, the reliability coefficient .60 when squared yields a percentage of 36%. This can readily be interpreted to indicate 36% similarity or consistency in results obtained from repeated administrations of the same test to the same population. Of course, the higher the correlation or percentage, the more reliable a test is.

In the same vein, when a correlation formula is used to determine test objectivity, the higher the objectivity coefficient, the greater the consistency among scorers of the same test. For instance, an objectivity correlation coefficient of .90 converted by squaring to 81% indicates that consistency among different scorers of the same test was 81%. Correlation coefficients are used to assess objectivity when scoring criteria, rather than scoring keys, are used to score tests in order to determine degree of consistency among the different scorers applying the criteria. Although this is a simplified explanation of the derivation and application of correlation coefficients, it serves the purpose of making a complicated issue more understandable.

Reliability and objectivity may be established much less formally without using statistical formulas. To obtain reliable test results, for example, a teacher constructs an exam to determine whether her students learned to spell recently taught words. She dictates sentences containing the words and asks students to write the sentences. Each taught word appears in two different sentences. When a student misspells the same word twice, it can be *reliably* concluded that the student has not yet learned to spell the word. Conversely, when a student correctly spells the same word twice, it can be *reliably* concluded that the student has learned how to spell the word. Students who spelled a word correctly once and incorrectly once may need to be tested further because the results are ambiguous. Or as a practical matter, it might be concluded that students who misspelled words once or twice have not sufficiently mastered the spelling of the words and require further instruction to attain mastery. The teacher might administer corrective instruction accordingly to ensure achievement of the learning objectives.

Objectivity of tests can be established informally by preparing a scoring key or scoring criteria and asking three qualified judges whether they agree with the key or criteria. If all three agree, objectivity has been established. If there is disagreement the judges can be asked to refine the scoring key or criteria until agreement is reached. When agreement is reached, objectivity can be claimed if the key or criteria are applied as specified.

In the preceding illustrations of how test reliability and objectivity can be facilitated it was not necessary to use statistics. Most often inconsistencies can be observed without the aid of statistics. Correlation coefficients are helpful because they precisely indicate degree of inconsistency. However inconsistencies are observed, to achieve reliability and objectivity, additional work must be done to reduce the inconsistencies before a test is ready to be used.

Statistics are used most extensively by psychometricians who construct tests for test publishers—typically copyrighted, complex, standardized, norm-referenced tests with national norms. Unfortunately, some of these tests attain a life of their own divorced from the instructional programs used to produce the achievement they are supposed to measure. When this happens the tests lose their usefulness as academic achievement tests.

Defending Your Use of a Test

It is not sufficient that you use a valid, reliable, and objective test. In addition, the test must be suitable for your purpose. That is, the test must assess the characteristics in the population you intend to assess. For instance, to defend the use of a math achievement test for fourth graders, you must show that the test you used (1) assessed math achievement (2) in fourth grade students. It would be more precise to show that the content of the test items covers the content of the school math curriculum for fourth graders, and that scores on the test indicated degrees of achievement of curriculum objectives.

Defending Your Administration of a Test

It is not only necessary to defend the test you use and its appropriateness for your purpose—it is also necessary to defend your administration of the test. To defend the administration of the test it would be necessary to show that (1) the test was administered according to test instructions, (2) test results were derived according to test instructions, and (3) the test was administered under favorable testing conditions (i.e., test takers were comfortable and not seriously ill; the environment was distraction-free; the room temperature was neither too hot nor too cold; the lighting was adequate, and students were given the supplies they needed to take the test).

Defending Your Conclusions

Ultimately, it is the conclusions educators draw about students that have the greatest repercussions. Failing students or reporting inadequate performance incites students, their parents, and lawyers to appeal in grievance proceedings and, if unsuccessful, in courts of law. Defending report card grades, for example, requires educators to show that grades were assigned correctly according to predetermined criteria that were shared with students and others, as appropriate, at the beginning of the term. One way to do this is to list the tests, projects, and assignments that are to be assessed during the term and the maximum number of points students can earn for each. These are added to show the maximum number of points that can be earned for the grading term. Points can then be converted to grades. For instance, 90% or more of maximum points earned is equivalent to an "A," 80% to 89% a "B," 70% to 79% a "C," 60% to 69% a "D," below 60% an "F." Establishing grading criteria beforehand not only helps educators defend the grades they assign, it helps them maintain objectivity in assigning grades. As much as educators may want to be unbiased in their grading of students, there is considerable evidence indicating that teacher expectations of student achievement significantly affects the grades they assign students. When teachers expect students to perform well they tend to grade students accordingly, and vice versa.

Reliability, in a more general sense, is a consideration when assigning grades to students. Not only do educators need to defend that the tests they used were reliable, they also need to defend that there was consistency in repeated assessments of student achievement of the same school learning objectives. When there is extensive variation in assessments of student achievement of the same objective, it is difficult to defend a grade assignment.

The aggregation procedure used to draw conclusions also needs to be defended. Different aggregation procedures can yield different conclusions. The above illustration shows how a point system can be used to score tests. (The tests can be weighted by assigning a greater number of points to tests deemed to be of greater value.) Points earned on individual tests can be totaled to yield total points earned for a grading term. Percentage of points earned can be used, as illustrated, to convert points to grades. Although the decision to use one aggregation procedure rather than another may be arbitrary, the selected aggregation procedure can be defended with respect to simplicity, logic, precedent, and plausibility. A simple procedure is more easily understood; a systematic procedure is inherently logical; precedent can be argued for a procedure that has become common practice; and plausibility can be argued for a procedure that seems reasonable. The aggregation procedure exemplified above was chosen because it is relatively simple. It follows a logical format and has been used before by many educators. It is also plausible in the sense that students who perform better on tests are assigned higher grades. Although seldom given the attention they deserve, aggregation procedures are an important consideration. They are used not only to assign grades; grades are often aggregated to decide whether or not students are to be promoted to the next grade.

Defending Test Selections: Guidelines

The following are guidelines for selecting tests.

Step 1: Define (1) the population you want to test and (2) the characteristics you want to describe in the population.

Populations are defined by listing the common characteristics of their members. In education the general population usually of interest is students. One characteristic may be sufficient to define a population (for example, third graders). The more characteristics specified the smaller and more specialized the population tends to be. A two-characteristic definition, such as (1) female (2) third graders, specifies a smaller, more specialized population of students. Characteristics are defined by naming them (for example, intelligence, math achievement, and musical aptitude). Being explicit in your definitions helps you identify appropriate tests.

Step 2: Identify tests that describe the characteristics in the population you have specified.

Most test manuals and reviews of tests specify the population for which the test is intended, and test validation and reliability studies summarized in test manuals indicate the populations in the studies. Test manuals also specify the characteristics assessed by the test. In addition, test reviews specify the characteristics assessed by each test, although the review formats are not the same. For instance, reviews in Buros' *Mental Measurements* yearbooks report characteristics in terms of the various scores a test yields. If you do not find the test you are looking for in the handbook, consult Buros' *Mental Measurements* yearbooks or one of the other publications referenced in the User's Guide. You may need more than one test to assess the characteristics you specify.

Step 3: Select from among the tests identified that serve your purpose those for which validity, reliability, and objectivity have been established.

The tests in the handbook meet minimum validity, reliability, and objectivity standards described previously, with few exceptions. The reviews of these tests in the handbook contain additional information on the validity, reliability, and objectivity of the tests. In reading these reviews, you can eliminate the tests that do not meet your standards.

In selecting a test, validity is the ultimate concern. Reliability and objectivity are important only insofar as they affect the validity of an assessment (Salvia and Ysseldyke, 2001). Therefore, if there is substantial evidence confirming the validity of a testing instrument, the instrument merits consideration even if evidence of reliability and objectivity is sparse or marginal. Following is an attempt to clarify the effect of reliability and objectivity on the validation of testing instruments.

It was said that a testing instrument is valid when it describes the characteristics in the population it was constructed to describe. To validate a testing instrument it is necessary to demonstrate that repeated administrations of the instrument to the population consistently describe the intended characteristics. Assessments of reliability and objectivity are important in establishing validity because they indicate inconsistencies in the results of repeated administrations of a testing instrument. If inconsistencies are excessive, the validity of an instrument cannot be established. In fact, extreme inconsistencies or fluctuations in results of repeated observations of any given event are difficult, if not impossible, to interpret, except perhaps to say that the results are highly variable.

Suppose, for example, a psychologist develops a mental measurement test to describe the intelligence (characteristic) of children (population) and wants to validate it. First, she might administer it to the same group of children twice to assess reliability. If the results of the two administrations are consistent, test-retest reliability has been established. Having established the reliability of her own observations, she is ready to establish objectivity. She teaches others to score the test, and then she has them score the tests she administered. If there is consistency in scoring, objectivity has been confirmed.

Having confirmed both the reliability and objectivity of the test, it has been shown that repeated administrations of the test yield consistent results, which in turn enables the test to be validated. Validation is achieved by comparing the characteristics described from the administration of the test to known characteristics of intelligence. If they are alike, evidence of the validity of the new intelligence test has been obtained. If they are not alike, there is evidence that the new test is invalid.

On the other hand, if reliability and objectivity studies have yielded inconsistent test results, validity cannot be established. The characteristics described by the new test have not been established, so there is nothing to compare to known characteristics of intelligence to assess the validity of the new test. In conclusion, reliability and objectivity studies should yield consistent results before attempts to validate a testing instrument are made. However, as a practical matter, attempts at validating tests are made before reliability and objectivity are established. Some credibility should be given to the results of these validation studies, especially if they have been replicated and yield consistent results.

Step 4: Select from the residual tests that meet your standards a test that is most feasible for you to obtain, administer, score, and interpret.

Feasibility is an important issue that is not often dealt with in test manuals or test reviews. However, it needs to be considered.

Feasibility Considerations

Although feasibility considerations may not carry much weight when educators need to defend the grades they assign students, they are frequently an issue when selecting a test. The amount of time teachers can allocate for testing is limited. They rarely have enough time to provide all their students with all the instruction they need, and they are beset with a slew of peripheral responsibilities which may include collecting picture, yearbook, lunch, and field trip money; obtaining permission and medical forms from parents; keeping students' permanent records up to date; filling out forms for vision and hearing screening; making photocopies for their classes; updating supplies; attending staff meetings and parent conferences; planning and participating in extracurricular activities; serving on cafeteria, bus, and recess duty; distributing fund-raiser information; and so on. The type of testing they do routinely is instructional prescription testing, which is an integral part of instruction. After each topic they must administer tests to determine whether students have learned the information and are ready to advance or need corrective instruction before proceeding. Other types of testing are less familiar to teachers and are an extra burden. They do learn how to construct and administer instructional prescription tests to some extent in their pre-service education and to a great extent on their own. In addition, they are capable of administering the standardized achievement tests required by their school, school district, or state. Still, they may not be qualified to analyze and interpret the test results as needed, and typically they have not been certified or licensed to administer and score tests that require special training, such as the Stanford-Binet Intelligence Test or the Rorschach Ink Blot Test. Published group tests are usually more feasible to use than individual tests. Group tests can often be machine-scored, and less time and money are required to test a whole class at one time than to test a class of students one at a time.

In addition to those discussed in the preceding guidelines for selecting tests, there are other issues that need to be considered.

Norm-Referenced and Criterion-Referenced Tests

A major consideration in selecting a test is whether a norm-referenced or criterion-referenced test is more suitable for your purpose. Norm-referenced tests are used to compare the test performance of individuals with a group of individuals with known characteristics who have taken the test. Using a norm-referenced test it can be concluded, for example, that an individual's test performance is above or at the 60th percentile when compared to norm-group members. Performance at the 60th percentile indicates that the individual's performance is equal to or better than 60 percent of the people in the norm group. The norm group used for comparison might be a school or a nation of individuals. Most standardized norm-referenced tests develop national norms for comparison. When choosing a norm-referenced test it is important to make certain that the norm group is not different from the individuals being tested on critical characteristics. For instance, comparing a learning disabled student's reading score to a nationally normed group of students can be misleading.

Norm-referenced tests are most useful when decisions based on status differentiation are being made pertaining to groups or individuals—for instance, when selecting students for scholarships, faculty for awards, or students for a school or program that has more applicants or nominees than can or will be accepted. Norm-referenced tests are also useful for comparing groups—for example, for comparing the performance of students in one state to other states on a nationally standardized norm-referenced achievement test.

Criterion-referenced tests are used to compare an individual's performance to a criterion to determine the extent to which the individual meets the criterion. For instance, conclusions drawn from a criterion-referenced test might be that a student achieved a course objective or answered 80% of the questions correctly on an achievement test. Since student achievement of learning objectives is a primary purpose of schools and the criterion for advancing in school, criterion-referenced tests are most appropriately used to determine the extent to which (1) schools meet accountability standards, (2) individual students are ready to be assigned the next more advanced lesson in a sequenced instructional program or need remedial instruction first, (3) students earn promotion to the next grade, (4) students meet the standards required for graduation, or (5) students meet entry criteria for a school or program. The criteria of greatest concern in academic achievement testing are learning objectives. Most criterion-referenced academic achievement tests are learning objective referenced.

Whether a norm-referenced or criterion-referenced test should be selected depends on the purpose of the educator. Following is a discussion of the use of norm- and criterion-referenced tests for admission, placement, instructional prescription, achievement certification, and referral decisions.

Admission Testing

School admission decisions are typically made on two levels. College admissions tests traditionally have been norm-referenced. Elite colleges that admit only a very small percentage of applicants, such as medical schools, use norm-referenced tests to identify the "cream of the crop" for admission. Colleges that admit a much higher percentage of their applicants use norm-referenced tests to cull out students who score low on the test.

Grade school admissions tests such as the Metropolitan Readiness Test attempt to determine whether preschoolers have developed and learned sufficiently to succeed in their first school experience. Both norm- and criterion-referenced tests can be used for this purpose; however, norm-referenced tests have usually been used. For instance, when considering student readiness to enter the first grade, norm-referenced tests are used to determine how a 6-year-old child compares to other 6-year-olds with respect to self-care, physical ability, learning readiness, and social maturity. Parents sometimes voluntarily delay their child's entry into school when their child is late in developing to improve the child's chances for initial success. On the other hand, schools not equipped to teach severely retarded children may deny admission to parents who apply and suggest appropriate alternatives. However, public schools are required by law to accommodate all age-eligible students or to arrange for accommodation.

Placement Testing

Norm-referenced tests are typically used to make placement decisions once students are admitted to school. Although other factors may be considered, students whose test scores are exceptionally high when compared with their peers frequently qualify for admission to accelerated programs, such as gifted programs. Also, students with low test scores frequently qualify for placement in programs for students with disability or learning difficulties. In addition, schools that ability group students use norm-referenced test scores to place their students. However, a substantial amount of research confirms that ability grouping does not enhance academic achievement (Friedman & Fisher, 1998).

Instructional Prescription Testing

Some diagnostic norm-referenced achievement tests are used to identify the readiness level of students as a basis for prescribing instruction for them. Primarily the tests are used to identify the grade level at which students are performing in various subject areas. They do not indicate how well students have learned a particular lesson as a basis for prescribing the next lesson. Criterion-referenced tests are most appropriate for determining the achievement of lesson objectives as a basis for deciding whether (1) students need corrective instruction to achieve the objective or (2) they are ready to be assigned the next more advanced lesson in a sequenced instructional program. Norm-referenced tests are inadequate for determining whether students achieve the instructional objectives of the particular instructional program they are being taught.

Teacher-made tests are most appropriate for making instructional prescription decisions. Whoever develops the curriculum, curriculum objectives, and curriculum-based tests, teachers are the ones who work day-to-day, lesson-by-lesson in their classrooms to make the ultimate achievement of curriculum objectives possible. They prepare lessons, they teach lessons, and they decide whether students achieve lesson objectives. They are in the best position to know what their lessons are expected to achieve and what the content of tests should be to assess the achievement of lesson objectives. However, although it is not difficult to construct simple instructional prescription tests to assess achievement of lesson objectives, many teachers have not been taught how. In-service training should be provided for teachers who have not learned how to construct simple, lesson-based instructional prescription tests.

Many published tests reviewed in the handbook are designed to be instructional prescription tests. They are constructed to pinpoint deficiencies in subskills needed to master a major skill being taught (e.g., reading) so that the deficiencies can be remediated through corrective instruction. It should be pointed out, however, that in many cases the whole is greater than the sum of its parts. Remediation of subskills needed to master a major skill such as reading does not ensure that students will be able to read.

Achievement Certification Testing

Achievement certification decisions are made before report cards are issued, promotion decisions are made, and graduation decisions are made. Test results (from what are usually called summative tests) typically play a major role in certifying student achievement. In some states, to prevent social promotion, students are required to score above a certain level on tests to meet minimum requirements for promotion and graduation.

To be able to defend achievement certification decisions, results of criterion-referenced tests must be used. The sole purpose of schooling is to instill desired learning, which is manifested in the attainment of school learning objectives. Learning objectives are in fact criteria that educators and students work together to eventually achieve. Therefore, criterion-referenced tests are most appropriate for certifying the achievement of school learning objectives.

Norm-referenced achievement tests indicate how the test performances of students who take the test compare with one another (e.g., their percentile ranking). However, they do not indicate the extent to which students achieve local learning objectives. Consequently, there is virtually no basis for determining and correcting inadequate student achievement of specific objectives. Grading on a normal curve requires that a normal distribution of grades be assigned, for instance, a normal distribution of "A's," "B's," "C's," "D's," and "F's." Under these conditions a certain number of students would be assigned an "A" even if, for example, the best students answered only 40% of the test questions correctly. Conversely, a certain number of students would be assigned an "F" even if, for example, they answered fewer than 20% of the test questions incorrectly. Using the normal curve, it is possible for students to receive an "A" without achieving learning objectives, and it is possible for students to receive an "F" even if they achieved learning objectives. Since grades are supposed to indicate achievement of school learning objectives, grading on a criterion-referenced basis is more defensible than grading on a norm-referenced basis. The "average" has been used to highlight the tyranny of norm-referenced conclusions. That is, people who have one foot on a hot stove and one in a freezer would, on the average, be comfortable.

Many states and school districts prompted by the motivation to excel naïvely establish goals requiring all their students to score above-grade-level norms on authorized achievement tests (e.g., state-developed accountability tests). In the long run, it is improbable, if not impossible, for all students to score above the average on a state test when the norms of the test are derived primarily from the scores of their own students.

Findings of a number of research studies indicate that norm-referenced achievement tests do not adequately assess the achievement of the learning objectives of local school curricula. A low norm-referenced test score may not indicate students' failure to achieve the learning objectives of the curriculum they were taught. Furthermore, students' scores on a norm-referenced achievement test, such as a reading test, may vary considerably depending upon the reading curriculum taught in their school. And students who were taught a given curriculum may score quite differently on different norm-referenced achievement tests that purport to assess achievement in the same subject area (Good & Salvia, 1989; Jenkins & Pany, 1978; Shapiro & Derr, 1987). When there is little or no correspondence between the content of achievement test items and the content of the curriculum taught, test results are meaningless.

Referral Testing

Criterion-referenced tests typically are used to make referral decisions. Students are referred for further testing because their actual criterion score on a screening test suggests they may have a functional impairment that, if not corrected, can prevent them from succeeding in school and otherwise. How a person's performance on a screening test compares to others is not usually the basis for making referral decisions. The important factor is that he or she is below a criterion level of adequate performance. The National Society for the Prevention of Blindness established criteria for referring students for further eye examination. Referral criteria have also been established for hearing and other basic functions. It should be noted, however, that in certain cases the norm may be the most useful criterion for making referrals. For instance, when attempting to determine whether a preschooler is developmentally delayed and not ready to begin school, the child's performance on significant developmental indicators is compared to the average child of the same age. There are a number of scales that have been constructed to enable young children's performance to be compared to the developmental norms of their age group.

Some published tests are constructed to be both norm-referenced and criterion-referenced. Most are standardized nationally normed achievement tests such as the Stanford Achievement Test Series. Census data is used to establish representative national norms, stratifying the norming sample on several variables, such as geographical region, urban-rural communities, socioeconomic status, and public-nonpublic status. School curricula are reviewed in a representative cross-section of regions of the nation in an effort to construct criterion-referenced tests for the nation. Test items are developed to represent the objectives and content common to the curriculum of American schools. However, the objectives and content common to the nation may not be sufficiently representative of the objectives and content of the curriculum of a particular school. In addition, the items on the test may have little relevance to the evaluation of student learning of the lessons teachers are teaching on a day-to-day basis.

In conclusion, two alerts need to be heeded. Since grades, promotion, and graduation implicitly, if not explicitly, certify achievement of school learning objectives, it is usually indefensible to base grades, promotion, or graduation on norm-referenced status alone. Furthermore, since nationally normed achievement tests are constructed to assess achievement of learning objectives common to the curriculum of American schools, they are most often inadequate for assessing achievement of lesson plan learning objectives of teachers and may well be inadequate for assessing the curricular learning objectives of schools. Tests that try to serve the purpose of all educators may not serve the purpose of any.

KEY TESTING ISSUES

Testing has never been given more attention than it is getting now, and testing issues have never been more volatile and provocative. Heated debates on accountability testing are taking place on the national level and in every state of the union. Teachers have always been questioned about their testing, but now teachers' competency to construct tests and assign grades based on student test performance is being challenged. The accuracy of admissions tests and intelligence tests in assessing student potential and predicting student success is being reevaluated. Following are discussions of major testing issues that educators must face and deal with.

Quantitative and Qualitative Description in Testing

As indicated, the purpose of a test is to describe particular characteristics in a particular population. Descriptions may be quantitative, qualitative, or a combination of the two. Quantitative descriptions are usually test scores; qualitative descriptions are usually words (used to describe categorical events). It is usually the case that published, nationally standardized tests constructed by psychometricians provide performance scores of the test taker and little else. However, both quantitative and qualitative description is important in testing. When teachers score tests and return them to students with marginal notes, the notes help students understand the mistakes they make. And when students are required to explain the answers they choose on a scored multiple-choice test, their explanations help teachers diagnose the causes of their mistakes, which in turn aids teachers in prescribing corrective instruction. It is important that educators understand the contributions of quantitative and qualitative description to testing and teaching and relevant issues that affect educational practice.

In recent years, qualitative descriptions of student performance have become more popular. Educators are being taught qualitative description techniques developed and promulgated by ethnographers. Many educators are eager to learn techniques of ethnographic description, partly because they see the limitations of using only test scores to describe student performance, and possibly because qualitative description programs are being offered as an alternative to quantitative description programs in college.

Many colleges of education are now teaching qualitative research methods as well as quantitative research methods in their introduction to educational research courses, and both are now being included in textbooks for such courses. Educators seeking advanced degrees are now finding that they can do either quantitative or qualitative research for their thesis or dissertation. Moreover, there are alternative qualitative and quantitative research tracks that have been developed at many colleges of education that offer advanced degrees. Educators can take courses in either track to prepare for the type of thesis or dissertation they choose. Educators who are not strong in math are welcoming a chance to do qualitative research. Colleges that have developed a qualitative research track to supplement their quantitative research track are adding qualitative research specialists to their faculty. They are naturally advocates of qualitative research and enlist students to enroll in their courses so that they can solidify their position on the faculty. This inevitably results in competition between those who practice and advocate qualitative research methodology and those who practice and advocate quantitative research methodology.

From my reading of qualitative research studies, it appears that ethnographers use only qualitative description, even when quantitative description could easily be added and would aid them in drawing warranted conclusions. Suppose, for example, an ethnographer were interviewing students to determine their attitude toward school. In one of their categorical comparisons they might choose to compare boy students' and girl students' attitude toward school. In a qualitative analysis they might report students' answers to the question, "How do you feel about school?" To make the comparison they might report the answers of boy students and girl students and make inferences from the comparison between their answers. Although quantitative comparisons could also be done to provide a more complete description and contrast, they omit adding quantitative analysis. As an illustration, they could simply determine the percentage of negative statements toward school made by boy students and by girl students and conduct a statistical test to determine whether there is a significant difference between them. This would make their comparison more complete.

Advocates of quantitative description argue that it is more discriminating and precise than qualitative description; that is, test scores better discriminate and more precisely describe student performance. Advocates of qualitative description argue that the quantitative descriptions of student performance are not nearly as discriminating and precise as they are proposed to be; the discrimination and precision is more pretended than real. The finely graded scores created to measure psychological phenomena such as learning are not nearly as accurate as those created to measure physical phenomena such as weight. Furthermore, test scores cannot describe the depth and breadth of student performance as well as qualitative description.

Teachers' comments about their students are often discredited as subjective, biased judgments, whether they are written in letters, on tests or report cards, or offered orally. They certainly should not be discredited if they accompany students' test scores or grades and provide diagnostic information to help students correct their misapprehensions and improve their performance. Furthermore, the judgments of well-trained professionals such as doctors, lawyers, and accountants are routinely accepted. Only when there is a need for a second opinion is one sought—for example, when the attending professional requests one, when there is client skepticism, or when there is a malpractice suit.

Although qualitative research became popular in education after quantitative research, from an evolutionary perspective qualitative description of phenomena tends to emerge before quantitative description. For instance, when Harvey discovered the circulatory system his descriptions of blood coursing through blood vessels were qualitative. As we learned more about blood over time, we were able to measure properties of the blood and supplement qualitative descriptions with quantitative description. Nowadays, we are able to quantitatively describe many properties of the blood. Before seeing a doctor for a periodic physical exam, a small sample of blood is extracted and analyzed to derive a large number of measurements of properties of the blood such as cholesterol and triglycerides. In addition, blood pressure is measured quantitatively. In short, quantitative descriptions generally add to the knowledge accumulated through qualitative description. Variables tend to be discovered and qualitatively labeled before quantities of the variable are measured.

Unfortunately, the schism that has developed between quantitative description and qualitative description in education has masked the advantages of combining the two. Suppose, for instance, that students were being taught what water is. Qualitative description might be used first to build on students' present knowledge. To begin with, water might be described as a liquid that people can often see through and drink to maintain their health, and that about 70% of the earth's surface is covered by water. Seventy percent, of course, is a quantitative description that adds to the qualitative description. To further students' knowledge, the components of water might be described. Students might be told that water is composed of hydrogen and oxygen. To use quantitative description to add precision and dimension to the qualitative description, the teacher might add that water consists of two parts of hydrogen to one part of oxygen between 32 degrees and 212 degrees Fahrenheit. As you can see, qualitative and quantitative description can complement each other to provide a more complete and accurate description. When teaching students about qualitative and quantitative description they need to be taught that qualitative variables vary in kind (e.g., male-female). Quantitative variables vary in amount or degree (e.g., length).

The extent to which educators use quantitative and qualitative description in testing depends on the type of decisions they need to make.

Admission Decisions

Some educational institutions use test scores to deprive applicants of admission. For instance, some colleges require that students exceed a minimum SAT score to qualify for admission. Other educational institutions may use both quantitative and qualitative information. They may use test scores and qualitative criteria such as whether or not applicants have worked, have participated in extracurricular activities, or have held leadership positions in organizations. They may also conduct interviews to obtain additional information to make an admission decision.

Placement Decisions

Test scores often count heavily toward making placement decisions. For example, IQ scores weigh heavily in determining whether a student is placed in classes for educable or trainable mentally retarded students. Qualitative description may count more toward making other placement decisions. For instance, teachers' written recommendations as well as student test scores and grades may count toward gifted class placement.

Instructional Prescription Decisions

When making instructional prescription decisions, teachers need to provide students with both quantitative and qualitative descriptions of their test performance to help them improve, when need be. Teachers can provide test scores and explain the test scores to students. They can explain to students what the test scores indicate in terms of achieving the learning objectives of the class. In addition, the teacher might explain to students how to correct the mistakes they made to help the students succeed. This qualitative information can be communicated to students in writing and/or in a personal conference.

Both qualitative and quantitative information provided by student test responses enable teachers to help students. Objective tests typically require students to choose the "correct answers" on a test in order to obtain the quantitative information necessary to score the test. If, in addition, students are required to explain their answers, their qualitative explanations can provide valuable diagnostic information. Such explanations often reveal the faulty thinking or procedures students used in deriving incorrect answers, which in turn enables teachers to provide more helpful feedback to students and to prescribe more effective corrective instruction for them. Both quantitative and qualitative information is valuable in providing feedback and planning corrective instruction.

Achievement Certification Decisions

Test scores usually count significantly in certifying student achievement. At the end of every report card period teachers are obliged to derive student grades from students' prior performance on tests. Qualitative comments may be added on report cards as space allows, and students are usually invited to arrange conferences with their teachers for further explanations of report card grades. However, the most propitious time for remediation is before report cards are issued to maximize students' opportunity to earn passing grades. Providing qualitative feedback after report cards are issued serves more to justify teachers' grades than to help students succeed. The aim should be to prevent failing grades rather than to explain them after the fact. Failure has a devastating effect on students, and a sizable amount of research demonstrates that failure breeds failure. Students who fail to be promoted or drop out of school have a history of previous failure (Friedman 2000, pp. 26, 27). Research also shows that the vast majority of students are able to achieve required learning objectives through high school. The primary difference among students is the amount of instruction they need to achieve the objectives (Block & Anderson, 1975). So the challenge is to provide all students all the instruction they need between report card periods to enable them to earn passing grades at the end of each report card period. This will reduce student failure, the dropout rate, and the need for social promotion. Corrective instruction based on diagnostic information derived from instructional prescription testing is the key to preventing student failure.

Referral Decisions

To make referral decisions, educators need to acquire both quantitative and qualitative information on underlying conditions that may be preventing student learning. Before any testing is done, teachers usually record qualitative information based on student observations that make them suspect an underlying ailment. For instance, a teacher may observe a student squinting and straining as he fails in an attempt to read aloud an assigned passage before the class. This may prompt the teacher to record the incident in a file and plan to administer a vision test such as a Snellen Eye Chart test. The teacher may then report the vision score and his anecdotal records to the student's parents, school administrators, and/or the student in an effort to encourage further diagnoses by a vision specialist.

In Defense of Teacher-Made Tests

Teacher-made tests are frequently discredited. Allegedly teachers' tests lack the technical adequacy of tests developed by psychometricians. More specifically, the validity, reliability, and objectivity of their tests are challenged, yet the facts do not confirm these allegations. In a study by Bloom and Peters (1961) it was demonstrated that teachers' high school grades are the best predictors of college grades when interschool differences in grading are statistically removed. The correlation between teachers' high school grades and college grades increases from about .50–.55 to .70–.75, making teachers' high school grades by far the best predictor of college success. Other evidence also confirms the adequacy of teachers' grades. Rank in high school class, which is based on teachers' grades, predicts college success better than the SAT. The SAT is developed by psychometricians given a substantial budget to establish (1) the technical adequacy of the test and (2) national norms which are reported in impressive comprehensive test manuals replete with statistical data. Teacher-made tests are developed by teachers who do not have the psychometric training that psychometricians do and cannot claim to be test experts. On the other hand, teachers know more about the learning objectives of their schools' curriculum and their own lesson plans, as well as the idiosyncrasies of their students, than the psychometricians who develop sophisticated standardized nationally normed tests. Not only are teacher-made tests defensible, they are in many ways superior to standardized, nationally normed tests. It's time for teachers to stop feeling inadequate when their tests are discredited and learn how to defend the achievement tests they construct. The following question-and-answer sequence addresses the major relevant issues.

Are Teacher-Made Tests Necessary?

Since teachers are not test experts, should they stick to teaching and let test experts do all the testing? The answer is no. Instructional prescription tests are best constructed by teachers. Instructional prescription tests are instruction-embedded tests that are constructed to determine whether students have sufficiently learned a recent topic they were taught and are ready to progress, or if they need corrective instruction before proceeding. Although teachers must pursue school learning objectives, they have a certain amount of academic freedom in planning lessons to achieve the objectives. Teachers are in the best position to develop tests to determine the extent to which their lessons have been learned. It has been shown previously that nationally normed tests do not adequately assess the learning instilled by particular lessons taught by particular teachers.

The overwhelming majority of commercially prepared norm-referenced tests are intended, first and foremost, to discriminate among test takers efficiently. Developers of norm-referenced tests try to strike a balance between including the minimum number of test items to allow reliable discrimination and including enough items to ensure content validity. The practice results in relatively insensitive tests that are unable to discriminate small changes in pupil performance. . . . Teachers who are concerned with pupil mastery of specific concepts and skills are in a better position to test a narrow range of objectives directly and frequently. . . . Teachers are the only ones who can match testing and instruction. (Salvia & Ysseldyke, 2001, p. 217)

So teacher-made tests are absolutely necessary to assess the learning of particular lessons planned and taught by the teacher.

There are other disadvantages of published achievement tests when compared to teacher-made tests. Many are scored exclusively by the publisher, and results may not be back for months. Most are paper-and-pencil tests, and therefore use only one mode to probe for student learning. Teachers can probe for learning in many additional ways, such as by orally questioning students, assigning projects, requiring students to produce products, and observing their actions when testing to see if students have learned a skill. Some students do not do well on paper-and-pencil tests because they are not accomplished readers and do not perform well under time pressure. Teachers when using their own tests can extend the time of testing to give students a chance to do their best. In addition, published tests that use a multiple-choice format, as many do, cannot adequately assess learning as well as teacher-made tests. In using oral questioning, observing students' actions, and evaluating student projects and products, teachers can assess learning in greater depth and breadth. Also, teacher-made tests usually provide more diagnostic information than published tests. Scores on published tests indicate the test items that were answered incorrectly, but they do not indicate why a student answered the test items incorrectly. Teachers can not only observe the correctness of students' answers, they can also observe the process students used to obtain the answers. This enables teachers to correct students' misapprehensions so that in the future they can answer correctly questions they previously missed. Finally, teacher-made tests enable teachers to provide more complete and valuable feedback to students than published tests; they allow teachers to provide qualitative as well as quantitative feedback. For example, on a teacher-made essay test, teachers can not only score the test, they can write suggestions for correcting mistakes in the margin for students to study and discuss with the teacher.

Teacher-made instructional prescription tests are almost always superior to published tests. One exception comes to mind; that is, when teachers are following an instructional program that prescribes lessons in small sequential increments and tests to assess the learning of the lessons. Some published programs of instruction are tightly structured in this way.

Should Teachers Construct Achievement Certification Tests?

Teachers do certify student achievement when they assign grades to students, and it is almost always the responsibility of teachers to assign grades. Teachers are most often able to assign grades based on the instructional prescription testing they do. To supplement instructional prescription testing, before report cards are issued, teachers can prepare achievement certification tests covering all lessons taught during the grading period. Whatever the teachers' testing plans may be for a grading period, as illustrated previously, teachers can establish and share with students their plan for testing, scoring tests, and assigning grades based on test performance. There is no apparent reason why teachers who have learned how to construct instructional prescription and achievement certification tests that cover their lesson plans should not continue to assign grades based on their test results. Teachers who have not learned how to construct instructional prescription tests and simple achievement certification tests to assess learning of their lessons, and how to derive grades from test scores, need to be taught these skills.

Whether teachers' tests and grades should be used to certify students for promotion or graduation is another matter. As you know, social promotions have become so common and so many illiterate students have graduated from high school that accountability legislation has been passed to curb social promotion and hold accountable educators who are responsible. Although teachers' grades have proven accurate in the past, nowadays their grades are suspect. Because society has become more litigious, teachers who issue failing grades are more likely to be challenged and sued. Not only are teachers apprehensive about being sued, they are apprehensive about their limited ability to defend their grades. As a rule, teachers are not test experts and have not been taught how to defend the tests they construct and the grades they assign. When they learn how they will be less likely to give social promotions and will be sufficiently qualified to certify who will be promoted and graduated. Then there will be no need to rely on inadequate nationally normed achievement test results for certification. The shortcomings of nationally normed achievement tests for certifying achievement of school learning objectives were evidenced by previously cited research. To reiterate, it was shown that students who were taught a given curriculum scored quite differently on different nationally normed achievement tests.

Teacher-made achievement tests might prove to be superior to norm-referenced tests for certifying students for promotion and graduation when teachers know enough about testing to confidently defend the achievement tests they construct. Meanwhile, with accountability legislation in place, state and nationally normed tests will be used to guard against social promotion.

Are Teacher-Made Tests Inferior Because "They Are Not Standardized"?

The allegation that teacher-made tests are not standardized is unreasonable. "They cannot be considered unstandardized because students usually receive the same materials and directions, and the same criteria usually are used in correcting student answers" (Salvia & Ysseldyke, 2001, p. 216). Teacher-made tests are also standardized in a way nationally normed tests cannot be. Standards are often set for the interpretations of teacher-made test results. For instance, standards can be designated indicating how student performance on a test will count toward their grade. Standardized nationally normed test results do not indicate how well students are progressing toward the achievement of their school's learning objectives, only how they compare to students in the nation who have taken the same test. This knowledge might make the students feel better or worse about themselves depending on how they compare, but it does not let them know the grade they will be assigned or specific inadequacies in achieving school objectives. Standards for comparison on norm-referenced tests, such as percentile rank, may not be relevant to achievement standards in a specific school.

Are Teacher-Made Tests Inadequate When They Are Not Norm-Referenced?

Since the primary purpose of teaching is to achieve learning objectives, and learning objectives are criteria, teacher-made tests certainly need to be criterion-referenced. Although norms can be derived for criterion-referenced tests, there does not appear to be a compelling reason for deriving norms for teacher-made tests.

Again, the advantage of a norm-referenced test is that it enables one to compare a student's performance with the performance of other students who have taken the test. It is implied, if not made explicit, that teacher-made tests do not permit such comparisons to be made. This allegation is patently untrue. Using criterion-referenced, teacher-made tests, one student's performance can indeed be compared to other students' performance on the same test. For instance, comparison can be made between a student who answered 10% of the questions on a test correctly and a student who answer 90% correctly, and such a comparison might be meaningful and useful to the teacher. If teachers were using peer tutoring to help underachieving students in their class, they would assign students who score high on their tests to tutor students who score low. On the other hand, it is no apparent functional advantage to teachers in their daily work to know how their students' performance compares to other students in the nation on a norm-referenced achievement test. Although it might boost teachers' vanity to know that their students performed well on a nationally normed test, it is doubtful that norm-referenced data could be used to improve the teacher's teaching or students' learning of lesson objectives. However, it can be of value for educators, school boards, and departments of education to use nationally normed test results to identify schools where student achievement is relatively poor—for example, in many isolated, indigent, rural areas and inner-city poverty pockets. In our mobile society, students need to be able to leave their neighborhood to compete for jobs or to attend school. In addition, they need to be able to compete for jobs when new industry moves to their locale and attracts outsiders to employment opportunities.

Can Teachers Construct Defensible Tests?

Prominent publishers of tests that are sold nationally provide funds that enable their psychometricians to conduct a number of research studies to establish the validity, reliability, and objectivity (inter-rater reliability) of the tests they publish and to report supportive statistical findings in their test manuals. Given sufficient funds, most tests can be tested and revised until they are valid, reliable, and objective. Test developers who may have the expertise but lack sufficient funds are often unable to amass sufficient data to convince test experts who review and critique their tests that their tests are valid, reliable, and objective. Although teachers do not have the time or money to conduct competitive studies, they can defend the achievement tests they construct if they learn how. Although teachers' defense of their tests will not include the sophisticated statistical findings that psychometricians can provide, teachers may have less difficulty than the psychometricians in communicating their corroborating findings to judges, juries, lawyers, and members of grievance committees in a language they can understand, that is, in plain English devoid of erudite psychometric terminology. It is not unusual for psychometricians, like experts in other highly technical fields, to set high technical standards for tests that only professionals with their training can meet. This tends to make it difficult for educators to construct tests that meet the standards without employing their expertise. However, it does not follow that teachers cannot develop quality defensible tests without using the sophisticated methods psychometricians use.

Consider the following example of how a teacher might defend a failing spelling grade—perhaps to a parent, a grievance committee, or a court of law. If teachers can learn to defend the failing grades they assign, they have the knowledge necessary to defend retaining the students in grade or preventing students from graduating.

First, the teacher would defend his method of arriving at the spelling grade. "The grade is given on the basis of students' performance on spelling tests. Students who spelled 90% or more of the words correctly earned an 'A,' 80% to 89% correctly earned a 'B,' 70% to 79% correctly earned a 'C,' 60% to 69% correctly earned a 'D,' below 60% correctly earned an 'F.' Johnathan earned an 'F' because he spelled only 75, or 50%, of the 150 words taught correctly." Educators can be enlisted to testify that it is not unusual to use these percentages to assign grades.

Next, the teacher would defend the adequacy of the spelling tests he constructed and used.

Defending the Validity of the Test

The teacher would defend the validity of his tests by showing how he established (1) test item validity and then (2) test response validity for her spelling tests. To establish test item validity he might say, "To achieve the assigned spelling objective students I teach must learn to spell 150 words. I constructed my spelling tests to include test items that require students to spell each of these words. Here are the words students are required to spell. Here are the test items that require students to spell each of the words. As you can see, the test items match curriculum requirements."

To demonstrate test response validity the teacher might say, "Here is proof that students' responses on the test indicate the extent to which they achieved the spelling objective, learning how to spell the 150 words. As you can see from inspecting the tests, the more words students spelled correctly, the higher the grade they earned."

Defending the Reliability of the Test

The teacher would defend the reliability of his spelling test by showing that students were given repeated opportunities to spell the 150 words and graded accordingly. "There were two test items constructed per word. If students answered both items correctly, I concluded that they knew how to spell the word correctly. If students answered both items incorrectly, I concluded that they did not know how to spell the word correctly. On the written test format, if students answered one correctly and one incorrectly I asked them to spell the word orally to settle the issue. Thus students were given repeated opportunities to spell the words before grades were assigned."

Defending the Objectivity of the Test

To defend the objectivity of his spelling test, the teacher would need to show that qualified test scorers agree on the scoring of the test. The teacher might say, "To avoid subjective bias in the scoring of the test, I developed a scoring key for scoring the test. Next, I asked a colleague of mine who teaches spelling at the same grade level as I do to critique the scoring key. I then met with her to discuss any disagreements we might have. To achieve agreement we changed the key until both of us were satisfied with the accuracy of the key." The collaborating teacher can testify that she helped develop and agrees with the accuracy of the final scoring key.

Most of the achievement tests teachers construct are one of two types: *scoring-key achievement tests*, just exemplified, and *scoring-criteria achievement tests*. For scoring-key achievement tests, a number of test items are constructed for which there is one correct or best answer. For each test item, students select an answer from at least four alternatives to reduce the chance of guessing the correct answer. Multiple-choice and matching-test items are examples. True-false items do not qualify because there is one chance in two of guessing the correct answer. A scoring key is developed that designates the correct or best answer for each test item. Typically, scoring-key achievement tests are paper-and-pencil tests that are completed by the student and can be scored either by hand or by machine. As indicated, all correct or best answers on the scoring key need to be reviewed by a qualified teacher who teaches the subject at the same grade level, and disagreements need to be reconciled.

For scoring-criteria achievement tests, scorers observe and compare student performance to criteria designating desirable performance. Scorers assign higher scores to students whose performance they judge conforms more closely to the established criteria. Scoring criteria are used to score essay exams, compositions, term papers, student projects, student products, oral exams, and other student performances for which a scoring key is not feasible or appropriate. When criteria are numerous and complex, scorers need to be trained to apply them correctly, and their competence needs to be certified before they are allowed to score student performance. Training and certification are required to administer and score many tests that require scorer judgment, such as the Thematic Apperception Test, a projective test, and some intelligence tests such as the Stanford-Binet.

It seems to serve the purpose of many professionals to argue that teachers are unable to construct valid, reliable, and objective tests. Psychometricians can argue that teachers do not know enough about measurement and statistics to competently design and conduct research studies to establish the validity, reliability, and objectivity of their tests. As well meaning as these allegations may be, they serve to elevate the need for and importance of their expertise without unduly demeaning teachers. Most teachers would readily admit that they have not taken courses in psychometrics and have not been trained to conduct sophisticated research, and many might add that they do not have a strong urge to learn how. Further, teachers and the school administrators who supervise them would argue that teachers do not have the time to conduct validation, reliability, and objectivity studies, even if they did have the expertise.

But times have changed. Teachers now need to be prepared to defend the tests they construct for their own peace of mind as well as to be prepared for the times they may be required to defend them. Teachers would be less reluctant to learn how to defend their tests if they knew that they did not need to be researchers and psychometricians to be able to defend them. They can learn how to defend them in a short time. Moreover, once they learned how, it would not take nearly as much additional time to prepare a cogent defense as test experts may claim. They can establish the validity and reliability of their tests by themselves. Validity can be provided for as they construct the tests. Reliability can be provided for by arranging for the repeated assessment of the achievement of learning objectives. Objectivity can be provided for by establishing a collaborative relationship with a colleague who teaches the same subjects at the same grade level, as explained. To build objective tests, it is only necessary to obtain agreement from a colleague that your scoring key or scoring criteria are accurate. However, it can be advantageous to extend cooperative efforts in building tests. Work can be cut in half if a partnership is formed in which each partner builds half the tests and the other ensures objectivity. In addition, each test can be used over and over again. So it is not necessarily true that teachers do not have time to build defensible tests. They may be able to save time if they learn how in college courses and in-service training.

Furthermore, cooperative efforts can extend beyond ensuring test objectivity. Each of the partners can critique the other's tests in their entirety. Test directions, the amount of testing time allowed, and the validity and reliability can be evaluated as well. In this way, each can testify in support of all aspects of the other's tests.

In conclusion, defending the adequacy of tests needs to be put in perspective. Teachers may be able to defend their tests to parents, grievance committees, and courts of law better than to psychometricians. Furthermore, teachers, more than psychometricians, may be better able to defend the tests they construct to parents, grievance committees, and courts of law. Teachers may not know as much about sophisticated measurement and statistical techniques as psychometricians, but these technical nuances are not always critical and are difficult to communicate to the untrained. On the other hand, teachers probably know more about the content of the subject they teach and test than psychometricians, and teachers are able to communicate about the subjects they teach in plain English. Grievance committee members, lawyers, judges, and members of juries probably were taught the same subjects when they went to grammar and high school but probably have not studied psychometrics.

Multiple Testing

Since many educational decisions are based on multiple test results, it is important to consider the pros and cons of multiple testing in its many forms. Multiple testing may apply to repeatedly administering the same test to corroborate findings, or it may apply to using different tests to abet or assess student performance. One previously discussed reason for multiple testing is to establish test-retest reliability. Grades are supposed to indicate the achievement of learning objectives in subject areas. To reliably assign grades to students, it is necessary that students' test performance consistently indicates the extent to which they have achieved a learning objective. This requires that students be tested a number of times so that inconsistencies in their performance can be reconciled within limits. Reliability cannot be established without multiple testing.

Multiple testing can also be used to maximize students' opportunity for success. Some students perform better in one test mode than another. On the other hand, test modes are adopted more for the benefit of educators than for the benefit of the students taking the test. Timed group paper-and-pencil tests with scoring keys or criteria are preferred by educators when feasible because they are easier to administer and score. However, some students do not do their best on this type of test and some do not function well under the pressure of timed tests and/or may be handicapped because they are poor readers. Such students, for instance, can be expected to perform better on an untimed oral test, or they might perform better when assigned to produce a product when they have a specific amount of time (say, two weeks) to complete it. Time limits are imposed on most school assignments, but none create more anxiety than being mandated to complete a paper-and-pencil test in a matter of minutes.

If student failure is to be reduced, students who fail conventionally administered tests need to be tested in modes that can be more favorable to them. Specifications of most academic learning objectives do not include time limitations on student responses. For instance, to manifest achievement of spelling objectives, students must be able to spell specified words correctly. There is usually no specification that students need to spell words within a time limit. Therefore, it is unnecessary and handicapping to students to limit their testing time on a spelling test to assess their achievement of a spelling objective. Only when an objective specifies that particular behaviors must be performed within a specified time is it necessary to consider response time when assessing achievement of the objective. For instance, an objective an athlete might need to achieve to make the team might be to run a specified distance under a specified time limit.

There are other ways testing procedures can be designed to help failing students succeed. When tests previously administered to students indicate the extent to which students achieve learning objectives but do not provide diagnostic information, diagnostic tests can be given to pinpoint student inadequacies so that they can be remediated. Effective corrective instruction cannot be prescribed if teachers do not know the student inadequacies that caused the student to fail an achievement test.

There is no need to abandon conventional testing procedures. However, there is a need to determine whether a student who fails a conventional timed test assessing achievement of a learning objective that does not specify time limits can pass the test if time limits are removed. Eliminating testing time limits might eliminate a sizable number of student failures. We should at least make an effort to find out. The cost of additional testing time is infinitesimal compared to the cost of the present student failure rate. Remediation of student failures is very costly, as is the rehabilitation of illiterate youth who have left school and are unemployable and frequently engaged in drug addiction and crime. It might also be beneficial in the long run to find out how many students who fail conventional written tests pass oral tests covering the same subject matter. Whether or not research proves that accommodating the testing mode to the student pays off, students are entitled to accommodations that enable them to pass the tests they are required to take. As difficult as it might be, such accommodations are frequently made for disabled students.

Students have a right to accommodations in testing. This right is derived mainly from the Fourteenth Amendment of the Constitution and expressed in the Americans with Disabilities Act of 1992. Modifications in testing that may be provided under the law and are provided by many states include extended testing time, individualized testing, and modifications of the test presentation or response format, such as oral testing. In a very real sense, student failures are disabled citizens who may become social wards if not given an adequate education. They are entitled to be tested in ways that enable them to show what they know.

Using one type of test rather than another to enable students to reveal their knowledge in toto does not need to compromise the validity, reliability, and objectivity of any specific test they may be given. All tests need to be valid, reliable, and objective. However, as multiple testing fads come and go, some stray from validity, reliability, and objectivity requirements (e.g., portfolio testing). Consider the following analysis of portfolio testing.

Feuer and Fulton (1993) defined portfolios as "collections of a student's work assembled over time" (p. 478). According to Airasian (1996), their purpose is "to collect a series of pupil performances or products that show the pupil's accomplishments or improvement over time" (p. 162). Portfolios have been used for a long time for evaluation in fields such as art, music, photography, journalism, commercial art, and modeling (Winograd & Gaskins, 1992). Presently the use of portfolios has extended beyond creative activities. Now they are used in academic areas such as reading, math, and science to document and evaluate student achievement and have been recognized as an evaluation tool in many states, including Vermont, Kentucky, California, and Pennsylvania.

A portfolio might include classroom assignments, work developed especially for the portfolio, a list of books that have been read, tests, checklists, journal entries, completed projects, response logs, artwork, and so on (Polin, 1991). Completed projects may be group as well as individual projects. A wide variety of work may be included in portfolios, depending on what students as well as teachers may want to include. Teachers also have been urged to allow students to establish their own performance standards (Tierney, Carter, & Desai, 1991; Winograd & Gaskins, 1992). Although teachers may be responsible for the evaluation of portfolios, many contend that the evaluation process should be broadened to include evaluations by the students themselves, their classmates, their parents, and other family members (Adams, 1991; Arter & Spandel, 1992; Salend, 1998; Tierney et al., 1991; Winograd & Gaskins, 1992). So it is quite possible that portfolio performance standards, the work included in portfolios, and evaluations of the work may not be directly related to required class learning objectives. What is equally troubling from a testing perspective is the questionable validity, reliability, and objectivity of many portfolio assessment formats. The reliance on the subjective judgments and evaluations of portfolio entries by students, their teachers, classmates, parents, and other family members casts doubt on the objectivity of portfolio assessment, and the inclusion in the portfolio of students' work that may not be relevant to the required class learning objectives casts suspicion on the validity of portfolio assessment. And the inclusion of such a diverse variety of student work makes it difficult to establish the reliability of portfolio testing. In short, portfolio assessment as it is frequently practiced does not conform to validity, reliability, and objectivity requirements.

Without specific criteria to guide the evaluation of multiple and complex samples of students' work, portfolio assessment is prone to subjective scoring. Dwyer (1993) indicates that testing reforms encourage subjective evaluations. Reform efforts allow "increasing tolerance for subjective judgment—even intuition—over precise decision rules and logical operations" (p. 269). Oosterhof (1994) also challenges the objectivity of portfolio assessment. In evaluating writing portfolios in Vermont, the average correlations among the scores of different raters ranged for .33 to .43 (Koretz, 1993, p. 2). McLoughlin and Lewis (2001) challenge the validity of portfolio assessment: "Validity is another concern, particularly the predictive validity of portfolio assessment in relation to future success in school and adult pursuits" (p. 156).

Furthermore, it can be a monumental and practically insurmountable task to aggregate the scores of the various student entries in a portfolio to derive a grade. For instance, suppose a teacher wants to assign a grade to a student based on the 16 items in the student's portfolio prepared for a zoology course. The portfolio contains one videotape of a student's class presentation on cats, two papers about snakes, six journal entries on the student's reactions to birds, three reports on frogs, lizards, and salamanders, one report and pictures of a field trip to the zoo, and three journal entries on the student's reactions to evolution. Scores are derived for each item on a scale from 1 to 6, 6 being the highest rating. How does the teacher combine the scores to assign a grade? Different aggregation procedures will yield different summary evaluations, which might result in the assignment of different grades.

To further complicate assigning grades to students, samples of group projects are frequently allowed to be included in students' portfolios. Report cards are generally issued to individual students, not groups of students. In order for report card grades to be valid they must be derived from the performance of individual students. And it is difficult, if not impossible, to determine individual performance from a group project.

It is important to recognize that although groups are taught in school, individual students are supposed to learn and do learn most subject matter that is taught. Group learning is primarily an issue when teamwork is taught—for instance, in sports and business. Teamwork learning is more a concern of athletic coaches and production line supervisors than school teachers.

As Salvia and Ysseldyke (2001) state, "Currently there appears to be more conviction than empirical support for the use of portfolios. Even given the most optimistic interpretation of the validity of portfolio assessment, we believe that the current literature provides an insufficient basis for an acceptance of portfolio assessment on any basis other than experimental" (p. 259). So many educators have made so many different recommendations for conducting portfolio assessment that it is difficult to determine exactly what portfolio assessment is and what it is not. There is no reason why a portfolio assessment format cannot be derived that is not subject to the criticisms levied against it. There is certainly nothing wrong with assembling samples of students' work as a basis for assigning grades to students. Still, in order to defend any multiple-testing technique, attention must be paid to validity, reliability, and objectivity requirements for each testing instrument used and to the aggregation of test scores to assign grades to students.

Since results of multiple testing are used to conclude about student performance, it might be helpful to review the sequence of conclusions that must be defended leading to the promotion of students.

Promotion: Promotion must be defended based on the grades students were assigned.

Grades: Grades must be defended based on student achievement of learning objectives.

Learning objectives: Achievement of learning objectives must be defended based on students' test results.

Test results: Test results must be defended based on the validity, reliability, and objectivity of the testing procedures used.

Validity, reliability, and objectivity: Test validity, reliability, and objectivity must be defended by showing that requirements for each have been met.

Educators need to learn how to make and defend the conclusions at all of these levels.

Assessing Student Academic Potential

Many of the decisions educators make are based on attempts to assess student academic potential. Admissions decisions are based on assessments of student potential both on the college and grade school level. The SAT, for example, is used to assess student potential to succeed in college. The Vane Kindergarten Test is used to assess students' potential to succeed in their initial entry to grade school. Attempts are also made to assess student potential for the purpose of making placement decisions once students have been admitted to school. The Stanford-Binet Intelligence Test has long been used to place students in programs for the mentally retarded and sometimes gifted programs. And, in a sense, student potential is assessed to make instructional prescription decisions. That is, teachers assess students' potential when on the basis of achievement test results they decide that students are ready to progress to a more advanced topic in an instructional sequence. Similarly, student potential is assessed when making achievement certification decisions. When students are promoted to the next grade, educators are certifying that they have the potential for success. However, when social promotions are given, certification is falsified. Finally, student potential is assessed to make referral decisions. When a teacher asks a student to identify letters on a reading chart, he is attempting to determine whether poor vision is impairing the student's potential to learn. There is little doubt that assessment of student academic potential is pertinent to most of the academic decisions educators make that affect students' schooling. However, there is a great deal of doubt about current methods of assessing student academic potential.

Aptitude tests are supposed to assess potential, and some do. For instance, if a person is tested to see if they are color-blind and they fail, it is unlikely that they have the potential to succeed as a color coordinator. And if a person fails miserably on a motor coordination test, it is unlikely that they have the potential to succeed as an airline pilot. Unfortunately, academic aptitude tests leave a lot to be desired in assessing students' academic potential. Furthermore, the distinction between academic aptitude and academic achievement tests is quite fuzzy. In many cases test items in academic achievement tests and so-called academic aptitude tests are quite similar. Frankel and Wallen (1996) clarify the problem:

> Aptitude tests are intended to measure an individual's potential to achieve; in actuality they measure present skills and abilities. . . . The same test may be either an aptitude or achievement test depending on the purpose for which it is used. A mathematics achievement test, for example, may also measure aptitude for additional mathematics. (p. 130)

Intelligence tests are often classified as aptitude tests because intelligence is supposed to be an inherent, stable trait that remains constant over the years. Intelligence tests are thought of in particular as being academic aptitude tests because it is thought that intelligence is required for academic achievement. Yet, there is a similarity between the items in some intelligence tests and academic achievement tests.

The Stanford-Binet Intelligence Test is a seminal work that has been used to assess academic potential for years. It is most effective in identifying mentally retarded students and distinguishing between the educable mentally retarded and the trainable mentally retarded, who have different learning potential and benefit from different instructional programs. The ultimate confirmation of any test of academic potential is how well it predicts academic success. It is interesting to note that the lower scores on the Binet are accurate in identifying students with low potential for achievement, but the higher scores on the test are not nearly as accurate in identifying students with exceptionally high potential for achievement. For instance, it cannot be predicted that students who score at the genius level on the test will make any great discoveries or inventions, or be outstanding in other mental achievements. It should be expected that the low end of the Binet scale is a more accurate predictor of achievement than the high end. Binet's original purpose in constructing his test was to distinguish students who are able to succeed in normal public school classes and those who cannot and need special education.

The Stanford-Binet test is often classified as an aptitude test because IQ scores of people tend to be stable over time. However, the stability of the IQ is an artifact of the way the scoring of the test was conceived:

$$IQ = Mental\ Age \div Chronological\ Age$$

The mental age functions as an achievement test score and increases each year, as achievement is supposed to. But it is devised to increase in proportion to a person's chronological age. For this reason, IQ tends to remain constant over time. Educators who use IQ tests to place students in special education classes base their decisions more on mental age scores than on IQ scores because mental age differentiates performance level more than IQ scores. So in many, if not most cases, mental age scores function as achievement scores and are more sensitive than IQ scores for making placement and other decisions.

It is also the case that test items on group paper-and-pencil IQ tests for older students are similar to the test items in achievement tests for older students. So it should be no surprise that measures of academic achievement predict future academic achievement at least as well, and often better, than academic aptitude tests. For example, of measures presently in use, rank in high school class is the best predictor of college success. Yet large sums of money are spent each year administering the SAT and the ACT, even though rank in high school class and other achievement records are available to colleges free of charge. Although aptitude tests may be valuable for some purposes, such as to identify mechanical aptitude, there is little reason to use measures of academic aptitude rather than measures of academic achievement to predict future academic success. Furthermore, there is every reason to reconsider previous conceptions of academic aptitude.

One of the more meaningful and distinct definitions of academic aptitude was conceived by Carroll (1963). He defines aptitude as the amount of time needed to learn a task under optimal conditions. He has shown through his research that most students can achieve high school learning objectives. The difference among students is the amount of instruction needed over time to achieve the objectives. So students with greater aptitude tend to achieve learning objectives in a shorter period of time with less instruction. From his perspective, students who learn more rapidly have greater aptitude for academic success. Carroll's conception seems most significant under usual classroom conditions. During regularly scheduled classes teachers do not have sufficient time to provide all students with all the instruction they need to succeed. Under these constraints academic success depends on speed of learning. On the other hand, if all students were given all the instructional time they need to achieve learning objectives, there would be very little difference in their academic achievement through high school.

It is well to remember that in America the purpose of assessing student academic potential is not to "weed out" students or to determine who shall be educated. Under our Constitution, all students have an equal right to receive an education to fulfill their potential, whatever that may be. Still, it is only since World War II that America has made an all-out effort to provide equal educational opportunity for all. Laws improving educational opportunities for minority and handicapped students were passed and enforced, making their constitutional rights more attainable. In the spirit of the Constitution, it is not acceptable to deny an education to students because they did not pass a test of academic potential, but rather to continue to teach students until they decide after coming of age not to further their education. Of course, after high school, tuition and attendant costs can be a deterrent. The purpose of assessing academic potential is to make better admission, placement, instructional prescription, achievement certification, and referral decisions.

In the final analysis, the most inexpensive and accurate way to assess student academic potential is on the basis of their previous academic achievement records. No additional testing should be necessary, with one exception: Assessment of academic potential should be obtained for preschoolers who are entering school for the first time to maximize their opportunity for success. Assessing their potential to succeed in school requires more than assessing academic potential; basic social and self-care skills need to be assessed as well.

Rather than continue to search for new tests to better assess academic potential, there is reason to believe that more can be gained by investigating new ways to use existing student academic records. Bloom's previously cited research (1961) serves as a case in point. It showed that high school grades are better predictors of college grades than was previously known. His research revealed that grades in different schools vary greatly. For instance, an "A" in one school is equivalent to a "C" in another school. By statistically removing interschool differences in grading, the correlation between high school and college grades increased substantially. This 1961 study shows compellingly that teacher grades can be credible. However, in this era of social promotion they may not be.

Accountability Testing

The accountability movement gained impetus after World War II, first from legislation to provide better educational opportunities for minority students and then handicapped students. Accountability initially focused on providing services. For example, busing was mandated as a service for minority groups, and Individual Education Plans

(IEPs) were mandated for handicapped students to enhance their education. Initially, schools were held accountable for providing these services, and an attitude of indulgence and permissiveness was extended to minority and handicapped students to be in compliance with the law, to compensate for previous injustices and neglect, and to assuage national guilt feelings. Educators were held responsible for providing the services. Slowly but surely, schools transformed to comply with the regulations, and educators were committed to make a special effort to help those students. To avoid problems, educators became more permissive in grading students. Failure creates problems for students and often for the educators who fail them.

Although programs for handicapped and minority students continued to be held accountable for providing legally mandated services, a new accountability dimension, outcome accountability, was added. Programs were held accountable for producing student benefits and achievement. For instance, programs for the handicapped were required to show that they produced measurable benefits for handicapped students. The new Individuals with Disabilities Act (IDEA) of 1997 required state departments of education to account for the educational outcomes of all students with disabilities. This tended to make failure more conspicuous and to increase social promotion. In short, social promotion entails promoting to the next higher grade students who have not achieved the required learning objectives of the previous grade.

At least three factors appear to underlie and provide incentive for social promotion: (1) pressure to be more indulgent and helpful to educationally neglected students, (2) reluctance and inability of educators to defend the failing grades they assign, and (3) pressure to show that educational programs are producing student success.

Social promotion enables educators to mask student failure and to show that they and their programs are effective. Students who previously might have failed are now succeeding, and parents and students are more pleased than ever. If image were everything, the illusion might have continued, but the euphoria based on the false certification of student achievement could not last. Too many youth produced by our schools were burdens to society. This gave rise to a new kind of outcome accountability.

Legislated achievement accountability emerged as a defensive reaction to the conspicuous consequences of social promotion. When illiterates and undereducated dropouts and high school graduates entered the job market, employers found them incapable of qualifying for any but the most menial jobs. Employers found it necessary to provide literacy training to prepare job applicants for entry-level positions. Business organizations had to invest large amounts of time and money for literacy training, even more during labor shortages. It became obvious that American schools were not doing their job, and consequently employers were being saddled with the costly responsibility of providing literacy education for American youths.

To remedy the problem the business community protested, and through powerful organizations that advocated their interests, such as their chambers of commerce, pressured government legislators to enact accountability laws to stop social promotions. Eventually, as the seriousness of the problem became more evident, accountability laws and testing were legislated. Schools were exposed and embarrassed by the legislation, and educators were now faced with either preparing students to pass accountability tests or suffering severe penalties. Educators whose students did not pass the tests could be discharged, and schools with a high percentage of their students failing the tests could be restaffed, even closed, depending upon the accountability laws in particular states.

Legislated accountability testing adds to the burden of previously established accountability legislation passed to ensure equal educational opportunity for all American youth. No nation in the history of the world had ever before embarked on such an enormous undertaking. All of the accountability legislation has been disruptive, requiring massive changes in educational practice, but few reforms have had as much of an impact on American education as accountability testing. Mandated restaffing and closing of schools that fail to meet standards and the discharging of teachers who fail to meet standards struck dread into educators and threatened school systems as they had never been threatened before.

Quite naturally, educators defended themselves by dredging up many of the hackneyed, knee-jerk objections used over the years:

- Teachers teach much more than is tested on accountability achievement tests. The tests lack validity.
- Parents have a much greater effect on student achievement than schooling.
- Student failure is attributed more to lack of student motivation and ability than teacher incompetence.
- Students fail despite the effective instructional techniques used by their teachers.
- The classroom is a jungle. Classroom violence and disruptions often make it impossible to teach.
- Teachers are given too many other assignments that keep them from teaching.
- Classes are much too large to permit effective teaching.
- Many students fail because they are absent too frequently.
- Academic freedom has diminished. Teachers are unable to take sufficient initiative to improve the achievement of their students.

And so on. Although there may be truth in some of these statements, they only explain student failure; they do not account for failures of the educational system. They are to a great extent nonresponsive to the accusation implicit in achievement testing accountability legislation, which suggests by innuendo that educators might be falsely elevating the achievement of their students to cover up their incompetence and to avoid recriminations. As brutal as this innuendo may be, it reflects the view of many reformers who have little difficulty documenting social promotions and the massive number of students who fail to achieve basic required learning objectives.

Since there are no records of social promotion, the best way to estimate its effects is to observe its aftermath in college and the workplace. In 1995, 29% of college freshmen were enrolled in remedial reading, writing, and math courses (U.S. Department of Education, 1998). In the workplace, employers report that they spend approximately 14.2% of their training time teaching elementary reading, writing, arithmetic, English language skills, and other fundamentals; 46.9% of employees reported receiving such remedial training during their current employment (Bureau of Labor Statistics, 1995).

The following illustrates the seriousness of the student failure problem.

Student failures are debilitated citizens suffering from a learning deficit that incapacitates them. Although student failures do not die from their malady, both they and society are handicapped by it. To better appreciate the size of the problem, consider that the United States has approximately 275 million citizens. Considering a dropout rate of from 10% to 15%, about 27 million to 40 million of our citizens are socially debilitated. Considering a student failure rate of over 30%, over 80 million of our citizens are socially debilitated. Considering the number of students who graduated high school by social promotion, the problem is even more severe. If over 80 million of our citizens were debilitated by a physical disease, we would declare an epidemic and a national emergency. But because student failures have no physical symptoms, they are much easier to ignore. (Friedman, 2000, p. 6)

As distasteful as it may be for professionals to have their competency assessed, educators are accustomed to being routinely evaluated by students, parents, superiors, and/or certification and accreditation agencies. But outcome accountability is different. First, educators are not being judged on their actions. They are being judged on the results they produce—the academic achievement of the students in their charge. Second, being held accountable is more like being publicly "on trial" than being evaluated. Third, outcome accountability is being imposed by government law to ensure that educational institutions do not falsify student achievement and pawn off on society citizens that can neither serve America's or their own best interests.

Most educators and other helping professionals are licensed based on their test performance and continue to hold a license based on their on-the-job performance. Outcome accountability is changing that. Increasingly, the competency of professionals is being determined not on their performance, but rather on the results they produce. Results that have not been publicized before are being recorded and exposed so that professionals may be held accountable. For instance, the success rate of surgeons is now being exposed and used as a criterion of their competency. It seems to be a sign of the times.

Extended government control of the quality of education is also a sign of the times. Many Americans are vehemently opposed to extending government authority to intervene in their affairs. Freedom is precious. However, they want and pay taxes for protection, a most fundamental function of government. Protection against harm extends beyond armed forces and police protection. Governments provide "watchdog" functions to protect people against harmful products and practices and establish agencies such as the Food and Drug Administration (FDA) to provide the protection. These agencies go beyond providing protection; they promote welfare. For example, the FDA advocates that Americans follow dietary recommendations specified on a food pyramid chart to promote their health. Such services are considered vital by many Americans because in the free enterprise system individuals and organizations can be counted on to serve the public interest only when it is in accord with their own interests. When there is a disparity the public is frequently slighted. The American Medical Association was formed to serve doctors, not patients. The National Education Association was founded to serve teachers and other school employees, not students or their parents. It is the job of government agencies to serve the public weal and to hold professionals and organizations accountable for the services and products they provide to the public. For this reason, government agencies issue permits, certificates, and licenses to practice and enforce laws that prohibit illicit practice.

Both federal and state governments have established departments of education to promote effective education—society's means of perpetuating and improving its culture. Since states have authority to provide education for its citizens, they issue permits, certificates, and licenses that allow schools and educators to practice. Although the federal government does not directly govern education, legislators pass laws and appropriate money that influences educational policy and practice. And recently the federal government began increasing its influence and promoting outcome accountability based on student test scores—for example, by passing the No Child Left Behind Act. On the state level, approximately 40 states have initiated outcome accountability testing in their schools and have developed their own accountability achievement tests. The tests are used not only to determine whether accountability standards have been met, but also by school administrators to make instructional and organizational decisions.

Unfortunately, promises made by ambitious political, civic, and educational leaders to achieve excellence in education have resulted in the establishment of unrealistic, even impossible, test achievement goals. For instance, some states have set as a goal that all of their students will be able to score above the grade level norms of a state-developed achievement test used in enforcing accountability legislation. This goal is unrealistic in the long run because the state norms for the test are derived from the scores of the students in the state. As the students' test scores improve, the norms will rise, too.

Accountability test scores are a driving force. When they serve as a basis for a state taking over and restaffing a school and also for paying bonuses to schools and faculty for raising test scores, educators are prompted to do what they can to boost scores. Attempts to elevate scores have been known to include improving instruction, teaching to the test, and giving students answers to the test questions ahead of time.

Since outcome accountability is here to stay, it is important for educators to understand it so that they can accommodate it. In outcome accountability the desired outcome is specified, and all those who contribute to the outcome are viewed as a work team responsible for achieving the outcome. An attempt is made to hold individual team members responsible for their contribution to the outcome to stop buck-passing, but there is always some overlap in responsibility, making it difficult to ascribe responsibility and to hold individuals accountable for their contribution to the outcome.

In education, the outcome sought is not elusive. The primary purpose of education is to instill desired learning—so the outcome sought is student achievement of learning objectives. Since educational institutions and the educators in them are responsible for the achievement of their students, they are to be held accountable for their students achieving required learning objectives. If their students fail, they have failed. When their students continue to fail over time, remedial action is initiated to enable students to succeed. Remediation includes an attempt to upgrade the skills of the educators responsible. If this does not work, the educators are replaced.

However large and complex an educational system may be, the basic accountability unit of concern is the school. Schools are where educators instill desired learning. The educators usually held accountable for student achievement are school administrators and teachers. School administrators are usually held accountable for student achievement in their schools; teachers are held accountable for student achievement in their classrooms. Accountability pressure creates dilemmas for both teachers and school administrators (see Haas, Haladyna, & Nolen, 1990).

School administrators are, of course, responsible for managing all aspects of schooling that make instruction possible. Some responsibilities have a more direct effect on student achievement than others. For instance, they are responsible for hiring and upgrading the skills of their teachers, and for implementing cogent admission and placement practices so that students in each class are capable of achieving class learning objectives.

Teachers are most directly responsible for student achievement. They manage the immediate milieu in which learning takes place and provide the instruction that produces student achievement. If educators are to make accountability work to their benefit, they must not lose sight of the overriding goal of education—student achievement of learning objectives—and they must keep in mind that teachers must provide the quality and quantity of instruction their students need to succeed. Other responsibilities notwithstanding, school administrators must focus on providing competent teachers to teach students who are ready to achieve the learning objectives they are assigned to achieve.

Educators need to do more than understand and accommodate outcome accountability; they need to take action to shape both educational practice and accountability testing. Outcome accountability may be the province of the state, but state governments are new at it and their groping efforts are presently creating as many problems as they are solving.

Unfortunately, in constructing their accountability testing programs some states have extended their testing objectives far beyond the accurate certification of student achievement to curb the devastating consequences of falsifying student achievement, social promotion, and graduating students who are ill prepared for college or modern job requirements. State accountability testing programs have tended to become much more encompassing in the breadth, depth, and amount of learning they attempt to assess, and the impact they are having on education. Must educators be held accountable for everything they teach? Are educators to have no discretion?

Accountability testing would be less of a problem for educators and state departments of education if accountability tests were used initially to determine whether *minimum* standards for promotion from grade to grade have been met. Each state could set its own minimum standards, which would at least ensure mastery of basic academic skills. They may or may not need to have their own achievement tests constructed to determine whether their minimum standards have been achieved. There are many nationally standardized achievement tests that are constructed to assess curriculum objectives common to most states. These tests cover all major subjects taught in grades K–12 in the United States. They can be administered in their entirety in about six hours and machine scored and analyzed by the publishers. Although published nationally, standardized tests may not be adequate for testing the achievement of all of the objectives of a particular curriculum, but they might well be sufficient for determining whether minimum standards have been met. Once states' testing programs have proven successful in ensuring that minimum standards for promotion have been met, social promotions will have been curbed and graduates will have the competencies that have been certified. Then state testing can be expanded as desired.

Teachers and schools could be encouraged to go beyond meeting minimum accountability standards to enrich their students' educations, but they would need to be held accountable for constructing adequate achievement tests to evaluate the achievement of the added learning objectives and for not promoting students who fail their tests. The achievement of enrichment learning objectives must be evaluated by adequate tests, and achievement certification must not be falsified.

Unfortunately, accountability regulations are not confined to assessing achievement of minimum standards and ensuring that educators are held accountable for testing and accurately reporting the achievement of learning objectives. Because limitations of accountability testing are not being circumscribed, to be safe educators must teach to the test. This throttles academic freedom and makes enrichment education too risky. Students are taught the answers to tests and graded on their recall of answers (Schnepel, 1991). In the final analysis, present accountability testing squelches both educator and student initiative and innovativeness. In the frenzy to stop the social promotion of academically inadequate students, the majority of students are being penalized. For education to serve America, it must enable students to learn more than the basics. All students should be given the opportunity to be educated to their full potential. All students who have the capability should be elevated to the cutting edge of knowledge so that they can extend it.

Innovation is the lifeblood of America's progress and leadership in the world. American business and industry invest a substantial portion of their profits in research and development to innovate better products and services to sell. Our federal government invests huge sums of money in research and development for innovations to improve public health and welfare in areas that are not profitable to private enterprise, and many charitable gifts are earmarked to find cures for debilitating and fatal diseases and to improve education.

It may be necessary for accountability testing to assess the achievement of minimum standards to ensure that our youth have the basic knowledge they need to survive in our society. It is both unnecessary and damaging to America's spirit and best interests to have accountability standards become the standards for American education.

Although in outcome accountability students are tested, it is not appropriate to use their test scores to make decisions pertaining to the students—not admission, placement, instructional prescription, achievement certification, or referral decisions. Each of these decisions needs to be based on test results relevant to the decision. One test score is seldom sufficient to make the decisions about individual students. The purpose of accountability testing is to enable decisions to be made about the educational institutions and educators whose job it is to educate the students in their charge. The problem is that at present they are not well designed for this purpose.

When accountability tests have been revamped, they will need to be used more judiciously in the evaluation of educator performance. Reward and punishment of educators will need to be based more on the achievement of students in their charge than is currently the practice. It is presently less difficult to discharge educators for overt bizarre or offensive actions towards colleagues, superiors, students, and parents than for instructional incompetence. If enough complainants attest to their undesirable actions, discharging the offender is easy to justify. In contrast, amassing evidence of instructional incompetence is much more difficult. It is necessary to prove that the students of allegedly incompetent educators do not achieve required learning objectives. Because learning is covert, evidence of educators' instructional incompetence must be inferred from the test scores of their students. To complicate matters, very instructionally competent educators may act offensively. With the emphasis on politically correct behavior, contentious, rude, nonconformist, yet instructionally competent educators are not likely to endure. On the other hand, educators whose students are not succeeding have been tolerated if they were "well liked" and adept at attributing their students' misfortune to circumstances beyond their control. It's not easy to judge educators solely on the basis of their students' learning.

Current accountability laws leave much to be desired. They tend to establish accountability standards, testing programs to determine whether the standards are met, and penalties for schools and educators that do not meet the standards, as exemplified previously. Penalties indicate incorrect action. They do not, in themselves, indicate correct practice. Until ineffective instructional practices are replaced by effective instructional practices, student achievement cannot be expected to increase appreciably. It's a shame because many educational practices that research shows are effective have not been adopted (see Friedman, 2000).

Educators need to work in their own behalf to instill educational practices that research shows increase academic achievement. They can no longer afford to defend the status quo, adopt the fad of the moment, or surrender to political pressure, artful sales pitches, or the personal opinions of would-be experts. Educators can shape their own destiny if they base more decisions on research results and learn how to construct and evaluate the tests they use.

REFERENCES

Adams, M. (1991). Writing portfolios, a powerful assessment and conversation tool. *Writing Teacher*, 12–15.

Aiken, L. R. (1988). *Psychological testing and assessment* (6th ed.). Boston: Allyn & Bacon.

Airasian, P. W. (1996). *Assessment in the classroom*. New York: McGraw-Hill.

Anastasi, A. (1988). *Psychological testing* (6th ed.). New York: Macmillan.

Arter, J., & Spandel, V. (1992, May). Using portfolios of student work in instruction and assessment. *Instructional Topics in Educational Measurement*, 36–44.

Block, J. H., & Anderson, L.W. (1975). *Mastery learning in classroom instruction*. New York: Macmillan.

Bloom, B. S., & Peters, F. (1961). *Use of academic prediction scales for counseling and selecting college entrants*. Glencoe, IL: Free Press.

Bureau of Labor Statistics. (1995). Washington, DC: Department of Labor.

Buros Institute of Mental Measurements. (2001, July). Announcement of their 14th yearbook.

Carroll, J. (1963). A model of school learning. *Teachers College Record 64*, 723–733.

Compton, C. (1984). *A guide to 75 tests for special education*. Belmont, CA: Fearon.

Dwyer, C. A. (1993). Innovation and reform: Examples from teacher assessment. In R. Bennett & W. Ward (Eds.), *Construction versus choice in cognitive measurement: Issues in constructed response, performance testing, and portfolio assessment*. Hillsdale, NJ: Erlbaum.

Feuer, M. J., & Fulton, K. (1993). The many faces of performance assessment. *Phi Delta Kappan 74*, 478.

Fitzpatrick, A. R. (1983). The meaning of content validity. *Applied Psychological Measurement 7*, 3–13.

Frankel, J. R., & Wallen, N. E. (1996). *How to design and evaluate research in education*. New York: McGraw-Hill.

Friedman, M. I. (2000). *Ensuring student success: A handbook of evidence-based strategies*. Columbia, SC: Institute for Evidence-Based Decision-Making in Education.

Friedman, M. I., & Fisher, S. (1998). *Handbook on effective instructional strategies: Evidence for decision-making*. Columbia, SC: Institute for Evidence-Based Decision-Making in Education.

Good, R., & Salvia, J. (1989). Curriculum bias in norm-referenced reading tests: Demonstrable effects. *School Psychology Review 17*(1), 51–60.

Haas, N. S., Haladyna, T. M., & Nolen, S. B. (1990). *War stories from the trenches: What educators say about the test*. Paper presented at the annual meeting of the American Educational Research Association, Boston.

Hammill, D. D., Brown, L., & Bryant, B. R. (1992). *A consumer's guide to tests in print*. Austin, TX: PRO-ED.

Jenkins, J., & Pany, D. (1978). Standardized achievement tests: How useful for special education? *Exceptional Children 44*, 448–453.

Kelley, T. L. (1927). *Interpretation of educational measurement.* Yonkers-on-Hudson, NY: World Press.

Keyser, D. J., & Sweetland, R. C. (Eds.). (1984–1994). *Test critiques.* 10 vols. Austin, TX: PRO-ED.

Koretz, D. (1993). New report on Vermont portfolio project documents challenges. *National Council on Measurement in Education Quarterly Newsletter 1*(4), 1–2.

McLoughlin, J. A., & Lewis, R. B. (2001). *Assessing students with special needs.* Upper Saddle River, NJ: Merrill/Prentice Hall.

Messick, S. (1989). Validity. In R. Linn (Ed.), *Educational measurement* (3rd ed., pp. 3–103). Washington, DC: American Council on Education.

Nunnally, J. C. (1978). *Psychometric theory.* New York: McGraw-Hill.

Oosterhof, A. (1994). *Classroom applications of educational measurement* (2nd ed.). New York: Merrill/Macmillan.

Polin, L (1991, January/February). Writing technology, teacher education: K–12 and college portfolio assessment. *The Writing Notebook*, 25–28.

Salend, S. (1998). Using portfolios to assess student performance. *Teaching Exceptional Children 31*(2), 36–43.

Salvia, J., & Ysseldyke, J. E. (2001). *Assessment* (8th ed.). Boston: Houghton Mifflin.

Sattler, J. M. (1988). *Assessment of children* (3rd ed.). San Diego: Author.

Schnepel, K. C. (1991). *An investigation of teachers' views of test preparation activities.* Dissertation, University of South Carolina.

Shapiro, E. S., & Derr, T. (1987). An examination of overlap between reading curricula and standardized reading tests. *The Journal of Special Education 21*(2), 59 n.67.

Sweetland, R. C., & Keyser, D. J. (1991). *Tests: A comprehensive reference for assessments in psychology, education and business.* Austin, TX: PRO-ED.

Tierney, R., Carter, M., & Desai, L. (1991). *Portfolio assessment in reading and writing classrooms.* New York: Christopher-Gorelon.

U.S. Department of Education. (1998). Washington, DC.

Winograd, P., & Gaskins, R. (1992). Improving the assessment of literacy: The power of portfolios. *Pennsylvania Reporter 23*(2), 1–6.

I

Admission Testing and Decision-Making

INTRODUCTION

Admission testing has been an educational ritual ever since the inception of schools and the education profession. To enhance the success of students, it is necessary to assess their readiness to undertake the educational challenges they are applying for. It is also necessary to assess the qualifications of the educators who undertake to teach the students. Education is a noble profession of high calling. Those who are entrusted to educate our youth are expected to be well prepared and qualified to meet high standards.

Still, the education profession seldom gives entry-level testing the attention it deserves. The emphasis seems to be on exit testing of students to determine whether they merit promotion and graduation. Admission testing deserves its due because the success of students depends on providing instruction in accordance with students' readiness to learn and teachers qualified to teach them. To improve education, we need to know more about admission testing and how to benefit from it.

Three types of admission tests will be reviewed in Part I of the handbook: (1) college admission tests, such as the Scholastic Assessment Test (SAT); (2) admission to the education profession: certification tests, such as the PRAXIS tests; and (3) early childhood school admission tests, such as the Metropolitan Readiness Tests.

College Admission Tests

Colleges and universities want to be successful and admit students who will be able to use the opportunity to persist and to perform adequately. Admitting students who cannot graduate is a poor use of resources, both for the school and for the individual. However, establishing admission policies that result in the selection of students who are able to succeed is no easy task. The great variation in the quality of secondary schools and, recently, the quality of home schooling make selection more difficult. This quandary was the motivation for the development of college admission instruments starting in the 1920s with the SAT. These instruments were to provide the uniform data on student performance that was unavailable earlier.

In its earliest form, the SAT was used by exclusive colleges in the Northeast to guide admissions. Later the usage broadened to become national but some regional flavor still remains. The ACT is more widely used in the central section of the United States, while the SAT is used by more students in the East and West.

These tests must be judged on their ability to perform one primary task: to predict college success as defined by grade point average (GPA).

Over the years, additional functions have been added. Colleges like to tout their "high standards" with the publication of average SAT or ACT scores for freshman classes. Comparisons abound. Clearly institutions like to boast if their scores are high. High schools publish their average admission test scores for senior classes. High schools may even find themselves evaluated on the basis of these same scores.

States compare themselves with other states on the basis of these scores. A great cry of dismay goes up in those states that find themselves on the bottom of any score ranking. It is clearly argued that these scores are an accurate measure of the academic quality of schools, and rarely does the discussion concern itself with the actual purpose of the test, which is prediction as opposed to an imagined purpose of academic achievement.

A whole industry has grown up around these tests. Publishers have produced a great number of thick "prep books." You have only to go to your nearest bookstore to see the great variety of expensive publications that can even include computer software. The number of classes and workshops held each year is astronomical. Thus, a great number of people have a stake in keeping these tests widely used.

What are the actual correlations of these tests with college performance? Both have very moderate correlations of about .40 (ACT = .43, SAT = .40). This is about the same correlation as high school grades have with GPA. Since high school GPA is already available, it would seem unnecessary to obtain either SAT or ACT scores.

If both tests were discontinued, the savings would be considerable. Test fees would be saved and materials, course costs, and all the expense of handling and interpreting the data on the part of high schools and colleges would be avoided. All this would be with no real loss of ability to predict college performance.

The wide adoption of undergraduate admission tests and the growth of graduate education led to the development of the Graduate Record Exam (GRE), which is purported to be appropriately used to select applicants for admission to graduate school, to select graduate fellowship applicants for awards, to award teaching and research assistantships, and for counseling applicants to graduate school.

Admission to the Education Profession: Certification Tests

Everyone agrees on the need for the best teachers in all classrooms. However, disagreements begin when the discussion turns to the best methods of achieving that result. Efforts range from making pay and benefits more attractive to restricting entrance into the profession through the administration of certification examinations. It is on these examinations that the following discussion will focus.

Every state jealously guards its long-held prerogative to set necessary minimum qualifications for teachers. These complex regulations are administered by a certification arm of the state department of education in each of the several states and in the District of Columbia. These regulations usually take the form of course requirements as well as test scores. Most educators find that satisfying the course requirements is an easier task than making the required test scores.

If a state decides to adopt a test (or tests) as part of its certification requirements, then there are a number of steps that usually follow. Some states have chosen to develop their own testing programs. There is some advantage to doing this because the locally developed tests have the possibility of being matched better to local requirements, values, and practices than a nationally developed instrument. The disadvantages are that this process is expensive and the development of high-quality, legally defensible tests is no easy task. Security issues also are a concern. In fact, some states, like Georgia and Florida, have abandoned their own tests in favor of nationally available instruments.

Once a state decides to adopt a national test for certification purposes, a long process begins. The state must then decide which of the many available PRAXIS tests to use. The usual process will select only a small percent of the available tests. This alone leads to confusion among test takers because the likelihood of signing up for the wrong test is rather high. The next step is to set cutoffs for each of the adopted tests. The process of setting passing scores is a conflict in itself. Since every state wants a high-quality pool of applicants for positions, this argues for a higher score. At the same time, each state wants an adequate number of persons in the applicant pool, so this argues for lower scores. Sometimes the score setting process is flawed and a score will be set unrealistically high. In some instances the scores are set as high as the 80th percentile, which has the effect of drying up the applicant pool and forcing the restructuring of college preparation programs. The score setting process may become political, where the pressure to choose higher scores in order to "raise educational standards" may be irresistible.

The Educational Testing Service (ETS) has long offered a comprehensive testing program to states for use in certification. Starting in the 1950s, the forerunners of the current tests became available as the National Teachers Exam (NTE). In its original form there were only two portions: a general test called the Commons and a limited array of specialty examinations in areas like elementary education and social studies. Typically states would require the Commons plus one specialty, and passing scores were set as the sum of the two separate tests, since both were on the same scale. Around 1982 the CORE Battery was introduced to replace the venerable Commons. The CORE was composed of three separate tests: General Knowledge (GK), Communication Skills (CS), and Professional Knowledge (PK). Three tests replaced one. States now elected to adopt up to three of these broad-based exams.

The most common usage in the 15 or so years that the CORE was in use was for all three of the tests to be adopted. The first two (GK and CS) were often used as admission tests into college education programs but not for certification. The PK and specialty exams were used for the actual certification procedure. All of these tests were known under the umbrella term NTE.

In the mid-1990s the title PRAXIS gradually supplanted the term NTE. This same period also saw the appearance of the present test forms under the terms PRAXIS I and PRAXIS II. The former took the form of three content exams covering reading, writing, and math administered in both paper-and-pencil (PPST) and computer (CBT) forms. These became the replacements for the discontinued GK and CS instruments and were also used most often as part of the admission process within educational institutions. Two tests became three. PRAXIS II was composed of the Principles of Learning and Teaching (PLT) as well as the growing number of specialty tests for different teaching areas.

The ETS offered the PLT test to states as a replacement for the old Professional Knowledge test. This came in three forms by grade level (K–6, 5–9, and 7–12). It has been fairly common for states to adopt all three forms but only one passing score. It is helpful to note here that the PLT illustrates the current movement toward tests that are more complex in nature by requiring students to answer both multiple-choice and essay questions on one test. It also illustrates the ETS movement toward more demanding reading passages through the incorporation of three case studies in the two-hour instrument.

At present, about two-thirds of the states, the District of Columbia, Guam, the Virgin Islands, and the Department of Defense Schools (DoD) use some form of PRAXIS. Two national organizations also use PRAXIS for national certification purposes. The American Speech-Language-Hearing Association (ASHA) requires passage of either the Audiology (10340) or Speech-Language Pathology (20330) test. The National Association of School Psychologists uses the School Psychology (10400) exam.

The ETS also publishes the School Leadership Series of tests, which includes the School Licensure Assessment, primarily required for the licensure of principals in a number of states, and the School Superintendent Assessment, used for the licensure of superintendents.

In spite of the wide adoption of these series of tests, some serious concerns remain. First, it is difficult to assess the quality of the instruments because of the extreme reluctance of the ETS to make available rather basic measures of the quality of an instrument, such as reliability and validity. Also, norming populations are not well described. Where some data has been released, its availability is extremely limited.

Second, these tests are inadequate for the purposes to which they are used. States use the results of these tests to make career-impacting decisions that hinge on a person's meeting a particular score. However, the tests are not able to measure with that degree of precision. For example, let's consider the widely used PLT, which contains six essay questions. Most states use a passing score of about 160–165. For this purpose, say 165. A testee scoring 164 fails, one making 165 passes. The ETS publishes a "standard error of scoring" as about 2 points (1.8 to 2.82). This means that there are about two chances in three (68%) that different readers for the essays would produce a score variation of about 4 points! To be 90% sure, the spread would be even broader.

Thus, despite their extensive adoption, it seems that the use of the PRAXIS, School Licensure Assessment, and School Superintendent Assessment exams for certifying and licensing educators is highly questionable. It is time for the whole education community to evaluate the use of exams for licensing educators. Professional educator organizations founded to serve the best interests of the educators who belong to them are obliged to take a more active part in evaluating these exams, exposing any inadequacies they find, and ensuring that their use in licensing educators is warranted by the evidence. Educator organizations that need to become more involved in evaluating licensure exams include the National Education Association, the American Association of School Administrators, the National Middle School Association, the National Association of Elementary School Principals, the National Association of Secondary School Principals, the American Federation of Teachers, and the American Association of Colleges for Teacher Education.

Early Childhood Admission Tests

Admitting children to school for the first time involves making very sensitive and significant decisions. Children are entering school at younger ages during the most vulnerable period of their lives. What children experience at that time is of utmost importance for the following reasons.

First, the amount of learning that takes place in the first five years is much greater than in any other five-year period in the span of life. Benjamin Bloom (1964) in his book *Stability and Change in Human Characteristics* demonstrated this rather conclusively. He scientifically analyzed data on human learning over much of the life span and established that learning during the first five years is greater in amount by far than during any comparable time period.

Second, early learning is potent. It takes place at a time when people are most impressionable. One of Freud's greatest contributions was explaining the enormous impact early learning has on people's lives and the trauma it can create. Freud's initial stages of emotional learning and development (the oral, anal, and phallic stages) occur during the first five years of life. Although his disciples add stages of emotional development through adulthood, he built his theory on the preeminence of experience and learning during the first five years. It seems that during the first five, years parents and guardians are responsible for ministering to their offspring and ensuring their survival. They are the primary teachers, and the young child, being aware of its own dependence, regards obeying their edicts to be a matter of life and death. Thus, the potency of early learning emanates from the abject dependence of the young child on its parents and other ministering adults for its very existence.

Third, early learning tends to be permanent. Later learning builds upon early learning rather than replacing it. Freud also offers an explanation for this contention. Although many early experiences are not available for immediate conscious recall, they reside in unconscious memory and continue to have an impact on people throughout their lives. Memories of very traumatic experiences remain repressed in the unconscious but disrupt the functioning of adults and can cause mental disorders. The clergy, too, seem to be aware of the permanence of early learning. Allegedly they have claimed something like the following, "Give a child to the church until he is six and he will belong to the church ever after." Yes, for the most part, early learning is indelible.

Although learning is lifelong, early learning is special. It provides the foundation for future development. A solid learning foundation provides a head start, opens the door to opportunity, and facilitates success in all of life's pursuits. Deficits in early learning form weak links in the chain of development that cause problems throughout life. Nothing is more important than understanding early learning and its consequences so that education can be planned to maximize its benefits and minimize its potential detriments.

There is substantial evidence demonstrating the long-term beneficial effects of more broadly conceived preschool programs. W. Steven Barnett (1995), in his scholarly review of 36 early childhood development programs, shows that they can produce large effects on IQ during the early childhood years and stable, persistent effects on grade retention, special education, high school graduation, and socialization. Fewer students in these programs are retained in grade, assigned to special education programs, or have behavior problems. More graduate high school. However, there is little or no evidence indicating that any gain in academic achievement that may result during preschool instruction is maintained over the long term. It is worth considering that any academic gain that might be generated by preschool programs cannot endure under present conditions, because children who are initially ahead academically are subjected to elementary school curricula that tend to reduce rather than maintain their lead. In classroom instruction, students who have a head start tend not to advance further academically until the rest of the class catches up to them. They can only maintain their lead if they continue to be taught more advanced content than they already know.

It is worth considering that many if not most preschool programs do not concentrate on teaching academic subjects. They focus more on developing social skills, such as cooperating with others and self-care skills such as eating, toileting, and dressing. This does not mean that preschoolers are not capable of learning academic subjects. Research shows that preschool instruction can be very effective in teaching subjects such as math, science language, social studies—even elementary problem solving (Friedman, 2000, pp. 217–226). Those who avoid teaching academic subjects to preschoolers because they contend that preschoolers are too young to learn them are misinformed. It is quite possible to begin teaching academic subjects at an earlier age and to accelerate the teaching of academic subjects from grade level to grade level.

At whatever level children begin school, their success depends on their readiness to learn what is being taught. For this reason the readiness tests children are given and their performance on the tests are of utmost importance. The tests ascertain the extent to which children are ready to enter school and the accommodations that need to be made for them to maximize their opportunity for success. Early childhood admissions tests need to reveal the following readiness information.

Self-help readiness including eating, toileting, dressing, and other self-care skills.

Psycho/social readiness including following the instructions of adults, cooperating with peers, knowing social rules, and not presenting a physical danger to themselves or others.

Language readiness including skill in visual and auditory discrimination, speaking, comprehending stories, and identifying body parts, colors, objects, actions, letters, sounds, and numbers.

Motor coordination readiness including both small and large motor movement capabilities.

Thinking readiness including understanding parts/whole relationships, space relationships, causality, means-end behavior, object permanence.

Although no one test adequately assesses all of the above readiness skills, many are relevant and some do a better job than others. It may be wise to use more than one test as well as caretaker questionnaires to obtain a more comprehensive, in-depth understanding of children's readiness to enter school. However, it should be recognized that it is no longer as legally acceptable as it once was to delay or deny school admission to children who are age-eligible. If parents are not willing to delay admission of their later-developing children, public schools are obliged to accept them and provide them with the appropriate placement and services (see Public Law 94-142, 1975).

The evaluation of preschoolers relies on their achievement of developmental benchmarks or norms. Assessment involves determining whether students are normal, advanced, or developmentally delayed for their age group. Thus, preschool achievement tests are usually norm-referenced. In addition, the procedures that need to be used to test preschoolers are different from procedures used to test older children and adults. Traditionally, test formats in which older students respond to examiners' written or oral questions are neither appropriate nor effective. Frequently in early childhood readiness tests children are given instructions to do something (e.g., touch their nose) and are scored on their ability to perform as instructed. Early childhood readiness testing is both unique and extremely important. In addition to revealing students' readiness for school, they reveal manifestations of inadequacies and disorders that were previously unknown. The earlier these problems are discovered, the less damage they are likely to do and the greater the opportunity to remedy the problems. Many children continue to suffer as adults when problems such as dyslexia go undetected early on. Even if schools are unable to treat problems initially indicated by readiness tests, proper referrals can be made to help the children and aid the often-startled parents.

There are a number of other tests reviewed elsewhere in the handbook that can be used to assess early childhood characteristics. Although they tend to be used for specialized purposes you may want to read about them. They include:

Under "Placement Testing and Decision-Making" (Part II): Brigance Screens; Kaufman Assessment Battery for Children; Learning Efficiency Test; Stanford-Binet Intelligence Scale: Fourth Edition; Woodcock-Johnson Psychoeducation Battery III.

Under "Instructional Prescription Testing and Decision-Making" (Part III): Brigance Diagnostic Comprehensive Inventory of Basic Skills-Revised; Comprehensive Receptive and Expressive Vocabulary Test; Test of Early Language Development, Third Edition.

Under "Achievement Certification Testing and Decision-Making" (Part IV): Mini-Battery of Achievement; STAR Early Literacy: Computer-Adaptive Diagnostic Assessment; Wechsler Individual Achievement Test-Second Edition.

REFERENCES

Barnett, W. S. (1995). Long-term effects of early childhood programs on cognitive and school outcomes. *The Future of Children 5*(3), 25–36.

Bloom, B. S. (1964). *Stability and change in human characteristics*. New York: Wiley.

Friedman, M. I. (2000). *Ensuring student success: A handbook of evidence-based strategies*. Columbia, SC: Institute for Evidence-Based Decision-Making in Education.

Public Law 94-142. Education for All Handicapped Children Act (1975).

College Admission Tests

American College Testing Assessment (ACT),
for testing groups of college-bound high school juniors and seniors
Reviewed by Charles W. Hatch, Ph.D., Educational Research and Measurement

---

Usefulness of the Test for Educators

Test Authors' Purpose

The ACT Assessment Program (AAP) is a comprehensive system of data collection, processing, and reporting designed to help high school students develop postsecondary educational plans and to help postsecondary institutions meet the needs of their students.

The ACT measures the knowledge, understanding, and skills that students have acquired throughout their education. Although the sum total of this knowledge cannot easily be changed, performance in a specific subject matter area can be affected by adequate preparation, especially if it has been some time since students have taken a course in that area.

Underlying the ACT tests of educational development is the belief that students' preparation for college is best assessed by measuring, as directly as possible, the academic skills that they need to perform college-level work.

Decision-Making Applications

High schools use ACT data in academic advising and counseling, evaluation studies, accreditation documentation, and public relations.

Colleges use ACT results for recruitment, admissions, course placement, and self-study.

Many state and national agencies that provide scholarships, loans, and other types of financial assistance to students tie such assistance to students' qualifications, as measured by ACT scores.

Many state and national agencies also use ACT assessment data to provide special recognition to academically talented students. (Wrightman & Jaeger, 1998, p. 4)

Relevant Population

College-bound high school juniors and seniors.

Characteristics Described

There are four content areas that are separately tested: English, mathematics, reading and science. In turn, each of these is broken down into subcategories as follows:

Content Area	*Number of Questions*
English	
Usage/Mechanics	
Punctuation	10
Basic Grammar and Usage	12
Sentence Structure	18
Rhetorical Skills	
Strategy	12
Organization	11
Style	12
Total	75
Mathematics	
Pre-Algebra	14
Elementary Algebra	10
Intermediate Algebra	9
Coordinate Geometry	9
Plane Geometry	14
Trigonometry	4
Total	60
Reading	
Prose Fiction	10
Humanities	10
Social Studies	10
Natural Sciences	10
Total	40
Science (Biology, Earth/Space Sciences, Chemistry, Physics)	
Data Representation	15

Research Summaries	18
Conflicting Viewpoints	7
Total	40

(ACT, 2001b, pp. 7–17)

Here are some sample questions from the four test sections.

English
   Then **there's** the Scotch bonnet, which ought to be called the scorch bonnet, since one walnut-sized pepper can heat a vat of salsa, with an SHU rating of 300,000.
      NO CHANGE
      theirs
      they're
      there are

Mathematics
   For what value of x is the equation $2(x - 6) + x = 18$ true?
      15
      10
      8
      4
      2

Reading
   The prompt is a reading passage of ten paragraphs and about 750 words.
   The passage suggests that one quality the narrator appreciated about the girls she met in India was their:
      feminist viewpoint
      taste in music
      adventurousness
      openness

Science
   All questions follow prompts with data presented in narrative, graphic, or tabular form.
   Prompt: Narrative discussions by two scientists concerning earthquake prediction.
   According to Scientist 2, which of the following assumptions about rocks is a major flaw in Scientist 1's view?
      All rocks react to pressure in an identical manner.
      The cracking of rocks causes an increase in rock volume.
      Radon gas is present in all types of rock.
      All rocks melt when subjected to pressure.
      (ACT, 2001d, pp. 22–45)

Test Scores Obtained

Each student receives a global score on a scale of 1 to 36 that summarizes performance across all four areas (English, mathematics, reading, and science). Each of these four areas also has a separate score reported, also on the 1–36 scale. The seven subscales are reported on a 1–18 scale. These subscales are as follows:

English
  Usage/Mechanics
  Rhetorical Skills

Mathematics
  Pre-Algebra and Elementary Algebra
  Intermediate Algebra and Coordinate Geometry
  Plane Geometry and Trigonometry

Reading
  Social Studies and Sciences
  Arts and Literature

Science
  No subscales

Technical Adequacy

Validity Confirmation

Test item validity provides no significant problems. The process by which the publisher develops items is well documented in the manuals. "First, the objectives for instruction for grades seven through twelve were obtained for all states in the United States that have published such objectives. Second, textbooks on state-approved lists for courses in grades seven through twelve were reviewed. Third, educators at the secondary and postsecondary levels were consulted to determine the knowledge and skills taught in grades seven through twelve prerequisite to successful performance in postsecondary courses. These three sources of information were analyzed to define a scope and sequence for each of the areas measured by the ACT Program" (ACT, 1999b, p. 4).

After items are written, they are "reviewed for accuracy, appropriateness, and fairness by independent content experts, teachers, and curriculum specialists at various high schools, junior colleges, colleges, and universities, as well as persons sensitive to issues of test and item fairness." Items are then pretested "on a representative sample of the ACT Assessment examinee population" (ACT, 1999b, p. 6).

In the area of *test response validity*, problems arise. The ACT has as its primary purpose the ability to predict college grades. It is on this basis that the test must be judged. The median correlation between the four ACT Assessment scores and freshman GPA is .43. This rises to .53 when high school subject grades are added (ACT, 1997, p. 56). Later in the validity discussion the publisher states, "a high degree of accuracy in making admissions can be achieved by using either ACT scores or HS grade average alone as admission criteria" (ACT, 1997, p. 66). This statement makes clear that ACT scores predict about as well as high school grades (correlations approximately .43) and that either adds only about 10% to the prediction strength. This weak relationship does not seem to justify the expense to individuals, high schools, or colleges.

Reliability Confirmation

The Technical Manual (ACT, 1997) reports generally high reliability figures for the ACT. The composite is naturally the highest (since it represents the largest number of items) with a figure of .96. The four tests range from .84 (science reasoning) to .91 (English and mathematics, a tie). The subscales vary from a low of .71 (intermediate algebra and coordinate geometry) to .85 (rhetorical skills). These figures are median reliabilities probably calculated to measure the stability of scores between two test forms taken by the same person (ACT, 1997, pp. 28–32).

These reliabilities are acceptable. The figures for the subscales are lower, but the decisions made from them are not so personally critical and are usually confined to a guidance or advisement function.

Objectivity Confirmation

Objectivity is not a concern with the ACT. All items are multiple choice and scored with a key. Thus there can be no variability in scoring as would happen if, for example, an essay response were included in the English test.

Statistical Confirmation

The Technical Manual and other publications by ACT contain adequate information. The norming populations are well described. It should always be remembered that there is not a single norming population since the revisions are ongoing and that new forms are in a constant process of development. These processes require the publisher to contract for the development of some 10,000 items annually (ACT, 1999b, p. 5). The items are then "pretested on a representative sample of the ACT Assessment examinee population" (ACT, 1999b, p. 6). This is important since the examinee population is *not* representative of the United States population. For example, the population of the eastern United States would be underrepresented on the ACT norms because most students and schools there opt for the SAT.

Special Features

Acronyms

ACT and ACT Assessment.

Levels of the Test

One.

Number of Test Forms

Many. Since the items are banked, the publisher can produce almost as many forms as desired.

Norm-Referenced?

Yes. The scale scores indicate this as well as the "percent at or below," which are percentiles (ACT, 2001, p. 8).

Criterion-Referenced?

No, but the content of the subscales is clearly defined and related to high school course content. This close relationship allows for remediation and feedback. For example, one of the subcategories under mathematics is plane geometry and trigonometry. Weakness here could be directly remediated by review of the content of the two relevant math courses. This directness could be contrasted with the difficulty in remediating a weakness on analogies from the SAT test.

Other Features

The ACT can be administered to students with a wide range of disabilities. Alternate test dates are also available to accommodate persons unable to test on the normal Saturday schedule for religious reasons.

A range of preparation materials is available for purchase from the test maker through their web site, www.act.org.

The publisher makes every effort to gather wide-ranging information from each test taker. This in turn is used to provide the testee and interested institutions with this data related to the testing performance.

Newly available is the CD-ROM preparation material called ACTive Prep, for use by schools ($495 for one school). This enables students to have an interactive response to their answers (ACT, 1999a).

Feasibility Considerations

Testing Time

English: 45 minutes; Mathematics: 60 minutes; Reading: 35 minutes; Science: 35 minutes; Total: 2 hours, 55 minutes.

For Testing Groups? Individuals?

Groups.

Test Administration and Scoring

The ACT is administered about six times a year. The registration fee includes both the administration and scoring. The reporting is detailed and helpful.

The publisher is careful to point out correctly that "It's important to keep in mind that test scores are just one of many indicators that ACT recommends colleges and scholarship agencies use" (ACT, 2001h, p. 2).

Also, to "encourage you not to overinterpret ACT scores, the Student Report gives the ranks of your scores as dashed lines ('bands') that roughly indicate the amount of measurement error involved" (ACT, 2001h, p. 3).

Clear interpretation of results is given for a band of score results. The following is part of the explanation of mathematics scores in the range 28–32, which is quite high on the scale: "Students can solve word problems containing several rates, proportions, or percentages. In probability, statistics and data analysis students can interpret and use information from figures, tables and graphs in coordinate plane; apply counting techniques; and compute probability when the event and/or sample space are not given or obvious" (ACT, 2001h, p. 5).

Test Materials and Approximate Costs

The basic charge for the four tests is $24.

Adequacy of Test Manuals

The published materials are adequate.

Excerpts from Other Test Reviews

"The core tests of the ACT Assessment cover a greater range of subject-matter content than do the SAT I: Reasoning Tests. . . . Another distinction between the ACT Assessment and the SAT Program is components of the ACT Assessment that provide information for guidance and counseling and, perhaps, student placement, in response to students' assessed vocational interests and reported academic strengths, needs and background experiences" (Wrightman & Jaeger, 1998, p. 48).

Ordering Information

Publisher

American College Testing, 2201 North Dodge Street, P.O. Box 168, Iowa City, IA 52243-0168; Phone: 319-337-1000; Fax: 319-339-3021; Web site: www.act.org.

Authors

ACT staff.

Publication Date

First administered in 1959 but has been constantly reviewed and updated since then.

Cautions and Comments

The ACT Assessment tests are more closely related to high school course content than is the SAT I. This allows students, families, and high schools to do preparation and review work in a more focused manner to improve test performance. The instrument gathers extensive information about the test takers to make counseling more effective not only on the part of the high school but also the college. The publisher is careful to present results in ranges, providing reasonable interpretation where possible.

The process of item development is clearly presented and allows a reviewer to approve that process.

The reliabilities estimated are satisfactory and the problems associated with objectivity on other instruments don't exist because this test is entirely multiple choice.

The ability of the ACT to predict college performance is the weak point of the instrument. In fact, this weakness calls into question whether the expenses involved are justified.

References

ACT. (1997). *ACT Assessment Technical Manual.* Iowa City, IA: The American College Testing Program.

ACT. (1998). *Helping students grow.* Iowa City, IA: The American College Testing Program.

ACT. (1999a). *ACTive Prep, the official electronic guide to the ACT Assessment.* Iowa City, IA: The American College Testing Program.

ACT. (1999b). *How the ACT Assessment Tests are constructed.* Iowa City, IA: The American College Testing Program.

ACT. (2000). *Fairness Report for the ACT Assessment Tests 1999–2000.* Iowa City, IA: The American College Testing Program.

ACT. (2001a). *About ACT.* Iowa City, IA: The American College Testing Program.

ACT. (2001b). *Content of the tests in the ACT Assessment.* Iowa City, IA: The American College Testing Program.

ACT. (2001c). *The High School Profile Report.* Iowa City, IA: The American College Testing Program.

ACT. (2001d). *Preparing for the ACT Assessment 2001–2002.* Iowa City, IA: The American College Testing Program.

ACT. (2001e). *Reporting services: Colleges and universities 2001–2002.* Iowa City, IA: The American College Testing Program.

ACT. (2001f). *Selected trends on ACT-tested students.* Iowa City, IA: The American College Testing Program.

ACT. (2001g). *User Handbook, 2001–2002.* Iowa City, IA: The American College Testing Program.

ACT. (2001h). *Using your ACT Assessment results, 2001–2002.* Iowa City, IA: The American College Testing Program.

Wrightman, L. F., & Jaeger, R. M. (1998). *High stakes and ubiquitous presence: An overview and comparison of the ACT Assessment Program and the SAT Program.* Washington, DC: A paper presented to a workshop on higher education admissions by the National Research Council.

Graduate Record Examination (GRE), for testing groups of college upperclassmen and graduates desiring admission to graduate school
Reviewed by Charles W. Hatch, Ph.D., Educational Research and Measurement

---

Usefulness of the Test for Educators

Test Authors' Purpose

"The General Test measures verbal, quantitative, and analytical skills that have been acquired over a long period of time and that are not related to any specific field of study" (ETS, 2001a, p. 8).

For the subject tests: "Each test deals with the subject matter that is emphasized in many undergraduate programs as preparation for graduate study in the field" (ETS, 2001b, p. 5).

Decision-Making Applications

The ETS *Guide to the Use of Scores* (2001b, p. 7) lists the following appropriate uses:

1. Selection of applicants for admission to graduate school

2. Selection of graduate fellowship applicants for awards

3. Selection of graduate teaching or research assistants

4. Guidance and counseling for graduate study

That publication also lists the following inappropriate uses:

1. Requirement of a minimum score on the General Test for conferral of a degree, credit by examination, advancement to candidacy, or any noneducational use.

2. Requirement of scores on the General Test, Subject Test, or Writing Assessment for employment decisions, including hiring, promotion, tenure, or retention.

3. Use of any measure involving a summation of verbal, quantitative and the analytical scores, or any subset of these scores without first conducting and documenting a validity study. (p. 7)

Relevant Population

College upperclassmen and graduates who desire admission to graduate school.

Characteristics Described

The General Test has three sections: Verbal, Quantitative, and Analytical (to be discontinued October 1, 2002).

"The verbal measure tests your ability to analyze and evaluate written material and synthesize information obtained from it, analyze relationships among component parts of sentences, and recognize relationships between words and concepts. The quantitative measure tests your basic mathematical skills and your understanding of elementary mathematical concepts, as well as your ability to reason quantitatively and solve problems in a quantitative setting. The analytical measure tests your ability to understand structured sets of relationships, deduce new information from sets of relationships, analyze and evaluate arguments, identify central issues and hypotheses, draw sound inferences, and identify plausible causal explanations" (ETS, 2001a, p. 8).

The Writing Assessment has two sections: "Present Your Perspective on an Issue" and "Analyze an Argument." This section will replace the Analytical part of the General Test after October 1, 2002 and will be titled "Analytical Writing."

The Subject Tests are available in eight areas: Biochemistry, cell and molecular theory; Biology; Chemistry; Computer Science; Literature in English; Mathematics; Physics; and Psychology.

Test Scores Obtained

Standard scores and percentiles are given for each part of the General Test (scale 200 to 800), the Writing Assessment (scale 0 to 6), and the Subject Tests (scale 200 to 980). Subscales are reported for the Subject Tests in Biochemistry, Biology, and Psychology.

Technical Adequacy

Validity Confirmation

The Technical Manual does not include information on *test item validity*. However, there is considerable evidence presented concerning *test response validity*. The General Test scores have only the most modest correlations with undergraduate and graduate GPAs (.22 to .48).

The Subject tests range from .27 to .51. None of these numbers is high enough to satisfy validity concerns.

Because the Writing Assessment is relatively new, validity confirmation is only in the preliminary stage. One publication from GRE discussed the problem and presents some data which is also not very compelling but shows a moderate relationship which is not quantified but only shown graphically among undergraduate GPA, undergraduate GPA in writing courses, undergraduate GPA in major courses, and the GRE Writing Assessment scores. However, the self-reported grades were restricted in range to "A's" and "B's" (ETS, 2000, p. 1).

Correlations among the three General Test scores ranged from .45 to .66, with the lowest figure between verbal and quantitative sections, which is to be expected. This would be reasonable evidence that the three sections are measuring discrete abilities.

Reliability Confirmation

The internal consistency reliabilities for all three General Test sections are .90 or above. These are excellent.

The lower reliability (.72) for the Writing Assessment is to be expected from the restricted scale (0–6) and the necessity that essays be read by different graders.

Reliabilities (also internal consistency) for the Subject Tests are also all above .90. The subscales with fewer items are slightly lower, and range from .84 to .89.

The *Guide for the Use of Test Scores* also contains extensive data on both the standard error of measure and the conditional standard error of measure.

Objectivity Confirmation

The ETS is to be commended for providing very good information on the objectivity of the GRE.

The Writing Assessment is reported as having a high degree of agreement (.94) between different graders of the same person's writing.

A further research study is reported where there was an exact agreement 59% of the time, within one point 39% of the time, and only 2% of the time was there a difference of over one point on a 0 to 6 point scale.

Statistical Confirmation

The Technical Bulletin contains a wealth of data presented in a very readable form with clear explanations.

Special Features

Acronym

GRE.

Levels of the Test

One.

Number of Test Forms

Many, because the General Test is given by computer and the presentation is adaptive. This means that a testee is given a question of moderate difficulty to start. If answered incorrectly, an easier question follows. If answered correctly, a more difficult question is presented. Thus, two persons taking the same test on the same computer will receive different questions. In some international locations paper-and-pencil forms are still given, which limits the form variety somewhat.

Norm-Referenced?

Yes, as evidenced by the standard scores and percentiles. Information on the norming groups is not presented, and thus no judgment can be made about how representative it may or may not be. It may well be that GRE simply uses data from subjects taking the test to build norms. In fact, tables 1 through 3 of the publication *Guide to the Use of Scores* all contain the phrase "Based on the performance of all examinees who tested between October 1, 1997 and September 30, 2000" (pp. 13–15). Each of these tables gives the relationship between percentile and scaled score for the various tests. The numbers range from a low of 6,753 persons on the Mathematics (rescaled) to 1,075,348 on each of the sections of the General Test.

Criterion-Referenced?

No, but GRE does offer what it calls diagnostic service. This is available on two levels: basic and enhanced. The first is free and the second is only $15. These help a test taker understand his or her weaknesses and provide answer analysis.

Other Features

The GRE is able to accommodate a wide range of handicapping conditions with an array of adjustments.

Users and potential users can access what GRE calls its free Powerprep software to aid preparation. It can even be downloaded from the ETS web site for nearly instantaneous use.

The GRE is a truly international test, offered in 45 different countries from Argentina to Zimbabwe.

Feasibility Considerations

Testing Time

Verbal: 30 minutes; Quantitative: 45 minutes; Analytical: 60 minutes; Writing Assessment: 1 hour, 15 minutes; Total: 2 hours, 50 minutes.

For Testing Groups? Individuals?

The computer forms of the General Test are individual by nature. The international forms of the same are group administered.

The Subject Tests are all paper-and-pencil formats, so they are all group administered but the group may be as small as one.

Test Administration and Scoring

Testees sign up separately for the General Test, Writing Assessment, and Subject Tests. When the General Tests are taken by computer, the scores are given at the conclusion of testing on a scale of 200 to 800. The paper-and-pencil versions are delayed but on the same scale. The Subject Tests are all paper-and-pencil tests on an overall scale of 200 to 980. However, it should be noted that specific tests do not cover that whole scale. For example, the Literature in English test is scaled 300 to 740, while the Physics test is scaled 420 to 980.

The Writing Assessment is reported on a scale of 0 to 6 where the scores on the two segments are averaged. (See ETS, 2001b, p. 23 for a complete description of each score.)

Test Materials and Approximate Costs

Current domestic charges are as follows: General Test $105; Writing Assessment $50; Subject Tests $130. International fees are somewhat higher.

Adequacy of Test Manuals

The test manuals are models for other test makers to emulate. The information is quite complete and presented in an organized, helpful manner. It is especially helpful to find information on how NOT to use the tests. The following quote illustrates this quality. "Regardless of the decision to be made, multiple sources of information should be used to ensure fairness and balance the limitations of any single measure of knowledge, skills, or abilities" (ETS, 2001b, p. 6).

Excerpts from Other Test Reviews

"The GRE General Test is a multiple-choice examination designed to measure the verbal, quantitative, and analytical skills you have developed in the course of your academic career. Because there is a strong correlation between high GRE scores and the probability of success in graduate school, many graduate schools require that their applicants take the GRE General Test" (Brownstein et al., 1992, p. 1).

Ordering Information

Publisher

Graduate Record Exam/Educational Testing Service, P.O. Box 6000, Princeton, NJ 08541-6000; Phone: 609-771-7780; Fax: 609-771-7165; Web site: www.gre.org.

Authors

GRE/ETS staff.

Publication Date

Continuously revised.

Cautions and Comments

The GRE has a long history of providing individuals and graduate schools with information to assist in decisions regarding graduate school admissions and related decisions like fellowships. It is easy to see how this information would aid in making decisions about applicants with wide-ranging abilities and backgrounds when such data as international transcripts would be so difficult to equate.

The test was changed in the year 2002 to eliminate the separate Writing Assessment and incorporate it under the General Test. The ability to administer this test by computer aids in two ways. It allows testees to have a wider range of dates in scheduling a test and it also provides almost instantaneous scores.

The published data is reasonably complete and helpful.

Preparation for this test can be successful and students can improve scores significantly by focusing on a number of areas, such as:

Time management on the test

Reading speed improvement

Reading comprehension improvement

Vocabulary enlargement

Review of relevant content

Understanding of test item formats (for example: Except)

In regard to the last area above, can you imagine the problems a person would have on the GRE if he or she used the meaning "to take" in every one of the many questions containing the word EXCEPT? That is, confusing except and accept.

References

Brownstein, S., Weiner, M., Green, S. W., & Hilbert, S. (1992). *How to prepare for the GRE.* Hauppage, NY: Barron's Educational Series.

Educational Testing Service (ETS). (2000). *GRE Dataviews: Early validity evidence for the writing assessment.* Princeton, NJ: Educational Testing Service.

Educational Testing Service (ETS). (2001a). *GRE Information and Registration Bulletin.* Princeton, NJ: Educational Testing Service.

Educational Testing Service (ETS). (2001b). *Guide to the Use of Scores.* Princeton, NJ: Educational Testing Service.

Preliminary SAT/National Merit Scholarship Qualifying Test (PSAT/NMSQT),
for testing groups of high school students prior to administering the SAT
Reviewed by Charles W. Hatch, Ph.D., Educational Research and Measurement

---

Note: From the test's beginnings in 1927 through 1994, the letters SAT stood for Scholastic Aptitude Test. At that point the name was changed to Scholastic Assessment Test. In 1997 that name was discontinued, and now the test is simply known as the SAT (Kagan & Gall, 1997, p. 1).

Usefulness of the Test for Educators

Test Authors' Purpose

PSAT/NMSQT scores indicate the readiness of high school students for college-level work. In addition to test scores, the Score Report PLUS provides personalized feedback on academic skills and information to help students prepare for college and for the SAT.

The tests assess many of the skills that are important to students' success in college. Because the subject matter of high school courses and high school grading standards vary widely, the tests have been established as a common standard against which student performance can be compared.

Decision-Making Applications

Over 2,000 colleges and universities use SAT scores as part of the admissions process. They use these scores as partial predictors of college success. The PSAT prepares students to take the longer, more complex SAT.

Relevant Population

High school students contemplating attending college. Most generally this test is taken in the junior year.

Characteristics Described

The Verbal section (52 questions) has three subsections:

1. Critical Reading (26 questions)
   Vocabulary in context
   Literal comprehension
   Extended reasoning
2. Sentence Completion (13 questions)
   Content
   Structure
   Functional skills
3. Analogies (13 questions)
   Content
   Abstraction of terms
   Functional skills

The Mathematics section (40 questions) has questions in four content areas:

1. Arithmetic
2. Algebra

3. Geometry

4. Miscellaneous (functions, number theory, statistics, geometric perception, and logical reasoning)

The Writing section (39 multiple-choice questions) has questions in three content areas:

1. Identifying sentence errors

2. Improving sentences

3. Improving paragraphs

The test items themselves are drawn from the SAT item banks. The items chosen are ones that are shorter, less difficult, and less complex than most of the others.

Here are some sample questions that illustrate the categories above:

Critical Reading

The reading prompt is 29 lines long.

Lines 1–10 suggest that Hemingway would most likely agree with which statement?

    A. Social injustice can be remedied through art.

    B. Living in troubled times shapes a writer's development as an artist.

    C. Nineteenth-century writers surpass modern writers in their descriptions of wars.

    D. The more personal tragedy writers endure, the more prolific they become.

    E. Historic events become more socially significant when interpreted by a skillful writer.

(College Board web site, 12/02/01)

Sentence Completion

Joshua's radical ideas were frowned on by most of his coworkers, who found them too _____ for their conservative tastes.

    A. heretical

    B. meticulous

    C. precise

    D. incoherent

    E. sagacious

(College Board web site, 12/02/01)

Analogy

JUDICIOUS : PRUDENCE

    A. deferential : scorn

B. malevolent : influence
C. indomitable : defeat
D. stoic : hardship
E. frivolous : giddiness
(College Board web site, 12/02/01)

Math—Multiple Choice

If a and b are integers greater than 100 such that a + b = 300, which of the following could be the exact ratio of a to b?

A. 9 to 1
B. 5 to 2
C. 5 to 3
D. 4 to 1
E. 3 to 2
(College Board web site, 12/02/01)

Math—Grid in

The sum of r and p is equal to twice s and p is 36 less than twice the sum of r and s. What is the value of r?
(College Board web site, 12/02/01)

Writing—Improving Sentences

The problem of antibiotic **resistance, frequently compounded in certain countries because** the sale and use of antibiotics are not tightly controlled.

A. resistance, frequently compounded in certain countries because
B. resistance, frequently compounded in certain countries and
C. resistance frequently compounded in certain countries when
D. resistance is frequently compounded in certain countries where
E. resistance is frequently compounded in certain countries and
(College Board web site, 12/02/01)

Test Scores Obtained

Test takers obtain three global scores (verbal, mathematical, and writing) on a scale of 20 to 80. An easy comparison may be made to SAT scores by simply adding a zero to each PSAT score.

Technical Adequacy

Validity Confirmation

Test item validity as relates to individual item development seems satisfactory. This development process is outlined in the technical publications and does include trial use. PSAT items are drawn from the SAT item pool. However, test items do not seem to be selected from that pool on the basis of their ability to differentiate between successful and unsuccessful college students, otherwise the tests would have greater predictive ability than is shown by current data.

Test response validity is a much more complex and vexing issue. Since the primary purpose of the SAT/PSAT is to provide colleges and universities with the means to predict a potential student's academic performance, the main validity concern is the extent to which it provides such data (predictive validity).

The following data refers to students graduating since 1980:

Correlations with Undergraduate GPA

SAT Verbal	.40
SAT Math	.41
Math + Verbal	.36
High school record	.42
Math + Verbal + HSR	.52

(The College Board, 2001b, p. 6)

All of these figures are modest and would not be sufficiently high to justify individual admissions decisions. It seems that the addition of SAT scores to the predictive ability of high school grades gives an increase of only about .10 (.42 to .52). Mathematically this accounts for only about a 9% increase!

Another important validity issue needs to be addressed, namely fallacious validity. There is a common but mistaken belief that the SAT/PSAT is a measure of the quality of high school instruction. That is, the focus is incorrectly changed from individual student performance to a quality measure of the high school, district, and state. This error is reflected in any number of newspaper articles where the performance of high schools, school districts, and states is compared. Several years ago, North Carolina was reported to have the lowest state mean SAT scores. That led to any number of radio and television programs, press releases, and newspaper articles, all of which incorporated a sound of alarm based on the fallacious assumption that SAT/PSAT scores were able to measure instructional performance.

Closely related to the above issues and clearly related to the test name changes is the issue of whether test coaching has any effect. Originally the publisher denied that coaching had any measurable effect on improving scores. Then when data would not support this position, the test name was changed from "aptitude" to "assessment."

Reliability Confirmation

The publisher quotes satisfactory reliabilities of between .91 and .93 for the SAT. Since the PSAT utilizes SAT questions but selects fewer, slightly easier questions, the reliability should be slightly lower but still satisfactory. The exact type of reliability calculation used is not clear (The College Board, 2000a, p. 27).

Objectivity Confirmation

Since the PSAT is entirely multiple choice, objectivity is not a serious concern.

Statistical Confirmation

There is strictly speaking no technical manual, but the various publications available from the publisher contain satisfactory statistical information.

Special Features

Acronym

PSAT/NMSQT.

Levels of the Test

One.

Number of Test Forms

Many; they are in a constant process of development.

Norm-Referenced?

Yes, the standard scores are on a scale of 20 to 80.

Criterion-Referenced?

No.

Other Features

Like other ETS tests, the PSAT has more than ample provision for handicapped test takers. The web site is among the best and provides all possible support and a great deal of information. Scores on the PSAT/NMSQT are the first step that students take in pursuit of a National Merit Scholarship as either a "Semi-Finalist" or "Commended Student." Test takers are given personalized recommendations on improving skills in the "Score Report Plus." Two or three skills are noted for improvement from each of the three sections and suggestions given for improvement. This is a valuable and helpful feature.

Feasibility Considerations

Testing Time

Two hours, 10 minutes.

For Testing Groups? Individuals?

Groups.

Test Administration and Scoring

The test is administered by local high schools on certain limited dates.

This publisher uses the correction for guessing in calculating scores. That is, a proportion of the wrong answers is subtracted from the number correct. This value ranges from one-fourth to one-half, depending on the number of answer choices.

In 1995, the scores were "re-centered." Originally the score of 50 was set as the midpoint on the scale, but over time the calculated midpoint gradually dropped. The re-centering amounted to raising the reported scores.

Test Materials and Approximate Costs

$9.50 for all three parts. Some study materials are now available directly from the publisher.

Adequacy of Test Manuals

The manuals are adequate.

Excerpts from Other Test Reviews

"Intended as a useful standard for comparing the abilities of students from widely different cultural backgrounds and types of schools, the test can also help students, their parents, and guidance counselors make decisions in the college application process" (Kagan & Gall, 1997, p. 1).

"Tests your experience, your familiarity with a set range of topics and terms, and your test-sense, your ability to steer a sensible course through the tricks and traps of a multiple-choice test, not your intelligence" (Brownstein, Weiner, & Green, 1994, p. 3).

Ordering Information

Publisher

The College Board, PSAT/NMSQT Program, P.O. Box 6720, Princeton, NJ 08541-6720; Phone: 609-771-7070; 888-477-PSAT (Counselor Hot-line); Fax: 609-530-0482; e-mail: psat@info.collegeboard.com; Web site: www.collegeboard.org.

Authors

College Board staff.

Publication Date

Continuously modified and updated.

Cautions and Comments

Taking the PSAT and SAT are time-honored traditions among high school students.

How many, many conversations between high school students and adults begin with an inquiry about these tests? The PSAT/SAT has gone through a great number of changes over the years and the process continues. The last major changes in 1994 included the following:

A. Emphasis on critical reading and reasoning skills

B. Reading material that is accessible and engaging

C. Passages ranging in length from 400 to 850 words

D. Use of double passages with two points of view on the same subject

E. Introductory and contextual information from the reading passages

F. Reading questions that emphasize analytical and evaluative skills

G. Passage-based questions testing vocabulary in context

H. Discrete questions measuring verbal reasoning and vocabulary in context

(The College Board, 2001a, p. 9)

The old familiar antonym question is no longer part of the PSAT. Here is an example of that type of question:

VIRTUE: (A) regret (B) hatred (C) penalty (D) denial (E) depravity
[Answer E]
(The College Board, 2001a, p. 4)

The reliability and objectivity of the PSAT have never really been in question (though more precise information would be welcomed on reliability). The problem is with validity. Because of its purpose, the tests must sink or swim on the basis of their ability to predict college performance. The correlation of SAT scores and undergraduate GPA is only about .40. When combined with high school records, it adds only about .10, bringing the correlation to about .50, which is still weak. The whole complex process of development, preparation, administration, and explanation doesn't justify a gain of only .10 in correlation. The costs for individual students are not considerable, but the expense to high schools is considerable. Often PSAT/SAT preparation courses are offered or required. In addition, colleges also experience considerable expense for little gain in predictive power. It would seem that the most practical course of action would be to abandon the PSAT/SAT in favor of currently available information, like high school rank or high school grades, for the purpose of predicting success. Then the function of the PSAT/SAT could be limited to a small population that would be using these scores in the pursuit of a National Merit Scholarship.

It is not difficult to see how a successful PSAT preparation program would be configured. There would be units that would address the following:

Increasing reading speed

Improving reading comprehension

Expanding vocabulary

Increasing geometry understanding

Improving performance on word problems

Reviewing the structures of analogy questions

Increasing awareness of critical clue words like "except"

Reviewing grammar, punctuation and expression

References

Brownstein, S. C., Weiner, M., & Green, S. W. (1994). *How to prepare for the SAT I*. Hauppage, NY: Barron's Educational Series.

Burdmman, P. (2001). A call to discard the SAT. *Black Issues in Higher Education*, March 15.

The College Board. (2000a). *Handbook for the SAT program 2000–2001*. Princeton, NJ: College Board SAT Program.

The College Board. (2000b). *Predictions of freshman grade-point average from the revised and recentered SAT I: Reasoning test*. Princeton, NJ: College Board SAT Program.

The College Board. (2000c). *The SAT I and high school grades: Utility in predicting success in college*. Princeton, NJ: College Board SAT Program.

The College Board. (2001a). *A historical perspective on the SAT 1926–2001*. Princeton, NJ: College Board SAT Program.

The College Board. (2001b). *Predicting success in college: SAT studies of classes graduating since 1980*. Princeton, NJ: College Board SAT Program.

The College Board. (2001c). *Recentering and realigning the SAT score distributions: How and why*. Princeton, NJ: College Board SAT Program.

College Board–sponsored study claims SAT is a good predictor of grades, graduation. (2001). *Black Issues in Higher Education*, May 24.

Hurd, H. (2000). Poor strategies continue to plague black test-takers. *Black Issues in Higher Education*, September 28.

Kagan, J., & Gall, S. (Eds.). (1997). SAT. *Gale encyclopedia of childhood and adolescence* (from Internet site).

Using a meta-analysis of more than 1,700 studies on the SAT, University of Minnesota researchers and a researcher from the Educational Testing Service have reported that the SAT predicts academic performance in college. (2001, Summer). *Gifted Child Magazine*.

SAT I, for testing groups of high school upperclassmen
Reviewed by Charles W. Hatch, Ph.D., Educational Research and Measurement

---

Note: From the test's beginnings in 1927 through 1994, the letters SAT stood for Scholastic Aptitude Test. At that point the name was changed to Scholastic Assessment Test. In 1997 that name was discontinued, and now the test is simply known as the SAT (Kagan & Gall, 1997, p. 1).

Usefulness of the Test for Educators

Test Authors' Purpose

The SAT Program is designed to assist students, parents, high schools, postsecondary institutions, and scholarship programs with educational planning and decision making and to provide a channel of communication during the transition from high school to college.

The SAT I and SAT II tests assess many of the skills that are important to students' success in college. Because the subject matter of high school courses and high school grading standards vary widely, the tests have been established as a common standard against which student performance can be compared.

Decision-Making Applications

Over 2,000 colleges and universities use these scores as part of the admissions process. They use SAT scores as partial predictors of college success.

Relevant Population

High school upperclassmen contemplating attending college. It should be noted, however, that some students are now taking the SAT in grades 7 and 8. The ETS, in fact, reported that 110,151 took the test in 1997–1998 as seventh or eighth graders (The College Board, 2000a, p. 27).

Characteristics Described

The Verbal section (78 questions) has three subsections:

1. Critical Reading (40 questions)
   Vocabulary in context
   Literal comprehension
   Extended reasoning

2. Sentence Completion (19 questions)
   Content
   Structure
   Functional skills

3. Analogies (19 questions)
   Content
   Abstraction of terms
   Functional skills

The Mathematics section (60 questions) has questions in four content areas:

5. Arithmetic

6. Algebra

7. Geometry

8. Miscellaneous (functions, number theory, statistics, geometric perception, and logical reasoning)

The following sample questions illustrate the content areas above:

Critical Reading

The reading prompt is 29 lines long.

Lines 1–10 suggest that Hemingway would most likely agree with which statement?

   F. Social injustice can be remedied through art.

   G. Living in troubled times shapes a writer's development as an artist.

   H. Nineteenth-century writers surpass modern writers in their descriptions of wars.

   I. The more personal tragedy writers endure, the more prolific they become.

   J. Historic events become more socially significant when interpreted by a skillful writer.

(College Board web site, 12/02/01)

Sentence Completion

Joshua's radical ideas were frowned on by most of his coworkers, who found them too _____ for their conservative tastes.

   F. heretical

   G. meticulous

   H. precise

   I. incoherent

   J. sagacious

(College Board web site, 12/02/01)

Analogy

JUDICIOUS : PRUDENCE

   F. deferential : scorn

   G. malevolent : influence

   H. indomitable : defeat

   I. stoic : hardship

   J. frivolous : giddiness

(College Board web site, 12/02/01)

Math—Multiple Choice

If a and b are integers greater than 100 such that $a + b = 300$, which of the following could be the exact ratio of a to b?

   F. 9 to 1

G. 5 to 2
H. 5 to 3
I. 4 to 1
J. 3 to 2
(College Board web site, 12/02/01)

Math—Grid in

The sum of r and p is equal to twice s and p is 36 less than twice the sum of r and s. What is the value of r?
(College Board web site, 12/02/01)

Writing—Improving Sentences

The problem of antibiotic **resistance, frequently compounded in certain countries because** the sale and use of antibiotics are not tightly controlled.
  F. resistance, frequently compounded in certain countries because
  G. resistance, frequently compounded in certain countries and
  H. resistance frequently compounded in certain countries when
  I. resistance is frequently compounded in certain countries where
  J. resistance is frequently compounded in certain countries and
(College Board web site, 12/02/01)

Test Scores Obtained

Test takers obtain two global scores (verbal and mathematical) on a scale of 200 to 800. It is common to sum these two scores.

Technical Adequacy

Validity Confirmation

Test item validity as relates to individual item development seems satisfactory. The development process is outlined in the technical publications and does include trial use. This accounts for the fact that there are more questions on any SAT than actually count for a score. Each testee is presented with one math and one verbal section that only contain questions in development, which do not count in the score calculation. This provides the publisher with an adequate supply of items at all times. However, test items do not seem to be selected from that pool on the basis of their ability to differentiate between successful and unsuccessful college students, otherwise the tests would have greater predictive ability than is shown by current data.

Test response validity is a much more complex and vexing issue. Since the primary purpose of the SAT is to provide colleges and universities with the means to predict a potential student's academic performance, the main validity concern is the extent to which it provides such data (predictive validity).

The following data refers to students graduating since 1980:

Correlations with Undergraduate GPA

SAT Verbal	.40
SAT Math	.41
Math + Verbal	.36
High school record	.42
Math + Verbal + HSR	.52

(The College Board, 2001b, p. 6)

All of these figures are modest and would not be sufficiently high to justify individual admissions decisions. It seems that the addition of SAT scores to the predictive ability of high school grades gives an increase of only about .10 (.42 to .52). Mathematically this accounts for only about a 9% increase!

Another important validity issue needs to be addressed, namely fallacious validity. There is a common but mistaken belief that the SAT is a measure of the quality of high school instruction. That is, the focus is incorrectly changed from individual student performance to a quality measure of the high school, district, and state. This error is reflected in any number of newspaper articles where the SAT performance of high schools, school districts, and states is compared. Several years ago, North Carolina was reported to have the lowest state mean SAT scores. That led to any number of radio and television programs, press releases, and newspaper articles, all of which incorporated a sound of alarm based on the fallacious assumption that SAT scores were able to measure instructional performance. This validity concern is not meant to reflect negatively on the test publisher but only to draw attention to an incorrect interpretation of SAT scores that is prevalent.

Closely related to the above issues and clearly related to the test name changes is the issue of whether test coaching has any effect. Originally the publisher denied that coaching had any measurable effect on improving scores. Then when data would not support this position, the test name was changed from "aptitude" to "assessment."

Reliability Confirmation

The publisher quotes satisfactory reliabilities between .91 and .93. The exact type of reliability calculation is not clear (The College Board, 2000a, p. 27).

Objectivity Confirmation

Since the SAT is almost entirely multiple choice, objectivity is not a serious concern. The only area of possible concern is with that section of the mathematics test, where the student supplies the answer to 10 questions. The answer grid provided greatly reduces objectivity concerns for these questions.

Statistical Confirmation

There is strictly speaking no technical manual, but the various publications available from the publisher contain satisfactory statistical information.

Special Features

Acronym

SAT-I.

Levels of the Test

One.

Number of Test Forms

Many; they are in a constant process of development.

Norm-Referenced?

Yes. The standard scores on the scale of 200 to 800 were among the first to be used. In fact, most common measurement textbooks contain reference to College Entrance Examination Board (CEEB) scores on the normal curve.

Criterion-Referenced?

No.

Other Features

Like other ETS tests, the SAT has more than ample provision for handicapped test takers. There are also many ways for the publisher to aid colleges and universities in their use of the test scores.

The web site is among the best and provides all possible support and a great deal of information.

Feasibility Considerations

Testing Time

Three hours.

For Testing Groups? Individuals?

Groups.

Test Administration and Scoring

The test publisher provides monitors, forms, and grading. It is only necessary for an individual to register and pay the necessary fees.

This test uses the correction for guessing in calculating scores. That is, a proportion of the wrong answers is subtracted from the number correct. This value ranges from one-fourth to one-half, depending on the number of answer choices.

In 1995, the scores were "re-centered." Originally the score of 500 was set as the midpoint on the scale, but over time the calculated midpoint gradually dropped. The re-centering amounted to raising the reported scores.

Test Materials and Approximate Costs

$25 for both parts. Some study materials are now available directly from the publisher.

Adequacy of Test Manuals

The manuals are adequate.

Excerpts from Other Test Reviews

"Intended as a useful standard for comparing the abilities of students from widely different cultural backgrounds and types of schools, the test can also help students, their parents, and guidance counselors make decisions in the college application process" (Kagan & Gall, 1997, p. 1).

"SAT I tests your experience, your familiarity with a set range of topics and terms, and your test-sense, your ability to steer a sensible course through the tricks and traps of a multiple-choice test, not your intelligence" (Brownstein, Weiner, & Green, 1994, p. 3).

Ordering Information

Publisher

College Board SAT Program, P.O. Box 6200, Princeton, NJ 08541-6200; Phone: 888-SAT-HELP (888-728-4357); e-mail: sat.help@info.collegeboard.com; Web site: www.collegeboard.org.

Authors

College Board staff.

Publication Date

First published in 1926 but continuously modified and updated since then.

Cautions and Comments

Taking the SAT is a time-honored tradition among high school upperclassmen. How many, many conversations between high school students and adults begin with an inquiry about this test? The SAT has gone through a great number of changes over the years and the process continues. The last major changes in 1994 included the following:

I. Emphasis on critical reading and reasoning skills

J. Reading material that is accessible and engaging

K. Passages ranging in length from 400 to 850 words

L. Use of double passages with two points of view on the same subject

M. Introductory and contextual information from the reading passages

N. Reading questions that emphasize analytical and evaluative skills

O. Passage-based questions testing vocabulary in context

P. Discrete questions measuring verbal reasoning and vocabulary in context

(The College Board, 2001a, p. 9)

The old familiar antonym question is no longer part of the SAT I. Here is an example of that type of question:

VIRTUE: (A) regret (B) hatred (C) penalty (D) denial (E) depravity
[Answer: E]
(The College Board, 2001a, p. 4)

The reliability and objectivity of the SAT I have never really been in question (though more precise information would be welcomed on reliability). The problem is with validity. Because of its purpose, the test must sink or swim on the basis of its ability to predict college performance. The correlation of SAT scores and undergraduate GPA is only about .40. When combined with high school record, it adds only about .10, bringing the correlation to about .50, which is still weak. The whole complex process of development, preparation, administration, and explanation doesn't justify a gain of only .10 in correlation. The costs for individual students are not considerable, but the expense to high schools is considerable. Often SAT preparation courses are offered or required. In addition, colleges also experience considerable expense for little gain in predictive power. It would seem that the most practical course of action would be to abandon the SAT in favor of currently available information like high school rank or high school grades for the purpose of predicting success. Then the function of the SAT could be limited to a small population that would be using these scores in the pursuit of a National Merit Scholarship.

In June 2002, the following changes (to be implemented in March 2005) were announced.

1. A third section will be added to the traditional verbal and quantitative sections. It will include both a handwritten essay and multiple-choice grammar items.

2. The verbal section will be renamed "Critical Reading" and expanded.

3. Analogy questions will be dropped.

4. In the quantitative section there will be two changes:

    a. More questions will be included in the Algebra II content range.

    b. The quantitative comparison items will be dropped. These are the ones that require a comparison of the relative value of mathematical expression or quantities in "Column A and Column B" format.

Some of the motivation for these changes came from the University of California's (UC) threat to discontinue use of the SAT I as an admission requirement for the whole UC system.

These changes, when and if implemented, will tend to have the following effects:

1. The objectivity of the new section containing the handwritten essay will probably be lower than the rest of the test.

2. The correspondence of the test items to the content of high school curriculum should increase.

3. With the modifications the test becomes less of a predictor of future academic achievement, as originally intended, and more of a measure of past academic achievement.

4. There will be further movement away from the original concept of the test as a measure of "aptitude," which was the original source of the letter "A" in SAT.

It is not difficult to see how a successful SAT preparation program would be configured. There would be units that would address the following:

Increasing reading speed

Improving reading comprehension

Expanding vocabulary

Increasing geometry understanding

Improving performance on word problems

Reviewing the structures of analogy questions

Surveying the grid for student-supplied math questions

Increasing awareness of critical clue words like "except"

References

Brownstein, S. C., Weiner, M., & Green, S. W. (1994). *How to prepare for the SAT I*. Hauppage, NY: Barron's Educational Series.

Burdmman, P. (2001). A call to discard the SAT. *Black Issues in Higher Education*, March 15.

The College Board. (2000a). *Handbook for the SAT Program 2000–2001*. Princeton, NJ: College Board SAT Program.

The College Board. (2000b). *Predictions of freshman grade-point average from the revised and recentered SAT I: Reasoning test.* Princeton, NJ: College Board SAT Program.

The College Board. (2000c). *The SAT I and high school grades: Utility in predicting success in college.* Princeton, NJ: College Board SAT Program.

The College Board. (2001a). *A historical perspective on the SAT 1926–2001.* Princeton, NJ: College Board SAT Program.

The College Board. (2001b). *Predicting success in college: SAT studies of classes graduating since 1980.* Princeton, NJ: College Board SAT Program.

The College Board. (2001c). *Recentering and realigning the SAT score distributions: How and why.* Princeton, NJ: College Board SAT Program.

College Board–sponsored study claims SAT is a good predictor of grades, graduation. (2001). *Black Issues in Higher Education*, May 24.

Hurd, H. (2000). Poor strategies continue to plague black test-takers. *Black Issues in Higher Education*, September 28.

Kagan, J., & Gall, S. (Eds.). (1997). SAT. *Gale encyclopedia of childhood and adolescence* (from Internet site).

Using a meta-analysis of more than 1,700 studies on the SAT, University of Minnesota researchers and a researcher from the Educational Testing Service have reported that the SAT predicts academic performance in college. (2001, Summer). *Gifted Child Magazine.*

SAT II, for testing groups of high school juniors and seniors
Reviewed by Charles W. Hatch, Ph.D., Educational Research and Measurement

---

Note: From the test's beginnings in 1927 through 1994, the letters SAT stood for Scholastic Aptitude Test. At that point the name was changed to Scholastic Assessment Test. In 1997 that name was discontinued, and now the test is simply known as the SAT (Kagan & Gall, 1997, p. 1).

Usefulness of the Test for Educators

Test Authors' Purpose

The SAT Program is designed to assist students, parents, high schools, postsecondary institutions, and scholarship programs with educational planning and decision making and to provide a channel of communication during the transition from high school to college.

The SAT I and SAT II tests assess many of the skills that are important to students' success in college. Because the subject matter of high school courses and high school grading standards vary widely, the tests have been established as a common standard against which student performance can be compared.

The SAT II: Subject Tests are designed to measure knowledge in specific subject areas and students' ability to apply that knowledge. Subject Tests are independent of particular textbooks or methods of instruction. Although the types of questions change little from year to year, the content of the tests evolves to reflect current trends in high school curricula.

Decision-Making Applications

"Many colleges use Subject Tests for admission, course placement, and advising students about course selection. Some colleges specify which Subject Tests are required for admission or placement; others allow applicants to choose" (The College Board, 2000a, p. 7).

The English Language Proficiency Test (ELPT) provides colleges with a measure to help in the admission of foreign students and placement information for their English language instruction.

Relevant Population

High school juniors and seniors contemplating attending college.

Characteristics Described

There are 22 separate tests included under SAT II. Here is a listing as of December 2001.

1. Writing
2. Literature
3. Unites States history
4. World history
5. Math level IC (C means calculator required)
6. Math level IIC (C means calculator required)
7. Biology (ecological/molecular)
8. Chemistry
9. Physics
10. French (reading only)
11. German (reading only)
12. Modern Hebrew (reading only)
13. Italian (reading only)
14. Latin (reading only)
15. Spanish (reading only)
16. Chinese (reading and listening)
17. French (reading and listening)
18. German (reading and listening)
19. Japanese (reading and listening)

20. Korean (reading and listening)
21. Spanish (reading and listening)
22. English language proficiency test (ELPT) (reading and listening)

As an example of the content of one test, the World history test covers the following chronological periods:

Period	Percentage
Pre-history to 500 A.D.	25
500–1500 A.D.	20
1500–1900 A.D.	25
Post-1900 A.D.	20
Cross-chronological	10

Looking at the same material from a geographical perspective yields these results:

Area	Percentage
Global or comparative	25
Europe	25
Africa	10
Southwest Asia	10
South and Southeast Asia	10
East Asia	10
Americas (not United States)	10

(The College Board, 2001d, p. 19)

Test Scores Obtained

Test takers for the first 21 tests obtain global scores on a scale of 200 to 800 and subscale scores on a scale of 20 to 80. However, scores on the ELPT are on a scale of 901 to 999 and the subscales (listening–short passage, listening–long passage, and reading) are reported on a scale of 1 to 50.

Technical Adequacy

Validity Confirmation

Test item validity seems entirely satisfactory. The whole process is outlined in the technical publications and does include monitoring and review by highly qualified development committees.

Test response validity is a more complex issue. However, the uses to which SAT II scores are put (generally course placement and course selection) are less technically demanding than when scores are used for admission (SAT I).

Even so, SAT II writing scores are more highly correlated with college English grades for eight out of nine reporting categories than SAT I Verbal scores (The College Board, 2000a, p. 39).

In addition, the correlation of SAT II writing scores with college GPA was .49, which is considerably higher than the correlations of SAT I verbal or math. This relationship held across racial and gender groupings, where the range was .31 (African-American male) to .51 (combined ethnic-female) (The College Board, 2000a, p. 39).

No data is presented on other SAT II tests and college GPA or college grades in the subject of the test.

Closely related to the above issues and clearly related to the test name changes is the issue of whether test coaching has any effect. Originally the publisher denied that coaching had any measurable effect on improving scores. Then when data would not support this position, the test name was changed from "aptitude" to "assessment."

One final concern needs to be voiced. The necessity for the ETS to make an additional "Security Charge" of $15 for testing in India and Pakistan strongly indicates that not all scores are obtained as the test makers desired. If there is any degree of irregularity, then test response validity concerns rise.

Reliability Confirmation

The publisher quotes satisfactory reliabilities of between .86 (Math IIC) and .97 (Chinese with listening). The exact type of reliability calculation made is not clear. Reliabilities are also reported for the subscales, which tend to be slightly lower, as would be expected since fewer questions are involved (The College Board, 2000a, pp. 36–37).

Objectivity Confirmation

Since the SAT II is almost entirely multiple choice, objectivity is not a serious concern. The only area of possible concern is with the writing sample of the Writing Test, which is holistically graded on a scale of 1 to 6 by two "experienced high school or college teachers." The degree of agreement is not reported.

Statistical Confirmation

There is strictly speaking no technical manual, but the various publications available from the publisher contain satisfactory statistical information.

Special Features

Acronym

SAT-II.

Levels of the Test

One.

Number of Test Forms

Many; they are in a constant process of development.

Norm-Referenced?

Yes. The standard scores on the scale of 200 to 800 were among the first to be used. In fact, most common measurement textbooks contain reference to College Entrance Examination Board (CEEB) scores on the normal curve.

Criterion-Referenced?

No.

Other Features

Like other ETS tests, the SAT II has more than ample provision for handicapped test takers. There are also many ways for the publisher to aid colleges and universities in their use of the test scores.

The web site is among the best and provides extensive support and a great deal of information.

Feasibility Considerations

Testing Time

Each of the tests is one hour.

For Testing Groups? Individuals?

Groups.

Test Administration and Scoring

The test publisher provides monitors, forms, and grading. It is only necessary for an individual to register and pay the necessary fees.

This test uses the correction for guessing in calculating scores. That is, a proportion of the wrong answers is subtracted from the number correct. This value ranges from one-fourth to one-half, depending on the number of answer choices.

In 1995, the scores were "re-centered." Originally the score of 500 was set as the midpoint on the scale, but over time the calculated midpoint gradually dropped. The re-centering amounted to raising the reported scores.

Test Materials and Approximate Costs

Writing Test: $11; Language tests with listening: $8; All others: $6. Students may take as many as three SAT II tests on one day. Some study materials are now available directly from the publisher.

Adequacy of Test Manuals

The manuals are adequate.

Excerpts from Other Test Reviews

"Intended as a useful standard for comparing the abilities of students from widely different cultural backgrounds and types of schools, the test can also help students, their parents, and guidance counselors make decisions in the college application process" (Kagan & Gall, 1997, p. 1).

"Tests your experience, your familiarity with a set range of topics and terms, and your test-sense, your ability to steer a sensible course through the tricks and traps of a multiple-choice test, not your intelligence" (Brownstein et al., 1994, p. 3).

Ordering Information

Publisher

College Board SAT Program, P.O. Box 6200, Princeton, NJ 08541-6200; Phone: 888-SAT-HELP (888-728-4357); e-mail: sat.help@info.collegeboard.com; Web site: www.collegeboard.org.

Authors

College Board staff.

Publication Date

First published in 1926 but continuously modified and updated since then.

Cautions and Comments

The reliability and objectivity of the SAT II have never really been in question (though more precise information would be welcomed on reliability and precisely which type is reported). Objectivity data should also be presented on the agreement of graders who evaluate the essay segment of the Writing Sample.

Validity is also not a great concern, since the items are well developed and monitored and the content is constantly in the process of modification and adjustment by qualified experts in their respective fields.

Using these tests for course placement, advisement, and remediation is well justified. In fact, this group of tests stands out among the SAT test array as the best.

The depth of support by The College Board will be appreciated both on the web site and through the use of published materials and study guides. The Essay Prep allows a person to get feedback from official readers to help prepare for the Writing Test.

The publication *Real SAT II: Subject Tests* contains 20 full-length tests plus practice for the Biology Ecological/Molecular and Korean language tests.

References

Brownstein, S. C., Weiner, M., & Green, S. W. (1994). *How to prepare for the SAT I.* Hauppage, NY: Barron's Educational Series.

Burdmman, P. (2001). A call to discard the SAT. *Black Issues in Higher Education*, March 15.

The College Board. (2000a). *Handbook for the SAT Program 2000–2001.* Princeton, NJ: College Board SAT Program.

The College Board. (2000b). *Predictions of freshman grade-point average from the revised and recentered SAT I: Reasoning test.* Princeton, NJ: College Board SAT Program.

The College Board. (2000c). *The SAT I and high school grades: Utility in predicting success in college.* Princeton, NJ: College Board SAT Program.

The College Board. (2001a). *A historical perspective on the SAT 1926–2001.* Princeton, NJ: College Board SAT Program.

The College Board. (2001b). *Predicting success in college: SAT studies of classes graduating since 1980.* Princeton, NJ: College Board SAT Program.

The College Board. (2001c). *Recentering and realigning the SAT score distributions: How and why.* Princeton, NJ: College Board SAT Program.

The College Board. (2001d). Unpublished manuscript. Princeton, NJ, College Board.

College Board–sponsored study claims SAT is a good predictor of grades, graduation. (2001). *Black Issues in Higher Education*, May 24.

Hurd, H. (2000). Poor strategies continue to plague black test-takers. *Black Issues in Higher Education*, September 28.

Kagan, J., & Gall, S. (Eds.). (1997). SAT. *Gale encyclopedia of childhood and adolescence* (from Internet site).

Using a meta-analysis of more than 1,700 studies on the SAT, University of Minnesota researchers and a researcher from the Educational Testing Service have reported that the SAT predicts academic performance in college. (2001, Summer). *Gifted Child Magazine*.

2

Admission to the Education Profession: Certification Tests

PRAXIS I: Pre-Professional Skills Tests (PPST and C-PPST),
for testing groups of college graduates or undergraduates who desire
admission to a teacher education program or certification in a state
Reviewed by Charles W. Hatch, Ph.D., Educational Research and Measurement

---

Note: Even though PRAXIS I is treated as if it were one instrument, it is actually a number of instruments and two formats under one umbrella title. The word PRAXIS itself, which appeared in the early 1990s for the first time replacing the venerable National Teachers Exam (NTE), doesn't really mean anything specific but seems to allude to educational practice.

Data for this review was not easy to obtain because the ETS seems reluctant to release data on reliability, validity, and objectivity. This is especially troubling since these tests are generally used for state teacher certification or admission to teacher education programs where specific cutoff scores are assigned and a person scoring one point too low is failed. The problem is especially critical on tests that have constructed response items like the essay on the writing tests. Here the variability introduced by the evaluation process (objectivity) could easily cause relatively large point swings.

Usefulness of the Test for Educators

Test Authors' Purpose

The PRAXIS I Assessments were designed to provide a system of thorough, fair, and carefully validated tests and assessments for states to use as part of their teacher licensure process.

"PRAXIS I: Academic Skills Assessments are designed to be taken early in your college career to measure your reading, writing and mathematical skills. The assessments are available in two formats, each measuring the same academic skills vital to all teacher candidates" (ETS, 2001b, p. 4).

Decision-Making Applications

These four instruments (reading, writing, listening, and mathematics) are intended for states to use as part of the certification process.

Another application would be for program evaluation and restructuring of college preparation programs. In this use, the test shortcomings would not be so crucial.

Relevant Population

College graduates or undergraduates who desire admission to a teacher education program or a particular state certification.

Characteristics Described

Reading (test 0710)
    Literal comprehension
    Critical and inferential comprehension

Writing (test 0720)
    Usage
    Sentence correction
    Essay

Mathematics (test 0730)
    Conceptual knowledge
    Procedural knowledge
    Representations of quantitative information
    Measurement and informal geometry
    Formal mathematical reasoning

Listening (test 0740)
    Retention and selection
    Identification of transactions and tone
    Analysis
    Critical evaluation

Test Scores Obtained

Testees obtain a single, global standard score on a scale of 150 to 190. In addition, the number correct is reported on each of the question subcategories (see "Characteristics Described" above).

Technical Adequacy

The ETS makes available only limited technical information. Most of what is available comes from the annual publication *Understanding Your PRAXIS Scores* (ETS,

2001d). The Background Papers in *Testing Teacher Candidates* (Mitchell et al., 2001) contains some further data. See below.

Validity Confirmation

The ETS has not generally released this data. However, the Committee on Assessment and Teacher Quality of the National Research Council was able to obtain some information.

The data on *test item validity* suggests that the items are generally developed in a satisfactory manner (Mitchell et al., 2001, pp. 349–460). It must be remembered that this process of item development for the PPST is always an ongoing activity, as items are constantly being added so that the multiple forms can be maintained. It is reported that results are used when response rates from a verification survey were as low as 16% (African-American and Hispanic teachers) (Mitchell et al., 2001, p. 352). Figures this low generally render the results unusable.

Test response validity presents greater problems. Correlations with other instruments are not given. Generalized procedures are released which describe the methods by which forms are equated and are adequate but not supported by data on specific test forms. The ETS uses a number of questions common across forms to provide the mathematical basis for equating (Mitchell et al., 2001, p. 364).

Possible breaches in test security would be a serious concern when considering test response validity. The ETS publishes guides for test administrations, but the challenge is great. One need look no further than the Bulletin of Information to see evidence that test security has been and continues to be a very serious problem. The administration of the PPST is severely limited in Louisiana. There is an additional security charge of $7 there because of previous security breaches (ETS, 2001a, pp. 11, 20).

Reliability Confirmation

The ETS has not generally released this information beyond the standard error of measurement, which varies from 2.1 to 2.7 for the reading and math. No figure is given for the writing. However, the Committee on Assessment and Teacher Quality of the National Research Council was able to obtain some information.

The reliability as an estimate of the unity of the test (internal consistency) was satisfactory and between .84 and .87 (Mitchell et al., 2001, p. 356).

Since these tests are used almost exclusively for critical career decisions and states assign cutoff scores, the most important set of figures would be reliability for pass/fail decisions. These are not given.

Objectivity Confirmation

PPST tests have two item types: multiple choice and essay. There is no objectivity problem with the multiple-choice questions. The problem lies with the essay portion of the Writing test. The ETS says the "Standard Error of Scoring" is 1.0. These would give, for example, + or –1 point on the essay raw scores, which would include two-thirds of graders. That interval would translate to an even greater interval on the standard score, which is derived from the raw score. To be 90% sure, the interval would be expanded. The ETS gives the objectivity data in an unusual format. It is more common to report inter-rater reliability.

The figure above is *not* low enough for individual decisions, let alone critical career decisions.

Statistical Confirmation

There is some statistical information contained in the publication *Understanding Your PRAXIS Scores*, but it is incomplete and inadequate because it is limited to possible score range, score interval, number of examinees, median, average performance range, standard error of measurement, and standard error of scoring.

The *Test at a Glance* publication (ETS, 2001b) gives only information on such test characteristics as number of items in a subcategory, topics covered, and some sample questions.

Further data is given in the very useful *Testing Teacher Candidates* (Mitchell et al., 2001). Information is found there which is not available elsewhere. However, readers should note carefully how many times those editors are forced to use phrasing like the following: "The absence of information on this element of the evaluation framework should not be interpreted to mean that it is ignored in the test development process. It should be interpreted to mean that no information about this aspect of test development was provided" (Mitchell et al., 2001, p. 356).

Special Features

Acronyms

PPST and C-PPST (computer version),

Levels of the Test

One. The content of the PPST and C-PPST is set at about eighth or ninth grade level.

Number of Test Forms

Questions are drawn from item banks, so the number of forms is almost unlimited.

Norm-Referenced?

Yes, the scores are reported in Standard Scores with a range of 150 to 190. However, no information is given on the norming sample, which would allow judgment concerning its representativeness.

Criterion-Referenced?

No. However, the test taker's performance is reported on a number of subcategories. This information allows a person to have enough information to initiate remediation. The PPST reports the number of questions answered correctly, the number of questions in the category, and the average performance range.

Other Features

The ETS is able to accommodate a wide range of handicapping conditions with specialized features like added time, readers, and large-print forms. Non-Saturday test dates are also available for persons who are unable to take a test on Saturday for religious reasons. C-PPST administrations are prescheduled through Prometric test centers (usually Sylvan Learning Centers) and are not very restricted on test dates or times.

Feasibility Considerations

Testing Time

One hour, unless the test taker applies for and is granted a time extension. This time extension is given to non-native speakers and some handicapped individuals.

For Testing Groups? Individuals?

The PPST is group administered, but sometimes the group is as small as one. The ETS is also willing to do an individual administration for an additional fee.

Test Administration and Scoring

The PPST is given on all of the regularly scheduled PRAXIS dates. Currently this is six times a year (January, March, April, June, September, and November).

The Registration Bulletin contains information on test sites.

The test taker obtains a single score on each part of the PPST. Performance is also given by subcategories (see "Characteristics Described" above).

Test Materials and Approximate Costs

Individuals, educational institutions, and states do not purchase the tests; individuals simply sign up to take the test. The cost for the PPST is $25 for each test, plus the $35 registration fee. The cost for the C-PPST is slightly higher.

Adequacy of Test Manuals

These are not available to the public. The ETS does make available its *Test at a Glance* booklet.

The annual publication *Understanding Your PRAXIS Scores* (ETS, 2001d) has as its primary purpose the listing of all the tests and the cutoff scores used by each state. Over 30 states use the PRAXIS I tests. This publication also includes possible score range, score interval, number of examinees, median, average performance range, standard error of measurement, and standard error of scoring. Omitted is helpful information on reliability, validity, norming groups, and objectivity. For this reason the publication is of only limited usefulness.

Excerpts from Other Test Reviews

"The PPST in Reading meets all of the review criteria. The test shows strong evidence of being technically sound. The procedures for test development, equating, reliability, and standard setting are consistent with current measurement practices. . . . However, since the job analysis on which the content is based is over 10 years old, a study should be conducted to examine whether the components included from the previous job analysis are still current and appropriate and whether additional skills should be addressed" (Mitchell et al., 2001, p. 87).

"PRAXIS I is the new name for the Pre-Professional Skills Test. These tests have been revised to match the preprofessional knowledge rated important by a large group of practicing teachers" (Postman, 1995, p. 4).

Ordering Information

Publisher

Educational Testing Service, Teaching and Learning Division, P.O. Box 6051, Princeton, NJ 08541-6051; Phone: 609-771-7395; Fax: 609-530-0581, 609-771-7906; Web site: www.teachingandlearning.org.

Authors

ETS staff.

Publication Date

Continuously revised.

Cautions and Comments

Objectivity concerns would mandate that the writing test *not* be used for individual certification decisions. For example, if a passing score is set at 173, there is considerable probability that a failing score of 172 would have been at least one point higher if graded by a different scorer. Likewise, there is no assurance that a passing score, say 173, would not be lower than passing if graded by another scorer.

Validity concerns would also argue against the use of PPST for individual decisions. The fact that the ETS is reluctant to share reliability and validity information must be taken into account in any evaluation or adoption process. This fact is evident in the work by the National Research Council (NRC) (Mitchell et al., 2001), where they note on page after page that certain information is not available and how this must be interpreted (see "Statistical Confirmation" above). The publication mode of this information further limits its dissemination. The NRC does list in the table of contents "Background papers provided to the committee" on pages 551–560 (Mitchell et al., 2001, xii). However, they are *not* published in the book and are only available through the NRC web site, www.nap.edu. Inquiry is further limited by the fact that each page in the unpublished section must be accessed and printed separately. Getting a hard copy takes time and persistence, since there are well over 100 pages.

On a historical note, the C-PPST was preceded by the Computer Based Testing (CBT), which was discontinued on December 31, 2001. Previous to the CBT/PPST, many states used the General Knowledge and Communication Skills tests for the same admission and certification purposes. Both were part of the CORE Battery, which was discontinued in the mid-1990s. The CBT was unique in that it was computer adaptive. This meant that the questions presented were "based on the responses made to previous questions." So when a test taker answered a question incorrectly, an easier question was presented. Likewise, answering correctly brought up a harder question. This technique was acceptable unless the examinee guessed a great deal; then the CBT would have trouble arriving at a correct score.

It should be noted that though most states use the PPST and C-PPST for admission to an education program, they are sometimes used for certification. Virginia uses these tests for that purpose. Whatever the purpose, each state decides on its own passing scores. Many educators find that they can be fully certified in one state, but have to meet different scores and/or take different tests when they move across state lines.

Preparation for this test can be successful and students can improve scores significantly by focusing on a number of areas:

Time management during the test

Reading speed improvement

Reading comprehension improvement

Vocabulary enlargement

Review of relevant math and grammar concepts

For example, in preparing for the 30-minute essay, students need to practice outlining and then writing a structured essay from the outline. Rigidly determining the length and number of paragraphs is a big help to some writers. There are also a number of web sites which help students master the content of the areas of PRAXIS I.

Here are some sample questions.

Mathematics

Which of the following fractions is least?
A. 11/10
B. 99/100
C. 25/24

D. 3/2
E. 501/500
(ETS, 2001b, p. 59)

Reading

Which of the following words, if substituted for the word "occult" in line 5, would introduce the LEAST change in the meaning of the sentence?
  legendary
  subtle
  invincible
  persuasive
  supernatural
(ETS, 2001b, p. 44) (Note: line 5 above refers to the passage that precedes the question.)

Writing

Sentence correction
  Martin Luther King, Jr., **spoke out passionately** for the poor of all races.
  A. spoke out passionately
  B. spoke out passionate
  C. did spoke out passionately
  D. has spoke out passionately
  E. had spoken out passionate
(ETS, 2001b, p. 52)

30-Minute Essay

Which of your possessions would be the most difficult for you to give up or lose? Discuss why. (ETS, 2001b, p. 55)

PRAXIS was known for many decades as the National Teachers Exam (NTE).

References

Boe, E. E., & Gilford, D. M. (Eds.). (1992). *Teacher supply, demand and quality: Policy issues, models and data bases*. Washington, DC: National Academy Press.

Committee on Assessment and Teacher Quality, National Research Council. (2000). *Tests and teaching quality, interim report*. Washington, DC: National Academy Press.

Educational Testing Service (ETS). (2001a). Bulletin of information. Princeton, NJ: ETS.

Educational Testing Service (ETS). (2001b). PRAXIS I: Academic Skills Assessments. In *Tests at a glance*. Princeton, NJ: ETS.

Educational Testing Service (ETS). (2001c). *Registration Bulletin, 2001–02*. Princeton, NJ: ETS.

Educational Testing Service (ETS). (2001d). *Understanding your PRAXIS scores*. Princeton, NJ: ETS.

Latham, A. S., Gitomer, D., & Ziomek, R. (1999). What the tests tell us about new teachers. *Educational Leadership 56*, 23–26.

Mitchell, K. J., Robinson, D. Z., Plake, B. S., & Knowles, K. T. (Eds.). (2001). *Testing teacher candidates: The role of licensure tests in improving teacher quality*. Washington, DC: National Academy Press.

Olebe, M., Jackson, A., & Danielson, C. (1999). Investing in beginning teachers: The California model. *Educational Leadership 56*, 41–44.

Pearlman, M. (1999). *Evaluating teachers' professional practice*. Invited paper for the Teachers of Latin America: New perspectives regarding the development and challenges in their professional development, June 28–30.

Postman, R. (1995), *How to prepare for the PRAXIS*. Hauppauge, NY: Barron's Educational Series.

PRAXIS II: Subject Assessment/Specialty Tests (PRAXIS II),
for testing groups of college graduates who desire certification in a state
Reviewed by Charles W. Hatch, Ph.D., Educational Research and Measurement
(There are approximately 138 different subject tests.)

Note: Even though PRAXIS II is treated as if it were one instrument, it is actually a large number of instruments under one umbrella title. The word PRAXIS itself, which appeared in the early 1990s for the first time replacing the venerable National Teachers Exam (NTE), doesn't really mean anything specific but seems to allude to educational practice. Closely related to PRAXIS II is the School Leadership Series of two tests, one for principals and one for superintendents. However, they are only used in a handful of states and the relevant population is relatively small. The ETS web site (www.teachingandlearning.org) has information on both of these tests.

Data for this review was not easy to obtain because the ETS seems reluctant to release data on reliability, validity, and objectivity. This is especially troubling since these tests are generally used for state teacher certification where specific cutoff scores are assigned and a person scoring one point too low is denied a teaching credential. The problem is especially critical on tests that are not multiple choice. Here the variability introduced by the evaluation process (objectivity) could easily cause relatively large point swings.

Usefulness of the Test for Educators

Test Authors' Purpose

The PRAXIS II Subject Assessments measure general and subject-specific pedagogical skills and knowledge. They provide a system of thorough, fair, and carefully validated tests and assessments for states to use as part of their teacher licensure process.

Decision-Making Applications

These instruments are intended for states to use as part of the certification process. Another application would be for program evaluation and restructuring of college preparation programs. In this use, the test shortcomings would not be so crucial.

Relevant Population

College graduates or undergraduates who desire a particular state certification.

Characteristics Described

Each of the tests covers its own unique range of content. The best source of a careful listing of the content categories is in the appropriate *Test at a Glance* (TAAG) booklet. For example, the test 0011 (Elementary Education: Curriculum, Instruction and Assessment) has the following content categories:

Reading and language arts	38 questions
Mathematics	22 questions
Science	11 questions
Social Studies	11 questions
Arts and Physical Education	11 questions
General information	17 questions

(ETS, 2001e, p. 23)

Test Scores Obtained

Testees obtain a single, global standard score on a scale 100 to 200 or 250 to 990. The older scale is the latter; it goes back to the very beginning of PRAXIS, then called the National Teachers Exam, in the 1950s. More recently developed tests are on the former scale. In addition, the number correct is reported on each of the question sub-categories (see "Characteristics Described" above).

In the above example (test 0011), the test taker receives a single score (scale 100 to 200) on the whole test. Additional data is provided on each of the above six subcategories, where the number answered correctly, number in the category, and the average score range are all given. Formerly the percent correct and number omitted were also included. Most states have set cutoffs that require a test taker get about 60% of the questions correct.

Technical Adequacy

The ETS makes available only limited technical information. Most of what is available is from the annual publication *Understanding Your PRAXIS Scores* (ETS, 2001o).

Validity Confirmation

The ETS has not generally released this data. However, the Committee on Assessment and Teacher Quality of the National Research Council was able to obtain some information.

The data on *test item validity* suggests that the items are generally developed in a satisfactory manner (Mitchell et al., 2001, pp. 349–460). It must be remembered that this process of item development for PRAXIS II is always an ongoing activity, as items are constantly being added so that the multiple forms can be maintained.

Test response validity presents greater problems. Correlations with other instruments are not given. Generalized procedures are released which describe the methods by which forms are equated and are adequate but not supported by data on specific test forms. The ETS uses a number of questions common across forms to provide the mathematical basis for equating (Mitchell et al., 2001, p. 364).

Possible breaches in test security would be a serious concern when considering test response validity. The ETS publishes guides for test administrations but the challenge is great. One need look no further than the Bulletin of Information to see evidence that test security has been and continues to be a very serious problem. The administration of the PRAXIS II is limited in Louisiana in both locations and dates. There is an additional security charge of $7 there because of previous security breaches (ETS, 2001c, pp. 11, 20).

The ETS has not released much validity information. General remarks are made concerning how tests and items are developed but these are not technically adequate.

Another serious concern lies with the pedagogy tests in various areas (for example, test 0043, English Language, Literature and Pedagogy). The assumption must be that the answers given by a test taker reflect how that person would teach the particular content. If a person were to answer in a manner to satisfy the grader that in no way reflected his or her teaching style, a passing score could be obtained that would completely lack validity. Related to this is the inability of test takers to anticipate what the graders are looking for as a "correct" answer for desired teaching techniques.

It is easy to imagine a situation where an experienced teacher answers questions just as he or she has taught successfully for decades, only to receive a failing grade because these methods do not match an unexpressed criterion. It also easy to see that the teacher above could retake the test and pass by giving the "correct" answers that in no way reflected that person's teaching practices.

An example may help clarify these points. The following is from the English, Reading and Composition TAAG booklet, p. 37. It refers to test 0043, English Language, Literature and Composition: Pedagogy.

Assume that you are planning to teach a unit on the "American Dream" to your eleventh grade American literature class of mixed ability and ethnic diversity. This unit will include the poem "Ellis Island," printed below.

Directions for your response:

First read the poem. Then, in a well-written essay, present ONE objective you would set for your students in studying the poem "Ellis Island."

Give a clear, detailed description of one activity you would use to help your students meet that objective in one or two class periods, and explain how the objective and activity are related.

Be sure to consider the context in which you will be using this activity.

Thus, there is no evidence presented that the scoring criteria for many of the PRAXIS II tests reflect effective teaching. This may be better assessed by an observation instrument than by a paper-and-pencil test.

Reliability Confirmation

The ETS has not released this information beyond the standard error of measurement, which varies from a low of only 4.1 on the German test (0181) to a high of 40 on Teaching speech to students with language impairments (0880). Since these tests are on different scales, the difference is not as great as it appears.

However, the Committee on Assessment and Teacher Quality of the National Research Council reports on three of the PRAXIS II tests:

A. Middle School: English/Language Arts

B. High School Mathematics Proofs, Models and Problems

C. Biology: Content Knowledge Parts 1 and 2

The reliability for the first is reported as .86, which is satisfactory. This is a measure of the unity (internal consistency) of the instrument (Mitchell et al., 2001, p. 399).

For the second, NRC reports that ETS does not calculate reliability for constructed response tests with fewer than six items (Mitchell et al., 2001, p. 421).

For the Biology tests, reliabilities range from .83 to .88, which are satisfactory. These numbers indicate reasonably unified tests (Mitchell et al., 2001, p. 443).

Objectivity Confirmation

PRAXIS II tests have two item types: multiple choice and essay. There is no objectivity problem with the multiple-choice questions. The problem lies with the essay tests. The ETS says the "Standard Error of Scoring" ranges from a low of 0.9 on the Middle school mathematics (0069) to 6.9 on the Social Studies analytical essays (0062). These would give, for example, + or − 6.9 points on the scores of test 0062, which would include two-thirds of graders. To be 90% sure, the interval would be expanded. The ETS gives the objectivity data in an unusual format. It is more common to report inter-rater reliability.

The figures above are *not* low enough for individual decisions to be made from most of the essay-driven tests, let alone critical career decisions.

The NRC reports that the agreement between different raters is .89 for the English test (Mitchell et al., 2001, p. 398) and .94 to .98 for the math test (p. 422). There is no objectivity concern with the biology tests because they are composed of multiple-choice items exclusively. These numbers are very good but inconsistent with the published Standard Error of Scoring. The ETS reports that to be 4.4 for the math test and 2.0 for the English test (ETS, 2001o, p. 20).

Statistical Confirmation

There is some statistical information contained in the publication *Understanding Your PRAXIS Scores,* but it is incomplete and inadequate because it is limited to possible score range, score interval, number of examinees, median, average performance range, standard error of measurement, and standard error of scoring.

The TAAG publications give information on test characteristics such as number of items, topics covered, and some sample questions. See the appropriate TAAG pamphlet for each test. (The references contain a listing of all TAAG publications.)

Further data is given in the very useful *Testing Teacher Candidates* (Mitchell et al., 2001). Information is found there which is not available elsewhere. However, readers should note carefully how many times those editors are forced the use phrasing like the following: "The absence of information on this element of the evaluation framework should not be interpreted to mean that it is ignored in the test development process. It should be interpreted to mean that no information about this aspect of test development was provided" (Mitchell et al., 2001, p. 426).

Special Features

Acronym

PRAXIS II.

Levels of the Test

One.

Number of Test Forms

Questions are drawn from item banks, so the number of forms for most tests is large. There seem to be a few tests that are not taken by many persons, which have only a few set forms.

Norm-Referenced?

Yes. The scores are reported in Standard Scores. Percentiles used to be reported by the ETS but are not at present. Stanines are also not reported.

Some norming samples are extremely small; 15 tests have samples of less than 100. Of these one test involved five persons (test 0097) and another just two (test 0482). This contrasts with others that approach 50,000 (ETS, 2001o, pp. 18–22).

Criterion-Referenced?

No. However, the test taker's performance is reported on a number of subcategories. This information allows a person to have enough information to initiate remediation. PRAXIS II reports the number of questions answered correctly, the number of questions in the category, and the average performance range.

Other Features

The ETS is able to accommodate a wide range of handicapping conditions with specialized features like added time, readers, and large-print forms. Non-Saturday test dates are also available for persons who are unable to take a test on Saturday for religious reasons.

Feasibility Considerations

Testing Time

One or two hours depending on the test, unless the test taker applies for and is granted a time extension. This time extension is given to non-native speakers and some handicapped individuals.

For Testing Groups? Individuals?

The PPST is group administered but sometimes the group is as small as one. The ETS is also willing to schedule an individual administration for an additional fee.

Test Administration and Scoring

The PRAXIS II is given on all of the regularly scheduled PRAXIS dates. Currently this is six times a year (January, March, April, June, September, and November).

The Registration Bulletin contains information on test sites.

The test taker obtains a single score on each test. Performance is also given by subcategories.

Test Materials and Approximate Costs

Individuals, educational institutions, and states do not purchase the tests. Individuals simply sign up to take the test. The cost for a PRAXIS II test ranges from $55 to $85 plus the $35 registration fee. The registration form is part of the Registration Bulletin. Online registration is also available through the web site for an additional fee of $25.

Adequacy of Test Manuals

These are not available to the public. The ETS does make available its TAAG booklets. These are extremely valuable sources of information about the test content to guide preparation study. Even though many people ignore it, the most instructive section is titled "Topics Covered."

The annual publication *Understanding Your PRAXIS Scores* (ETS, 2001o) has as its primary purpose the listing of all the tests and the cutoff scores used by each state. Some specific tests are used by almost three dozen states, while others may be only used by one. For each of the approximately 138 PRAXIS II tests this publication includes possible score range, score interval, number of examinees, median, average performance range, standard error of measurement, and standard error of scoring. Omitted is helpful information on reliability, validity, norming groups, and objectivity. For this reason the publication is of only limited usefulness.

Excerpts from Other Test Reviews

"Overall the test [Middle school English/language arts] is well constructed and has moderate to good psychometric properties. The procedures for test development are all consistent with current measurement practices. No information was provided on equating alternate forms of the test, and validity evidence is limited to content-related evidence" (Impara, 2000, quoted in Mitchell et al., 2001, p. 93).

"Subject assessments are the revised form of the old Specialty Area tests. Subject Assessments have been extensively revised and are all based on a job analysis. These tests feature a modularized format that usually includes modules for Content Knowledge, Content Essays, and Pedagogy (a combination of multiple choice and short answer). States may require some or all of these modules for certification" (Postman, 1995, p. 7).

Ordering Information

Publisher

Educational Testing Service, Teaching and Learning Division, P.O. Box 6051, Princeton, NJ 08541-6051; Phone: 609-771-7395; Fax: 609-530-0581, 609-771-7906; Web site: www.teachingandlearning.org.

Authors

ETS staff.

Publication Date

Continuously revised.

Cautions and Comments

Objectivity concerns would mandate that the essay tests *not* be used for individual certification decisions. For example, if a passing score is set at 173, there is considerable probability that a failing score of 172 would have been at least one point higher if graded by a different scorer. Likewise, there is no assurance that a passing score, say 173, would not be lower than passing if graded by another scorer.

Validity concerns would also argue against the use of the PRAXIS II for individual decisions. The fact that the ETS is reluctant to share reliability and validity information must be taken into account in any evaluation or adoption process.

Many educators find that they can be fully certified in one state but have to meet different scores and/or take different tests when they move across state lines.

The exact number of PRAXIS II exams changes constantly, so the number 138 given at the beginning is close but it may not be exact. The ETS posts discontinued tests on its web site. This information is probably the most current.

Test takers must be *very* careful to take the correct test. They must match both the name and the test number to the state requirements. The ETS has a state-by-state listing of the test name, code, and required score for all states using the PRAXIS. It is common for persons to take the wrong test. One common mistake is to take the test that closely matches a college major even when that test is not used by the state desired.

Preparation for these tests can be successful and students can improve scores significantly by focusing on a number of areas:

Time management on the test

Reading speed improvement

Reading comprehension improvement

Vocabulary enlargement

Review of relevant content

Understanding of test item formats (for example: Except)

In regard to the last area above, can you imaging the problems a person would have on the PRAXIS II if he or she used the meaning "to take" in every one of the many questions containing the word EXCEPT? That is, confusing except and accept.

PRAXIS was known for many decades as the National Teachers Exam (NTE).

References

Boe, E. E., & Gilford, D. M. (Eds.). (1992). *Teacher supply, demand and quality: Policy issues, models and data bases.* Washington, DC: National Academy Press.

Committee on Assessment and Teacher Quality, National Research Council. (2000). *Tests and teaching quality, interim report.* Washington, DC: National Academy Press.

Educational Testing Service (ETS). (2001a). Art, music and theatre. In *Tests at a glance.* Princeton, NJ: ETS.

Educational Testing Service (ETS). (2001b). Biology and general science. In *Tests at a glance.* Princeton, NJ: ETS.

Educational Testing Service (ETS). (2001b). Bulletin of information. Princeton, NJ: ETS.

Educational Testing Service (ETS). (2001d). Business and technology. In *Tests at a glance.* Princeton, NJ: ETS.

Educational Testing Service (ETS). (2001e). Education. In *Tests at a glance.* Princeton, NJ: ETS.

Educational Testing Service (ETS). (2001f). Education of students with disabilities. In *Tests at a glance*. Princeton, NJ: ETS.

Educational Testing Service (ETS). (2001g). English, reading and communication. In *Tests at a glance*. Princeton, NJ: ETS.

Educational Testing Service (ETS). (2001h). Guidance, administration and school services. In *Tests at a glance*. Princeton, NJ: ETS.

Educational Testing Service (ETS). (2001i). Languages. In *Tests at a glance*. Princeton, NJ: ETS.

Educational Testing Service (ETS). (2001j). Mathematics. In *Tests at a glance*. Princeton, NJ: ETS.

Educational Testing Service (ETS). (2001k). Middle school. In *Tests at a glance*. Princeton, NJ: ETS.

Educational Testing Service (ETS). (2001l). Physical science. In *Tests at a glance*. Princeton, NJ: ETS.

Educational Testing Service (ETS). (2001m). *Registration Bulletin, 2001–02*. Princeton, NJ: ETS.

Educational Testing Service (ETS). (2001n). Social Sciences. In *Tests at a Glance*. Princeton, NJ: ETS.

Educational Testing Service (ETS). (2001o). *Understanding your PRAXIS scores*. Princeton, NJ: ETS.

Impara, J. C. (2000). *An evaluation of the middle school: English/language test*. Technical Report. Paper commissioned by the Committee of Assessment and Teacher Quality, Center for Education, National Research Council.

Latham, A. S., Gitomer, D., & Ziomek, R. (1999). What the tests tell us about new teachers. *Educational Leadership 56*, 23–26.

Mitchell, K. J., Robinson, D. Z., Plake, B. S., & Knowles, K. T. (Eds.). (2001). *Testing teacher candidates: The role of licensure tests in improving teacher quality*. Washington, DC: National Academy Press.

Olebe, M., Jackson, A., & Danielson, C. (1999). Investing in beginning teachers: The California model. *Educational Leadership 56*, 41–44.

Pearlman, Mari. (1999). *Evaluating teachers' professional practice*. Invited paper for the Teachers of Latin America: New perspectives regarding the development and challenges in their professional development, June 28–30.

Postman, R. (1995). *How to prepare for the PRAXIS*. Hauppauge, NY: Barron's Educational Series.

PRAXIS: Principles of Learning and Teaching (PLT),
for testing groups of college graduates who desire certification in a state
Reviewed by Charles W. Hatch, Ph.D., Educational Research and Measurement

---

Usefulness of the Test for Educators

Test Authors' Purpose

"To provide a system of thorough, fair, and carefully validated tests and assessments for states to use as part of this teacher licensure process" (ETS, 2001, p. 4).

"These assessments use a case study approach to measure your general pedagogical knowledge at three grade levels" (ETS, 2001a, p. 5).

Decision-Making Applications

The PLT is intended for states to use as part of the certification process. That is, states set minimum scores for candidates to meet for licensure.

Another application would be for program evaluation and restructuring. States could use PLT results for feedback to colleges and universities so that their course offerings would be more directly aligned with the test content. For this use, the test's shortcomings would not be so crucial.

Relevant Population

College graduates or undergraduates who desire a particular state certification.

Characteristics Described

The PLT is designed to assess a beginning teacher's knowledge of a variety of job-related criteria. Such knowledge is typically obtained in undergraduate preparation in such areas as educational psychology, human growth and development, classroom management, instructional design and delivery techniques, evaluation and assessment, and other professional preparation. These broad content areas are reported in five subcategories (see "Test Scores Obtained" below).

Test Scores Obtained

Testees obtain a single, global standard score on a scale of 100 to 200. Previously the ETS reported percentiles, but this is no longer true. No stanines are reported. In addition, scores are reported on the following subcategories:

1. Organizing content knowledge for student learning

2. Creating an environment for student learning

3. Teaching for student learning

4. Teacher professionalism

5. Short answer (discussion questions)

Examples

A multiple-choice question related to a case study:

Which of the following characteristics of Burns (a gifted student in the preceding case study) is most indicative of giftedness?
   A. Taking structured and careful notes
   B. Attempting to gain teacher approval
   C. Demonstrating academic resourcefulness
   D. Intending to pursue a professional career
(ETS, 2001b)

A discussion question related to the same case study:

> List either three characteristics of, or three strategies for, effective use of questioning during a lecture in order to increase students' learning. Explain the importance of one of the strategies you have listed above. (Scored 0–3) (ETS, 2001b)

A multiple-choice question *not* related to case study:

> In a sixth grade social studies unit on election, groups of students develop a political platform, debate the issues, and vote for candidates of their choice. The teacher of this class is using which of the following approaches?
> A. Cooperative
> B. Work-study
> C. Stimulation
> D. Inquiry
> (ETS, 2001b)

Technical Adequacy

The ETS makes available only limited technical information. Most of what is available comes from the annual publication *Understanding Your PRAXIS Scores*. The Background Papers in *Testing Teacher Candidates* (Mitchell et al., 2001) contain some further data. See below.

Validity Confirmation

The ETS has not generally released this data. However, the Committee on Assessment and Teacher Quality of the National Research Council was able to obtain some information.

The data on *test item validity* suggests that the items are generally developed in a satisfactory manner (Mitchell et al., 2001, pp. 349–460). It must be remembered that this process of item development for PLT is always an ongoing activity, as items are constantly being added so that the multiple forms can be maintained. It is reported that results are used when response rates from a verification survey were as low as 3% (state agency officials) (Mitchell et al., 2001, p. 373). Figures this low generally render the results unusable.

Test response validity presents greater problems. Correlations with other instruments are not given. Generalized procedures are released which describe the methods by which forms are equated and are adequate but not supported by data on specific test forms. The ETS uses a number of questions common across forms to provide the mathematical basis for equating (Mitchell et al., 2001, p. 378).

Possible breaches in test security would be a serious concern when considering test response validity. The ETS publishes guides for test administrations, but the challenge is great. One need look no further than the Bulletin of Information to see evidence that test security has been and continues to be a very serious problem. The administration of the PRAXIS is limited in Louisiana. There is an additional security charge of $7 there because of previous security breaches (ETS, 2001a, pp. 11, 20).

Test item validity is a continuing concern because the makers assume that one test is able to reflect accurately the instruction that occurs in each of the many preparation programs across the United States.

Another validity concern would be the degree to which PLT scores differentiate between successful and unsuccessful teacher candidates.

Reliability Confirmation

The ETS has not released information beyond the standard error of measurement, which varies from 6.0 to 6.8 for these three PLT tests. However, the Committee on Assessment and Teacher Quality of the National Research Council was able to obtain some information.

The estimates of the consistency of scores from different forms were only between .72 and .76. These figures are low, even considering that PLT contains essay responses as well as multiple choice (Mitchell et al., 2001, p. 377).

Objectivity Confirmation

The PLT has two item types: multiple choice and discussion. There is no objectivity problem with the 45 multiple-choice questions. The problem lies with the six short-answer questions. The ETS says the "Standard Error of Scoring" is 1.9 (grades K–6), 1.8 (grades 5–9), and 2.82 (grades 7–12). These would give, for example, + or – 1.9 points on the short-answer raw scores, which would include two-thirds of graders. To be 90% sure, the interval would be expanded to 2.43 for the K–6 form, 2.3 for the 5–9 form and 2.82 on the 7–12 form. This is a range of over four points!

The NRC reports exact agreement on the six short-answer questions between 72% and 78%, and agreement within one point to be 99% (Mitchell et al., 2001, p. 377). These are excellent but not consistent with the standard error of scoring reported by the ETS.

The standard error of scoring figures is *not* low enough for individual decisions, let alone critical career decisions, to be made from the PLT alone.

Statistical Confirmation

There is some statistical information contained in the publication *Understanding Your PRAXIS Scores*, but it is incomplete and inadequate because it is limited to possible score range, score interval, number of examinees, median, average performance range, standard error of measurement, and standard error of scoring. The TAAG publications only give information on test characteristics such as number of items, topics covered, and some sample questions.

Further data is given in the very useful *Testing Teacher Candidates* (Mitchell et al., 2001). Information is found there which is not available elsewhere. However, readers should note carefully how many times those editors are forced to use phrasing like the following: "The absence of information on this element of the evaluation framework should not be interpreted to mean that it is ignored in the test development process. It should be interpreted to mean that no information about this aspect of test development was provided" (Mitchell et al., 2001, p. 356).

Special Features

Acronym

PLT.

Levels of the Test

Three levels are administered: kindergarten–grade 6 (test 0522), grade 5–grade 9 (test 0523), and grade 7–grade 12 (test 0524).

Number of Test Forms

Questions are drawn from item banks, so the number of forms is almost unlimited.

Norm-Referenced?

Yes. The scores are reported in Standard Scores with a range of 100 to 200. The only information on the norming sample is the number. The K–6 test form is based on 40,960 responses, the 5–9 test is based on 5,552 responses, and the 7–12 form is based on 25,045 responses. Though no further information is provided these individuals are assumed to be simply those persons who signed up to take the test and were *not* a group selected to be nationally representative.

Criterion-Referenced?

No. However, the test taker's performance is reported on a number of subcategories. This information allows a person to have enough information to initiate remediation. PLT reports the number of questions answered correctly, the number of questions in the category, and the average performance range. The reporting categories are:

Organizing content knowledge for student learning

Creating an environment for student learning

Teaching for student learning

Teacher professionalism

In addition, the short-answer performance is also recorded.

Other Features

The ETS is able to accommodate a wide range of handicapping conditions with specialized features like added time, readers, and large-print forms. Non-Saturday test dates are also available for persons who are unable to take a test on Saturday for religious reasons.

Feasibility Considerations

Testing Time

Two hours, unless the test taker applies for and is granted a time extension. This time extension is given to non-native speakers and some handicapped individuals.

For Testing Groups? Individuals?

The PLT is group administered but sometimes the group is as small as one. The ETS is also willing to do an individual administration for an additional fee.

Test Administration and Scoring

The PLT is given on all of the regularly scheduled PRAXIS dates. Currently this is six times a year (January, March, April, June, September, and November). The *Registration Bulletin* (ETS, 2001c) contains information on test sites.

The test taker obtains a single score on the PLT.

Performance is also given by subcategories (see "Criterion-Referenced?" above).

Test Materials and Approximate Costs

Individuals, educational institutions, and states do not purchase the tests. Individuals simply sign up to take the test. The cost is $80 (test fee) + $35 (registration fee) for a total of $115. The registration form is part of the *Registration Bulletin*. Online registration is also available through the web site for an additional fee of $25.

Adequacy of Test Manuals

These are not available to the public. The ETS does make available, at no charge, its TAAG booklets. This is an extremely valuable source of information about the test content to guide preparation study.

The annual publication *Understanding Your PRAXIS Scores* contains limited technical information on the following: possible score range, score interval, number of examinees, median, average performance range, standard error of measurement, and standard error of scoring. Of more benefit to most test takers is the listing of all the states using each test and the passing score required by each. Although it contains some useful information, it is inadequate for critical evaluation.

Excerpts from Other Test Reviews

"The test seems to be well constructed and has moderate-to-good psychometric qualities. The procedures reportedly used for test development, standard setting, and validation are all consistent with sound measurement practices. The fairness reviews and technical strategies used are also consistent with sound measurement practices. . . . No information was provided on equating alternate forms of the test. This is a problem as equating tests that combine both multiple-choice and constructed response items may not be a straightforward process. It appears that the test has been getting easier as later forms are developed, suggesting that the equating process may have to deal with differences in score distribution" (Mitchell et al., 2001, p. 391).

Ordering Information

Publisher

Educational Testing Service, Teaching and Learning Division, P.O. Box 6051, Princeton, NJ 08541-6051; Phone: 609-771-7395; Fax: 609-530-0581; Web site: www.teachingandlearning.org.

Authors

ETS staff.

Publication Date

Around 1994. Although the test originally appeared some years ago, the ETS has the capacity to constantly update questions to keep the test content current to within about 18 months of a test administration date.

Cautions and Comments

The PLT is the successor to the Professional Knowledge (PK) test formerly offered by the ETS as part of the CORE Battery. This was in turn preceded by the Commons Exam. Many states that used the PK test in the certification process simply switched to the PLT in the mid-1990s.

Objectivity concerns would mandate that this test *not* be used for individual certification decisions. For example, if a passing score is set at 165, there is considerable probability that a failing score of 164 would have been at least one point higher if graded by a different scorer. Likewise, there is no assurance that a passing score, say 166, would not be lower than passing if graded by another scorer.

Validity concerns would also argue against the use of PLT for individual decisions.

The test requires that an examinee prepare carefully and have a plan developed before answering the first question. Since the test requires the test taker to read three case studies, to answer 45 multiple-choice questions, and to write six discussion answers within two hours, careful time management is a must.

The fact that the ETS is reluctant to share more complete reliability, validity, and objectivity information must be taken into account in any evaluation or adoption process.

Preparation for this test can be successful and students can improve scores significantly by focusing on a number of areas:

Time management during the test

Reading speed improvement

Reading comprehension improvement

Vocabulary enlargement

Review of educational psychology

Understanding statistics and educational measurement

References

Boe, E. E., & Gilford, D. M. (Eds.). (1992). *Teacher supply, demand and quality: Policy issues, models and databases*. Washington, DC: National Academy Press.

Committee on Assessment and Teacher Quality, National Research Council. (2000). *Tests and teaching quality, interim report*. Washington, DC: National Academy Press.

Educational Testing Service (ETS). (2001a). PRAXIS I: Academic Skills Assessments. In *Tests at a glance*. Princeton, NJ: ETS.

Educational Testing Service (ETS). (2001b). Principles of learning and teaching. In *Tests at a glance*. Princeton, NJ: ETS.

Educational Testing Service (ETS). (2001c). *Registration Bulletin, 2001–02*. Princeton, NJ: ETS.

Latham, A. S., Gitomer, D., & Ziomek, R. (1999). What the tests tell us about new teachers. *Educational Leadership 56*, 23–26.

Mitchell, K. J., Robinson, D. Z., Plake, B. S., & Knowles, K. T. (Eds.). (2001). *Testing teacher candidates: The role of licensure tests in improving teacher quality*. Washington, DC: National Academy Press.

Olebe, M., Jackson, A., & Danielson, C. (1999). Investing in beginning teachers: The California model. *Educational Leadership 56*, 41–44.

Pearlman, M. (1999). *Evaluating teachers' professional practice*. Invited paper for the Teachers of Latin America: New perspectives regarding the development and challenges in their professional development, June 28–30.

3

Early Childhood Admission Tests

Boehm Test of Basic Concepts: Third Edition (BOEHM-3),
for testing groups or individuals from 5 through 7 years of age
Reviewed by Charles W. Hatch, Ph.D., Educational Research and Measurement

Usefulness of the Test for Educators

Test Author's Purpose

The test "was devised to determine whether relational concepts commonly used in primary-school curricular materials and teacher directions, often assumed present at time of school entrance, were possessed by young children" (Boehm, 2001).

Decision-Making Applications

The BOEHM-3 is suited for admission and for the identification of at-risk children. It may also serve as a guide in the planning of instruction for remediation. Since the results are in terms of the number of mastered relational concepts, children may be ranged easily from the least number satisfactorily answered to the most. Providing data for instructional prescriptive decisions would be an important function for the BOEHM-3. Instruction itself is facilitated by the nature of the relational concepts themselves. For example, it would be far less difficult to instruct a child lacking the concept "top" from BOEHM-3 than, say, to teach a second child who has weak performance on a global characteristic obtained from another test.

Relevant Population

Kindergarten through grade 2 (ages 5–7).

Characteristics Described

Knowledge of essential relational words and phrases such as "next to," "few," and "after." The words/phrases are grouped under the following classifications:

Spatial (example: next to)

Quantitative (example: few)

Temporal (example: after)

Miscellaneous (example: other)

Test Scores Obtained

Students are assessed on a pass/fail basis for each of the 50 words. In addition, overall percentile rank and ranking on individual items is obtained. Separate scales are provided twice for each of the three grade levels, at the beginning and end of each year. It is also possible to compare performance to students of similar socioeconomic status (SES).

Technical Adequacy

Validity Confirmation

Test item validity: The concepts measured were chosen because of the frequency with which they were used in primary curricula, particularly in directions given to the pupil, and the relative lack of emphasis within standard textbooks and workbooks.

Test response validity: Correlations with other achievement tests range from .38 to .64 (median .40). These figures are certainly not compelling.

Reliability Confirmation

Comparison of scores from children taking two different forms of the test: reliability coefficients = .82 at kindergarten, .77 at grade 1, .65 at grade 2.

As above but with the same form repeated after one year, reliability coefficients = .55 to .88 (only 2 over .80).

A split half comparison of scores from children taking one form of the test: reliability coefficients = .55 to .87 (only 10 over .80).

These figures are satisfactory but not convincingly high.

Objectivity Confirmation

Keys are available from the publisher. Use of these should provide satisfactory agreement between different scorers evaluating the same student's answers.

Statistical Confirmation

The manual provides adequate information on reliability, validity, and norming population.

Special Features

Acronym

BOEHM-3. The earlier versions were known as the BTBC and the BTBC-R (for the revised version).

Levels of the Test

There are three levels: kindergarten, grade 1, and grade 2.

Number of Test Forms

There are two current forms: E and F. Still able to be purchased are forms C and D (of BTBS-R). These would still be useful to support a testing program that has invested heavily in the BTBS-R. The publisher should be encouraged for providing this kind of continued support.

Norm-Referenced?

Yes. This is a norm-referenced test with norming tables presented for the beginning and end of each grade covered (total of 6). Additionally, percentile rank is reported with reference to either the total sample or by SES. The norming sample is reasonably representative of U.S. schoolchildren, but some problems and potential problems need to be noted.

The norming sample was composed only of public school children in regular classes. These are limitations. Additionally, districts were asked to choose schools for inclusion that "would provide a sample representative of the range of schools within the district." Self-selection is thus another potential problem.

Criterion-Referenced?

Although the BOEHM-3 is a norm-referenced instrument, pass/fail results are available for each child by individual word. This detailed reporting allows precise remediation to be undertaken. Thus, a teacher could know *exactly* which words or phrases each child missed. This would allow for effective group and individual remediation.

Other Features

The BOEHM-3 may be administered in both English and Spanish.

Feasibility Considerations

Testing Time

Thirty to 40 minutes for the two booklets.

For Testing Groups? Individuals?

The BOEHM-3 is a group-administered test, but it can be administered individually.

Test Administration and Scoring

The test is administered in the form of two booklets in which the child makes responses. There are three practice questions. Then, starting with easy concepts, the child proceeds to more complicated concepts. For each question the subject is asked to indicate the picture that correctly indicates the desired relationship. For example, "Mark the one where the book is **next to** the horse." Keys are provided for ease of grading and increased agreement between scorers.

Test Materials and Approximate Costs

All of the following prices are available from the web site but should be verified before ordering.

Examination Set (015-4020-80X-WP199)	$55
Test Kit (25 forms)	
Form E (015-8020-804-WP199)	$75
Form F (015-8020-812-WP199)	$75
Examiner's Manual (015-8020-820-WP199)	$49
Keys (E & F) (015-8020-863-WP199)	$5 each
Directions for Administering (015-8020-88X-WP199)	$15

In addition, the BOEHM-R (forms C and D) may still be purchased.

Adequacy of Test Manuals

The manual is adequate, but caution needs to be exercised because some quoted data is from the original BTBC and the subsequent BTBC-R.

Excerpts from Other Test Reviews

"Although there is some evidence for the importance of the words (and hence for the use of the test as a criterion-referenced device), the device has inadequate reliability and norms for purposes other than screening" (Salvia & Ysseldyke, 2001).

"The BOEHM Test of Basic Concepts can be used as an aid in pinpointing specific areas where a child can benefit from remedial help" (Gale, 1998).

Ordering Information

Publisher

The Psychological Corporation, 19500 Bulverde Road, San Antonio, TX 78259; Phone: 800-228-0752; Fax: 210-339-5873; Web site: www.psychcorp.com.

Author

Ann E. Boehm.

Publication Dates

BOEHM-3, 2000; BTBC-R, 1986.

Cautions and Comments

The BOEHM-3 has exceptional practicality, which derives from its conceptual basis. The measurement of single instructionally important words and concepts provides directly relevant information for educators and parents. The ability to gain important information from this instrument along with supporting data from other instruments can lead to productive intervention that cannot fail to have a long-term positive outcome.

The norming sample has problems of being too narrowly defined (public schools, regular classrooms) and not being as representative as it might have been if the factor of self-selection had been removed (see "Norm-Referenced?" above).

Because of some weakness in the reliability and validity data, the test may be better suited to screening than for individual decision-making on the basis of this single data source.

References

Boehm, A. E. (1966). *The development of comparative concepts in primary school children.* Unpublished doctoral dissertation, Teachers College, Columbia University, New York.

Boehm, A. E. (2001). Self-profile. www.mayfieldpub.com/psychtesting/profiles/boehm, August 20.

Cohen, L. G., & Spenciner, L. J. (1994). *Assessment of young children.* New York: Longman.

Gale encyclopedia of childhood and adolescence. (1998). Gale Research. Available on the Internet at looksmart.com.

Genishi, C. (Ed.). (1992). *Ways of assessing children and curriculum: Stories of early childhood practice.* New York: Teachers College Press.

McCullough, V. (1992). *Testing and your child: What you should know about 150 of the most common medical, educational and psychological tests.* New York: Plume.

Pierangelo, R., & Giuliani, G. (2000). *Special educator's guide to 109 diagnostic tests.* New York: Prentice Hall.

Salvia, J., & Ysseldyke, J. (2001). *Assessment* (8th ed.). Boston: Houghton Mifflin.

Sattler, J. M. (2001). *Assessment of children: Cognitive applications* (4th ed.). La Mesa, CA: Jerome M. Sattler Publications.

Bracken Basic Concept Scale-Revised (BBCS-R), for testing
individuals from 2 years, 6 months through 7 years, 11 months of age
(Formerly Bracken Basic Concept Scale [BBCS])
Reviewed by Charles W. Hatch, Ph.D., Educational Research and Measurement

---

Usefulness of the Test for Educators

Test Author's Purpose

The BBCS-R is "a developmentally sensitive measure of children's basic concept acquisition and receptive language skills" (Nellis, 2001, p. 162) and "is used to assess the basic concept development of children in the age range of 2 years 6 months through 7 years 11 months" (Bracken, 1998).

Decision-Making Applications

Assessment

As an independent measure of a child's concept acquisition

For addressing the receptive component when contrasting a child's receptive and expressive language skills

For examining the relationship between a child's language development and his or her cognitive functioning when used in conjunction with other tests

For pairing results with specific intervention strategies (Bracken, 1998, p. 6)

Screening

For possible developmental delay

For possible cognitive-related exceptionalities (e.g., learning disability [LD], mental retardation [MR], giftedness [GT]) (Bracken, 1998, p. 6)

School Readiness (using the School Readiness Composite)

Useful for preschool screening

For kindergarten "roundup"

For decision-making when retention is an issue (Bracken, 1998, p. 6)

Clinical and Educational Research

Program evaluations

Contrasted group studies

Studies of children's developmental progression (Bracken, 1998, p. 7)

This instrument seems well suited for making admission, placement, instructional prescription, achievement certification, and referral decisions. For further discussion, see "Cautions and Comments" below. Other instruments listed in that section could be used in supporting the above decision-making process.

Relevant Population

Children ages 2 years, 6 months through 7 years, 11 months.

Characteristics Described

The following 11 concepts are assessed separately in the order listed: (1) Colors; (2) Letters; (3) Numbers/counting; (4) Sizes; (5) Comparisons; (6) Shapes; (7) Direction/position; (8) Self-/social awareness; (9) Texture/material; (10) Quantity; (11) Time/sequence. The first six comprise the School Readiness Composite (SRC).

Test Scores Obtained

The following are reported:

A. Raw scores (for each of the 11 concepts and total)

B. Scaled scores (for the SRC and each of the concepts 7–11)

C. Standard scores (for the SRC and total)

D. Percentile ranks (for scaled scores and standard scores)

E. Concept age scores (by age level)

F. Global summary (examples: delayed, very delayed)

G. 95% confidence interval on scaled and standard scores

Technical Adequacy

Validity Confirmation

The author reported that the *test response validity* was satisfactorily high. Correlations were reported with the following:

BBSC (former version)	.55 to .89
Wechsler (WPPSI-R)	.72 to .88
Differential Ability Scales	.69 to .88
BOEHM-R	.73 and .89
Preschool Language Scale	.46 to .84

Evidence for *test item validity* concerned the development process for the items. Initial concepts were drawn from

> a wide variety of resource materials . . . included commonly used psycho-educational tests, which either employ concepts in test directions . . . or in test items. In addition to tests of academic, language, and cognitive ability, early childhood language arts worksheets, workbooks, texts, and other curricular materials were examined. . . . After obvious omissions were addressed, the entire list of concepts was reviewed by early childhood professionals (school counselors, preschool and elementary teachers, school psychologists) to identify missing concepts. (Bracken, 1998, p. 11)

The author asserts that the resulting 258 basic concepts "formed the most comprehensive collection of basic language concepts ever compiled in one source" (Bracken, 1998, p. 11).

Reliability Confirmation

The reliabilities reported are more than adequate for applying results to individual children and for making decisions about their placement and instruction.

Internal consistency for the total test ranged from .96 to .99. The subtests were generally lower because of fewer items; these ranged from .78 to .97. Internal consistency reliability estimates the degree to which a test is measuring one characteristic. The range is 0 to 1, where the closer to 1 the figure is, the more reliable the test.

When the same test was administered to the same children twice with a one- to two-week interval, the correlations were .78 to .88. This reliability estimates the stability of the test scores over time.

Objectivity Confirmation

Not addressed in the technical information.

The answer key is actually integral to the recording sheet. That is, the test administrators can see whether a given response is correct or not. However, there is often a degree of subjectivity in the interpretation of responses because of the age of the children involved. A measure on inter-rater agreement would be welcome, and the lack of this information detracts from the completeness of the technical information for this superior test.

Statistical Confirmation

The Examiner's Manual contains a wealth of information on the standardization sample as well as reliability and validity.

Special Features

Acronym

BBCS-R. The Bracken Basic Concept Scale (BBCS) was an earlier form of the test.

Levels of the Test

One, but some modification of administration to accommodate the youngest children.

Number of Test Forms

Two: English and Spanish.

Norm-Referenced?

Yes, as evidenced by the reporting of scaled scores, standard scores, percentile ranks, and age equivalents.

The norming populations are extensively described in the Examiner's Manual and are representative of the U.S. population in 1995.

Criterion-Referenced?

No, but certain specific information can be obtained by conceptual domain that could guide the planning of individual instruction and remediation.

Other Features

The availability of this test in both English and Spanish forms is a plus. The Examiner's Manual contains a wealth of information, both technical and practical.

Feasibility Considerations

Testing Time

The total BBCS-R should take about 30 minutes, and the SRC should take about 10–15 of that total. A very young child may need to have the testing broken down into several sessions.

For Testing Groups? Individuals?

Individuals.

Test Administration and Scoring

The author stresses that since the test is standardized, the conditions of each child's testing be as similar as possible and that the testing be conducted "in a quiet, well-lit, and properly ventilated room removed from distractions and disruptions. Seat the child next to you at a table so both of you can easily see the *Stimulus Manual*" (Bracken, 1998, p. 25).

The qualifications to administer the BBCS-R are reasonable. It "was designed to be administered by professionals knowledgeable in the administration and interpretation of educational instruments. Also, individuals who are involved with psychoeducational assessment or screening (e.g., school psychologists, educational diagnosticians, speech-language pathologists, and special education teachers)" (Bracken, 1998, p. 5).

The record form is clear and complete. The progression from the individual items to the subtest totals and finally to the scaled scores, confidence interval, percentile rank, normative classification, and concept age equivalent is orderly.

A classroom teacher should be able to administer this test with no trouble. A few trial sessions after reading the manual should be sufficient as training. The processes of calculating a basal, establishing a ceiling, and calculating raw scores, while explained in the manual, will be greatly clarified by going through the process.

Test Materials and Approximate Costs

BBCS-R complete kit: $239; English Record Forms (15): $18; Spanish Record

Forms (15): $18; Stimulus Manual: $185; Examiner's Manual: $59. The BBCS Record forms (package of 25: $35) can still be ordered. This last item is encouraging, since it shows the publisher's willingness to support the earlier edition and not force previous users to use the new form unwillingly.

Adequacy of Test Manuals

The Examiner's Manual (212 pages) is a model of what can be included in a clear, usable format.

Excerpts from Other Test Reviews

"The BBCS-R is a well-developed, psychometrically sound instrument that will likely continue to serve a solid role in the assessment of young children" (Nellis, 2000, p. 164).

"Overall, the BBCS-R presents as a bigger and better version of the BBCS with an improved manual and testing format. . . . This test continues to be one of the most comprehensive means of determining a preschooler, kindergartener, or a first-grader's level. The BBCS-R is a sound method of providing a link with assessment and the formation of remedial education interventions" (Solomon, 2001, p. 165).

Ordering Information

Publisher

The Psychological Corporation, 19500 Bulverde Road, San Antonio, TX 78259; Phone: 800-228-0752; Fax: 210-339-5873; Web site: www.psychcorp.com.

Author

Bruce A. Bracken.

Publication Dates

BBCS-R, 1998; BBCS, 1984.

Cautions and Comments

The BBCS-R can be recommended practically without reservation. It has wide application for admission, placement, instructional prescription, achievement, and referral decisions. As with all test-based decisions, the best course is to use information from more than one test source. This cautious approach would be especially relevant when making admission and placement decisions. Other instruments that could be used in decision-making might be:

Wechsler Preschool and Primary Scale of Intelligence (WPPSI-R)

Differential Ability Scales (DAS)

Peabody Picture Vocabulary Test, Third Edition (PPVT-III)

Boehm Test of Basic Concepts-Revised (BOEHM-R)

Boehm Test of Basic Concepts-Preschool Version

Preschool Language Scale-3 (PLS-3)

(Bracken, 1998, pp. 69–74)

The materials are attractive and the Examiner's Manual is extensive and helpful. The references that are included (pp. 209–212) would provide further reading for anyone. The author even elected to list all the tryout and standardization examiners with location (pp. 205–207).

One cautionary note needs to be made concerning the Spanish version. Less than 200 subjects were in that standardization sample, so decisions made from this version need to be more cautious than ones made from the English form.

Lack of objectivity data is a problem that could be easily remedied. It does, however, indicate the necessity for test administrators to study the manual carefully before administering the test and to conduct several practice administrations.

Test results for the standard scores on the SRC and the total score are reported in numbers that are like IQ scores. Nowhere is it asserted that these scores are measures of intelligence, thus the possibility of confusion should be eliminated by reporting the scores on another scale.

References

Bracken, B. A. (1998). *Examiner's manual*. San Antonio, TX: The Psychological Corporation.
Nellis, L. M. (2001). Review of the Bracken Basic Concept Scale-Revised. In B. S. Plake & J. C. Impara (Eds.), *The Fourteenth Mental Measurements Yearbook* (pp. 162–164). Lincoln, NE: The Buros Institute of Mental Measurements.
Solomon, R. H. (2001). Review of the Bracken Basic Concept Scale-Revised. In B. S. Plake & J. C. Impara (Eds.), *The Fourteenth Mental Measurements Yearbook* (pp. 164–165). Lincoln, NE: The Buros Institute of Mental Measurements.

Cognitive Skills Assessment Battery: 2nd Edition (CSAB),
for testing individuals in kindergarten and prior to kindergarten
Reviewed by Charles W. Hatch, Ph.D., Educational Research and Measurement

---

Note: Previously the CSAB was known as (1) the Inventory of Cognitive Skills and Visual-Motor Functioning and (2) the Kindergarten Assessment Battery.

Usefulness of the Test for Educators

Test Authors' Purpose

"The Cognitive Skills Assessment Battery (CSAB) was developed to provide teachers of pre-kindergarten and kindergarten children with information regarding children's progress relative to teaching goals in the cognitive and physical-motor areas" (Diamond, 1985, p. 356).

"The CSAB was developed to include tasks that would provide the teacher with information most useful in curriculum planning throughout the school year and can be supplemented through ongoing teacher observation" (Boehm & Slater, 1981).

Decision-Making Applications

The CSAB "may best be classified as an instructional screening measure which is intended to be used by teachers to make goal-referenced decisions" (Boehm & Slater, 1981, p. 2). The authors are clear that this instrument is not intended for admission decisions or to make decisions about possible developmental delays. They assert that this test is best used to provide a guide for the planning of both class and individual instruction. They are further adamant that the performance *not* be added to form a total score (Boehm & Slater, 1981, p. 8).

Relevant Population

Pre-kindergarten and kindergarten students.

Characteristics Described

The CSAB includes the following five competency areas:

1. Orientation toward one's environment
2. Discrimination of similarities and differences
3. Comprehension and concept formation
4. Coordination
5. Immediate and delayed memory

Test Scores Obtained

Response is recorded for each question/task. These are summed into totals for portions of each of the five competency areas. For example, the second competency area, discrimination of similarities and differences, has five subcategories. They are: color identification, shape identification, symbol and letter discrimination, visual-auditory discrimination, and auditory discrimination.

In addition, similar scores are obtained for a whole class so that a teacher can plan both individual and class activities.

Technical Adequacy

Validity Confirmation

Test item validity: The authors developed the included items from a broad range of sources: curricular materials, teacher interviews, classroom observations, and research.

For the second edition the authors reexamined the content to see whether classroom requirements had changed. They surveyed 51 professionals for input on needed competencies. Table 8 in the Assessor's Manual correlates the competency areas with the appropriate CSAB area (Boehm & Slater, 1981, p. 34).

Reliability Confirmation

The authors administered the test twice with a two- to three-week interval to 16 pre-kindergarten children and 32 kindergarten students. Overall agreement was 79.7% for the younger children and 85% for the older (Boehm & Slater, 1981, pp. 31–33). These numbers are acceptable considering the age of the children and the variability inherent with any measure of young children.

Objectivity Confirmation

Not addressed. This is clearly an area where data is needed, since there is a degree of subjectivity throughout the test. That is, the test administrator is continually required to rate a child's responses across a scale of options. Judgment is involved in these ratings.

Statistical Confirmation

The Assessor's Manual (Boehm & Slater, 1981) contains adequate information.

Special Features

Acronym

CSAB.

Levels of the Test

One.

Number of Test Forms

One.

Norm-Referenced?

No. The authors clearly intended that this test not be norm-referenced.

Criterion-Referenced?

Yes. The specific intent of the authors is for a test that does not have as its purpose differentiating between individuals, but is intended to give instructional information on achievement of particular content and developmental objectives. The data from extensive field testing is included in tabular form in the Assessor's Manual (Boehm & Slater, 1981).

Other Features

The easel/test form is easy to use, portable, and nearly foolproof. It is placed so that the student sees one side and the test administrator sees the other. Each has necessary prompts. Also included are the recording forms.

Feasibility Considerations

Testing Time

Twenty to 25 minutes. May be given in two sessions if the child lacks the attention span to do it in one sitting.

For Testing Groups? Individuals?

Individuals, because the administrator needs to interact with each child individually to elicit responses.

Test Administration and Scoring

"The CSAB is administered to each child individually by a teacher, a school psychologist, a teacher aid, or other school staff" (Boehm & Slater, 1981, p. 5).

The location of the testing is also not critical. "A quiet corner of the regular classroom, an adjoining room, or a corridor are satisfactory places to administer the battery" (Boehm & Slater, 1981, p. 5).

A few minutes should suffice as preparation time before a person administers the test for the first time. It is also necessary for this person to establish rapport with the child before the test starts. Thus, time restraints need to be relaxed.

In addition to the publisher's materials, the following will need to be supplied before testing may start:

1. Eight blocks of the same color, size, and shape.
2. A watch with a sweep second hand or a digital watch that displays seconds.
3. Several primary-size pencils.
4. Blank pieces of paper.
5. A clipboard or other smooth surface on which to attach the Pupil Response Sheet. (Boehm & Slater, 1981, p. 6)

Test Materials and Approximate Costs

The CSAB Kit is $51.95; the CSAB Sampler is $3.95.

Adequacy of Test Manuals

The manuals are satisfactory; the easel is especially good.

Excerpts from Other Test Reviews

"Overall, the CSAB appears to be a useful instrument for purposes of rough, informal assessment of children's developmental level in the five areas represented. Any attempt to go beyond this type of assessment and make more in-depth inferences cannot be justified until there is stronger evidence of validity and reliability" (Diamond, 1985, p. 356).

"In summary, the CSAB seeks to fulfill a definite need in assessing skills that are prerequisite to grade school. However, little psychometric development accompanies the instrument to evaluate its quality. This reviewer cannot recommend the test for routine assessment" (Embretson, 1985, p. 357).

Ordering Information

Publisher

Teachers College Press, 525 West 120th Street, Box 303, New York, NY 10027; Phone: 212-678-3929; Fax: 212-678-4149; Web site: www.tc.columbia.edu.

Authors

Ann E. Boehm and Barbara R. Slater (the former is also the author of the excellent Boehm Test of Basic Concepts [BOEHM-3]).

Publication Date

1981.

Cautions and Comments

The CSAB is now an older instrument that has not been updated. It needs more current field data in addition to objectivity information. In spite of these drawbacks, it is still an excellent instrument for its intended purpose of supplying information to assist in the planning of instruction for an individual or a group.

It is not uncommon for this instrument to be misused. In direct contradiction to the Assessor's Manual (Boehm & Slater, 1981, p. 8), scores are summed for a total score in many schools and at least one state.

The authors also warn about another common misuse of the CSAB: " 'teaching to the test' or allowing the CSAB to 'set goals' is not advisable and would limit the variety of learning experiences prekindergarten and kindergarten children ought to have" (Boehm & Slater, 1981, p. 11). This misuse by educators has come about through the use of CSAB as a school evaluation instrument, which was never the authors' intent.

If this test were to be given to first graders, this too would be a test misuse since the CSAB is intended only for children younger than that, and the *only* data available is for those younger children.

References

Bergen, D., Reid, R., & Torelli, L. (2001). *Instructor's manual for educating and caring for very young children: The infant/toddler curriculum.* New York: Teachers College Press.

Boehm, A. E. (1971). Out of the classroom. *Exceptional Children 37*, 523–527.

Boehm, A. E., & Slater, B. R. (1981). *Cognitive Skills Assessment Battery assessors manual.* New York: Teachers College Press.

Diamond, E. E.. (1985). Review of the Cognitive Skills Assessment Battery. In J. V. Mitchell (Ed.), *The Ninth Mental Measurements Yearbook* (pp. 355–356). Lincoln: University of Nebraska Press.

Embretson, S. (1985). Review of the Cognitive Skills Assessment Battery. In J. V. Mitchell (Ed.), *The Ninth Mental Measurements Yearbook* (pp. 356–357). Lincoln: University of Nebraska Press.

Slater, B. R. (1971). Perceptual development at the kindergarten level. *Journal of Clinical Psychology 27*, 263–266.

Denver Developmental Screening Test (Denver II),
for testing individuals from birth through 6 years of age
Reviewed by Aileen C. Lau-Dickinson, Ed.D., Special Education Administration

---

Usefulness of the Test for Educators

Test Authors' Purpose

The purpose of the original Denver Developmental Screening Test, published in 1967, was to "help health providers detect developmental problems in young children" (Technical Manual, p. 1). This continues to be the major purpose of the Denver II, published in 1990.

Decision-Making Applications

Public Law 99-457 was passed by Congress and extends special education services down to birth for children at risk or with developmental delays. For this reason alone, the Denver II can provide the needed diagnosis for placement of young children into special programs for the developmentally delayed, thus meeting the requirements of Public Law 99-457.

Relevant Population

The Denver II is designed to be used with "apparently well children between birth and six years of age" (Training Manual, p. 1).

Characteristics Described

The Denver II consists of 125 test items. There are four developmental areas that are included in the screening. Developmental areas include Personal-Social, Fine Motor-Adaptive, Language, and Gross Motor. All test items are on a developmental hierarchy. There are also five "Test Behavior" items that are completed after the test has been administered. These items include Compliance, Interest in Surroundings, Fearfulness, Speech, and Attention Span. These items are rated on a 3-point scale by the examiner.

Test materials are included in the test kit.

Description of Developmental Areas

Personal-Social: getting along with people and caring for personal needs. Test items range from "regard face" to" prepare cereal."

Fine Motor-Adaptive: eye-hand coordination and manipulation of small objects, as well as problem solving. Test items range from "grasp rattle" to "copy shapes."

Language: hearing, understanding, and using speech. Test items range from "simple vocalizations" to "verbalization of opposites."

Gross Motor: sitting, walking, jumping, and overall large muscle movement. Test items range from" lifting head" to "heel-to-toe walking."

Test Scores Obtained

There is a one-page response form to record responses to test items. An age scale is across the top of the form with ages ranging from birth to 6 years. Each space between age marks on the scale represents three months. Each of the 125 test items is represented on the form by a bar that spans the ages at which 25%, 50%, 75%, and 90% of the norming sample passed that item. After the examiner calculates the chronological age, an "age line" is drawn from the top of the form to the bottom. Scoring is "P" = Pass, "F" = Fail, "N.O." = No Opportunity (this is only used on "report" items—items reported by parent), "R" = Refusal (child refuses to respond). The test only gives the percentages of the standardization group that "passed" the test item. If a child passes an item that falls to the right of the age line, he or she is considered "advanced" compared to his chronological age. If a child fails or refuses to respond to an item and this falls to the right of the age line, the child's development is considered "normal." If the child fails or refuses to respond to an item and the "age line" falls on or between the 75th or 90th percentile, a "caution" is indicated on the test form by writing a "C" to the right of the bar. When a child fails or refuses to respond to an item that falls completely to the left of the age line, this is considered a "Delay" and the right end of the bar is colored in. The "No Opportunity" items are not considered in the interpretation of the test.

Technical Adequacy

Validity Confirmation

Test item validity: The DDST which was published in 1967 was revised and updated. The total number of potential items for the Denver was 336. The final selection of the 125 test items was determined by a group composed of a pediatrician, a psychologist, statisticians, research assistants, and a consultant from the Colorado State Health Department's Health Screening Program. Statistical data was reviewed and criteria selected, which resulted in the final selection of the 125 test items. According to the Technical Manual, "The validity of the Denver II rests upon its standardization: i.e., it simply presents the age at which children in this sample are able to do a variety of tests" (p. 17).

Test response validity: The Technical Manual does not report any studies relating the Denver II with other developmental screening tests.

Reliability Confirmation

The Denver II was administered twice to 38 children (three per age group and eight extras). The interval between the test administrations was 7 to 10 days. Four examiners who alternated between testing and observing the child being tested were used. Percent of agreement for test-retest reliability for the same tester with 7 to 10 days between testings was 89%. For test-retest, reliability with different testers and 7 to 10 days between testings assessment was 87.5%. Five- to 10-minute delay test-retest reliability was also reported for this sample. This involved same-day, different-examiner responses. Better than 90% (90.8%) of agreement between different examiners was reported when test items were repeated after only 5- to 10-minute intervals.

Objectivity Confirmation

Percentage of agreement between scorers was 99.7% for 141 test items.

Statistical Confirmation

The Technical Manual offers statistical information regarding reliability, objectivity, and standardization.

Special Features

Acronym

Denver II.

Levels of the Test

One level, with developmental test items ranging from birth to 6 years of age.

Number of Test Forms

One.

Norm-Referenced?

Yes. The standardization sample was composed of 2,096 children (1,039 from Denver and 1,057 not from Denver). The age range was from 0 to 6 years, 6 months and divided into 10 age groups. The demographic makeup of the sample was metropolitan, nonmetropolitan, urban, semi-rural, and rural; all were from the state of Colorado. For those children in the sample from Denver county, the independent variables were ethnicity and maternal education. Variables and data are presented in Appendixes G and H of the Technical Manual.

Criterion-Referenced?

No.

Other Features

The Denver II includes a Behavior and Speech Rating which is completed after the administration of the test. These items include (1) Compliance, (2) Alertness, (3) Fearfulness, (4) Speech, and (5) Attention.

Feasibility Considerations

Testing Time

Testing time will vary with the age of the child, but generally should not take more than 20 minutes.

For Testing Groups? Individuals?

Individuals.

Test Administration and Scoring

The Denver II does require training and practice administering the test items and determining the Pass or Fail of the item. However, with repeated administrations with children of varied ages, the test should become fairly easy to administer. The Training Manual describes in detail the training required for examiners of the Denver II. The authors recommend that potential examiners pass a proficiency test before using the test for clinical purposes. There is a videotape that is recommended for potential examiners. The video gives demonstrations of administration of test items to children of different ages. Practice testing of children of various ages should help the potential examiner become comfortable with the administration of the Denver II.

Test Materials and Approximate Costs

Complete kit: $84; Pad of 100 response forms: $23.

Adequacy of Test Manuals

There are two manuals: Technical Manual and Training Manual. The manuals are easy to follow. The Training Manual gives very clear and explicit directions for administration of each test item; the Technical Manual has a chapter on training for examiners, which includes a proficiency test for potential examiners. Chapter III provides information on how to set up a community screening program utilizing the Denver II.

Excerpts from Other Test Reviews

No reviews of the Denver II were found. However, the DDST (Denver Developmental Screening Test, 1990) was reviewed in Salvia and Ysseldyke (1995): "The test's reliability and validity are adequate for a screening device, although the norms are both questionable and very dated" (p. 676). McLoughlin and Lewis, in a review of the DDST, state, "best used with younger children having severe delays" (p. 529).

Ordering Information

Publisher

Denver Developmental Materials, Inc., P.O. Box 371075, Denver, CO 80237-5075; Phone: 800-419-4729, Fax: 303-344-5622.

Authors

W. K. Frankenburg, Josiah Dodds, Philip Archer, Beverly Bresnick, Patrick Maschka, Norma Edelman, and Howard Shapiro.

Publication Dates

1967 and 1990.

Cautions and Comments

The Denver II is useful for screening purposes to make determinations regarding developmental levels of young children as compared to chronological age. It is not a difficult test to administer for examiners who have knowledge and experience determining developmental milestones in young children. The Denver II has been restandardized, primarily with children from Colorado. The authors indicate that "comparing the Colorado composite (or average) 90% norms with the theoretical U.S. composite norms, there were no clinically significant differences" (Technical Manual, p. 10). It would seem that a national sample would give the test additional credibility. The test is brief and the reliability is adequate, but correlations with the Denver II and other tests that focus on a child's development are not reported in the Technical Manual.

References

McLoughlin, J. A., & Lewis, R. B. (1990). *Assessing special students* (3rd ed.). Columbus, OH: Merrill.

Salvia, J., & Ysseldyke, J. E. (1995). *Assessment* (6th ed.). Boston: Houghton Mifflin.

**Developmental Indicators for the Assessment of Learning,
Third Edition (DIAL3 or DIAL-3),**
for testing individuals from 3 years through 6 years, 11 months of age
Reviewed by Charles W. Hatch, Ph.D., Educational Research and Measurement

Usefulness of the Test for Educators

Test Authors' Purpose

"Developmental Indicators for the Assessment of Learning-Third edition (DIAL-3) is an individually administered developmental screening test designed to identify young children in need of further diagnostic assessment" (Fairbank, 2001, p. 398).

"DIAL-3 items assess developmental skills that are the foundation for academic learning. They relate directly to successful classroom functioning or they sample behaviors clearly associated with the domain measured" (Mardell-Czudnowski & Goldenburg, 1998d).

Decision-Making Applications

The DIAL-3 is designed as a screening instrument to select children in need of further assessment by other instruments. Tables are provided by the authors to identify students as developmentally delayed (Mardell-Czudnowski & Goldenburg, 1998d, pp. 110–113).

Limitations to this screening function are imposed by the marginal reliabilities of the subtests (see "Reliability Confirmation" below).

The authors are most helpful when they specifically discuss possible misuses of the DIAL-3.

1. It is neither an intelligence test nor a diagnostic test
2. It does not measure innate abilities or identify those children with brain dysfunction
3. It should not be used for instructional planning
4. Nor should the results be used to track children into ability groups (Mardell-Czudnowski & Goldenburg, 1998d, p. 7)

Relevant Population

Children from 3 years through 6 years, 11 months of age.

Characteristics Described

The DIAL-3 provides data from three subtests, which they term areas. The first is the Motor area, which includes:

Catching a beanbag (one and two hands)

Hop-skip-jump

Building with blocks

Twiddling thumbs and sequentially touching fingers

Cutting with scissors

Copying four geometric shapes and four letters

Writing own name (Mardell-Czudnowski & Goldenburg, 1998d, pp. 18–19)

This is followed by the Concepts subtest, which includes:

Identification of body parts

Identification of colors

Rapid color naming

Counting

Placing a block in various positions (front, back, etc.)

Concept identification (big, little, etc.)

Shapes (sorting by shape and by color and by both) (Mardell-Czudnowski & Goldenburg, 1998d, pp. 19–21)

The last tested area is that of Language, which includes:

Giving personal data

Articulation of sounds (t, ng, r, etc.)

Objects and Actions (relating nouns correctly with verbs)

Letters and sounds (naming letters and correct sounds)

Rhyming and I Spy

Problem solving ("What do you do when . . ."?)

Intelligibility (Mardell-Czudnowski & Goldenburg, 1998d, pp. 21–23)

In addition to the above data gathered from each child, the parent questionnaire yields two additional scores. The first is a Self-Help rating, which assesses a child's ability to perform 15 functions, such as dressing and eating, on a scale that ranges from "most of the time, with no help" to "not allowed to or not asked to" (Mardell-Czudnowski & Goldenburg, 1998g, p. 2). The second is a Social Development rating, which rates the child on a scale from "Always or almost always" to "Never or almost never." Here the parent is responding to 20 prompts like "Accepts limits without getting upset" (Mardell-Czudnowski & Goldenburg, 1998g, p. 3)

The following is an example of a task included in the Motor subtest:

The test administrator builds a pyramid of six blocks (three on the bottom, two above those and one on top where the two lower layers have spaces between the blocks) and says "Now, you do it." The child is given two points for a correct construction with spaces, one point for a pyramid without spaces and no points for any other response. (Mardell-Czudnowski & Goldenburg, 1998e, p. 14)

One for the concept area in counting might be (after placing 12 blocks on the table):

To request that the child "Take THREE blocks and put them here."
Then, "Take SEVEN blocks. Put them here."
And finally, "Take ELEVEN blocks. Put them here."

The scoring is as follows: 0 = no success; 1 = counting three blocks; 2 = counting seven blocks; 3 = counting eleven blocks (Mardell-Czudnowski & Goldenburg, 1998a, p. 13).

An item illustrative of the Language area is as follows:

The administrator has an easel with a movable circular opening that shows one picture at a time. He or she says "OK, (child's name), now we are going to play a game. I'm going to show you some pictures and say a word. Then you will say the same word." A picture of a cup is shown and the administrator says "**cup**." If there is no response, he or she says "Now, you say **cup**." Twelve more words follow.

The scoring is as follows: 2 = for each word pronounced correctly; 1 = for each word with one error; 0 = for each word with more than one error (Mardell-Czudnowski & Goldenburg, 1998c, p. 9).

Test Scores Obtained

For each of the three subtests (Motor, Concepts, and Language), raw scores are converted to scale scores. The scale scores are summed into the total score. All of the above are converted by table into percentiles with cutoffs indicating developmental delay. The two raw scores from the parent questionnaire (self-help and social development) are also converted to scale scores, percentiles, and developmental delay. Use of the ASSIST computer program should be considered, especially where a large number of assessments are needed.

Technical Adequacy

Validity Confirmation

"Some claim can be made for the content validity of the DIAL-3 because of the careful selection and field testing of the items" (Salvia & Ysseldyke, 2001, p. 629). The preceding supports *test item validity*. The following supports *test response validity*:

Some evidence for criterion-related validity comes from the modest (that is, .25 to .45) correlations with similar subtests on the Early Screening Profile, moderate (that is, .30 to .55) correlations with similar subtests on the Battelle Screening Test, and fairly strong correlations of the total score on the Brigance Preschool Screen with Concepts, Language, and the DIAL-3 total (that is .53 to .79), and on Language with the Peabody Picture Vocabulary Test. The Self-Help and Social ratings were also correlated with parent ratings of social skills on the Social Skills Rating System. Finally, children with disabilities who were identified by means other than the DIAL-3 earned lower normalized standard scores. (Salvia & Ysseldyke, 2001, p. 629)

Thus, the authors present reasonable evidence for both test item validity and test response validity in the extensive data included in the DIAL-3 Manual.

Reliability Confirmation

The authors present the following median reliabilities for the test subscales and total:

Motor	.66
Concepts	.84
Language	.77
Total	.87
Self-Help	.78
Social Development	.85

These figures are estimates of the unity of each portion; that is, they are measures of the internal consistency of that portion of DIAL-3 (Mardell-Czudnowski & Goldenburg, 1998d, p. 80).

Figures on the stability of test scores are also given. These are correlations of scores for the same child retested after a mean interval of 28 days. Separate results are given for younger children (3 years, 6 months to 4 years, 5 months) and older ones (4 years, 6 months to 5 years, 10 months).

Test	Age Group	Stability Reliability
Motor	younger	.69
Concepts	younger	.85
Language	younger	.85
Total	younger	.88
Self-Help	younger	.75
Social Development	younger	.77

Test	Age Group	Stability Reliability
Motor	older	.67
Concepts	older	.74
Language	older	.78
Total	older	.84
Self-Help	older	.79
Social Development	older	.85

(Mardell-Czudnowski & Goldenburg, 1998d, p. 81)

The total scores have reliabilities above .80 and are satisfactory for screening deci-sions. The subtests vary considerably and should probably not be used for decision-making.

Standard errors of measurement are greatest for the Total score (about three to four scale score points). The subtests have SEMs of about two points (Mardell-Czudnowski & Goldenburg, 1998d, p. 81).

Objectivity Confirmation

No data is presented on objectivity. This is an issue since many scores are based on a test administrator's judgment of a response. For example, on the word repetition segment the errors are judged as none, one, or more than one. Different persons may "hear" a different number of errors. Data here would be welcomed.

Statistical Confirmation

The *DIAL3 Manual* contains extensive data on reliability, validity, norms, and scor-ing. Objectivity data is lacking.

Special Features

Acronym

DIAL3 or DIAL-3.

Levels of the Test

One, but norms are broken down by age.

Number of Test Forms

One. However, a subset of items termed the Speed DIAL is available, which consti-tutes another form.

Norm-Referenced?

Yes, as evidenced by the scale scores and percentiles. The norming populations are well detailed and based on the 1994 U.S. Census. The following population variables were reported: sex, race/ethnicity, geographic region, and parental educational level.

Criterion-Referenced?

No.

Other Features

The availability of the Speed DIAL (see below) is a plus and allows the testing time to be cut in half.

The availability of a Spanish version complete with norms, training video, test forms, parent questionnaire, and conversion tables is a plus. Usually the Spanish version is bound with the English and requires the administrator only to flip the guide over to switch languages.

The materials come in attractive, color-coded totes for each of the three content areas. This makes keeping up with the various test items a simple process.

The Parent Questionnaire could be used without the rest of the DIAL-3 test items. It could be a valuable adjunct to any preschool program if used this way.

Feasibility Considerations

Testing Time

Thirty minutes (only 15 minutes for the Speed DIAL).

For Testing Groups? Individuals?

Individuals, but the procedures are set up so three administrators (each one doing a single subtest) could screen a fairly large group of children quickly.

Test Administration and Scoring

There are no special requirements for administration beyond a careful reading of the manuals and a couple of trial administrations. The whole process is scripted in detail.

The scoring tables are contained in the *DIAL3 Manual* and are clear. The ASSIST computer program from the publisher will greatly assist in the scoring of the DIAL-3.

Test Materials and Approximate Costs

Complete kit with ASSIST: $487.95; Complete kit: $388.95; Complete kit with Spanish forms: $388.95; Speed DIAL forms (50): $28.95; Training video: $78.95; Parent Questionnaire (50): $20.95. These prices are current as of December 2001 from the American Guidance Service web site (www.agsnet.com).

Adequacy of Test Manuals

The manuals are excellent and quite complete.

Excerpts from Other Test Reviews

"The DIAL-3 is an individually administered screening device assessing develop-ment in motor, conceptual, language, self-help and social domains. The norms are generally representative, the reliability for the total score is generally adequate (al-though the reliabilities of the subtests usually are not), and the validity appears clearly established. Users are urged to make screening decisions based on the total score" (Salvia & Ysseldyke, 2001, p. 629).

"Overall, the new version of the DIAL represents an improvement over the previ-ous version and compared to some of the alternatives that exist for accomplishing its purpose, the DIAL-3 provides a defensible way to help educators identify children at risk for school failure resulting from developmental delays. . . . This instrument will appeal to those who seek a quick method of screening young children who may need additional assessment for developmental delays in five key areas" (Cizek, 2001, p. 398).

"The DIAL-3 appears to be a stronger and better standardized screening instrument than the earlier editions. The authors have addressed concerns and incorporated changes suggested by earlier reviewers. The DIAL-3 is a useful tool in developmental screen-ing programs, but should be used only as a screening instrument with caution taken in overinterpreting the results" (Fairbank, 2001, p. 400).

Ordering Information

Publisher

American Guidance Service, Inc., 4201 Woodland Road, Circle Pines, MN 55014-1796; Phone: 800-328-2560; Fax: 800-471-8457; Web site: www.agsnet.com.

Authors

Carol Mardell-Czudnowski and Dorothea S. Goldenburg.

Publication Date

1998. This third edition is based on the DIAL-Revised (1983, 1990).

Cautions and Comments

The DIAL-3 is most attractively packaged and presented by the publisher. Test subsections come in individual canvas totes, which contain all the necessary accesso-ries for test administration like blocks, presentation easels, and complete directions in both English and Spanish. Statistical data is also included in the manual for the Span-ish form. This is a real plus.

There is also an option called Speed DIAL, which is a short form of the DIAL-3 consisting of only 10 items and requiring about 15 minutes (half the time of the complete battery). Making it even more attractive are satisfactory reliabilities (.80 for unity and .82–.84 for stability). It too has a Spanish version.

Users screening a large number of students will want to investigate the use of the ASSIST computer program for scoring that is available from AGS.

The user should probably limit the use of the DIAL-3 to the total score because the reliabilities of the subtests are more variable and tend to be lower. The Speed DIAL is a very attractive alternative.

The following quote from the authors shows one successful application of the DIAL-3 with a large number of testees: "The Wichita, Kansas Schools used the DIAL-3 district-wide during the 1999–2000 school year to pre-test 4000 kindergarten children in the fall and then for post-testing in the spring. The results were so positive that program administrators expanded DIAL-3 screening to include pre-K students for the current school year" (Mardell-Czudnowski & Goldenburg, 2001, p. 1).

References

Cizek, G. J. (2001). Review of the Developmental Indicators for the Assessment of Learning, Third Edition. In B. S. Plake & J. C. Impara (Eds.) *The Fourteenth Mental Measurements Yearbook* (pp. 395–398). Lincoln, NE: The Buros Institute of Mental Measurements.

Fairbank, D. (2001). Review of the Developmental Indicators for the Assessment of Learning, Third Edition. In B. S. Plake & J. C. Impara (Eds.), *The Fourteenth Mental Measurements Yearbook* (pp. 398–400). Lincoln, NE: The Buros Institute of Mental Measurements.

Mardell-Czudnowski, C., & Goldenburg, D. (1998a). *DIAL3 Concepts Area*. Circle Pines, MN: American Guidance Service.

Mardell-Czudnowski, C., & Goldenburg, D. (1998b). *DIAL3 English and Spanish Training Packet*. Circle Pines, MN: American Guidance Service.

Mardell-Czudnowski, C., & Goldenburg, D. (1998c). *DIAL3 Language Area*. Circle Pines, MN: American Guidance Service.

Mardell-Czudnowski, C., & Goldenburg, D. (1998d). *DIAL3 Manual*. Circle Pines, MN: American Guidance Service.

Mardell-Czudnowski, C., & Goldenburg, D. (1998e). *DIAL3 Motor Area*. Circle Pines, MN: American Guidance Service.

Mardell-Czudnowski, C., & Goldenburg, D. (1998f). *DIAL3 Speed Dial Operator's Handbook*. Circle Pines, MN: American Guidance Service.

Mardell-Czudnowski, C., & Goldenburg, D. (1998g). *DIAL3 Parent Questionnaire*. Circle Pines, MN: American Guidance Service.

Mardell-Czudnowski, C., & Goldenburg, D. (1998h). *DIAL3 Record Form*. Circle Pines, MN: American Guidance Service.

Mardell-Czudnowski, C., & Goldenburg, D. (2001). *Wichita schools DIAL-3 for successful preschool screening*. Downloaded December 22 from www.speechandlanguage.com.

Salvia, J., & Ysseldyke, J. E. (2001). *Assessment* (8th ed.). Boston: Houghton Mifflin.

Early Childhood Behavior Scale (ECBS),
for testing individuals from 36 through 72 months of age
Reviewed by Charles W. Hatch, Ph.D., Educational Research and Measurement

---

Usefulness of the Test for Educators

Test Author's Purpose

"Designed to objectively and efficiently document those behaviors most indicative of early childhood emotionally disturbed/behaviorally disordered students and the behavior problems which exceed the norm of any student in the school environment" (McCarney, 1992, p. 1).

Decision-Making Applications

The ECBS was developed primarily as a selection tool to identify individuals in need of intervention. A secondary function was to guide in the delivery of intervention services. This selection function could take the form of admission decisions into intense remedial programs based on ECBS performance. Individuals scoring below a certain level, say, the 10th percentile, might be accepted.

Placement decisions could be made between regular and remedial programs. Analysis of an individual's scores could lead to prescriptive recommendations—for example, there are many activities to enhance both short- and long-term memory.

After completing a program of remediation, the ECBS could function as a measure of achievement and indicate a previously low-scoring child's readiness to enter a regular curriculum. Extremely low scores might indicate the need for referral for more evaluation and extensive professional assistance.

Relevant Population

Children from 36 through 72 months of age.

Characteristics Described

Three characteristics are described. They are academic progress, social relationships, and personal adjustment.

Academic progress (10 items) includes items to assess a characteristic which includes both memory (example: Has difficulty with short-term memory) and academic performance. This second aspect includes motivation (example: Is not motivated by rewards) and classroom interactions (example: Has little or no interaction with adults).

Social relationships (12 items) also has two facets, as reflected in the items, namely aggressive behavior (example: Fights with other children) and anti-social behavior (example: Makes inappropriate comments to adults).

Personal adjustment (31 items) has three aspects: behavior (example: Is unpredictable in behavior), maturity (example: Does not accept changes in established routine), and concentration (example: Is tired, listless, apathetic, unmotivated, and not interested in activities).

Test Scores Obtained

The ECBS provides raw scores and standard scores on each of the three subscales. From the summing of the three standard scores, a percentile is obtained.

Technical Adequacy

Validity Confirmation

Test item validity: The test items were developed by a survey of literature in the field and from diagnosticians and educators. The resulting pool of items was reduced through continued professional review and mathematical analysis from trial administrations.

Test response validity: The test results were analyzed mathematically to see whether the test did indeed measure *one* characteristic and whether the three subscales were confirmed mathematically. These desired results were not clearly demonstrated. The author alludes to this problem when he describes the "factorial conplexity" of the results.

Fifty-seven individuals were administered the ECBS and the appropriate form of the Child Behavior Checklist (CBCL). The correlations ranged from .62 to .71. These results are not compelling for either test item validity or test response validity.

Reliability Confirmation

When subjects were administered the test twice with a 30-day interval, the correlations ranged from .81 to .91. These are satisfactory considering the young age of the participants.

Another measure of reliability considers the correlation of subscales of the test with each other. The figures obtained range from .90 to .94, which is more than satisfactory.

Objectivity Confirmation

When two observers rated the same child, the correlations obtained were .81 to .88. These figures indicate satisfactory agreement among raters observing the same child.

Statistical Confirmation

The Technical Manual contains information on reliability, validity, objectivity, and the norming populations.

Special Features

Acronym

ECBS.

Levels of the Test

One.

Number of Test Forms

One.

Norm-Referenced?

Yes. The scores obtained are standard scores and percentiles. The norming population (1990–1991) was composed of 1,314 children in the following five age groups: boys, 3, 4, and 5 (three groups); girls, 3 and 4–5 (two groups). All were from public schools in 17 states. They seem to be reasonably representative of the U.S. population, except that white-collar families were seriously underrepresented at 43% (the United States has 88%). However, this data may be in error since the total percent is only 82, not 100. The missing 18% may not even have been classified.

Criterion-Referenced?

No.

Other Features

Users may purchase the Quick Score computer program, which simplifies calculations and formats output. The program is neither complex nor multifaceted. It is very basic.

Feasibility Considerations

Testing Time

Thirty to 90 minutes.

For Testing Groups? Individuals?

Individuals. The test administrator observes the behavior and indicates the frequency.

Test Administration and Scoring

The ECBS test requires that the administrator be quite familiar with the child being evaluated for longer than 30 days. The Test Manual states, "This person (e.g., teacher, counselor, etc.) may not spend extended periods of time with the student, but may, over a period of several weeks to several months, have a measure of 'familiarity' with the child" (p. 17).

The test administrator must indicate a response from the following scale for each of the 53 items.

0 = Not in my presence
1 = One time

2 = Several times

3 = More than one time a month, up to one time a week

4 = More than one time a week, up to once a day

5 = More than once a day, up to once an hour

6 = More than once an hour

The directions caution not to leave any item blank.

The items in each subscale are summed and a standard score reported from the appropriate table. These standard scores are summed for the overall percentile score.

Test Materials and Approximate Costs

Complete kit (01450): $89.50; Technical Manual (01400): $12.50; Rating forms (50) (01410): $31; Intervention Manual (01420): $20; Quick Score program (IBM) (01401): $20.

Adequacy of Test Manuals

The manuals are sufficient and provide the necessary statistical information and tables.

Excerpts from Other Test Reviews

"An instrument that combines a careful quantitative approach with sensitivity to the nuances of young children's development is needed. If revised and interpreted within a developmental context consistent with current policy, the ECBS could meet this need" (Paget, 2001, p. 383).

"This scale probably meets the minimum standards for measures of this kind, but it is not the best measure available for identifying emotionally disturbed or behaviorally disturbed children. . . . More data should be collected on this measure" (Sandoval, 2001, p. 384).

Ordering Information

Publisher

Hawthorne Educational Services, 800 Gray Oak Drive, Columbia, MO 65201; Phone: 800-542-1673; Fax: 800-442-9509.

Author

Stephen B. McCarney.

Publication Date

1992.

Cautions and Comments

Validity is a potential weakness of the ECBS, which will limit the usefulness of the instrument. Results should be confirmed by further testing before making individual decisions.

In spite of the published data, objectivity remains a concern because of the complexity of decisions regarding the rating scale.

Different scorers of the same child would have problems agreeing whether a particular behavior was evidenced "one time" or "several times" over several months when the observations may have been very limited in duration in one instance and extensive in the other.

As the three scales are described in the Technical Manual, it is difficult to see how the author is able to differentiate closely related concepts. For example, concentration and memory, though on separate subscales, seem to be closely related. It is also hard to understand why motivation and memory are on the same subscale.

Items were retained on the test which had only the weakest correlation with subscale totals. These low numbers include one item on the academic progress subscale with .50, one on the social relationships subscale with .38, and three below .35 on the personal adjustment subscale (.28, .31 and .33)!

References

Brown, L., Branston, M. B., Hamre-Neitupski, S., Pumpian, I., Certo, N., & Grunewald, L. (1979). A strategy for developing chronological age appropriate and functional curriculum content for severely handicapped adolescents and adults. *Journal of Special Education 13*, 81–90.

McCarney, S. B. (1992). *Early Childhood Behavior Scale* (ECBS). Columbia, MO: Hawthorne Educational Services.

Mercer, C. D., & Mercer, A. R. (1993). *Teaching students with learning problems* (4th ed.). Englewood Cliffs, NJ: Merrill.

Paget, K. D. (2001). Review of the Early Childhood Behavior Scale. In B. S. Plake & J. C. Impara (Eds.), *The Fourteenth Mental Measurements Yearbook* (pp. 382–383). Lincoln, NE: The Buros Institute of Mental Measurements.

Sandoval, J. (2001). Review of the Early Childhood Behavior Scale. In B. S. Plake & J. C. Impara (Eds.), *The Fourteenth Mental Measurements Yearbook* (pp. 383–384). Lincoln, NE: The Buros Institute of Mental Measurements.

Ysseldyke, J. E., & Olsen, K. R. (1997). *Putting alternative assessments into practice: What to measure and possible sources of data* (Synthesis Report No. 28). Minneapolis: University of Minnesota, National Center on Educational Outcomes. Retrieved September 27, 2001 from the World Wide Web: http://education.umn.edu/nceo/onlinepubs/synthesis28.htm.

High/Scope Child Observation Record (COR),
for testing individuals from 2 years, 6 months through 6 years of age
Reviewed by Aileen C. Lau-Dickinson, Ed.D., Special Education Administration

---

Usefulness of the Test for Educators

Test Authors' Purpose

The authors state: "Its purpose was to achieve three major goals: (1) to make it useful for all early childhood teachers, whether or not they use the High/Scope Curriculum; (2) to establish the new COR as a reliable, valid instrument; and (3) to demonstrate the feasibility of its use in 64 Head Start programs located in southeastern Michigan" (Information for Decision Makers, p. 1). The new High/Scope COR "focuses on the important developmental experiences that should be observable in all developmentally appropriate early childhood programs" (Information for Decision Makers, p. 1).

Decision-Making Applications

According to the authors, "High/Scope Child Observation Record (COR) aids teachers in planning developmentally appropriate goals for young children, provides an assessment of individual children over time in a variety of situations, emphasizes strengths and abilities rather than skills, helps teachers write anecdotal notes about a child and gives parents information regarding the child's progress, and helps teachers learn more about organizational skills and child development" (Information for Decision Makers, pp. 6–7). The COR can be used alone or as part of an assessment profile. The COR also can be used for developmental screening of children and, therefore, identifying children for referral and additional assessment.

Relevant Population

The COR is designed for young children ages 2 years, 6 months through 6 years of age who attend a developmentally appropriate early childhood program.

Characteristics Described

Six categories are observed by teachers and/or trained observers as children proceed through their daily activities in an early childhood program.

1. Initiative
    A. Expressing choices
    B. Solving problems
    C. Engaging in complex play
    D. Cooperating in program routines

2. Social Relations
   - E. Relating to adults
   - F. Relating to children
   - G. Making friends with other children
   - H. Engaging in social problem solving
   - I. Understanding and expressing feelings

3. Creative Representation
   - J. Making and building
   - K. Drawing and painting
   - L. Pretending

4. Music and Movement
   - M. Exhibiting body coordination
   - N. Exhibiting manual coordination
   - O. Imitating movements to a steady beat
   - P. Following music and movement directions

5. Language and Literacy
   - Q. Understanding speech
   - R. Speaking
   - S. Showing interest in reading activities
   - T. Demonstrating knowledge about books
   - U. Beginning reading
   - V. Beginning writing

6. Logic and Mathematics
   - W. Sorting
   - X. Using the words not, some, and all
   - Y. Arranging materials in graduated order
   - Z. Using comparison words
   - AA. Comparing numbers of objects
   - BB. Counting objects
   - CC. Describing spatial relations
   - DD. Describing sequence and time

The COR provides ongoing observations of young children, and these are conducted by teachers and observers throughout the program year. The observation record form gives the general categories for observing the child as listed above, followed by the subareas. There are five choices and three observations over time.

Test Scores Obtained

There is a Summary of Scores Response Form available in the Observation Record, which allows the examiner to obtain a score for each category. However, the manual does not describe how this score would be used. The manual does not contain norm tables. The uses for the observation records appear to be anecdotal rather than providing derived scores, such as percentiles and standard scores. Anecdotal note cards are to be used by observers to record observational behaviors.

Technical Adequacy

Validity Confirmation

Test item validity: The COR measures the developmental status of young children aged 2 years, 6 months through 6 years of age. This measurement is dependent on the child's attendance in a child development center that provides a developmentally appropriate curriculum. There is no information provided in the Information for Decision Makers on how the categories were selected and whether these items measure the developmental categories observed. However, the authors claim that the COR "embodies dimensions of child development that should be evident in early childhood programs that engage in developmentally appropriate practice as defined by the National Association for the Education of Young Children (NAEYC)" (Educational and Psychological Measurement, p. 447). The High/Scope Foundation has focused on early childhood developmental experiences for over 20 years. Their experience has resulted in the creation of the COR. The observational items used in the COR are based on the 20 years of experience using the High/Scope model in which young children "learn by doing."

Test response validity: During the spring of 1990, the McCarthy Scales of Children's Abilities was administered to 98 children. Correlations between the COR ratings and the McCarthy scores were made, and these correlations ranged from .27 to .66 . The highest correlation was between language and literacy (COR) and perceptual performance (McCarthy Scales). Correlations of each scale of the COR are listed in the Information for Decision Makers (p. 21). The correlations are moderate, and further correlation studies need to be conducted to further validate this instrument.

A study of COR ratings of children's behavior was conducted with 64 teams of Head Start teachers and assistant teachers in southeastern Michigan. This study demonstrated that COR was a feasible instrument to be used to measure development of young children in Head Start Centers.

Reliability Confirmation

A study of internal consistency was conducted in the fall of 1990 with 50 teachers and 50 teacher assistants and 484 children. Correlations ranged from .93 for teachers to .91 for assistants for Logic and Mathematics. Other correlations averaged .67 to .72 for each scale of the COR. No test-retest studies were reported for the COR.

Objectivity Confirmation

The correlations between the ratings of two observers are reported. Correlations ranged from .29 (Understanding Speech) to .60 (Spatial Relations). Sixty teachers and 354 children were included in these correlations. These correlations were moderate at best. Additional studies of inter-rater correlations need to be conducted to confirm test objectivity.

Statistical Confirmation

Limited statistical data on validity and reliability can be found in the Information for Decision Makers.

Special Features

Acronym

COR.

Levels of the Test

One.

Number of Test Forms

One.

Norm-Referenced?

Yes. A study was conducted in the spring and fall of 1990–1991 school year using the COR. There were 51 teachers and 484 children in the fall data collection and 54 teachers and 415 children in the spring data collection. Factor-loading data was collected in the fall of 1990 and the rest of the data collected in the spring of 1991. Fall-spring correlations were made for each of the test observational items. Correlations ranged from .29 (Understanding Speech) to .60 (Spatial Relations). Factor loading of items on the six COR scales ranged from .57 to .82, with only Expressing Feelings, Body Coordination, Beginning Reading, and Beginning Writing falling below a correlation of .70. The authors claim that the COR "emerges from this study as a psychometrically acceptable tool for the assessment of children's development in all developmentally appropriate early childhood programs" (Information for Decision Makers, p. 24). The children in the COR study were "like the population" served by Head Start nationally.

Criterion-Referenced?

No.

Feasibility Considerations

Testing Time

Teachers and caregivers score the COR two or three times a year. The first set of ratings is usually completed after the first six weeks of the program year. Other ratings are taken throughout the year. The authors state that "observation of the child over a prolonged period of time, while the child is engaged in the varied activities typical of an appropriate early childhood program, can give you a well-rounded and accurate picture of that child's performance" (Information for Decision Makers, p. 4).

For Testing Groups? Individuals?

Individuals.

Test Administration and Scoring

The COR is an observational instrument. The observer dates each observation and checks whether the item is accomplished. Scores are added and divided by the number of items under the category to obtain the overall score. There is no explanation on how this score is to be used or what it means. There are no norm tables or derived scores. According to the authors, training is highly recommended. "High/Scope training provides in-depth information on the individual COR items, scoring, guidance, and practice with anecdotal note taking; and exploration of observation strategies for parents, teachers, caregivers, and administrators" (Information for Decision Makers, p. 9).

Test Materials and Approximate Costs

Complete kit, which includes COR Manual, COR Assessment Booklets (25), COR Anecdotal Note Cards (4 sets of 25 cards), COR Parent Report Forms (2 sets of 25 forms), and COR Poster: $90.95.

Adequacy of Test Manuals

The Information for Decision Makers test manual is brief and clearly written. Additional information would be helpful on the standardization procedures. There is an excellent discussion on the "Advantages of Observational Assessment" which is important information for teachers and others planning on conducting such assessments.

Excerpts from Other Test Reviews

No test reviews were located for the COR.

Ordering Information

Publisher

High/Scope Press, 600 North River Street, Ypsilanti, MI 48198-1898; Phone: 800-40-PRESS; Fax: 800-442-4FAX; Web site: info@highscope.org.

Authors

High/Scope Educational Foundation.

Publication Date

1992.

Cautions and Comments

The COR has been revised over the past decade to the present form of the observational instrument. The focus of the COR is on observation of the young child while participating in developmentally appropriate activities in a child development program. The COR provides for systematic observation of children in day-to-day activities. This is an alternative to conventional standardized testing, which requires the child to respond to specific tasks on subtests. The COR is an "informal" test that observes the child as he "goes about his business" rather than a test that is rigid and requires specific procedures. The COR is not a "standardized test," even though there is some evidence reported relative to reliability and validity. There are no norms that relate the test to a national population. It appears that the authors' intent is to assess young children with developmental categories in an informal setting.

It should be noted here that the High/Scope Foundation publishes a High/Scope Program Quality Assessment. This assessment is designed to evaluate the quality of early childhood programs. Finally, the High/Scope Foundation publishes the High/Scope COR for Infants and Toddlers, which is an observational instrument that provides a well-rounded, systematic assessment in programs serving children from six weeks to three years of age.

Metropolitan Readiness Tests: Sixth Edition (MRT6), for testing individuals (Level 1) and groups (Level 2) from pre-kindergarten through grade 1
Reviewed by Charles W. Hatch, Ph.D., Educational Research and Measurement

---

Usefulness of the Test for Educators

Test Authors' Purpose

Levels 1 and 2 of the Metropolitan Readiness Tests: Sixth Edition (MRT6) are an integral part of the Metropolitan Early Childhood Assessment Program, a complete assessment program designed to assess the readiness skills of children in pre-kindergarten, kindergarten, and grade 1.

While both Levels 1 and 2 include measures of auditory, visual, language, and quantitative processes, the content of each level varies slightly to accommodate the differences in the stages of development that generally exist from ages 4 to 6 years.

Decision-Making Applications

The authors have designed this instrument for a wide range of decisions. Admission, placement, instructional prescription, achievement certification, and referral decisions can be made using their scoring format. Many of the above are inferred from the Content Referenced Scores, where student responses are placed in the following three categories:

Plus   proficient

Check   learning and instruction should continue

Minus   needs instruction but may never have received instruction in these skills, may need to be re-taught, or may need instruction in prerequisite skills (Nurss & McGauvran, 1995c, p. 13)

However, the severe shortcomings of the MRT6 make all of the above intentions irrelevant. The test should only be used to provide supporting data to another more valid and reliable instrument for any individual student decision.

Relevant Population

Pre-kindergarten through grade 1.

Characteristics Described

The tests have items covering the following areas:

1. Beginning Reading

   Visual Discrimination (Level 1 only)

   Beginning Consonants

   Sound-Letter Correspondence

   Aural Cloze with Letter (Level 2 only)

2. Story Comprehension

3. Quantitative Concepts and Reasoning

The following item examples will illustrate the above categories:

Visual Discrimination: These items ask a child "to discriminate among visual symbols by asking the child to match single letters and letter series, single numbers and number series, and words" (Nurss & McGauvran, 1995c, p. 11). That is, the child is given a letter, perhaps "B," followed by several letters including "B." Marking the space under the correct match is counted as a correct response. The same is done for numbers and simple words.

Beginning Consonants: The child is presented with a row of four picture prompts, for example, girl, duck, hand, and frog. The child is asked to choose the picture of the word that best matches the initial sound in the word DOG.

Sound-Letter Correspondence: The child is presented with a picture of a mouse and then chooses from four letter choices (s, m, u, or o) which one matches the initial consonant of mouse.

Aural Cloze with Letter: The student is presented with a letter, say "P," followed by three pictures: towel, pencil, and pillow. The test administrator then says, "This _____ is very soft. Mark under the picture that begins with the sound of the letter in the black box and makes sense (belongs) in the sentence" (Nurss & McGauvran, 1995a, p. 27).

Story Comprehension: The administrator begins by reading a story from the Story Comprehension Big Book, showing the pictures. Then the child is given three picture choices. The student might be asked to indicate "the picture that shows something Emily usually ate after school" (Nurss & McGauvran, 1995a, p. 33).

Quantitative Concepts and Reasoning: The child is presented with four pictures of ponds with three, four, five, and six ducks. The test administrator asks the subject to indicate "the group that has four ducks" (Nurss & McGauvran, 1995a, p. 41).

Test Scores Obtained

Raw scores are reported for each area and subtest. Then the Beginning Reading and Story Comprehension are combined to form the Prereading Composite, and the Total Test Composite is obtained by adding all subtests. For each of the above, percentiles and stanines are calculated and then a performance rating is given.

The reporting is slightly complicated by the fact that the two test levels have slightly different components. Only Level 1 contains the visual discrimination section. However, only Level 2 contains the Aural Cloze with Letter section.

Technical Adequacy

Validity Confirmation

This instrument has serious problems both in the area of *test item validity* and *test response validity*.

The following quote describes problems with the former:

The content selection methods are described as follows. "An extensive review of the literature was conducted prior to the tests' development to provide evidence that the results are assessing those skills that are important to early learning" (p. 48). The results of this analysis are provided in the Manual for Interpreting where the performance objectives and associated items are listed. These stated objectives, however, are not listed on any of the content-referenced interpretive charts provided. The interpretive charts and record forms include only subtest ratings of performance and norm-referenced scores by subtests, thereby deemphasizing analyses by instructional objective. If, in fact, the content is usefully organized by instructional objective it would seem reasonable to in some way assist the user in applying this information to instructional design. (Kamphaus, 2001, p. 748)

That is, the test authors do not provide information on test item development or classification by instructional objective.

The problems in the area of test response validity are summarized by Kamphaus below.

The MRT6, like its most recent predecessor, has limited evidence of validity. A mere two pages of validity evidence is reported. Two of the three investigations reported in the Norms Book are predictive validity studies where Level 2 of the MRT6 is used as a predictor of Metropolitan Achievement Tests and Stanford Achievement Test scores. Level 2 scores correlated moderately with the Metropolitan scores (coefficients in the .50s) and better with the Stanford (coefficients in the .60s and .70s). The last study reported is a table of intercorrelations for the Level 2 subtests accompanied by the following explanation: "Further evidence of the validity of the MRT can be derived from the intercorrelations among the subtests and Skill Areas of the MRT." In other words, the test developers present no validity evidence for Level 1 and virtually none for Level 2. (Kamphaus, 2001, p. 748)

Since test response validity is such a complex concept, a test author almost can't give it too much attention. The authors of the MRT6 have failed to give enough attention and the data cited is far from convincing.

Reliability Confirmation

[Reliabilities] for subtests and the Total Test Composite for Level 1 were calculated for two prekindergarten samples (tested at midyear, or spring) and three kindergarten samples (tested at fall, midyear, or spring); for Level 2, they were calculated for two kindergarten samples (midyear and spring) and for first-graders in the fall. Five of the eight internal-consistency estimates for the Total Score Composite equaled or exceeded .90; 2 of the 40 internal consistencies of subtests equalled or exceeded .90 and 25 were less than .80. Test-retest reliability was estimated using 124 undescribed students who were retested with Level 2 after an unspecified period. Only the stability of the Total Test Composite was greater than .90; two subtests had stabilities less than .80. Thus, only the reliabilities of the composite is occasionally high enough for making important decisions for individual students. (Salvia & Ysseldyke, 2001, p. 630)

Since reliability is only an estimate of the consistency of test scores, it should be measured in a number of different ways. Thus, the authors failed to provide convincing evidence that the subtest scores are consistent enough for decisions about individual students. However, the composite does seem to have reliability high enough to justify individual decisions.

Reliability concerns must certainly limit the usefulness of scores obtained.

Objectivity Confirmation

Even though this is not really a multiple-choice test, objectivity is only a minor concern because the directions and response sheets are designed so that there is little judgment necessary on the part of the test administrator. That being said, actual data would be welcome, especially for Level 1, where the test administrator records the answers given by the child (Nurss & McGauvran, 1995c, p. 17).

Statistical Confirmation

The Norms Book contains some information, but there are several areas where more adequate data would be welcomed.

Special Features

Acronym

MRT6.

Levels of the Test

Two.

Number of Test Forms

One form for each level.

Norm-Referenced?

Yes. The results are given in age percentiles and stanines as well as grade percentiles and stanines.

Criterion-Referenced?

No, but the Norms Book gives what it calls "Content-Referenced" results where performance is listed in three categories: "Plus," "Check," and "Minus" (see "Decision-Making Applications" above). These three categories seem to create more problems than they solve.

Ratings are based on raw scores and justified purely on the basis of the authors' judgment. As reported in the Manual for Interpreting, Performance Ratings may not always coincide with Stanine Classifications, which assign Above Average, Average or Below Average labels according to normative standards. A good example of how different the resulting pictures of students might be can be drawn from the sample class data provided in the Norms Book (pp. 22–24). Raw scores of 8 and 9 on the Story Comprehension subtest yield percentiles and stanines of 1; however, the Performance Rating of one is considered to be in the acquisition stage, whereas the second is considered to need instruction in this skill area. (Novak, 2001, p. 750)

Other Features

The materials are printed in attractive colors, and the test items themselves use colorful presentation to enhance the student understanding. The Parent-Teacher Conference Report is a nice touch, though many parents would want much more detailed information.

The Directions for Administering Level 2 are clear and should present few problems. The grading directions in the Norms Book are also fully adequate, with worked examples for illustration.

Feasibility Considerations

Testing Time

About 100 minutes, plus 15 minutes for practice questions in four sittings.

For Testing Groups? Individuals?

Level 1 is administered individually. Level 2 is group administered.

Test Administration and Scoring

Scoring is straightforward and is adequately delineated in the Norms Book. The publisher does not specifically list the qualifications for administration and scoring, but the demands are not great and should be able to be handled by professionals in the field. It would be necessary to invest some time prior to the actual administration looking over the Directions for Administering.

Test Materials and Approximate Costs

Level 1: Complete kit: $101; p-t conference forms and student record forms (25 of each): $26.75; Manual: $25.25; Stimulus Manual: $47; Exam Kit: $24.50.

Level 2: Complete kit: $135.25; test booklets (25): $67.50; Answer Key: $24.50; Manual: $33.75; Norms Book: $25.25; Exam Kit: $14.

Adequacy of Test Manuals

The manuals provide adequate information on administering and grading. There are technical areas where the materials are inadequate (see "Technical Adequacy" above).

Excerpts from Other Test Reviews

"There are at least two valuations that may be assigned to the MRT6. Either it is a good test that is simply poorly documented, or it is unusable due to poor design at every phase of development. The answer to this question is unknown based upon reading the manuals. As such it is probably most reasonable to assume that it is unusable unless locally validated" (Kamphaus, 2001, p. 749).

"The MRT6 provides information that could be useful in determining early academic or 'readiness' skills in reading and math. However, users are cautioned against overinterpretation for individual students particularly in relation to profile analysis of strengths and weaknesses" (Novak, 2001, p. 751).

"The sixth edition of the MRT is the latest version of a test originally published in 1933. The technical qualities are marginal. The reliability of the total composite is usually sufficient for making important decisions for individual students; the other scores are usually not reliable enough for that purpose. The norming procedures are poorly described. Validity evidence is largely absent" (Salvia & Ysseldyke, 2001, p. 631).

Ordering Information

Publisher

The Psychological Corporation, Harcourt Educational Measurement, 19500 Bulverde Road, San Antonio, TX 78259-3701; Order Service Center: P.O. Box 708906, San Antonio, TX 78270-8906; Phone: 800-872-1726; Fax: 800-232-1223; Web site: www.psychcorp.com.

Authors

Joanne R. Nurss and Mary E. McGauvran.

Publication Date

First published in 1933; the current edition appeared in 1995.

Cautions and Comments

The technical shortcomings in the areas of validity and reliability do much to limit the usefulness of the MRT6. If an instrument is weak in both of these areas, professionals must realize that another instrument would be a better choice unless the MRT6 would only be used to lend support to other test data and not stand on its own for individual student decisions.

Another practical consideration is whether the MRT6 justifies the amount of time necessary to administer. This time investment concern is especially relevant with the Level 1 form that is individually administered.

It may well be that this test has been revised and supported beyond its useful life span. This view is supported by R. A. Kamphaus' review where the *Standards for Educational and Psychological Testing* (1999) is used as an appropriate measuring tool (Kamphaus, 2001, pp. 747–749).

A glaring discrepancy exists between the MRT6 and the *Test Standards* in the former's lack of attention to fairness. Topics such as proper populations for application of the MRT6, preparation for testing for children from diverse backgrounds, statistical analyses of bias, appropriateness of test content for children from diverse backgrounds, and interpretation of results for non-English or limited-English speakers are given so little attention. This shortcoming makes the MRT6 inadequate by modern standards, given that an entire chapter of the *Test Standards* is now devoted to issues of fairness. (Kamphaus, 2001, p. 749)

References

Kamphaus, R. W. (2001). Review of the Metropolitan Readiness Tests, Sixth Edition. In B. S. Plake & J. C. Impara (Eds.), *The Fourteenth Mental Measurements Yearbook* (pp. 747–749). Lincoln, NE: The Buros Institute of Mental Measurements.

Novak, C. (2001). Review of the Metropolitan Readiness Tests, Sixth Edition. In B. S. Plake & J. C. Impara (Eds.), *The Fourteenth Mental Measurements Yearbook* (pp. 749–751). Lincoln, NE: The Buros Institute of Mental Measurements.

Nurss, J. R., & McGauvran, M. E. (1995a). *Metropolitan Readiness Tests, Sixth Edition, Directions for administering, Level 2.* New York: Harcourt Brace.

Nurss, J. R., & McGauvran, M. E. (1995b). *Metropolitan Readiness Tests, Sixth Edition, Level 2.* New York: Harcourt Brace.

Nurss, J. R., & McGauvran, M. E. (1995c). *Metropolitan Readiness Tests, Sixth Edition, Norms Book.* New York: Harcourt Brace.

Salvia, J., & Ysseldyke, J. E. (2001). *Assessment* (8th ed.). Boston: Houghton Mifflin.

Mullen Scales of Early Learning (MSEL),
for testing individuals from birth through 68 months of age
Reviewed by Charles W. Hatch, Ph.D., Educational Research and Measurement

---

Usefulness of the Test for Educators

Test Author's Purpose

"A developmentally integrated system that assesses language, motor and perceptual abilities" (AGS, 2001).

Decision-Making Applications

The MSEL may be used in conjunction with other instruments for admission, program planning, and intervention. The MSEL could be used as a partial determinant for the admission of either high- or low-functioning individuals to specific programs aimed at each group. Probably the best data to use for this purpose would be the Gross Motor Skills scores for younger children (birth through 33 months) and the Early Learning Composite score for older children (birth through 68 months). This latter scale is derived from the four cognitive scales (see "Characteristics Described" below).

Test data from the MSEL could also be used to design instruction based on group weaknesses, as seen most easily on the four discrete cognitive scales.

Intervention on an individual basis would be based on patterns of weakness indicated by the MSEL and other instruments. In this regard the test author asserts that the test is able to differentiate between children with and without developmental delays. (See "Cautions and Comments" below for a discussion of the useful data that can be reported for this purpose.)

Relevant Population

Children from birth through 68 months of age.

Characteristics Described

Gross motor skills (birth through 33 months)

Visual recognition, fine motor skills, receptive language, expressive language (birth through 68 months)

Visual recognition (VRO Scale) includes such tasks as tracking, scanning, distinguishing forms, and matching letters.

Fine motor skills (VEO Scale) measures eye-hand coordination and control with such tasks as copying a vertical line, stringing beads, and copying a square.

Receptive language (LRO Scale) assesses auditory discrimination with activities like showing comprehension of action words, following unrelated commands, and differentiating right and left.

Expressive language (LEO Scale) tests verbal expression by the child's ability to use two-word phrases, to formulate questions, and to repeat sentences.

Further discussion of the scales is incorporated in the discussion of ASSIST output in "Cautions and Comments" below.

Test Scores Obtained

Scores are on each of the above plus a composite score. The results for the individual scales are expressed in T-scores, percentile rank, developmental stage, and age equivalent.

Early learning composite is reported in a scale with a mean of 100 and a standard deviation of 15. (See "Cautions and Comments" below for further discussion.)

Technical Adequacy

Validity Confirmation

Test response validity was investigated by correlating the MSEL test scores with the Bayley Scales of Infant Development scores, reported as follows:

Composite   .70
Four cognitive scales   .53–.59

Also, MSEL Gross Motor Skills scores were correlated with Bayley's Psychomotor Development Index yielding .76.

The above figures are correlation coefficients which indicate whether scores obtained on both instruments by the same individuals are similar or different. A higher number indicates that the instruments are measuring the same or closely related characteristics.

The developer presents further data in support of test response validity by measuring the stability of child responses. The interval was 11 days and the correlations for the younger group (1–24 months) ranged from .82 through .96. The results for the older group (25–56 months) were somewhat lower, .71 through .79.

The method that the author of the MSEL used to select and develop test items is very unclear. Data is not presented in the manual that would allow a reviewer to decide on the adequacy or inadequacy of the procedures used. The reference to content validity below corresponds to this volume's use of the term "test item validity."

"Although test items seem to represent the target domains, the author presents no specific information about how specific items were selected. Therefore, test users must judge the MSEL's content for themselves" (Salvia & Ysseldyke, 2001, p. 625).

"Content validity is not directly mentioned" (Chittooran, 2001, p. 794).

Reliability Confirmation

Repeated administrations of the test at two age levels yielded the following reliability coefficients:

1–24 months   .82–.96
25–56 months   .71–.79

Again, higher numbers are desirable.

Objectivity Confirmation

Agreement among different scorers who scored the test was .91–.99.

Statistical Confirmation

The Test Manual contains information on reliability, validity, objectivity, and norming populations.

Special Features

Acronym

MSEL.

Levels of the Test

There are two levels of this test, which are necessitated by the extremely young age of some of the subjects. The ways the cognitive functioning of a newborn may be assessed are much different from those of, say, a 5-year-old.

1. Gross motor skills, 1 score, birth through age 33 months.
2. Cognitive scales, 4 scores on 144 items, birth through age 68 months. In addition, a composite score which encompasses the four cognitive scales may be reported.

Number of Test Forms

One.

Norm-Referenced?

Yes, as evidenced by the age equivalents, percentile ranks, derived IQ scores, and T-scores. Norm tables are available for the following ages (in months): 22, 25, 28, 31, 36, 42, 48, 54, 60, and 66.

Criterion-Referenced?

No.

Other Features

Earlier tests from which the MSEL developed were titled the Infant Mullen Scales of Early Learning and the Preschool Mullen Scales of Early Learning.

The product listing on the American Guidance Service web site provides products that upgrade either of the above to the MSEL for $281.95. The order number for the former is AC11160 and for the latter is AC11170. The ability of the publisher to offer such a product illustrates how closely related the three instruments are.

The optional ASSIST computer program is also able to suggest extensive activities for both program planning and individual intervention.

Feasibility Considerations

Testing Time

Fifteen to 60 minutes, depending on the age of the child (15 minutes for a 1-year-old, 25–35 minutes for a 3-year-old, 40–60 minutes for a 5-year-old).

For Testing Groups? Individuals?

Individuals.

Test Administration and Scoring

The test administration is not too demanding and can be performed by most professionals in the field with ease. According to the publisher (AGS), "test administrators should have completed graduate training and have experience in clinical infant assessment." The scoring is also not very difficult. The ASSIST computer program would be very helpful in this regard. Its cost would be well justified if the MSEL were to become a regular feature of any educational program. (See "Cautions and Comments" below for a discussion of the computer output.)

Test Materials and Approximate Costs

Training Video: $99.95; Mullen Manual: $60.95; ASSIST (IBM, Macintosh, Windows): $149.95; Complete kit (with ASSIST): $734.95; Complete kit (without ASSIST): $635.95; record forms (25): $28.95.

ASSIST is a computer program to aid in calculating and printing score reports and suggested remediation activities.

It is important to note here that prices do change often and that the best way to obtain current pricing information is to consult the web site (www.agsnet.com).

Adequacy of Test Manuals

Reviewers were impressed by the quality of the test manuals. "Directions have numerous diagrams to aid comprehension and are of superior quality" (Kessler, 2001, p. 795).

"Scoring and interpretation are enhanced by the inclusion of clearly organized tables, case studies and ASSIST software" (Chittooran, 2001, p. 793).

Excerpts from Other Test Reviews

"The Mullen appears to be a satisfactory alternative to other measures of functioning for early childhood populations, particularly if it is used as part of a comprehensive assessment battery" (Chittooran, 2001, p. 794).

"I highly recommend this assessment tool when the examiner is interested in measuring a young child's cognitive abilities and gross motor base for learning" (Kessler, 2001, p. 795).

Ordering Information

Publisher

American Guidance Service, Inc., 4201 Woodland Road, Circle Pines, MN 55014-1796; Phone: 800-328-2560; Fax: 800-471-8457; Web site: www.agsnet.com.

Author

Eileen M. Mullen.

Publication Date

1992.

Cautions and Comments

A test administrator needs to supply some materials *not* included in the kits, such as paper and coins. Some items in the kit may not be stout enough for continued use with children.

Because of some limitations in the reliability and validity data, caution needs to be exercised in the interpretation of data for older children as well as children with exceptionalities and/or non-English speakers.

Data is not presented on the sufficiency or insufficiency of item selection or refinement. Therefore, users must decide on test item validity themselves for their own application.

It would seem that an assessment instrument aimed at children only a few weeks or months old might be overly ambitious. The suggestion by Salvia and Ysseldyke that the test apply to children ages 21–63 months seems reasonable.

Since the Early Learning Composite scores are reported on a scale with a mean of 100 and a standard deviation of 15, they have the appearance of IQ scores. There are so many problems associated with IQ scores that it seems unwise to report scores from the MSEL in a way that may well lead to further misunderstanding and are liable to misinterpretation.

The ASSIST program provides extensive output, which greatly enhances the value of the MSEL. Purchase is advised. This program provides extensive reporting of each subscale in terms of raw score, T-score, 90% confidence interval, percentile rank, developmental stage, and age equivalent. The composite is reported in standard score, 90% confidence interval, and percentile rank. In addition, each has a descriptive category like "below average" appended. Graphical presentations and verbal summaries follow. Most users will greatly appreciate the "Recommended Activities" section. It lists many activities appropriate to the child tested. One example of an activity might be "have your baby imitate you while you clap your hands or blow a kiss." Though a parent or caregiver could plan activities inferred from the ASSIST output, there are two activity books sold by the publisher that describe appropriate activities (*You and Your Small Wonder*, books one and two).

The web site (www.agsnet.com) has a sample ASSIST output that a potential user may print out to evaluate. Doing this is strongly recommended.

References

American Guidance Service (AGS). (2001). www.agsnet.com. Retrieved August 19, 2001 from the World Wide Web.

Bradley-Johnson, S. (1997). Review of the Mullen Scales of Early Learning. *Psychology in the Schools 34*, 379–382.

Chittooran, M. M. (2001). Review of the Mullen Scales of Early Learning, AGS Edition. In B. S. Plake & J. C. Impara (Eds.), *The Fourteenth Mental Measurements Yearbook* (pp. 792–794). Lincoln, NE: The Buros Institute of Mental Measurements.

Eisert, E. M., & Lamorey, S. (1996). Play as a window on child development: The relationship between play and other developmental domains. *Early Education and Development 7*, 221–235.

Griffith, E. M., Pennington, B. F., Wehner, E. A., & Rogers, S. J. (1999). Executive functions in young children with autism. *Child Development 70*(4), 817–832.

Kessler, C. E. (2001). Review of the Mullen Scales of Early Learning, AGS Edition. In B. S. Plake & J. C. Impara (Eds.) *The Fourteenth Mental Measurements Yearbook* (pp. 794–795). Lincoln, NE: The Buros Institute of Mental Measurements.

Morrison, D., & Villareal, S. (1993). Cognitive performance of prenatally drug-exposed infants. *The Transdisciplinary Journal 3*, 211–220.

Salvia, J., & Ysseldyke, J. E. (2001). *Assessment* (8th ed.). Boston: Houghton Mifflin.

Schrader, B. D. (1993). Assessment of measures to detect preschool academic risk in very-low-birth-weight children. *Nursing Research 42*, 17–21.

Schrader, B. D., Heaverly, M. A., & Rappaport, J. (1990a). Temperament, behavior problems, and learning skills in very-low-birth-weight preschoolers. *Research in Nursing & Health 13*, 27–34.

Schrader, B. D., Heaverly, M. A., & Rappaport, J. (1990b). The value of early home assessment in identifying risk in children who were very low birth weight. *Pediatric Nursing 16*, 268–272.

Vohr, B. R. (1991) Preterm cognitive development: Biologic and environmental influences. *Infants and Young Children 3*, 20–29.

Vohr, B. R., Garcia-Coll, C., Mayfield, S., Brann, B., Shaul, P., & Oh, W. (1989). Neurologic and developmental status related to the evolution of visual-motor abnormalities from birth to 2 years of age in preterm infants with intraventicular hemorrhage. *The Journal of Pediatrics 115*, 296–302.

Vohr, B. R., Garcia-Coll, C., & Oh, W. (1988). Language development of low-birthweight infants at two years. *Developmental Medicine and Child Neurology 30*, 608–615.

Vohr, B. R., Garcia-Coll, C., & Oh, W. (1989). Language and neurodevelopmental outcome of low-birthweight infants at three years. *Developmental Medicine and Child Neurology 31*, 582–590.

Pre-Kindergarten Screen (PKS), for testing individuals 4 and 5 years of age
Reviewed by Charles W. Hatch, Ph.D., Educational Research and Measurement

---

Usefulness of the Test for Educators

Test Authors' Purpose

"The Pre-Kindergarten Screen (PKS) is designed to be a quick screening instrument for children between the ages of 4 years 0 months and 5 years 11 months who may be at risk for early academic difficulty" (Webster & Matthews, 2000a).

Decision-Making Applications

"It identifies deficiencies in several skill areas shown by recent research to be indicators of a child's later academic success. . . . Each of the nine brief subtests consists of items designed to differentiate between children who have the skills necessary for early school success and those who may require additional efforts during kindergarten in preparation for subsequent entry into first grade" (Webster & Matthews, 2000a, p. 5).

On the basis of scores on the PKS, children could be placed in the first grade or retained in kindergarten, referred for further evaluation, or provided with additional instruction and help in areas of weakness.

Relevant Population

Four- and 5-year-old children who have not entered first grade.

Characteristics Described

Gross Motor Skills (6 tasks)
   Example: The child is asked to walk a 6-foot tape without help.

Fine Motor Skills (5 tasks)
   Example: The child is asked to copy a circle in the space provided.

Following Directions (4 tasks)
   Example: The child is asked to "point to your right foot."

Block Tapping (4 tasks)
   Example: The child is asked to reproduce a series of motor sequences without language. Using the first of the test plates, the administrator silently indicates a sequence of printed blocks, say, first then third. The child reproduces the sequence.

Visual Matching (4 tasks)
   Example: The child is asked to match a given figure or letter with a matching one from a choice of four.

Visual Memory (5 tasks)
   Example: The child is presented with a figure or pair of figures, the image is removed, and the child indicates a match from a choice of three.

Imitation (5 tasks)
   Example: The child is asked to mimic hand and finger sequences like clapping.

Basic Academic Skills (5 tasks)
   Example: The child is asked to write his or her name.

Delayed Gratification (1 task)
   Example: The child is presented with two treats and asked to wait to eat. The administrator leaves for two minutes but observes the child's behavior.

Test Scores Obtained

A raw score is obtained for each of the nine subtests and a total score, which is the sum of the subtests. The total score (range 1–95) is converted to a standard score (mean = 100, standard deviation = 15) as well as percentile. The tables are set up separately for each two-month age span covering the two-year focus of the instrument (4- and 5-year-olds).

Technical Adequacy

Validity Confirmation

Test response validity is supported by the data. Obtained scores moved consistently upward with increased age. A screening instrument which aims at measuring developmental progress should have that characteristic.

Other data presented to support test response validity was adequate but not compelling. The test was able to distinguish between students already identified as needing intervention, low performing, and high performing. Since the groups are compared by means, it is not possible to see whether any individual students would have been misclassified by PKS scores.

When the PKS was related to end of kindergarten outcome, the result was that of 392 students, 98.7% were correctly classified. The categories used were Special Education Referral, Retained in Grade, Provisionally Passed, and Promoted (Webster & Matthews, 2000a, p. 36). This latter data is strong evidence for satisfactory test response validity.

Reliability Confirmation

The authors report that when administration of the PKS was repeated with the same children (58) after an interval of 115 to 135 days, a reliability of .78 was obtained for the total score. This number is satisfactory. The subtests ranged from .31 to .89, but it should be remembered that these young children change dramatically in their functioning over four or five months.

When the authors focused on the unity of the test (internal consistency), the reliability figures ranged from .67 to .90, but most were between .81 and .90. The median reliability was .825. Interestingly, the oldest children (5 years, 6 months through 5 years, 11 months) showed the lowest reliabilities, .67 and .68.

Objectivity Confirmation

The authors report that the agreement among examiners was 92%, and no disagreement was more than one point. It should be noted, however, that only 12 children were involved in this calculation. The simplicity of the directions and observations, as well as the well-laid-out record form, would lead to a satisfactorily high level of agreement.

Statistical Confirmation

The PKS Manual contains well-thought-out tables and sufficient data.

Special Features

Acronym

PKS.

Levels of the Test

One.

Number of Test Forms

One.

Norm-Referenced?

Yes. The results are converted to standard scores which resemble IQ scores and percentiles. The norming sample is not discussed in great detail but was composed of 679 children from across the country. Ethnicity was stated to be "70 percent 'White,' and 30 percent 'Other Ethnicities,' which closely matches the U.S. population (1998, U.S. Census Bureau)" (Webster & Matthews, 2000a, p. 28).

Criterion-Referenced?

No.

Other Features

The PKS Manual does a commendable job of explaining concepts before providing data. The segments on reliability and validity are clear without being too complex or jargon filled. The references are quite usable and relevant to a further understanding of the testing issues surrounding young children.

Feasibility Considerations

Testing Time

Ten to 15 minutes.

For Testing Groups? Individuals?

Individuals.

Test Administration and Scoring

The directions for administration and scoring in the PKS Manual are really simple and straightforward. Many manuals promise that this is true but for the PKS it is a reality. Training for the administration of this instrument is not required.

The test administrator does need to supply some materials for the testing. Not included are the six-foot tape, crayons, pencils, and treats (for the delayed gratification item).

Test Materials and Approximate Costs

The web site offers the following materials: PKS kit (8150-9): $65; test forms (50) (8153-5): $25. Any part of the kit may be ordered separately.

Adequacy of Test Manuals

The PKS Manual is well designed and easy to follow. Test administrators will have little trouble using the test for the first time. The well-planned recording sheet also aids test administration.

Excerpts from Other Test Reviews

No reviews were found for the PKS.

Ordering Information

Publisher

Academic Therapy Publications, 20 Commercial Boulevard, Novato, CA 94949-6191; Phone: 800-422-7249; Fax: 888-287-9925; Web site: www.academictherapy.com.

Authors

Raymond E. Webster and Angela Matthews.

Publication Date

2000.

Cautions and Comments

This is an excellent instrument for its intended screening purpose. The speed and simplicity of the administration process, as well as the superior quality of the printed material, argue for adoption consideration. However, the use of IQ-like standard scores is a drawback because of the possibility of confusion and misinterpretation.

The inclusion of the unique delayed gratification item is another positive characteristic of this instrument.

References

Webster, R. E., & Matthews, A. (2000a). *Pre-Kindergarten Screen Manual.* Novato, CA: Academic Therapy Publications.

Webster, R. E., & Matthews, A. (2000b). *Pre-Kindergarten Screen Record Form*. Novato, CA:
    Academic Therapy Publications
Webster, R. E., & Matthews, A. (2000c). *Pre-Kindergarten Screen Test Plates*. Novato, CA:
    Academic Therapy Publications.

Preschool Evaluation Scale (PES),
for testing individuals from birth through 72 months of age
Reviewed by Charles W. Hatch, Ph.D., Educational Research and Measurement

---

Usefulness of the Test for Educators

Test Author's Purpose

"To contribute to the early identification of students with developmental delays"
(Technical Manual).

Decision-Making Applications

The PES may be used in conjunction with other instruments for admission, program planning, and intervention.

Since the PES is based on the specific deficit areas enumerated in Public Law 99-
457, it is primarily designed to identify individuals who exhibit developmental delays
as defined in the above public law.

Educators could use PES results along with data from other instruments to make
admission and instructional decisions.

Relevant Population

Children through age 72 months in two stages, birth through 35 months and 36
through 72 months.

Characteristics Described

Each child is evaluated on the following six characteristics: cognitive, physical,
language and speech, psychosocial, and self-help. The cognitive segment has items,
for example, that assess a child's ability to demonstrate pre-reading and pre-math
skills. The physical segment is broken down into separate scores on gross motor skills
and fine motor skills. The language and speech segment contains items that indicate
whether a child is able to name objects and pictures. The psychosocial segment assesses such skills as the choice of appropriate play behavior and knowledge of social
rules. The self-help segment indicates the child's ability to dress and feed.

Test Scores Obtained

For each of the items (94 or 85, depending on the form), the child is given the following rating: 0 = cannot perform the behavior; 1 = performs the behavior success-fully but on an inconsistent basis; 2 = performs the behavior successfully and inde-pendently.

The six subscales are derived from the items included in each (see "Characteristics Described" above). In addition, a total is obtained. Scaled scores are given for the subscales and percentiles are given for the total. The subscale standard scores are obtained by use of data from one of 14 norming groups in the Technical Manual. Through age 35 months the tables yield standard scores which combine both sexes in small age increments (example: 25–28 months of age). For older children, 36 through 72 months, the tables cover a greater age span but have separate tables for males and females.

The total performance percentiles are obtained from additional tables with the same age and sex divisions as were used on the subscale standard scores.

Technical Adequacy

Validity Confirmation

Test item validity: Since the instrument was developed specifically to measure the specified categories of Public Law 99-457, that to a large degree determined the subscales and items.

> For the purpose of the development of the Preschool Evaluation Scale, develop-ment descriptors were gathered for the educational environment from diagnosti-cians and preschool educators working with developmentally delayed and nondevelopmentally delayed children. These behavioral descriptors were clus-tered and factor analyzed according to domains of cognitive thinking, large muscle/small muscle, language, social/emotional and self-help. (PES Technical Manual, 1992, p. 6)

Factor analysis is a mathematical sorting process. Test item validity is satisfactory.

Test response validity: Scores obtained for 60 children on the younger form PES subscales (birth–35 months) were compared with the Early Learning Accomplish-ment Profile (ELAP). The correlation figures ranged from .58 to .71. In a second study, 58 older children (36–72 months) were compared on the PES and the Learning Accomplishment Profile (LAP). Here the figures ranged from .61 to .80. The data is not compelling that the tests measure similar characteristics, merely suggestive.

It would seem that if the subscales were indeed discrete and measured different characteristics, then mathematical interrelations between the subscales would be low. This was not the case. On the surface it would seem that, for example, the social/emotional scale would be relatively unrelated to fine motor skills. For younger chil-dren (birth through 35 months) the figures were .83 to .92. However, for the older children (36–72 months) the correlations were lower, .60 to .83.

Reliability Confirmation

When the test was administered twice to the same 391 children, the subscales exhibited correlations of .80 to .92, and the total was .88. These are satisfactory figures but the description of the 391 children is lacking. Even the proportions taking each of the two forms are unclear.

Objectivity Confirmation

The publisher provides data on the degree of agreement for two observers of the same child. These figures ranged from .80 to .89. However, a caution needs to be expressed that the three-point scale (0-1-2) requires an evaluator to use some judgment in rating a behavior, especially when deciding whether a behavior is a "1" or a "2." For example, one of the items is "can share toys in a reciprocal fashion." The evaluator may have some difficulty deciding whether the observed behavior is a "1" or a "2."

Statistical Confirmation

Statistical data on validity, reliability, and norms is available in the Technical Manual for the PES.

Special Features

Acronym

PES.

Levels of the Test

Two levels: birth–35 months and 36–72 months.

Number of Test Forms

There only seems to be one form for each of the two levels.

Norm-Referenced?

Yes. The PES is norm-referenced as evidenced by the percentile rank reported on the total score. In addition, standard scores are given for each of the subscales.

Criterion-Referenced?

No. See "Norm-Referenced?" above.

Other Features

A computer program is available to provide standardized output. The order number is 01801 and the cost is $20. *Note*: the program in not very refined and only provides a basic minimum of output.

Feasibility Considerations

Testing Time

Twenty to 25 minutes.

For Testing Groups? Individuals?

Individuals.

Test Administration and Scoring

The PES should be administered by "professional educators with primary observational opportunities. These persons would usually be early childhood educators who work directly with the child during preschool or related situations" (Test Manual). The test administrator fills in a test booklet with a 0-1-2 rating for each described behavior. The subscales are summed and a standard score obtained from the Technical Manual (or by computer program). Then the total is calculated and the percentile obtained from the Technical Manual.

It is not difficult to imagine a test administrator bringing a form outside with the children at recess and filling in the form as a child plays.

Test Materials and Approximate Costs

Complete kit (01850): $74.50; Technical Manual (01800): $12.50; forms (birth through 35 months) (50) (01810): $31; forms (36–72 months) (50) (01811): $31; PES Quick score (computer program) (01801): $20.

Adequacy of Test Manuals

The manuals seem adequate.

Excerpts from Other Test Reviews

"PES norms are generally representative. Reliability information is incompletely reported for internal consistency and stability, although the information that is presented suggests adequate reliability. Nonetheless, users should interpret PES results cautiously" (Salvia & Ysseldyke, 2001).

"Overall, this measure has some good features and several rather undesirable ones. At this point, the PES is probably best used as a screening measure of functioning in young children, as an adjunct to other measures like the Battelle Developmental Inventory, the Bayley Scales of Infant Development, Second Edition, and the Early Learning Accomplishment Profile or as the starting point for the development of instructional objectives. In any event, results obtained with this instrument should be interpreted with some caution" (Chittooran, 2001).

"The PES may be considered psychometrically sound, although further establishment of criterion-related validity is desirable. . . . the PES would be a nice addition to the evaluation of young children" (Gaddis, 2001).

Ordering Information

Publisher

Hawthorne Educational Services, 800 Gray Oak Drive, Columbia, MO 65201; Phone: 800-542-1673; Fax: 800-442-9509.

Author

Stephen B. McCarney.

Publication Date

1992.

Cautions and Comments

This instrument will probably do just what it was designed to do: indicate developmental delays as per Public Law 99-457. It is probably not realistic to expect it to do much more. For example, it is probably not sufficient in itself and should be supplemented by other instruments. It does not provide outlines for remedial action as given by the Mullen Scales of Early Learning.

The publisher does not provide the kind of broad support that is found in so many other instruments. The Internet dimension is missing and the computer program is basic at best. The reliability and validity data is not compelling and some questions remain on objectivity.

References

Chittooran, M. M. (2001). Review of the Preschool Evaluation Scale. In B. S. Plake & J. C. Impara (Eds.), *The Fourteenth Mental Measurements Yearbook* (pp. 779–781). Lincoln, NE: The Buros Institute of Mental Measurements.

Gaddis, L. R. (2001). Review of the Preschool Evaluation Scale. In B. S. Plake & J. C. Impara (Eds.), *The Fourteenth Mental Measurements Yearbook* (pp. 781–782). Lincoln, NE: The Buros Institute of Mental Measurements.

Salvia, J., & Ysseldyke, J. E. (2001). *Assessment* (8th ed.). Boston: Houghton Mifflin.

Preschool Language Scale (PLS-3), for testing individuals from birth through 6 years, 11 months of age (Formerly PLS [1969] and PLS-R]1979]) Reviewed by Charles W. Hatch, Ph.D., Educational Research and Measurement

---

Usefulness of the Test for Educators

Test Authors' Purpose

"The original *Preschool Language Scale* was developed in 1969 because clinicians needed a diagnostic instrument capable of measuring the language development of young children" (Zimmerman, Steiner, & Pond, 1992).

"The Scale proved to be especially useful for measuring early language development because it tapped a broad range of language skills" (Zimmerman et al., 1992).

Decision-Making Applications

"PLS-3 can be used to assess receptive and expressive language skills in infants and young children. Two subscales, Auditory Comprehension and Expressive Communication, enable you to evaluate a child's relative ability in receptive and expressive language. When comparing the scores, you can determine whether deficiencies are primarily receptive or expressive in nature, or if they reflect an overall delay or disorder in communication. PLS-3 also assesses behaviors considered to be language precursors" (Zimmerman et al., 1992, p. 5).

Therefore, the main applications of this instrument are for instructional prescription and individual referral. The newest edition (PLS-3) was motivated by the passage of Public Law 94-142 in 1975 as well as Public Law 99-457 in 1986 and provides data consistent with both acts.

The literature of the American Hyperlexia Association notes that the PLS-3 is a valuable tool in screening for the hyperlexia disorder, which is characterized by precocious reading abilities. "When testing the young child, the Zimmerman Pre-School Language Scale is a useful instrument since it evaluates both receptive and expressive language skills and includes both rote and analytic items. Usually on this test you will find that the receptive and expressive language skills are approximately commensurate but that his rote skills are far superior to the analytic ones" (Kupperman, Bligh, & Barouski, 2002, p. 8).

Relevant Population

Children from birth through 6 years, 11 months of age.

Characteristics Described

Language Precursors
    Attention
    Vocal Development
    Social Communication
Semantics (Content)
    Vocabulary
    Concepts
        Quality
        Quantity
        Spatial
        Time/Sequence

Structure (Form)

Morphology

Syntax

Integrative Thinking Skills

For most but not all of the above there are "items" that fall in both the auditory discrimination and expression communication categories.

Attention has items only in the auditory category. Example: "Looks intently at speaker."

Vocal development has items only in the expressive communication area. Example: "Produces at least four consonant sounds."

Social Communication (expressive only) contains items like the following: "Vocalizes when talked to."

All the following areas are represented by items in both auditory and expressive categories:

Vocabulary

Auditory: "Responds to no-no"

Expressive: "Names objects"

Quality

Auditory: "Understands descriptive concepts (big, wet, little)"

Expressive: "Uses adjectives to describe people or objects"

Quantity

Auditory: "Understands quantity (3, 5)"

Expressive: "Uses words for quantity (empty, more)"

Spatial

Auditory: "Understands spatial concepts (in, off, out of)"

Expressive: "Uses prepositions (on, behind, next to, front)"

Time/Sequence

Auditory: "Understands time concepts (night, day)"

Expressive: "Answers WHEN questions"

Morphology

Auditory: "Understands pronouns (me, him, my, your)"

Expressive: "Uses pronouns"

Syntax

Auditory: "Understands passive voice"

Expressive: "Repeats complex sentences"

"Each of two 48-item subscales, Auditory Comprehension (AC) and Expressive Communication (EC), includes 4 items (tasks) at each of the 14 age levels. Age levels span 6 months, except the last two, which span 12 months" (Grill, 1998, p. 783).

Test Scores Obtained

A child is given raw scores on the AC and EC scales, as well as a Total Language Score. These three are followed by standard scores, percentile rank, and age equivalents for each. Confidence intervals (68, 80, or 90%) can be obtained for each of the above.

The standard scores reported are on a scale which is set up with a mean of 100 and a standard deviation of 15, which gives them the appearance of IQ scores. This appearance can lead users to serious misinterpretations, which could be avoided by using some other scale. It is entirely possible, for example, that a user might think of the standard scores as IQ scores and explain them using that conception, when there is no explicit presentation by the publisher that IQ scores may actually be obtained from the PLS.

Technical Adequacy

Validity Confirmation

The authors approached *test item validity* by detailing the extensive developmental process for items. Information and feedback from previous forms also allowed for further item refinement. Data on the characteristics of the field test subjects is reported and follows the U.S. Census data for 1980. In terms of race/ethnicity, however, the sample underrepresents "Whites" and "Other" (not White, African-American, or Hispanic) while African-American and Hispanic are over-represented (Zimmerman et al., 1992, p. 80).

Test response validity presents a problem. The authors report that the test did not perform very well when used to differentiate previously diagnosed language-disordered children from others. Accuracy was only 66% for age 3 children, 80% for age 4 children, and 70% for age 5 children (Zimmerman et al., 1992, p. 93).

Reliability Confirmation

Discussion of the reliability of this instrument is made more complex because there exist 14 age groups and three obtained scores for each age level (auditory, expressive, and total). Reliability as a measure of the unity (internal consistency) of the test ranged from .47 to .88 on auditory, from .68 to .91 on expressive, and from .74 to .94 on total. Using .80 as a criterion, only 6 reliabilities were satisfactory on auditory, 8 on expressive, and 12 on total. This is only about 62% of the reported figures (Zimmerman et al., 1992, p. 89).

When the authors reported on the stability of obtained scores (test-retest reliability) with an interval of two days to two weeks between test administrations, the figures were .82 to .94. These are satisfactory especially considering that the children were only 3 to 5 years old (Zimmerman et al., 1992, p. 90).

Objectivity Confirmation

Agreement between two raters of the same child was reported as 89%. This is satisfactory, but on an instrument like this, administered to very young children, the possibility for objectivity problems is high. For example, did the child produce four consonant sounds (meeting the criteria) or was it just three?

Statistical Confirmation

The Examiner's Manual contains extensive statistics as well as tables for score conversion.

Special Features

Acronym

PLS-3 (the previous editions were known as the PLS-R and PLS).

Levels of the Test

Fourteen levels, by child's age.

Number of Test Forms

One.

Norm-Referenced?

Yes. This is evidenced by the use of percentile rank, age equivalents, and standard scores that are scaled exactly like IQ scores. The authors intended to have the norming sample reflect the 1980 U.S. Census, but their percentages are not very close. For example, the norming sample was 56.3% White while the census shows 69.6%. In general, the norming sample overrepresents both African-American and Hispanic subjects (Zimmerman et al., 1992, p. 80).

Criterion-Referenced?

No.

Other Features

A Spanish version of the test is available.
Directions are given for modification to suit children with severe developmental delays, physical impairments, and hearing impairments.

Feasibility Considerations

Testing Time

Thirty to 60 minutes.

For Testing Groups? Individuals?

Individuals.

Test Administration and Scoring

The administration process is covered well in the Examiner's Manual. The process itself is not simple and will require considerable preparation on the part of the administrator. Quite a number of necessary supplies for administration are *not* included in the kit. For example, the administrator will need a sheet of cellophane and a teddy bear. Training will be needed before a person will feel comfortable administering the PLS-3.

Test Materials and Approximate Costs

PLS-3
   Complete kit (015-8659-309-ws199): $159
   Record forms (12) (015-8659-333-ws199): $31.50
   Picture Book (015-8659-325-ws199): $99
   Examiner's Manual (015-8659-317-ws199): $55

PLS-R
   Record forms (12) (015-8659-171-wp199): $55.00

It should be noted that the publisher continues to support the previous edition with the sale of record forms. This action speaks well of the publisher's willingness to prolong the useful life of an expensive purchase and adds to the test's value.

Adequacy of Test Manuals

The Examiner's Manual contains extensive information on the test development, administration and scoring, design and standardization, reliability and validity, test interpretation, supplemental measures, and references. There is also a useful section titled "After Assessment: The Next Step," which includes follow-up assessment, treatment suggestions, and resources.

Excerpts from Other Test Reviews

"In summary, the PLS-3 examiner's manual is especially valuable with clear, concise, usable information on assessing children's language. But the test is flawed. More items, more naturally distributed over the targeted age ranges, might resolve the reliability and validity problems. The PLS-3 may be used best as a quick language assessment tool for 3-, 4- and 5-year-old children, but should not be used alone to obtain a thorough language evaluation" (Grill, 1998, p. 784).

"In summary, the PLS-3 has many positive features in its test design and scoring. Considerable effort was made to create a language test that could reliably make initial decisions regarding the presence or absence of a language disorder in preschool children. However, findings of construct validity suggest that the test may not adequately discriminate between children with and without language disorders, rendering this test of limited use for its stated purposes" (Norris, 1998, p. 786).

Ordering Information

Publisher

The Psychological Corporation, 19500 Bulverde Road, San Antonio, TX 78259; Phone: 800-228-0752; Fax: 210-339-5873; Web site: www.psychcorp.com.

Authors

Irla Lee Zimmerman, Violette G. Steiner, and Roberta Evatt Pond.

Publication Date

1992.

Cautions and Comments

This is an attractive, well-documented instrument supported by a strong company. There are some problems with both reliability and validity that argue against using results from this test alone to make referral or remediation decisions. The use of scaled scores that have the appearance of IQ scores may lead to misinterpretation or overinterpretation.

References

Grill, J. (1998). Review of the Preschool Language Scale. In J. C. Impara & B. S. Plake (Eds.), *The Thirteenth Mental Measurements Yearbook* (pp. 782–784). Lincoln, NE: The Buros Institute of Mental Measurements.

Kupperman, P., Bligh, S., & Barouski, K. (2002). *Hyperlexia.* Retrieved March 22, 2002 from the World Wide Web: www.hyperlexia.org.

Norris, J. A. (1998). Review of the Preschool Language Scale. In J. C. Impara & B. S. Plake (Eds.), *The Thirteenth Mental Measurements Yearbook* (pp. 784–786). Lincoln, NE: The Buros Institute of Mental Measurements.

Zimmerman, I. L, Steiner, V. G., & Pond, R. E. (1992). *Preschool Language Scale-3 Examiner's Manual.* San Antonio, TX: The Psychological Corporation.

Pre-School Screening Instrument (PSSI),
for testing individuals 4 and 5 years of age
Reviewed by Charles W. Hatch, Ph.D., Educational Research and Measurement

---

Usefulness of the Test for Educators

Test Author's Purpose

"In psychological and educational settings the need has been recognized for adequate screening instruments which will detect children with potential learning disabilities prior to comprehensive diagnostic testing" (Cohen, 1979a).

"The PSSI was designed with a format for the screening of large populations of children quickly and accurately" (Cohen, 1979a).

Decision-Making Applications

"Early screening should not be used to diagnose or label children. Rather, it gives the examiner an estimate of the child's task proficiency and stimulates a more detailed evaluation to identify specific problem areas in order that appropriate services may be integrated into the child's curriculum" (Cohen, 1979a, p. 5).

The intended use of the PSSI is thus as a five- to eight-minute screening instrument to select those students for more detailed testing to determine problems in "speech and language development, visual perceptual, fine and gross motor skills as well as behavior" (Cohen, 1979a, p. 5).

Since the test is intended to be a screening instrument used to determine whether more in-depth testing is needed, it is not designed for making admission, placement, instructional prescription, achievement certification, or referral decisions. However, because of insufficient evidence of its validity, reliability, and objectivity, as you will see, it is doubtful that it will serve as an adequate screening instrument.

Relevant Population

Children 4 and 5 years of age.

Characteristics Described

The PSSI records results in the following content/performance categories: (1) human figure drawing, (2) visual motor perception/fine motor skills, (3) gross motor skills, (4) language development, (5) speech, and (6) behavior.

For human figure drawing, the child is asked to draw a human figure (large pencils supplied) in the test instrument. Each drawing is scored 0–10 on the number of characteristics present (head, hair, eyes, etc.).

For visual motor perception/fine motor skills, the child is asked to draw a circle, a cross, and a square. Using the supplied blocks, the child copies a pattern of five blocks shaped in an "L" and builds a tower.

For gross motor skills, the child is required to jump, balance on one foot, throw a ball, bounce a ball, and hop.

For language development, the child is evaluated through the use of a series of questions including the following areas: knowing name, explaining a picture, explaining a word like "runs" or "burns," and explaining a word like "apple" or "cup."

For speech, the child is evaluated by the examiner on a three-point scale going from 1 = clear to 3 = unclear.

For behavior, the child is evaluated again on the same three-point scale, looking at activity, impulsiveness, attention span, and distractibility.

Test Scores Obtained

The Instruction Manual contains four tables for converting performance scores to "estimated range of developmental level." These scores go from 3.0 to 5.0 in five steps.

The language development score is obtained by taking the total score and converting it to a three-point scale (0–2). For example, 13 or 14 points would be rated "2."

The speech performance is recorded on the 1–3 scale as explained above. The same is true for the behavior scale.

The author provides a sample feedback letter to provide screening information for parents (Cohen, 1979a, p. 34). It seems to provide enough information to be useful without being too quantitative and thus confusing to many.

Technical Adequacy

Validity Confirmation

Information from the publisher regarding *test response validity* was based on the ability of the test to predict kindergarten problems. The degree of agreement was 87%, which means that most of the time a predicted problem area from the test was also observed in the classroom by "their kindergarten teacher and a learning specialist (who had no previous information concerning the findings of the PSSI)" (Cohen, 1979a, pp. 5–6). It is also reassuring from the point of view of its projected use as a screening instrument that the errors above included more false positives (10% overreferrals) than false negatives (3% underreferrals). If a test of this type is to be in error, it is better to report more children for referral than absolutely necessary; that is, to err on the side of caution. However, this data was obtained in the mid-1970s, and validity needs to be reexamined along with expansion to include comparison with other instruments.

No information was presented by the publisher concerning *test item validity*. Thus, there is no information on the item selection or development process beyond some vague references in the Review of Literature (Cohen, 1979a, pp. 3–4). The author does note that the revisions of 1977–1978 were "based on direct experience with the instrument, comments of knowledgeable individuals in the field, statistical analysis, and research" (Cohen, 1979a, p. 5). Therefore, there is no evidence presented to assure that items were developed to "detect children with potential learning disabilities," which is the author's stated purpose (Cohen, 1979a, p. 3).

Reliability Confirmation

Reliability is a problem. The author states, "Although no test-retest reliability data are presently available, it is expected to be in the same range as other tests of intelligence and learning" (Cohen, 1979a, p. 5). Lack of any firm reliability data probably removes the test from serious adoption consideration.

Objectivity Confirmation

Objectivity is reported to be .95 to .96 for subtest items. This would mean that two persons observing the same behavior were almost always in agreement. This would be excellent. However, the publisher says these numbers were obtained from only 20 children and four examiners. The small size of the sample makes the result questionable, especially when the subjective nature of many items is considered. For example, in the human figure drawing, are the arms attached or within the general area? This is often a judgment call. Objectivity can only be judged satisfactory when the above numbers are confirmed by further research.

Statistical Confirmation

What scant information is available is in the Instruction Manual. More data would be welcomed on validity, reliability, objectivity, and norming population.

Special Features

Acronym

PSSI.

Levels of the Test

One.

Number of Test Forms

One.

Norm-Referenced?

Probably. The test scores indicate whether a child falls into the following developmental categories:

Level 1	0 to 5 months behind age level
Level 2	6 to 11 months behind age level
Level 3	12 or more months behind age level

Exactly how these levels were determined is not made clear.

The norming population is described as "504 children between the ages of four and five whose socio-economic range is from upper middle to lower class, but with no serious deprivation" (Cohen, 1979a, p. 5). Clearly, expansion and updating are required.

Criterion-Referenced?

There is a clear criterion-referenced component to the scores, and instruction could be planned easily around many of the test item concepts if the instructional objective was to teach the concepts or skills from the test. These could range from ball playing to drawing to reading aloud.

Other Features

The chief feature is the speed with which the PSSI may be administered to an individual child—less than 10 minutes. This would allow a reasonably large group, like a class, to be assessed in one day.

The parental questionnaire is useful and would provide any program a great deal of useful information about a young child. In fact, a school might well adopt the parental questionnaire without adopting the PSSI itself.

Here are some examples from the parental questionnaire:

Age at which your child was able to:
    Sit alone
    Begin to walk
    Say first words
    etc.

Does your child
    Pay attention to the reading of a short story?
    Answer simple questions and talk about the story?
    Converse easily with family and friends?
    etc.

Behavioral Characteristics: Check items that describe your child.
    Friendly
    Shy
    Cooperative
    etc.

Medical history
    Hearing, vision, accidents, etc.

Experiences and interests
(Cohen, 1979b)

Feasibility Considerations

Testing Time

About 7–8 minutes.

For Testing Groups? Individuals?

Individuals.

Test Administration and Scoring

Administration is not difficult because the directions in the Instruction Manual are clear. An administrator would need to read the relevant sections and do a couple of trial evaluations; none of this would be very time consuming or require background experience and training in testing. However, most similar manuals include a thoroughly worked out example; this one does not. It does have examples of sample evaluations for some of the drawing sections (five human figures are included), but that is all.

Test Materials and Approximate Costs

Pre-School Screening Instrument (PSSI) Kit (32142): $75; PSSI Manual (32142-M): $20; PSSI Record Forms (32142-R) (25): $30; PSSI Parental Questionnaire (32142-Q) (25): $20. These prices are as of December 2001 from the Stoelting web site, www.stoeltingco.com.

Adequacy of Test Manuals

The publisher provides enough information to administer the test with little trouble. However, a worked form would be useful. The data on reliability, validity, objectivity, and norming population is weak.

Excerpts from Other Test Reviews

"In summary, the PSSI might be quite useful if potential users are aware of its statistical shortcomings and use it only as a screening instrument and not to replace a formal evaluation. The author recommends the development of local norms and this would certainly be appropriate. The instrument appears to have promise, but will need continuing improvement to reach its full potential" (Schwarting, 1985, p. 1193).

Ordering Information

Publisher

Stoelting Company, 620 Wheat Lane, Wood Dale, IL 60191; Phone: 630-860-9700; Fax: 630-860-9775; Web site: www.stoeltingco.com/tests.

Author

Stephen Paul Cohen.

Publication Date

1979.

Cautions and Comments

The technical shortcomings seem to preclude the use of the PSSI. There is no reliability data at all, and the objectivity data is based on only 20 subjects.

The parental questionnaire is very useful and might be used independently of the PSSI test itself.

The test might be useful primarily because of the short administration time and the ability to provide screening information if its more serious problems were addressed.

References

Cohen, S. P. (1979a). *Pre-School Screening Instrument. Instruction Manual.* Wood Dale, IL: Stoelting Company.

Cohen, S. P. (1979b). *Pre-School Screening Instrument. Parental Questionnaire.* Wood Dale, IL: Stoelting Company.

Schwarting, G. (1985). Review of the Pre-School Screening Instrument. In J. W. Mitchell (Ed.), *The Ninth Mental Measurements Yearbook* (vol. II, p. 1193). Lincoln, NE: The Buros Institute of Mental Measurements.

Tests of Basic Experiences, Second Edition (TOBE 2),
for testing individuals and groups from pre-kindergarten through grade 1
Reviewed by Charles W. Hatch, Ph.D., Educational Research and Measurement

---

Usefulness of the Test for Educators

Test Author's Purpose

The TOBE 2 is designed to measure the differences in children's awareness of the world around them. An underlying assumption of the TOBE 2 is that children's experiences and learning opportunities vary considerably. To succeed in school, children must master certain concepts before they can begin to participate in formal educational programs. The TOBE 2 can evaluate the richness of a child's experiences.

The TOBE 2 is neither a reading readiness test nor a test of readiness to learn. Instead, it measures factors that contribute to readiness.

Decision-Making Applications

"TOBE 2 provides educators with an impartial, reliable gauge of the effectiveness of instructional programs. Curriculum can then be developed or revised, and general teaching goals and strategies can be established. . . . Since TOBE 2 has both fall and spring norms, it can be used in a pretest-posttest model to provide a measure of student growth. . . . TOBE 2 results can be used as a guide to grouping students according to common needs or as a starting point for determining individual instructional needs" (Moss, 1979g, p. 2).

From the above it can be seen that the author recommends the test be used for placement, instructional prescription, achievement certification, and program evaluation purposes.

Relevant Population

Children in pre-kindergarten, kindergarten, and grade 1.

Characteristics Described

The following four subjects with their ambitious content subcategories are covered by the TOBE 2.

Mathematics
   Order of Numbers
   Counting
   Geometry
   Time and Money
   Weight, Volume, and Linear Measurement
   Properties and Operations
   Fractions
Language
   Visual Discrimination
   Alphabet Knowledge
   Initial Sounds
   Final Sounds
   Rhyming
   Space and Location
   Verb Tense
   Sentence Sense
   Context
   Comprehension
   Reading Terminology
Science
   Electricity and Magnetism
   Force, Motion, and Mechanics

Light, Optics, and Sound

Chemistry

Earth Science and Astronomy

Animal Reproduction and Development

Animal Behavior and Characteristics

Plant Life

Social Studies

Geography and Travel

Environment and Use of Natural Resources

Human Relations and Behavior

Occupations and the World of Work

Sociocultural Geography

History and Chronology

Health and Safety

Money and Consumer Behavior

Here are examples of questions used and the ingenious ways the author assesses a student's experience and learning. The students each have a response booklet with answer choices in the form of pictures or simple words. They mark in the booklets.

Language
The test administrator directs, "Mark the one that is different." The choices are COME, COME, CAME, AND COME (Moss, 1979b, p. 24).

Mathematics
The child is directed, "Mark the one that shows ten o'clock."
Four clocks are shown with eight o'clock, one o'clock, ten o'clock, and five o'clock (Moss, 1979b, p. 20).

Science
The administrator directs, "Mark the one that makes water boil."
Four pictures are seen: a cooking pot, a water faucet, a gas burner, and a measuring cup (Moss, 1979b, p. 29).

Social Studies
"Mark the one a plumber uses" is the prompt. The four pictures that follow are a rake, a saw, a paint brush, and a pipe wrench (Moss, 1979b, p. 32).

Test Scores Obtained

Each of the four content areas, the combined math and language, and the total score are reported as raw score, percentile rank, stanine, and normal curve equivalents.

Technical Adequacy

Validity Confirmation

It is in the area of validity that the greatest problems arise. *Test item validity* is reasonably well covered and the process of item development is outlined in the Norms and Technical Data Book (Moss, 1979g, pp. 3–11).

It is in the area of *test response validity* where sufficient data is lacking. The publisher has many pages of test intercorrelations. That is, each subsection (4) and summed section (2) is related to the others. Sometimes figures like this are difficult to interpret because if different subsections, say, social studies and mathematics, are found to have a relatively low correlation, it may simply be that the content is not closely related so a low figure (.64) would make perfect sense. On the other hand, a high figure, say .95, would again make perfect sense if the two components were mathematics/language and mathematics where one section is simply a component of the other (Moss, 1979g, pp. 12–15).

The expected correlations with other instruments were never presented.

Reliability Confirmation

The publisher gives four tables containing reliability figures for both Level K and Level L. The range of reliabilities for the younger children (Form K) was .66 (Social Studies) to .86 (total battery). The older children (Form L) showed a wider range— .64 (Language) to .87 (total battery). Some of the figures for subtests were somewhat low, but the figures for the summed portions (Mathematics/Language and total battery) were consistently satisfactory. This increase is largely explained by the fact that more items were included in these two portions. The range for the Mathematics/Language scores across forms was .77 to .81, while the corresponding figures for the total battery were .84 to .87. All of the above figures were calculated from testing done in 1977 and 1978. The reliabilities were measures of the unity of the test (internal consistency) (Moss, 1979g, pp. 28–30).

Objectivity Confirmation

There is little concern that an objectivity problem exists because the questions are really in a multiple-choice format and there is virtually no judgment exercised by the grader. The only instance might be where two answers are marked or where one choice is only partially erased.

Statistical Confirmation

The Norms and Technical Data Book contains adequate information on item development processes and reliability but is inadequate for validity data.

Special Features

Acronym

TOBE 2.

Levels of the Test

Two levels: K (kindergarten) and L (grade 1).

Number of Test Forms

One for each level.

Norm-Referenced?

Yes. The percentiles, stanines, and normal curve equivalents clearly indicate this. Information on the norming groups is given in the Norms and Technical Data Book (pp. 16–25) but this needs to be updated since the figures are from 1977 and 1978.

Criterion-Referenced?

No, but the content of the subtests is sufficiently clear to allow instructional and curriculum decisions to be made both for groups and individuals. For example, if a child were to miss the clock question above, the remedial instruction could be planned easily.

Other Features

The test allows for easy fall and spring administration so that a year's progress may be ascertained at both grade levels.

From the information given about the norming sample, the TOBE 2 seems to have been widely used in Head Start programs.

The author presents attempts to assure fairness with the following: "All items in the tryout study were reviewed for ethnic, cultural and sex bias by members of the educational community" (Moss, 1979g, p. 3). The Spanish version was reviewed by native speakers from Puerto Rico, Cuba, and Mexico.

Feasibility Considerations

Testing Time

Thirty to 45 minutes for each of the four test books, plus 30 minutes for the practice test. The publisher recommends spreading the testing over three or four days without an intervening weekend.

For Testing Groups? Individuals?

The TOBE 2 is group administered but the group could be as small as one. Groups should not be very large, since it is important for the test administrator to monitor each child with great regularity.

Test Administration and Scoring

The Examiner's Manual is very detailed and scripts what the administrator should say at every point. The training requirements are not especially onerous but would require some study before the test session.

Scoring may be done by hand or forms may be sent to the publisher for machine scoring.

Test Materials and Approximate Costs

Hand-scorable practice tests (30): $30.80; Subject tests (30) (Levels K or L): $79.50; Examiner's Manual (Levels K or L): $14.40; Instructional Activities Kit: $196; Classroom Evaluation Record: $2.60; Individual Evaluation Records (30) (Levels K or L): $30.80; Norms and Technical Data Book: $16.10.

Adequacy of Test Manuals

The manuals are adequate and provide a wealth of information. There is even a section that deals with a number of issues in a question-and-answer format.

Excerpts from Other Test Reviews

"Problems in creating a group test of basic concepts for young children of widely different cultural backgrounds may be intrinsically insoluble. Questions are raised about the content of some test items, but otherwise the design of the test and conditions of its administration are probably as good as can be obtained" (Cazden, 1972, p. 34).

Ordering Information

Publisher

CTB/McGraw Hill, 20 Ryan Ranch Road, Monterey, CA 93940-5703; Phone: 800-538-9547; Fax: 800-282-0266; Web site: www.ctb.com.

Author

Margaret H. Moss.

Publication Date

1979. First appeared in 1968 as the Test of Basic Experiences (TOBE), which was a development of the Test of Basic Information (1965) and Items of Space and Location (no date given).

Cautions and Comments

The TOBE 2 is an intriguing instrument which has fascinating items that measure complex ideas in novel ways. It even manages to meet the challenge of measuring very young children between the ages of 4 and 6. That being said, there are some problems that the publisher needs to address: (1) data from the late 1970s needs to be updated; (2) test response validity needs to be addressed by a number of studies with an array of other instruments. This instrument deserves to be validated and updated because of the underlying quality of the concepts and items.

References

Cazden, C. B. (1972). Review of the Tests of Basic Experiences. In O. C. Buros (Ed.), *The Seventh Mental Measurements Yearbook* (pp. 33–34). Highland Park, NJ: The Gryphon Press.

Moss, M. H. (1979a). *Tests of Basic Experiences, Second edition. Level K Examiner's Manual.* Monterey, CA: CTB/McGraw-Hill.

Moss, M. H. (1979b). *Tests of Basic Experiences, Second edition. Level L Examiner's Manual.* Monterey, CA: CTB/McGraw-Hill.

Moss, M. H. (1979c). *Tests of Basic Experiences, Second edition. Language, Level K.* Monterey, CA: CTB/McGraw-Hill.

Moss, M. H. (1979d). *Tests of Basic Experiences, Second edition. Language, Level L.* Monterey, CA: CTB/McGraw-Hill.

Moss, M. H. (1979e). *Tests of Basic Experiences, Second edition. Mathematics, Level K.* Monterey, CA: CTB/McGraw-Hill.

Moss, M. H. (1979f). *Tests of Basic Experiences, Second edition. Mathematics, Level L.* Monterey, CA: CTB/McGraw-Hill.

Moss, M. H. (1979g). *Tests of Basic Experiences, Second edition. Norms and Technical Data Book.* Monterey, CA: CTB/McGraw-Hill.

Moss, M. H. (1979h). *Tests of Basic Experiences, Second edition. Science, Level K.* Monterey, CA: CTB/McGraw-Hill.

Moss, M. H. (1979i). *Tests of Basic Experiences, Second edition. Science, Level L.* Monterey, CA: CTB/McGraw-Hill.

Moss, M. H. (1979j). *Tests of Basic Experiences, Second edition. Social Studies, Level K.* Monterey, CA: CTB/McGraw-Hill.

Moss, M. H. (1979k). *Tests of Basic Experiences, Second edition. Social Studies, Level L.* Monterey, CA: CTB/McGraw-Hill.

II

Placement Testing and Decision-Making

INTRODUCTION

The recent trend is to place and educate a greater number of students in regular classrooms. The enactment of laws mandating the education of disabled students in the least restrictive environment is mainly responsible for the trend. Many disabled students who in the past would have been placed in self-contained classrooms are now taught in regular classrooms. This, of course, increases the burden on regular classroom teachers who must teach these students. Their classes are more heterogeneous and they must accommodate handicapping conditions and adjust their teaching to the special needs of these students, which often reduces time available for teaching. Their new responsibilities require that teacher training be expanded. Classroom teachers need to be taught how to accommodate various handicapping conditions as well as how to provide the specialized instruction and services these students need.

Still, there is only so much regular classroom teachers can be expected to do. When disabled students need more than can be provided in a regular classroom, other arrangements need to be made.

Federal law allows for a number of alternative placements to be made with one guiding proviso: *Disabled students' personal and educational needs are to be provided in the least restrictive environment.* Placement alternatives include instruction in regular classrooms, special classes, special schools, home instruction, and instruction in hospitals and institutions. When being placed in a regular classroom, provisions must be made as needed for supplementary services such as resource room, itinerant instruction, and other related services. Although fewer disabled students are placed outside of regular classrooms of late, legal regulations require that placement decisions be made with care.

Following is a guide for making placement decisions. Instructional support can be provided for disabled students in the following ways, ranging from the least to the most restrictive.

1. Instructional support can be provided by a special education teacher in a regular classroom.

2. Instructional support can be provided by a special education teacher in a resource room. Students leave the regular classroom a portion of the day to receive specialized instruction in their areas of difficulty from a special education teacher in a special education resource room.

3. Part-time instruction can be provided in a special education classroom. Students spend part of the day in a special education classroom receiving the specialized instruction they need in their areas of difficulty and the rest of the day in regular classrooms.

4. Full-time instruction can be provided in a special education classroom with limited integration. Students are integrated with nondisabled peers for some activities such as lunch, recess, and assemblies.

5. Full-time instruction can be provided in a special education classroom, without integration.

Generally speaking, more intense, time-consuming interventions are needed to educate more severely disabled students. More restrictive environments are usually required to administer more intense, time-consuming educational interventions. To make placement decisions more complicated, all of the five options may not be provided in one school, or one school district, for that matter.

Federal law governs eligibility and placement decisions. In 1975 the Education for All Handicapped Children Act was passed, entitling every disabled child a free appropriate education designed to meet its needs as stipulated in Public Law 94-142. This law was revised. Currently two laws govern placement decisions: the Individuals with Disabilities Education Act (IDEA, Public Law 101-47 and Public Law 101-17) and Section 504 of the Rehabilitation Act of 1973, a civil rights law. Eligibility requirements for services under Section 504 tend to be the less stringent of the two. However, to become eligible for both services children must undergo assessment procedures which often involve taking a number of published standardized tests. Testing must be multidisciplinary, nondiscriminatory, and at no cost to the parent.

After students become eligible, a planning team meets to evaluate test results and historical and environmental information to determine a plan of services for the child. Under IDEA, the plan is called an IEP (Individual Education Plan). Under Section 504 the plan is called a 504 Plan or "ED Plan."

Approximately 70% of students with disabilities receive special education and related services in general education classrooms. General education teachers need to be aware of federal laws and regulations that guide special education services in the schools.

To be eligible for services under IDEA, students must qualify in one or more of the following diagnostic categories and must require special education.

Autism

Specific learning disability

Speech and language impairment

Emotional disturbance

Traumatic brain injury

Visual impairment

Hearing impairment

Deafness

Mental retardation

Multiple disabilities

Orthopedic impairment

Other health impairment

Children aged 3 through 9 may be found eligible if they demonstrate developmental delays in one or more of the following areas: physical development, cognitive development, communication development, social or emotional development, or adaptive development. The disabling condition must adversely affect the student's educational performance.

Attention deficit/hyperactivity disorder (ADD/ADHD) is not a discrete category under IDEA; however, these students may be served under IDEA if certain conditions are met. These conditions include emotional disturbance or criteria for OHI (Other Health Impaired). Most of these students are eligible for services under Section 504.

In order to be found eligible for services under Section 504, the student must be considered a "qualified handicapped person," which is "a handicapped person (1) who is of an age in which non-handicapped persons are provided such services, (2) of any age in which it is mandatory under state law to provide such services to handicapped persons, or (3) to whom a state is required to provide services under IDEA." Often this is an easier standard to meet than the IDEA's.

There has never been a greater need for placement testing than there is now in order for educators to determine eligibility for IDEA and Section 504. Placement decisions must be based on eligibility requirements and regulations of IDEA, Section 504, and state statutes.

An important reason to educate more students in regular classrooms is because a compelling amount of research shows that ability grouping students does not increase academic achievement, as once thought (Friedman & Fisher, 1998, p. 230). There is no justification for continuing any of the ability grouping practices that were devised to enhance learning. Ability grouping does not work whether ability grouped students are taught in separate classrooms or separate schools, or grouped across grade levels or within the same classroom—with one notable exception.

Research indicates that enriched and accelerated pullout programs for gifted and talented students do increase students' academic achievement. So there is reason to continue to place the gifted and talented in pullout programs, provided that the curriculum is enriched and instruction is accelerated. There is no evidence, however, that such pullout programs develop special talents of individual students or enhance student creativity. The evidence does seem to suggest that students capable of learning at a faster rate than the present pace of instruction allows will learn more if they are placed in an enriched, accelerated pullout program. Moreover, the evidence does not indicate that gifted and talented students would gain any additional benefit from being placed in a school for the gifted or in a class for the gifted the entire school day.

Selecting students to participate in gifted programs is not an easy matter. The identification of the gifted emanates from the work of Lewis Terman (1916, 1925). Because he advocated teaching children commensurate with their mental ability and identified mental ability as intelligence derived from scores on an IQ test, intelligence became the criterion for identifying giftedness, and IQ tests became the vehicles for identifying superior intelligence. The identification of the intellectually gifted expanded as a result of J. P. Guilford's work (1959, 1967). He identified a total of 120 possible intellectual abilities embodied in a three-dimensional model, which he called the "structure of the intellect." He also used his model to highlight creative intelligence. In the early 1960s Torrance (1962) and Getzels and Jackson (1962) increased our awareness of creativity as a trait of the gifted. Getzels and Jackson reported research that validated the distinction between creativity and IQ. They also suggested other criteria for identifying giftedness, including criteria for moral giftedness. During the 1960s Kohlberg (1960, 1971) offered his own version of moral development.

As criteria for defining giftedness expanded beyond intellectual abilities, they became increasingly more numerous. Giftedness became associated with the various content areas taught in school. As a result, giftedness can be defined as superiority in any subject area one wishes to name. The U.S. Office of Gifted and Talented, recognizing the need for an identification guide, assigned the Council for Exceptional Children to prepare a composite list of gifted characteristics without reference to particular content areas. This resulted in a publication entitled *Characteristics of the Gifted and Talented*. The list contains four sections: (1) general characteristics, (2) creative characteristics, (3) learning characteristics, and (4) behavioral characteristics. Each section contains a list of at least 10 characteristics.

As the list of characteristics proliferates, the selection of students for gifted and talented programs becomes more difficult. On the other hand, if one were selecting students for an enriched, accelerated pullout program to increase their academic achievement, as previously discussed, it would be simple and justifiable to select students who presently earn the highest academic achievement scores and grades. Past success often predicts future success in a given area. Otherwise, it becomes necessary to derive a definition of giftedness to use as a criterion for making a selection.

There is an available giftedness test that is reviewed in this section. However, before deciding to use a test you must determine whether the test authors' concept of giftedness agrees with the criterion you are using.

As students grow older, placement decisions need to be made for them less frequently. Older students learn to manage their disabilities better and to use compensatory aids, such as wheelchairs, with less need for assistance. In addition, older students are able to and are more often given the prerogative to make their own educational program decisions and select more of the courses they take. When students enter college they can choose a major, a minor, and electives. And most college students attend regular classrooms, even if they may need special accommodations, such as test-taking accommodations. Besides, disabled college students can take advantage of accommodations made for nondisabled students, such as television, computer, and mail-order instruction opportunities.

PLACEMENT TESTS

When placements are made, all of the data in the student's file needs to be taken into account and evaluated. Missing data is obtained by subjecting students to additional testing. Many of the additional tests need to be administered by clinicians who are trained and licensed. Physical exams are given by doctors, nurses, and/or vision, hearing, and motor coordination specialists. Psychological tests are given by licensed psychologists to identify mental ability and psychological disorders. Assessments of students' academic achievement status are often conducted by special education assessment specialists. However, teachers can assess academic achievement status if the tests they use do not require training to administer and score. Tests included in Chapter 4, "Placement Tests," are fundamentally diagnostic tools designed to identify students' level of functioning and impediments to learning. Once placements are made, further testing can be done to determine the instructional prescriptions appropriate for students (see Part III, "Instructional Prescription Testing and Decision-Making"). In Part V, "Referral Testing and Decision-Making," simple screening instruments that can be used by teachers to make referral decisions are reviewed. These tests are used for the initial detection of vision, hearing, adaptation, behavior, and psychomotor deficits.

Federal law strongly influences and complicates the testing that needs to be done to determine whether students fit specified diagnostic categories that qualify them for disability services. For example, federal law indicates that students with a learning disability often have a significant discrepancy between achievement and intellectual ability in one or more of the following areas: oral expression, listening comprehension, written expression, basic reading skill, reading comprehension, mathematics, calculation, and mathematics reasoning. This one legal stipulation has enormous implications for eligibility testing. To determine whether students fit the diagnostic category "learning disabled," they must be given tests that assess both intellectual ability and achievement. Many of the IQ and other ability tests reviewed in Part II are used to assess intellectual ability. Many of the achievement tests listed under "Instructional

Prescription Testing" and "Achievement Certification Testing" are used to assess level of achievement. Since the law refers to achievement in several areas, testing needs to be done in those areas. This requires giving students a multi-skill achievement test and/or several single-skill achievement tests. After the intellectual ability and achievement tests have been administered, scores are compared and interpreted. If a significant discrepancy is found between students' intellectual ability score and their score in one or more achievement test areas, they qualify to be diagnosed as "learning disabled." Each state has developed its own discrepancy formula for the identification of learning disabilities. Extensive testing and analysis needs to be done to diagnose students as learning disabled.

Following is a sample of tests that are reviewed in this handbook and can be used to assess intellectual ability and achievement. The Woodcock-Johnson Psychoeducational Battery III assesses both. It consists of two test batteries: Test of Cognitive Abilities and Tests of Achievement. The Wechsler Individual Achievement Test II is designed to be used in conjunction with any of the Wechsler Scales of Intelligence to derive a discrepancy. The Cognitive Abilities Test is designed to be used in conjunction with the Iowa Tests of Achievement. However, discrepancies can be derived using most norm-referenced tests of achievement in conjunction with most norm-referenced tests of intellectual ability appropriate for the students to be tested.

The diagnosis of mental retardation also requires the administration of two different types of tests: an intellectual ability test and an adaptive behavior test. However, a discrepancy between the two is not derived for the diagnosis of mental retardation. To be diagnosed as mentally retarded students must score low on both an intellectual ability test, indicating an intellectual deficit, and an adaptive behavior test, indicating coping limitations. Tests that can be used to assess intellectual ability are reviewed in Part II. Adaptive behavior tests are reviewed in Part V.

The American Association of Mental Retardation's (AAMR) definition of mental retardation has been accepted as the federal definition:

> Mental retardation refers to substantial limitations in present functioning. It is characterized by significantly sub-average intellectual functioning, existing concurrently with related limitations in two or more of the following applicable adaptive skills areas: communication, self-care, home living, social skills, community use, self-direction, health and safety, functional academics, leisure, and work. Mental retardation manifests before age 18. (AAMR, Definition of Mental Retardation)

There is more to the diagnosis of disabilities than meets the eye. Some diagnoses are more common than others. Of all the students having academic difficulty, a great many are diagnosed as learning disabled because so many children with normal or above-average intelligence are low achievers in particular academic areas. Some diagnoses tend to be more tolerable to parents than others, and parents' input is considered in deriving a diagnosis. For instance, parents tend to find a diagnosis of learning disabled more acceptable than more severe disorders, such as mental retardation. Perhaps it is because a learning disability tends to be regarded as an almost normal, no-fault diagnosis. Many parents worry about their possible contribution to their children's problems. A diagnosis of mental retardation can give parents pause to wonder if they might have been responsible for a contributing brain injury or genetic predisposition.

In the final analysis, placement of students is an arduous, complex undertaking. In many cases extensive testing needs to be done to determine eligibility for special education services. If eligible, placement teams are obliged to consider, in addition to diagnostic test results, parents' and teachers' input, medical records, historical data, and other data in students' files. After eligibility requirements have been met, the team must find the least restrictive environment in which students can receive the academic and supportive services they need to be successful.

REFERENCES

Friedman, M. I., & Fisher, S. P. (1998). *Handbook on effective instructional strategies: Evidence for decision-making*. Columbia, SC: Institute for Evidence-Based Decision-Making in Education.

Getzels, J. W., & Jackson, P. W. (1962). *Creativity and intelligence*. New York: John Wiley & Sons.

Guilford, J. P. (1959). Traits of creativity. In H. Andersen (Ed.), *Creativity and its cultivation*. New York: Harper.

Guilford, J. P. (1967). *The nature of human intelligence*. New York: McGraw-Hill.

Kohlberg, L. (1960). *The psychology of character development*. New York: John Wiley & Sons.

Kohnberg, L. (1971). Stages of moral development as a basis for moral education. In C. M. Beck, B. S. Crittenden, & E. V. Sullivan (Eds.), *Moral education: Interdisciplinary approaches*. New York: Newman Press.

Terman, L. M. (1916). *The measurement of intelligence*. Boston: Houghton.

Terman, L. M. (1925). *Genetic studies of genius: Mental and physical traits of a thousand gifted children* (vol. 1). Stanford, CA: Stanford University Press.

Torrance, E. B. (1962). *Guiding creative talent*. Englewood Cliffs, NJ: Prentice-Hall.

4

Placement Tests

Brigance Screens,
for testing individuals from birth through 7 years, 6 months of age
Reviewed by Aileen C. Lau-Dickinson, Ed.D., Special Education Administration

Usefulness of the Test for Educators

Test Author's Purpose

The Brigance Screens are designed to "quickly and accurately screen key developmental and early academic skills."

Decision-Making Applications

These screening tests are most appropriate for making referral and placement decisions for infants, toddlers, and young children. Children found to perform poorly on these screens are referred for further testing to determine their eligibility for special services. Many of these children could be placed in special programs to further diagnostically assess their developmental or early academic skills. These are screening tests and do not probe developmental skills or early academic skills in depth. Additional testing will be needed to assess and identify error patterns. These screens can also be used as admission measures. In addition to identifying children who may have special learning needs, the Brigance Screens may be useful for improving learning and instruction. Teachers will find the screens helpful when writing Individual Education Plans.

Relevant Population

The Brigance Screens include the Infant & Toddler Screen, the Early Preschool Screen, the Preschool Screen, and the K & 1 Screen. These screens are designed for children from birth through the end of first grade (7 years, 6 months).

1. Brigance Infant & Toddler Screen (2002): Infant (for children from birth through 11 months of age); Toddler (for children from 12 through 23 months of age).

2. Brigance Early Preschool Screen (1998–1999): 2-Year-Old Child (for children from 1 year, 9 months through 2 years, 2 months of age); 2 1/2-Year-Old Child (for children from 2 years, 3 months through 2 years, 8 months of age).

3. Preschool Screen (1985–1998): 3-Year-Old Child (for children from 2 years, 9 months through 3 years, 8 months of age); 4-Year-Old Child (for children from 3 years, 9 months through 4 years, 8 months of age).

4. K & 1 Screen (1982, 1987, 1992, 1997): Kindergarten Child (children from 4 years, 9 months through 5 years, 8 months of age); First Grade Child (for students 5 years, 9 months of age or older); End of First Grade Child (for students ending their first grade year or beginning second grade).

Characteristics Described

Developmental levels are described by the basic assessments in the following developmental domains for the Brigance Infant & Toddler Screen (see Table 1-1 of the test). Developmental levels include the domains of fine motor, gross motor, self-help, social-emotional, receptive, and expressive language.

Basic assessments for the 2-year-old child and higher include domains of visual/fine/and graphomotor, gross motor, quantitative concepts, personal information, receptive vocabulary, prereading/reading skills, expressive vocabulary, and articulation/verbal fluency/syntax (see Table 1-2 of the test).

Test Scores Obtained

Point values assigned to each assessment in the Brigance Screens allow for a total score of 100. A point value is assigned to each subtest, and the number correct is multiplied by the point value to obtain the raw score. The total raw score is calculated by adding the numbers for each subtest. Cutoff scores have been established for detecting children likely to have developmental disabilities or academic delays and for children who may be gifted or academically talented. Accuracy of responses and criteria for correct or incorrect responses is given for each test item. Some test items require a basal of three correct and a ceiling of three incorrect. Other test items have no basal or ceiling requirements. This may be confusing for the examiner and requires careful administration to avoid errors in basals and ceilings. Percentiles, quotients, and age-equivalents are also available in the Technical Report.

Technical Adequacy

Validity Confirmation

Test item validity was "based on the authors' extensive reading of developmental and readiness literature and on collaboration with numerous other educators who assisted in item selection."

Brigance selected items for the Brigance Screens from the Brigance Inventory of Early Development (IED). Several studies were conducted, and the results indicated that test items were retained when 90% of the professionals nominated that test item. Extensive field testing was conducted, and the results of field trials were used to finalize item selection and clarify item content. No evidence of statistical evaluation of test items was reported. Validity of the final choice of test items can be questioned.

Test response validity was established for the Brigance Infant & Toddler Screen through correlations with other criterion measures. These criterion measures included measures of cognitive skills, expressive language skills, receptive language skills, fine motor skills, gross motor skills, global motor development, daily living skills, and social-emotional skills. Correlations greater than .30 were significant at $p < .05$. These correlations can be found in the Technical Report.

For children 2 years of age and older, achievement correlations were established using the Woodcock-Johnson Psycho-Educational Battery—Test of Achievement (WJ RA) and the Child Development Inventory. The correlations appear somewhat modest, even though significance was found with all children on specific criterion measures. These correlations can be found in the Technical Report.

According to the Technical Report, "the domains, subtests, and factors are highly correlated with diagnostic measures of development, academics, intelligence, and teacher/examiner ratings."

Reliability Confirmation

Initial evidence of test-retest reliability of the Brigance Screens comes from the test-retest reliability of the Brigance Inventory of Early Development (IED). Correlations ranged from .53 to .99 when administering the assessment one to four months later; 1,156 students stratified by geographic region, gender, and ethnicity were used in the repeated test administration of the IED subtests used to create the Brigance Screens. The test-retest reliability of Brigance Screen items as drawn from the IED revealed a high degree of reliability. Other types of reliability confirmation are included in the Technical Manual.

Objectivity Confirmation

Several studies are reported to determine objectivity of the Brigance Screens. Inter-examiner correlations were determined in 1993 and 1999 with a sample of 134 children and were .90 or higher. For the 2001 study, objectivity of the Brigance Infant & Toddler Screen was assessed by having a second examiner retest 36 children, and the correlations were .98 and .99. No 2001 objectivity correlations were obtained for the other three Brigance Screens.

Statistical Confirmation

Statistical data on validity, reliability, and norms is available in the Technical Report for the Brigance Screens.

Special Features

Acronym

None.

Levels of the Test

Infant & Toddler Screen, Early Preschool Screen, Preschool Screen, and K & 1 Screen-Revised.

Number of Test Forms

One.

Norm-Referenced?

Yes. Test items for the four Brigance Screens were taken from the IED, which was standardized on 1,156 children ranging in age from 1 year, 1 month to beyond 6 years. The norming group was stratified by gender, geographic locations, and socioeconomic levels.

Criterion-Referenced?

Yes. Each subtest contains between 2 and 24 related items or skills. The screens are criterion-referenced measures designed to sample a range of skills essential for school success. Specific learning objectives have been established for each skill area. Refer back to Tables 1-1 and 1-2 in this review.

Feasibility Considerations

Testing Time

Testing time for all four Brigance Screens is estimated at 15 minutes to administer and one to two minutes to score.

For Testing Groups? Individuals?

Individuals.

Test Administration and Scoring

Tests can be machine scored. A CD-ROM for easy scoring is included in test materials. No special training is required for test administration; however, training in early childhood development would be helpful and is recommended. The Technical Manual indicates that "it is critical that all examiners become familiar with the directions and scoring procedures and that they administer the test in strict accordance with the directions accompanying each basic assessment" (p. 11). The test materials include a videotape that demonstrates test administration techniques.

Test Materials and Approximate Costs

Brigance Infant & Toddler Screen: $110
  Data Sheets (30): $31
Brigance Early Preschool Screen: $89
  Data Sheets (2-Year-Old (30): $31
  Data Sheets (2 1/2-Year-Old (30): $31
Brigance Preschool Screen: $89
  Data Sheets (3-Year-Old (30): $31
  Data Sheets (4-Year-Old (30): $39
Brigance K & 1 Screen-Revised: $89
  Data Sheets (30): $39
  End of Grade 1 Data Sheets (30): $31

Data sheets in Spanish are also available.

Adequacy of Test Manuals

Each of the four Brigance Screens includes an overview of the screens and clear screening directions including general recommendations for screening procedures, format, materials, directions for completing data sheets (including scoring), and cut-off score information. The screens use color-coded tabs for locating test items easily. The Technical Report for the Brigance Screens, written by Frances Page Glascoe, Ph.D., has technical information along with tables to locate percentile ranks, quotients, and age equivalents.

In addition, the Technical Report includes the following appendixes: Appendix A: Sample Data Sheets; Appendix B: Registration and Background Information Form; Appendix C: Consideration When Testing Defined Populations; Appendix D: Information Sheets for Parents; Appendix E: Comparison of the Brigance Screens with Other Screening Tests; Appendix F: Percentile Ranks, Quotients and Age Equivalents for Total Scored on the Brigance Screens; and Appendix G: Optional Scoring for Programs Requiring Percentages of Delay or Standard Deviations from the Mean by Developmental Domain.

Excerpts from Other Test Reviews

The Brigance K & 1 Screen was reviewed by McLoughlin and Lewis (1990), and they report that the screen "needs further study, especially its cutoff points" (p. 543).

The Brigance Preschool Screen (BPS) was reviewed by Heil in the twelfth edition of the Buros Institute's *Mental Measurements Yearbook*. This was before the BPS had been standardized. She states, "the Brigance Preschool Screen appears to be a very cost-effective instrument, both in terms of time of administration and personnel utilization. Its special use would be in conducting preschool screening of large numbers of children for possible consideration for referral for in-depth testing."

The Brigance K & 1 Screen-Revised (1982–1992) was reviewed in the same edition of the *Mental Measurements Yearbook* by Berk. He states, "statements by the author suggest the scores on the Screen be used primarily to classify students into the appropriate grade level (K and 1) and instructional groups, particularly those students who may have disabilities requiring special placement."

Ordering Information

Publisher

Curriculum Associates, Inc., 153 Rangeway Road, P.O. Box 2001, North Billerica, MA 01862-0901; Phone: 800-225-0248; Fax: 800-366-1158; e-mail: cainfo@ curriculumassociates.com; Web site: www.curriculumassociates.com.

Author

Albert H. Brigance.

Publication Dates

1997, 1998, and 2002.

Cautions and Comments

These four Brigance Screens can be useful for placement (especially the Brigance K & 1 Screen) and referral (especially the Brigance Infant & Toddler Screen, the Brigance Early Preschool Screen, and the Brigance Preschool Screen). The Brigance K & 1 Screen is useful for ranking students in kindergarten and first grade and subsequently grouping them using the cutoff scores. The author suggests that those with a cutoff score below 60 should have further testing. Caution should be used when using the screens as the only placement instrument. The screens can be helpful for obtaining initial information about a student. The Screens can provide useful information when part of a evaluation includes parent interview, observation, and other testing.

References

Berk, R. A. (1995). Review of the Brigance K & 1 Screen. In J. C. Conoley and & J. E. Impara (Eds.), *The Twelfth Mental Measurements Yearbook*. Lincoln, NE: The Buros Institute of Mental Measurements.

Heil, E. S. (1995). Review of the Brigance K & 1 Screen. In J. C. Conoley & J. C. Impara (Eds.), *The Twelfth Mental Measurements Yearbook*. Lincoln, NE: The Buros Institute of Mental Measurements.

McLoughlin, J. A., & Lewis, R. B. (1990). *Assessing special students* (3rd ed.). Columbus, OH: Merrill.

Clinical Evaluation of Language Fundamentals-Third Edition (CELF-3),
for testing individuals from 6 through 21 years of age
Reviewed by Aileen C. Lau-Dickinson, Ed.D., Special Education Administration

Usefulness of the Test for Educators

Test Authors' Purpose

"Clinical Evaluation of Language Fundamentals-Third Edition (CELF-3) . . . is an individually administered clinical tool for the identification, diagnosis, and follow-up evaluation of language skill deficits in school-age children, adolescents, and young adults" (Examiner's Manual, p. 1).

Decision-Making Applications

The CELF-3 is best suited for making diagnostic and placement decisions for school-age children, adolescents, and young adults who are suspected of having deficits in language. It is also possible to identify students' strengths and weaknesses in form and content of the language and develop language objectives and intervention programs. The CELF-3 is widely used by speech and language pathologists to identify and place students in remedial speech and language programs.

Relevant Population

The CELF-3 is designed for children from 6 through 21 years of age.

Characteristics Described

The core subtests of the CELF-3 measure syntax, semantics, and memory, and supplementary subtests measure receptive and expressive language and rapid automatic naming. There are 11 subtests in the entire battery. Six subtests are required to compute the composite scores: receptive language, expressive language, and total language.

The core subtests are Sentence Structure, Word Structure, Concepts and Directions, Formulating Sentences, Word Classes, Recalling Sentences, Sentence Assembly, and Semantic Relationships.

The supplementary subtests are Word Associations, Listening to Paragraphs, and Rapid, Automatic Naming.

Description of Subtests

Sentence Structure (Receptive—Ages 6–8): When presented four stimulus pictures, the child must respond to a verbal sentence by pointing to the appropriate picture. (Assesses acquisition of English structural rules)

Word Structure (Expressive—Ages 6 years–8 years, 11 months): When presented a picture stimulus, the child must complete orally presented sentences. (Assesses acquisition of English morphological rules)

Concepts and Directions (Receptive—Ages 6 years–21 years, 11 months): When presented with an oral direction, the examinee must identify pictured geometric shapes. (Assesses the ability to interpret, recall, and execute oral commands of varying length and complexity)

Formulating Sentences (Expressive—Ages 6 years—21 years, 11 months): When presented a target word orally that is appropriate to a stimulus picture, the examinee must formulate a sentence. (Assesses the ability to formulate compound and complex sentences that have semantic and syntactic constraints)

Word Classes (Receptive—Ages 6 years–21 years, 11 months): When presented two of four verbally presented words, the examinee must select two words that go together. (Assesses the ability to perceive associative relationships between words)

Recalling Sentences (Expressive—Ages 6 years–21 years, 11 months): When presented a sentence orally, the examinee must recall the sentence. (Assesses the ability to recall and reproduce sentence surface structures of varying length and syntactic complexity)

Sentence Assembly (Expressive—Ages 9 years–21 years, 11 months): When presented words and word clusters, visually and auditorially, the examinee must produce two semantically and syntactically intact sentences. (Assesses the ability to assemble syntactic structures into syntactically and semantically acceptable sentences)

Semantic Relationships (Receptive—Ages 9 years–21 years, 11 months): When presented a list of facts auditorially, the examinee selects two choices from four visually presented options, two of which are correct. (Assesses the ability to interpret different semantic relationships in sentences)

Word Associations (Expressive—Ages 6 years–21 years, 11 months): The examinee must list targeted categories of words within one minute. (Assesses the ability to recall labels of members of a semantic class within a time limit)

Listening to Paragraphs (Receptive—Ages 6 years–21 years, 11 months): When presented a spoken paragraph, the examinee must answer questions about the paragraph. (Assesses the ability to interpret factual and inferential information presented in spoken paragraphs)

Rapid, Automatic Naming (Optional subtest) (Ages 6 years–21 years, 11 months). The examinee must name colors, shapes, and color-shape combinations while being timed. (Assesses the ability to produce "automatic speech") (Adapted from Technical Manual, pp. 8–25)

Test Scores Obtained

Several normative scores are available. Raw scores are converted to standard scores based on the student's age. Standard scores can be converted to percentile ranks, stanines, or normal curve equivalents. The Receptive Language standard score is computed by summing the standard scores of the Sentence Structure (ages 6–8), Concepts and Directions, Word Classes, and Semantic Relationships (ages 9+) subtests. The Expressive Language standard score is computed by summing the standard scores of the Word Structures (ages 6–8), Formulating Sentences, Recalling Sentences, and Sentence Assembly (ages 9+) subtests. The CELF-3 Total Language score is computed by summing the Receptive and Expressive standard scores. An Age Equivalent score is also available. There is a CELF-3 software scoring program available, Clinical Assistant, which scores the test and produces a narrative report of the results.

Technical Adequacy

Validity Confirmation

Test item validity: The CELF-3, as did its predecessor, CELF-R, purports to measure two dimensions of language: content and form. Discussions were held with professionals in the field. In addition, focus groups gathered information about the use and function of the CELF-R in various settings. A national tryout of the CELF-3, using two parallel forms of the test, was undertaken. This tryout testing was conducted by 225 nationally certified and/or state-licensed speech-language pathologists who were experienced in test administration. Subjects included 800 children and adolescents without a diagnosis of language impairment and 143 individuals who had been identified as language impaired. Final item selection was based on appropriateness of content, item difficulty, item discrimination, lack of item bias, and ease and reliability of scoring. The final items were reordered according to a hierarchy of difficulty.

Test response validity was established by comparing scores on the CELF-3 with other measures of language ability. First the CELF-3 and the CELF-R were compared using 300 examinees ages 6 to 16. Correlation coefficients were established between each subtest and composite scores. Composite scores of Receptive Language, Expressive Language, and Total Language Scores ranged from .72 to .79. The relationship of the CELF-3 and the CELF Preschool was made using 101 children aged 6 years to 6 years, 11 months. The composite scores of Receptive Language, Expressive Language, and Total Language Scores are .49, .59, and .63, respectively. Finally, the CELF-3 and the WISC-III were compared using 203 children and adolescents. The correlations between CELF-3 and WISC-III composite standard scores for Receptive Language and Verbal IQ was .70, Performance IQ was .58, and Total Language was .71; for Expressive Language and Verbal IQ was .72, Performance IQ was .56, and Total Language was .60. Finally, the Total Language Score was compared to the Verbal IQ, Performance IQ, and Full Scale IQ with correlations of .75, .60, and .75. These correlations were only moderate.

Reliability Confirmation

A study using 152 examinees that were part of the standardization sample was made. These examinees repeated the test with one week to one month between testings;

both tests were administered by the same examiner. The correlation coefficients for the Receptive Language Score, Expressive Language Score, and Total Language Score were .80, .92, and .93, respectively. These correlations were for the Total Language Score and the two composite scores; the individual subtest correlations were lower. The Technical Manual reports reliability correlations for internal consistency.

Objectivity Confirmation

Examiner judgement is required for scoring the Word Structure, Formulated Sentences, Recalling Sentences, Sentence Assembly, and Word Association subtests. These judgments may also require decisions in regard to dialect. Two trained raters were selected to independently score 590 protocols, and these scorers concentrated on two subtests, Formulated Sentences and Word Associations. Correlations between raw scores for the Formulated Sentences and Word Association subtests by two independent scorers for three age groups ranged from .97 to .99.

Statistical Confirmation

Statistical data on validity and reliability is available in the Technical Manual and norms data is available in the Examiner's Manual.

Special Features

Acronym

CELF-3.

Levels of the Test

There is one level of the test. Each subtest clearly indicates the ages for which the subtest is designed. The CELF-3 is designed to be given to students aged 6 years through 21 years, 11 months.

Number of Test Forms

One.

Norm-Referenced?

Yes. The CELF-3 was nationally normed on 2,450 individuals in 1994–1995. The norming sample was stratified to represent the U.S. population of individuals between the ages of 6 and 21 years and stratified across age, gender, race/ethnicity, geographic region, and parent education level. The sample was limited to non-language-impaired individuals. No individual used in the sample had been diagnosed with a language impairment or disability. Thirty percent of the sample was reported to have dialectal differences.

Criterion-Referenced?

No.

Other Features

Chapter 4 of the Examiner's Manual offers extension testing. According to the authors, "you use extension testing to establish the conditions under which the student can respond correctly" (p. 115). This chapter presents "extension testing objectives" for each CELF-3 subtest, followed by instructional objectives that can be used in the Individual Education Plans.

Feasibility Considerations

Testing Time

The six subtests used for a Total Language Score require 30 to 45 minutes. All 11 subtests can be administered in under an hour.

For Testing Groups? Individuals?

Individuals.

Test Administration and Scoring

Scoring guidelines are clearly stated in the Technical Manual and the Examiner's Manual. Tables for converting raw scores are available in Appendixes D through H. Chapter 3 offers information on Test Interpretation, including CELF-3 Scores for Diagnosis and Establishing Objectives for Intervention and Case Studies. For those examiners who are experienced in using CELF test materials, the authors offer a "Quick Start" which allows the examiner to move quickly into testing. Training exercises are offered in appendixes for scoring the Formulated Sentences and Word Associations subtests. A software scoring program, Clinical Assistant, is available to score the test and produce a narrative report of the results.

Examiners should have experience and training in the administration of individually administered standardized tests.

Test Materials and Approximate Costs

CELF-3, complete kit: $360; Record Forms (12): $27; Record Forms (50): $95; Set of two Stimulus Manuals: $179; Examiner's Manual: $75; Technical Manual: $79; Clinical Assistant: $129.

Adequacy of Test Manuals

There are two manuals: a Technical Manual and an Examiner's Manual. The Technical Manual focuses on Purposes and Design, Development and Standardization, Reliability, and Validity. The Examiner's Manual includes Information of Characteristics, Test Instructions, Test Interpretation, Extension Testing, and Instructional Objectives, as well as norm tables. These manuals are user-friendly and provide specific directions for the examiner.

Excerpts from Other Test Reviews

"The CELF-3 should be used with caution. . . . Neither the design nor the purpose of the CELF-3 are supported by the reliability and validity studies reported in the technical manual. . . . The CELF-3 should not be used to diagnose language impairment" (Gilliam, 2001, p. 262).

"Unfortunately, it suffers from marginal subtest reliability, which limits ability to individually interpret subtest scores, particularly at adolescent and young adult age ranges" (MacDonald, 2001, p. 263).

Ordering Information

Publisher

The Psychological Corporation, 19500 Bulverde Road, San Antonio, TX 78259; Phone: 800-228-0752; Fax: 210-339-5873; Web site: www. psychcorp.com.

Authors

Eleanor Semel, Elizabeth H. Wiig, and Wayne A. Secord.

Publication Date

1995.

Cautions and Comments

Reviews of the CELF-3 indicate concerns over the reliability and validity of the measure. The test-retest correlations for the Receptive and Expressive Language Scores and Total Language Scores appear to be adequate, but correlations for individual subtests were less than adequate with ranges for all ages in the low .70s, with the exception of the Recalling Sentences subtest, which was .87. Test response validity was limited to correlations with the CELF-3 and the CELF-R and the WISC-III. One would expect the correlation between the CELF-3 and the CELF-R to be high, but they were only modest. The correlations with the WISC-III indicate that those correlations with the Verbal IQ support that the CELF-3 does measure general verbal ability. Additional comparisons of the CELF-3 with other measures of expressive and receptive language would add to the validity of this measure.

Overall, the CELF-3 manuals and materials are well designed and written and directions for administering the instrument are clear; however, the educator and speech and language pathologist would be wise to use caution when making placement and diagnostic decisions from the test results. Further reliability and validity studies should be undertaken.

References

Gillam, R. B. (2001). Review of the Clinical Evaluation of Language Fundamentals, Third Edition (CELF-3). In B. S. Plake & J. C. Impara (Eds.), *The Fourteenth Mental Measurements Yearbook* (pp. 261–262). Lincoln, NE: The Buros Institute of Mental Measurements.
MacDonald, J. (2001). Review of the Clinical Evaluation of Language Fundamentals, Third Edition (CELF-3). In B. S. Plake & J. C. Impara (Eds.), *The Fourteenth Mental Measurements Yearbook* (pp. 262–263). Lincoln, NE: The Buros Institute of Mental Measurements.

Cognitive Assessment System (CAS),
for testing individuals from 5 through 17 years of age
Reviewed by Aileen C. Lau-Dickinson, Ed.D., Special Education Administration

---

Usefulness of the Test for Educators

Test Authors' Purpose

The CAS was developed to "evaluate Planning, Attention, Simultaneous and Successive (PASS) cognitive processes of individuals between the ages of 5 and 17" (Interpretive Handbook, p. 1).

Decision-Making Applications

The educator may find the CAS useful for diagnosing learning abilities and disabilities and for making placement decisions. Classification of children for purposes of eligibility for special placement such as learning disabilities, attention deficit disorder, mental retardation, and giftedness is a major end product of the CAS.

Relevant Population

The CAS is designed for children between the ages of 5 and 17.

Characteristics Described

The CAS has two forms: a Standard Battery and a Basic Battery. The Standard Battery has three subtests in each scale, and the Basic Battery has two subtests in each scale.

The CAS is based on the Cognitive Abilities Theory. The major components of this theory are listed below.

Planning is a process by which the individual plans, selects, evaluates, and solves problems.

Attention is a process by which the individual focuses on particular stimuli while inhibiting responses that compete with that stimuli.

Simultaneous Processing is a process by which the individual demonstrates his ability to take separate stimuli and develop a single whole or group.

Successive Processing is a process by which the individual is able to serialize stimuli to form a chain-like progression.

Planning Subtests

Matching Numbers (MN). This is a four-page paper-and-pencil subtest that requires the subject to underline the two numbers in each row that are the same. Children between 5 and 7 years of age are given the first two items; children between 8 and 17 years of age are administered the last three items. This is a timed subtest. This subtest is included in the Standard and Basic Batteries.

Planned Codes (PCd). This requires the subject to fill in corresponding letter codes in empty boxes. A legend at the top of each page shows a correspondence of letters to specific codes (e.g., A, B, C, D to OX, XX, OO). The child is required to translate letters into specific codes. This is a timed subtest. This subtest is included in the Standard and Basic Batteries.

Planned Connections (PCn). This subtest contains eight items. The first six items require the subjects to connect numbers in sequential order, and the last two items require subjects to connect both numbers and letters in sequential order, alternating the numbers and letters. This is a timed subtest. This subtest is included in the Standard Battery only.

Attention Subtests

Expressive Attention (EA). There are two sets of different items. Children ages 5–7 are presented a stimulus consisting of pictures of common animals, large and small. Children are asked to identify whether each animal depicted in the item is large or small. The object is for the children to respond based on the size of the animals in real life, ignoring the size of the animals in the picture. Children 8 years of age and older are presented colors or color names. Children must name the color in which the word is printed. The distractor is that the word "red" might be printed in blue. 180 seconds are allowed per item. This subtest is included in the Standard and Basic Batteries.

Number Detection (ND). Children are presented a page of numbers and are asked to underline specific numbers that match numbers that appear at the top of each page. Children are required to find the numbers on a page with a variety of distractors. 150 seconds are allowed per item. This subtest is included in the Standard and Basic Batteries.

Receptive Attention (RA). This test is a two-page paper-and-pencil subtest written in two versions. For children ages 5–7, the task is to underline pairs of objects that are the same. First the children must underline objects that are identical, and then they must underline objects that have the same name. Children 8 and above are required to underline pairs of letters that are physically the same, and then the children are required to underline pairs of letters that have the same name. Distractors include pairs of objects or letters that do not match or are not the same. 120 seconds are allowed for Items 1–5 and 180 seconds for Item 6. This subtest is included in the Standard Battery only.

Simultaneous Processing Subtests

Nonverbal Matrices (NvM). This is a 33-item multiple-choice subtest that utilizes shapes and geometric elements that are interrelated. The child is asked to decode the relationships among the parts of the item and respond by choosing the best of six options. This subtest is included in the Standard and Basic Battery.

Verbal-Spatial Relations (VSR). This is a 27-item subtest that requires the comprehension of logical and grammatical descriptions of spatial relationships. The child is required to select the option that matches a verbal description of six drawings. The examiner reads a question that appears at the bottom of the page. Thirty seconds are allowed per item. This subtest is included in the Standard and Basic Battery.

Figure Memory (FM). This is a 27-item paper-and-pencil subtest in which the child is asked to identify a geometric design (previously shown them for five seconds) that is embedded within a larger figure. Stimulus is exposed for five seconds. This subtest is included in the Standard Battery only.

Successive Processing Subtests

Word Series (WS). This subtest has 27 items that are read aloud by the examiner. The examiner reads nine single-syllable high-frequency words: Book, Car, Cow, Dog, Girl, Key, Man. The examiner reads aloud from two to nine words in sequence and the child is asked to repeat the words in the same sequential order as presented by the examiner. This subtest is not timed. This subtest is included in the Standard and Basic Battery.

Sentence Repetition (SR). This 29-sentence subtest requires the child to repeat a sentence that has "little meaning" exactly as it was presented. Each sentence uses color names in place of content words. This subtest is not timed. This subtest is included in the Standard and Basic Battery.

Speech Rate (SpR), Ages 5–7. This eight-item timed subtest requires the child to repeat a three-word series in order until the examiner tells them to stop. Thirty seconds are given per item. This subtest is included in the Standard Battery only.

Sentence Questions (SQ), Ages 8–17 only. This 21-item subtest requires the child to respond to a question about a sentence read to the child. This requires the child to comprehend the question based on the serial placement of the words. Content words are replaced by color words. This subtest is not timed. This subtest is included in the Standard Battery only.

Test Scores Obtained

The CAS Standard Battery is composed of three subtests in each of the four PASS scales. The Basic Battery is composed of two subtests in each of the four PASS scales. The CAS Full Scale score is obtained from the sum of the standard scores for the 8 (Basic Battery) and 12 (Standard Battery PASS) scale subtests. Subtest Scaled Scores are combined to obtain PASS Scale Scores with a mean of 100 and a standard deviation of 15. The CAS Full Scale and PASS Scales both yield standard scores.

Descriptive Categories of PASS and Full Scale Standard Scores

Standard Score	Classification
130 and above	Very Superior
120–129	Superior
110–119	High Average
90–109	Average
80–89	Low Average
70–79	Below Average
69 and below	Well Below Average

Source: Administration and Scoring Manual, Table C.1, p. 193. Reproduced with permission.

Technical Adequacy

Validity Confirmation

Test item validity: The CAS was developed using "non-traditional" approaches to intelligence. It is based on "recent findings about intelligence as a group of cognitive processes." The CAS attempts to evaluate Planning, Attention, Simultaneous, and Successive (PASS) cognitive processes. The subtests and test items of the CAS are based on the cognitive processes that many professionals do not consider to be synonymous with intelligence. In contrast, the PASS theory has been researched and developed by the authors of the CAS. Their study and development of the CAS has covered a 20-year period. According to the authors, the CAS subtests "followed a sequence of item generation, examination, revision, and reexamination until the instructions, items and other dimensions were refined" (Intepretive Handbook, p. 14).

Test response validity: This was established through relating the PASS scales to tests of achievement and intelligence. Correlations were obtained between the CAS and the Woodcock-Johnson Revised Tests of Achievement (WJ R). 1,600 children were in a large-scale study between the WJ R and the CAS Standard Battery and the Basic Battery. The correlations of standard scores ranged from .61 to .74. Correlations were also made between the CAS and the Wechsler Intelligence Scale for Children (WISC-III) using three different samples of students: students in regular education (n

= 46), students with learning disabilitites (n = 80), and students with mental retardation (n = 80). The WISC-III Verbal IQ was not significantly correlated with Planning or Attention for students in regular education or students with mental retardation. Also, the WISC-III Performance IQ (PIQ) and the CAS did not significantly correlate with Successive Processing for students with learning disabilities. However, significant correlations were found for other test relationships. The Full Scale CAS and the WISC-III Full Scale IQ correlated significantly with each measure of achievement for the sample of children with learning disabilities. Using 53 children in gifted educational programs, the CAS and the SAT were administered. The CAS Full Scale scores correlated significantly with both SAT Verbal and Math (Verbal = .49, Math = .56) .Other studies and correlations are reported in the Interpretive Manual with special populations. Differences in PASS scale performance were found for these groups, supporting the test's ability to discriminate between special groups.

Reliability Confirmation

The test-retest reliability of the CAS standard scores was examined with a sample of 215 children selected from the standardization sample. Each child was administered the CAS twice, with 9 to 73 days between test administrations. The sample was divided into three age groups: 5–7, 8–11, and 12–17. The test-retest correlations for the 5–7 age group ranged from .63 to .89; for the 8–11 age group the correlations ranged from .67 to .93; and for the 12–17 age group the correlations ranged from .71 to .92. The averages of these correlations for the Full Scale Basic Battery and the Standard Battery were .90–.91. Reliability of the instrument appears to be good.

Objectivity Confirmation

There is a Scoring Templates Booklet with scoring transparencies used for objective scoring. The following subtests are to be scored using the templates: Matching Numbers, Planned Codes, Number Detection, and Receptive Attention. Expressive Attention does not require the use of a template. The accuracy score is the number of correct responses. For Planned Connections and Speech Rate the raw score is the sum of the time in seconds to complete all items for the subtest. The raw score for the remaining subtests is the number of correct items. The authors do not report reliability coefficients for standard scores when scoring is performed by two independent evaluators.

Statistical Confirmation

Statistical data on validity, reliability, and norms can be found in the Interpretive Handbook and the Administration and Scoring Manual.

Special Features

Acronym

CAS.

Levels of the Test

There are two levels of the test: the Standard Battery and the Basic Battery. The Standard Battery has 12 subtests that comprise the PASS Scale, and the Basic Battery has eight subtests that comprise the CAS Full Scale.

Norm-Referenced?

Yes. The normative sample was made up of 2,200 children, and an additional 872 children participated in reliability and validity studies. The normative sample was selected from both regular education and special education settings. To ensure a sample that was representative, the 1990 U.S. Census was used. The sample was stratified according to variables of age, gender, race, Hispanic origin, geographic region, parental educational attainment, and community setting. The special populations included Learning disabled (5.1%), Speech/language impaired (1.1%), Emotionally disturbed (0.8%), Mentally retarded (1.3%), and Gifted (4.4%).

Criterion-Referenced?

No.

Feasibility Considerations

Testing Time

Basic Battery (8 subtests): 40 minutes; Standard Battery (12 subtests): 60 minutes.

For Testing Groups? Individuals?

Individuals.

Test Administration and Scoring

The Administration and Scoring Manual gives detailed instructions for the administration of each subtest. All directions to be read aloud by the examiner are printed in blue. Scoring guidelines vary from subtest to subtest, which may be confusing for some examiners. Four subtests use Scoring Templates, which make scoring much easier. Some subtests are timed so a stopwatch is necessary.

The authors recommend that all those who administer the CAS have experience in testing. Those with credentials as psychologists, certified specialists, and other trained professionals are qualified to administer the CAS.

Test Materials and Approximate Costs

CAS complete kit with carrying case: $655; Administration and Scoring Manual: $53; Intepretive Handbook: $53; Record Forms (5–17) (25): $29.50; Response Booklets (5–7 and 8–17) (25): 18.50; Scoring Template: $12.

Adequacy of Test Manuals

Test manuals include an Interpretive Handbook and an Administration and Scoring Manual. These are readable and contain general information about the CAS, including a discussion of PASS Theory. The Administration and Scoring Manual includes the norm tables, interpretive tables, and CAS/WJ-R achievement comparison tables. The Interpretive Handbook includes a chapter devoted to intervention and remediation programs. The PASS Remedial Program (PREP) is described in the Interpretive Handbook (p. 118). The procedures for administration and scoring of the CAS are explicit and easy to follow.

Excerpts from Other Test Reviews

"Evidence for CAS's validity is difficult because the model of intelligence is so different from the models used by other tests of intelligence. . . . CAS does correlate well with other intelligence measures, and it does predict scores on standardized achievement tests" (Salvia & Ysseldyke, 2001).

Ordering Information

Publisher

Riverside Publishing Company, 425 Spring Lake Drive, Itasca, IL 60143-2079; Phone: 800-323-9540; Fax: 630-467-7192; Web site: www.riverpub.com.

Authors

Jack A. Naglieri and J. P. Das.

Publication Date

1997.

Cautions and Comments

The CAS is a different approach to assessing intelligence through cognitive processing. The extensive research that the authors have undertaken over the past 20 years can only support this approach to intelligence. The standardization of the instrument appears adequate and supportive of the validity and reliability of this measure of intelligence. Perhaps the CAS can best be used for "screening," as suggested by Salvia and Ysseldyke (2001). In any case, it can be an valuable assessment tool for the professional's repertoire that may provide additional information regarding cognitive abilities of students 5 through 17 years of age.

Reference

Salvia, J., & Ysseldyke, J. E. (2001). *Assessment* (8th ed.). Boston: Houghton Mifflin.

Detroit Tests of Learning Aptitude (DTLA-4),
for testing individuals from 6 years through 17 years, 11 months of age
Reviewed by Aileen C. Lau-Dickinson, Ed.D., Special Education Administration

---

Usefulness of the Test for Educators

Test Author's Purpose

The DTLA-4 can be thought of as a "battery that measures a variety of developed abilities" (Examiner's Manual, p. 9). The DTLA-4 has four principal uses (purposes): "(a) to determine strengths and weaknesses among developed mental abilities; (b) to identify children and youths who are significantly below their peers in important abilities; (c) to make predictions about future performance; and (d) to serve as a measurement device in research studies investigating aptitude, intelligence, and cognitive behavior" (Examiner's Manual, p. 24).

Decision-Making Applications

The results of the DTLA-4 can be used to "estimate general cognitive functioning (intelligence), predict future success (aptitude), or show mastery of particular content and skills (achievement)" (Examiner's Manual, p. 9). The DTLA-4 may be used to qualify individuals for placement in special education programs for mental retardation, learning disabilities, or other disabling conditions. The DTLA-4 can also be used to determine a student's future performance and subsequent placement or advancement into college, trade schools, and regular school classes. In that context, it could be considered an Achievement Certification test.

Relevant Population

The DTLA-4 is appropriate for students ages 6 years through 17 years, 11 months who are able to understand directions, are familiar with printed pictures and forms, and can pass the practice items.

Characteristics Described

The DTLA-4 is a battery of 10 subtests that purport to measure different but interrelated mental abilities. Following is the description of each of the 10 subtests:

1. Word Opposites: A stimulus word is presented orally and the examinee must respond with a word that means the direct opposite. (Vocabulary knowledge)

2. Design Sequences: The examinee must reproduce a previously shown design sequence presented for five seconds by the examiner. (Visual discrimination and memory)

3. Sentence Imitation: The examinee must reproduce a sentence following the oral presentation of the stimulus sentence. (Spoken syntax and grammar)

4. Reversed Letters: The examinee must write each letter in reversed order after he is presented a series of letters by the examiner. (Auditory memory for spoken letters)

5. Story Construction: The examinee must tell a story about a picture shown to him. (Ability to conceptualize and orally express a meaningful story)

6. Design Reproduction: The examinee is shown a picture of a geometric form for a short period of time. After removal of the stimulus, the examinee is asked to draw the form from memory. (Visual Memory Ability)

7. Basic Information: The examinee gives oral answers to questions from everyday situations. (Knowledge of commonly known facts)

8. Symbolic Relations: The examinee must select a missing design from six pictured possibilities after being shown a visual problem involving a series of designs in which one design is missing. (Nonverbal reasoning ability)

9. Word Sequences: The examinee must repeat a series of unrelated and isolated words presented orally by the examiner. (Auditory attention)

10. Story Sequences: The examinee must indicate the correct order of a series of pictures presented to him. He places number chips under the pictures to denote the correct order. (Organizational and conceptual ability)

Test Scores Obtained

The DTLA-4 yields five types of scores: raw scores, subtest standard scores, composite standard scores (quotients), percentiles, and age equivalents. Based on a mean of 10 and standard deviation of 3, subtest standard scores are converted from raw scores. The composite quotients are derived by adding the designated subtest standard scores and converting each sum to a quotient. The author indicates that the most useful values derived from the DTLA-4 are composite quotients. A description of the composite quotients generated from the DTLA-4 is described below.

Global Composites

General Mental Ability Quotient (GMAQ): Refers to an individual's general aptitude for schoolwork or basic intelligence. The GMAQ is a combination of the standard scores of all 10 subtests on the battery.

Optimal Composite: The four largest standard scores are combined to obtain the Optimal Composite. Refers to the best estimate of an individual's "potential."

Domain Composite

Refers to a composite of the individual's linguistic, attending, and motor abilities (first described by Baker and Leland in the original 1934 DTLA). The Domain Composite combines the standard scores of the Verbal Quotient (VBQ), the Nonverbal Quotient (NVQ), the Attention-Enhanced Quotient (AEQ), the

Attention-Reduced Quotient (ARQ), the Motor-Enhanced Quotient (MEQ), and the Motor-Reduced Quotient (MRQ).

Theoretical Composite

Refers to composites of constructs used by theorists to explain intelligence. The author posits that these constructs "are provided mostly for those examiners who are interested in studying the particular cognitive constructs that are represented by the quotients" (Examiner's Manual, p. 79). The theorists and their constructs are:

Catell and Ham: (1) Fluid Intelligence (Nonverbal Operations) and (2) Crystallized Intelligence (Acquired Skills). Scores that contribute to Fluid Intelligence are: Design Sequences, Reversed Letters, Design Reproduction, and Symbolic Relations. Scores that contribute to Crystallized Intelligence are: Word Opposites, Sentence Imitation, Story Construction, Basic Information, Word Sequences, and Story Sequences.

Das: (1) Simultaneous Processing (stimuli are arranged in a concurrent manner to make a decision) and (2) Successive Processing (stimuli are arranged in a sequential order to make a decision). Scores that contribute to Simultaneous Processing are: Word Opposites, Sentence Imitation, Story Construction, Design Reproduction, Basic Information, and Symbolic Relations. Scores that contribute to Successive Processing are: Design Sequence, Reversed Letters, Word Sequences, and Story Sequences.

Jensen: (1) Associative Level (provides a high correspondence between the form of the stimulus input and the form of the response output) and (2) Cognitive Level (involves transformation of the stimulus input; the stimulus is manipulated to formulate a correct output). Scores that contribute to Associative Level are: Design Sequences, Sentence Imitation, Reversed Letters, Design Reproduction, and Word Sequences. Scores that contribute to the Cognitive Level are: Word Opposites, Story Construction, Basic Information, Symbolic Relations, and Story Sequences.

Wechsler: (1) Verbal Scale (involves spoken words and letters) and (2) Performance Scale (spoken words are not included). Scores contributing to the Verbal Scale are: Word Opposites, Sentence Imitation, Story Construction, Basic Information, and Word Sequences. Scores contributing to the Performance Scale are: Design Sequences, Reversed Letters, Design Reproduction, Symbolic Relations, and Story Sequences.

For ease in converting raw scores into standard scores and composites, a computerized program for IBM-compatible PCs is available.

Technical Adequacy

Validity Confirmation

Test item validity was established by qualitative evidence for the DTLA-4 in that the author details the content validity by relating the subtests of the DTLA-4 to (1) theories of intellect, (2) Salvia & Ysseldyke's behaviors/abilities measured by most tests of intelligence and aptitude (Salvia & Ysseldyke, 1998), and (3) detailed rationale underlying the selection of formats and items for the subtests. Quantitatively, the DTLA-4 was subject to item discrimination and item difficulty analysis. Based on the item discrimination and item difficulty statistics, unsatisfactory items were deleted from the test. This analysis was performed using the entire normative sample as subjects.

Test response validity was established by relating the various scores on the DTLA-4 to a number of similar assessments. Four studies (Hammill, 1991; Hishinuma & Yamakawa, 1993; McGhee, 1991; Sorrell, 1993) were conducted which correlated the DTLA-4 to such tests as the DTLA-2, the Kaufman Assessment Battery for Children, Scholastic Aptitude Scale, the Peabody Picture Vocabulary Test-Revised, the Wide Range Achievement Test-Revised, the WISC-III, the Woodcock-Johnson Psycho-Educational Battery-Revised, and the Test of Nonverbal Intelligence-Second Edition. In all cases, raw scores were converted to standard scores, which were correlated with the composite scores of these tests on intelligence or aptitude. The resulting correlations are reported in the Examiner's Manual (p. 141) and appear to be sufficiently high to support test response validity. The correlation coefficient with the Woodcock-Johnson Psycho-Educational Battery-Revised and the GMAQ (General Mental Ability Quotient) ranged from .90 to .91.

Reliability Confirmation

Reliability was investigated by testing 96 children residing in Austin, Texas. Testing was conducted twice with a one-week period between tests. The subjects ranged from first through twelfth grade and attended an elementary school, a junior high school, and a high school. All schools were considered to be low socioeconomic status and were multicultural in their student composition. Raw scores for the two tests were converted into standard scores and quotients. Correlations for test-retest reliability were divided by grades 1–3 (N = 24), grades 4–6 (N = 36), and grades 7–12 (N = 36). All correlations were above .60 and significant at the .05 level of probability. Correlations were also conducted on the entire sample of 96 in grades 1–12, and the resulting correlations for the subtests and composite scores were found to range from .73 to .99. These coefficients confirm test-retest reliability.

Objectivity Confirmation

Detailed guidelines governing scoring are included in administration procedures in the Examiner's Manual. Two staff persons in the publisher's research department independently scored a set of 30 completed protocols. These protocols were randomly selected from the normative sample. The sample ranged from third through twelfth graders. Raw scores were converted to standard scores, then correlated. These coefficients ranged from .95 to .98.

Statistical Confirmation

Statistical data on validity, reliability, objectivity, and norms can be found in the Examiner's Manual for the DTLA-4.

Special Features

Acronym

DTLA-4.

Levels of the Test

One.

Number of Test Forms

One.

Norm-Referenced?

Yes. The DTLA-3 and the DTLA-4 test items are identical and the norming process included data from 1998–1999 and 1996–1997. The DTLA-4 were normed on a total sample of 1,350 persons in 37 states and persons ranging in age from 6 years through 18 years, 11 months. Students with disabilities who were enrolled in general classes were included in the normative sample. The normative sample was representative of geographic region, gender, race, rural or urban residence, ethnicity, family income, educational attainment of parents, and disability. Demographic information was stratified by age. The description of the normative sample and procedures for developing norms are confusing in the Examiner's Manual. It was unclear as to which norming procedures were being described, the DTLA-3 or the DTLA-4.

Criterion-Referenced?

No.

Feasibility Considerations

Testing Time

Testing time for the DTLA-4 varies from approximately 50 minutes to two hours. The examiner is encouraged to request that the examinee respond in 10 seconds of presentation of the item. The DTLA-4 can be completed in one testing session; however, for some individuals the testing may be divided into two sessions.

For Testing Groups? Individuals?

Individuals.

Test Administration and Scoring

It is recommended that examiners have some formal training in assessment. Supervised practice in using mental abilities tests is also desirable. Test examiners should be knowledgeable concerning federal and state regulations regarding qualification of individuals for special programs. Specific directions for administering the DTLA-4 are clearly presented in the Examiner's Manual. Abbreviated instructions are included in the Examiner Record Booklet.

Test Materials and Approximate Costs

Complete kit: $329; Examiner's Manual: $79; Picture Book 1: $94; Picture Book 2: $34; Profile/Summary Forms (25): $24; Examiner Record Booklets (25): $44; Response Forms (25): $24; Story Sequence Chips: $20; Designs Sequence Cubes: $29; Software Scoring and Report System: $109.

Adequacy of Test Manuals

The complete kit for the DTLA-4 includes an Examiner's Manual, Picture Books 1 and 2, Profile/Summary Forms, Examiner Record Booklet, Response Forms (Design Reproduction), Story Sequence Chips, and Design Sequence Cubes. These materials are user-friendly and clearly written, with more than adequate test administration procedures.

Excerpts from Other Test Reviews

Smith (2001) and Traub (2001) are both concerned with the 16 composite scores. Smith recommends that the "16 scores be reduced to 3, eliminating all but the General, the Verbal, and the Nonverbal." Smith feels that "the rest of the composites are either too similar to one another to be useful, or are simply indications that the DTLA-4 subtests can be combined to look like other theoretical approaches to measuring intelligence."

Traub (2001) is also concerned about the 16 composite scores. He states: "For the recommended composites to possess the interpretations ascribed to them, the specific components of the 10 subtests must account for a substantial amount of variance, and elicit the unique mental qualities said to be assessed by each composite."

Salvia & Ysselydyke (2001) are critical of the normative sample: "While the description of the normative sample is substantially better than in previous editions, it remains less than complete. . . . no data are presented to show that the sample is representative at each age."

Ordering Information

Publisher

PRO-ED, 8700 Shoal Creek Boulevard, Austin, TX 78757-6897; Phone: 800-897-3202; Fax: 800-397-7633; Web site: http://www.proedinc.com.

Author

Donald D. Hammill.

Publication Date

1998.

Cautions and Comments

The DTLA was originally introduced in 1935 by Henry J. Baker and Bernice Leland and was the first test of mental ability that measured intraindividual strengths and weaknesses. The DTLA-2 and DTLA-3 were revisions of the original test and revised by Donald Hammill. In the DTLA-4 Hammill made "improvements" which included the characteristics of the normative sample, new reliability data computed for subgroups, new validity studies with attention to subgroups, reevaluated test items, and an increased number of cases in the test-retest study.

Several test reviewers agree that the Composite Scores in the DTLA-4 are confusing and may not be useful or understood by the educator. Of particular concern is the Optimal Composite, which is a composite of the student's four highest scores. These scores will vary from student to student. There is a question of the purpose and value for such a composite. The manual indicates that this score reflects the "best estimate of the individual's potential." However, the GMAQ (General Mental Ability Quotient) that combines the standard scores of all 10 subtests may be of most value to the educator. According to the Examiner's Manual, the GMAQ "is a numeric representation of an examinee's overall performance on the particular abilities measured by the DTLA-4 subtests. Therefore, it may be the best predictor of the student's achievement and the best estimate of an individual's current ability to process information" (p. 14). Overall, the DTLA-4 provides an unbiased measure of general intelligence that assesses multiple abilities.

References

Hammill, D. D. (1991). *Detroit Tests of Learning Aptitude-Third Edition*. Austin, TX: PRO-ED.

Hishinuma, E. S., & Yamakawa, R. (1993). Construct and criterion-related validity of the WISC III for exceptional students and those who are "at risk." *Journal for Psychoeducational Assessment*. WISC III Monograph (94-104).

McGhee, R. (1991). A comparison between the DTLA-3 and the WJ-R: A validity study. Unpublished manuscript.

Salvia, J., & Ysseldyke, J. E. (1998). *Assessment* (7th ed.). Boston: Houghton Mifflin.

Salvia, J., & Ysseldyke, J. E. (2001). *Assessment* (8th ed.). Boston: Houghton Mifflin.

Smith, J. K. (2001). Review of the Detroit Tests of Learning Aptitude, Fourth Edition. In B. S. Plake & J. C. Impara (Eds.), *The Fourteenth Mental Measurements Yearbook* (pp. 382–383). Lincoln, NE: The Buros Institute of Mental Measurements.

Sorrell, A. L. (1993). Aptitude IQ-achievement discrepancy and behavior among students classified as dyslexic and students classified as learning disabled: A comparison. Unpublished doctoral dissertation.

Traub, R. E. (2001). Review of the Detroit Tests of Learning Aptitude, Fourth Edition. In B. S. Plake & J. C. Impara (Eds.), *The Fourteenth Mental Measurements Yearbook* (pp. 384–386). Lincoln, NE: The Buros Institute of Mental Measurements.

Diagnostic Achievement Battery-Third Edition (DAB-3),
for testing individuals from 6 years through 14 years, 11 months of age
Reviewed by Aileen C. Lau-Dickinson, Ed.D., Special Education Administration

---

Usefulness of the Test for Educators

Test Author's Purpose

"The DAB-3 is an achievement test that makes an important contribution in identifying children's strengths and weaknesses in listening, speaking, reading, writing, and mathematics" (Assessment Probes, p. 1).

Decision-Making Applications

The DAB-3 is best suited for identifying children with possible learning disabilities. The basic constructs of the test were derived from the Individuals with Disabilities Education Act of 1990 (IDEA), originally known as the Education for All Handicapped Children Act of 1975 (Public Law 94-142). This law named five ability areas—listening, speaking, reading, writing, and mathematics—as germane to the identification of learning disabilities. The DAB-3 addresses all five ability areas described by the IDEA. The inclusion of spoken language skills (listening and speaking) is a particularly important aspect of the DAB-3. Basically, the DAB-3 identifies students who are significantly below their peers in spoken language (listening and speaking), written language (reading and writing), and mathematics. It is difficult to label it a "placement" test, as it can only be a part of the testing required to identify and label a child "learning disabled." However, it is a component of that process.

The DAB-3 may also be useful as an Achievement Certification tool, as it does document progress in both regular and special class settings and can be evidence that the child is "ready" or "not ready" for another program or educational setting.

Finally, the DAB-3 does measure various academic dimensions, and this allows the educator to determine his academic strengths and weaknesses. Therefore, the DAB-3 can be used for Instructional Prescription Applications. The author explored commonly used curricula and teaching programs in order to understand the scope and sequence of skills in specific academic areas. This information was incorporated into the DAB-3 subtests. The DAB-3 provides the educator with enough information regarding academic skills to identify strengths and weaknesses, but does not probe each academic area in depth to identify specific error patterns.

Relevant Population

The DAB-3 is designed for children ages 6 years through 14 years, 11 months. There are 14 short subtests to determine a child's strengths and weaknesses across several areas of achievement.

Characteristics Described

Characteristics of the DAB-3

Composite	*Subtests*
Listening	Story Comprehension, Characteristics
Speaking	Synonyms, Grammatic Completion
Reading	Alphabet/Word Knowledge, Reading Comprehension
Writing	Capitalization and Punctuation, Spelling, Writing: Contextual Language and Writing: Story Construction
Mathematics	Mathematics Reasoning, Mathematics Calculation
Spoken Language	Story Comprehension, Characteristics, Synonyms, Grammatic Completion
Written Language	Alphabet/Word Knowledge, Reading Comprehension, Capitalization and Punctuation, Spelling, Writing: Contextual Language and Writing: Story Construction
Supplemental Subtest	Phonemic Awareness
Total Achievement	First 13 Subtests

A brief description of each subtest follows:

Subtest 1: Story Comprehension (Listening). In the 35-item subtest, the examiner reads aloud brief stories and asks the student to answer questions about the story.

Subtest 2: Characteristics (Listening). In the 35-item subtest, the student listens to a brief statement and decides whether it is true or false. Relational-meaning theory is tapped here.

Subtest 3: Synonyms (Speaking). In this 25-item subtest, the examiner says a word and the child must supply a word that has the same meaning.

Subtest 4: Grammatic Completion (Speaking). In this 27-item subtest, the examiner measures the ability to understand and use certain common morphological forms in English.

Subtest 5: Alphabet/Word Knowledge (Reading). In this 63-item subtest, the student identifies letters and words that are different from others but similar in appearance, points to letters, names letters, and recognizes words beginning and ending with specific phonemes presented by the examiner. The higher levels of this subtest require students to read aloud written words that increase in level of difficulty.

Subtest 6: Reading Comprehension (Reading). In this subtest, the student is required to read short stories silently and to answer a series of questions. Comprehension questions are asked by the examiner.

Subtest 7: Capitalization and Punctuation (Writing). In this subtest, 28 sentences containing no capital letters or punctuation marks are presented to the students. The student must supply the correct capitals and punctuation.

Subtest 8: Spelling (Writing). In this subtest, 27 words are dictated to the student and the task is to write the words correctly.

Subtest 10–11: Wrting: Contextual Language and Writing: Story Construction (Writing). In this subtest, the student is presented three pictures that represent the fable "The Tortoise and the Hare." The student must write a story with a beginning, middle, and ending based on the pictures. The quality of the writing is measured by 11 aspects of story construction and 14 aspects of contextual language.

Subtest 12: Mathematics Reasoning (Mathematics). In this 30-item subtest, the student must respond to a mathematical problem presented orally.

Subtest 13: Mathematics Calculation (Mathematics). In this subtest, the student must mathematically calculate 36 problems presented to the student on a worksheet. The problems are arranged in hierarchical order.

Subtest 14: Phonemic Analysis (Supplemental). In this 40-item subtest, the student is asked to segment words into phonemic units.

Test Scores Obtained

To shorten testing time as much as possible, entry points, basals, and ceilings are used. The entry point may be the first item in a subtest or the age of the student. A basal must be established and is usually represented by five consecutive correct answers. The ceiling is five consecutive incorrect answers. The raw score is determined by adding the number of correct items. The Entry Points and Basals and Ceiling Criteria are displayed in Table 2.1, found in the Examiner's Manual (p. 16) Helpful examples of determining basals and ceilings are found in the Examiner's Manual (pp. 17–22).

The DAB-3 yields five types of scores: raw scores, standard scores, percentiles, composite quotients, and age and grade equivalents The Total Achievement Quotient (TAQ) is the estimate of global achievement. The standard scores for all 13 subtests are added and transformed into the TAQ by consulting the table in Appendix B (Examiner's Manual).

Guidelines for Interpreting DAB-3 Quotients and Percentile Ranks

Percentile Rank	Quotient	Description	Percentage Included
> 98	> 130	Very Superior	2.34
91–98	121–130	Superior	6.87
76–90	111–120	Above Average	16.12
26–75	90–110	Average	49.51
10–25	80–89	Below Average	16.12
3–9	70–79	Poor	6.87
0–2	< 70	Very Poor	2.34

Source: Examiner's Manual, Table 3.3, p. 45.

The author cautions that test scores should be shared with persons who are legally eligible to receive the information, including other professionals, parents, and the examiner. The author suggests that reporting of test scores should be accompanied by any of the following that are applicable: "The examiner's personal interpretation of what the scores mean, reports of any other diagnostic work, alternative interpretations of the results, suggestions of areas that need instructional change of emphasis, and recommendations of potential intervention programs that might be appropriate for the student" (Examiner's Manual, p. 56).

Technical Adequacy

Validity Confirmation

Test item validity: The DAB-3 is comprised of 14 subtests. For the most part, test items were taken from or modified from the DAB and DAB-2. The only new item, Subtest 14: Phonemic Analysis, was not included in the previous editions of the DAB. Forty experimental items were developed for this subtest. Some items omitted the initial word (such as "boy" for "cowboy") or sound (such as the "c" in "cat"). Other items omitted the final word or sound. These 40 items were field tested and an item analysis was conducted. As a result, all 40 items were retained in the subtest.

The rationale underlying the use of each test item in the 13 other subtests and information about their development is described in the Examiner's Manual (pp. 78–84). Many of the test items were taken from former versions of the DAB-3 (DAB and DAB-2). An item analysis of all subtest items was undertaken using the entire normative sample as subjects. Only 1% of DAB-3 test items were found to be potentially biased. Test items were statistically analyzed in regard to item discrimination and item difficulty. The "good" items were placed in easy-to-difficult order to compose the final norming version of the DAB-3. Other items were reordered based on this statistical analysis.

Test response validity: The DAB-3 was correlated with the Stanford Achievement Test-Ninth Edition (SAT-9) with 70 students (ages 7–12) in the study. The standard scores of the SAT-9 and the raw scores of the DAB-3 were correlated. Seventy-five percent of the correlation coefficients were found to be in the "high range" (.60–.80). The Total Achievement correlations ranged from .70 to .84, and these coefficients are in the "high" to "very high" range. The correlations between the SAT-9 and the DAB-3 suggest that the DAB-3 is another measure of school achievement. No other correlations were reported as evidence of test response validity.

Reliability Confirmation

Test-retest correlation was used to study the reliability of the DAB-3. One group of elementary children (35) and another group of middle school students (30) were used to conduct a test-retest study. The DAB-3 was administered twice to the samples with approximately two weeks between tests. The scores were correlated and the correlations for Total Achievement ranged from .97 for the elementary students to .98 for the middle school students.

Objectivity Confirmation

Two members of the publisher's staff independently scored a set of 33 completed protocols drawn randomly from the students in the normative sample. They ranged in age from 7 to 14. The results of the correlated scores ranged from .95 to .98.

The writing sample of the DAB-3 is scored as two subtests, Writing: Contextual Language and Writing: Story Construction. The procedures for scoring these subtests were revised for the DAB-3. Two trained individuals independently scored 30 randomly selected writing samples using the new scoring procedures. The correlation for the Writing: Contextual Language and Writing: Story Construction subtests was .85. This correlation indicated that the new scoring procedures aided the examiners in consistent scoring.

Statistical Confirmation

Statistical data on validity, reliability, and norms can be found in the Examiner's Manual to the DAB-3.

Special Features

Acronym

DAB-3.

Levels of the Test

There is one level of the test, with norms for children ages 6 through 14.

Number of Test Forms

One.

Norm-Referenced?

Yes. The DAB-3 was normed in 1997 through 2000. The DAB-3 was standardized on a sample of 1,094 students in 13 states. The sample is representative of the national population with regard to gender, race, ethnicity, geographic region, and urban/rural residence.

Criterion-Referenced?

No.

Reports Available

The author suggests that results of the testing should be shared with "persons who are legally eligible to review the information including other professionals, parents and the examiner" (p. 56).

The Profile/Examiner Record Booklet displays the Subtest Scores, Composite Quotients, Record of Other Test Scores, Profile of Scores, and Interpretations and Recommendations. This booklet would be helpful to others interested in the test results.

Feasibility Considerations

Testing Time

The DAB-3 has no set time limits. However, the time to administer the entire test may vary from 90 to 120 minutes. Selected subtests may be administered with testing time shortened considerably.

For Testing Groups? Individuals?

Individuals.

Test Administration and Scoring

The DAB-3 includes a Student Booklet that includes Stimuli for Subtest 1 (Story Comprehension—an audiotape—is also available for Story Comprehension), Subtest 5 (Alphabet/Word Knowledge), Subtest 6 (Reading Comprehension), and Subtest 12 (Mathematics Reasoning). This booklet is colorful and easy for the student to follow. The directions for administering the test are explicit and clear. The Student Response Booklet is used by the student to record his responses and is written with the student in mind. The Profile/Examiner Booklet is written with the examiner in mind. However, the print is small, which requires the examiner to be careful when recording responses in the spaces provided. The specific administration instructions are included in the Examiner's Manual as well as the Profile/Examiner Record Booklet.

The DAB-3 includes a supplemental manual, Assessment Probes, to be used with students who do poorly on the DAB-3. The author refers to this procedure as Adaptive Assessment. Adaptive Assessment may include verbal probes for test items that appear to be incorrect due to the student's lack of understanding of the task. The Assessment Probes includes probes for all 14 subtests. The original test scores are not altered after the administration of probes, but these probes can provide the examiner insight into the child's "comprehension of the instruction, their thinking processes, and their potential for learning" (Assessment Probes, p. 1).

The author suggests that examiners who use the DAB-3 should have training in standardized assessment. Supervised practice is also desirable.

Test Materials and Approximate Costs

Complete kit: $244; Software Kit (Manual and CD-ROM): $109; Manual: $69; Student Booklet: $39; Profile/Examiner Record Booklets (25): $54; Student Response Booklets (25): $39; Audiotape: $14; Assessment Probes: $34.

Adequacy of Test Manuals

The DAB-3 provides the Examiner's Manual, the Student Booklet, and the Assessment Probes Manual. The material is user-friendly and easy to follow. The Examiner's Manual provides tables for converting subtest raw scores to percentiles, standard scores, age, and grade equivalents.

Excerpts from Other Test Reviews

No test reviews were found for the DAB-3. However, the DAB was reviewed in *A Consumer's Guide to Tests in Print* (Hammill, Brown, & Bryant, 1989) and by Deni (1985) and Webster (1985). The DAB-2 was reviewed by Bernier and Hebert (1995), Brown (1995), Cohen and Spenciner (1998), Compton (1996), Hammill et al. (1992), and Salvia and Ysseldyke (1998).

Ordering Information

Publisher

PRO-ED, 8700 Shoal Creek Boulevard, Austin, TX 78757-6897; Phone: 800-897-3202; Fax: 800-397-7633; Web site: www.proedinc.com.

Author

Phyllis Newcomer.

Publication Date

2001.

Cautions and Comments

Overall, the DAB-3 appears to be a useful test for determining achievement levels for children from ages 6 through 14 in five areas of Listening, Speaking, Reading, Writing, and Mathematics. It appears that this revision of the original DAB (1984) and the DAB-2 (1990) has addressed many of the criticisms that were made by reviewers of the DAB and DAB-2. Specifically, new studies were conducted which addressed validity and reliability issues, and evidence is now provided by gender, disability, and ethnicity. Various subtests have been shortened and clarified, and on the whole the DAB-3 has been made more user-friendly.

The writing subtests may be a problem for some examiners. The criteria for scoring may not be as objective as it could be; that is, it may be difficult for the examiner to judge such criteria as "composition is composed of" and "vocabulary selection." There are 14 different criteria that must be judged by the examiner that could lead to examiner differences. However, based on new scoring criteria—correlations based on two independent scorers—scoring the writing subtest indicated adequate objectivity. Examiners should have practice in scoring the writing subtest under supervision of an experienced examiner.

Overall, the uniqueness of the DAB-3 is that it is does attempt to measure achievement in the areas of Listening, Speaking, Reading, Writing, and Mathematics that are identified by federal law (IDEA) and to be pertinent in identifying learning disabled students.

References

Bernier, J. J., & Hebert, M. (1995). Review of the Diagnostic Achievement Battery-Second Edition. In J. C. Conoley & J. C. Impara (Eds.), *The Twelfth Mental Measurements Yearbook* (pp. 294–295). Lincoln, NE: The Buros Institute of Mental Measurements.

Brown, R. (1995). Review of the Diagnostic Achievement Battery-Second Edition. In J. C. Conoley & J. C. Impara (Eds.), *The Twelfth Mental Measurements Yearbook* (pp. 295–296). Lincoln, NE: The Buros Institute of Mental Measurements.

Cohen, L. G., & Spenciner, L. J. (1998). *Assessment of children and youth.* New York: Longman.

Compton, C. (1996). *A guide to 100 tests for special education.* Palo Alto, CA: Globe Fearon.

Deni, J. R. (1985). Diagnostic Achievement Battery. In D. J. Keyser & R. C. Sweetland (Eds.), *Test critiques* (vol. 2, pp. 235–240). New York: Test Corporation of America.

Hammill, D. D., Brown, L., & Bryant, B. R. (1989). *A consumer's guide to tests in print.* Austin, TX: PRO-ED.

Salvia, J., & Ysseldyke, J. (1998). *Assessment* (7th ed.) Boston: Houghton Mifflin.

Webster, W. J. (1985). Review of the Diagnostic Achievement Battery. In J. V. Mitchell (Ed.), *The Ninth Mental Measurements Yearbook* (pp. 474–475). Lincoln, NE: The Buros Institute of Mental Measurements.

Goldman-Fristoe Test of Articulation-Second Edition (GFTA-2),
for testing individuals from 2 years through 21 years, 11 months of age
Reviewed by Aileen C. Lau-Dickinson, Ed.D., Special Education Administration

---

Usefulness of the Test for Educators

Test Authors' Purpose

"GFTA-2 is a systematic means of assessing an individual's articulation of the consonant sounds of Standard American English" (Manual, p. 1).

Decision-Making Applications

The GFTA-2 provides speech and language pathologists a primary measure for assessing articulation. The normed information can be used for determining eligibility for speech therapy services in the schools. The test meets the requirements of Public Law 94-142, now the Individuals with Disabilities Education Act (IDEA).

Relevant Population

The test is appropriate for children aged 2 years through 21 years, 11 months and provides age-based standard scores.

Characteristics Described

The first section of the GFTA-2, Sounds-in-Words, has 34 picture plates and 53 target words to elicit the articulation of 61 consonant sounds. These sounds appear in either the initial, medial, or final position of words. In addition, 16 consonant blends in the initial position are assessed. The second section, Sounds-in-Sentences, measures spontaneous articulation. The third section, Stimulability, assesses the examinee's ability to correctly produce a misarticulated sound when asked to watch and listen to the examiner's production of the sound.

Sounds-in-Words: The examinee is required to name the picture or to answer a question about the picture.

Sounds-in-Sentences: The examinee is asked to retell a story using picture plates which illustrate both the gist of the story and the target words. This is an attempt to approximate conversational speech and thus to measure the child's ability to use target sounds spontaneously or in connected speech.

Stimulability: The examinee is asked to repeat a previously misarticulated target sound after being given a correct production of that sound.

The International Phonetic Alphabet (IPA) is used to identify target words on the GFTA-2. On the GFTA-2 Response Form, the target words are listed first by their Standard English spellings and then using the IPA symbols An attempt was made to test the target sounds in developmental order, even though there are conflicting views on the order of acquisition of initial consonant sounds. The GFTA-2 uses the terms initial, medial, and final consonants in describing the position of consonant sounds in words. Other approaches may still be used by speech pathologists when using the GFTA-2.

Test Scores Obtained

Target sound errors are noted on the target sounds (IPA words or Standard English) by the examiner after the examinee responds. The raw score is determined by counting the number of articulation errors. The normative scores provided by the GFTA-2 include Standard Scores, Percentile Ranks (converted from Standard Scores), and Test-Age Equivalents.

Technical Adequacy

Validity Confirmation

Test item validity: The GFTA-2 measures 23 of the 25 consonant sounds in Standard American English. It attempts to obtain a spontaneous sample of the examinee's sound production in words and sentences.

Test response validity: The GFTA-2 was not correlated with any other similar test of sound production. However, an attempt was made to determine whether the measurement of sound production measures age differentiation, given the fact that children learn to articulate sounds on a continuum up to age 8. The attempt to measure age differentiation reveals steady decreases in mean raw scores as measured by the number of articulation errors throughout the age range from 2 to 21.

Reliability Confirmation

To investigate test-retest reliability, 53 children ranging in age from 4 years, 6 months through 7 years were tested. They were retested with an interval of the same day to 34 days, with a median interval of 14 days. All retesting was performed by the same examiner who had tested the children originally. Sounds-in-Words was used in the test-retest study. Correlations were not calculated, but test-retest reliability was measured by percent of agreement for a presence of an error for Sounds-in-Words. Most agreements were 100%, and the least agreement was with the initial (89%) and medial (79%) for the voiceless "th" sound and with the medial (89%) voiced "th" sound. Total agreement was in the 98% range.

Objectivity Confirmation

Objectivity was established by having two different examiners test the same sample of 30 examinees twice using a counterbalanced order of testing. The results were measured as percent of agreement for presence of error for Sounds-in-Words. Agreements ranged from 70% to 100%, and the least agreement was with the initial "dr" (70%), the medial "s" (73%), and the final "r" (73%).

Statistical Confirmation

Statistical data on validity, reliability, and norms can be found in the Manual for the GFTA-2.

Special Features

Acronym

GFTA-2.

Levels of the Test

There are three test levels: Sounds-in-Words, Sounds-in-Sentences, and Stimulability.

Number of Test Forms

One.

Norm-Referenced?

Yes. The Goldman-Fristoe Test of Articulation has been used by speech and language pathologists for over 30 years. Normative data was added in 1972, and this edition, GFTA-2, was renormed and standardization was completed in 1999. A representative sample of 2,350 examinees aged 2 years through 21 years, 11 months was tested at over 300 sites nationally. Of the three sections of the GFTA-2, the Sounds-in-Words section is the only one with normative data. The standardized sample was designed to separate subjects by gender and age. The GFTA-2 standardization sample was designed to match the U.S. Census data of March 1998. The female and male samples were stratified within each age group by the following variables: race/ethnic group, geographic region, and socioeconomic status.

Criterion-Referenced?

Yes. In the sense that age of acquisition of speech sounds occurs at different ages, developmental acquisition of sounds may be considered a criterion or a learning objective. For example, the learning objective may be stated as: "Billy will produce the target sound in isolation and in the initial position of words with 100% accuracy."

Feasibility Considerations

Testing Time

Testing time ranges from 5 to 15 minutes for the Sounds-in-Words section of the GFTA-2.

For Testing Groups? Individuals?

Individuals.

Test Administration and Scoring

The test items are presented in an easy-to-administer easel format, but knowledge of the presence of sound production errors is vital to the administration of the test. Only persons who have had training in listening and interpreting error sounds should administer this test. This is a test to be administered by the trained "ear." As the authors recommend, "This type of discriminative evaluation should be done only by those persons who have had training in phonetics and in the nature of articulation disorders" (Manual, p. 5). The authors recommend that the test is one that can only be interpreted by persons with "training in speech pathology" (Manual, p. 6).

Test Materials and Approximate Costs

Complete kit: $189.95; Response Forms (25): $21.95; Easel: $153.95; Manual: $35.95.

Adequacy of Test Manuals

The Manual is well-written and concise. The directions for administering and scoring the test are adequate.

Excerpts from Other Test Reviews

Two reviews of the 1968, 1972, and 1986 versions of the Goldman-Fristoe Test of Articulation are included in *A Consumer's Guide to Tests in Print* (Hammill, Brown, & Bryant, 1992). The overall rating for all three reviews is that the test is not recommended and does not meet the criteria set by the *Consumer's Guide* guideline. The GFTA-2 is not included in this edition of the *Consumer's Guide*.

Salvia & Ysseldyke (2001) state, "There are no objective measures of validity reported. . . . This lack of validity data is a weakness in the instrument. . . . Reliability data are inadequately reported but do appear adequate for at least half of the sample" (p. 486).

Ordering Information

Publisher

American Guidance Service, Inc., 4201 Woodland Road, Circle Pines, MN 55014-1796; Phone: 800-328-2560; Fax: 800-471-8457; Web site: www.agsnet.com.

Authors

Ronald Goldman and Macalyne Fristoe.

Publication Date

2000.

Cautions and Comments

The Goldman-Fristoe Test of Articulation has been used by speech and language pathologists for over 30 years to test the articulation skills of children and to determine whether those children require treatment for their misarticulations. The more recent editions of the Goldman-Fristoe Test of Articulation and the most recent GFTA-2 now are standardized and have test-age equivalents and percentiles. These derived scores are needed for eligibility requirements for the IDEA (Individuals with Disabilities Education Act). Assessing acquisition of consonant sounds is based on developmental acquisition and represents a hierarchy of skill development. The GFTA-2 accomplishes that task. However, the authors of the GFTA-2 have wanted to offer a norm-referenced test, which is not an easy task for consonant acquisition. Even though the validity and reliability information is limited, the test has merit for clinical usage by the speech and language pathologist.

References

Hammill, D. D., Brown, L., Bryant, B. R. (1992). *A consumer's guide to tests in print* (2nd ed.). Austin, TX: PRO-ED.
Salvia, J., & Ysselydyke, J. E. (2001). *Assessment* (8th ed.). Boston: Houghton Mifflin.

Kaufman Assessment Battery for Children (K-ABC),
for testing individuals from 2 years, 6 months through 12 years, 6 months of age
Reviewed by Aileen C. Lau-Dickinson, Ed.D., Special Education Administration

---

Usefulness of the Test for Educators

Test Authors' Purpose

"The K-ABC is intended for psychological and clinical assessment, psychoeducational evaluation of learning disabled and other exceptional children, educational planning and placement, minority group assessment, preschool assessment, neuropsychological assessment and research" (Administration & Scoring Manual, p. 1).

Decision-Making Applications

The K-ABC is appropriate for making placement decisions for children suspected of having learning disability or other special needs. The K-ABC is primarily a clinical instrument for the evaluation of preschool and elementary school children. The test includes both intellectual ability and achievement tasks. The authors state, "the inclusion of intelligence and achievement scales in a single battery provides the ideal circumstance for comparing ability to achievement for children suspected of having learning disability" (pp. 10–11). The battery allows the examiner to identify, label, and determine placement required by federal law. The battery is not only useful for determining learning disability but is useful for identifying children with reading disability, mental retardation, and emotional disturbance.

The K-ABC also has a Nonverbal Scale with separate norm tables. This scale can be used with children with hearing, speech, or language disorders who are low verbal or nonverbal, as the tasks can be administered in pantomime and responded to motorically.

Some states question whether the K-ABC can legitimately serve as the measure of intelligence for diagnostic and placement purposes because it does not yield an IQ. The authors indicate that they "wrestled with the pros and cons of labeling as IQs the scores yielded by the intelligence scales, but felt it was wrong to perpetuate what has become to many an offensive term."

There is a Minority Group Assessment, a Preschool Assessment, and a Neuropsychological Assessment.

The K-ABC comprises four Global Scales, each yielding standard scores having a mean of 100 and a standard deviation of 15. These scales include Sequential Processing, Simultaneous Processing, Mental Processing Composite, and Achievement.

Relevant Population

The K-ABC is designed for children from 2 1/2 to 12 1/2 years of age with norms for nonverbal, minority (Black and Hispanic), preschool, and brain-injured children.

Characteristics Described

The K-ABC comprises 16 subtests, although a maximum of 13 are administered to any one child. The K-ABC is shorter for young children in terms of both the testing time and the number of subtests. The descriptions of the subtests of the K-ABC are as follows:

Sequential Processing Scale

Hand Movements (ages 2 years, 6 months–12 years, 5 months): Child performs a series of hand movements in the same sequence as the examiner performed them.

Number Recall (ages 2 years, 6 months–12 years, 5 months): Child repeats a series of digits in the same sequence as the examiner said them.

Word Order (ages 4 years–12 years, 5 months): Child touches a series of silhouettes of common objects in the same sequence as the examiner said the names of the objects.

Simultaneous Processing Scale

Magic Window (ages 2 years, 6 months–4 years, 11 months): Child identifies a picture which the examiner exposed by slowly moving it behind a narrow window, making the picture only partially visible at any one time.

Face Recognition (ages 2 years, 6 months–4 years, 11 months): Child selects from a group photograph the one or two faces that were exposed briefly on the preceding page.

Gestalt Closure (ages 2 years, 6 months–12 years, 5 months): Child names an object or scene pictured in a partially completed "inkblot" drawing.

Matrix Analogies (ages 5 years–12 years, 5 months): Child selects the meaningful picture or abstract design which best completes a visual analogy.

Spatial Memory (ages 5 years–12 years, 5 months): Child recalls the placement of pictures on a page that was exposed briefly.

Photo Series (ages 6 years–12 years, 5 months). Child places photographs of an event in chronological order.

Achievement Scale

Expressive Vocabulary (ages 2 years, 6 months–12 years, 5 months): Child names the object pictured in a photograph.

Faces & Places (ages 2 years, 6 months–12 years, 5 months): Child names the well-known person, fictional character, or place pictured in a photograph or drawing.

Arithmetic (ages 3 years–12 years, 5 months): Child demonstrates knowledge of numbers and mathematical concepts, counting and computational skills, and other school-related arithmetic abilities.

Riddles (ages 3 years–12 years, 5 months): Child infers the name of a concrete or abstract concept when given a list of its characteristics.

Reading/Decoding (ages 5 years–12 years, 5 months): Child identifies letters and reads words.

Reading/Understanding (ages 7 years–12 years, 5 months): Child demonstrates reading comprehension by following commands that are given in a sentence.

Age-by-Age Grouping of Subtests on the K-ABC

Ages	*2 1/2*	*3*	*4*	*5*	*6*	*7–12 1/2*
Scale & Subtests						
Sequential						
Hand Movements	X	X	X	X	X	X
Number Recall	X	X	X	X	X	X
Simultaneous						
Magic Window	X	X	X			
Face Recognition		X	X	X		
Gestalt Closure	X	X	X	X	X	

Ages	2 1/2	3	4	5	6	7–12 1/2
Triangles			X	X	X	X
Matrix Analogies				X	X	X
Spatial Memory				X	X	X
Achievement						
Expressive Vocabulary	X	X	X			
Faces & Places		X	X			
Arithmetic		X	X	X	X	X
Riddles		X	X	X	X	X
Reading/Decoding				X	X	X
Reading/Understanding					X	

Test Scores Obtained

For each subtest, items are grouped in units, which are easily identified in the Individual Test Record booklet. "Starting points" are clear and are based on the child's chronological age. A hand indicating "stop" delineates the "stopping point." However, children who have "passed" all items in a unit may move to the next unit and the examiner continues testing until the child misses one item. The examiner must "discontinue" testing when the child misses every item in a unit. A summary of starting and stopping rules is given in the Administration and Scoring Manual (p. 36). Correct scores are given a 1 and incorrect scores are given a 0. The total raw score on each subtest is obtained by subtracting the number of errors (the total number of items scored 0) from the ceiling item (the highest item administered). Directions for converting subtest raw scores to scaled scores and standard scores are given in the Administration and Scoring Manual (p. 53). K-ABC ASSIST is available on CD-ROM for automated scoring and interpreting standard scores. With ASSIST, the examiner enters raw scores and identification data and the software automatically gives the derived scores.

Technical Adequacy

Validity Confirmation

Both test item and test response validation procedures were used to validate the test battery. *Test item validity* was established initially by the development of a pool of 50 mental processing and achievement tasks. These experimental tasks were piloted in 10 separate studies, where about 600 children were tested in Georgia, Illinois, Nebraska, Arizona, and South Carolina. Item analyses and factor analyses were also conducted to identify the best items and tasks for the K-ABC.

Test response validity was established by relating the scores from the K-ABC to scores on such tests as the Wechsler, the WISC-R, and the Stanford-Binet (see the K-ABC Interpretative Manual).

Age differentiation is a major criterion used to validate intelligence tests. According to the authors, "tests that purport to measure intelligence, achievement or other aspects of functioning that bear a clear cut and consistent relationship to chronological development have to demonstrate significant age differentiation to support any claim of construct validity" (p. 100). Significant correlations were found with age for each K-ABC subtest. No significant differences were found in the correlations obtained for females and males, for children from different races, for ethnic groups (black, Hispanic, or white), or for preschool children.

Reliability Confirmation

The K-ABC was administered twice to 246 children who spanned the entire 2 1/2- to 12 1/2-year age range. The interval between testing was two to four weeks. Test-retest reliability improved with increasing age, particularly with the Mental Processing Subtests. Test-retest reliability was .80 or above for all ages on the Achievement Tests. Other types of reliability confirmation are also provided in the Technical Report.

Objectivity Confirmation

Appendix A covers specific criteria for scoring correct verbal responses in English (p. 69) and Appendix B covers specific criteria for scoring correct verbal responses in Spanish (p. 85). The subtests are presented in an easel format, and criteria for correct and incorrect responses are clear. Sample and teaching items are provided in each subtest to help the child understand the required task. No study is reported of a correlation between different scorers of the same test. The authors take note of "objectivity," indicating that objectivity results when all examiners adhere to the rules each time the test is administered (Administration and Scoring Manual, p. 17).

Statistical Confirmation

Statistical data on validity, reliability, and norms is available in the Administration and Scoring Manual of the K-ABC.

Special Features

Acronym

K-ABC.

Levels of the Test

There are 16 subtests. These subtests are divided into "mental processing" and "achievement" areas. However, not all subtests are administered to all children from ages 2 1/2 to 12 1/2. This has been described earlier in this review.

Number of Test Forms

One.

Norm-Referenced?

Yes. The test battery was nationally normed and standardized. The national standardization program included more than 2,000 children tested in 34 test sites in 24 states. The sample was stratified within each age group by sex, geographical region, socioeconomic status, race or ethnic group, community size, and normal and exceptional children. The multi-subtest battery yields standard scores with a mean of 100 and a standard deviation of 15.

Criterion-Referenced?

No.

Feasibility Considerations

Testing Time

Ages:	2 1/2	3	4	5	6	7–12 1/2
Minutes:	35	40–45	45–55	50–60	60–70	75–85

For Testing Groups? Individuals?

Individuals.

Test Administration and Scoring

Testing directions are clear and appear on each subtest. Individual Test Records are easy to follow and scores recorded are either 1 (correct) or 0 (incorrect). Tables to obtain scaled scores, Global scaled scores, percentile ranks, grade equivalents, age equivalents, and stanines are found in the Administration and Scoring Manual. Minority and Out-of-Level norms are also available in the manual. Out-of-Level norms are for children who are mentally retarded or developmentally delayed and are administered subtests below their chronological age level. The authors are clear that administration of the K-ABC requires "a competent, trained examiner, well versed in psychology and individual intellectual assessment, who has studied carefully both the K-ABC Interpretative Manual and K-ABC Administration and Scoring Manual" (p. 4). The K-ABC ASSIST software program offers numerous report options, including score summary, narrative, graphic profile, composite comparisons, high/low analysis, shared/unique abilities, and a parent letter. The authors indicate that "experience in individual psychological or psychoeducational assessment" is preferred for individuals who plan to administer the K-ABC.

Test Materials and Approximate Costs

Complete K-ABC kit: $412.95; K-ABC ASSIST kit: $199.95; Complete K-ABC kit with ASSIST: $511.95.

Adequacy of Test Manuals

There are two test manuals: the Administrative and Scoring Manual and the Interpretative Manual. They are complete with detailed information regarding description, background, and psychological analysis of each subtest. Test development and standardization, administration, scoring, and norm tables are also included. The manual also carries instructional suggestions for teaching academic skills by using students' sequential or simultaneous processing strengths.

Excerpts from Other Test Reviews

McLoughlin and Lewis (1990) indicate that "the K-ABC appears to be a promising measure of intellectual performance with several interesting features, including a nonverbal scale and tests of two types of processing abilities."

Criticism has been leveled at the K-ABC in reference to its theoretical base (Sternberg, 1984), its sequential-simultaneous factor structure (Strommen, 1988), and its relevance to instructional planning (Salvia & Hritcko, 1984). Further validation of the intervention approach is needed (McLoughlin & Lewis, 1990). Hammill, Brown, and Bryant gave an "F" to the overall rating for the subtests Hand Movement, Magic Window, and Face Recognition. Reliability issues were a concern in regard to these subtests.

Ordering Information

Publisher

American Guidance Service, Inc., 4201 Woodland Road, Circle Pines, MN 55014-1796; Phone: 800-328-2560; Fax: 800-471-8457; e-mail: agsmail@agsnet.com; Web site: www. agsnet.com.

Authors

Alan S. Kaufman and Nadeen L. Kaufman.

Publication Date

1983.

Cautions and Comments

Since the K-ABC can only be administered by trained school psychologists, the educator's role is one of utilizing the results primarily for placement. Interpretation of the results is left to the school psychologist.

The nonverbal scale may allow the psychologist to gain valuable information on the intellectual and academic functioning of children who are low verbal or whose verbal intelligibility is poor. In addition, the battery is sensitive to the testing of preschool, minority, and exceptional groups.

Even though there has been some criticism of the lack of validity for the remedial program found in the Interpretative Manual, the methods and examples could be useful to teachers for carrying out instruction. The authors have reviewed the research and given justification for the remedial techniques included in the Interpretative Manual.

References

Hammill, D. D., Brown, L., & Bryant, B. R. (1992). *A consumer's guide to tests in print* (2nd ed.). Austin, TX: PRO-ED.

McLoughlin J. A., & Lewis, R. B. (1990). *Assessing special students* (3rd ed.). Columbus, OH: Merrill.

Salvia, J., & Hritcko, T. (1984). The K-ABC and ability testing. *Journal of Special Education 18*, 345–356.

Sternberg, R. J. (1984). What should intelligence tests test? Implications of a triachic theory of intelligence for intelligence testing. *Educational Researcher 13*(1), 5–15.

Strommen, E. (1988). Confirmation factor of the *Kaufman Assessment Battery for Children*: A reevaluation. *Journal of School Psychology 26*, 13–23.

Learning Efficiency Test (LET-II),
for testing individuals from 5 through 75 years of age
Reviewed by Aileen C. Lau-Dickinson, Ed.D., Special Education Administration

---

Usefulness of the Test for Educators

Test Author's Purpose

"The LET-II is a norm-referenced diagnostic test which examines how effectively and efficiently a person processes and retains information presented visually and auditorily" (Manual, p. 7).

Decision-Making Applications

According to the author, the LET-II tests the student's ability to transfer information from Short-Term Memory (STM) to Long-Term Memory (LTM). The LET-II purports to predict success in performance of reading and mathematics. "Its high predictive validity for classroom performance is particularly important in light of Public Law 94-142, which recommends that diagnostic instruments have a direct relationship to subsequent instructional programming" (Manual, p. 8). Therefore, it could be useful as part of the battery of tests that the educator uses to make placement decisions for individuals with learning disabilities or other learning problems. For the older populations, the LET-II can provide information regarding memory loss and the modality that is most depressed, visual or auditory.

Relevant Population

The LET-II is designed for individuals from 5 through 75 years of age. The author states that it is not appropriate for the severely hearing impaired, deaf, trainable mentally retarded, or severely or profoundly mentally retarded. Blind and visually impaired students can take the auditory sections of the LET-II.

Characteristics Described

The LET-II has two modality-specific tests: Visual Memory and Auditory Memory. There are six subtests for each modality, which evaluate varying levels of the individual's ability to recall a string of letters with and without verbal interference. The letters used as stimulus items are serial strings of non-rhyming or phonetically non-confusable consonants. Each string of letters ranges in length from two to nine letters.

Information processes are assessed for each subtest under three different recall conditions: immediate recall, short-term recall, and long-term recall.

Immediate Recall: This is the amount of information the individual recalls without verbal interference and without drill or repetition of the information.

Short-Term Recall: This is the amount of information the individual recalls after the introduction of irrelevant verbal material.

Long-Term Recall: This is the amount of information the individual recalls after transferring the information from short-term recall to long-term recall after the presentation of additional verbal interference. "The basic factor distinguishing STM from LTM is the length of time the information is held while further interference is presented" (Manual, p. 10).

Immediate Recall

For the Visual Memory test, each item (letter) in the stimulus string is visually presented using visual stimulus cards for two seconds before moving to the next item in the string.

For the Auditory Memory test, each item is read from the Record Form with a one-second pause between items. The examinee is asked to recall the letters in the order presented or as many letters as possible regardless of order.

Short-Term Recall

Following the Immediate Recall test, the examinee counts aloud as indicated on the Record Form and then must state the letters presented earlier in the correct order or the letters regardless of order.

Long-Term Recall

After the Short-Term Recall test, the examinee is asked to repeat a sentence that appears on the Record Form and then is asked to recall as many of the original letters in the serial string as possible, either in correct order or in any order.

Scoring of correct responses is recorded on the Record Form, and one point is given for each letter recalled in the correct serial order. Testing is discontinued when the examinee fails to recall correctly two consecutive letter strings during the Ordered

Immediate Recall Test. However, the remaining two subtests for Short-Term Recall and Long-Term Recall are still administered.

Test Scores Obtained

Scoring procedures for the LET-II are detailed in the Manual (p. 45). Norm tables convert raw scores to scaled scores. Summed raw scores are converted to standard scores for the Visual Modality and Auditory Modality. The Global Memory Factor score is obtained by summing the two raw scores from the Visual and Auditory Modality Factors and transforming this score into a standard score using age-adjusted tables in the Appendixes. Standard scores are converted to percentile ranks, which are found on the back cover of the Record Form.

Relationship of Scaled Scores, Percentile Ranks, and Levels of Performance

Scaled Scores	Percentile Ranks	Classification
16–19	96+	Superior (4% of population)
13–15	77–95	Above Average (19% of population)
8–12	23–76	Average (54% of population)
5–7	4–22	Below Average (19% of population)
1–4	< 4	Low (4% of population)

Source: Manual, Figure 8.

Technical Adequacy

Validity Confirmation

Test item validity: According to the author, test item validity was established by "(1) using non-rhyming letters as stimulus items to provide a relatively unrestricted response domain, (2) allowing for examination of the full range of memory capacity by including serial strings which range from two through nine items, and (3) utilizing a testing methodology consistent with the two-store model of memory to assess immediate recall as well as short term and long term recall" (Manual, p. 29). Further, a detailed discussion of the Two-Store Model of Memory, Memory Span Capacity, Short-Term Memory and Learning Disabilities, Verbal Interference Effects, and Learning is offered. The Aptitude-by-Treatment Interaction and a review of studies that demonstrate the usefulness of the LET in distinguishing atypical-disabled learners from non-LD learners is also provided (Manual, pp. 11–23).

Test response validity: Several studies were reported that attempted to relate the LET-II to the California Achievement Test and the Kuhlmann-Anderson Test. Criterion variables were (1) actual grade level in reading and (2) actual grades earned in reading, mathematics, and social studies and the end of the school year. "LET-II test performance was significantly predictive of student performance on nearly all of these criteria" (Manual, p. 32). The LET-II was compared to the Woodcock-Johnson Tests of Cognitive Ability using a sample of 120 students. Correlations of the Woodcock-Johnson Broad Cognitive Index score and the LET-II factor scores ranged from .47 (Auditory Modality factor) to .63 (Visual Modality factor). The Manual did not give tables of the correlations, and for the most part correlations were low. No correlations were reported between scores on the LET-II and scores on another test of Memory, such as the Wide Range Assessment of Memory and Learning.

Reliability Confirmation

Fifty-three learning disability students in grades 4 through 12 were involved in a test-retest study which yielded coefficients from .71 to .86 for the 12 subtests, both modalities. No detail was given concerning the intervals between testing or other variables of the sample. A second test-retest study was reported using 40 secondary students with identified learning and behavior problems. There was a period of one to six weeks between the tests. Correlations were calculated for Ordered and Unordered Visual and Auditory Memory and for Immediate, Short-Term, and Long-Term Recall. Correlations were high, above .90 except for Short-Term Visual Memory, which was .81. Global Memory correlations were not reported.

Several other small studies of test-retest reliability are reported in the Manual with a broad range of correlations (Manual, pp. 28–29).

Objectivity Confirmation

Scoring is dependent on the number of letters recalled by the examinee. The recall is distinguished by the degree and type of verbal interference presented, and the length of time between initial presentation of the serial string and verbal recall. There was no evidence reported in the Manual that two independent scorers reviewed test protocols in order to establish test result objectivity.

Statistical Confirmation

Statistical data on validity, reliability, and norms can be found in the Manual for the LET-II.

Special Features

Acronym

LET-II.

Levels of the Test

One.

Number of Test Forms

One.

Norm-Referenced?

Yes. A total of 1,126 children and adults between the ages of 5 years and 85 years, 4 months comprised the sample to standardize the LET-II. All students were enrolled in public schools and the adults were volunteers obtained from community centers or social agencies. The sample was randomly selected by teachers. All students were functioning on grade level and stratified according to age, socioeconomic status, gender, and race. No students identified for special services were included in the sample.

Criterion-Referenced?

No.

Other Features

The Manual includes a section of Remedial Strategies to Enhance Learning. These include strategies to enhance memory. These strategies are based on extensive research of memory-enhancing interventions. The educator would find these strategies helpful particularly for young students (Manual, pp. 91–106).

Feasibility Considerations

Testing Time

The LET-II takes about 10 minutes to administer and 10 minutes to score.

For Testing Groups? Individuals?

Individuals.

Test Administration and Scoring

Test administration is straightforward, and instructions given to the student are explicit. The examiner introduces the testing by saying:

> I want to find out how well you can remember letters that are shown to you for a short period of time. Your job is to remember the letters in the same order as you saw them. If you cannot remember them in the same order, try to remember as many of them as you can in any order [for the Visual Memory Subtests]. Now I want to see how well you remember letters when you hear them. They will be said one at a time. Your job is to remember these letters in the same order as you heard them. If you cannot remember them in the same order, try to remember as many of them as you can in any order [for the Auditory Memory Subtests]. (Manual, p. 41)

The Manual does not give qualifications for examiners.

Test Materials and Approximate Costs

Test Kit: $92; Manual: $40; Stimulus Cards: $22; Record Forms (50): $30; Specimen Set (Manual and Sample Forms): $40; LET-II Scoring System (Software): $50.

Adequacy of Test Manuals

The Test Manual is adequate and gives an overview of the test and its development and standardization. A very helpful portion of the Manual includes three case studies and a useful section on remedial strategies. Conversion tables are included in the Appendixes.

Excerpts from Other Test Reviews

A test review of the 1981 edition of the Learning Efficiency Test was located in *A Consumer's Guide to Tests in Print* (Hammill, Brown, & Bryant, 1992). The result was an overall rating of "Not Recommended." According to the *Consumer's Guide*, a "Not Recommended" rating is that the test did not meet minimum criteria for technical adequacy. This edition of the LET (LET-II) is expanded including norms to include ages 5 through 75. No other test reviews were located for the LET-II.

Ordering Information

Publisher

Academic Therapy Publications, 20 Commercial Boulevard, Novato, CA 94949-6191; Phone: 800-422-7249; Fax: 888-287-9925; Web site: www.academictherapy.com.

Author

Raymond E. Webster.

Publication Date

1998.

Cautions and Comments

The LET-II gives the educator useful information concerning visual and auditory information processing characteristics. A number of learning deficits may be related to information processing difficulties. Additional studies are warranted to give the educator more information concerning validity, reliability, and objectivity of the LET-II. The expanded age norms should be helpful for those working with the young child as well as those who need to evaluate memory loss in older adults. The Manual can be helpful for the educator when looking at the effects of memory on learning. The Manual also contains some specific instructional strategies that would be beneficial for students in the classroom and for planning Individual Education Plans.

Reference

Hammill, D. D., Brown, L., & Bryant, B. R. (1992). *A consumer's guide to tests in print* (2nd ed.). Austin TX: PRO-ED.

Leiter International Performance Scale-Revised (Leiter-R),
for testing individuals from 2 years through 20 years, 11 months of age
Reviewed by Aileen C. Lau-Dickinson, Ed.D., Special Education Administration

---

Usefulness of the Test for Educators

Test Authors' Purpose

"The goal of developing this instrument was to construct a reliable and valid non-verbal measure of intellectual ability, memory and attention that could be used to assess children, adolescents and young adults who could not be reliably and validly assessed with traditional intelligence tests" (Examiner's Manual, p. 1).

Decision-Making Applications

The Leiter-R is best suited for making placement decisions for specialized groups of children. The Leiter-R can be used to identify young children (2- to 5-year-olds) with cognitive delays so that these children will qualify for special services under the Individuals with Disabilities Education Act (IDEA). There is also a need to identify cognitive ability in children with communication disorders, motor impairments, or those with English as a second language. The Leiter-R provides a test of cognitive abilities both for children with disabilities for those who are gifted.

Relevant Population

The Leiter-R assesses cognitive functions in children and adolescents ages 2 years through 20 years, 11 months. It has been designed for children and adolescents with significant communication disorders, cognitive delay, English as a second language, hearing impairments, motor impairments, traumatic brain injury, attention deficit disorder, and other types of disabilities.

Characteristics Described

The Leiter-R comprises 20 subtests with two batteries: the Visualization and Reasoning (VR) Battery and the Attention and Memory (AM) Battery. The Leiter-R is available with stimulus items in an easel format. The response cards and easel pictures and designs are in color. The brief description of the 20 subtests is found below.

Visualization and Reasoning Battery

1. Figure Ground (FG): Subject identifies embedded figures or designs within a complex stimulus. (Visualization)

2. Design Analogies (DA): Subject identifies "matrix analogies" using geometric shapes. (Reasoning)

3. Form Completion (FC): Subject demonstrates ability to recognize a "whole object" from a randomly displayed array of its fragmented parts. (Visualization)

4. Matching (M): Subject matches response cards or manipulative shapes to easel stimuli. (Visualization)

5. Sequential Order (SO): Subject must select related stimuli that progress in a corresponding order. (Reasoning)

6. Repeated Patterns (RP): Subject supplies "missing" portion of pattern by moving response cards into alignments with easel. (Reasoning)

7. Picture Context (PC): Subject must recognize a pictured object that has been removed from a larger display using visual contextual clues. (Visualization)

8. Classification (C): Subject must categorize objects or geometric designs. (Reasoning)

9. Paper Folding (PF): Subject must demonstrate the ability to mentally "fold" an object displayed in two dimensions—unfolded—and to match it to a target. (Visualization)

10. Figure Rotation (FR): Subject must mentally rotate a two- or three-dimensional object or geometric figure. (Visualization)

Attention and Memory Battery

11. Associated Pairs (AP): Subject must recall meaningful and non-meaningful associations. (Memory)

12. Immediate Recognition (IR): Subject must demonstrate ability to discriminate between present and absent objects after a stimulus array of picture objects is shown for five seconds. (Memory)

13. Forward Memory (FM): Subject must demonstrate ability to remember a sequence of pictured objects to which the examiner points in a given sequence. (Memory)

14. Attention Sustained (AS): Subject must demonstrate ability to find and cross out all squares found in an array of geometric shapes printed on a page. There are three parallel forms: a preschool form with smiling faces, an animal pictures form, and a more complex array of geometric shapes. (Attention)

15. Reverse Memory (RM): Subject must demonstrate ability to remember a sequence of pictured objects in the opposite order from that in which the examiner pointed. (Memory)

16. Visual Coding (VC): Subject must recall a nonverbal version of a symbol to digit coding task, using pictorial and geometric objects as well as numbers. (Memory)

17. Spatial Memory (SM): Subject must demonstrate the placement of cards on the correct spatial location on a blank matrix grid after an array in a matrix format is shown for 10 seconds and then removed. (Memory)

18. Delayed Pairs (DP): Subject must demonstrate the ability to recognize objects associated in the AP subtest after a 30-minute delay. (Memory)

19. Delayed Recognition (DR): Subject must demonstrate the ability to recognize the objects present in the IR subtest after a 30-minute delay. (Memory)

20. Attention Divided (AD): Subject must divide his/her attention between pointing to objects in a cardboard sheath and sorting cards. (Attention)

Note: Not all subtests are administered at each given age. See the Examiner's Manual for age groupings and subtests administered.

Supplemental Characteristics

In addition to the 20 subtests of the Leiter-R, there are four rating scales: Examiner Rating, Parent Rating, Teacher Rating, and Child's Self Rating. The ratings are on a Likert scale ranging from 1 to 3 points (parent, teacher, and self rating) and 0 to 3 points (examiner). These scales include the domains of attention, activity level, organization/impulse control, sociability, sensory reactivity, emotions, anxiety, and mood.

Test Scores Obtained

IQ Scores: Two IQ estimates are available based on the scaled scores of the VR Battery: a Brief IQ Screener composed of four subtests and a Full Scale IQ composed of six subtests that are slightly different for preschool versus school-aged children. These IQ scores are intended as measures of "g" or general nonverbal intelligence.

Composite Scores: The VR Battery also offers Composite Scores for Fluid Reasoning, Fundamental Visualization, and Spatial Visualization.

Diagnostic Scores and Composite Scores: There are eight special Diagnostic Scores for the AM Battery subtests that are available for an in-depth analysis of the child's performance. Diagnostic Scores are discussed in the Examiner's Manual (pp. 85–87). The AM Battery offers composite scores for Memory Screening, Associative Memory, Memory Span, Attention, Memory Process, and Recognition Memory.

Tables for converting raw scores to scaled scores are found in the Examiner's Manual. Scaled scores are converted to IQs. Percentiles and Age Equivalents are also available.

Growth Scores: Criterion-Referenced Growth Scores are calculated by converting raw scores for each subtest, each composite, and each IQ estimate to a Growth Scale score. Using the Growth Scale, the child's growth or development can be compared to performances on multiple occasions or testings. The Growth Scores will allow for estimation of the difficulty that items may have for the child, which can then be used to target skills for appropriate intervention.

Rating Scales: Scaled scores can be obtained for the four Rating Scales. Two composite scores can also be calculated for the Rating Scales, Cognitive/Social and Emotions/Regulations.

Computer Scoring Software: A Computer Scoring Software System and User's Guide can be purchased separately, and after raw scores are entered they are automatically converted to scaled scores and IQs. Two report versions can be generated: a five-page summary of tables of the results and a nine-page report containing tables and profiles.

Technical Adequacy

Validity Confirmation

Test item validity: The revision of the Leiter has been a multiyear effort with extensive field testing. The Tryout Phase and the Standardization Phase followed careful scrutiny of test items by 174 examiners. These examiners were particularly concerned with the administration of test items in a nonverbal and nonlanguage mode. Subtests were deleted that required verbalization during test administration or in the responses of children. The Leiter-R was designed on the basis of a unifying model of nonverbal cognitive abilities. The Examiner's Manual discusses the careful selection of items based on "review of the literature, factor verification, expert review, and empirical studies of internal consistency" (p. 169) used to select the items for the subtests. In addition, the Rating Scales underwent careful development and review by experts and examiners in both Tryout and Standardization Editions.

Test response validity was established by correlating the Leiter-R VR Battery with the original Leiter. A sample of 124 children and adolescents, ages 2–19, were given both batteries. The correlation for the Leiter IQ and the Leiter-R Brief IQ was .85, and the Leiter IQ and the Leiter-R Full IQ was also .85. The Leiter-R was also correlated with the WISC-III using a sample of 126 children (ages 6 to 16). The correlations for the Leiter Brief IQ and Leiter Full Scale IQ with the WISC-III Full Scale IQ and Performance IQ ranged from .85 to .86. These results suggest that a global factor "g" is common between the two test batteries. Other correlation studies can be found in the Examiner's Manual (pp. 181–182).

Reliability Confirmation

A sample of 163 children and adolescents (ages 2 to 20) were administered the VR Battery, and 45 children were administered the AM Battery on two occasions (time between testings was not reported in the Examiner's Manual). Coefficients for the VR Battery were high (.96) for Full IQ and Brief IQ. Composites ranged from .86 to .96, and individual subtest correlations were lower, ranging from .65 to .90. Coefficients for the AM battery ranged from .55 to .85, and coefficients for the Examiner Rating Scales ranged from .76 to .94 across three age groups (2–5, 6–10, and 11–20).

Objectivity Confirmation

The Examiner's Manual does not report any attempt to correlate agreement between two interpreters of test results.

Statistical Confirmation

Statistical data on validity, reliability, and norms is in the Examiner's Manual.

Special Features

Acronym

Leiter-R.

Levels of the Test

There are two test batteries: (1) Visualization and Reasoning (VR) and (2) Attention and Memory (AM). The Leiter-R is divided by four age groupings (2–3, 4–5, 6–10, and 11–20). Not all subtests are administered to all age groups. There are also four rating scales: Examiner Rating, Parent Rating, Teacher Rating, and Child's Self Rating.

Number of Test Forms

One.

Norm-Referenced?

Yes. The Tryout Edition was administered to 550 children and adolescents in 1994–1995. The Tryout Edition included 704 items in 23 subtests. The subjects included 225 typical children and 325 children with disabilities. Subjects ranged in age from 2 years to 22 years, 7 months. The children were representative of all four Census regions of the United States. Data from the Tryout Edition was analyzed and the optimal set of items was selected for the Standardization Edition of the Leiter-R. The Leiter-R was standardized on 1,719 typical children and adolescents and 692 atypical/disabled children and adolescents in 1996. The Leiter-R standardization sample includes the same proportions of ethnicity as found in the 1993 U.S. Census update survey. Standardization was carefully constructed to accurately represent the child's age, gender, and socioeconomic status.

Criterion-Referenced?

Yes. The criteria used for the Leiter-R are Growth Scales. These scales are criterion-referenced as each subtest item carries a growth value. These values range from

380 to 560 and explain the relative item difficulty of each item. The Growth Scale scores provide a quantitative measure of the child's nonverbal cognition on a scale that is referenced to the domain of all skills tapped by the Leiter-R, rather than referenced to the norm sample.

Feasibility Considerations

Testing Time

The Leiter-R is an untimed test. The Brief IQ Screener can be administered in approximately 25 minutes, and the Full Scale IQ can be administered in about 40 minutes. The AM Battery can be administered in about 40 minutes, and the Brief Memory Process Screener can be administered in about 25 minutes.

For Testing Groups? Individuals?

Individuals.

Test Administration and Scoring

Administration of the test and recording scores on the Record Forms and Examiner's Rating Scale is clearly covered in the Examiner's Manual. The Teaching Trials for each age group are noted on each easel page with suggestions relative to administration. Only nonverbal gestures and cues are used by the examiner and the subjects respond by pointing, gesturing, or eye pointing.

The Leiter-R has been developed for a wide variety of user groups, experienced psychologists, occupational therapists, speech and language pathologists, educational diagnosticians, special educators, and resource teachers. All professionals who use the Leiter-R are expected to adhere to the ethical standards or competencies developed by their professional organizations. Professional supervision in the administration and interpretation of the Leiter-R is suggested by the authors. In addition, users would benefit from "workshops on intelligence assessment or in the interpretation of other cognitive batteries similar to Leiter-R" (Examiner's Manual, p. 13).

Test Materials and Approximate Costs

Complete kit: $850; Record Forms, VR and AM Batteries (20): $25; Attention Sustained Booklet A, Ages 2–3 (20): $15; Attention Sustained Booklet B, Ages 4–5 (20): $15; Attention Sustained Booklet C, Ages 6–21 (20): $15; Growth Profile Booklet (20): $25; Manual: $75.

Adequacy of Test Manuals

The Examiner's Manual is user-friendly and clearly written. Examiners are encouraged to read the manual from cover to cover before attempting to administer the Leiter-R.

Excerpts from Other Test Reviews

"Excellent test materials, along with a comprehensive Examiner's Manual that also serves as a technical manual, go a long way toward making the Leiter-R a solid measurement instrument" (Marco, 2001).

"The Leiter-R is recommended as an excellent contemporary test of nonverbal intellectual ability . . . careful attention has been paid to all aspects of its development and psychometric qualities" (Stinnett, 2001).

"The test is adequately standardized. And there is good evidence the IQs and composite scores are reliable" (Salvia & Ysselydyke, 2001, p. 332).

Ordering Information

Publisher

Stoelting Company, 620 Wheat Lane, Wood Dale, IL 60191; Phone: 630-860-9700; Fax: 630-860-9775; Web site: www.stoeltingco.com/tests.

Authors

Gale H. Roid and Lucy J. Miller.

Publication Date

1997.

Cautions and Comments

The original Leiter Scale was constructed in 1929 for the purpose of assessing the intellectual abilities of special needs children who might have difficulty responding verbally. Five revisions were published between 1934 and 1948. Grace Arthur published an adaptation of the original Leiter in 1949. The Leiter-R has gone through extensive revisions from these earlier versions, but has maintained the overall goal of providing a much-needed instrument to be used with children who have difficulty "responding verbally." Stinnett (2001) indicates that the Leiter-R "represents a significant modernization and upgrade of an historic icon" (p. 687). The authors caution that the interpretation of the Leiter-R should not be just a look at "scores," but the examiner must look at the whole child in context with his environment. Of course, the Leiter-R can provide the necessary placement information required by federal and state regulations. When an examiner must evaluate a child who is nonverbal or has limited English agility, the Leiter-R can easily "fit the bill" and provide the educator with the information needed and required for placement.

References

Hammill, D. D., Brown, L., & Bryant, B. R. (1992). *A consumer's guide to tests in print* (2nd ed.). Austin, TX: PRO-ED.

Marco, G. L. (2001). Review of the Leiter International Performance Scale-Revised. In B. S. Plake & J. C. Impara (Eds,), *The Fourteenth Mental Measurements Yearbook* (pp. 683–687). Lincoln, NE: The Buros Institute of Mental Measurements.

Salvia, J., & Ysseldyke, J. E. (2001). *Assessment* (8th ed.). Boston: Houghton Mifflin.

Stinnett, T. A. (2001). Review of the Leiter International Performance Scale-Revised. In B. S. Plake & J. C. Impara (Eds.), *The Fourteenth Mental Measurements Yearbook* (pp. 687–692). Lincoln, NE: The Buros Institute of Mental Measurements.

Naglieri Nonverbal Ability Test (NNAT),
for testing groups from kindergarten through grade 12
Reviewed by Aileen C. Lau-Dickinson, Ed.D., Special Education Administration

---

Usefulness of the Test for Educators

Test Author's Purpose

"The Naglieri Nonverbal Ability Test (NNAT) is a brief, culture-fair, nonverbal measure of school ability" (Multilevel Technical Manual, p. 1).

Decision-Making Applications

According to the authors, the NNAT is "appropriate as a measure of general ability and as a predictor of scholastic achievement for children in all grades" (Multilevel Technical Manual, p. 4). The NNAT can be used to make educational decisions for those students who have hearing, language, or motor impairments, and for children with impaired color vision. The NNAT would also be useful for children with limited English proficiency. The NNAT is a revision of the expanded and short forms of the Matrix Analogies Test.

Relevant Population

There are seven levels, designed for children from kindergarten through grade 12: Level A (kindergarten), Level B (grade 1), Level C (grade 2), Level D (grades 3–4), Level E (grades 5–6), Level F (grades 7–9), and Level G (grades 10–12) (Multilevel Technical Manual, p. 2).

Characteristics Described

All test items follow the same format, in which the student examines the relationships among the parts of a design (matrix) and "decide[s] which response is the correct one based on the information inherent in the item" (Multilevel Technical Manual, p. 2). All of the information needed to solve each item is included in the item. "The geometric shapes composing NNAT items are universal, so NNAT can be used with diverse population of students" (Multilevel Technical Manual, p. 1). Each level of the NNAT has 38 test items. NNAT clusters include Pattern Completion (PC), Reasoning by Analogy (RA), Serial Reasoning (SR), and Spatial Visualization (SV). The clusters are assigned to NNAT levels.

Description of Test Items

Pattern Completion (PC) Items: The student is asked to look at a design within a large rectangle from which a portion is missing and to determine which response completes the pattern.

Reasoning by Analogy (RA) Items: The student is asked to recognize a logical relationship between several geometric shapes.

Serial Reasoning (SR) Items: The student is asked to recognize the sequence of shapes (e.g., circle-square-triangle) and how the sequence changes on the lower rows.

Spatial Visualization (SV) Items: The student is asked to recognize how two or more designs would look if combined.

Test Scores Obtained

Norm-referenced scores obtained include scaled scores converted from the raw scores. Grade-based percentile ranks, stanines, and normal curve equivalents (NCE) scores are all based on the scaled score. The total raw score for each level is used to obtain the Nonverbal Ability Index (NAI). The NAI is a standard score and can be converted to corresponding percentile ranks and stanines. Raw scores can also be converted to cluster scores by level and by grade. Cluster scores are items that were constructed in the same manner and have been combined in the NNAT to form clusters. The NNAT yields between two and four cluster scores at every level. Not every item belongs to a scorable cluster.

NNAT Levels and Assigned Clusters

Level	PC	RA	SR	SV
A	Yes	Yes	No	No
B	Yes	Yes	Yes	No
C	Yes	Yes	Yes	Yes
D	Yes	Yes	Yes	Yes
E	Yes	Yes	Yes	Yes
F	No	Yes	Yes	Yes
G	No	Yes	Yes	Yes

Technical Adequacy

Validity Confirmation

Test item validity was established by using items found in the Matrix Analogies Test-Expanded Form (MAT-EF) and the Matrix Analogies Test-Short Form (MAT-

SF). Many new items were developed, but the "original attributes" of those in the MAT were retained. Once the items were developed, two large-scale experiments were conducted to try out the new items. Approximately 6,000 students from grades K–4, 6, 8, and 10 were included in the tryouts. Statistical analyses followed the tryout to select the 38 items for each level for the standardization phase.

Test response validity was established for the NNAT by showing the relationship between the NNAT (school ability) and academic achievement. Correlations were established between the NNAT and the Stanford Achievement Test, Form S for the fall standardization sample for grades K–12. For the complete battery, correlations ranged from .58 to .69. Correlations between Aprenda: La Prueba De Logros En Espanol (2nd ed., 1997) (APRENDA2) and NNAT for the spring standardization sample were made using raw scores, and the correlation coefficients ranged from .26 to .67 for the Basic Battery comparisons. Total reading correlations ranged from .07 to .51 for grades K–12. These correlations are low to moderate. No other comparative studies were reported in the Multilevel Technical Manual.

Reliability Confirmation

No effort was made to repeatedly administer the test or test levels over time to correlate scores from different administrations. However, item responses of the test were correlated with one another to obtain reliability coefficients. Correlations were in the .80s and .90s in terms of raw scores from different grades K–12.

Objectivity Confirmation

The Multilevel Response Key contains the correct response number and the corresponding cluster for each item of Levels A through G.

The Side by Side Key contains separate keys for levels A through D, with copies of test booklet pages and the correct responses filled in, as well as the corresponding cluster for each item.

In the Key for Hand-Scorable Answer Document, stencils are placed on the answer document for Levels D through G, showing correct or incorrect responses and clusters.

There is no report of scorer correlations showing agreement between scorers who scored the same protocols. A scoring service is available from Harcourt Brace Educational Measurement.

Statistical Confirmation

Statistical data on validity and reliability is found in the Multilevel Technical Manual, and spring and fall norms are found in the Multilevel Norms Booklets.

Special Features

Acronym

NNAT.

Levels of the Test

There are seven levels of the test, with each level designed for a different grade or grades (see "Characteristics Described" above).

Number of Test Forms

One.

Norm-Referenced?

Yes. The NNAT was administered to 22,600 children in grades K–12 in the fall of 1995 and 67,000 children in grades K–12 in the spring of 1996. Standardization occurred at the same time as the SAT-9 and APRENDA-2. School districts were selected through use of a stratified random sampling technique. The stratification was done by state. Schools were selected that represented socioeconomic status, urbanicity, and ethnicity typical of the national school population.

Criterion-Referenced?

No.

Feasibility Considerations

Testing Time

Approximately 30 to 45 minutes.

For Testing Groups? Individuals?

Groups.

Test Administration and Scoring

Users of the test can purchase a scoring service from Harcourt Brace Educational Measurements or may score the test in the district using a reflected light scanner. A guide is available for interpreting the scores. The Multilevel Technical Manual and the Multilevel Norms Booklets give no guidelines for those persons administering the test. It is assumed that educators giving the test would have experience in the administration of group tests.

Test Materials and Approximate Costs

Technical Manual: $78.50.

Examination Kits (includes one copy each of Machine-Scorable or Reusable Test Booklets, Multilevel Directions for Administering, and Machine-Scorable Answer Document for Levels E–G): $23.50.

Machine Scorable Test Booklets, Levels A–D (includes directions) (25): $87.50.

Reusable Hand-Scorable Test, Booklets Levels E–G (includes directions) (25): $63.50.

Hand-Scorable Test Booklets, Levels A–D (includes directions) (25): $63.50.

Side-by-Side Keys for Hand-Scorable Test Booklets, Levels A–D: $44.50.

Stencil Keys for Hand-Scorable Answer Documents, Levels D–G: $22.

Response Keys (list of correct responses—all levels): $30.

Norms Books (spring and fall): $60.

Adequacy of Test Manuals

Two manuals are available: the Multilevel Norms Booklets (Spring and Fall) and the Multilevel Technical Manual. It would seem that these manuals could easily be combined, as there is a good bit of repetition. The manuals provide limited information on the administration of the test itself and no item-by-item descriptions. Overall, the manuals are adequate but lack detail.

Excerpts from Other Test Reviews

"The NNAT could be an acceptable instrument for users who need a quick, narrow-score estimate of nonverbal general intellectual ability" (Stinnett 2001, pp. 819–822).

Trevisan (2001) offers the following three cautions and criticisms regarding the NNAT: "The NNAT may not be accepted by many states for placing students into special programs . . . the NNAT does not provide any connection or information about a student's verbal ability . . . the validity evidence for the NNAT is insufficient" (p. 824).

Ordering Information

Publisher

The Psychological Corporation, 19500 Bulverde Road, San Antonio, TX 78259; Phone: 800-228-0752; Fax: 210-339-5873; Web site: www.psychcorp.com.

Author

Jack A. Naglieri.

Publication Date

1996–1997.

Cautions and Comments

The NNAT is an extension and revision of the Matrix Analogies Test-Short Form published in 1985. It is an attempt to screen general nonverbal ability and to identify gifted students for whom English is a second language or other students with limited

English proficiency, low verbal or nonverbal at-risk students with potential academic problems, and students with learning disability. The NNAT was standardized on more than 90,000 students, but test-retest reliability is not reported and validity studies are limited. There are several "nonverbal ability/intelligence tests" on the market that could provide important correlations with the NNAT. Validity studies with such tests as the Leiter International Performance Scale-Revised (Leiter-R), the Universal Non-verbal Intelligence Test (UNIT), the Test of Non-Verbal Intelligence (TONI-3), and the Stoelting Brief Nonverbal Intelligence Test (S-BIT) would be advantageous.

The manuals that accompany the NNAT offer only limited details regarding psychometric data. Little detailed information is offered in the manuals regarding test item descriptions and administration and scoring of test items. For those educators who need information about nonverbal ability for large groups of students, the NNAT may be considered for inclusion in the test repertoire.

References

Stinnett, T. A. (2001). Review of the Naglieri Nonverbal Ability Test. In B. S. Plake & J. C. Impara (Eds.), *The Fourteenth Mental Measurements Yearbook* (pp. 819–822). Lincoln, NE: The Buros Institute of Mental Measurements.

Trevisan, M. S. (2001). Review of the Naglieri Nonverbal Ability Test. In B. S. Plake & J. C. Impara (Eds.), *The Fourteenth Mental Measurements Yearbook* (pp. 822–824). Lincoln, NE: The Buros Institute of Mental Measurements.

Otis-Lennon School Ability Test, Seventh Edition (OLSAT 7),
for testing groups from kindergarten through grade 12
Reviewed by Aileen C. Lau-Dickinson, Ed.D., Special Education Administration

---

Usefulness of the Test for Educators

Test Authors' Purpose

"OLSAT 7 is designed to measure those verbal, quantitative, and figural reasoning skills that are most closely related to scholastic achievement" (Technical Manual, p. 7).

Decision-Making Applications

The OLSAT 7 is designed "to assess examinees' ability to cope with school learning tasks, to suggest their possible placement for school learning functions, and to evaluate their achievement in relation to the talents they bring to school learning situations" (Directions for Administering, p. 5). It is difficult to ascertain specific uses of the OLSAT 7 that are warranted. Hence, using it for educational decision-making is precarious. It would not be appropriate to use the OLSAT 7 test for placing or assigning students to particular grades and/or special programs.

Relevant Population

There are seven levels of the OLSAT 7 that collectively assess the range of ability of students from kindergarten through grade 12. Levels and grade equivalents are listed below:

Levels A and B (kindergarten and grade 1): Test items are dictated.

Level C (grade 2): First two parts are self-administered/others are dictated.

Levels D, E, F, and G (grades 3–12): All parts are self-administered.

Characteristics Described

Test items are divided into five clusters: Verbal Comprehension, Verbal Reasoning (Verbal Tasks), Pictorial Reasoning, Figural Reasoning, and Quantitative Reasoning (Nonverbal Tasks).

Description of Content of Levels A , B, and C (Grades K, 1, 2)

Verbal Comprehension: Items assess understanding of the nature of language. Subtest involves Following Directions.

Verbal Reasoning: Items assess the complex thought processes required at higher cognitive levels. Subtests include Aural Reasoning and Arithmetic Reasoning.

Pictorial Reasoning: Items assess an important nonverbal dimension in children who do not yet read fluently. Subtests include Picture Classification, Picture Analogy, and Picture Series.

Figural Reasoning: Items assess the ability to use geometric figures, to infer relationships, to perceive progressions, and to predict what would be the next step in those progressions. Subtests include Figural Classification, Figural Analogy, Pattern Matrix, and Figural Series.

Description of Content of Level D (Grade 3)

Verbal Comprehension: Items assess understanding of the nature of language. Subtests include Antonyms, Sentence Completion, and Sentence Arrangement.

Verbal Reasoning: Items assess the complex thought processes required at higher cognitive levels. Subtests include Arithmetic Reasoning, Logical Selection, Word/Letter Matrix, Verbal Analogy, and Verbal Classification.

Figural Reasoning: Items assess the ability to use geometric figures to infer relationships, to perceive progressions, and to predict what would be the next step in those progressions. Subtests include Figural Classification, Figural Analogy, Pattern Matrix, and Figural Series.

Quantitative Reasoning: Items comprise various types, including classifying, solving analogies, and completing numeric series.

Description of the Content of Levels E, F, and G (Grades 4–5, 6–8, and 9–12)

Verbal Comprehension: Items assess understanding of the nature of language. Subtests include Antonyms, Sentence Completion, and Sentence Arrangement.

Verbal Reasoning: Items assess the complex thought processes required at higher cognitive levels. Subtests include Arithmetic Reasoning, Logical Selection, Word/Letter Matrix, Verbal Analogy, Verbal Classification, and Inference.

Figural Reasoning: Items assess the ability to reason with geometric figures. Subtests include Figural Analogy, Pattern Matrix, and Figural Series.

Quantitative Reasoning: Items assess the ability to use numbers in order to infer relationships, deduce computational rules, and predict outcomes. Subtests include Number Series, Numeric Inference, and Number Matrix.

(*Note*: Complete descriptions are found in the Directions for Administering for each level.)

Clusters /Test Items	Levels That Test These Clusters/Test Items						
Cluster/Item Type	A	B	C	D	E	F	G
VERBAL							
Verbal Comprehension							
Following Directions	X	X	X				
Antonyms				X	X	X	X
Sentence Completion				X	X	X	X
Sentence Arrangement				X	X	X	X
Verbal Reasoning							
Aural Reasoning	X	X	X				
Arithmetic Reasoning	X	X	X	X	X	X	X
Logical Selection				X	X	X	X
Word/Letter Matrix				X	X	X	X
Verbal Analogy				X	X	X	X
Verbal Classification				X	X	X	X
Inference					X	X	X
NONVERBAL							
Pictorial Reasoning							
Picture Classification	X	X	X				
Picture Analogies	X	X	X				
Picture Series	X	X	X				
Figural Reasoning							
Figural Classification	X	X	X	X			
Figural Analogy	X	X	X	X	X	X	X
Pattern Matrix	X	X	X	X	X	X	X
Figural Series	X	X	X	X	X	X	X

Clusters /Test Items	Levels That Test These Clusters/Test Items						
Cluster/Item Type	A	B	C	D	E	F	G
Quantitative Reasoning							
Number Series					X	X	X
Numeric Inference					X	X	X
Number Matrix					X	X	X

Source: OLSAT Content Outline, Directions and Administration, Figure 1.

Test Scores Obtained

According to the authors, the total score (total of verbal and nonverbal part scores) is the best indicator of students' learning ability (Directions for Administering, p. 6).

The OLSAT 7 provides scaled scores that can be converted to the School Ability Index (SAI: mean of 100 and standard deviation of 16), age- or grade-based percentile ranks, stanines, and normal curve equivalents. Scoring can be done by using hand-scored forms (norms can be located in the MultiLevel Fall or Spring Norms Manuals) or by using machine-scorable test booklets. The publisher will score the tests and prepare the reports. Instructions for Preparing Machine-Scorable Documents for Scoring are found in the Directions for Administering Manual for each test level. This service is particularly useful for schools that administer hundreds of tests.

Technical Adequacy

Validity Confirmation

Test item validity: The Technical Manual of the OLSAT 7 reports that the test items used in the test are a compilation of items from the fifth and sixth editions, as well as newly developed test items. All test items were reviewed and edited by editorial staff, measurement specialists, and psychologists for clarity, appropriateness of content, accuracy of correct answers, and overall quality. The Item Tryout took place in February 1994 with approximately 10,000 students from schools across the country. Test items selected for the standardization of the OLSAT 7 were those that met certain statistical criteria.

Test response validity: The Technical Manual reports that the OLSAT 7 was correlated with former editions of the OLSAT, the idea being that the same complex of skills that has been assessed in the past would correlate positively with those assessed by the OLSAT 7. Correlations were made between the OLSAT seventh edition and the OLSAT sixth edition and ranged from .77 to .82 for total scores at all levels of the OLSAT. The lowest correlation was found on Level F; here the Total Correlation was .77, the Verbal Correlation was .77, and the Nonverbal Correlation was .68. The Technical Manual Supplement reports additional evidence of the test response validity of the OLSAT 7. Correlations were determined by subtest and total scores of four achievement batteries and the OLSAT 7 verbal, nonverbal, and total scores. The achievement batteries included the Iowa Tests of Basic Skills, Tests of Achievement and Proficiency, the Comprehensive Test of Basic Skills, and the California Achievement Test. Data used for these correlations was collected from schools participating in the OLSAT Standardization Program. Four correlations were above .80, and these were total scores of OLSAT 7 and the Math Concepts and Problem Solving subtests from the Tests of Achievement and Proficiency and Math subtest from the California Achievement Test. The best correlations were found between the OLSAT 7 and the Comprehensive Test of Basic Skills, with correlations of total scores of ranging from .66 to .78 (see the Technical Manual Supplement for Tables of Correlations). In summarizing validity information, it appears that the OLSAT 7 relates to academic achievement. There are no validity studies reported relating the OLSAT 7 to the WISC-III or other intelligence tests.

Reliability Confirmation

No effort was made to repeatedly administer the test or levels of the test over time in order to correlate scores of repeated administrations. Reliability coefficients were reported reflecting the interrelationships of test items (internal consistency reliability of the OLSAT 7). This data was related to Total, Verbal, and Nonverbal scores and for the clusters on OLSAT 7. The reliabilites were generally in the .80s and .90s.

Objectivity Confirmation

No correlations of two independent hand scorings of the OLSAT 7 were reported in the Technical Manual.

Machine-test booklets are available at each level. After testing, these are sent to the publisher for scoring. Instructions for Preparing Machine Scorable Documents for Scoring are provided in the Directions and Administering Manual for each level of the OLSAT 7.

Statistical Confirmation

Statistical data on validity, reliability, and norms can be found in the Technical Manual, Technical Manual Supplement, Multilevel Fall Norms, and Multilevel Spring Norms booklets.

Special Features

Acronym

OLSAT 7.

Levels of the Test

There are seven levels of the OLSAT 7 to be used from kindergarten through grade 12.

Number of Test Forms

One for each level.

Norm-Referenced?

Yes. Approximately 150,000 students from 1,000 school districts across the nation participated in the spring standardization of the OLSAT 7 from April 3 to April 28, 1995, and approximately 200,000 students participated in the fall standardization of the OLSAT 7 from September 18 to October 13, 1995. The schools in the sample were chosen through a stratified random sampling technique, stratifying by state. Within each state, the samples were selected to be representative of the national school population based on data from the National Center for Education Statistics, U.S. Department of Education, 1992–1993.

Criterion-Referenced?

No.

Feasibility Considerations

Testing Time

The Practice Tests for each level are given separately approximately one week before the actual testing.

Level A, Grade K: Time 70 minutes over 2 sessions.

Level B, Grade 1: Time 70 minutes over 2 sessions.

Level C, Grade 2: Time 70 minutes over 2 sessions.

Level D, Grade 3: Time 60 minutes over 1 session.

Level E, Grades 4–5: Time 60 minutes over 1 session.

Level F, Grades 6–8: Time 60 minutes over 1 session.

Level G, Grades 9–12: Time 60 minutes over 1 session.

For Testing Groups? Individuals?

Groups.

Test Administration and Scoring

The test can be hand scored as well as scored by the publisher. The examinee fills in the answer in the Test Booklet directly below each test item. Training for testing is described and practiced with the Directions for Administering Practice Test and the Practice Test booklet. The Practice Test is administered one week prior to administering the complete test. The Administration of the Group Tests is described in the Directions for Administering and in the Test Booklet. The examiner's verbal directions to the students are color coded and numbered for easy administration. Directions are clear and spelled out for the examiner. According to the Directions for Administering, the "person responsible for administering OLSAT 7 does not need special training but must be able to carry out standard examination procedures . . . the examiner must become thoroughly familiar with these procedures before attempting to administer the test" (Directions for Administration, p. 9).

Test Materials and Approximate Costs

Technical Manual: $62.25; Norms Book: $62.50; Form 3, Levels A–G Machine-scorable test booklets including Directions for Administration (25): $83.50 (each level); Form 3, Levels A–D Test booklets (specify reusable or hand scorable, and level): $60.50 (each level); Scoring Keys (specify type): $22; Form 3, Practice Tests (25) (specify level) (includes Directions for Administration): $25.

Adequacy of Test Manuals

Several manuals are available with the OLSAT 7. There is a Technical Manual that includes information on Test Development, Standardization, Scores and Norms, and Technical Information. In addition there are two Multilevel Norm Manuals (Spring and Fall), and for each level there are Directions for Administering Practice Tests and Level Tests. These manuals are complete and user-friendly.

Excerpts from Other Test Reviews

DeStefano (2001) states a number of concerns regarding the OLSAT 7: "Perhaps the most serious weakness of the Seventh Edition of the OLSAT is the validity evidence presented in the Technical Manual. . . . the interpretation of OLSAT scores is an ambiguous endeavor and thus increased the risk of misuse. . . . in light of recent advances in cognitive theory, the theoretical foundations of the OLSAT 7 should be questioned. . . . No data relating to stability of OLSAT scores over time are currently available."

According to Goldman (2001), "Raw scores can be converted to School Ability Indexes, but there is no explanation of what these indexes are, although they resemble IQs. . . . Until a more complete technical manual addressing the doubts raised by this review is prepared to replace the Preliminary Technical Manual, one should proceed with caution in using this instrument."

Salvia and Ysseldyke (2001) state, "There is no support for stability. Evidence for validity is limited."

Ordering Information

Publisher

Harcourt Educational Measurement, 19500 Bulverde Road, San Antonio, TX 78259-3701; Phone: 800-211-8378; Fax: 877-576-1816; Web site: www.hemweb.com.

Authors

Arthur Otis and Roger T. Lennon.

Publication Date

1997.

Cautions and Comments

The first in the Otis series of ability tests, based on Dr. Arthur Otis' graduate work at Stanford University, was published in 1918. This is the seventh edition of the Otis-Lennon School Ability Test. The name was changed from Otis-Lennon Mental Ability Test to School Ability test to indicate that the test evaluates achievement in relation to the "talents" that students bring to school learning situations. However, the authors state that the OLSAT 7 is "based upon the same theory of the nature and organization of cognitive abilities and seeks to serve the same purposes as earlier editions in the Otis series" (Technical Manual, p. 7). This statement is confusing and makes it difficult to distinguish between testing of "mental abilities" and/or "school abilities." The use of "school abilities" to define "talents" or "ability to cope with learning tasks" is not clear. It is difficult to determine just what the OLSAT 7 does measure and for what purpose. The authors have attempted to address the validity issues that have been raised by other reviewers by publishing a Technical Manual Supplement (1998) in which they have presented correlations between the OLSAT 7 and scores on various achievement test batteries. Reliability was not confirmed by correlating scores of repeated test administrations of the same levels of the test.

References

DeStefano, L. (2001). Review of the Otis-Lennon School Ability Test, Seventh Edition. In B. S. Plake & J. C. Impara (Eds.), *The Fourteenth Mental Measurements Yearbook* (pp. 875–881). Lincoln, NE: The Buros Institute of Mental Measurements.

Goldman, B.A. (2001). Review of the Otis-Lennon School Ability Test, Seventh Edition. In B. S. Plake & J. C. Impara (Eds.), *The Fourteenth Mental Measurements Yearbook* (pp. 875–881). Lincoln, NE: The Buros Institute of Mental Measurements.

Salvia, J., & Ysseldyke, J. E. (2001). *Assessment* (8th ed.). Boston: Houghton Mifflin.

Peabody Picture Vocabulary Test-III (PPVT-III),
for testing individuals from 2 years, 6 months through 90+ years of age
Reviewed by Aileen C. Lau-Dickinson, Ed.D., Special Education Administration

---

Usefulness of the Test for Educators

Test Authors' Purpose

The authors state that there are two purposes for the PPVT-III. First, "the PPVT-III is designed as a measure of an examinee's receptive (hearing) vocabulary. Second, the PPVT-III serves as a screening test of verbal ability, or as one element in a comprehensive test battery of cognitive processes" (Examiner's Manual, p. 2).

Decision-Making Applications

The PPVT-III is useful for making decisions regarding the detection of a language impairment at all ages. In that sense, the PPVT-III can be considered a placement assessment for language therapy. For adults it can be used to determine the degree of aphasia and, in selected geriatric cases, the extent of vocabulary deterioration. In that context, placement in language remediation would be appropriate. The PPVT-III is also useful for testing preschool children, where vocabulary acquisition is so important as an indicator of a child's linguistic and cognitive development. Therefore, the PPVT-III can be considered a placement assessment for placing a child or adult into language therapy.

Relevant Population

The PPVT-III is designed for persons aged 2 years, 6 months through 90+. It is relevant for all populations, but can be especially helpful when information is needed for the following specific populations:

Preschool populations: Vocabulary acquisition is an important factor.

English as a Second Language: PPVT-III provides a measure of English language proficiency.

Autistic and withdrawn populations: No need to speak or interact verbally with the examiner.

Cerebral palsy: Response to the test can be a signal of "yes or no" as the examiner points to each choice.

Visual disabilities: Because the pictures are black-and-white line drawings and are free of fine detail, individuals with visual disability are not penalized.

Characteristics Described

The PPVT-III is an individually administered, untimed, norm-referenced, wide-range test available in two parallel forms: Form IIIA and Form IIIB. There are 204 test items grouped into 17 sets of 12 items per set. Items are arranged in order of increasing difficulty and include a good balance of gerunds, nouns, and descriptors. Twenty categories are included to ensure some degree of balance in context. These categories are: (1) actions; (2) adjectives; (3) animals; (4) body parts; (5) books, stationery, and school and office equipment; (6) buildings and outdoor structures; (7) clothing and accessories; (8) emotions and facial expressions; (9) foods, except produce; (10) fruits and vegetables; (11) geographical scenes; (12) household objects; (13) musical instruments; (14) references to people or humanoid forms; (15) plants; (16) shapes, signs, and symbols; (17) tools, machinery, and scientific apparatus; (18) toys and recreational items; (19) vehicles and their parts; (20) workers, such as carpenter.

There are four stimulus pictures on each PicturePlate and three detractors in each PicturePlate. The examinee selects the named picture from the examiners verbal stimulus. For example: Point to _____, Show me _____.

Test Scores Obtained

Test scores obtained include standard score equivalents by age, percentile ranks, normal curve equivalents, stanines, and age equivalents. Raw scores are easily obtained establishing the number of errors and subtracting these from the ceiling item. Using the tables, raw scores are converted to deviation-type norms (standard score, percentile rank, normal curve equivalent, and stanine) and developmental-type norms (age equivalent). A graphic display of deviational-type norm scores can be shown on the front of the Performance Record. The ASSIST software program is available for computer-assisted preparation or reports.

Technical Adequacy

Validity Confirmation

Test item validity was established by choosing an item pool which began in the 1950s with an examination of all entries in the 1953 edition of *Webster's New Collegiate Dictionary*. 3,885 words were selected whose meanings could be clearly illustrated with black-and-white line drawings. The original PPVT (1959) utilized 300 stimulus words from this initial pool, and an expanded item pool of possible stimulus words was assembled in the 1970s. The primary source for the new words was the *Webster's New Collegiate Dictionary*. Of the 300 original words, 144 words were retained. These decisions were based on numerous studies. The item pool was further expanded for the PPVT-III. Various resources were used to identify potential words for the PPVT-III. 240 field test items were selected for each of the two new forms so that the weakest items per form could be deleted. The 480 words were used in the carefully controlled national tryout or field test of the PPVT-III. 908 subjects (505 females and 403 males) aged 2 years, 6 months through 21 years with equal representation by gender, region of the country, and the major racial/ethnic groups were included in the national tryout. Item analyses were conducted with the responses to identify poorly discriminating items. The tryout data and subsequent item analyses provided the necessary item calibrations so that the remaining items could be ordered into two parallel test forms with smooth and equal progressions of difficulties. Using the data from the national tryout, the 480 test items were reduced to the final 408 items. Two parallel test forms were constructed from this reduced item pool, each consisting of 204 items, divided into 17 sets of 12 items. A national testing program was conducted at 240 test sites, and these were balanced across central cities, suburban and small town communities, and rural areas. 650 examiners took part in the testing. Following standardization, all item responses were entered and scored by computer. Items were analyzed using the classical item statistics of difficulty and discrimination or item-to-total correlation. The items were calibrated for difficulty, and all items were determined to have good discrimination and good fits. No items were deleted, and all 204 items in each form were retained for the final test. Items were also submitted to a bias review panel to ensure that none of the items contained racial, ethnic, or gender biases.

Test response validity was established by relating the PPVT-III to the Wechsler Intelligence Scale for Children-Third Edition (WISC-III). 41 children aged 7 years, 11 months through 14 years, 4 months were administered the two tests in counterbalanced order. The correlations ranged from .82 to .92. Further, 28 adolescents aged 13 years through 17 years, 8 months were administered the PPVT-III and the Kaufman Adolescents and Adult Intelligence Test (KAIT). The correlations ranged from .78 to .91. In addition, the PPVT-III and the Kaufman Brief Intelligence Test (K-BIT) were administered to 80 adults aged 18 years through 71 years, 1 month. The correlations ranged from .62 to .82. Finally, the PPVT-III and the Oral and Written Language Scale (OWLS) were administered to 41 children aged 3 years through 5 years, 8 months and 43 children aged 8 years, 1 month through 12 years, 10 months. The correlations ranged from .63 to .83. Additional information on studies using the PPVT-III with special groups such as gifted, mild mental retardation, learning disabilities, or language impairments can be found in the Technical References.

Reliability Confirmation

Alternate forms reliability was established by administering both forms to all subjects in the standardization sample. All persons in the standardization sample (2,725 subjects) took both test forms (Forms IIIA and IIIB) in a counterbalanced design in one session. Alternate-forms reliability coefficients computed from standard scores ranged from .88 to .96 with a median value of .94. Alternate-forms reliability coefficients computed from raw scores ranged from .89 to .99 with a median value of .95.

Objectivity Confirmation

The PPVT-III is objective in that there is only one correct answer for each test item. These correct answers have been established through extensive field and standardization testing of the test items. (See the section on test item validity in the Examiner's Manual.) There is no evidence of inter-rater reliability coefficients given in the Examiner's Manual.

Statistical Confirmation

Statistical data on validity, reliability, and norms can be found in the Examiner's Manual for the PPVT-III and the Norms Booklet for the PPVT-III.

Special Features

Acronym

PPVT-III.

Levels of the Test

Even though there is only one level of the test, the items are arranged in order of increasing difficulty and the test has been standardized for individuals from persons aged 2 years, 6 months to 90+ years of age.

Number of Test Forms

There are two parallel test forms, designated as Form IIIA and Form IIIB. Each form contains four training items and 204 test items grouped into 17 sets of 12 items each. The items are arranged in order of increasing difficulty. Each item consists of four black-and-white illustrations arranged on a page called a PicturePlate. The task of the test taker is to select the picture that best represents the meaning of a stimulus word presented orally by the examiner.

Norm-Referenced?

Yes. The PPVT-III was normed in 1997. The norming sample totaled 2,275 individuals and stratified into the 25 age categories ranging from 2 years, 6 months to 90+ years of age. This grouping can be found in Table 3.1 (Examiner's Manual, p. 41). The standardized sample was selected to match proportionately the U.S. census data from the March 1994 *Current Population Survey*. The sample represented geographical regions, education levels, race or ethnic groups, and special education groups.

Criterion-Referenced?

No.

Other Features

Features of the PPVT-III include:

1. individual administration
2. two parallel forms
3. clear black-and-white line drawings
4. wide-range use
5. quick administration
6. untimed administration
7. no reading required by examinee
8. no oral or written response required
9. objective, rapid scoring
10. norm-referenced interpretation and norms range from ages 2 years, 6 months to 90+ years
11. only items over critical range administered
12. training items provided to ensure initial success
13. 204 test items in each form
14. test items grouped into 17 sets of 12 in each form
15. locator tabs identify the 17 sets of test items

16. a portable TestKit that provides efficient transporting and storage of test materials

Feasibility Considerations

Testing Time

Testing time averages only 11 to 12 minutes. Time requirements will vary among examinees.

For Testing Groups? Individuals?

Individuals.

Test Administration and Scoring

Training items are provided in the TestKit to introduce the test. Test items are administered in sets of 12. The examiner starts with the first item in each set and administers items to obtain a basal, which is one or no errors in a set. The examiner tests until eight or more errors are found in a set. The total number of errors is then recorded on the Performance Record. Subtracting the number of errors from the ceiling item (the last item in the Ceiling Set) establishes the raw score. Raw scores are converted to standard scores, percentiles, normal curve equivalents, stanines, and age equivalents, and these are found in the Norms Booklet. The ASSIST CD-ROM is available to convert raw scores into standard scores. ASSIST will generate group reports by score, school, grade, or age.

No certification is required to administer the PPVT-III. However, it is wise for the examiner to receive supervision when administering the test for the first time.

Test Materials and Approximate Costs

PPVT-IIIA and IIIB TestKits with EVT (Expressive Vocabulary Test): $369.95; PPVT-IIIA and IIIB TestKits with ASSIST: $245.95; PPVT-IIIA and IIIB TestKits with EVT and ASSIST: $567.95.

Adequacy of Test Manuals

The Examiner's Manual is clearly written with detailed information for administration. A more comprehensive treatment of the PPVT-III standardization procedures can be found in the Technical References for the PPVT-III (Williams & Wang, 1997).

Excerpts from Other Test Reviews

The PPVT-III has been reviewed by Bessai (1998) and Wasyliw (1998). Bessai states, "PPVT-III has a wide range and can be used as readily with preschool children as it can with adolescents and adults" (p. 909). Wasyliw complimented the test by saying, "The PPVT-III is one of the most user-friendly psychometric instruments of its kind I have yet seen . . . it is much easier to administer than the PPVT-R. . . . the PPVT-III has improved reliability and updated norms" (p. 910).

Ordering Information

Publisher

American Guidance Service, Inc., 4201 Woodland Road, Circle Pines, MN 55014-1796; Phone: 800-328-2560; Fax: 800-471-8457; Web site: www.agsnet.com.

Authors

Lloyd M. Dunn and Leota M. Dunn.

Publication Date

1997 (original edition 1959).

Cautions and Comments

The PPVT has a long and successful history. The first edition was published in 1959 as a "brief intelligence test." It was widely used for that purpose; unfortunately, some children were misplaced into special education programs based on the results of the PPVT. The PPVT-R was published in 1981 and its use as an "intelligence" test was abandoned and it was described as a "receptive vocabulary test." Dunn and Dunn observe that the PPVT-R "is not a comprehensive test of general intelligence." The PPVT-III (1997) is a welcome revision of the original PPVT published in 1959. Standardization procedures have been carefully followed, and the validity and reliability of the test appears to be more than adequate. Care must be taken that the PPVT-III tests receptive (listening) vocabulary. However, the authors indicate that it can be used as a screening device for verbal ability, which is one element in a comprehensive test battery of cognitive processes.

References

Bessai, F. (1998). Review of the Peabody Picture Vocabulary Test-III. In J. C. Impara & B. S. Plake (Eds.), *The Thirteenth Mental Measurements Yearbook* (pp. 908–910). Lincoln, NE: The Buros Institute of Mental Measurements.

Wasyliw, O. (1998). Review of the Peabody Picture Vocabulary Test-III. In J. C. Impara & B. S. Plake (Eds.), *The Thirteenth Mental Measurements Yearbook* (pp. 910–911). Lincoln, NE: The Buros Institute of Mental Measurements.

Williams, K. T., & Wang, J. (1997). *Technical Reference to the Peabody Picture Vocabulary Test-Third Edition (PPVT-III)*. Circle Pines, MN: American Guidance Service.

Screening Assessment for Gifted Elementary and Middle School Students (SAGES-II), for testing individuals and groups from 5 years through 14 years, 11 months of age
Reviewed by Aileen C. Lau-Dickinson, Ed.D., Special Education Administration

---

Usefulness of the Test for Educators

Test Authors' Purpose

"The SAGES-II was developed to address the need for a technically adequate measure that is not biased and that identifies potentially gifted students in two of the most frequently served areas: intelligence and achievement" (Examiner's Manual, p. 14).

Decision-Making Applications

Multiple abilities have been emphasized in definitions of giftedness. In 1972, Marland indicated that general intellectual abilities included verbal, number, spatial, memory, and reasoning factors most often associated with superior performance in school and on intelligence tests. Definitions of giftedness vary from state to state: 49 states recognize intelligence and achievement, 41 recognize creativity, 35 recognize artistic abilities, and 30 recognize leadership (Coleman & Gallager, 1995).

The SAGES-II emphasizes intelligence and achievement and is designed and useful for identifying children for gifted classes. The SAGES-II meets the criteria required by 49 states. In that sense, the SAGES-II can be considered a placement test for identifying gifted children. It is also a screening instrument for a group of children being considered for gifted programs or as a second-level screening instrument for only the nominated group. The SAGES-II provides norms for those children in general education classes and those already identified as gifted.

Relevant Population

The SAGES-II has been developed for children in kindergarten through eighth grade. It is appropriate for students ranging in age from 5 years to 14 years, 11 months. Two levels of the test are available (K–3 and 4–8), and there are three subtests in each level.

Characteristics Described

The subtests within each level are as follows:

Subtest 1: Mathematics/Science. This subtest samples achievement in mathematics and science. Subtest items require recall, understanding, and application of ideas and basic concepts in the content areas.

Subtest 2: Language Arts/Social Studies. This subtest samples achievement in language arts and social studies. Items require the student to recall, understand, and apply ideas and basic concepts.

Subtest 3: Reasoning. This subtest samples one aspect of intelligence or aptitude—problem solving. This subtest requires the child to solve new problems by identifying relationships among figures and pictures. The child must recognize pictures or figures, deduce relationships, and then find other pictures or figures that relate to the stimulus in the same way. These are analogies that require "second-order relations."

Test Scores Obtained

This is a norm-referenced test and provides percentiles and quotients for both the normal and the gifted normative samples. Quotients allow examiners to make comparisons across subtests and can give the examiner information for interpreting the "probability of giftedness"; percentile ranks indicate the child's ranking as compared to the standardized sample.

Guidelines for Interpreting Quotients Obtained from the Normative Sample

Quotient	Probability of Giftedness	Percent Included
> 130	Very Likely	2.34
121–130	Likely	6.87
111–120	Possibly	16.12
90–110	Unlikely	49.51
80–89	Very Unlikely	16.12
70–79	Very Unlikely	6.87
< 70	Very Unlikely	2.34

Source: Examiner's Manual, Table 3.3, p. 49.

A Profile/Scoring Sheet is provided, and the child's scores can be profiled. The examiner can get a gross estimate of the student's strengths and weaknesses across subtests by visually scanning the profile.

Technical Adequacy

Validity Confirmation

Test item validity was established for this test by first reviewing tests and the professional literature. Then an experimental edition of the test, with 25 items in each of the core areas for each of the three levels (K–2, 3–5, and 6–8), was developed. These items were submitted to university professors, graduate students, teachers of the gifted, gifted students, and other professionals for critical review. The original items were administered to 1,465 gifted and normal students in grades K–2, 1,500 gifted and normal students in grades 3–5, and 1,485 gifted and normal students in grades 6–8. Item discriminating power and item difficulty were ascertained for each item at each of the three levels. Following this analysis, items were revised or discarded. The norming version of the SAGES-II was created.

Test response validity was established by correlations between the SAGES-II and the Wechsler Intelligence Scale for Children-Third Edition (WISC-III), the Otis-Lennon School Ability Test (OLSAT), and the Stanford Achievement Test-Ninth Edition (SAT-9). Correlations with the WISC-III ranged from .71 to .89, with the OLSAT from .49 to .64, and with the SAT-9 from .47 to .53. Correlations are high enough to give support for the validity of the SAGES-2 scores.

Reliability Confirmation

Sixty children were tested twice, with a two-week period between testings. The children ranged in age from 6 through 14 and attended an elementary school and a junior high school. Correlations ranged from .78 to .97. These correlations established sufficient confidence in the test scores' stability over time.

Objectivity Confirmation

Level K–3: There is no separate answer sheet for the K–3 level of the SAGES-II: children mark their responses directly on their test booklets. The examiner reads all test items aloud. There are no basals, and ceilings are achieved when the child misses three out of five consecutive items. A scoring key is provided for the multiple-choice test.

Level 4–8: A scoring key for the SAGES-II: 4–8 is available for scoring the multiple-choice test items. The child selects a letter, which he places on the line next to the corresponding test item number in Section VI, Student Response Form. After the examiner reads the examples, the children read the questions to themselves. A Scoring Transparency is used for scoring the responses. There are no basals, and ceilings are achieved when the child misses three out of five consecutive items.

Two staff persons at PRO-ED's research department independently scored a set of 72 completed protocols. The protocols were randomly selected from the normative sample. The sample ranged in age from 5 through 14 years. Correlations were reported by age intervals, and the correlations ranged from .91 to .99. These correlations provide convincing evidence of high scorer agreement.

Statistical Confirmation

Statistical data on validity, reliability, and norms can be found in the Examiner's Manual for the SAGES-II.

Special Features

Acronym

SAGES-II.

Levels of the Test

There are two overlapping levels: K–3 and 4–8.

Number of Test Forms

One.

Norm-Referenced?

Yes. The SAGES-II was normed on a sample of 5,313 persons in 28 states. The samples used to prepare the SAGES-II norms were tested in 1998–1999. There were two norming samples: "the normal sample" and the "gifted sample." The samples were representative of the following demographics: geographic area, gender, race, residence, ethnicity, family income, educational attainment of parents, and disability status. The percentages for these characteristics were compared with those reported in the *Statistical Abstract of the United States* (1997). The "normal sample" included 3,023 students and the "gifted sample" included 2,290 students.

Criterion-Referenced?

No.

Feasibility Considerations

Testing Time

Thirty to 45 minutes should be allowed for each subtest, or a total of 90 or 135 minutes for the entire test. For younger children, individual subtests can be administered on different days to reduce fatigue.

For Testing Groups? Individuals?

Groups and individuals. The SAGES-II can be administered to groups as large as 30 children. Smaller groups of 10 to 15 are recommended when testing younger children.

Test Administration and Scoring

The SAGES-II: K–3 test is administered by the examiner reading aloud the directions for each test item and the child or children marking the correct answer in the Student Response Booklet. There is no separate answer sheet for the K–3 subtest. The examiner then transfers the answers to the Profile/Scoring Sheet. Ceilings are determined when the child misses three out of five consecutive items. The raw score is determined by counting all correct answers below the ceiling. Examples of scoring the SAGES-II: K–3 are found in the Examiner's Manual (pp. 21–22).

The SAGES-II: 4–8 test requires the student to mark responses in Section VI on the back of the Profile/Response Sheet by placing the letter of the correct response next to its corresponding item number. The examiner scores the responses using the SAGES-II: 4–8 Scoring Transparency.

The authors suggest that examiners who give the SAGES-II should have some formal training in assessment and supervised practice in using the test. Knowledge of the local school policies and state regulations is desirable when the purpose of testing is to qualify a child for a special program.

Test Materials and Approximate Costs

Complete Kit, which includes Examiner's Manual, Response Forms for K–3 and 4–8 (10), K–3 Profile/Scoring Sheets (50), 4–8 Profile/Scoring Sheets (50), and a 4–8 Scoring Transparency: $179; Response Booklets (K–3 and 4–8) (10): $14; Profile/Scoring Sheets (K–3) (pad of 50): $24; Profile/Scoring Sheets (4–8) (pad of 50): $24.

Adequacy of Test Manuals

The Examiner's Manual includes specific administration instructions. For the SAGES-II: K–3 test, the teacher reads each question to the children and the children select the best answer. These instructions are color-coded in the Examiner's Manual and are specific and clear. For the SAGES-II: 4–8 test, the students read the items silently from the SAGES-II: 4–8 Student Booklets and record their answers on the Profile/Scoring Sheet.

The Student Response Booklets are easy to follow and user-friendly for both levels of the test.

Excerpts from Other Test Reviews

Screening Assessment for Gifted Elementary Students (SAGES) and Screening Assessment for Gifted Elementary Students-Primary (SAGES-P), earlier versions of the SAGES-II, were reviewed by five different reviewers. "An excellent feature of the SAGES and SAGES-P is that they provide normative tables for both gifted and normal children, allowing for two types of group-referenced comparisons" (Lewandowski & Sussman, 1988; Moore, 1993; Urbina, 1995). Lewandowski and Sussman (1988, p. 714) reported that "the reliability data of the SAGES are impressive." Overall, the reviewers of the earlier versions felt that there was a scarcity of validity studies, including no information on the intercorrelations of the SAGES-P subtests (Urbina, 1995), no factor analysis (Coleman & Kim, 1989), and no prediction of group membership (Lewandowski & Sussman, 1988; Moore, 1993).

The authors report that they considered the reviewers' suggestions for improvement and took these suggestions into account when developing the SAGES-II (see pages ix–x of the Examiner's Manual).

No current reviews were located regarding SAGES-II.

Ordering Information

Publisher

PRO-ED, 8700 Shoal Creek Boulevard, Austin, TX 78757-6897; Phone: 800-897-3202; Fax: 800-397-7633: Web site: http://www.proedinc.com.

Authors

Susan K. Johnsen and Anne L. Corn.

Publication Date

2001.

Cautions and Comments

The authors have taken into account criticisms of the earlier versions of the SAGES-II and have made a number of excellent improvements. The normative data is current, as all new normative data was collected in the fall and spring of 1998–1999. Test-retest studies have been added, new validity studies have been conducted, and special attention has been paid to showing the test to be valid for a wide variety of subgroups as well as for a general school population. New federal and state guidelines concerning gifted education have been considered in the rationale for the SAGES-II.

School districts should find the SAGES-II an excellent instrument for identifying gifted students.

References

Coleman, L. J., & Kim, K. S. (1989). Review of Screening Assessment for Gifted Elementary Students. *Journal of Psychoeducational Assessment 7*, 272–277.

Coleman, M. R., & Gallagher, J. J. (1995). Gifted education: Historical perspectives and current concepts. In J. L. Genshaft, M. Gireley, & C. L. Hollinger (Eds.), *Serving gifted and talented students: A resource for school personnel* (pp. 3–16). Austin, TX: PRO-ED.

Lewandowski, L. J., & Sussman, K. R. (1988). Screening Assessment for Gifted Elementary Students (SAGES). *Reading Teacher 41*, 712–716.

Marland, S. (1972). *Education of the gifted and talented: Volume 1. Report to Congress of the United States by the U.S. Commissioner of Education.* Washington, DC: U.S. Government Printing Office.

Moore, S. D. (1993). Review of the SAGES and SAGES-P. *Roeper Review 16*, 54–57.

Urbina, S. (1995). Review of Screening Assessment for Gifted Elementary Students-Primary versions. In J. C. Conoley & J. C. Impara (Eds.), *The Twelfth Mental Measurements Yearbook* (pp. 935–936). Lincoln, NE: The Buros Institute of Mental Measurements.

Slosson Intelligence Test for Children and Adults-Revised (SIT-R),
for testing individuals from 4 through 18+ years of age
Reviewed by Aileen C. Lau-Dickinson, Ed.D., Special Education Administration

---

Usefulness of the Test for Educators

Test Authors' Purpose

"The SIT-R can be used in situations where a quick estimate of general verbal cognitive ability is needed" (Manual, p. 1).

Decision-Making Applications

The SIT-R is designed as a screening instrument and should not be used for making placement decisions. However, it can be most helpful in providing a "quick estimate of ability," "a tentative diagnosis of cognitive ability," and "confirmation of other test results" (Manual, p. 1).

Relevant Population

The SIT-R is designed for children and adults from 4 through 18+ years of age, and standardization included individuals with disabilities with no speech or hearing impairments. The authors stress that command of the English language is essential. During the standardization, the SIT-R was administered to blind, learning disabled, cerebral palsied, orthopedically handicapped, emotionally disturbed, mentally handicapped, and behavior disordered individuals. The number of disabled individuals in the standardized sample is not reported in the Manual.

Characteristics Described

The SIT-R uses a question-and-answer format. The difficulty of the questions increases. There are 187 questions; the age of the individual determines which question the examiner asks first. Ten consecutive correct answers are required to establish a basal, and 10 consecutive incorrect answers establish the ceiling. The following six domains of items are included on the SIT-R: Vocabulary, General Information, Similarities and Differences, Comprehension, Quantitative Knowledge, and Auditory Memory. These domains are described below:

Vocabulary (V): This domain reflects the examinee's ability to use, understand, and define words orally. Example: (8). What is a door?

General Information (GI): These items reflect the "learning of cultural knowledge." Example: (11) How many legs does a person have?

Similarities and Differences (SD): These items reflect the examinee's ability to determine common and uncommon attributes of two dissimilar things or concepts. Example: (15) Which is bigger, a cat or a mouse?

Comprehension (CO): These items reflect the examinee's ability to use "common sense" and the ability to interpret proverbs and sayings. Example: (20) Why do we have clocks?

Quantitative Knowledge (QN): This domain reflects the examinee's ability to do mental calculations, remember essential numbers, determine the arithmetic process required, and calculate the correct answers. Example: (24) What number comes just after eight?

Auditory Memory (AM): This domain reflects the examinee's ability to remember and repeat a series of digits, both forwards and backwards, and recall sentences. Example: (30) Say these numbers the way I say them when I finish. 2, 9, 5, 3.

Test Scores Obtained

Scores obtained include the Mean Age Equivalent (MAE, similar to Mental Age). For example, the Raw Score of 103 has an MAE of 12.3 years. The Total Standard Score (TSS) replaces the IQ found on the original SIT. TSS scores can be converted to stanines, percentiles, Wechsler Scales, Z scores, CEEB (College Entrance Exam Board), GATB (General Aptitude Test Battery) Standard Scores, T-scores, and NCEs. The SIT-R Computer Report is available. This report scores and prints an individual three-page report using the TSS scores and computes the Severe Discrepancy Level to determine learning disabilities under federal guidelines.

Technical Adequacy

Validity Confirmation

Test item validity was established by taking the test items from the original SIT and including these with 600 new items that were developed, tested, and analyzed. Item difficulties and ability levels were estimated for each age group separately; these analyses produced a continuous range of item difficulties for all age groups.

Test response validity was established by correlating the TSS scores of the SIT-R with the WISC-R. 234 subjects between the ages of 6 and 16 were used. The correlation coefficients between the SIT-R and the Full Scale WISC-III were .82. The correlation coefficients for the SIT-R and the WISC-III range from .92 for the WISC-III FSIQ for ages 6–8, .61 for ages 9–11, .74 for ages 12–14, and .84 for ages 15–16. These correlations support test response validity between the WISC-III and the SIT-R. Additional test response validity studies with such tests as the K-ABC and the WJ-R Cognitive would add to test response validity.

Reliability Confirmation

The SIT-R was administered twice to a sample of 41 individuals with administrations one week apart. The correlation was .96, which supports the reliability of repeated administrations of the instrument. The sample is small and the characteristics of the sample were not given in the Technical Manual.

Objectivity Confirmation

No evidence of agreement among test scorers or Scoring Keys is reported in the Manual for the SIT-R. Scoring Criteria for each test question are located below each test question, but for many test questions the Scoring Criteria are imprecise and sometimes ambiguous. Correctness of responses is left to the judgment of the examiner, and judgments among examiners can vary considerably.

Statistical Confirmation

Statistical data on validity, reliability, and norms is in the Manual for the SIT-R.

Special Features

Acronym

SIT-R.

Levels of the Test

One.

Number of Test Forms

One.

Norm-Referenced?

Yes. The current revision of the SIT-R was completed in 1998. Examiners for the standardization were individuals who had been users of the original SIT, as well as other professionals interested in assessment. Examiners selected subjects in given age ranges without regard to gender, ethnicity, or educational or occupational level. Completed protocols were collected on 2,400 individuals, and from this number the authors selected 1,854 individuals to match the U.S. population as closely as possible (*World Almanac*, 1990). More effort was placed on matching the population of the sample in terms of educational and social characteristics rather than by geographic representation. The sample, although sufficiently large, was not randomized.

Criterion-Referenced?

No.

Feasibility Considerations

Testing Time

The SIT-R is untimed. However, the average amount of time for administration of the test is approximately 10 to 15 minutes. For the person who may be slower, the administration may take as long as 30 minutes.

For Testing Groups? Individuals?

Individuals.

Test Administration and Scoring

The SIT-R is an easy test to administer. Test questions are straightforward and require simple responses, which are marked correct (1) or incorrect (2). Ten consecutive correct answers are required for a basal, and 10 consecutive incorrect answers are required for a ceiling.

Test Materials and Approximate Costs

Complete kit: $99.95; Score sheets (pads of 50): $33.50; Norm Tables/Technical Manual: $45; Manual: $45.

Adequacy of Test Manuals

The Manual contains the test questions and Administration and Scoring Details. There is a Helpful Checklist for Test Examiners. This checklist is excellent, with 25 clearly written ideas for quick and easy administration (Manual, p. 10). The Technical Manual includes the Validity, Reliability, and Standardization Information, as well as norm tables for the Total Standard Scores by Age Level (TSS) and the Mean Age Equivalent (MAE).

Excerpts from Other Test Reviews

A Consumer's Guide to Tests in Print (1992) gave an Overall Rating of "F" to the SIT-R as well as "F" ratings for Demographics, Total Norms, and Stability. Kamphaus states that "although the SIT-R is not fatally flawed as a screener there are many good alternatives available with better psychometric properties" (p. 239). Kamphaus (1994) suggests that the Kaufman Brief Intelligence Test (K-BIT) would be a better screener due to good validity and less dependence on verbal responses. Further, Watson (1994) states that the "SIT-R may be used cautiously as a preliminary screening device to crudely estimate overall IQ" (p. 241).

Ordering Information

Publisher

Slosson Educational Publications, Inc., P.O. Box 280, East Aurora, NY 14052-0280; Phone: 888-756-7766; Fax: 800-655-3840; Web site: www.slosson.com.

Authors

Richard L. Slosson; revised by Charles L. Nicholson and Terry L. Hibpshman.

Publication Dates

1990, 1991 Revised Norms (Slosson), 1998.

Cautions and Comments

Reviews of the SIT-R are in agreement that the test has limitations. It is clear that the demographic information used to select individuals for the standardization is limited. The procedure used required the examiners to select the sample based on age, and later the authors selected the subjects from that pool of individuals. No attempt was made to randomize the sample.

There is no data on the number of individuals with disabilities in the standardization sample, although the Manual states that the SIT-R "can be given to certain handicapped individuals" (Manual, p. 9).

Test-retest reliability information reported is vague and incomplete, and sample sizes are small.

The Scoring Criteria are not objective, and there is no agreement among different scorers (inter-rater reliability) of the test. Caution should be used when including this test in diagnostic decisions relating to placement. The authors are commended for stating that this test is primarily for screening purposes and provides only a "quick estimate of ability." The fear is that some educators may find the SIT-R such a "quick" test that they may use it for placement purposes rather than screening. Finally, the following table can be misleading in that regard for the educator: the table assumes that diagnostic decisions can be made based on the Total Standard Scores (TSS).

Very Superior: TSS = 148 and above

Superior: TSS = 132–147

High: TSS = 120–131

Above Average: TSS = 110–119

Below Average: TSS = 90–109

Borderline M/H: TSS = 80–89

Mild M/H: TSS = 69–79

Moderate M/H: TSS = 36–51

Severe/ Profound M/H: TSS = 35 and below

Source: Manual, p. 7.

References

Hammill, D. D., Brown, L., & Bryant, B. R. (1992). *A consumer's guide to tests in print* (2nd ed.). Austin, TX: PRO-ED.

Kamphaus, R. (1994). Review of the Slosson Intelligence Test for Children and Adults. In J. C.

Impara & L. L. Murphy (Eds.), *Psychological assessment in the schools* (pp. 237–239). Lincoln, NE: The Buros Institute of Mental Measurements.

Watson, S. (1994). Review of the Slosson Intelligence Test for Children and Adults. In J. E. Impara & L. L. Murphy (Eds.), *Psychological assessment in the schools* (pp. 239–241). Lincoln, NE: The Buros Institute of Mental Measurements.

Stanford-Binet Intelligence Scale: Fourth Edition (SB-IV),
for testing individuals from 2 through 23 years of age
Reviewed by Aileen C. Lau-Dickinson, Ed.D., Special Education Administration

---

Usefulness of the Test for Educators

Test Authors' Purpose

In 1905, Alfred Binet and Theodore Simon published the first version of an assessment to measure intelligence. The third edition of the Stanford-Binet Scale, Form L–M, was published in 1960. The fourth edition of the Stanford-Binet was published in 1986 as a result of changes and new research in cognitive psychology. The major purpose is to assess intelligence and cognitive abilities.

Decision-Making Applications

The measurement of intellectual ability has been a vital concern for educators. The Individuals with Disabilities Education Act (IDEA) requires that school-aged children undergo intellectual evaluation before placement decisions can be made. Further, the authors indicate that there are four purposes for the Fourth Edition: "(1) To help differentiate between students who are mentally retarded and those who have specific learning disabilities, (2) to help educators and psychologists understand why a particular student is having difficulty learning in school, (3) to help identify gifted students, [and] (4) to study the development of cognitive skills of individuals from ages 2 to adult" (Guide for Administering and Scoring the Fourth Edition, p. 2).

Relevant Population

The Fourth Edition is norm-referenced for persons between the ages of 2 and 23.

Characteristics Described

The authors have adopted a three-level hierarchical model of the structure of cognitive abilities with the general reasoning factor, *g*, at the top. The levels are listed below:

First Level: *g* represents the "general reasoning factor."

Second Level: Crystallized Abilities, Fluid-Analytic Abilities, and Short-Term Memory. Crystallized Abilities are influenced by schooling and scholastic-academic factors. Fluid-Analytic Abilities are cognitive skills necessary for solving new problems. Short-Term Memory allows the individual to retain new information temporarily and to hold information drawn from long-term memory that is being used for an ongoing task.

Third Level: includes Verbal Reasoning, Quantitative Reasoning, and Abstract/Visual Reasoning.

There are 15 tests in which items of the same type are grouped. Four broad areas of cognitive abilities are evaluated by the 15 tests: Verbal Reasoning, Abstract/Visual Reasoning, Quantitative Reasoning, and Short-Term Memory. The Vocabulary Test and the chronological age are used to determine the level on each test at which testing should begin.

The Test Descriptions

Verbal Reasoning

Vocabulary: The examinee is required to give a dictionary definition or synonym of a word after being shown a picture or presented an oral stimulus. There are 14 picture vocabulary items and 32 oral items. The oral items are presented to older examinees. The vocabulary test is an important test as it determines the level at which examinees enter all remaining tests on the Fourth Edition.

Comprehension: The examinee is required to give one correct reason in response to an oral question, such as: Why do people use umbrellas? There are 42 comprehension items.

Absurdities: The examinee must tell what is absurd about a picture or why parts of the picture are absurd. Example: Picture of an adult drinking from a baby bottle. There are 13 test items.

Verbal Relations: The examinee must explain how a concept is different after being presented three concepts that are alike and the fourth one different. There are 18 test items.

Quantitative Reasoning

Quantitative: For Levels A–H the examinee is asked to place counting blocks in the counting-blocks tray to match, count, add, subtract, or form logical series. For Levels I–V the examinee is asked to answer quantitative items presented visually and orally to the examinee. There are 48 test items.

Number Series: The examinee must determine the correct number in a series after seeing a series of number sequences. The examinee is given two minutes to solve the sequence. There are 26 test items.

Equation Building: The examinee must arrange a sequence of numbers and mathematical symbols in a way that forms a valid equation. There are 18 test items. The examinee is asked to move on after spending two minutes on a problem.

Abstract/Visual Reasoning

Pattern Analysis: A three-hole form board is used with young children. The examinee is asked to place geometric forms in the correct holes. For older individuals, the examinee is required to duplicate a geometric design using nine cubes. There are time limits for duplication of cube designs.

Copying: The examinee is required to copy designs of increasing complexity. At the lower levels the designs are copied using blocks, and at the higher levels the designs are drawn with a pencil. There are 28 test items.

Matrices: The examinee is asked to fill in the item that belongs in the matrices shown in the record booklet. There are 26 test items.

Paper Folding and Cutting: The examinee must respond to a multiple-choice subtest that consists of pictures. The examinee must determine which response option is correct after looking at a picture and the subsequent folding and cutting. There are 18 subtest items.

Short-Term Memory

Bead Memory: The younger examinee is required to look at one bead for two seconds and then correctly identify the bead on a card containing assorted pictures of beads. The older examinee is required to look for five seconds at a picture of colored beads of different shapes strung on a stick, and then must reproduce the design with his or her beads and stick.

Memory for Sentences: The examinee must repeat a sentence read by the examiner with no errors. There are 42 sentences in a hierarchy.

Memory for Digits: The examinee must repeat a series of digits forwards, then repeat a series of digits backwards.

Memory for Objects: The examinee must select pictures in the order of their appearance after being presented a picture of a common object for one second and then another picture of a different object for one second. There are 14 test items.

Test Scores Obtained

Raw scores are converted to the Standard Age Scores using the SAS Conversion tables. The Standard Age Scores (SAS) for the Area Scores and for the total test composite have a mean of 100 and a standard deviation of 15. The composite score, based upon assessment of all four areas, represents the best estimate of *g*. Percentile ranks and age equivalents are also available.

A Four Score Computer Scoring Program is also available for the Fourth Edition. This software calculates chronological age and provides SAS Scores, Age Equivalents, and Percentile Ranks for each subtest, area, and composite score.

Technical Adequacy

Validity Confirmation

Test item validity was established by retaining many of the item types from the Form L-M Scale. Through item analyses, some item types were rejected. New item types were developed for the Fourth Edition. All item types were subjected to a series of tryouts. Standard item analyses were conducted to identify the most appropriate items for the final form of the Fourth Edition. All items for the Fourth Edition were reviewed for bias and any imbalance in ethnic and gender representation.

Test response validity was well established and documented in the Technical Manual. Five studies are reported which correlated the Fourth Edition with the following intelligence tests: the Stanford-Binet Intelligence Scale: Form L-M, the Wechsler Intelligence Scale for Children-Revised (WISC-R), the Wechsler Adult Intelligence Scale-Revised (WAIS-R), the Wechsler Preschool and Primary Scale of Intelligence (WPPSI), and the Kaufman Assessment Battery for Children (K-ABC). The examiners for these administrations were all psychologists associated with schools, clinics, or universities. The examinees were students from regular schools or preschool programs. Following is a list of the composite correlations for these tests:

Fourth Edition (SAS) and Stanford-Binet Intelligence Scale: Form L-M-IQ: N = 139, Composite Correlation = .81.

Fourth Edition (SAS) and WISC-R Full Scale IQ: N = 205, Composite Correlation = .83.

Fourth Edition (SAS) and WPPSI Full Scale IQ: N = 75, Composite Correlation = .80.

Fourth Edition (SAS) and WAIS-R Full Scale IQ: N = 47, Composite Correlation = .91.

Fourth Edition (SAS) and K-ABC (N = 175): Correlations for 4 K-ABC and 4 SAS subtest composite scores ranged from .82 to .89.

Note: The above correlation studies were conducted with non-exceptional children.

Additional correlation studies are reported in the Technical Manual for exceptional students including samples of gifted, learning disabled, and mentally retarded. Discussion of correlations and results of these studies can be found in the Technical Manual (pp. 69–83).

Reliability Confirmation

Reliability was investigated by testing 112 children. There were two groups of children tested, 57 children aged approximately 5 years and 55 children aged 8 years. The test-retest interval was two to eight months. The correlations for the test-retest scores were sufficiently high for both groups to confirm reliability. The reliability coefficient for composite scores was .91 for the younger group and .90 for the older group. Internal consistency and test-retest reliability correlations are reported in the Technical Manual with composite correlations of .91 for the younger group and .90 for the older group.

Objectivity Confirmation

Scoring keys are used to score most of the subtests of the Fourth Edition except for the Vocabulary, Comprehension, Absurdities, Copying, and Verbal Relations subtests. These tests require examiner judgment. Examples of acceptable, ambiguous, and unacceptable responses are provided for these tests in the appendixes. Inter-rater agreement of test scores was not reported in the Technical Manual.

Statistical Confirmation

Statistical data on validity, reliability, and norms is available in the Technical Manual of the Fourth Edition.

Special Features

Acronym

SB-IV or Fourth Edition.

Levels of the Test

Levels are determined by Multi-Stage testing. In the first stage, the examiner gives the routing (vocabulary test), which determines the entry level. Each of the remaining 14 tests continues to use adaptive-testing procedures to adjust difficulty level for the examinees.

Number of Test Forms

One.

Norm-Referenced?

Yes. Standardization of the Fourth Edition was conducted in 1985. More than 5,000 subjects were part of the standardization. The design for standardization was based on the 1980 U.S. Census and the variables were geographic region, community size, ethnic group, age, and gender. School districts participating in the standardization were randomly selected. For rural regions, psychologists randomly selected examinees who represented the standardization profile.

Criterion-Referenced?

No.

Other Features

Abbreviated test batteries are offered in the Fourth Edition. Recommendations for

Abbreviated Batteries can be found in the Guide for Administering and Scoring the Fourth Edition (p. 36).

Feasibility Considerations

Testing Time

Time varies depending on the ages and purpose for the testing. The Technical Manual indicates that the administration should not take more than one hour except for young children. Of course, the examiner must be sensitive to the examinee and adjust administration time according to test reactions.

For Testing Groups? Individuals?

Individuals.

Test Administration and Scoring

Explicit and easy-to-follow instructions for administering all of the subtests of the Fourth Edition are provided in the Guide for Administering and Scoring the Fourth Edition. The Record Booklet and the Item Books give additional information for test procedures and scoring. The order of the presentation of the tests is offered in the Record Booklet. The authors suggest that examiners become familiar with the *Examiner's Handbook: An Expanded Guide for Fourth Edition Users* as well as Part II of the *Standards for Educational and Psychological Testing* by the American Psychological Association.

Test Materials and Approximate Costs

Stanford-Binet IV Examiner's Kit: $777.50; Guide for Administering and Scoring: $79.50; Technical Manual: $55; Record Booklets (35): $81.50; Informal Abilities and Influences Charts (50): $21.50; *Examiner's Handbook*: $42; VHS Videotape: $75.50; Four Score Computer Scoring Program: $261.50.

Adequacy of Test Manuals

The two manuals, The Technical Manual and the Guide for Administering and Scoring the Fourth Edition, are excellent. They are clearly written and user-friendly. Each manual provides information, directions, scoring guidelines, and norms for understanding the intent of the Fourth Edition and administering and scoring the tests in the Fourth Edition.

Excerpts from Other Test Reviews

Salvia and Ysseldyke (2001) summarize their remarks of the Fourth Edition by stating, "Not only does the SB provide the technical data needed to evaluate the adequacy of its reliability and norms, but the data indicate a well-normed and highly reliable device" (p. 318).

Hammill, Brown, and Bryant (1992) give an overall "B" rating for the Fourth Edition. They give an "F" rating for test stability for individual subtests and ratings of "A" for "test composite" stability (reliability) and "B" for overall reliability.

Ordering Information

Publisher

Riverside Publishing Company, 425 Spring Lake Drive, Itasca, IL 60143-2079; Phone: 800-323-9540; Fax: 630-467-7192; web site: www.riverpub.com.

Authors

Robert L. Thorndike, Elizabeth P. Hagen, and Jerome M. Sattler.

Publication Date

1986.

Cautions and Comments

The Fourth Edition of the Stanford-Binet Intelligence Scale is an excellent measure for determining cognitive abilities in children and young adults. The measure has been standardized with a large sample of children and young adults, and the validity and reliability issues are well documented and researched. This Fourth Edition is one that Alfred Binet would be proud of in every respect. Based on this review, the Fourth Edition is highly recommended for determining placement of children with disabilities.

References

Hammill, D. D., Brown, L., & Bryant, B. R. (1992). *A consumer's guide to tests in print* (2nd ed.). Austin, TX: PRO-ED.

Salvia, J., & Ysseldyke, J. E. (2001). *Assessment* (8th ed.). Boston: Houghton Mifflin.

Stoelting Brief Nonverbal Intelligence Test (S-BIT),
for testing individuals from 6 years through 20 years, 11 months of age
Reviewed by Aileen C. Lau-Dickinson, Ed.D., Special Education Administration

---

Usefulness of the Test for Educators

Test Authors' Purpose

"The goal of developing this instrument was to construct a reliable and valid nonverbal, non-language measure of intellectual ability useful for brief screening of general-ability level" (Examiner's Manual, p. 1).

The authors state that the uses (purposes) of the S-BIT include: "1) A quick assessment of general cognitive ability in non-English speakers. 2) Screening individuals who have been referred for evaluation of giftedness or disabilities. 3) Assessment of intellectual ability in the context of a larger battery of tests. 4) Supplemental second or third assessment or any re-evaluation of individuals previously tested with full-scale IQ tests of cognitive batteries. 5) Brief assessment in research projects, dissertations and theses. 6) Quick assessment of nonverbal cognitive ability for individuals with speech or hearing impairments in the context of neuropsychological testing or evaluations of memory or achievement" (Examiner's Manual, p. 1).

Decision-Making Applications

Intellectual assessments are required by the Individuals with Disabilities Education Act (IDEA) for screening and identification purposes. Certain federal programs such as SSI have "degree of impairment" categories for inclusion and "gifted and talented" children require standardized scores for inclusion. In those cases, the use of the S-BIT may demonstrate that the individual is "eligible" to receive the support or service. The S-BIT fits this requirement. The authors indicate that the S-BIT and other brief screening tests should not be used alone to identify learning disabilities or cognitive impairments. The S-BIT can be used for placement purposes; however, it is essential that it be part of a battery of assessments.

Relevant Population

The test is an individually administered screening test designed to assess cognitive functions in children, adolescents, and young adults ages 6 years through 20 years, 11 months. In addition, the criterion-referenced "growth scores" can be used with individuals of any age and can be converted to age-equivalent scores (see Appendix N in the Examiner's Manual).

Characteristics Described

The S-BIT is completely nonverbal. The individual does not read, write, speak, or listen to any material. The examiner uses pantomime or gestures to indicate instructions and the individual responds by pointing or placing a card into the correct position.

The S-BIT includes four subtests: Figure Ground, Form Completion, Sequential Order, and Repeated Patterns. The S-BIT was developed as a subset of tasks within the standardization version of the Leiter-R (Roid & Miller, 1997).

The primary abilities measured by each subtest are described below:

Visualization Subtests

1. Figure Ground (PG): This subtest requires the examinee to identify embedded figures or details of objects depicted on response cards. The details increase in difficulty.

2. Form Completion (FC): This subtest requires the examinee to recognize a "whole object" from a randomly displayed array of its fragmented parts.

Reasoning Subtests

3. Sequential Order (SO): This subtest requires the examinee to select related stimuli from a logical progression of pictorial or figural objects to complete the sequence.
4. Repeated Patterns (RP): This subtest requires the examinee to supply "missing" portions of a pattern by moving response cards into alignment with the easel patterns.

Test Scores Obtained

The Nonverbal IQ (S-BIT-IQ) score provides a measure of nonverbal intelligence. This score includes two prominent factors of cognition: fluid reasoning and visual ability. The S-BIT raw scores (sum for each of the S-BIT four subtests' correct responses) can be converted to normalized scaled scores with a mean of 10 and a standard deviation of 3. Fluid Reasoning and Visualization Scales are composite scores. The subtests included for Fluid Reasoning and Visualization Composite Scales are found below.

Subtest Composition of the S-BIT IQ, Fluid Reasoning, and Visualization Composites

Score	Subtests in Score
S-BIT IQ	Figure Ground (PG)
	Form Completion (FC)
	Repeated Patterns (RP)
	Sequential Order (SO)
Visualization	Figure Ground (PG)
	Form Completion (FC)
Fluid Reasoning	Sequential Order (SO)
	Repeated Patterns (RP)
	(count twice)

Source: Examiner's Manual, Figure 4.3.

Fluid Reasoning and Visualization Composite Scores

The authors caution that the Fluid Reasoning and Visualization composite scores should not be equated with IQ as they are only one factor of intellectual ability and more specific than general ability. The General Ability score is comprised of the sums of the scaled scores for the subtests Figure Ground, Form Completion, Repeated Patterns, and Sequential Order (FG, FC, RP, and SO). Appendix B (in the Examiner's Manual) presents the normalized standard score equivalents (M = 100, SD = 15). These scores apply to all age groups, resulting in a single norm table rather than the age group tables used for scaled scores. Percentiles are also available for each standard score and are found in the conversion tables in Appendix B; age equivalency scores are also available. The authors do not recommend the use of age equivalency scores unless such scores are needed or required to determine that the child is eligible for specific placement decisions as required by state regulations. Criterion-Referenced Growth Scales are also included in the S-BIT. These scores include both item difficulty and growth-level estimates on a criterion-referenced scale. The individual's skill level is defined by the tasks she or he can typically master. The tables in Appendix L allow the examiner to convert raw scores for each subtest, each composite, and each IQ estimate to Growth Scale Scores. Growth Scale Scores are three-digit numbers, ranging from approximately 420 to 550, which provide an index sensitive to the rate at which the individual is growing. The scores give the educator or other professionals information relative to improvement in the cognitive skills. This allows parents, teachers, or other professionals to measure the progress of the child (growth) across time. (See Figure 3.5, Sample Growth Scale Record Form, for a sample profile of Growth Scale Scores.)

Finally, the S-BIT offers an Examiner Rating Scale. This scale has 49 items and is presented in a four-choice Likert rating format. It is suggested that the scale be completed by the examiner at the end of the testing session.

Directions for scoring are provided on the Examiner Rating Scale. The S-BIT Examiner Rating Scales also provide two composite scores, Cognitive/Social and Emotions/Regulations. Norm tables in Appendix E provide the standard score equivalents for these composite scales.

Technical Adequacy

Validity Confirmation

Test item validity: The authors indicate that "nonverbal intellectual abilities are defined as those mental and cognitive skills and aptitudes that can be tested with pictures, figural illustrations, and coded symbols, for purposes of 'culture fair' assessment." The S-BIT has been derived from the Leiter-R. Sixty examiners in the Tryout Phase and 114 examiners in the Standardization Phase carefully evaluated each test item to ensure that these items could be administered in a nonverbal and nonlanguage mode. Finally, a number of items were eliminated. Pilot versions of each subtest were examined and administered to 550 individuals, ages 2 to 20 (Tryout Edition) and 983 typical individuals and 562 atypical individuals, ages 6 to 20 (Standardization Edition). Further, all items were inspected by content experts and psychologists, and items with poor ratings by examiners and experts were eliminated from the final published version of the test. The Examiner Rating Scale underwent careful development and review by experts and examiners in both the Tryout and Standardization Editions of the S-BIT. Therefore, test item validity was established by careful item analysis, expert review, and empirical studies of internal consistency.

Test response validity was established by correlating the S-BIT with the original Leiter. A sample of 81 children and adolescents, ages 6 to 19, were given the original Leiter and the S-BIT. This sample was representative of each U.S. region and ethnic backgrounds, and 69% typical cases and 30% atypical cases. The correlation between the original Leiter and the S-BIT IQ was .87; it was .80 for the Fluid Composite and .84 for the Visual Composite. Correlations between the Leiter-R and the S-BIT were found to be .98 for the S-BIT IQ, .94 for the Fluid Composite, and .93 for the Visual Composite.

The Growth Scale Scores correlate more highly with the Mental Age score of the original Leiter, where correlations ranged from .63 to .77. Further, Test Response Validations were made using a sample of 122 children, ages 6 to 16, who were given both the S-BIT and the WISC-III. The testing was conducted predominantly in the midwest and the south with normative cases (47%), cognitive delay (18%), gifted (9%), and ESL-Spanish (23%). Correlations were made between the S-BIT and the WISC-III Full Scale scores. These correlations ranged from .75 (Composite Scores) to .78, and with the S-BIT IQ the correlation was .85. All of these high correlations support test response validity of the S-BIT.

Reliability Confirmation

A sample of 106 children and adolescents, ages 6 years, 1 month through 20 years, 9 months, were administered the S-BIT or two occasions. The average time between testing was 14 days. The test-retest correlations were divided into two age groups (ages 6–10 and 11–20).

Correlations for the S-BIT IQ were .91 for ages 6–10 and .96 for ages 11–20. Composites ranged from .83 to .87 for ages 6–10 and .92 for ages 11–20. The Growth Scale correlations were .93 for ages 6–10 and .96 for ages 11–20. Test-retest reliability coefficients conducted on the Examiner Rating Scales Correlations for ages 6–10 ranged from .72 to .89, and for ages 11–21 coefficients ranged from .68 to .79.

Statistical Confirmation

All statistical data on validity, reliability, and norms is available in the Examiner's Manual for the S-BIT.

Special Features

Acronym

S-BIT.

Levels of the Test

The test has one level divided into four subtests required to determine the S-BIT

IQ. Composite scores are determined from combinations of the scores of the four subtests. The Examiner's Rating Scale is another component of the S-BIT.

Number of Test Forms

One.

Norm-Referenced?

Yes. The norming process for the S-BIT included a Tryout Phase, which is discussed completely in chapter 6 of the Examiner's Manual. The standardization of the S-BIT was conducted in 1995 and 1997. The sample of 983 typical individuals was carefully selected to be representative of the population of individuals between the ages of 6 years and 20 years, 11 months. The S-BIT standardization sample included proportions of Caucasians, African Americans, Asian Americans, Hispanics, and Native Americans similar to those found in the population survey gathered by the U.S. Bureau of the Census (1993). This sample was obtained from all four geographic regions of the continental United States. The S-BIT standardization of 983 individuals included 11.2% rural residence. Further, the S-BIT was standardized on age-group subsamples with approximately equal numbers of boys and girls in each age group. In the standardization of the S-BIT, atypical individuals in various exceptional categories were included. The categories and numbers of individuals in each category are listed below.

	N	*Description of Category*
1.	65	Severe Speech or Language Impairment
2.	44	Severe Hearing Impairment
3.	39	Severe Motoric Delay or Deviation
4.	3	Traumatic Brain Injury
5.	84	Significant Cognitive Delay (mental retardation)
6.	111	Attention Deficit Disorder with or without Hyperactivity
7.	67	Gifted
8.	29	Learning Disability Category A
9.	39	Learning Disability Category B
10.	56	English as a Second Language (Spanish)
11.	25	English as a Second Language (Asian)

Source: Examiner's Manual, pp. 78–79.

The detail presented on the special groups was gratifying, as the S-BIT is a test that is primarily designed for atypical populations. Each of the above categories is defined in Appendix H of the Examiner's Manual.

Criterion-Referenced?

Yes. The authors consider the S-BIT to be criterion-referenced based on the use of the Growth Scale. Each test item is given a growth value. These values explain the relative item difficulty of each item passed and failed by the individual. These Growth Scale Scores have values from 429 to 522, and the Growth Scale is located on the Record/Profile Form. The Growth Scale Scores provide criterion-referenced ability estimates and are available for all subtests of the S-BIT, the Composites, and the IQ. The Growth Scale can reflect the growth of the individual over time when presented with intensive training related to problem solving and academic activities. The authors give an example of "Rosa," a hearing-impaired individual, who demonstrated improvement in cognitive development after two years of job training. The Growth Scores on the second administration of the S-BIT reflected improvement, increasing 16 points on the Sequential Order subtest and 12 points in the Fluid Reasoning area. The job training emphasized both problem solving and academic strategies.

Other Features

The Examiner Rating Scale is an example of a special feature of the S-BIT. This Likert scale can provide the educator with the individual's "activity level, attention, impulse control, and other emotional characteristics" that may have an effect on test results. This information may be helpful to the educator when interpreting the results of the S-BIT to parents. The Examiner Rating Scale includes the following subdomains and composite scores.

Sub-Domains	Number of Items	Composites
Attention	10 items	
Organization/Impulse Control	8 items	
Activity Level	4 items	
Sociability	5 items	
	Total 27 items	Cognitive/Social
Energy and Feelings	6 items	
Regulation	6 items	
Anxiety	6 items	
Sensory Reactivity	4 items	
	Total 22 items	Emotions/Regulations

Source: Examiner's Manual, p. 42.

Feasibility Considerations

Testing Time

The subtests of the S-BIT are untimed. If the individual does not respond after approximately three minutes, the "pacing rule" is applied. The examiner gestures to the individual that it is time to "move ahead." According to the authors, experienced examiners of the S-BIT should be able to administer the test in about 25 minutes.

For Testing Groups? Individuals?

The S-BIT is an individually administered screening test to assess cognitive functions in children, adolescents, and young adults.

Test Administration and Scoring

Explicit and easy-to-follow instructions for administering all of the subtests of the S-BIT are provided in the Examiner's Manual. In addition, the S-BIT Record/Profile Form and the Easel/Picture Book give specific directions for administering and scoring each subtest. These directions are easy to follow. The Examiner's Manual has excellent guidelines for administrating the S-BIT and should be read completely before the examiner administers the test. The authors suggest that those using the S-BIT have formal assessment training, especially in the interpretation of scores. The administration of the S-BIT is straightforward and user-friendly, but the difficult part is the scoring and interpretation.

Test Materials and Approximate Costs

Complete kit: $319; Examiner's Manual: $54; Record Forms (25): $24; Easel/Picture Book: $174; Response Cards: $74.

Adequacy of Test Manuals

The complete kit contains the Examiner's Manual, 25 Record Forms, Easel/Picture Book, and Response Cards, all attractively packaged and including a convenient carrying case for the traveling professional. Clear directions are included in the Easel/Picture Book. Each subtest includes the following information for administration: Starting Points, Stop Rule (ceiling), Scoring, Materials, Position, Teaching Trials, and General Administration. Pictures in the easel and response cards are brightly colored and should interest the youngest subject. The S-BIT Record/Profile Form is also well done with color-coded scoring blanks for easy placement of score. The Examiner's Manual has tables for converting the raw scores to Scaled Scores, Percentile Ranks, Scaled Scores, Normal Curve Equivalents, and Standard Scores, and Conversion of Raw Scores to Standard Score Equivalents for the Examiner Rating Scale Composite Scores. Growth Scale Scores can be recorded on the Profile included in the Record/Profile Form. Easy-to-follow instructions are included on the profile.

Excerpts from Other Test Reviews

No test reviews were found for the S-BIT.

Ordering Information

Publisher

Stoelting Company, 620 Wheat Lane, Wood Dale, IL 60191; Phone: 630-860-9700; Fax: 630-860-9775; Web site: www.stoeltingco.com/tests.

Authors

Gale H. Roid and Lucy J. Miller.

Publication Date

1999.

Cautions and Comments

Roid and Miller revised the Leiter-R in 1997, and the S-BIT was normed as a subset of the Leiter-R. The original Leiter International Performance Scale was developed by Russell Leiter in 1979. The authors of the S-BIT employed the strategy of "taking apart" the items of the original Leiter and matching them to documented cognitive abilities (Examiner's Manual, p. 6). Subtests of the S-BIT are used to estimate intellectual ability. The S-BIT doesn't give a "Full Scale" IQ, so the authors recommend that additional subtests could be used to provide a profile of nonverbal attention and memory abilities. Overall, the S-BIT is a user-friendly measure of intelligence for atypical individuals who are difficult to test including Cognitively Delayed, Disadvantaged, Nonverbal or Non-English Speaking, English as a Second Language, and Speech or Hearing Impaired. There are two aspects of the S-BIT that make it appealing to the educator: the brevity of the test and the nonverbal format. The S-BIT should be useful to educators, speech and language pathologists, and psychologists who need cognitive information regarding "hard-to-test" individuals.

Test of Nonverbal Intelligence (TONI-3),
for testing individuals from 6 years through 89 years, 11 months of age
Reviewed by Aileen C. Lau-Dickinson, Ed.D., Special Education Administration

---

Usefulness of the Test for Educators

Test Authors' Purpose

The TONI-3 is a language-free and motor-free test to assess aptitude, intelligence, abstract reasoning, and problem solving. Therefore, "the TONI-3 can be used with confidence (a) to estimate aptitude and intellectual functioning; (b) to identify subjects who are believed to have intellectual impairments, or to rule out intellectual impairment, especially with subjects whose test performance may be confounded by concurrent language and motor impairments; (c) to verify the validity of referrals for treatment, therapy, or special services; (d) to formulate hypotheses that may guide intervention or further evaluation; and (e) to conduct research" (Examiner's Manual, p. 32).

Decision-Making Applications

The TONI-3 can be appropriately used to identify those persons with low intellectual functioning and is therefore appropriate to determine placement in Special Education or as an instrument for referral for further assessment. Since the test is language-free and motor-reduced, the test is designed to use with hard-to-test subjects.

Relevant Population

The TONI-3 is designed for subjects from 6 years through 89 years, 11 months. The TONI-3 can be used to assess the intelligence levels of persons with acquired or developmental aphasia; persons who are low-verbal or nonverbal; persons who are deaf or hearing impaired; persons who have low English language proficiency or who cannot read and write standard English; and persons who have cognitive, language, or motor impairments resulting from cerebral palsy, stroke, disease, or head trauma.

Characteristics Described

There are two equivalent forms (A and B) of the TONI-3; therefore, it can be used for pre- and post-testing and test-retest purposes. Since the TONI-3 is language-free, there are no items that require reading, writing, speaking, or listening. The subject's responses can be through finger pointing, eye pointing, head or stick pointing, or other mechanisms that would allow the subject to respond. The examiner's instructions are nonverbal; the examiner uses pantomime, gestures, and eye-pointing to communicate the requirements of the test. There are preliminary practice items that are used to teach the examinee the procedure and response options. The Examiner's Manual recommends that the practice items be readministered if the examinee does not understand what is expected.

The test focuses on problem solving, a mental ability that is hypothesized to be an overarching component of intelligence. All items require the examinee to solve problems related to novel abstract figures. Test items are situations that the examinee must problem solve in order to demonstrate what he would do in that situation (test responses). Figural matrixes are arranged in order of difficulty from the easiest to the most difficult. The test items range from simple matching problems to extremely complex, multifaceted problems. There are five types of problem-solving items: simple matching, analogies, classification, intersection, and progressions. The abstract figures of the TONI-3 contain one or more of the following "constituent characteristics: shape, position, direction, rotation, contiguity, shading, size and movement" (Examiner's Manual, p. 31).

The TONI-3 test items are contained in a picture book with one item per page. The administration of the test does not begin until a series of five practice items are administered to ensure that the examinee understands the pantomimed directions and can respond by pointing, gesturing, head-pointing, and so on.

Test Scores Obtained

Raw scores are converted to deviation quotients and percentile ranks. These scores are determined by counting the number of correct responses from Item 1 to the ceiling. The table for converting the raw scores for both forms of the TONI-3 into deviation quotients is found in Appendix A of the Examiner's Manual. Appendix B has the table for converting deviation quotients into percentile ranks for both forms of the TONI-3. Age equivalents are also available in Appendix C. However, the authors do not recommend the use of "Age Equivalents," since such scores have been "criticized by virtually every reputable psychometrist" (Examiner's Manual, p. 60). The authors indicate that "Age equivalents have only been provided in the TONI-3 for administrative purposes for school-age subjects" (Examiner's Manual, p. 60).

Guidelines for Interpreting TONI-3 Quotients and Percentile Ranks

Percentiles	Deviation Quotients	Descriptions	% Included
> 98	> 130	Very Superior	2.34
91–98	121–130	Superior	6.87
74–97	111–120	Above Average	16.87
25–73	90–110	Average	49.51
9–14	80–89	Below Average	16.12
2–8	70–79	Poor	6.87
< 2	< 70	Very Poor	2.34

Source: Examiner's Manual, Table 4.2.

Technical Adequacy

Validity Confirmation

Test item validity for the TONI-3 must show that the test measures abilities associated with intelligence. The authors concentrate on problem solving. They report that there is ample empirical evidence of the power and complexity of problem solving as a predictor of intelligence. The Examiner's Manual details in Chapter 1 the research that has been conducted on problem solving. The challenge for the authors was to create test items that were free of language and yet required problem solving. Test items were built around abstract figures that would reduce the linguistic and motoric requirements of the subjects. Further, the instructions are pantomimed and not read by the test takers or given to them orally by an examiner. The item pool was a total of 307 items. These items were reviewed by knowledgeable professionals. Subsequently, the item pool was reduced to 183 items. The 183 items were subjected to item analytic techniques and the result was a 100-item test divided into two equivalent 50-item test forms. In this third edition of the TONI, additional item analytic techniques were used to reduce the number of items and to exclude items that showed bias with regard to gender, ethnic, and diagnostic characteristics. The final TONI-3 was slimmed down to a 45-item test with two equivalent forms.

Test response validity was established by correlating the TONI-3 with three intelligence tests: the Comprehensive Test of Nonverbal Intelligence (CTONI), the Wechsler Intelligence Scale for Children-Third Edition (WISC-III), and the Wechsler Adult Intelligence Scale-Revised (WAIS-R). Five hundred fifty individuals ranging in age from 19 to 50 whose geographic, racial, socioeconomic, linguistic, disability, and cultural demographics were the same as those reported in the 1990 census were used in the correlation studies for the TONI-3 and the CTONI. These correlations ranged from .64 to .74 on the equivalent forms. The WISC-III and the WAIS-R study used 53 subjects enrolled in the Winston School in Dallas, Texas. All subjects had been diagnosed with learning disability using the guidelines established by the Texas Education Agency. Ages ranged from 7 to 19. Correlations for the WISC-III ranged from .56 to .63. Correlations for the WAIS-R ranged from .51 to .71. The TONI-3 correlates in the moderate to high range with the Wechsler scores. Other studies are reported in the Examiner's Manual correlating the earlier editions of the TONI and TONI-2 with a variety of measures of general, verbal, and nonverbal aptitude. These correlations are presented in Table 7.7 of the Examiner's Manual.

Reliability Confirmation

Reliability confirmation was investigated by testing 170 students residing in Texas, Washington, and South Dakota, ages 13, 15, and 29–40. The time lapse between the two testings was one week. The test-retest results were greater than .90 for both forms of the test at all ages tested. In addition, the two forms of the TONI-3 were administered at the same time and correlated with 20 different age intervals using the test performance of the entire normative sample (3,451). The resulting correlations range from .79 to .95. These correlations indicate that there is a high correlation between the two forms of the TONI-3 (A and B).

Objectivity Confirmation

To avoid test error due to variability in scoring the TONI-3, two staff members of the publishers independently scored a set of 25 pairs of completed protocols for both forms, randomly selected from the normative sample. This sample ranged in age from 8 to 18 years. The correlation coefficients were .99 for both forms, A and B. This correlation provides sufficient evidence that there is little variability in scoring of the TONI-3 and its two equivalent forms.

Statistical Confirmation

Statistical data on validity, reliability, objectivity, and norms can be found in the Examiner's Manual for the TONI-3.

Special Features

Acronym

TONI-3.

Levels of the Test

One.

Number of Test Forms

Two test forms (A and B).

Norm-Referenced?

Yes. The TONI-3 was normed in 1995 and 1996 on a sample of 3,451 individuals residing in 28 states. Major standardization sites were selected in each of the four geographic regions designated by the U.S. Census Bureau. All children in the normative sample attended school in general education classes; children with disabilities who were enrolled in these classes were included in the normative sample. At the six sites, 2,060 individuals were tested. Further normative testing was done in smaller test sites. 67 individuals from 22 states volunteered and tested an additional 1,391 individuals. In reviewing the tables describing the normative sample, there was a limited number with disabilities. Eleven percent of the subjects in the school-age sample were disabled, and 8% of the subjects in the adult sample were disabled. Since the purpose of the TONI-3 is to test individuals whose cognitive, linguistic, or motor skills may adversely affect their performance on traditional tests of intelligence, the representative group for this population appears to be limited.

Criterion-Referenced?

No.

Other Features

The unique feature of the TONI-3 is the language-free administration by the examiner and the language-free responses by the examinee. This is a valuable feature when testing those individuals who are unable to respond in a conventional manner.

Feasibility Considerations

Testing Time

The TONI-3 is not a timed test. Generally, it takes about 15 minutes to administer one form of the TONI-3.

For Testing Groups? Individuals?

Individuals.

Test Administration and Scoring

The TONI-3 may be administered by professional diagnosticians, psychologists, educators, speech and language pathologists, and others with professional experience in assessment. The authors recommend that qualified professionals have knowledge of general testing procedures and formal coursework in assessment. The Examiner's Manual (pp. 35–40) gives 19 administration procedures that should lead to conformity in administration.

Test Materials and Approximate Costs

Complete kit: $249; Examiner's Manual: $66; Picture Book: $109; Form A and B Answer Booklets and Record Forms: $39 each.

Adequacy of Test Manuals

The Examiner's Manual is clearly written and user-friendly. The manual provides a discussion of earlier editions of the TONI and a discussion of basic concepts in nonverbal intelligence testing. The discussion includes theories of intelligence, historical definitions of intelligence, intelligence testing, measuring intelligence nonverbally, and measuring abstract reasoning and problem solving in nonverbal, language-free ways. Appendix A provides tables for converting raw scores to deviation quotients, Appendix B provides a table for converting quotients to percentile ranks, and Appendix C provides a table for converting raw scores to age equivalents for school-age subjects.

Excerpts from Other Test Reviews

Atlas (2001) reviewed the TONI-3 and indicated, "A limitation of the TONI-3 is the two-fold problem that special placement decisions do continue to be based primarily on Intellectual Quotient (IQ) scores derived from groundbreaking instruments such as the Wechsler scales, and that the TONI-3 manual overstates the value of its concurrent validity. . . . Correlations ranging from .53 and .63 between the TONI-3 and the Wechsler Intelligence for Children, Third Edition (WISC-3), the primary assessment for the exceptional population served, are at best moderate." However, Atlas does point out that "the TONI-3 is probably the best instrument we have in making some sort of comparison to the standard Wechsler scale when it cannot be administered due to sensory limitations of the subject" (p. 1259). DeMauro (2001) reports in his review that "TONI-3 offers much evidence to support its use" (p. 1260). Salvia and Ysseldyke (2001) report the "Evidence for the reliability and validity of this test is good."

Ordering Information

Publisher

PRO-ED, 8700 Shoal Creek Boulevard, Austin, TX 78757-6897; Phone: 800-897-3202; Fax: 800-397-7633; Web site: http://www.proedinc.com.

Authors

Linda Brown, Rita J. Sherbenou, and Susan K. Johnsen.

Publication Dates

1982 (TONI); 1990 (TONI-2); 1997 (TONI-3).

Cautions and Comments

The TONI-3 appears to be an excellent assessment tool for determining aptitude and intelligence of sensory impaired individuals, non-English-speaking individuals, and those individuals with neurologically related deficits. Since the WISC-R has been the primary test to determine aptitude and intelligence, but does not serve this purpose for sensory impaired individuals, the TONI-3 fills the void. Perhaps additional validity studies should be conducted with a larger sample of subjects with disabilities.

References

Atlas, J. A. (2001). Review of the Test of Nonverbal Intelligence, Third Edition. In B. S. Plake & J. C. Impara (Eds.), *The Fourteenth Mental Measurements Yearbook* (pp. 1259–1260). Lincoln, NE: The Buros Institute of Mental Measurements.

DeMauro, G. E. Review of the Test of Nonverbal Intelligence, Third Edition. In B. S. Plake & J. C. Impara (Eds.), *The Fourteenth Mental Measurements Yearbook* (pp. 1260–1261). Lincoln, NE: The Buros Institute of Mental Measurements.

Jensen, A. R. (1980). *Bias in mental testing*. New York: Free Press.

Salvia, J., & Ysseldyke, J. E. (2001). *Assessment* (8th ed.) Boston: Houghton Mifflin.

Universal Nonverbal Intelligence Test (UNIT),
for testing individuals from 5 through 17 years of age
Reviewed by Aileen C. Lau-Dickinson, Ed.D., Special Education Administration

---

Usefulness of the Test for Educators

Test Authors' Purpose

The UNIT is "designed to measure fairly the general intelligence and cognitive abilities of children and adolescents from ages 5 years through 17 years who may be disadvantaged by traditional verbal and language-loaded measures" (Examiner's Manual, p. 1).

Decision-Making Applications

The UNIT is a test that has implications for clinical and educational placement decisions, especially for special groups. Recent federal data (U.S. Department of Education, 1995) reports that 5.7% of children in special programs have been diagnosed as learning disabled, approximately 2.4% are identified with speech of language impairments, 1.3% with mental retardation, and 1.0% with serious emotional disturbance. Gifted students comprise 6.2% of the school population. Since large numbers in these populations lack language skills, a nonverbal test such as the UNIT can be particularly useful for determining intellectual functioning and subsequently provide information for making placement decisions. The UNIT identifies individuals who are mentally retarded or intellectually gifted. The intellectual functioning of individuals with learning disabilities can also be differentiated. According to the authors, "the UNIT is diagnostically useful and sensitive to common clinical and exceptional conditions."

Relevant Population

The UNIT is a test of intelligence specially developed for children and adolescents between the ages of 5 and 17 who may be "disadvantaged by traditional verbal and language loaded measures" (Examiner's Manual, p. 1). This measure can be used for children and adolescents in the "general" population and for special groups such as deaf and hearing impaired, individuals from different cultural backgrounds, individuals who are intellectually gifted, individuals with learning disabilities, individuals with limited English proficiency, individuals with mental retardation, individuals with serious emotional disturbance or psychiatric disorders, and individuals with speech and language impairments. Each of these special populations is described in the Examiner's Manual (pp. 5–7).

Characteristics Described

Three batteries and six subtests comprise the UNIT: Abbreviated Battery (includes first two subtests), Standard Battery (includes first four subtests), and Extended Battery (includes all six subtests). The Standard Battery is used primarily for making educational placement decisions, the Abbreviated Battery is used for screening purposes, and the Extended Battery is used for more in-depth diagnostic assessments.

Abbreviated Battery Subtests: (1) Symbolic Memory; (2) Cube Design.

Standard Battery Subtests: (1) Symbolic Memory; (2) Cube Design; (3) Spatial Memory; (4) Analogic Reasoning.

Extended Battery Subtests: (1) Symbolic Memory; (2) Cube Design; (3) Spatial Memory; (4) Analogic Reasoning; (5) Object Memory; (6) Mazes.

Hand signals and gestures used to administer the subtests include Head Nodding, Head Shaking, Open-Handed Shrugging, Palm Rolling, Pointing, Hand Waving, Stop, and Thumbs Up (Examiner's Manual, pp. 48–50).

Descriptions of the UNIT Subtests

1. Symbolic Memory: The individual is required to recreate a sequence of universal symbols for "baby," "girl," "boy," "woman," and "man" after viewing the stimulus for five seconds. There are 30 scored items, 4 demonstration items, 4 sample items, and Symbolic Memory Response Cards.

2. Cube Design: The individual is required to reconstruct a cube design while viewing the stimulus within a specified time limit. There are 15 scored items, 3 demonstration items, and 3 sample items.

3. Spatial Memory: The individual is required to recreate a pattern by placing green and black circular chips on a response grid after viewing the stimulus for five seconds. There are 27 scored items, 5 demonstration items, and 5 sample items.

4. Analogic Reasoning: The individual is required to point to one of four response options after a stimulus is presented which is an incomplete conceptual or geometric analogy in matrix format. There are 31 scored items, 4 demonstration items, and 4 sample items.

5. Object Memory: The individual is presented a stimulus which is a random pictorial array of common objects for five seconds. After a second array of pictorial objects is presented containing the previously presented pictorial objects and additional objects serving as foils, the individual must recognize and identify the objects presented in the first pictorial array by placing response chips on those stimulus figures previously presented. There are 30 scored items, 2 demonstration items, and 2 sample items.

6. Mazes: The individual uses a pencil to draw a path from the center of the maze to the exit using the correct path. There are 13 scored items, 3 demonstration items, and 3 sample items.

Test Scores Obtained

Norm-referenced data includes scaled and standard scores, confidence intervals, percentile ranks, and test-age equivalents (level of performance of the "typical" child of that given age). Full Scale IQ (FSIQ) scores are available for all three batteries: Abbreviated, Standard, and Extended.

Descriptive Classifications of UNIT Scale Standard Scores

Standard Scores	Classification
130 and above	Very Superior
120–129	Superior

Standard Scores	*Classification*
110–119	High Average
90–109	Average
80–89	Low Average
70–79	Delayed
69 and below	Very Delayed

Other norm scores are also available, such as scale score differences, intraindividual score differences, and frequency of a discrepancy between two scores.

Technical Adequacy

Validity Confirmation

Test item validity: The UNIT follows two primary constructs (memory and reasoning) and two secondary processes (symbolic and nonsymbolic internal mediation). The six subtests were designed as a measure of complex short-term memory or a measure of reasoning. Also, each subtest was developed to capture one of two mediational processes (symbolic and nonsymbolic) when applied to the demands of the task. Therefore, test items were based on the basic theory underlying the UNIT. During pilot testing, test items were retained "if participant performance appeared centrally related to the constructs under study such as (ability to reason) and not other factors such as (comprehension of instructions)" (Examiner's Manual, p. 123). Test items were also retained if their nonverbal administration was sufficiently "easy and effective." For the standardization edition of the UNIT, every test item was examined for "adequacy of fit." In the final standardization edition of the UNIT, all test items demonstrated adequate fit.

Test response validity: The UNIT was correlated with other measures of intelligence including the Wechsler Adult Intelligence Scale-Third Edition (WISC-III), the Tests of Cognitive Ability of the Woodcock-Johnson Psycho-Educational Battery-Revised (WJ-R), the Kaufman Brief Intelligence Test (K-BIT), the Matrix Analogies Test (MAT), the Standard Progressive Matrices (Raven's SPM), and the Test of Nonverbal Intelligence-Second Edition (TONI-2).

Correlations between the UNIT and the WISC-III are reported here. The sample used for this study included special populations: learning disabilities (n = 61), mental retardation (n = 59), intellectually gifted (n = 43), and Native American (n = 34). Strong correlations were reported for the group with learning disabilities using FSIQ scores of the WISC-III and the FSIQ scores from the three batteries of the UNIT (Abbreviated, Standard, and Extended) (.78, .84, and .83). The UNIT Abbreviated, Standard, and Extended FSIQ (Full Scale IQ) scores and the WISC-III FSIQ scores were correlated and reported as .86, .84, and .88, respectively for the examinees with mental retardation. For the intellectually gifted group, the WISC-III PIQ scores were compared to the FSIQ scores of the Abbreviated, Standard, and Extended Batteries of the UNIT. The UNIT Abbreviated, Standard, and Extended FSIQs correlated .78, .83, and .89, respectively with the WISC-III PIQ scores. It should be noted that gifted children are usually quite verbal and scored lower on the UNIT, which emphasizes nonverbal responses. The reported correlations for the Native American group between the WISC-III FSIQ scores and with the UNIT FSIQ scores were .87, .81, and .65. The correlations between the UNIT Extended Battery FSIQ and the WISC-III FSIQ were considerably lower than the other correlations. For the most part the correlations between the batteries of the UNIT and the WISC-III were consistent, except for the single correlation of .65 for the Native American sample. Tables of additional correlations between the four groups and the WISC-III and the UNIT are found in the Examiner's Manual, as well as correlations between the UNIT, the WJ-R, BATERIA-R, K-BIT, and three Progressive Matrices. The UNIT correlates well with other measures of intelligence and across samples of special populations. However, samples used in the validity studies were small. Additional studies with larger samples would be helpful.

Reliability Confirmation

Test-retest correlations were reported in a study with 197 subjects who were administered the UNIT twice over an interval of approximately three weeks. Correlations were reported for four age groups and for each of the three batteries: Standard Battery, Extended Battery, and Abbreviated Battery.

For the entire group of subjects, the test-retest correlation for the Abbreviated Battery was .79, for the Standard Battery was .84, and for the Extended Battery was .81. Each of the four age group test-retest scores was correlated by subtest and battery. The highest correlations for Full Scale scores were found for the 11–13 age group. For the Abbreviated Battery the Full Scale correlation was .86, for the Standard Battery the Full Scale correlation was .90, and for the Extended Battery the Full Scale correlation was .87. Additional correlations for each subtest are available in the Examiner's Manual (Table 5.6, pp. 108–109).

Full Scale Test-Retest Correlations for Four Age Groups

	Abbreviated Battery	Standard Battery	Extended Battery
Ages 5–7	r.81	r.84	r.80
Ages 8–10	r.64	r.83	r.81
Ages 11–13	r.86	r.90	r.87
Ages 14–17	r.83	r.83	r.75

Objectivity Confirmation

Scoring criteria are listed after each subtest description found in the Examiner's Manual (pp. 53–90). The examiner scores each subtest based on the directions found in the Examiner's Manual. There is nothing reported in the Examiner's Manual regarding scoring agreement between pairs of scorers.

Statistical Confirmation

Statistical data on validity, reliability, and norms is found in the Examiner's Manual.

Special Features

Acronym

UNIT.

Levels of the Test

There are three overlapping levels of the test: Abbreviated Battery, Standard Battery, and Extended Battery (see "Characteristics Described" for details).

Number of Test Forms

One.

Norm-Referenced?

Yes. Normative data was collected using 2,100 children and adolescents (ages 5 years through 17 years, 11 months) and an additional 1,765 children and adolescents were included in the technical studies. The random sample was representative of the U.S. population and stratified by sex, race, national origin, region, community setting, classroom placement, special education services, and parental educational attainment.

Criterion-Referenced?

No.

Feasibility Considerations

Testing Time

Abbreviated Battery: 10 to 15 minutes; Standard Battery: 30 minutes; Extended Battery: 45 minutes.

For Testing Groups? Individuals?

Individuals.

Test Administration and Scoring

The UNIT requires the examiner to adhere closely to the directions found in the Administering and Scoring section in the Examiner's Manual. Specific, clear, and detailed directions are stated for the examiner to follow. However, it may be difficult for the examiner to manipulate all of the materials required for administration at the same time: Examiner's Manual, Record Form, and Stimulus Book (1 and 2), and other materials including Stop Watch (supplied by examiner), Symbolic Memory Response Cards, Cube Design Cubes, Cube Design Response Mat, Response Chips, Response Grid, and Mazes Response Booklet. All the materials and books are attractive and clearly written. Perhaps the test publishers could include the specific directions on the Record Form or in the Stimulus Books for more efficient administration. In terms of scoring, a computer scoring program with interpretative reports would add to a more efficient reporting of the results of the UNIT.

Demonstration and Sample Items are available for each subtest.

The UNIT includes a laminated page of gestures to be used by the examiner when administering the test.

Test Materials and Approximate Costs

Complete kit: $460; Record Forms (25): $35; Abbreviated Record Forms (25): $17; Maze Response Booklets (25): $39; Examiner's Manual: $67.

Adequacy of Test Manuals

The Examiner's Manual is clear and written in a readable fashion. It is attractive using a green and white motif. It is spiral bound, which makes for easy page turning. Chapter 7 of the Examiner's Manual is entitled "Interpretation of UNIT Performance" and gives valuable information for the educator, especially when testing special populations. Appendix A has the conversion tables for Scaled Score Equivalents and Appendix B has the conversion table for Standard Score Equivalents from the sums of Scaled Scores. Other tables are included in Appendixes C–F.

Excerpts from Other Test Reviews

Bandalos (2001) summarizes her review by saying, "It is a carefully developed instrument with excellent reliability and impressive evidence of validity for use as a supplement to or substitute for more traditional measures such as the WISC-III. Although additional validity evidence based on larger groups, as well as studies of predictive validity for school grades or other classroom achievement measures would be desirable, the evidence presented in the manual is both appropriate and convincing" (p. 1298). Salvia and Ysseldyke (2001) state, "Evidence for test-retest reliability is limited, and validity evidence is sufficient for use of IQ scores obtained for the full battery only. . . . Reliance on subtest scores or subscale scores for diagnostic purposes is precarious" (p. 344).

Ordering Information

Publisher

Riverside Publishing Company, 425 Spring Lake Drive, Itasca, IL 60143-2079; Phone: 800-323-9540; Fax: 630-467-7192; Web site: www.riverpub.com.

Authors

Bruce A. Bracken and R. Steve McCallum.

Publication Date

1998.

Cautions and Comments

The test reviews are favorable to this test and indicate that the UNIT has strengths for testing special populations. Physically disabled subjects may find the measure difficult, since they may be unable to manipulate materials manually such as cubes, chips, and symbolic cards. The test directions for administration are explicit and clear and are located in the Examiner's Manual. The publisher may find it easier for the examiner if these directions were located on the Record Forms or Stimulus Books (1 and 2). Finally, additional validity studies would be helpful with larger samples. However, the test response validity with special populations is impressive. Separate norms for these populations would be valuable information for educators who must make decisions for these populations.

References

Bandalos, D. L. (2001). Review of the Universal Nonverbal Intelligence Test. In B. S. Plake and J. C. Impara (Eds.), *The Fourteenth Mental Measurements Yearbook* (pp. 1295–1298). Lincoln, NE: The Buros Institute of Mental Measurements.

Salvia, J., & Ysseldyke, J. E. (2001). *Assessment* (8th ed.). Boston: Houghton Mifflin.

Wechsler Adult Intelligence Scale-Third Edition (WAIS-III),
for testing individuals from 16 through 89 years of age
Reviewed by Aileen C. Lau-Dickinson, Ed.D., Special Education Administration

---

Usefulness of the Test for Educators

Test Authors' Purpose

"The WAIS-III is an individually administered clinical instrument for assessing the intellectual ability of adults aged 16 through 89" (Administration and Scoring Manual, p. 1).

Decision-Making Applications

The authors indicate that the quantitative and qualitative information provided by the WAIS-III should be interpreted in light of the individual's history and other known information. The purposes for the use of the WAIS-II vary, from placement decisions to diagnostic decisions related to neurological and psychiatric disorders that may affect intelligence for secondary and postsecondary school planning. Federal and state regulations require that individuals receiving special services be reevaluated on a prescribed schedule.

The WAIS-III is an instrument used to diagnose mental retardation as these individuals must demonstrate "general intellectual functioning significantly below average" (Full Scale IQ < 70) along with significant adaptive impairments in at least two areas. Finally, the WAIS-III can be used for diagnosing neuropsychological impairments and giftedness.

Relevant Population

The WAIS-III is an instrument to be used with individuals aged 16 through 89.

Characteristics Described

The WAIS-III was revised from the WAIS-R (1981) and reflects the views of David Wechsler on the nature of intelligence. Wechsler considered intelligence as a multidimensional construct and defined intelligence as the "capacity of the individual to act purposefully, to think rationally, and to deal effectively with his environment" (Technical Manual, p. 1). Each subtest measures a different aspect of intelligence. Wechsler believed that intelligence is global, including both verbal and performance tasks. The WAIS-III has 14 subtests with 12 subtests retained from the WAIS-R and two new subtests, Matrix Reasoning and Letter-Number Sequencing.

Description of WAIS-III Subtests

Picture Completion: Performance Scale. The examinee must identify the missing part of a set of colored pictures.

Vocabulary: Verbal Scale. The examinee must define orally a series of orally and visually presented words.

Digit Symbol—Coding: Performance Scale. The examinee writes the symbol, using a key, corresponding to its number after being presented a series of numbers, each of which is paired with its own corresponding hieroglyphic-like symbol.

Similarities: Verbal Scale. The examinee must explain the similarity of common objects or concepts after a series of orally presented pairs of words is presented.

Block Design: Performance Scale. The examinee replicates two-dimensional geometric patterns that have been modeled or printed using two-color cubes.

Arithmetic: Verbal Scale. The examinee solves a series of arithmetic problems mentally and responds orally.

Matrix Reasoning: Performance Scale. The examinee points to or says the number of the correct response to complete a gridded pattern from five possible choices when presented a series of incomplete gridded patterns.

Digit Span: Verbal Scale. The examinee repeats verbatim either forwards or backwards a series of digits presented orally.

Information: Verbal Scale. The examinee answers a series of orally presented questions that tap the examinee's knowledge of common events, objects, places, and people.

Picture Arrangement: Performance Scale. The examinee arranges a series of mixed-up pictures into a sequential order.

Comprehension: Verbal Scale. The examinee answers a series of questions orally that require him to understand and articulate social rules and concepts or solutions to everyday problems.

Symbol Search: Performance Scale. [*Note*: If Digit Symbol-Coding subtest is spoiled, Symbol Search subtest can be substituted.] The examinee marks the "yes" or "no" box after he scans two groups of symbols: "a target group (composed of two symbols) and a search group (composed of five symbols) and indicates whether either of the target symbols matches the symbols in the search group" (Administration and Scoring Manual, p. 165). A time limit of 120 seconds is imposed.

Letter-Number Sequencing: Verbal Scale. [*Note*: If the Digit Span subtest is spoiled, the Letter-Number Sequencing subtest can be substituted.] The examinee must repeat a series of orally presented sequences of letters and numbers with the numbers in ascending order and the letters in alphabetical order.

Object Assembly: Performance Scale. [*Note*: If any Performance Scale subtest is spoiled, the Object Assembly subtest can be substituted, but only for individuals aged 16 to 74.] The examinee assembles a set of puzzles of common objects, each presented in a standardized configuration.

WAIS-III Subtests Grouped According to Verbal and Performance Scales

Verbal	*Performance*
Vocabulary	Picture Completion
Similarities	Digit Symbol—Coding
Arithmetic	Block Design
Digit Span	Matrix Reasoning
Information	Picture Arrangement
Comprehension	Symbol Search
Letter-Number Sequencing	Object Assembly

Source: Adapted from Administration and Scoring Manual, Table 1.2, p. 3.

WAIS-III Subtests Grouped According to Index Scores

Verbal Comprehension: Vocabulary, Similarities, Information.

Perceptual Organization: Picture Completion, Block Design, Matrix Reasoning.

Working Memory: Arithmetic, Digit Span, Letter-Number Sequencing.

Processing Speed: Digit Symbol—Coding, Symbol Search.

Test Scores Obtained

As with the WISC-III, the WAIS-III yields the same three composite IQ scores: Verbal (VIQ), Performance (PIQ), and Full Scale (FSIQ), as well as four Index scores: Verbal Comprehension, Perceptual Organization, Working Memory, and Processing Speed. The WAIS-III has been co-normed with the Wechsler Memory Scale-Third Edition, and the results from these two tests when combined can give the examiner a more complete psychological assessment.

Technical Adequacy

Validity Confirmation

Test item validity: "Wechsler viewed his intelligence scales as clinical instruments that sample an individual's abilities" (Technical Manual, p. 2). Wechsler also believed that intelligence should be measured through verbal and performance tasks. The subtests of the WAIS-III reflect both verbal and performance tasks. Test item validity was established by ensuring that the content of test items was valid by having all proposed test items reviewed by numerous neuropsychologists as well as clinical and school psychologists. In developing the content for the WAIS-III, a review of existing items, development of new items, pilot testing of the revised and new items, a national tryout study to examine item difficulties and item bias, and finally restandardization of the instrument were included in the content development. Detailed information of the modification of test items from the WAIS-R to the WAIS-III is available in the Technical Manual.

Test response validity was established by correlating the WAIS-III with other tests of intelligence such as the WAIS-R, the WISC-III, Standard Progressive Matrices (SPM), the Stanford-Binet Intelligence Scale-Fourth Edition, and with a standardized measure of achievement, the WIAT-II.

The WAIS-R and the WAIS-III were administered to 192 adults ages 16–72, and the correlation coefficients of the sample's performances on the two tests were found to be .94, .86, and .93 for VIQ, PIQ, and FSIQ. The WISC-III and the WAIS-II were administered in counterbalanced order to a sample of 184 16-year-olds. The correlation coefficients between the two scales were .88, 78, and .88 for the VIQ, PIQ, and FSIQ. Twenty-six adults were administered the SB-IV (Stanford-Binet-IV) and the WAIS-III, and the correlation between the WAIS-III Full Scale IQ score and the global SB-IV composite score was .88. This was consistent with other correlation studies with Wechsler scales and the Stanford-Binet-IV. Other correlation coefficients can be found in the Technical Manual. Also, the Technical Manual provides results of studies that show how individuals with neurological disorders such as Alzheimer's, Huntington's, and Parkinson's diseases, traumatic brain injury, and Korsakoff's syndrome perform on the WAIS-III.

Reliability Confirmation

The WAIS-III was administered twice to 394 adults with approximately 30 individuals from each of 13 age groups. Test intervals ranged from 2 to 12 weeks. Correlation coefficients were calculated for four pooled age groups: 16–29, 30–54, 55–74, and 75–89. VIQ, PIQ, and FSIQ correlations were all in the .90s. Subtest and index correlations across groups can be found in the Technical Manual (pp. 58–61). These results indicate that the WAIS-III scores are sufficiently consistent across time and for all age groups.

Objectivity Confirmation

Pairs of trained scorers were used to confirm agreement between scorers in a study that targeted three of the WAIS-III subtests: Vocabulary, Similarities, and Comprehension. Sixty protocols were scored, and the agreement between scores was very high: .95 for Vocabulary, .93 for Similarities, and .91 for Comprehension. The authors state that since scoring criteria for the WAIS-III subtests is "simple and objective," agreement between two trained scorers would be exceptionally high.

Statistical Confirmation

Statistical data on validity, reliability, objectivity, and norms can be found in the Technical Manual.

Special Features

Acronym

WAIS-III.

Levels of the Test

One.

Number of Test Forms

One.

Norm-Referenced?

Yes. The WAIS-III was standardized on adults aged 16 to 89. The stratified sample included 2,450 adults. Stratification was based on variables of age, sex, race/ethnicity, education level, and geographic region as defined in the 1995 U.S. Census.

Criterion-Referenced?

No.

Feasibility Considerations

Testing Time

Total testing time varies, depending on the age of the examinee. For administration of the 11 WAIS-III subtests that yield IQ scores, testing time is estimated at 60 to 90 minutes. Administration of the 11 WAIS-III subtests that yield the four index scores requires approximately 45 to 75 minutes. For administration of the 13 subtests to obtain IQ scores and index scores, the range is 65 to 95 minutes. It is recommended that testing take place in one session, but if two sessions are required, testing should not be more than one week apart.

For Testing Groups? Individuals?

Individuals.

Test Administration and Scoring

Since criteria for scoring are clear, simple, and objective, administration of the subtests is straightforward. Scores can be entered into the WAIS-III Writer to be calculated. A statistical report that provides scaled scores, IQ and Index scores, percentiles, and confidence intervals is available. In addition, the WAIS-III Writer generates an Interpretive Report, Clinical Review, and Client Report.

The authors suggest that examiners using the WAIS-III have experience in testing and interpretation of standardized tests. In addition, experience in testing specific individuals with cultural, linguistic, and educational differences is helpful. A training video is available which can be used to facilitate training for the examiners.

Test Materials and Approximate Costs

WAIS-III Complete Set in Box: $700; WAIS-III Complete Set/Attache or Soft-Side Case: $750; Administration and Scoring Manual: $82; WAIS-III Technical Manual: 47; Response Books (25): $79; Training Video: $54; WAIS-III Writer: $398.

Adequacy of Test Manuals

The Technical Manual and Administration and Scoring Manual are clearly written with background information on Concepts of Intelligence and Development of the Scales. The Technical Manual also includes information regarding the Wechsler Memory Scale-III (WMS-III), a companion test that is not included in this review. A training video is available for examiners to view before administering the WAIS-III or the WMS-III.

Excerpts from Other Test Reviews

Hess (2001) comments on the Technical Manual: "The WAIS-III technical manual is a model of how a test manual should be composed. . . . It reviews the theoretical rationale and the extensive procedures and data upon which the WAIS-III is constructed" (p. 1333). Further, Hess states, "The psychometric excellence of the WAIS-III blended with the continuing emphasis on the rich clinical material that makes a psychological examination portrait of a person, would delight David Wechsler" (2001, p. 1336). Rogers (2001) states, "The scores from the test are reliable enough to be used in all of the designated age ranges and the validity evidence gives confidence that the test scores measure those intellectual constructs that it purports to measure"

(p. 1340). According to Salvia and Ysseldyke (2001), "The WAIS-III contains more evidence of validity than its predecessors" (p. 322).

Ordering Information

Publisher

The Psychological Corporation, 19500 Bulverde Road, San Antonio, TX 78259; Phone: 800-228-0752; Fax: 210-339-5873; Web site: www.psychcorp.com.

Authors

The Psychological Corporation.

Publication Date

1997.

Cautions and Comments

Like its predecessors, the WAIS-III has included a group of different subtests that contribute to global IQ scores. The structure of the WAIS-III is true to the original Wechsler-Bellevue Intelligence Scale (1939) only now with updated norms, outdated test items replaced, and scoring rules changed. Clinical group studies are now included in the Technical Manual. The WAIS-III has now been co-normed with the Wechsler Memory Scale-III to help examine the important relationship between intellectual functioning and memory (a review of the Wechsler Memory Scale-III is not included here). Norms now reflect an expanded age range for adults 74 through 89 years of age, reflecting increased average life expectancy. Evidence of test-retest reliability is high for the overall scores of VIQ, PIQ, and FSIQ. Test response validity studies indicate very acceptable correlations between other Wechsler intelligence measures as well as the Stanford-Binet-IV and Standard Progressive Matrices. Additional studies of test response validity and correlations with other tests of intelligence such as the Woodcock-Johnson Test of Cognitive Abilities would provide helpful validity information.

References

Hess, A. K. (2001). Review of the Wechsler Adult Intelligence Test-Third Edition. In B. S. Plake & J. C. Impara (Eds.), *The Fourteenth Mental Measurements Yearbook* (pp. 1332–1336). Lincoln, NE: The Buros Institute of Mental Measurements.

Rogers, B. G. (2001). Review of the Wechsler Adult Intelligence Test-Third Edition. In B. S. Plake & J. C. Impara (Eds.), *The Fourteenth Mental Measurements Yearbook* (pp. 1336–1340). Lincoln, NE: The Buros Institute of Mental Measurements.

Salvia, J., & Ysseldyke, J. E. (2001). *Assessment* (8th ed.). Boston: Houghton Mifflin.

Wechsler Intelligence Scale for Children-Third Edition (WISC-III),
for testing individuals from 6 years through 16 years, 11 months of age
Reviewed by Aileen C. Lau-Dickinson, Ed.D., Special Education Administration

Usefulness of the Test for Educators

Test Author's Purpose

The WISC-III is the third edition of the Wechsler Intelligence Scale for Children. It is a "clinical instrument for assessing the intellectual ability of children aged 6 years through 16 years" (Manual, p. 1).

Decision-Making Applications

Decisions can be made regarding planning and placement for school-age children. Diagnosis of exceptionality and other clinical and neuropsychological considerations can be determined using the WISC-III. Children receiving special services in the schools must be reevaluated every three years, according to the standards set by the Individuals with Disabilities Education Act (IDEA). The WISC-III is a frequently used assessment instrument to meet this requirement. The WISC-III can be used as a part of diagnosis of mental retardation. The definition of mental retardation requires evidence of below-average functioning in regard to intellectual level, and the WISC-III can provide the necessary evidence. The WISC-III may also be used to determine giftedness, as the identification of giftedness includes assessment of intellect as well as other talents and skills. The WISC-III can provide the needed information regarding the intellectual functioning of students with learning disability, learning problems, and other cognitive deficits. When the WISC-III is linked with the Wechsler Individual Achievement Test-Second Edition (WIAT-II), ability/achievement discrepancies can be obtained to aid educators with the necessary federal or state requirements for eligibility for special services.

Relevant Population

The WISC-III was developed for school-age children 6 years through 16 years, 11 months of age. There is an overlap between the Wechsler Preschool and Primary Scale of Intelligence-Revised (WPPSI-R) at the lower levels and the Wechsler Adult Intelligence Scale-Revised (WAIS-R) at the upper levels.

Characteristics Described

Thirteen subtests comprise the WISC-III. There are two scales: Performance and Verbal. Seven subtests comprise the Performance Scale and six subtests comprise the Verbal Scale. Two subtests are considered supplementary: Mazes and Digit Span. They are not required to obtain an IQ and are used if time permits. They may be substituted for one Verbal and one Performance subtest.

Descriptions of the WISC-III Subtests

Performance Subtests

Picture Completion: The child is asked to identify a missing and important part of a set of colorful pictures of common objects and scenes. Twenty-second time limit.

Coding: The child is asked to draw the symbol using Code A or a corresponding number using Code B according to a key. Code A and Code B are included on a single perforated sheet in the Record Form. 120-second time limit.

Picture Arrangement: The child is asked to rearrange in a logical story sequence a set of colorful pictures presented in mixed-up order.

Block Design: The child is asked to replicate a set of printed two-dimensional geometric patterns using two-color cubes. Record time.

Object Assembly: The child is asked to assemble a set of puzzles of common objects, each presented in a standardized configuration to form a meaningful whole. Various time limits.

Symbol Search: The child is asked to scan two groups of a series of paired groups of symbols, each pair consisting of a target group and a search group and marks the appropriate box (whether or not a target symbol appears in the search group). The child responds to as many items as possible within a 120-second time limit.

Mazes: The child is asked to solve increasingly difficult mazes, printed in a response booklet. (Time limits for each maze.)

Verbal Subtests

Information: The child is asked to answer specific factual questions.

Similarities: The child is asked to explain the similarity of pairs of words presented to him orally.

Arithmetic: The child is asked to solve a series of arithmetic problems mentally.

Vocabulary: The child is asked to define a series of words presented to him.

Comprehension: The child is asked to solve everyday problems and/or social problems presented to him orally.

Digit Span: The child is asked to repeat verbatim a series of orally presented number sequences both forwards and backwards. (Adapted from Manual, Table 1.1, p. 6)

Test Scores Obtained

Raw scores are converted to scaled scores based on the child's age. A Verbal IQ (VIQ), Performance IQ (PIQ), and a Full Scale IQ (FSIQ) can be converted from the child's scaled score. Index Scores are available for Verbal Comprehension, Perceptual Organization, Freedom from Distractibility, and Processing Speed. Percentile equivalents and confidence intervals can also be found in the norms tables (Manual). Raw scores can also be converted to test-ages in Table 1.9 (Manual).

Scoring is simple and straightforward; however, simple errors in scoring can occur and the author has prepared a list of cautions and reminders for the examiner to make scoring accurate and correct (Manual, p. 57). For ease in scoring, the WISC-III Writer: The Interpretive Software is available to the examiner. The software calculates Scaled Scores, Percentiles, Index Scores, Composites, and Confidence Intervals.

Technical Adequacy

Validity Confirmation

Test item validity: The Wechsler scales have a long history. The Wechsler Scale of Intelligence was developed in 1930 as the Wechsler-Bellevue Intelligence Scale. The WISC (Wechsler Scale of Intelligence) and the WISC-R (Wechsler Scale of Intelligence-Revised) followed. These scales have been respected for years for their psychometric features and quality of standardization. The WISC-III maintains the original content and structure of the WISC-R. According to the author, "more than 73% of the WISC-R items (not including the Coding subtest) were retained either in original or slightly modified form" (Manual, p. 19). In an attempt to remove bias from the test items, item analyses and a review panel composed of psychologists reviewed test items and recommendations were made to remove any bias from WISC-III items. Detailed information for revising each of the Verbal and Performance items from the WISC-R to the WISC-III is available in the Manual (pp. 14–19).

Test response validity: A number of studies are reported in the Manual comparing the WISC III with other measures of intelligence including the Otis-Lennon School Ability Test, the Wechsler Primary and Preschool Scale of Intelligence-Revised (WPPSI-R), the Wechsler Adults Intelligence Scale-Revised (WAIS-R), the Wechsler Intelligence Scale for Children-Revised (WISC-R), and Differential Ability Scales. Full Scale IQ correlations reported were in the .70s and .80s (Manual, pp. 197–205) for all tests. Correlation with the WISC-R FSIQ was .89, with the WAIS-R was .86, and with the WPPSI-R was .85. Other correlations were made for the Index Scores of the WISC-III and the Otis-Lennon School Ability Test Scores, and the Differential Ability Scale Cognitive and Achievement Standard Scores. These correlations vary but are acceptable and can be found in the Manual (pp. 203–205).

Reliability Confirmation

A study using 353 children who were tested twice with the WISC-III was conducted. The interval between test administrations ranged from 12 to 63 days. This test-retest study used three age groups: ages 6–7 (n = 111), ages 10–11 (n = 119), and ages 14–15 (n = 123). For group one, the correlations for VIQ, PIQ, and FSIQ were .90, .86, and .92; for group two, correlations for VIQ, PIQ and FSIQ were .94, .88, and .95; and for group three, correlations for VIQ, PIQ, and FSIQ were .94, .87, and .94.

These correlations indicate that the WISC-III remains stable when test-retests are conducted.

Objectivity Confirmation

Scoring agreement was checked between pairs of scorers with scoring agreement found to be in the high .90s. Since several subtests require more evaluator judgment, the Similarities, Vocabulary, Comprehension, and Mazes subtests were submitted to four scorers for comparison. Sixty protocols were randomly selected from the standardization sample (20 from each age group). The four scorers independently scored all four of the subtests for all 60 cases. Reliabilities were .94 for Similarities, .92 for Vocabulary, .90 for Comprehension, and .92 for Mazes. These results indicate that test protocols can be scored consistently by different scorers.

Statistical Confirmation

Statistical data on validity, reliability, and norms is in the WISC-III Manual.

Special Features

Acronym

WISC-III.

Levels of the Test

One.

Number of Test Forms

One.

Norm-Referenced?

Yes. The standardization sample was representative of the U.S. population of children. The random sampling was stratified using the following variables: age, gender, race/ethnicity, geographic region, socioeconomic status, and parent education. The sample of 2,200 children included 200 children in each of 11 age groups ranging from 6 years, 6 months through 16 years, 6 months.

Criterion-Referenced?

No.

Feasibility Considerations

Testing Time

Administration of the regular battery of 10 subtests requires 50 to 70 minutes; three supplemental subtests require approximately 10 to 15 minutes.

For Testing Groups? Individuals?

Individuals.

Test Administration and Scoring

The Manual provides step-by-step directions for starting and discontinuation points, determining raw scores, and converting raw scores to scaled scores, IQ scores, Index scores, and Test-Age Equivalents. The examiners who use the WISC-III should have had prior experience with the Wechsler intelligence scales. In addition, examiners should have had graduate training in testing children as well as children with diverse backgrounds and educational histories. Examiners usually have credentials and graduate training in psychological testing. The WISC-II Writer provides the examiner with software that reduces the burden of hand-scoring.

Test Materials and Approximate Costs

Complete Kit with Attache Case: $725; Basic Kit (packaged in box): $675; Manual: $80; Stimulus Booklet: $102; Mazes Response Booklets (25): $42; (100): $150; Symbol Search Response Booklets (25): $42; (100): $150; Record Forms (25): $75; (100): $300; Object Assembly Puzzles: $225; WISC-III Writer: The Interpretive Software System (CD-ROM): $398.

Adequacy of Test Manuals

The WISC-III test manual is excellent and clearly written. The Manual includes information on the development of the WISC-III and underlying conceptions of intelligence. In addition, Norm Conversion Tables are included in the Manual.

Excerpts from Other Test Reviews

A Consumer's Guide to Tests in Print (Hammill, Brown, & Bryant, 1992) reviewed the WISC-III and gave various subtests of the WISC-III the score of "F" for stability or test-retest reliability. The following subtests were singled out: Arithmetic, Comprehension, Picture Arrangement, Block Design, Object Assembly, Digit Span, Symbol Search, and Mazes. The standards for test-retest reliability used in *A Consumer's Guide* are correlations of .90 or above. Many of the test-retest correlations for the subtests were well below .90. Validity was rated A and B across all subtests and total scores. Salvia and Ysseldyke (2001) question the representativeness of the normative sample: "The sample was stratified, but insufficient attention was paid to cross-tabulations" (p. 321).

Ordering Information

Publisher

The Psychological Corporation, 19500 Bulverde Road, San Antonio, TX 78259; Phone: 800-228-0752; Fax: 210-339-5873; Web site: www.psychcorp.com.

Author

David Wechsler.

Publication Date

1991.

Cautions and Comments

The Wechsler Intelligence Scale for Children-Revised (WISC-R) has been used by psychologists and professionals for many years. In 1991, the WISC-III version of the scale was developed with revised test items and updated norms. The WISC-III can be used for diagnosing mental retardation, giftedness, and neuropsychological impairments with school-aged children. The WISC-III links with the WIAT-II (Wechsler Individual Achievement Test-II) in order to determine ability-achievement discrepancies based on both of these measures. The WISC-III Writer: The Interpretive Software System not only calculates scores for the WISC-III, but provides three report formats: the extensive Interpretive Report, a Parent Report, and a Tables and Graphs Report. The software will also calculate ability-achievement discrepancies between the WISC-III and WIAT-II.

References

Hammill, D. D., Brown, L., & Bryant, B. R. (1992). *A consumer's guide to tests in print* (2nd ed.). Austin, TX: PRO-ED.

Salvia, J., & Ysseldyke, J. E. (2001). *Assessment* (8th ed.). Boston: Houghton Mifflin.

Wide Range Assessment of Memory and Learning (WRAML),
for testing individuals from 5 through 17 years of age
Reviewed by Aileen C. Lau-Dickinson, Ed.D., Special Education Administration

---

Usefulness of the Test for Educators

Test Authors' Purpose

The test battery allows "the user to evaluate a child's ability to actively learn and memorize a variety of information" (Administration Manual, p. 9).

Decision-Making Applications

The test is most appropriate for making placement and referral decisions. The General Memory Index can be converted to standard scores and percentiles for age-based performance comparisons. There are three major divisions within the WRAML. The first division makes a distinction between "memory and learning"; that is, each memory subtest requires immediate recall of a discrete amount of information, and each learning subtest involves the acquisition of new information over trials.

The second division is based upon the modality of the information presented; that is, both visual and verbal scales progress from rote memory demands to memory demands with increasingly meaningful material. The third WRAML division examines the length of time between task administration and recall demand; that is, some subtests require short-term recall and several subtests also allow for delayed recall.

Since memory plays an essential role in school success, the WRAML is helpful to the educator in identifying suspected memory weaknesses. In addition, the WRAML may be helpful in determining placement of some children with memory deficits in classes for the learning disabled and attention deficit disorder. The WRAML can also be useful for referral purposes—for example, if a child demonstrates below-average memory scores, referral to a speech and language pathologist, audiologist, or psychologist is suggested for further testing.

Relevant Population

The test is appropriate for children ages 5 through 17. The WRAML examines relevant memory issues with the school-aged population.

Characteristics Described

The WRAML is divided into four subareas: (1) Verbal Memory Scale, (2) Visual Memory Scale, (3) Learning Scale, and (4) Delayed Recall Subtests. There are four subtests that can be used for screening purposes. These subtests sample varied aspects of visual and verbal memory and verbal learning.

Verbal Memory Scale

There are three subtests under this heading: Number/Letter Memory, Sentence Memory, and Story Memory. These subtests allow the examiner to assess the child's capabilities on a rote memory task and to compare that performance with tasks that increase in semantic complexity.

Number/Letter Memory: Here the child is asked to repeat a group of both numbers and letters presented randomly.

Sentence Memory: Here the task requires the child to repeat meaningful sentences which increase in length and complexity.

Story Memory: Two short stories are read and the child is asked to recall as many parts of each story as can be remembered.

Visual Memory Scale

There are three subtests included here: Finger Windows Subtest, Design Memory Subtest, and Picture Memory Subtest. Each subtest increases in meaningfulness.

Finger Windows Subtest: The child is asked to reproduce spatial sequences after the examiner has pointed to a series of locations found on a card.

Design Memory Subtest: Four designs are presented, and following a 10-second delay the child is asked to draw the designs remembered.

Picture Memory Subtest: The child is required to point to altered elements of a picture which was previously presented and then altered.

Learning Scale

Three subtests are in this scale: Verbal Learning Subtest, Visual Learning Subtest, and Sound Symbol Subtest.

Verbal Learning Subtest: The child is read a list of simple words and must recall as many of these words as possible immediately following the reading of the list.

Visual Learning Subtest: The child is asked to recall a fixed number of visual stimuli presented over four trials. This test requires immediate feedback.

Sound Symbol Subtest: This test requires the child to recall sounds associated with various abstract figures. Again, four discrete trials are administered.

Delayed Recall Subtests

Delayed recall subtests are included for Verbal Learning, Visual Learning, Sound Symbol, and Story Memory subtests. These subtests are optional but demand a relatively small amount of time and may provide important information as to the rapid decay of memory. According to the authors, rapid decay may suggest an important learning problem.

Test Scores Obtained

Raw scores are obtained by scoring one point for each correct response for all subtests, except for Sentence Memory, for which 0, 1, or 2 points can be assigned. Scaled scores conversions are made for each subtest. The scaled scores tables differ by six-month intervals, beginning at 5 years and extending to 13 years, 11 months. Starting at age 14, the tables increase by yearly intervals. The General Memory Index (GMI) is obtained by adding the sum of scaled scores for the Verbal, Visual, and Learning indexes. Conversions are made by using the Table of the Sum of All Scaled Scores to the GMI. This index score can then be converted to percentiles, stanines, T-scores, and scaled score equivalents. A measure of memory decay or "forgetting" may be obtained for the Verbal Learning, Story Memory, Sound Symbol, and Visual Learning subtests. This memory decay is called the difference score. Since difference scores cannot be derived in a psychometrically sound manner, the examiner is provided with a descriptive ranking for each child. Level of performance can be described as Bright Average, Average, Low Average, Borderline, or Atypical.

Technical Adequacy

Validity Confirmation

Test item validity: Each subtest was constructed to measure a relatively specific component of memory determined by varying visual-verbal, rote-meaningful, and learning-memory dimensions. Two separate item analysis studies were conducted to determine the relevance of the items in each domain. Fourteen original subtests were developed in the 1980s which covered the different facets of memory thought to be important to learning and to the diagnosis of learning disabled children. There was an excess of items in these subtests. They were given to over 200 children at three age levels from grade 1 through high school. Subtests items were analyzed and either edited, dropped, or replaced to provide a graduated scale of item difficulty for children 5 through 17 years of age. The final nine subtests were fine-tuned to provide satisfactory item and person separation characteristics.

Test response validity: Three studies were designed to determine the relationship of the WRAML with other instruments which have been commonly used to assess memory in children. These instruments included the McCarthy Scales of Children's Abilities Memory Index, the Stanford-Binet: Fourth Edition Short-Term Memory, and the Wechsler Memory Scale-Revised Index Scores.

Correlations between these tests and the WRAML General Memory Index ranged from .54 to .80. Correlations generally are strongest among the WRAML and measures of short-term verbal memory and attention/concentration.

Reliability Confirmation

According to the authors, "Using test-retest measures of reliability for a memory test has inherent problems. The nature of all memory tests is to evaluate how much information has been retained. The very process of the first measurement affects the second measurement because of the carry-over. Since individuals may retain differing amounts of learned information the correlation of these two measures may not give an accurate estimate of the ability of the test or estimate the true score" (Manual, p. 85). Despite this caution of assessing reliability by repeatedly administering the WRAML to the same people, such reliability studies were conducted. The test-retest reliability of the index scores was sufficiently high for all subtests/indexes to confirm reliability. Total test-retest reliability scores ranged from .61 to .84.

Objectivity Confirmation

Scoring criteria are detailed for the Design Memory and Story Memory subtests. In all subtests one point is given for each correct response; criteria for correct or incorrect responses is detailed at the end of each subtest. The examiner must become familiar with each subtest and its criteria before administration of the test so that validity and objectivity can be preserved. Eight of the nine WRAML subtests require minimal judgment in assessing the accuracy of the child's response. The Design Memory subtest requires the examiner to make judgments; a detailed description for scoring has been developed to minimize inter-scorer differences. Eighty-two children were randomly selected from the normative sample to assess inter-scorer reliability. An inter-scorer reliability coefficient of .996 between the total scores received was obtained.

Statistical Confirmation

Statistical data on validity, reliability, and norms is available in the Technical Data section of the WRAML Manual.

Special Features

Acronym

WRAML.

Levels of the Test

WRAML subtests are slightly different for children from 5 through 9 years of age and for those from 9 through 17 years of age. The examiner must be mindful of the age limitations when administering the test. Also, four subtests can be used for screening (WRAML-S). They take about 10 to 15 minutes to give and will result in a Memory Screening Index.

Number of Test Forms

One.

Norm-Referenced?

Yes. The test has national norms. The norm sample was selected according to a national, stratified norm model based on demographic data available from the 1980 U.S. Census and the *1988 Rand McNally Commercial Atlas and Marketing Guide*. Twenty-one age groups were selected between the ages of 5 years and 17 years, 11 months. All items in the WRAML were administered to all children in the sample. 2,363 children, representative of the U.S. population in regard to sex, race, geographic, region, and parental occupation were included.

Criterion-Referenced?

No.

Feasibility Considerations

Testing Time

Testing time for the WRAML is approximately 45 minutes. If the Delayed Recall tasks are presented, the time should be extended to approximately 60 minutes. The four subtests of the screening test/short form should take approximately 10 to 15 minutes.

For Testing Groups? Individuals?

Individuals.

Test Administration and Scoring

Step-by-step test directions are available in the Manual. Supervised training in the administration of the test items is desirable. However, a teacher or trained technician may learn how to administer the tests in the WRAML. Interpretation of test results should be made by a professional with training and experience in the area of cognitive assessment and experience with the interpretation of the test results of the WRAML.

Test Materials and Approximate Costs

The complete kit, which includes all test materials, 25 examiner forms, 25 response forms, and one general manual, all in a sturdy briefcase: $375.

Adequacy of Test Manuals

The Administration Manual is essential for following test administration instructions. Scoring tables located in the manual provide the General Memory Index, which can be converted to standard scores and percentiles for age-based performance comparisons. Test pictures, designs, and other materials are colorful and clear for easy use.

Excerpts from Other Test Reviews

The WRAML has been reviewed by *A Consumer's Guide to Tests in Print* (Hammill, Brown, & Bryant, 1992) and was given ratings ranging from "A" to "F." The authors assigned an "F" (unacceptable) rating for stability reliability to all subtests of the WRAML. Due to the inherent problems associated with memory tasks discussed earlier, test-retest reliability may never be adequate.

Medway (1992) indicates that "the test appears to be a better measure of immediate recall and concentration than of evaluation of memory strategies. . . . Future studies are needed in which the WRAML is given to clinical samples with known deficient memories such as children with diffuse brain damage, Turner's Syndrome, mental retardation, and autism."

Cautions and Comments

WRAML interpretations need to be integrated with data from other standardized tests, teacher observations, and the child's medical and clinical history. These subtests are most appropriate for testing children who are suspected of having attentional, distractible, and observed short-term memory deficits. Even though disabled children were not part of the standardization sample, the WRAML can be useful for children with suspected memory deficits. Further research is needed with disabled children.

Ordering Information

Publisher

Western Psychological Services, 12031 Wilshire Boulevard, Los Angeles, CA 90025-1251; Phone: 310-478-2061; Fax: 310-478-7838; Web site: http://www.wpspublish.com.

Authors

David Seslow and Wayne Adams.

Publication Date

1990.

References

Hammill, D. D., Brown, L., & Bryant, B. R. (1992). *A consumer's guide to tests in print* (2nd ed.). Austin, TX: PRO-ED.

Medway, F. (1992). Review of the Wide Range Assessment of Memory and Learning. In J. J. Kramer & J. C. Conoley (Eds.), *The Eleventh Mental Measurements Yearbook*. Lincoln, NE: The Buros Institute of Mental Measurements.

Woodcock-Johnson Psychoeducation Battery III: Tests of Cognitive Abilities and Tests of Achievement (WJ III, WJ III ACH, WJ III COG),
for testing individuals from age 2 to the geriatric level
Reviewed by Aileen C. Lau-Dickinson, Ed.D., Special Education Administration

---

Usefulness of the Test for Educators

Test Authors' Purpose

"The Woodcock-Johnson III consists of two distinct, co-normed batteries: WJ III Tests of Cognitive Abilities (WJ III COG) and the WJ III Tests of Achievement (WJ III ACH). Together, these batteries comprise a wide age-range, comprehensive system for measuring general intellectual ability (g), specific cognitive abilities, oral language, and academic achievement" (Technical Manual, p. 1).

Decision-Making Applications

The WJ III is an in-depth measurement of cognition and achievement and can be used for comprehensive evaluation when an individual scores poorly on a screening test. The WJ III is especially useful for making placement decisions for children with learning problems. Discrepancies between cognitive ability and achievement levels can be determined and the procedures for establishing discrepancies are clearly spelled out for the examiner. In the field of learning disabilities, discrepancy information is used as part of the decision-making process when determining placement for learning disability (LD) or for determining placement in special programs. Further, the WJ III ACH tests can be useful for assisting in vocational planning as valuable information can be gleaned about reading, writing, and mathematics performance. Instructional needs of the individual can also be gleaned from the WJ III ACH for developing Individual Education Plans (IEPs).

Relevant Population

The WJ III can be used from the preschool level to the geriatric level to obtain information of general intellectual ability, specific cognitive abilities, oral language, and achievement. The WJ III is designed particularly for the school-aged population, but there is a broad range of measurement extending from age 2 to the geriatric level.

Characteristics Described

There are 42 WJ III tests contained in the total battery: 20 cognitive tests and 22 achievement tests. Test items are grouped under clusters (i.e., "set of two or more tests that, after combining scores, can be interpreted with derived scores") (Technical Manual, p. 1). The clusters forming the WJ III COG battery include Comprehension-Knowledge, Long-Term Retrieval, Visual-Spatial Thinking, Auditory Processing, Fluid Reasoning, Processing Speed, and Short-Term Memory. Clusters that form the WJ III ACH battery include Reading, Writing, Mathematics, Comprehension-Knowledge, Auditory Processing, and Long-Term Retrieval. Table 2.2 displays the "Broad and Narrow Abilities Measured by the WJ III COG and WJ III ACH" (Technical Manual, pp. 13–14). The WJ III refers to Broad Abilities as those abilities that are based on a multifaceted picture and Narrow Abilities as those based on a single ability.

WJ III ACH Tests of Achievement

1. *Letter-Wood Identification*: The examinee is asked to identify letters and to pronounce words correctly. Narrow Abilities Measured: Reading decoding.

2. *Reading Fluency*: The examinee is asked to read simple sentences in the Subject Response Booklet and to decide if the statement is true or not true. Narrow Abilities Measured: Reading speed.

3. *Story Recall*: The examinee is asked to recall as many details as possible from a story that was presented to him using an audio recording. Narrow Abilities Measured: Language development, Listening ability.

4. *Understanding Directions*: The examinee is asked to follow directions given by an audio recording by pointing to various objects in a colored picture. Narrow Abilities Measured: Language development, Listening ability.

5. *Calculation*: The examinee is asked to write single numbers and perform addition, subtraction, multiplication, and division problems as well as geometric, trigonometric, logarithmic, and calculus operations. Problems

presented increase in difficulty and are presented in the Subject Response Booklet. Narrow Abilities Measured: Math achievement.

6. *Math Fluency*: The examinee is asked to solve addition, subtraction, and multiplication problems quickly. The time limit is three minutes and the problems are found in the Student Response Booklet. Narrow Abilities Measured: Math achievement, Numerical facility.

7. *Spelling*: The examinee is asked to demonstrate prewriting skills, upper and lower case letters, and to spell words correctly. Item difficulty increases. Narrow Abilities Measured: Spelling ability.

8. *Writing Fluency*: The examinee is asked to formulate and write simple sentences quickly after being presented with a stimulus picture. There is a seven-minute time limit. Narrow Abilities Measured: Writing speed.

9. *Passage Comprehension*: The examinee is asked to match a rebus with a picture or object (easiest level). On the next level, the examinee is asked to point to the picture represented by a phrase. Finally, the examinee is asked to read a passage and identify a missing key word that makes sense for that passage. Narrow Abilities Measured: Reading comprehension, Verbal (printed) language comprehension.

10. *Applied Problems*: The examinee is asked to listen to a math problem and then to solve the problem. Narrow Abilities Measured: Quantitative reasoning, Math achievement, Math knowledge.

11. *Writing Samples*: The examinee is asked to produce written sentences of increasing complexity. Narrow Abilities Measured: Writing ability.

12. *Story Recall-Delayed*: The examinee is asked to recall elements of the story presented in Item 3 after 30 minutes and not more than a delay of eight days. Narrow Abilities Measured: Meaningful memory.

13. *Word Attack*: The examinee is asked to produce sounds of letters, nonsense words, and low-frequency words. Item difficulty increases. Narrow Abilities Measured: Reading decoding, Phonetic coding: Analysis and synthesis.

14. *Picture Vocabulary*: The examinee is asked to identify pictures and objects. Item difficulty increases. Narrow Abilities Measured: Language development, Lexical knowledge.

15. *Oral Comprehension*: The examinee is asked to supply a missing word after being presented an audio-recorded passage. Item difficulty increases. Narrow Abilities Measured: Listening ability.

16. *Editing*: The examinee is asked to recognize errors in punctuation, spelling, capitalization, and inappropriate word usage in a written passage. Passages increase in difficulty. Narrow Abilities Measured: Language development, English usage.

17. *Reading Vocabulary*: The examinee is asked to supply synonyms, antonyms,

and analogies after reading words and incomplete analogies. Narrow Abilities Measured: Verbal (printed) language comprehension, Lexical knowledge.

18. *Quantitative Concepts*: The examinee is asked to count and identify numbers, shapes, and sequences in the first subtest. In the second subtest, the examinee is asked to look at a series of numbers, figure out the pattern, then provide the missing number in a series. Narrow Abilities Measured: Math knowledge, Quantitative reasoning.

19. *Academic Knowledge*: The examinee is asked to demonstrate knowledge in the areas of Science, Social Studies, and Humanities. Narrow Abilities Measured: General information, Science, Cultural, and Geography information.

20. *Spelling of Sounds*: The examinee is asked to write single letters of sounds and letter combinations after listening to an audiotape. Item difficulty increases. Narrow Abilities Measured: Spelling ability, Phonetic coding, Analysis.

21. *Sound Awareness*: The examinee is asked to demonstrate knowledge of phonological awareness using rhyming, deletion, substitution, and reversal techniques. Item difficulty increases. Narrow Abilities Measured: Phonetic coding: Analysis and Synthesis.

22. *Punctuation and Capitalization*: The examinee is required to punctuate or capitalize items correctly. Narrow Abilities Measured: English usage.

WJ III Tests of Cognitive Abilities

1. *Verbal Comprehension*: The examinee is asked to identify pictures of familiar and unfamiliar objects. Item difficulty increases. Narrow Abilities Measured: Lexical knowledge, Language development.

2. *Visual-Auditory Learning*: The examinee is asked to learn and recall rebuses. Narrow Abilities Measured: Associative memory.

3. *Spatial Relations*: The examinee is asked to identify the two or three pieces that form a complete target shape. Test item increases. Narrow Abilities Measured: Visualization, Spatial relations.

4. *Sound Blending*: The examinee is asked to blend phonemes or syllables into words. Narrow Abilities Measured: Phonetic coding, Synthesis.

5. *Concept Formation*: The examinee is asked to derive the rule for each complete stimulus item presented. Narrow Abilities Measured: Induction.

6. *Visual Matching*: The examinee is asked to point to the two matching shapes in a row of four or five shapes (version one, preschool or students with developmental delays). Two-minute time limit. In Version two, the examinee is asked to locate and circle the two identical numbers in a row of six numbers. Item difficulty increases. Three-minute time limit. Narrow Abilities Measured: Perceptual speed.

7. *Numbers Reversed*: The examinee is asked to hold a series of numbers in his memory and then to reverse the sequence. Narrow Abilities Measured: Working memory.

8. *Incomplete Words*: The examinee is asked to identify a complete word after listening to an audiotape of words with missing phonemes. Narrow Abilities Measured: Phonetic coding, Analysis.

9. *Auditory Working Memory*: The examinee is asked to listen to a series of digits and words and then to reorder the information, repeating first the objects and then the sequence of digits. Narrow Abilities Measured: Working memory.

10. *Visual-Auditory Learning-Delayed*: The examinee is asked to relearn the associations presented in Test 2 with a 30-minute or up to eight-day delay. Narrow Abilities Measured: Associative memory.

11. *General Information*: The examinee is asked to respond to two subtests that contain "where" and "what" questions. Narrow Abilities Measured: General (verbal) information.

12. *Retrieval Fluency*: The examinee is asked to name as many examples as possible from a given category in one minute. Narrow Abilities Measured: Ideational fluency.

13. *Picture Recognition*: The examinee is asked to recognize a subset of previously presented pictures within a field of detractors. Item difficulty increases. Narrow Abilities Measured: Visual memory.

14. *Auditory Attention*: The examinee is asked to listen to a word while looking at four pictures and then to select the correct picture for the word. Narrow Abilities Measured: Speech-sound discrimination, Resistance to auditory stimulus distortion.

15. *Analysis-Synthesis*: The examinee is given instructions on how to perform an increasingly difficult task, and then he is asked to perform the task. Narrow Abilities Measured: General sequential reasoning.

16. *Decision Speed*: The examinee is asked to locate two pictures that appear in a row that are most similar. Three-minute time limit. Narrow Abilities Measured: Semantic processing speed.

17. *Memory for Words*: The examinee is asked to repeat lists of unrelated words in the same sequence. Narrow Abilities Measured: Memory span.

18. *Rapid Picture Naming*: The examinee is asked to name pictures when presented in the same sequence. Two-minute time limit. Narrow Abilities Measured: Naming facility.

19. *Planning*: The examinee is asked to trace a pattern without removing the pencil from the paper or retracing the lines. Narrow Abilities Measured: Spatial scanning, General sequential reasoning.

20. *Pair Cancellation*: The examinee is asked to locate and mark a repeated pattern as quickly as possible. Three-minute time limit. Narrow Abilities Measured: Attention and concentration.

Test Scores Obtained

The WJ III must be scored by a computer program. (WJ III Compuscore and Profiles Program, 2001). Scores for General Intellectual Ability are (g) (GIA) general intelligence scores, and Predicted Achievement Scores are provided by the computer program. The Predicted Achievement Scores are scores that provide the best possible prediction for success in four areas of achievement (Reading, Mathematics, Written Language, and Knowledge). These scores account for developmental differences between cognitive abilities and achievement domains. Age equivalents, percentiles, and standard scores are provided through the computer scoring program. Discrepancy norms are available, and these norms are the differences between an actual score obtained by a subject and some predicted score for that same individual. There are two sets of discrepancy information: ability/achievement discrepancies and intra-ability discrepancies. Administering both the WJ III COG and the WJ III ACH batteries will provide discrepancy scores necessary for identification of individuals with learning disabilities. A Brief Intellectual Ability (BIA) score is also available for screening purposes.

Technical Adequacy

Validity Confirmation

Test item validity was established for the tests by basing the content of WJ III on the Cattell-Horn-Carroll (CHC) theory of cognitive abilities (Technical Manual, pp. 10–12).

WJ III ACH test item validity was justified as follows: "test and cluster content were designed to cover core curricular areas and areas of oral language competency and achievement specified in federal legislation" (Technical Manual, p. 50). In developing test items, contributions were made by experienced teachers and psychologists. The 22 WJ III ACH test items sample achievement in reading, mathematics, written language, oral language, and curricular knowledge. The authors state that the "item content in these tests was based primarily on the principle of providing a broad sampling of achievement rather than an in-depth assessment in a relatively narrow area" (Technical Manual, p. 52). According to the Technical Manual (p. 51), "To ensure that all items in a test measured the same narrow ability or trait, the process of item selection employed stringent fit-criteria based on the Rasch model. . . . This process also helped to avoid selecting items that measured processes extraneous to the intended construct." All test items were reviewed, and any item that was identified as potentially biased was eliminated or revised. The 20 WJ III COG tests provide a representative sampling of the complex set of abilities considered to constitute intellectual ability using CHC theory. For detailed information on the cognitive functions included in the CHC theory, see Chapter 2 of the WJ III.

Test response validity was established for the WJ III COG by correlating scores with other measures of intelligence. These measures included the Wechsler Intelligence Scale for Children-III (WISC-III), the Differential Ability Scale (DAS), the Wechsler Adult Intelligence Scale-III (WAIS-III), and the Leiter-R. The WJ III, General Intellectual Ability (GIA) correlations with the WPPSI-R and the WISC-III Full scale IQ scores consistently ranged from .71 to .76. Correlations with the WAIS-III were slightly lower (.67).

Reports of correlations using the WJ III ACH Battery and other achievement measures, such as the Wechsler Individual Achievement Tests (WIAT), the Kaufman Tests of Educational Achievement (KTEA), and the Wide Range Achievement Test-III (WRAT-III), suggest that the WJ III ACH measures academic skills and abilities similar to those measured by other achievement tests. Correlations for the WIAT and the WJ III ACH were .65 and for the WIAT and the KTEA were .79.

Reliability Confirmation

Two studies were reported that established test-retest reliability for the WJ III. The first study reports that eight cognitive (WJ III COG) and achievement (WJ III ACH) speeded tests were administered to 165 subjects in three age groups. The test interval was one day. The correlations for the speeded tests ranged from .76 to .87 for ages 7–11, from .73 to .89 for ages 14–17, and from .70 to .94 for ages 26–79. The correlations for the Math Fluency subtest were the highest across all age groups. A second test-retest study using a sample of 457 students ranging in age from 4 to 17 was conducted, with a test interval of one year. The test-retest correlations for 17 WJ III ACH and 12 clusters gave a median test-retest reliability for all ages of .94.

Since the WJ III has a form A and B, alternate form reliability procedures were undertaken. The median alternate form reliability correlation was .85 across the 11 age groups, with the majority of the correlations ranging from .85 to .96.

Objectivity Confirmation

Scoring keys are available for WJ III ACH Test 2: Reading Fluency, Test 6: Math Fluency, and Test 11: Writing Samples. The WJ III Compuscore and Profiles Program (Riverside Publishing Co., 2001) is a microcomputer program used to assist examiners in scoring the WJ III. The program calculates scores and provides norm-referenced and proficiency-based descriptions of a subject's performance on the assessments. The examiner enters the scores from the WJ III COG and WJ III ACH batteries into the computer program. Objectivity of norm-referenced results is ensured.

Three tests of the WJ III ACH (Writing Samples, Writing Fluency, and Handwriting) require a subjective evaluation, so inter-rater objectivity studies for these measures were conducted. Six raters scored the writing tests and the correlations were about .90. These were for grades 2, 9, and 16. A second study for grade 3 and high school and college using trained raters gave correlations in the high .90s, and a third study using a learning disabled sample revealed a reliability coefficient of .93. These studies suggest that trained raters for writing tests are consistent in their scoring.

Statistical Confirmation

Statistical data on validity, reliability, and standardization procedures can be found in the Technical Manual.

Special Features

Acronyms

WJ III, WJ III COG, and WJ III ACH.

Levels of the Test

One level for Cognitive and one for Achievement.

Number of Test Forms

There are two equivalent forms of the WJ III: A and B.

Norm-Referenced?

Yes. Extensive information is given in Chapter 2 of the Technical Manual regarding the standardization and norming procedures for the WJ III. A large nationally representative sample of 8,818 subjects was used as the normative sample. All subjects were given both the cognitive and achievement batteries so that the normative data would be based on a single sample. Subjects were randomly selected within a stratified sampling design that controlled for 10 specific community and subject variables.

Criterion-Referenced?

No.

Feasibility Considerations

Testing Time

Testing time will vary between very young subjects and those with special needs. However, with experienced examiners, approximately 60–70 minutes would be required for each battery: Cognitive and Achievement.

For Testing Groups? Individuals?

Individuals.

Test Administration and Scoring

As indicated earlier, the WJ III must be scored by computer. Examiners enter identifying information, raw score, and "Test Session Observations Checklist" directly into the computer program. The Compuscore and Profiles Program calculates all derived scores and discrepancies and generates a summary narrative report, age/grade profiles, and standard and percentile rankings. It is suggested that novice examiners study the Examiner's Manual, Test Books, Test Record, Subject Response Booklet, and Examiner Training Workbook. Several practice tests should be administered before the novice examiner can be proficient in the administration of the WJ III.

Test Materials and Approximate Costs

WJ III: Complete Battery: $925; Tests of Achievement (Form A): $425; Tests of Achievement (Form A) with Carrying Case: $500; Tests of Achievement (Form B): $425; Tests of Achievement (Form B) with Carrying Case: $500; Tests of Cognitive Abilities: $575; Tests of Cognitive Abilities with Carrying Case: $650; Leather Carrying Case: $150; Compuscore and Profiled Program: $99; Technical Manual: $50; Report Writer for the WJ III: $295.

WJ III ACH: Test Records and Subject Response Books (Form A) (25): $55; Test Records and Subject Response Books (Form B) (25): $55.

WJ III COG: Test Records and Subject Response Booklets (25): $55; Brief Intellectual Ability (BEA) Test Records (25): $25.

Adequacy of Test Manuals

The WJ III has three manuals available for the consumer: the Technical Manual and two Examiner's Manuals (one for Cognitive and one for Achievement). These manuals are well written and specific in regard to test procedures and scoring. The Examiner's Manuals are not needed for actual testing as clear, well-written directions for the administration of each subtest are included on the test easels.

Excerpts from Other Test Reviews

"The WJ III's norms, reliability, and validity appear adequate. . . . Although the domains assessed and their interpretations are well within the mainstream of modern testing, the methodology used to develop the test is quite different from that used to develop most other tests" (Salvia & Ysseldyke, 2001, p. 614).

Ordering Information

Publisher

Riverside Publishing Company, 425 Spring Lake Drive, Itasca, IL 60143-2079; Phone: 800-323-9540; Fax: 630-467-7192; Web site: www.riverpub.com.

Authors

Richard W. Woodcock, Kevin S. McGrew, and Nancy Mather.

Publication Date

2001.

Cautions and Comments

The WJ III is a comprehensive battery of two norm-referenced assessments to measure cognition and achievement. Discrepancy scores between ability and achievement give the information needed to meet IDEA (Individuals with Disabilities Education Act) eligibility requirements for the diagnosis and subsequent placement of students with learning disabilities into special programs. Because the WJ III Tests of Achievement and Tests of Cognitive Abilities are co-normed, intra-individual discrepancies and intra-cognitive discrepancies scores are available for professionals to determine strengths and weaknesses, identify language and learning disabilities, and assist in intervention planning. The WJ III can be helpful in rehabilitation centers for gathering information necessary in planning habilitation and rehabilitation programs. The standardization, validity, and reliability procedures appear to be adequate. The average educator may be intimidated by the extent of the test and find that interpreting the derived scores may be difficult. Only with repeated administrations of the WJ III will the educator find the battery user-friendly.

The Report Writer for the WJ III, developed by Dr. Richard Woodcock, is a valuable resource. The program produces an accurate and comprehensive report for the educator. This computer program is an extension of the WJ III Compuscore and Profiles Program and can be helpful for the practitioner in creating more comprehensive and understandable reports.

Reference

Salvia, J., & Ysseldyke, J. E. (2001). *Assessment* (8th ed.). Boston: Houghton Mifflin.

III

Instructional Prescription Testing and Decision-Making

INTRODUCTION

Once students are placed in instructional programs, instruction begins. After instruction prescribed to achieve learning objectives is completed, instructional prescription testing is done as a basis for prescribing subsequent instruction. Test results are used to make one of two decisions: (1) students have achieved the learning objective and are ready to pursue the next, more advanced learning objective in the program or (2) students have not yet achieved the learning objective and need corrective instruction to be ready to advance. In other words, students have learning deficiencies in need of remediation.

To be useful in making instructional prescription decisions, instructional prescription tests must indicate achievement of learning objectives so that students who achieve them can be advanced and students with deficiencies that need to be remediated can achieve the learning objectives. The more an instructional prescription test reveals about student deficiencies, the more useful it is in prescribing remedial instruction. As indicated in the User's Guide, the accountability testing movement was initiated largely because students with learning deficiencies were being promoted and graduated despite their inability to contribute to their own or society's best interests. Although accountability testing legislation may be successful in preventing social promotion and graduation, dire consequences could result. The failure rate could increase substantially.

To solve the problem, students who fail to achieve learning objectives must receive remedial instruction so that they can earn promotion. In order for remedial instruction to be effective, it must be prescribed to correct particular learning deficiencies that caused the students to fail. This requires that instructional prescription tests reveal student academic deficiencies.

The least an instructional prescription test must be able to do is to indicate the degree of deficiency of the characteristic or skill being assessed. This tends to indicate the amount of corrective instruction needed for students to achieve the learning objective. Students with greater deficiencies need more corrective instruction over time to achieve the objective. Plans can be made to reteach the skills students failed to master using various instructional techniques shown by research to be effective (see Friedman & Fisher, 1998) and by varying instruction so that students do not become bored.

Instructional prescription tests can be more effective to the extent that they reveal deficiencies in subskills that contribute to the performance of the primary skill being taught. For example, if the skill being taught is solving basic arithmetic story problems, students might exhibit a deficiency in choosing the appropriate procedure (addition, subtraction, multiplication, or division) or the deficiency might be in calculation. An instructional prescription test that not only reveals the degree of deficiency in solving arithmetic story problems but, in addition, reveals whether the deficiency results from choosing the correct arithmetic procedures, executing the calculations correctly, or both, is more useful in prescribing corrective instruction because it indicates subskill deficiencies that must be remediated to increase student overall performance on an arithmetic story problem test.

An instructional prescription test that assesses subskills must include test items that reveal deficiencies in performing each of the subskills. So the greater the number of subskills tested, the more test items needed on the test. Moreover, a number of test items need to be constructed to assess the performance of each subskill. For example, a student could miss one test item that assesses a subskill by chance. However, if the student misses three or more test items that assess the same subskill, a pattern emerges and it becomes more evident that the student is deficient in performing the subskill. An instructional prescription test that assesses performance of subskills usually yields a score for the major skill being assessed, as well as a score for each of the subtests. For example, the Woodcock Reading Mastery Tests (WRMT-R), reviewed in this part of the handbook, assess reading and the following subskills: (1) visual-auditory learning, (2) letter identification, (3) word identification, (4) word attack, (5) word comprehension, and (6) passage comprehension. A number of test items are included to assess each subskill, and the tests yield composite scores as well as subtest scores.

Since the purpose of instructional prescriptions is to achieve learning objectives, objective-referenced tests are needed to assess the effectiveness of instructional prescriptions. Objective-referenced tests are a type of criterion-referenced test in which the criteria of achievement are learning objectives. Such tests typically indicate the extent to which achievement of learning objectives have been mastered. Level of mastery of each objective is assessed in terms of test performance—for instance, (1) 0%–50% of the test items answered correctly might be reported as "not mastered," (2) 51%–75% as "partially mastered," and (3) 76%–99% as "mastered." Corrective instruction would be prescribed for students whose test results are reported as "not mastered" or "partially mastered" until the students' performance reaches the level of "mastery."

Norm-referenced tests are not as suitable as criterion-referenced tests for instructional prescription testing because they do not typically indicate deficiencies in performing skills and subskills being taught. Rather, they indicate level of achievement when compared to other students who have taken the test. For example, percentile level of performance indicates the percentage of students who perform below the level of the student being assessed. Level of achievement is reported for performance on the test as a whole. And if there are subtest components, profiles can be derived showing student performance on the various subtests. A profile reveals variations in level of subskill achievement. Profiles are often interpreted to reveal students' "weaknesses" when in fact they reveal only level of performance as compared to peers who took the test. For instance, it is quite possible for students to be above average in performing a skill in comparison to their classmates or a norm group and still not have mastered the skill. Also, it is quite possible for students to be below average in performing a skill when compared to their classmates or a norm group and not be deficient in performing the skill. So it is unwarranted to conclude that students who perform a skill below average on a norm-referenced test have a weakness or deficiency. The most accurate way of identifying deficiencies is by using objective-referenced tests. There are, however, times when the norm is the desired objective. For instance, when assessing motor development in early childhood, the most useful criterion is the norm for the students' age group. In such instances, degree of deficiency is assessed in terms of how far students' performance is below the norm for their age group.

Although objective-referenced tests are usually more suitable for assessing deficiencies, they are not as suitable as norm-referenced tests for assessing superiority in performing a skill. The higher the student's score is above average, the more superior the student can be said to be in performing the skill. Results of objective-referenced tests can indicate only deficiencies in performing a skill or absence of deficiencies. If the goal is to reduce the number of student failures by remediating their deficiencies, then objective-referenced tests are more appropriate. If the goal is to make a decision based on student group status, then norm-referenced tests are more appropriate when one wishes to reward superior status or to cull out students of lower status.

It should also be noted that to stop social promotion and the graduation of illiterates and students who are qualified for only the most menial jobs, students must achieve all required learning objectives, regardless of what their relative status may be in their class or school.

The individual differences in student readiness in a class at the beginning of a school term have always presented a challenge to classroom teachers. They are challenged to meet the needs of all students, ranging from students with learning deficiencies to precocious students. Practices such as social promotion and the mainstreaming of disabled students markedly increase the number of students with learning deficiencies in each regular classroom, exacerbating teachers' problems. Students with learning difficulties not only require more instruction, they often require special instruction targeted to their specific deficiencies. It is the primary purpose of instructional prescription testing to reveal student deficiencies.

Commercial tests are available and can be used to diagnose specific learning deficiencies in most basic skill areas, including reading, math, spoken language, and written language. Tests will be reviewed in each of these areas. Some are more effective diagnostic instruments than others. Tests that have more than one form to serve as pre-test and post-test can also be used to evaluate the effectiveness of remedial instruction.

Educators must become proficient in diagnosing academic deficiencies in subjects they teach so that they have a basis for prescribing corrective instruction. They should be able to devise, administer, score, and interpret instructional prescription tests in their academic fields of expertise, but they should not be held responsible for diagnosing underlying causes of students' failure to learn. For example, they should not be held responsible for diagnosing behavior, psychomotor, adaptation, vision, or hearing problems that hamper learning and must be remediated to enable students to overcome their academic deficiencies. On the other hand, educators should learn how to administer and score tests that enable them to make enlightened referrals to clinicians who can diagnose and treat underlying causes of failure to learn.

Educators can learn how to make observations and administer tests that enable them to make referrals with more confidence than most presently have. It behooves educators to read Part V, "Referral Testing and Decision-Making," in order to learn about observation techniques, informal assessments, and published tests they can use to make enlightened referrals. Although they are not qualified to use these techniques to diagnose specific causes of failure to learn, they can interpret test results well enough to decide when a referral is warranted. Rules of thumb are cited that enable educators to make referrals confidently and to provide evidence to support their decisions with respect to psychomotor, vision, hearing, adaptation, and behavior problems.

In short, educators should know how to diagnose and remediate academic learning deficiencies in the fields they teach. They should not presume to be able to diagnose or treat underlying causes of students' failure to learn what they teach. They should, however, be able to use test results and signs of primary underlying causes of academic failure to refer students for in-depth clinical diagnoses and possible treatment.

REFERENCE

Friedman, M. I., & Fisher, S. P. (1998). *Handbook on effective instructional strategies: Evidence for decision-making*. Columbia, SC: Institute for Evidence-Based Decision-Making in Education.

Brigance Diagnostic Comprehensive Inventory of Basic Skills-Revised (CIBS-R), for testing individuals from 5 through 13 years of age
Reviewed by Aileen C. Dickinson, Ed.D., Special Education Administration

---

Usefulness of the Test for Educators

Test Authors' Purpose

The purpose of the CIBS-R is to simplify and combine the processes of assessing, diagnosing, record keeping, and instructional planning for elementary and middle school students.

Decision-Making Applications

The CIBS-R is primarily a criterion-referenced measure with over 154 assessments in readiness, speech, listening, reading, spelling, writing, research and study skills, and math. These assessments are based on curriculum content and objectives and can be used to identify the student's strengths and weaknesses in pre-academic and academic areas.

The CIBS-R can be used for diagnostic placement decisions as well as for instructional planning. However, only a portion of the test has been standardized. The standardized portions of the CIBS-R are designed to meet state and federal assessment requirements and can be used to meet eligibility requirements for placement in special education. Children who demonstrate extensive strengths or weaknesses in specific areas would require additional testing to establish the diagnosis of learning disability or giftedness. These assessments can be most helpful in planning instruction for those students identified with specific weaknesses. The CIBS-R has been used for many years to identify strengths and weaknesses across skill areas. Components of the standardized portions of the CIBS-R include Readiness Assessments, First-Grade through Sixth-Grade Assessments, and the CIBS-R screener.

Readiness Assessments

The 27 Readiness Assessments of the CIBS-R are designed for kindergarten students. All 27 assessments have been standardized and validated. These assessments fall under the following composites: general knowledge, language, gross-motor skills, graphomotor and writing skills, reading skills, and math skills. Since these assessments may be used to determine a child's readiness skills for kindergarten or first grade, they can also be used as admissions tests for kindergarten or first grade.

First-Grade through Sixth-Grade Assessments

Ten assessments, designed for first grade through sixth grade students, were included in the national standardization and validation study. The 10 assessments include Basic Reading Skills, Reading Comprehension, Mathematics, Written Expression, and Listening Comprehension. In addition, three assessments, when timed, can generate separate scores on a critical and central aspect of information processing and its efficiency (i.e., processing speed in the areas of reading rate, computational rate, and rate of written expression). Alternate forms of the assessment are also available for several areas to permit pre- and post-testing of skill development.

CIBS-R Screener

Three of the 10 First-Grade through Sixth-Grade Assessments can be used as a quick screening tool to determine whether additional testing is needed. The screening portion of the test would not be useful for placement purposes. The screening assessment could be used to refer students for further in-depth testing in their weakest areas. The screening tests includes Comprehends Passages, Sentence Writing, and Computational Skills.

Relevant Population

The standardized and validated portions of the CIBS-R (27 assessments—Readiness, 10 assessments—First-Grade through Sixth-Grade) have been standardized and validated on children 5 through 13 years of age. The criterion-referenced entire test can be used for children from pre-kindergarten through grade 9.

Characteristics Described

Student achievement is assessed through the subtest scores obtained through the following composites for the Readiness and the First Grade-Sixth Grade portions of the CIBS-R. Figures 1.1 and 1.2 show the relationship of assessments to composites for the Readiness Assessments and for the First-Grade through Sixth-Grade portions of the CIBS-R.

Test Scores Obtained

Both norm-referenced and criterion-referenced data are provided. Correct responses are circled and incorrect responses are underlined. The number of correct responses are recorded as the raw score. However, this is not clearly stated in the Technical Manual, Student Record Book, or the Standardized Scoring Sheets.

Raw scores are the number of items that the student successfully completed. Total raw scores are converted to standard scores. Norm-referenced data includes percentile ranks, quotients, and grade-equivalent and age-equivalent scores.

Technical Adequacy

Validity Confirmation

Test item validity: There is no evidence of the test item validity based on an analysis of test items. It is stated that "there is abundant support for the content validity (test items) of the CIBS-R and for its applicability in educational settings" (Standardization and Validation Manual, p. 39). The test items were selected by the author through his research of readiness literature and educational development and in collaboration with "hundreds of educators across the US who assisted in item selection" (p. 39).

Test response validity: Correlations were established between the CIBS-R Readiness Assessments and the Woodcock-Johnson Psycho-Educational Battery. The correlations ranged from .10 to .79 for 115 students. According to the authors, "the range of performance on some CIBS-R assessments is restricted, correlations are by nature restricted" (Standardization and Validation Manual, p. 49).

The correlations between the CIBS-R and the WISC-II for the First-Grade through Sixth-Grade Assessments range from .43 to .72. Data was collected from 78 students.

Partial correlations (after adjustment for ages) between reading and written language subtests from group achievement tests (Iowa Tests of Basic Skills, California Achievement Test, and the Stanford Achievement Test) and the CIBS-R First-Grade

Figure 1.1
Relationships between Readiness Assessments and Composites

Assessments	General Knowledge and Language	Gross-Motor Skills	Graphomotor and Writing Skills	Reading	Math
A-2 Recognizes Colors (s)	X				
A-3 Self-help Skills (s)	X				
A-1 Personal Data Response	X				
A-7 Identifies Body Parts	X				
A-26 Understands Directional and Positional Concepts	X				
A-25 Running and Skipping Gross-Motor Skills (s)		X			
A-23 Standing Gross-Motor Skills		X			
A-24 Walking Gross-Motor Skills		X			
A-4 Draws a Person (s)			X		
A-5 Visual Motor Skills—Forms (s)			X		
A-12 Prints Lowercase Letters in Sequence (s)			X		
A-13 Prints Uppercase Letters Dictated (s)			X		
A-14 Prints Lowercase Letters Dictated (s)			X		
A-11 Prints Uppercase Letters in Sequence			X		
A-15 Prints Personal Data			X		
A-22 Writes Numerals in Sequence			X		
A-6 Visual Discrimination—Forms, Letters, and Words (s)				X	
A-8 Recites Alphabet (s)				X	
A-9 Reads Uppercase Letters (s)				X	
A-10 Reads Lowercase Letters				X	
A-27 Readiness for Reading				X	
A-20 Joins Sets (s)					X
A-21 Numeral Comprehension (s)					X
A-16 Rote Counting					X
A-17 Understands Quantitative Concepts					X
A-18 Counts Objects					X
A-19 Reads Numerals					X

(s) = supplemental. Supplemental assessment scores are not included in the composite scores.
Source: Standardization and Validation Manual. Reprinted by permission.

Figure 1.2
Relationships between First-Grade through Sixth-Grade Assessments and Composites

Assessments	Basic Reading Composite	Reading Comprehension Composite	Math Composite	Written Expression Composite	Listening Comprehension Indicator	Information Processing
H-4 Warning and Safety Signs (supplemental)*	X					
D-1 Word Recognition Grade-Placement Test	X					
G-1 Word-Analysis Survey	X					
F-1 Reading Vocabulary Comprehension Grade-Placement Test		X				
F-2 Comprehends Passages**		X				
M-1 Computational Skills Grade-Placement Test**			X			
M-2 Problem-Solving Grade-Placement Test			X			
I-1 Spelling Grade-Placement Test				X		
J-3 Sentence-Writing Grade-Placement Test**				X		
C-4 Listening Vocabulary Comprehension Grade-Placement Test					X	
Math Information Processing***						X
Writing Information Processing***						X
Reading Information Processing***						X

*This assessment is not included in the Basic Reading Composite score.

**These assessments comprise the CIBS-R Screener.

***These assessments are not administered separately. Scores are derived by applying separate scoring criteria to previously administered assessments.

Source: Standardization and Validation Manual. Reprinted by permission.

through Sixth-Grade Assessments were made. These correlations revealed a strong relationship between criterion measures and like assessments on the CIBS-R. Correlations were particularly strong, with the basic reading composite having the strongest correlation with spelling (.84) and the weakest with word analysis (.04).

Reliability Confirmation

Test reliability was assessed by correlating scores obtained from administering the test to the same students at different times. Test-retest reliability was established in 1998 with 41 students in kindergarten through sixth grade. Reliability ranged from .63 to .89 between the first and second administration.

Test-retest reliability for the CIBS-R Readiness Assessments also demonstrates high reliability, ranging from .82 to .99 when retesting occurs over a short interval of time.

Reliability was also established by correlating scores obtained from administering the alternate forms of the CIBS-R to the same population. There are no alternate forms for the CIBS-R Readiness Assessment. Therefore, evidence of alternate form reliability cannot be reported.

Objectivity Confirmation

Following each subtest of the CIBS-R Readiness Assessment and the First-Grade through Sixth-Grade Assessments, criteria for scoring the response correct are listed under "Accuracy" of response. For two subtests, Visual Motor Skills-Forms and Prints Personal Data, "Scoring Criteria" are detailed. The evaluator has the responsibility of making judgments of test item responses which may not be in agreement with other evaluators. There may be discrepancies in judging "correct" responses by evaluators, as there are no clear-cut criteria. Basals and ceilings vary from subtest to subtest. The basal establishes the highest point at which students can be assumed to have mastered all previous items/skills. The ceiling indicates the instructional level at which students will experience failure and frustration. According to the authors, "absence of a basal and/or ceiling with young or delayed students does not interfere with valid scoring of an assessment" (Standardization and Validation Manual, p. 10). Caution should be taken when scoring items correct/incorrect, since examiner judgment can differ from examiner to examiner. The 1998 study involved two different examiners (classroom teachers and an educational examiner administered the CIBS-R) and the correlation coefficients were high in regard to different examiners obtaining identical results. No correlation coefficients were given in the Manual to support these results.

Statistical Confirmation

Statistical data on validity, reliability, and norms for the CIBS-R Readiness Assessment and the standardized portions of the First-Grade through Sixth-Grade Assessment can be found in the CIBS-R Standardization and Validation Manual prepared by Frances Page Glascoe.

Special Features

Acronym

CIBS-R.

Levels of the Test

The standardized portions of the CIBS-R include the entire Readiness Assessment, 10 composites of the First-Grade through Sixth-Grade Assessment, and three Screening Assessments.

Number of Test Forms

Forms A and B for the First-Grade through Sixth-Grade Assessments. The Readiness Assessment has no alternate forms.

Norm-Referenced?

Yes. The Readiness Assessment and the 10 composites of the First-Grade through Sixth Grade Assessment are norm-referenced. National sampling was conducted in six sites representing the broad geographic regions of the continental United States. Within each site, one or two schools were identified that had a balance of children from backgrounds of high, middle, and low socioeconomic status. The sample was overwhelming urban (83%) and 17% rural. 1,121 students were used in the standardization study. It is reported that the characteristics of participating students closely approximates U.S. demographics.

Criterion-Referenced?

Yes. 154 assessments in readiness, speech, listening, research and study skills, reading, spelling, writing, and math are included in the entire CIBS-R. All skill areas are sequenced and the sequence determines the grade levels at which skills are taught and which level competency is expected. Related skill sequences appear at the end of many sections. Learning objectives are the criteria for each skill area. These are clearly stated.

Readiness Assessments: Skills being sampled in each assessment.

General Knowledge

Personal Data: Gives personal data verbally.

Recognizes Colors: Identifies and names 11 colors of objects.

Self-Help Skills: Independently performs self-help skills.

Identifies Body Parts: Points to or touches body parts as named by someone else.

Understands Directional and Positional Concepts: Shows ability to follow verbal prompts such as "front/back," "inside/outside," "right/left," and so on.

Graphomotor and Writing Skills

Draws a Person: Draws a person with recognizable, distinct body parts.

Visual-Motor Skills—Forms: Copies forms; prints uppercase letters in sequence; prints lowercase letters in sequence; prints uppercase letters dictated; prints lowercase letters dictated; prints personal data.

Writes Numerals in Sequence: Writes numerals in sequence from memory from 1 to 100.

Reading

Visual Discrimination—Forms, Letters, and Words: visually discriminates which one of four printed symbols is different; recites alphabet; reads uppercase letters; reads lowercase letters.

Readiness for Reading: Reads some common words, shows interest in reading, and so on.

Math

Rote Counting: Counts by rote; understands quantitative concepts.

Counts Objects: Counts a group of objects with quantities from 3 to 24 pictures of objects.

Reads Numerals: Reads numerals from 2 to 100 when presented out of order.

Joins Sets: Combines and counts two groups of objects.

Numeral Comprehension: Shows quantities to match symbols.

Gross Motor Skills

Standing Gross-Motor Skills: Stands on each foot, toe to toe, and so on.

Walking Gross-Motor Skills: Walks on a straight line, heel-to-toe, and so on.

Running and Skipping Gross-Motor skills: Runs and skips.

First-Grade through Sixth-Grade Assessment (Standardized Portions)

Basic Reading Composite

Word Recognition Grade Placement Test: Pronounces at least 5 out of 10 words at grade level.

Word Analysis Survey: Distinguishes if pairs of words sound alike or different; identifies initial consonants; substitutes sounds; reads word parts; and divides word into syllables.

Warning and Safety Signs: Reads common safety and warning signs, such as "don't walk" and "exit."

Reading Comprehension Composite

Reading Vocabulary Comprehension Grade-Placement Test: Reads three lists of five words and identifies the word in each list that does not belong.

Comprehends Passages: Reads a selection silently and answers question presented orally with at least 80% comprehension accuracy.

Math Composite

Computational Skills Grade-Placement Test: Computes at least three of four problems at grade level.

Problem Solving Grade-Placement Test: Solves at least one of two problems at grade level.

Written Expression Composite

Spelling Grade-Placement Tests: Spells words at grade level with 60% accuracy.

Sentence-Writing Grade Placement Test: Constructs and writes sentences at grade level.

Listening Comprehension Indicator

Listening Vocabulary Comprehension Grade-Placement Test: Listens to a selection with a designated readability level and responds orally to five comprehension questions with at least 80% comprehension accuracy.

Information processing deficits can be assessed by:

1. Math: Counting the number of computational problems completed in 60 seconds.
2. Writing: Counting the number of correctly written sentences completed in 120 seconds.
3. Reading: Using a stopwatch while students read passages on the Reading Comprehension Assessment.

The entire CIBS-R First-Grade through Sixth-Grade Assessment may be used, but it is not recommended to administer the entire criterion-referenced assessment. There is a CIBS-R student record book which includes all 184 test items.

There are two CIBS-R Standardized Scoring Sheets to be used for recording the raw scores from the 10 standardized test items from the First-Grade through Sixth-Grade Assessments and the 27 Readiness Assessments. An important goal of the standardized administration of the CIBS-R is to identify students' ability to demonstrate skills independently and to answer such questions as "Which skills are mastered?" and "Which continue to need instructional attention?"

Feasibility Considerations

Testing Time

If administering all standardized assessments, the CIBS-R Readiness battery requires approximately 75 minutes and the First-Grade through Sixth-Grade battery takes 45 to 60 minutes. The CIBS-R battery is rarely administered in its entirety. Teachers pick and choose assessments to suit individual student needs.

For Testing Groups? Individuals?

Individuals.

Test Administration and Scoring

The standardized assessments must be scored by the examiner by counting the number of correctly completed items to obtain the raw scores. It is noted that the basals and ceilings for test items vary. Basal levels range from 3 to 10 consecutive correct responses, and ceiling levels range from 2 to 10 incorrect responses. No information is given in the manual to justify these variations. There is room for examiner error due to the variability of determining basals and ceilings.

Extensive training in the administration and scoring of the CIBS-R should be required in order to avoid administration and scoring errors. A CD-ROM scoring software program is available. This program automatically converts raw scores to quotients, percentiles, grade equivalents, age equivalents, and instructional ranges. The raw scores that have been recorded on the scoring sheet can easily be entered into the computer by a paraprofessional.

Screener: Three of the First-Grade through Sixth-Grade assessments are used as a screening tool. There is an arrow symbol on the scoring sheet to identify those test items that are used in the screening. The screening results will provide the teacher the necessary information needed to determine the child's need for further testing. A Screener Test Booklet is available.

Test Materials and Approximate Costs

CIBS-R components include: Inventory: $159; Student Record Book (100 pack): $329; Class Record Book: $14; Placement Test Booklet (100 pack): $199; CIBS-R Inservice Video: $15.95; CIBS-R Standardization and Validation Manual: $40; Screener Test Booklet (100 pack): $260; Standardized Scoring Sheets (100 pack, Readiness or 1–6): $70; Standardized Scoring Conversion Software on CD-ROM: $29.95.

Adequacy of Test Manuals

The test inventory has well defined and sequenced skill levels. Each assessment includes a clear description of its administration, including the exact words to use, followed by an instructional objective. The Student Record Book details the procedure for recording responses. There is an excellent section in the Inventory (pp. xviii–xix) on Do's and Don'ts. The Class Record Book allows the teacher to compile data for an entire class. Specific directions are given for effective recording of skills introduced and not achieved and skills achieved. Standardized scoring sheets for the CIBS-R Readiness Assessment and the First-Grade through Sixth-Grade Assessment are concise, which allows for easy recording of the scores. The CIBS-R Standardization and Validation Manual is helpful and includes detailed descriptions of the standardization procedure. The Inventory has "boxes" which give specific directions for obtaining basals and ceilings for the portions of the inventory that are standardized.

Excerpts from Other Test Reviews

The CIBS-R has been reviewed by McLellan (2001). She states that "this test provides one of the most extensive selections of items of achievement batteries available. . . . The addition of derived standard scores in the key areas of achievement marks a major addition to the measure." However, she cautions, "the standardized edition should be used with caution when determining eligibility of students for special education services" (p. 176). Cizek (2001) also reviewed the inventory. He comments that "the materials should be revised to make them easier to work with and more technically accurate, and some attention might be directed toward understanding how the assessment functions for students who are not native speakers of English. . . . The CIBS-R is an improvement over its previous edition. The revision demonstrates greater attention to validity, and users can now derive norm-referenced scores. . . . The CIBS-R attempts to do too much by attempting to satisfy the needs of those interested in both objectives- and norm-referenced assessment" (p. 175).

Ordering Information

Publisher

Curriculum Associates, Inc., 153 Rangeway Road, P.O. Box 2001, North Billerica, MA 01862-0901; Phone: 800-225-0248; Fax: 800-366-1158; Web site: www.curriculumassociates.com.

Authors

Albert H. Brigance and Frances Page Glascoe.

Publication Dates

1983, 1999.

Cautions and Comments

The standardized portions of the CIBS-R may be useful for the special education teacher, psychologist, or education evaluator when considering students for special education placement. However, additional measures should be included in the battery of tests to determine placement in special education. The CIBS-R may be best used for pinpointing student skills and, therefore, selecting objectives and planning instruction for special needs students. The CIBS-R Standardization and Validation Manual provides ways that the CIBS-R results can be interpreted by the teacher and used for placement and planning instruction.

The CIBS-R Readiness Assessment is examiner-friendly and can be administered with ease. However, the CIBS-R First-Grade through Sixth-Grade Assessment is not as easy to administer, as the test Student Record Book does not follow the order of the CIBS-R Standardized Record Form and the examiner must continually locate the correct subtest. A separate standardized testing manual would facilitate the test procedure.

It must be noted that the "Brigance System" includes a variety of criterion measures such as Brigance Screens (e.g., Early Preschool Screen, Preschool Screen, and K & 1 Screen Revised). The Brigance Screens have been standardized and provide cutoff scores, percentiles, and age equivalents. (The Brigance Screens are reviewed elsewhere in this handbook). Technical information for the screens can be found in the Technical Report for the Brigance Screens. Other inventories include the Inventory of Early Development-Revised, Assessment of Basic Skills-Spanish Edition, Inventory of Essential Skills, Life Skills Inventory, and the Employability Skills Inventory. These inventories are not standardized and therefore do not have validity, reliability, or objectivity information; thus they are not included in the handbook. All of the Brigance Systems are useful to the classroom teacher and/or special education teacher for assessing pre-academic and academic skills, pinpointing strengths and weaknesses, and setting developmental and academic objectives. A Goals and Objectives Writer software is available on CD-ROM. This software allows the teacher to quickly create, edit, and print Individual Educational Plans (IEPs).

References

Cizek, Gory J. (2001). Review of the Brigance Diagnostic Comprehensive Inventory of Basic Skills-Revised. In B. S. Plake & J. C. Impara (Eds.), *The Fourteenth Mental Measurements Yearbook* (pp. 172–175). Lincoln, NE: The Buros Institute of Mental Measurements.

Glascoe, F. P. (1999). *CIBS-R Standardization and Validation Manual*. North Billerica, MA: Curriculum Associates.

McLellan, M. (2001). Review of the Brigance Diagnostic Comprehensive Inventory of Basic Skills-Revised. In B. S. Plake & J. C. Impara (Eds.), *The Fourteenth Mental Measurements Yearbook* (pp. 175–176). Lincoln, NE: The Buros Institute of Mental Measurements.

5

Reading Tests

Usefulness of the Test for Educators

Test Authors' Purpose

The authors of the ERDA say that it is a simple diagnostic tool to help teachers identify strengths and weaknesses in reading skills in students already recognized as having reading difficulties. The results will help teachers plan instruction that is targeted to the specific needs of each student. The authors say that the ERDA measures a broad range of reading readiness and early reading skills, including phonological awareness, alphabetic principles, word recognition, oral reading accuracy, and comprehension of text. They say that this reading diagnostic instrument is designed to identify strengths as well as weaknesses for specific intervention planning. When used as a further assessment of children identified as having reading difficulties, they say that the ERDA will prescribe and assess the progress of reading interventions for students in grades K–3.

Decision-Making Applications

The ERDA can be used to make diagnostic and prescriptive decisions about early reading skills and reading readiness for students in grades K–3. The ERDA can be used to make decisions about placing students in instructional reading programs and/or remedial reading programs. Also, it can be used to refer students to speech therapy or learning disabilities programs if needed. The ERDA can be used to assess the effectiveness of intervention that has already been implemented. As with any diagnosis of strengths and weaknesses in academic skills, the more information the teacher has, the better, so the ERDA would probably be best used in conjunction with teacher-made diagnostic tools and/or other standardized diagnostic or prescriptive assessment instruments.

Relevant Population

The ERDA was developed for students in grades K–3 who are having reading difficulties.

Characteristics Described

The ERDA subtests were derived from the Wechsler Individual Achievement Test (WIAT), the Wechsler Individual Achievement Test-Second Edition (WIAT-II), and the Process Assessment of the Learner-Test Battery for Reading and Writing (PAL-RW). The subtests of the ERDA are meant to measure the following reading skills: Concept of Print, Phonological Awareness, Listening Comprehension, Letter Identification, Language Development, Reading Comprehension, Oral Reading, Word Recognition, Word Analysis, and Rapid Automatized Naming. In the Rhyming subtest, the child is asked to discriminate between words that are read to him that have the same ending sounds and to generate real words that have the same ending sounds. In the Syllables subtest, the student is asked to repeat a polysyllabic word and then to say the remaining syllables when a targeted syllable is omitted. In the Phonemes subtest, the student is asked to repeat a monosyllabic or polysyllabic word and then to say the remaining phonemes when a targeted phoneme is omitted. In the Rimes subtest, the student is asked to repeat the portions of a monosyllabic or polysyllabic word when the targeted rime is omitted. In the Story Retell subtest, the student must listen to a narrative, respond to comprehension questions, then retell the narrative in his or her own words. In the Listening Comprehension subtest, the student is asked to look at a picture, listen to a passage, and answer comprehension questions. The student responds orally. In the Vocabulary subtest, the student must select, from a choice of four, the picture that best represents the spoken vocabulary word. In the Letter Recognition subtest, the student is asked to name the letters of the alphabet. In the Reading Comprehension subtest, the student is asked to read sentences or passages then answer questions about them orally.

Test Scores Obtained

Figure 1.1
ERDA Subtests and Composite Scores by Skill

Content	Grade K	Grade 1	Grade 2	Grade 3
Concept of Print	Concept of Print	Concept of Print		
	Observation Checklists	Observation Checklists		

Figure 1.1 (continued)

Content	Grade K	Grade 1	Grade 2	Grade 3
Phonological Awareness	Rhyming Syllables Phonemes	Syllables Phonemes Rimes	Syllables Phonemes Rimes	Syllables Phonemes Rimes
Listening Comprehension	Story Retell	Listening Comprehension		
Letter Identification	Letter Recognition	Letter Recognition		
Language Development	Vocabulary	Vocabulary		
Reading Comprehension	Reading Comprehension	Reading Comprehension	Reading Comprehension	Reading Comprehension
Oral Reading	Reading Sentences Aloud	Reading Sentences Aloud Word Reading Pseudoword Decoding	Reading Sentences Aloud Word Reading	Reading Sentences Aloud Word Reading
Word Recognition			Word Reading	Word Reading
Word Analysis			Pseudoword Decoding	Pseudoword Decoding
Rapid Automatized Naming			RAN-Digits RAN-Letters RAN-Words RAN-Words & Digits	RAN-Digits RAN-Letters RAN-Words RAN-Words & Digits

Source: Manual, Table 1.1, p. 2.

Raw scores (number correct) are computed for each subtest given. Then composite scores are computed using the raw scores of all subtests for that level and that skill.

Technical Adequacy

Validity Confirmation

Test item validity for the ERDA is supported by first determining the curriculum objectives within each of the curriculum areas in state department of education standards. These curriculum objectives in turn defined the content of the ERDA subtests. Thus, the items of each subtest were matched to the curriculum objectives for that subtest.

In order to show *test response validity*, 26 students from grades K–2 were administered the ERDA along with selected subtests from the WIAT: Basic Reading, Reading Comprehension, and Oral Expression. The WIAT Basic Reading subtests were strongly correlated with most of the ERDA subtests. For example, Listening Comprehension correlated significantly with Oral Expression but not with Basic Reading or Reading Comprehension, as expected; Word Reading and Pseudoword Decoding were correlated with Basic Reading and Reading Comprehension. The skills associated with Phonological Awareness are more closely related to reading skills than to oral expression, and the correlations support that. Reading Comprehension approached significance with WIAT Reading Comprehension, but because grade K students did not take these subtests, the reduced study size affected significance level. The authors say that the results show that the ERDA is a valid measure of the constructs found in similar reading test batteries. The correlations of the standard scores on the WIAT with the ERDA subtest scores are shown in Figure 1.2.

Reliability Confirmation

Test-retest reliability was assessed in a study of 61 students who were tested twice. The sample was drawn from grade 1 students in the WIAT-II standardization sample, because this grade received the majority of the subtests available in the ERDA battery, as opposed to the kindergarten and grade 2–3 subtest sets. The interval between testings ranged from 7 to 28 days, with a median retest interval of 7 days. As the information in Figure 1.3 demonstrates, ERDA subtest scores possess adequate stability across time. Thus, the authors say that teachers can have confidence that the scores obtained on these subtests are reliable over time.

Objectivity Confirmation

Two studies were conducted to assess inter-scorer objectivity. The first study involved scoring the Reading Comprehension subtest. Reading Comprehension was analyzed according to the subtest items that required judgment in scoring: items that comprise Reading Comprehension (as opposed to Reading Sentences Aloud). A total of 600 students' responses (200 each from grade 1, grade 2, and grade 3) on the Reading Comprehension subtests were scored independently by at least two scorers. The correlations between pairs of scores were .97 for grade 1, .98 for grade 2, and .98 for grade 3. The second study involved scoring the Story Retell Subtest. The responses from 199 kindergarten students were scored independently by at least two scorers. The correlation between pairs of scores was .96. The authors tell us that the results of these scoring studies show that responses in those subtests that require scorer judgment can be scored very objectively.

Statistical Confirmation

Statistical confirmation for validity, reliability, objectivity, and norms of the ERDA can be found in the Examiner's Manual.

Figure 1.2
Correlations of ERDA and WIAT Subtests

Subtest/Composite	WIAT Basic Reading	WIAT Reading Comprehension	WIAT Oral Expression
Letter Recognition	.27	.09	.19
Listening Comprehension	.06	−.05	.75**
Phonological Awareness Composite	.57**	.40	.24
Pseudoword Decoding	.82**	.71**	.48
Reading Sentences Aloud	.77**	.81**	.30
Reading Comprehension	.70**	.54*	.37
Story Retell	.47	.28	.45
Word Reading	.75**	.71**	.17

*p < .05; **p < .01.

Source: Manual, Table 5.10, p. 80.

Figure 1.3
Stability Coefficients of the Subtests and Composites for Grade 1

Subtests/Composites

Letter Recognition	.46
Pseudoword Decoding	.91
Reading Comprehension	.95
Reading Sentences Aloud	.92
Vocabulary	.79
Word Reading	.94

Source: Manual, Table 5.3, p. 74.

Special Features

Acronym

ERDA.

Levels of the Test

One.

Number of Test Forms

One.

Norm-Referenced?

Yes. The normative data for the ERDA is based on the test performance of 1,320 children in grades K, 2, and 3 and those same 1,320 children plus 343 in grade 1 for a total of 1,663. The samples that were used for the ERDA were taken from the standardization samples which were collected during the 1999–2000 school year for the original WIAT (Wechsler Individual Achievement Test—only six Listening Comprehension items), the WIAT-II (Wechsler Individual Achievement Test-Second Edition), and the PAL-RW (Process Assessment of the Learner-Test Battery for Reading and Writing). The samples closely approximate the school-aged population of the United States as reported in the October 1998 Census data.

Criterion-Referenced?

Yes. The items of the ERDA subtests are referenced to the curriculum objectives for each subtest.

Other Features

1. Pseudoword Audiotape for Examiners is an audiotape giving the examiner correct pronunciation of the list of pseudowords. The audiotape is not intended for use during the testing session.
2. Large-print versions of student materials are available.
3. Information is provided in the Examiner's Manual for planning and implementing effective intervention.

Feasibility Considerations

Testing Time

Administration of all subtests within the ERDA requires approximately 45 minutes for students in kindergarten and approximately 60 minutes for students in grades 1–3, although not all subtests are administered to all students. Every effort should be made to complete the testing in one session. However, some students, especially younger ones, may need to be tested in two sessions because of fatigue or inadequate motivation. Also, testing of students in grades 2–3 requires scoring Word Reading, Pseudoword Decoding, and Reading Comprehension subtests in order to determine if the follow-up subtests are necessary, so a short break between testing sessions may occur.

For Testing Groups? Individuals?

Individuals.

Test Administration and Scoring

Instructions for administering the subtests of the ERDA are provided in the Examiner's Manual. Training modules have been developed in conjunction with the manual to assist the classroom teacher in developing appropriate test administration, scoring, reporting, and interpretation skills. The authors suggest that the teacher should practice administering and scoring the tests.

Test Materials and Approximate Costs

The ERDA kit for grades K–1 administration includes the following materials: Manual; Stimulus Booklet for grades K–1; Record Forms for grades K–1; Word Card; Pseudoword Audiotape for Examiners; Parent Report for grades K–1.

The ERDA kit for grades 2–3 administration includes the following materials: Manual; Stimulus Booklet for grades 2–3; Record Forms for grades 2–3; Word Card; Pseudoword Audiotape for Examiners; Parent Report for grades 2–3.

Prices for the materials can be obtained from the publisher.

Adequacy of Test Manuals

The Examiner's Manual explains the administration of the test clearly and the technical information given is adequate. The directions for scoring the subtests is confusing and rather involved.

Excerpts from Other Test Reviews

No test reviews were found for the ERDA.

Ordering Information

Publisher

The Psychological Corporation, 19500 Bulverde Road, San Antonio, TX 78259; Phone: 800-228-0752; Fax: 210-339-5873; Web site: www.psychcorp.com.

Authors

The research and development team of the Psychological Corporation.

Publication Date

2000.

Cautions and Comments

The ERDA is intended to be a simple diagnostic tool to help teachers identify strengths and weaknesses in students already recognized as having reading difficulties. It also can be used to prescribe and assess the progress of reading interventions for students in grades K–3. The scoring and interpretation of scores does seem to be rather complex and not necessarily easily done by a classroom teacher not trained in assessment.

Gates-MacGinitie Reading Tests, Forms S & T (GMRT),
for testing groups from preschool through adulthood
Reviewed by Katherine C. Schnepel, Ph.D.,
Educational Research and Measurement

Usefulness of the Test for Educators

Test Authors' Purpose

The test authors state that the basic premise of the GMRT is that it is useful for teachers and schools to know the general level of reading achievement of individuals throughout their school careers. The objective information obtained from the tests, complemented by teachers' evaluations and other sources of information, is an important basis for

1. Selecting students for further individual diagnosis and special instruction;
2. Planning instructional emphases;
3. Locating students who are ready to work with more advanced materials;
4. Making decisions about grouping students;
5. Talking with students about their progress in reading;
6. Deciding which levels of instructional materials to use with new students;
7. Evaluating the effectiveness of instructional programs;
8. Reporting to parents and the community. (Directions for Administration Manual, p. 2)

Decision-Making Applications

The GMRT can be used by the classroom teacher to pinpoint weaknesses and deficiencies in specific reading skills measured by the subtests. These diagnoses of deficiencies can help the teacher to plan instruction needed to improve these skills in individuals and groups.

Relevant Population

The GMRT is meant to be used with children who are pre-reading through beginning readers, grades 1–12, and adults.

Characteristics Described

See Figure 1.1.

Figure 1.1
Test Content

Level	Test or Subtest	Content
PR	Literacy Concepts	Measures the student's understanding of the nature and uses of written English, such as what and why people read and write, what words and letters look like, and words and phrases that are commonly used in reading instruction, such as *first* letter, *same as*, *ends with*, and *next* word.
	Oral Language Concepts (Phonological Awareness)	Measures the student's ability to attend to the basic structure of spoken English words, including phoneme matching and rhyme.
	Letters and Letter-Sound Correspondences	Measures the student's ability to recognize letters and to relate them to sounds. It contains four sections: Visual Discrimination (matching letters and words), Letter Recognition (letter names), Letter-Sound Correspondences, and Initial Spelling Concepts (sound-to-letter correspondences).
	Listening (Story) Comprehension	Measures the student's ability to attend to important elements in a story, integrate information from different parts of a story, and make inferences about story developments.
BR	Initial Consonants and Consonant Clusters	Include questions that ask the student to choose the picture with a name that begins with or ends with the letter(s) in the box and the word that goes with the picture in the box. To make the directions to the student for these two types of questions as simple as possible, the content of these three subtests is divided between the first two testing sessions.
	Final Consonants and Consonant Clusters	
	Vowels	
	Basic Story Words	Measures the student's ability to read words commonly used in stories and other writing.
1	Word Decoding	Primarily a test of decoding skills. The student's task for each question is to identify, from among words that look much alike, the one word that fits the picture. Students' answers can be analyzed for clues to decoding skills that the students still need to learn. Decoding Skills Analysis Forms are available to help teachers who hand score the tests organize this information; a Decoding Skills Analysis Report can be obtained through the Riverside Scoring Service.
	Comprehension	Consists of stories and nonfiction passages, each divided into short segments. The student's task is to choose the picture that illustrates a segment or that answers a question about it.

Figure 1.1 (continued)

Level	Test or Subtest	Content
2	Word Decoding	Similar to the Level 1 Word Decoding test, but the decoding skills required are more difficult and usually learned later than the skills required by Level 1.
	Word Knowledge	A test of reading vocabulary. It has the same format as the Word Decoding test, but the test words are less familiar. The student's task is to choose among the answer choices on the basis of their meanings rather than their letter "sounds."
	Comprehension	Similar to the Level 1 Comprehension test, but the passages are longer and more challenging.
3–10/12	Vocabulary	A test of word knowledge. The student's task is to choose the word or through phrase that means most nearly the same as the test word.
	Comprehension	Consists of prose passages selected from published works. The passages are fiction and nonfiction, from various content areas, and written in a variety of styles.
AR	Vocabulary	Similar to the Vocabulary test for Levels 3–10/12, but more wide-ranging in difficulty.
	Comprehension	Similar to the Comprehension test for Levels 3–10/12. Passages represent a wide range of difficulty and have content appropriate for mature individuals.

Source: Directions for Administration Manual, p. 5.

Test Scores Obtained

Figure 1.2
Scores Provided

		Type of Score				
Level	Test or Subtest	NCE	PR	Stanine	GE	ESS
PR	Total	X	X	X	X	X
	Literacy Concepts			X		
	Oral Language Concepts (Phonological Awareness)			X		
	Letters and Letter-Sound Correspondences			X		
	Listening (Story) Comprehension			X		
BR	Total	X	X	X	X	X
	Initial Consonants			X		
	Final Consonants			X		
	Vowels			X		
	Basic Story Words			X		
1	Total	X	X	X	X	X

Figure 1.2 (continued)

Level	Test or Subtest	NCE	PR	Stanine	GE	ESS
				Type of Score		
	Word Decoding	X	X	X	X	X
	Comprehension	X	X	X	X	X
2	Total	X	X	X	X	X
	Word Decoding	X	X	X	X	X
	Word Knowledge	X	X	X	X	X
	Comprehension	X	X	X	X	X
3–	Total	X	X	X	X*	X
10/12	Vocabulary	X	X	X	X*	X
	Comprehension	X	X	X	X*	X
AR	Total	X	X	X	X*	X
	Vocabulary	X	X	X	X*	X
	Comprehension	X	X	X	X*	X

Notes: NCE = Normal Curve Equivalent; PR = Percentile Rank; GE = Grade Equivalent; ESS = Extended Scale Score.
* up to 12.9.
Source: Directions for Administration Manual, p. 7.

Technical Adequacy

Validity Confirmation

The authors give as evidence of *test item validity* an in-depth description of the design and development of the test. They state that the validity of the GMRT is rooted in the overall design of the series, which measures the progression of students' understandings and skills in reading from kindergarten through high school (Technical Report, p. 70).

As evidence of *test response validity*, the authors start by correlating the total scores of the Third Edition and the Fourth Edition. The correlation coefficients ranged from .58 through .93, with just two coefficients below .80. Then, they correlate the Third Edition with the PSAT Verbal section, SAT Verbal section, and ACT English test, and they show the relationships between scores on the Third Edition of the GMRT and teacher-assigned course grades. The authors suggest that the results of these studies of the Third Edition are relevant to the validity of the Fourth Edition because (1) the total score correlations between the Third Edition and the Fourth Edition were very high, (2) the design of the two editions was very similar, and (3) the procedures for developing the Fourth Edition tests were essentially the same as those for developing the Third Edition. This evidence shows very weak support for the validity of the GMRT.

Reliability Confirmation

The authors give as evidence of stability reliability correlations between fall and spring Total Test Raw Scores at each level. The correlation coefficients ranged from

.58 to .91 with just two coefficients below .70. Also presented are correlations between alternate forms of the test (Form S and Form T). Except for grades 9 and 11, the total score correlations are all .90 or higher. The anomalous correlation at grade 11 and the high correlations at grade 12 are based on relatively small samples. The alternate-form correlations for the individual tests (e.g., Vocabulary, Comprehension) are also excellent. All, except those at grade 11, are .80 or higher. Also given are inter-correlations of all subtests at all levels. These correlation coefficients range from .76 to .95, with just two coefficients below .80.

Objectivity Confirmation

No statistical information is given for inter-rater objectivity. However, very clear directions for administering are given and a scoring key is presented for hand scoring. Machine scoring by the publisher is also available. The authors make no suggestion that examiners should have specific training.

Statistical Confirmation

Statistical data on reliability and norms can be obtained from the Technical Report, Forms S and T.

Special Features

Acronym

GMRT.

Levels of the Test

Eleven.

Number of Test Forms

Two.

Norm-Referenced?

Yes. The norming followed a stratified random sampling design. Three stratifying variables were used to classify public school districts across the nation: (1) geographic region (East, Midwest, South, and West), (2) district enrollment, and (3) district socioeconomic status. The sample was chosen to be representative of the national school population. There was both a fall and a spring standardization. The authors tell us that for the fall standardization 29,525 students from 45 states were used and for the spring standardization 32,475 students were used.

Criterion-Referenced?

Yes. The GMRT subtests are referenced to specific reading skills and can be used to diagnose deficiencies or weaknesses in those skills.

Other Features

Linking Testing to Teaching: A Classroom Resource for Reading Assessment and Instruction. This series shows the examiner how to use the scores as part of a comprehensive assessment of reading and how to use the scores to guide instruction by level.

Feasibility Considerations

Testing Time

These are not speed tests, and most students will have time to try all the questions. However, examiners are told that the norms will apply to the students in their class only if the time allowances for the tests are followed exactly. The total time for the Word Decoding Test is about 35 minutes, for the Word Knowledge Test about 30 minutes, and for the Comprehension Test about 50 minutes.

For Testing Groups? Individuals?

Groups.

Test Administration and Scoring

There is a separate administration booklet for each level. Clear and detailed directions for administering are given in the manuals. Both machine-scorable and hand-scorable answer forms are available. Instructions for preparing the answer forms for machine scoring as well as instructions for hand scoring are also in the manuals. The authors state that no specific training or certification is required for examiners or scorers.

Test Materials and Approximate Costs

Machine-scorable test booklets for PR level (includes administration directions and machine-scorable materials) (35): $132; Machine-scorable test booklets, per level, for all other levels (includes administration directions and machine-scorable materials) (35): $111.25; Hand-scored test booklets (includes administration directions, scoring key, and class summary sheet), per level (35): $73.50; Mark Reflex Answer Sheets, per level (100): $106; Mark Reflex Answer Sheets (includes one class summary sheet), per level (25): $40; Self-Scorable Answer Sheets, per level (250): $355.50; Class summary and record forms, per level: $11.50; Booklet scoring key, per level: $9; Scoring Template for Mark Reflex Answer Sheets, per level: $24.50; Administration directions, per level: $10; Manual for scoring and interpretation, per level: $19.50; Technical Report: $24; Linking Testing to Teaching, per level: $9; GMRT Score Converting and Reporting Software: $475.

Adequacy of Test Manuals

For each level of the test there is a Directions for Administration Manual, a Manual for Scoring and Interpretation, a Linking Testing to Teaching Manual, and a Technical

Report. The Administration and Scoring and Interpretation manuals are clearly written and easily understood by the teacher not trained in testing. However, the Technical Report is confusing and not easily understood. Linking Testing to Teaching is clear and seems to be a helpful tool for the classroom teacher.

Excerpts from Other Test Reviews

The GMRT, Fourth Edition has not been reviewed in the Buros Institute's annual *Mental Measurement Yearbooks*, nor has it been reviewed by Salvia and Ysseldyke in any of their editions of *Assessment*. However, in the manual of the GMRT, Fourth Edition, the authors show the strong correlation of the Fourth Edition with the GMRT, Third Edition. They then give the correlations of the Third Edition with several other instruments that are assumed to measure the same constructs of Reading Vocabulary and Comprehension. These tests include general achievement screening batteries such as the Iowa Tests of Basic Skills (ITBS), Tests of Achievement and Proficiency (TAP), the Comprehensive Tests of Basic Skills (CTBS), the California Achievement Test (CAT), the Metropolitan Achievement Test (MAT), the Survey of Basic Skills (SBS), and the Verbal and Mathematics sections of the Preliminary Scholastic Social Science, Natural Science, and Composite sections of the American College Testing Program (ACT). The GMRT, Third Edition was reviewed by Swerdlik (1992), who states that "validity data are not provided for the major uses for which the test is recommended such as selecting students who may benefit from additional instruction or different types of reading instruction. No validity data unique to the purposes of level PR (pre-reading) are provided. . . . Based on the information presented above, the GMRT is recommended for use as a screening test."

Ordering Information

Publisher

Riverside Publishing Company, 425 Spring Lake Drive, Itasca, IL 60143-2079; Phone: 800-323-9540; Fax: 630-467-7192; Web site: www.riverpub.com.

Authors

Walter H. MacGinitie, Ruth K. MacGinitie, Katherine Maria, and Lois G. Dreyer.

Publication Date

2002.

Cautions and Comments

The GMRT seems to be an effective instrument for use by the classroom teacher for diagnosing deficiencies in specific reading skills, thus enabling the teacher to prescribe remedial instruction. However, because of its weak validity evidence, it might be prudent to combine it with other means of diagnosing weaknesses. Also, because of questionable validity confirmation, the test's norm-referenced uses are probably limited.

Reference

Swerdlik, M. E. (1992). Review of the Gates-MacGinitie Reading Tests, Third Edition. In J. J. Kramer & J. C. Conoley (Eds.), *The Eleventh Mental Measurements Yearbook* [Electronic version]. Retrieved March 15, 2002 from Buros Institute's Test Reviews Online web site: http://www.unl.edu/buros.

Gray Oral Reading Test, Fourth Edition (GORT-4),
for testing individuals from 6 years through 18 years, 11 months of age
Reviewed by Katherine C. Schnepel, Ph.D.,
Educational Research and Measurement

Usefulness of the Test for Educators

Test Authors' Purpose

The authors state that the GORT-4 is intended to accomplish four purposes: (1) to help identify those students who are significantly below their peers in oral reading proficiency and who may profit from supplemental help; (2) to aid in determining the particular kinds of reading strengths and weaknesses that individual students possess; (3) to document students' progress in reading as a consequence of special intervention programs; and (4) to serve as a measurement device in investigations where researchers are studying the reading abilities of school-aged students (Examiner's Manual, p. 4).

Decision-Making Applications

The GORT-4 seems to be very useful and effective for identifying children with reading deficiencies and for identifying where those deficiencies lie. Also, the GORT-4 could be used for pinpointing strengths as well as weaknesses in reading skills. The test can certainly be used to recommend reading skill areas in need of remediation. However, it might be useful for the teacher to use the student's homework, quizzes, and class test results as corroboration for prescribing remedial instruction.

Relevant Population

The GORT-4 is appropriate for individuals ages 6 years through 18 years, 11 months.

Characteristics Described

The GORT-4 describes oral reading rate, accuracy, fluency, and comprehension. The test also describes oral reading miscues made in five areas:

1. Meaning Similarity—the appropriateness of the student's word error in regard to meaning within the story.

2. Function Similarity—the appropriateness of the student's word error in regard to the grammatical correctness of the word substituted in the sentence.

3. Graphic/Phonemic Similarity—the appropriateness of the student's word error as to its similarity to the look and sound of the printed word.

4. Multiple Sources—the student's word error that has a combined meaning, function, and graphic-phonemic similarity to the printed word.

5. Self-Correction—a word error that is immediately corrected by the student.

The GORT-4 contains 14 separate stories. Five multiple-choice comprehension questions follow each story. The student is asked to read the stories and respond to the comprehension questions. The amount of time taken by the student to read a story results in the Rate Score. The student's ability to pronounce each word in the story correctly results in the Accuracy Score. The student's Rate and Accuracy Scores combined result in the Fluency Score. The appropriateness of the student's responses to questions about the content of each story read results in the Comprehension Score. A combination of a student's Fluency and Comprehension Scores results in the Overall Reading Ability Score.

Test Scores Obtained

Rate, Accuracy, Fluency, and Comprehension results are reported as standard scores. The overall oral reading composite score is reported as a quotient. Age equivalents, grade equivalents, and percentiles are also provided. The frequency of each of the five reading errors is reported as a percentage.

Technical Adequacy

Validity Confirmation

The authors give evidence of *test item validity* by providing an extensive rationale for the GORT-4's format and content. They describe (1) the rationale for using a story reading format to assess oral reading, (2) the factors considered in composing the stories, (3) the way in which the comprehension questions were developed, (4) the measurement of fluency on the GORT-4, (5) the manner in which the stories were sequenced, and (6) the analysis of deviations from print. Also, two item analysis techniques were used (i.e., item discrimination and item difficulty). The resulting item discrimination coefficients and item difficulties for comprehension are reported in the Examiner's Manual. For the most part, the test items provide evidence of test item validity.

Test response validity is supported by correlating the GORT-4 with the Gray Diagnostic Reading Tests-Second Edition (Letter-Word Recognition, Phonetic Analysis,

Reading Vocabulary, Reading Comprehension Quotient, Decoding Quotient, and Total Reading Quotient) and the Gray Silent Reading Tests. Also, the GORT-4 is correlated with the GORT-3 and the GORT-R. The GORT-3 was correlated with the Tests of Word Reading Efficiency (Sight Word Efficiency and Phonemic Decoding Efficiency), the Iowa Tests of Educational Development (Total Reading), the California Achievement Tests-Fifth Edition (Total Reading), the Gray Oral Reading Tests-Diagnostic (Total Reading), and the Diagnostic Achievement Battery-Second Edition (Reading Quotient). The GORT-R was correlated with the Woodcock Reading Master Tests-Revised (Word Attack) and the Wide Range Achievement Test-Revised (Reading). The median correlations for all studies range from .45 to .75.

Reliability Confirmation

Stability reliability is supported by using the Alternate Forms (immediate) technique, the Alternate Forms (delayed) technique, and the Test-Retest technique. The two forms of the GORT-4 were administered in one testing session. The coefficients depicting the relationship between Form A and Form B exceed .71. Fifty percent of the coefficients are .90 or above; another 34% are between .80 and .89. A delayed Alternate-Forms Correlation was computed for Form A and Form B. The delayed Alternate-Forms coefficients range from .78 to .95. The Test-Retest technique was used by administering both forms of the test twice to the sample; the intervening time was approximately two weeks. The resulting coefficients ranged from .85 to .95 with just one coefficient being .78 (comprehension).

Objectivity Confirmation

Inter-scorer objectivity was investigated by having two members of the PRO-ED research staff independently score a set of 30 completed protocols. The protocols were drawn randomly from the children in the normative sample. The standard scores of the scorings were correlated. These coefficients ranged from .94 to .99.

Statistical Confirmation

All of the statistical data for validity, reliability, objectivity, and norms is presented very clearly and succinctly in the Examiner's Manual.

Special Features

Acronym

GORT-4.

Levels of the Test

Levels are determined by the use of basals and ceilings. If examiners know the general reading ability of the student being tested, they should use the information in selecting the entry-level story. For example, if they know that the student is a very poor reader, the examiner should begin testing at the lower levels. In general, however, testing should begin at the story level that corresponds to the student's grade level. Starting points are as follows:

Grades	*Starting Points*
Grades 1 and 2	Story 1
Grades 3 and 4	Story 3
Grades 5 through 8	Story 5
Grades 9 through 12	Story 9

Source: Examiner's Manual, p. 10.

The test yields four scores: Rate, Accuracy, Fluency, and Comprehension. However, only the Fluency and Comprehension Scores are used to ascertain basals and ceilings. Examiners should note that basals and ceilings are computed separately for Fluency and Comprehension Scores and must be computed and considered during testing to assure correct test administration. The ceiling for the Comprehension Score is reached when the student misses at least three of five comprehension questions for any one story. The ceiling for the Fluency Score occurs when the reader achieves a Fluency Score of 2 or less for a story. The Rate and Accuracy Scores are added to get the Fluency Score.

Number of Test Forms

Two.

Norm-Referenced?

Yes. The GORT-4 was normed on a sample of 1,677 persons in 28 states. The entire sample was collected between Fall 1999 and Fall 2000. Standardization sites were selected in each of the four major geographic regions as designated by the U.S. Bureau of the Census. The sample is representative of the nation as a whole. The percentage of the characteristics of the sample with regard to geographic region, gender, race, rural or urban residence, ethnicity, family income, educational attainment of parents, and disability are comparable to the percentages of these characteristics in the general school-age population. All students tested attended general classes. Students with disabilities who were enrolled in general classes were included in the normative sample. Several hundred students in grades 1 through 12 were tested at each major site.

Criterion-Referenced?

The GORT-4 is referenced to reading skills, but is not referenced to specific curricular or instructional skills.

Feasibility Considerations

Testing Time

The GORT-4 can be given in about 15 to 45 minutes, depending on the student's reading ability. Although the test is best administered in one session, two sessions are sometimes required (e.g., in cases where the reader becomes fatigued or uncooperative) (Examiner's Manual, p. 10).

For Testing Groups? Individuals?

Individuals.

Test Administration and Scoring

Both general administration guidelines and specific instructions for administration and scoring are given in the Examiner's Manual. These are easily followed. However, the authors do recommend that examiners who give and interpret the GORT-4 should have some formal training in assessment. They suggest that this training should result in a basic understanding regarding testing statistics and general procedures governing test administration, scoring, and interpretation.

Test Materials and Approximate Costs

Complete kit, which includes Examiner's Manual, Student Books for Form A and Form B, and Profile/Examiner Record for Form A and Form B: $189; Examiner's Manual: $69; Student Books (25) (specify Form A or Form B): $46; Profile/Examiner Record Forms (25) (specify Form A or Form B): $39.

Adequacy of Test Manuals

The Examiner's Manual is very clear and specific about administration of the GORT-4 and interpretation of the results. It also provides an overview of the test and its development. The Examiner's Manual also very clearly presents the technical information (i.e., validity, reliability, and norming data).

Excerpts from Other Test Reviews

No test reviews were found for the GORT-4.

Ordering Information

Publisher

PRO-ED, 8700 Shoal Creek Boulevard, Austin, TX 78757-6897; Phone: 800-897-3202; Fax: 800-397-7633; Web site: http://www.proedinc.com.

Authors

J. Lee Wiederholt and Brian R. Bryant.

Publication Date

2001.

Cautions and Comments

The GORT-4 is useful for identifying children who are significantly below their peers in oral reading proficiency and who may benefit from supplemental help. It also can be used to determine students' strengths and weaknesses in oral reading. Also, the GORT-4 is well suited to document progress of students who are in remediation programs. The two equivalent forms of the test allow examiners to test reading skills periodically. The only caution about the GORT-4 would be that, just as with any diagnostic test, it should be not be used for purposes beyond its capabilities (e.g., the sole basis for instructional intervention). After strengths and weaknesses are identified with the GORT-4, further diagnostic assessment should be done in order to prescribe specific instruction.

Group Reading Assessment and Diagnostic Evaluation (GRADE), for testing individuals and groups from pre-kindergarten through young adulthood
Reviewed by Katherine C. Schnepel, Ph.D.,
Educational Research and Measurement

Usefulness of the Test for Educators

Test Author's Purpose

The author states that the GRADE can be used in several ways in school settings:

1. Placement and Planning—Results from the GRADE could be used to place students in appropriate instructional groups within a classroom or into pull-out programs that provide enrichment or remedial assistance outside of the classroom environment. Since the GRADE can also be given individually or to small groups, results could be used by special educators to develop annual Individual Education Plans (IEPs). Because the GRADE can be used with older students, it can also help with vocational and postsecondary educational planning.

2. Understanding the Reading Skills of Students—The diagnostic analyses provided for each of the GRADE subtests can be used to analyze reading

strengths and weaknesses by classroom or student. These analyses could help teachers develop group or individual instruction plans to more closely match areas that need skill improvement.

3. Testing on Level and Out of Level—Because the reading skills of a typical classroom of students can vary widely, the GRADE content at each level was designed to assess overlapping ranges of reading performance.

4. Monitoring Growth—Because the levels of the GRADE are psychometrically linked, results can be used to monitor progress from grade to grade, year after year, from elementary school to the postsecondary years. With two parallel forms for each test level, the GRADE can be used as a pre- and post-test to measure growth following a remediation or enrichment program.

5. Research—The growth scale values of the GRADE can be used for gathering longitudinal research data using the same metric across the multiple test levels (Technical Manual, pp. 3–4).

Decision-Making Applications

The GRADE can be used effectively by the classroom teacher to diagnose weaknesses and deficiencies in the reading skills assessed by the subtests. These diagnoses then enable the teacher to develop instruction plans that address the areas that need skill improvement. Also, the two parallel forms on each level can be used to measure the effectiveness of remediation for individual students or groups.

Relevant Population

Pre-kindergarten children through young adult postsecondary students.

Characteristics Described

Figure 1.1
GRADE Components and Subtests

Component	Subtest	P	K	1	2	3	4	5	6	M	H	A
Pre-Reading	Picture Matching	X										
	Picture Differences	X										
	Verbal Concepts	X										
	Picture Categories	X										
Reading	Sound Matching	X	X									
Readiness	Rhyming	X	X									
	Print Awareness		X									
	Letter Recognition		X									
	Same and Different Words		X									
	Phoneme-Grapheme Correspondence		X									

Figure 1.1 (continued)

		Level										
Component	*Subtest*	P	K	1	2	3	4	5	6	M	H	A
Vocabulary	Word Reading		X	X	X	X						
	Word Meaning			X	X							
	Vocabulary					X	X	X	X	X	X	X
Comprehension	Sentence Comprehension		X	X	X	X	X	X	X	X	X	X
	Passage Comprehension		X	X	X	X	X	X	X	X	X	X
Oral Language	Listening Comprehension	X	X	X	X	X	X	X	X	X	X	X

Source: Technical Manual, Table 2.1, p. 12. Reproduced with permission.

Each Picture Matching item consists of a picture in a box followed by four pictures, one target and three distracters. The teacher points to the picture in the box and asks the students to find the picture that is the same. The students mark the one that is the same as the picture in the box (Technical Manual, p. 12).

Each Picture Differences item consists of four pictures. The teacher explains that three of the pictures are the same and one is different. The students are instructed to look at the four pictures in their Student Booklets and mark the one that is different from the others (Technical Manual, p. 14).

For each item on the Verbal Concepts subtest, the teacher reads a sentence aloud that tells the students which picture to mark. The students listen while they look at a set of four pictures in their Student Booklets. The teacher then repeats the sentence and instructs the students to mark the picture that best goes with what was read by the teacher (Technical Manual, p. 15).

Each Picture Categories item includes four pictures. The teacher points to them and indicates that three of the pictures go together and one of them does not belong. The students look at the four pictures in their Student Booklets and mark the picture that does not belong (Technical Manual, p. 17).

Sound Matching consists of two sections: "Begins with" and "Ends with." Each item within a section contains four pictures representing three distracter words and the target word. The teacher names the four pictures as the students look at them in their Student Booklets and then says a stimulus word. For the "Begins with" section, the students are told to mark the picture that has the same beginning sound as the stimulus word. For the "Ends with" section, students are instructed to mark the picture that ends with the same sound as the stimulus word the teacher says (Technical Manual, p. 19).

For each Rhyming item, the teacher names four pictures as the students look at the pictures in their Student Booklets. The students are then instructed to mark the picture that rhymes with the word the teacher says (Technical Manual, p. 21).

For each Print Awareness item, the teacher reads a sentence that tells the students what to mark. Students listen to the sentence while they look at a set of four boxes in their Student Booklets. The sentence is repeated, and the students are then instructed to mark the picture that best fits what the teacher has read (Technical Manual, p. 24).

For each Letter Recognition item, the teacher says a letter name as the students look at a set of five letters in their Student Booklets. The students are instructed to mark the letter named (Technical Manual, p. 25).

Same and Different Words consists of two sections: "Same Words" and "Different Words." For each Same Words item, the teacher points to a word in a box and asks the students to find the word that is the same. The students look at a set of four words in their Student Booklets and mark the word that is the same as the one in the box. For each Different Words item, students look at four words and mark the word that is different from the other three (Technical Manual, p. 27).

The Phoneme-Grapheme Correspondence subtest consists of two sections. In the first section, the teacher instructs the students to mark the letter that makes the sound they hear at the beginning of a word. In the second section, the students are to mark the letter that makes the sound they hear at the end of a word (Technical Manual, p. 29).

For each item in the Word Reading subtest, the teacher reads a target word, reads a sentence that contains the word, and then repeats the word. The student picks the target word from a list of four or five choices (Technical Manual, p. 30).

For each Word Meaning item, the students silently read a target word and look at a set of four pictures. Students then mark the picture that best tells the meaning of the word (Technical Manual, p. 34).

For the Vocabulary subtest, the student reads a phrase or short sentence in which one of the words is printed in bold type (the target word) and then picks the meaning of that word from a list of four or five choices (Technical Manual, p. 36).

Each Sentence Comprehension item includes a single sentence with a missing word represented by a blank (_____). Four or five single-word choices are then listed, which comprise three or four possible distracters and one clearly correct answer (Technical Manual, p. 39).

Passage Comprehension requires the student to read a passage of one or more paragraphs and to answer three, four, or five multiple-choice questions about the passage (Technical Manual, p. 44).

For each Listening Comprehension item, the teacher reads a sentence aloud to the class. The students are asked to mark one of four pictures that best goes with what was read by the teacher (Technical Manual, p. 51).

Test Scores Obtained

Raw scores from GRADE subtests can be converted to stanines. Composite and Total Test raw scores can be converted to these types of scores:

1. Standard Scores—With this common metric, comparisons can be made between GRADE scores and scores earned on tests of cognitive ability, oral language, and other measures of academic achievement.

2. Stanines, percentiles, normal curve equivalents (NCEs), and grade equivalents.

3. Growth scale values (GSVs; for Total Test only)—These values provide a means for tracking reading growth when the student is given different GRADE levels over the years (Technical Manual, p. 3).

Technical Adequacy

Validity Confirmation

The author addresses *test item validity* by considering how completely the 16 GRADE subtests assess the various skill areas of pre-reading and reading, by considering how the items in each subtest assess these areas, and by considering the appropriateness of the subtest formats and item types. She addresses the same four topics for each of the 16 subtests: (1) Subtest Description, (2) Skill Measurement, (3) Format and Item Types, and (4) Interpreting Results.

To give evidence of *test response validity*, the author correlated the GRADE Total Test Scores with scores from two different group-administered achievement tests, the Iowa Tests of Basic Skills (ITBS) and the California Achievement Test (CAT). She also correlated the GRADE total test scores with scores from one group-administered reading test, the Gates-MacGinitie Reading Tests (GMRT), and with scores from one individually administered achievement test, the Peabody Individual Achievement Test-Revised (PIAT-R). The correlation coefficients of the GRADE and the ITBS for three grade levels ranged from .69 to .71. The coefficients of the GRADE and the CAT at levels 1 and 2 were .82 and .87, respectively; the correlation coefficients of the GRADE scores and the GMRT at levels 1 and 2, 3, 6, and M ranged from .86 to .90; and the correlations of the GRADE level 5 with the PIAT-R scores ranged from .74 to .80. The GRADE scores levels 2, 4, and 6 were also correlated with the Standard Scores of the TerraNova, a nationally standardized achievement battery. Those three correlation coefficients were .76, .77, and .86, respectively. The author contends that "this information provides substantial evidence that the GRADE does indeed measure what it purports to measure and that appropriate inferences from test results can be made" (Technical Manual, p. 103).

Reliability Confirmation

Stability reliability was supported by the author by means of the test-retest procedure. "A sample of 816 students took part in a test-retest reliability study of the GRADE. For each of the 16 grade-enrollment groups . . . the students were tested twice with the same form of the appropriate GRADE level" (Technical Manual). The average number of days between testings ranged from 3.5 days to 42 days. Correlation coefficients for the 12 groups taking Form A of the appropriate level during both testings range from .77 to .98. The correlation coefficients for the four groups taking Form B during both testing sessions are .83, .90, .96, and .96. Also presented are Alternate-Form reliabilities (derived from the administration of two different but parallel test forms to a group of students). The correlation coefficients of Form A and Form B of the GRADE at all levels ranged from .81 to .94. Also given are split-half reliabilities, which indicate internal consistency of the items on the test. The split-half procedure involves correlating one-half of the items with the other half of the items, usually the odd-numbered items with the even-numbered items. The correlation coefficients resulting from this procedure were very high on all levels for all subtests. Most of those coefficients were over .90, with only a few at the higher grade levels between .70 and .80. The author states that "the reliability information . . . provides substantial evidence for a high degree of consistency in the measurement of GRADE scores" (Technical Manual, pp. 77–88).

Objectivity Confirmation

There is no statistical evidence given to support inter-rater objectivity. However, complete directions with answer keys for hand scoring the GRADE are provided in the GRADE Teacher's Scoring & Interpretive Manuals.

Statistical Confirmation

Statistical data for validity, reliability, and standardization is given in the Technical Manual.

Special Features

Acronym

GRADE.

Levels of the Test

Eleven.

Number of Test Forms

Two.

Norm-Referenced?

Yes. The author tells us that "During the spring of 2000, a nationwide sample of preschool through twelfth-grade students was tested at 122 sites using the 11 levels of standardization edition of the GRADE. In the fall of 2000, a second sample was collected using the same materials. This time the testing included postsecondary students at 12 additional sites. . . . The purpose of the two national standardizations was to develop separate spring and fall normative scores for students in preschool through Grade 12 and a single set of normative scores for postsecondary students." In an effort to ensure representation of the national student population, the GRADE standardization sites were chosen based on community size or type (urban, suburban, or rural). The percentage of students receiving free lunch at each site was considered to monitor socioeconomic status. A total of 33,432 preschool through postsecondary students were tested (Technical Manual, pp. 67–68).

Criterion-Referenced?

Yes. The GRADE is referenced to the individual reading skills measured by each subtest. Thus, each subtest enables the diagnosis of a specific inadequacy.

Feasibility Considerations

Testing Time

Generally forty-five minutes to one hour. The GRADE is not a timed test. Students are to be given sufficient time to attempt all items so that a diagnostic analysis of strengths and needs can be completed.

For Testing Groups? Individuals?

Groups and individuals.

Test Administration and Scoring

Clear and specific directions for administration are given in the Teacher's Administration Manuals. The scoring keys and directions for scoring are provided in the Teacher's Scoring & Interpretive Manuals. The author suggests that the GRADE can be administered and scored by persons from a wide range of educational backgrounds (i.e., paraprofessionals, assistants, etc., as long as they are working under supervision). It is suggested that the examiner practice by reading aloud the Listening Comprehension items for all levels and the item-by-item instructions for the lower levels. Also, only individuals who are involved in educational testing and/or have specific training in the teaching of reading (i.e., classroom teachers, reading specialists, etc.) should interpret GRADE test results.

Test Materials and Approximate Costs

Scoring & Reporting Software (individual use): $299.95; Scoring & Reporting Software (multi-user network): $9,995.

Level P: Student Booklets (10) (Form A or B): $26.95; Administration Manual (Form A or B): $11.95; Scoring & Interpretive Manual: $39.95; Classroom set (Form A): $122.95; Classroom set (Forms A and B): $209.95; Resource Library (CD-ROM): $99.95.

Level K: Same as Level P.

Level 1: Same as level K except: Classroom set (Forms A and B): $189.95; Administration Manual (Form A or B): $9.95.

Level 2: Same as Level 1.

Level 3: Same as Level 2.

Level 4: Same as Level 3 except: Classroom set (Form A): $169.95; Classroom set (Forms A & B): $279.95; Hand scoring template (Forms A & B): $39.95.

Level 5: Same as Level 4.

Level 6: Same as Level 5.

Levels M, H, and A: Same as Level 6.

Elementary Resource Specialist Set (P, K, 1, 2, 3, 4, 5, and 6): $899.95.

Secondary Resource Specialist Set (M, H, and A): $429.95.

Technical Manual (all levels): $49.95.

Adequacy of Test Manuals

All of the information needed by the examiner is given in the three manuals provided; the Teacher's Administration Manual (for each level), the Teacher's Scoring & Interpretive Manual (for each level), and the Technical Manual (for all levels). All of the manuals are clearly written and user-friendly.

Excerpts from Other Test Reviews

No test reviews were found for the GRADE.

Ordering Information

Publisher

American Guidance Service, Inc., 4201 Woodland Road, Circle Pines, MN 55014-1796; Phone: 800-328-2560; Fax: 800-471-8457; Web site: www.agsnet.com.

Author

Kathleen T. Williams.

Publication Date

2001.

Cautions and Comments

The GRADE is a psychometrically sound test which can be used effectively either as a criterion-referenced diagnostic assessment or as a norm-referenced instrument. It is particularly useful for monitoring growth and progress from grade to grade because the levels are psychometrically linked from pre-kindergarten through postsecondary.

Standardized Reading Inventory, Second Edition (SRI-2),
for testing individuals from 6 years through 14 years, 6 months of age
Reviewed by Katherine C. Schnepel, Ph.D.,
Educational Research and Measurement

Usefulness of the Test for Educators

Test Author's Purpose

The author states that the components of the SRI-2 can be used for five specific purposes: (1) to identify deficiencies in the reading vocabularies of groups of children; 2) as a survey test by determining a student's reading levels; (3) as a diagnostic test by providing evidence of specific strengths and weaknesses in reading strategies, knowledge, and skills; (4) to document overall progress in reading as a consequence of intervention programs; and (5) as a measure of research into children's reading.

Decision-Making Applications

The SRI-2 can be used to identify reading vocabulary deficiencies. Educators can first screen groups of students for reading problems by using just the Vocabulary in Context (VOC) subtest. Students who are identified as deficient on the VOC can be administered the individualized components of the SRI-2 to explore the depth and degree of their reading difficulties. The SRI-2 can be used to give the teacher an indication of a student's general level of competence in the skills of word recognition and comprehension (i.e., reading level). The SRI-2 can be used to identify a student's specific reading strengths and weaknesses. This information can be used to prescribe instruction or remediation. The teacher can use the SRI-2 to monitor the progress of students in instructional programs to ensure that they are responding to the instruction. For that purpose, the test should be used in conjunction with teacher opinion or clinical judgment.

Relevant Population

The SRI-2 is designed to be given to children from 6 years through 14 years, 6 months of age.

Characteristics Described

The Word Recognition in Context subtest is a measure of the extent to which the reader deviates from print when reading. Passage comprehension, the ability to construct meaning from text, is measured by the Passage Comprehension subtest. The Vocabulary in Context subtest assesses vocabulary knowledge. There is a supplemental subtest called Predictive Comprehension, which involves the ability to synthesize the material in the reading passages and to identify or predict the sentence (from five choices) that could logically fit into the passage. The student is asked to read aloud or silently and then asked to respond orally or in writing to questions about what was read.

Test Scores Obtained

	Passage Comprehension (PC) Subtest	Word Recognition Accuracy (WRA) Subtest
PP	X	X
P	X	X
1	X	X
2	X	X
3	X	X
4	X	X
5	X	X
6	X	X
7	X	X
8	X	X

	PC	WRA	Vocabulary in Context (VOC) Subtest
Raw Score	X	X	X
Age Equivalent	X	X	X
Grade Equivalent	X	X	X
Percentile	X	X	X
Standard Score	X	X	X
Sum of Standard Scores for PC + WRA =	X		
Percentile	X		
Reading Quotient (RQ)	X		

Source: Examiner's Manual, Section II, Figure 4.1, p. 13.

Technical Adequacy

Validity Confirmation

The author demonstrates *test item validity* in several ways. First is a discussion of the structure and content of the passages and comprehension questions. Second, the rationale and strategies for the development of the supplemental SRI-2 subtests (i.e., Vocabulary in Context and Predictive Comprehension) are presented. Third, the rationale for assigning reading levels to the passages that comprise the SRI-2 is discussed. Fourth, the validity of the items is supported by the results of "classical" item analysis procedures and analysis used to show the absence of bias (pp. 41–48).

Test response validity support is given by correlating the appropriate subtests of the SRI-2 with the Gray Silent Reading Test (GSRT), the Comprehensive Test of Phonological Processes (CTPP), and the Test of Word Reading Fluency (TOWRE). All of the subtests of both forms of the SRI-2 correlate adequately with both forms of the GSRT. However, most of the correlations of the SRI-2 subtests with the subtests of the CTPP are too low to indicate test response validity. Correlations of the Word Recognition Accuracy subtest with the subtests of the TOWRE are acceptable, but correlations of the Vocabulary in Context subtest with the TOWRE subtests are too low to be of value. The reading quotient obtained from the SRI-2 and the TOWRE range from .33 to .60, so are probably not strong support for test response validity.

Reliability Confirmation

To establish stability reliability, both forms of the original SRI at levels 2, 3, and 4 were administered during the second week of October 1984 to 30 third grade, on-level readers (8 years, 1 month through 8 years, 11 months) attending an elementary school in Pennsylvania. Approximately two weeks later, the students again were given levels 2, 3, and 4 of both forms of the test. The resulting values were correlated. The coefficients ranged from .83 to .92, thus allowing confidence in the test scores' stability over time.

Objectivity Confirmation

Scorer objectivity was established in two ways. First, 30 test protocols obtained by the author were scored both by the author and by a colleague who was an expert in the use of reading inventories. The resulting levels of agreement for estimating instructional level were 97% for Passage Comprehension and 97% for Word Recognition Accuracy. Second, tape recordings were made of the actual testing of 20 randomly selected students who were part of the standardization sample. Both the author and the same colleague were required to record responses independently. The extent of agreement for instructional level was 95% for Form A and 90% for Form B for Passage Comprehension and 90% for both forms of Word Recognition Accuracy. Specific instructions for scoring and scoring criteria are given for each subtest. The SRI-2 can be administered by anyone who is competent in the administration of reading tests. The author recommends that examiners should take the time to practice administering the SRI-2 several times before using the test to obtain reading scores for instructional purposes.

Statistical Confirmation

Statistical confirmation for the validity, reliability, objectivity, and norms of the SRI-2 can be found in the Examiner's Manual.

Special Features

Acronym

SRI-2.

Levels of the Test

Ten levels: pre-primary, primary, 1, 2, 3, 4, 5, 6, 7, and 8.

Number of Test Forms

Two.

Norm-Referenced?

Yes. Normative data was collected from 1,099 students from 28 states. The students ranged in age from 6 to 14. The number of students at each age ranged from 60 to 197. An attempt was made to compare the demographic characteristics of the norming sample with 1997 Census data. However, the norm group appears to be slightly over-represented by white, middle-income northeasterners.

Criterion-Referenced?

Yes. The SRI-2 is referenced to specific reading abilities, errors, vocabulary proficiency, and predictive comprehension.

Feasibility Considerations

Testing Time

The SRI-2 is not timed, so the testing time can range from 30 to 90 minutes, depending on the level and the number of subtests used.

For Testing Groups? Individuals?

Individuals.

Test Administration and Scoring

There is no computer scoring available for the SRI-2, but detailed administration procedures and scoring directions are provided in the Examiner's Manual. No formal training is required to administer the SRI-2, although the author recommends that the examiner have experience in administering reading tests.

Test Materials and Approximate Costs

Complete kit, including Examiner's Manual, Story Book, Forms A and B Vocabulary Sheets (25), Forms A and B Record Booklets (25), and Profile Scoring Forms (50): $224; Vocabulary Sheets (25) (specify form): $13; Record Booklets (25) (specify form): $49; Profile Scoring Forms (50): $21; Story Book: $36; Examiner's Manual: $47.

Adequacy of Test Manuals

The Examiner's Manual is clearly written, giving detailed administration procedures and scoring directions along with considerable technical information.

Excerpts from Other Test Reviews

The SRI-2 was reviewed by Solomon (2001) and Stevens (2001). Solomon says, "The SRI provides teachers with a useful assessment procedure in terms of presenting a series of passages designed to assess a student's reading ability efficiently. However, most teachers can construct, administer, and score meaningful informal reading inventories on their own" (p. 1170). Stevens suggests that "the author has attempted to address and respond to a number of criticisms aimed at its first edition. . . . The author has revised its format and clarified its administration procedures. . . . It now provides more information about a student's specific reading abilities, errors, vocabulary proficiency, and predictive comprehension skills. . . . It now provides a way to compare a student to his age and grade level peers. . . . This edition has taken a large step toward being a more frequently used and more valued reading inventory" (pp. 1170–1172).

Ordering Information

Publisher

PRO-ED, 8700 Shoal Creek Boulevard, Austin, TX 78757-6897; Phone: 800-897-3202; Fax: 800-397-7633; Web site: http://www.proedinc.com.

Author

Phyllis L. Newcomer.

Publication Date

1999.

Cautions and Comments

The SRI-2 can provide a useful instrument for assessing a student's reading ability. However, experienced teachers could certainly construct meaningful informal reading inventories on their own. In fact, these teacher-made inventories might be referenced more specifically to the textbooks and instruction being used by the teacher.

References

Solomon, A. (2001). Review of the Standardized Reading Inventory, Second Edition. In B. S. Plake & J. C. Impara (Eds.), *The Fourteenth Mental Measurements Yearbook* (p. 1170). Lincoln, NE: The Buros Institute of Mental Measurements.

Stevens, B.A. (2001). Review of the Standardized Reading Inventory, Second Edition. In B. S. Plake & J. C. Impara (Eds.), *The Fourteenth Mental Measurement Yearbook* (pp. 1170–1172). Lincoln, NE: The Buros Institute of Mental Measurements.

Stanford Diagnostic Reading Test, Fourth Edition (SDRT-4),
for testing groups grades 1.5 through 13
Reviewed by Katherine C. Schnepel, Ph.D.,
Educational Research and Measurement

Usefulness of the Test for Educators

Test Authors' Purpose

The authors tell us that the SDRT-4 is intended to diagnose students' strengths and weaknesses in the major components of the reading process. They say that its results can be used to challenge students who are doing well and to provide special help for others who lack some of the essential reading skills. They also say that the results can be used to identify trends in the reading levels of the students in the district, provide information about the effectiveness of instructional programs, measure changes that have taken place over an instructional period, and keep the community and school board informed about students' overall progress in reading (Directions for Administering, p. 5).

Decision-Making Applications

The SDRT-4 can be used effectively to diagnose students' weaknesses and deficiencies in reading. However, it would probably not be appropriate to use the results of the test as the only basis for developing instructional interventions for students experiencing reading difficulties. In other words, teachers should not go directly from looking at SDRT-4 results to developing instructional intervention. Rather, the test's results should serve as a guide to further exploration and diagnosis. Also, it would not be appropriate to use the SDRT-4 to identify trends in the reading skills of students in a district or to measure changes that have taken place over an instructional period. The SDRT-4 should not be used to monitor the effectiveness of instructional programs or to inform the community and/or school board about students' progress in reading. All of these purposes would be better served using an achievement instrument. Neither would it be appropriate to use the SDRT-4 to challenge students who are doing well.

Because of the nature of the test, it should be used only for below-average students who are suspected of having deficiencies in reading.

Relevant Population

Red Level—Grades 1.5–2.5; Orange Level—Grades 2.5–3.5; Green Level—Grades 3.5–4.5; Purple Level—Grades 4.5–6.5; Brown Level—Grades 6.5–8.9; Blue Level—Grades 9–13.

Characteristics Described

Red Level—measures pre-reading skills: phonetic analysis, auditory vocabulary and word recognition, comprehension of sentences, riddles, cloze, and short paragraphs with questions.

Orange Level—measures pre-reading skills in phonetic analysis, auditory vocabulary, reading vocabulary, comprehension of cloze, and paragraphs that reflect informational, recreational, and functional types of text.

Green Level—assesses phonetic analysis, reading vocabulary, and comprehension of paragraphs involving the various kinds of selections.

Purple Level—measures reading vocabulary, comprehension of different kinds of text, and scanning text to locate information without reading the text first.

Brown Level—measures fluency in reading vocabulary, reading comprehension, and scanning.

Blue Level—measures reading vocabulary, reading comprehension, and scanning.

Test Scores Obtained

Red Level—Yields 19 scores: Phonetic Analysis (Consonants-Single, Consonants-Blends, Consonants-Digraphs, Consonants Total, Vowels-Short, Vowels-Long, Vowels Total, Total), Vocabulary (Word Reading, Listening Vocabulary, Nouns, Verbs, Others, Total), Comprehension (Sentences, Riddles, Cloze, Total), Paragraphs with Questions.

Orange Level—Yields 19 scores: Phonetic Analysis (Consonants-Single, Consonants-Blends, Consonants-Digraphs, Consonants Total, Vowels-Short, Vowels-Long, Vowels Total, Total), Vocabulary (Listening Vocabulary, Reading Vocabulary, Synonyms, Classification, Total), Comprehension (Cloze, Total), Paragraphs with Questions, Recreational Reading, Textual Reading, Functional Reading.

Green Level—Yields 22 scores: Phonetic Analysis (Consonants-Single, Consonants-Blends, Consonants-Digraphs, Consonants Total, Vowels-Short, Vowels-Long, Vowels-Other, Vowels Total, Total), Vocabulary (Listening Vocabulary, Reading Vocabulary, Synonyms, Classification, Word Parts, Content Area Words, Total), Comprehension, Paragraphs with Questions, Recreational Reading, Textual Reading, Functional Reading, Initial Understanding, Interpretation, Critical Analysis and Reading Strategies.

Purple Level—Yields 16 scores: Vocabulary (Reading Vocabulary, Synonyms, Classification, Word Parts, Content Area Words, Total), Comprehension, Paragraphs with

Questions, Recreational Reading, Textual Reading, Functional Reading, Initial Understanding, Interpretation, Critical Analysis, Reading Strategies, Scanning.

Brown Level—Yields 16 scores: Same as Purple Level.

Blue Level—Yields 16 scores: Same as Purple Level.

Technical Adequacy

Validity Confirmation

In order to support *test item validity*, the authors give a detailed description of the objectives and items in the SDRT-4. They tell us that, "as items were written and received from item writers, they went through an internal review process by content experts who made sure that the items were actually assessing the content objectives they were assigned to; measurement experts who reviewed the items for correct test item properties; and editorial specialists who made sure that the items were free of grammatical and typographical errors" (Multilevel Norms Book, p. 8).

As evidence of *test response validity*, the authors provide high correlations between performance on the SDRT-4 and the Third Edition. However, no correlations between the SDRT-4 and other well-accepted measures of reading achievement are given. Moderate intercorrelations among the SDRT-4 subtests and correlations between these subtests and the Otis-Lennon School Ability Test, Sixth Edition are also given as evidence of test response validity. These correlations are typical of what would be expected for these types of tests.

Reliability Confirmation

Evidence of stability reliability is provided by reporting alternate-form reliability. The alternate-form reliability coefficients for the components range from .62 to .82, and they range from .86 to .88 for the total scores. No evidence of the stability of the scores over time, such as test-retest reliability coefficients, is provided. Internal consistency measures, KR20 and KR21, are reported. The KR20 coefficients range from .79 to .94 for the four major components of the SDRT-4, and KR20 coefficients range from .95 to .98 for the total scores; the KR21 coefficients are comparable.

Objectivity Confirmation

There are no free response items on the SDRT-4. All of the items are multiple choice. Therefore, no evidence to support inter-rater objectivity is needed and none was reported.

Statistical Confirmation

Statistical data on validity, reliability, and norms can be obtained from the 1995 Multilevel Norms Book and Technical Information. This data could be summarized more effectively and could be made more clear for the classroom teacher who is not measurement trained.

Special Features

Acronym

SDRT-4.

Levels of the Test

Six. Red Level—Grades 1.5–2.5; Orange Level—Grades 2.5–3.5; Green Level—Grades 3.5–4.5; Purple Level—Grades 4.5–6.5; Brown Level—Grades 6.5–8.9; Blue Level—Grades 9–13.

Number of Test Forms

One for Red, Orange, and Green levels; two for Purple, Brown, and Blue levels.

Norm-Referenced?

Yes. Normative data was collected during the fall of 1994 (approximately 33,000 examinees) and the spring of 1995 (approximately 20,000 examinees). The norms for college freshmen were based on approximately 2,000 students. The samples were collected using a stratified random sampling technique based on geographical region, socioeconomic status, urbanicity, ethnicity, handicapping condition, and nonpublic schools to be representative of the national school population. The fall and spring samples approximate the national school population on most variables. However, the fall sample is overrepresented with students attending private schools and underrepresented with Hispanic students for both the spring and fall norming. The spring sample is underrepresented with urban school districts and overrepresented with rural school districts. No descriptive information on the 2,000 college freshmen comprising the fall norms is provided. Thus, the test user should be cautious in using these norms and the test for norm-referenced comparisons.

Criterion-Referenced?

Yes. Selection of items was based, in part, on a review of the literature in reading education, diagnosis, and instruction, and on the most recent state and district school curricula and educational objectives. However, the authors say that test users must determine the extent to which the SDRT-4 reflects their own local curriculum.

Other Features

The SDRT-4 includes three optional informal assessments. The Reading Questionnaire assesses a student's attitudes toward reading, reading habits and interests, and familiarity with topics and important concepts involved in the Reading Comprehension subtest. The Reading Strategies Survey is a self-report measure of a student's use of desirable and counterproductive reading strategies. The Story Retelling subtest assesses comprehension ability by having students reconstruct a story either orally or in writing. These informal assessments help the test user to diagnose more fully a student's strengths and weaknesses in conjunction with the more formal standardized component of the SDRT-4 or other standardized reading tests. Also, practice tests, with their own administration booklets, are available for each level.

Feasibility Considerations

Testing Time

Red Level: 105 (110) minutes; Orange Level and Green Level: 100 (105) minutes; Purple Level, Brown Level, and Blue Level: 85 (90) minutes.

For Testing Groups? Individuals?

Groups.

Test Administration and Scoring

There is a separate administration booklet for each level. Clear and detailed directions for administering the SDRT-4 are given in the manuals. Both machine-scorable and hand-scorable answer forms are available. Instructions for preparing the answer forms for machine scoring as well as instructions for hand scoring are also given in the manuals.

Test Materials and Approximate Costs

Examination kit, including multiple-choice test booklet and directions for administering, practice test and directions for administering, answer document, class record form, Reading Questionnaire, Reading Strategies Survey, Story Retelling (Story and Response Form), and directions for each (specify level): $37.50.

Practice tests and directions for administering (25) (specify Red, Orange, Green, Purple, or Brown level): $17.

Machine-scorable test booklets, type 1, and directions for administering (25) (specify Red, Orange, or Green level): $111.

Hand-scorable test booklets, directions for administering, and class record forms (25) (specify Red, Orange, or Green level): $76.

Reusable test booklets and directions for administering (25) (specify Purple, Brown, or Blue level and Form J or K): $55.

Reading Questionnaires and directions for administering (25) (specify level and form): $37.50.

Reading Strategies Surveys and directions for administering (25) (specify Red/ Orange, Green/Purple, or Brown/Blue levels): $37.50.

Story Retelling manual (1995, 15 pages) and Story and Response forms (25) (specify Red/Orange, Green/Purple, or Brown/Blue levels): $44.50.

Machine-scorable answer documents, type 1 (for Purple/Brown/Blue levels): $37.50.

Hand-scorable answer documents with blackline master of student record form and class record forms (25) (for Purple/Brown/Blue levels): $30.

Side-by-side keys for hand-scorable test booklets with blackline master of student record form (specify Red, Orange, or Green level): $15.

Response keys (specify level and form): $15.

Stencil keys for hand-scorable answer documents (specify Purple, Brown, or Blue level and Form J or K): $22.

Class record forms (specify Red, Orange, Green, or Purple/Brown/Blue levels) (25): $6.50.

Row markers (25): $6.90.

Fall or Spring Multilevel norms booklet (1996, 103 pages): $52.

Teacher's manual for interpreting (specify Red/Orange level [1996, 67 pages], Green/Purple level [1996, 68 pages], or Brown/Blue level [1996, 62 pages]): $22.

Test directions for administering (specify Red, Orange, Green, or Purple/Brown/Blue level): $10.

Practice test directions for administering (specify Red, Orange, Green, Purple, or Brown level): $6.50.

Reading Questionnaire directions for administering: $6.50.

Reading Strategies Survey directions for administering: $6.50.

Story Retelling manual: $9.

Price information for scoring services is available from the publisher.

Adequacy of Test Manuals

There is an administration manual for each level of the test, an administration manual for each practice test, and administration manuals for each of the informal assessments. There are interpretation manuals for the teacher and two norms and technical information books. The administration and interpretation manuals are clearly written and easily understood by the teacher who is not trained in testing. However, the norms and technical manual is not easily understood by persons without a testing background. It would be helpful if the norms tables and the validity and reliability information could be summarized and presented more clearly.

Excerpts from Other Test Reviews

The SDRT-4 was reviewed by Engelhard (1998), Swerdlik and Bucy (1998), and Salvia and Ysseldkye (2001). Engelhard says that "the SDRT-4 reflects sound professional test development, administration, and scoring strategies, and appears to offer a useful measure of reading."

Swerdlik and Bucy state that "The SDRT-4 is a generally well developed diagnostic measure to assess reading strengths and weaknesses of students experiencing reading difficulties in grades 1 through 12. The college norms, which are not adequately described, should be interpreted with caution as should the three informal assessments as no reliability or validity evidence is provided. The test user should also avoid interpreting some areas of strength and weakness due to the low reliability of some clusters. Despite these limitations, the SDRT-4 could prove particularly useful for classroom teachers and reading specialists who want to evaluate large numbers of students and want to assess the effectiveness of instructional programs. As is true of most diagnostic reading tests, the usefulness of the SDRT-4 in developing effective interventions for students experiencing reading difficulties is yet to be documented. In addition, as is also true of all diagnostic reading tests, test users must carefully assess the correspondence of the test content to the reading curriculum in which their students were instructed and if a close match does not exist the use of the SDRT-4 would not be recommended."

Salvia and Ysseldyke say that "Validity for the SDRT-4, as for any achievement measure, must be judged relative to the content of local curricula" (p. 440).

Ordering Information

Publisher

Harcourt Educational Measurement, 19500 Bulverde Road, San Antonio, TX 78259-3701; Phone: 800-211-8378; Fax: 877-576-1816; Web site: www. hemweb.com.

Authors

Bjorn Karlsen and Eric F. Gardner.

Publication Date

1996.

Cautions and Comments

The SDRT-4 is a diagnostic test, not an achievement test. Diagnostic tests place more emphasis on the lower achiever who is having problems. Thus, they contain more easy questions than do general mathematics achievement tests, which are intended to measure the broad range of ability of the entire student population. The authors say that the SDRT-4 can also be used to "challenge students who are doing well" (Multilevel Norms Booklet, p. 7). This reviewer does not recommend this because it would seem that a good student might think that she or he knows more about those concepts measured than she or he really does. So, the SDRT-4 should probably be used only with below-average students or with students who are suspected of having deficiencies. Also, using this test for program evaluation or to measure change might not be appropriate because the subtests are very specific in their coverage of instructional areas. A survey achievement test, which is broader in scope, would be more appropriate for these purposes.

References

Engelhard, G., Jr. (1998). Review of the Stanford Diagnostic Reading Test, Fourth Edition. In J. C. Impara & B. S. Plake (Eds.), *The Thirteenth Mental Measurements Yearbook* (pp. 939–941). Lincoln, NE: The Buros Institute of Mental Measurements.

Salvia, J., & Ysseldyke, J. E. (2001). *Assessment* (8th ed.). Boston: Houghton Mifflin.

Swerdlik, M. E., & Bucy, J. E. (1998). Review of the Stanford Diagnostic Reading Test, Fourth Edition. In J. C. Impara & B. S. Plake (Eds.), *The Thirteenth Mental Measurements Yearbook* (pp. 941–943). Lincoln, NE: The Buros Institute of Mental Measurements.

Test of Early Reading Ability, Third Edition (TERA-3),
for testing individuals from 3 years, 6 months through 8 years, 6 months of age
Reviewed by Katherine C. Schnepel, Ph.D.,
Educational Research and Measurement

Usefulness of the Test for Educators

Test Authors' Purpose

The authors state that the TERA-3 has five purposes: (1) to identify those children who are significantly below their peers in reading development and thus may be candidates for early intervention, (2) to identify strengths and weaknesses of individual children, (3) to document children's progress as a consequence of early reading intervention programs, (4) to serve as a measure in research studying reading development in young children, and (5) to accompany other assessment techniques (Examiner's Manual, p. 8).

Decision-Making Applications

The TERA-3 seems to be very useful for identifying children with early reading deficiencies and for identifying where those deficiencies lie. Also, the TERA-3 would be useful for pinpointing strengths as well as weaknesses in early reading skills. The test can be used to recommend further diagnostic assessment and/or the results of the test can be used as the basis for development of instructional intervention.

Relevant Population

The TERA-3 measures early reading in children ages 3 years, 6 months through 8 years, 6 months (Examiner's Manual, p. 7). It can be used with children who vary widely in the style of English they speak (Examiner's Manual, p. 11).

Characteristics Described

Early reading is measured by the TERA-3 by means of three subtests: (1) Alphabet, which measures children's knowledge of the alphabet and sound-letter correspondence; (2) Conventions, which measures children's familiarity with the conventions of print; and (3) Meaning, which measures children's ability to comprehend the meaning of printed material. The Alphabet subtest responses are measured by showing the child a picture or printed letters and asking him or her to point to a letter or word and name it. The Conventions subtest involves asking the child what comes next in a printed context. In the case of the Meaning subtest, the child is asked to tell something about the meaning of the picture or words he/she saw.

Test Scores Obtained

Subtests	Raw Score	Age Equiv.	Grade Equiv.	Std. Score	%ile	SEM	Conf. Int.	Std. Sc. Rge
Alphabet	X	X	X	X	X	X	X	X
Conventions	X	X	X	X	X	X	X	X
Meaning	X	X	X	X	X	X	X	X
Reading Quotient				X	X	X	X	X

Source: Examiner's Manual, p. 20.

Raw scores are simply the number of items scored correct on each subtest. The Age and Grade Equivalents are figured from the Raw Score Using the table in Appendix D of the Examiner's Manual. The Standard Scores are converted from raw scores using the tables in Appendix A. Percentiles represent values that indicate the percentage of the norming distribution that is equal to or below a particular score. The percentile is generated for the subtests and composites using tables in Appendixes A and B, respectively. The Reading Quotient is the standard score for the composite. The composite score is derived by adding the subtest standard scores and converting the sum to a composite score using Appendix B.

Technical Adequacy

Validity Confirmation

Test item validity was supported by the authors by:

1. Reviews of existing research, commercial and noncommercial curriculum materials (including scope-and-sequence charts and state standards), and popular tests showing that the TERA-3 items reflect the current state of knowledge.
2. Comparison of existing lists of emergent reading behaviors.
3. Having experts examine the items.
4. The results of conventional item analysis procedures and item response theory procedures used to choose items during the developmental stages of test construction.
5. The results of differential item functioning analysis used to show the absence of bias in the test's items.

As evidence of *test response validity* the authors correlated the scores of the TERA-3 with those of selected criterion reading tests from the Stanford Achievement Test

Series, Ninth Edition (SAT-9) and the Woodcock Reading Mastery Test-Revised-Normative Update (WRMT-R-NU). As further evidence of test response validity the TERA-3 was correlated with teacher ratings of students on general reading ability, oral reading, reading comprehension, decoding, spelling, and punctuation. Correlations of the TERA-3 with the reading tests of the SAT-9 and the WRMT-R-NU ranged from .36 to .67, with just four correlations below .40. Correlations of the TERA-3 with teacher judgments ranged from .43 to .71, with just four correlations below .50.

Reliability Confirmation

Stability reliability is supported by using the test-retest procedure and the alternate forms procedure. In the test-retest procedure, the first testing and the second testing with two weeks in between were done on two groups of children: one group of 30 normally achieving children ages 4 to 6 and another group of 34 normally achieving children ages 7 to 9. Both forms of the test were administered twice to the samples. After the testing was completed, the subtest scores and total scores were correlated. The resulting coefficients ranged from .86 to .99. The alternate forms procedure was accomplished by administering both forms of the test during one testing session. Then Form A and Form B subtests were correlated at six age intervals using the test performance of the entire normative sample as subjects. The resulting correlations ranged from .82 to .95. Internal consistency reliability evidence was also provided. All of the resulting reliability coefficients were greater than .80. All of the procedures used provide strong evidence of the reliability of the TERA-3.

Objectivity Confirmation

In order to show inter-scorer objectivity of the TERA-3, one of the TERA-3's authors and two advanced graduate students in special education at the University of Texas independently scored a set of 40 completed protocols drawn randomly from the children in the normative sample. The results were correlated. In all instances, the resulting coefficients rounded to .99, giving strong evidence supporting the TERA-3's inter-scorer objectivity.

Statistical Confirmation

Statistical data supporting validity, reliability, objectivity, and norms is presented clearly in the Examiner's Manual.

Special Features

Acronym

TERA-3.

Levels of the Test

Four. Levels are determined by the use of basals and ceilings. Testing begins at the entry point noted for each subtest (basal) and continues until a child misses three items in a row (ceiling). The entry points are shown below.

		Subtest	
Ages	*Alphabet*	*Conventions*	*Meaning*
3 years, 6 months to 5 years, 11 months	Item 1	Item 1	Item 1
6 years to 6 years, 11 months	Item 10	Item 5	Item 5
7 years to 7 years, 11 months	Item 15	Item 10	Item 10
8 years to 8 years, 6 months	Item 20	Item 15	Item 15

Source: Examiner's Manual, Table 2.1, p. 15.

The entry points are the same for the subtests of both forms of the test.

Number of Test Forms

Two.

Norm-Referenced?

Yes. The normative sample is made up of 875 children residing in 22 states. The selection procedures used resulted in a normative sample that is representative of the nation as a whole with regard to geographic region, gender, race, residence, ethnicity, family income, educational attainment of parents, and disabling condition.

Criterion-Referenced?

The TERA-3 is referenced to reading skills, but is not referenced to specific curricular or instructional skills.

Feasibility Considerations

Testing Time

The time required to administer the entire TERA-3 varies from approximately 15 minutes to 45 minutes. The TERA-3 is not a timed test; therefore, no precise time limits are imposed on the children being tested. Usually the TERA-3 can be completed in one testing session. However, for some individuals the testing may have to be conducted during several sessions.

For Testing Groups? Individuals?

Individuals.

Test Administration and Scoring

Both general administration guidelines and specific instructions for administration and scoring are given in the Examiner's Manual. These are easily followed. However, the authors do recommend that examiners who give and interpret the TERA-3 should have some formal training in assessment. They suggest that this training should result in a basic understanding regarding testing statistics and general procedures governing test administration, scoring, and interpretation.

Test Materials and Approximate Costs

Complete kit, which includes Examiner's Manual, Picture Books for Form A and Form B, and Profile/Examiner Record Forms for Form A and Form B: $229; Examiner's Manual: $79; Picture Book (specify Form A or Form B): $54; Profile/Examiner Record Forms (25) (specify Form A or Form B): $24.

Adequacy of Test Manuals

The Examiner's Manual is very clear and specific about administration of the TERA-3 and interpretation of the results. It also provides an overview of the test and its development. The Examiner's Manual includes technical information (i.e. validity, reliability, and norming data).

Excerpts from Other Test Reviews

No test reviews were found for the TERA-3.

Ordering Information

Publisher

PRO-ED, 8700 Shoal Creek Boulevard, Austin, TX 78757-6897; Phone: 800-897-3202; Fax: 800-397-7633; Web site: http://www.proedinc.com.

Authors

D. Kim Reid, Wayne P. Hresko, and Donald D. Hammill.

Publication Date

2001.

Cautions and Comments

The TERA-3 is useful for identifying children who have reading problems and for detecting their strengths and weaknesses in reading. The TERA-3 provides an efficient, standardized assessment of a young child's reading ability.

Woodcock Reading Mastery Tests-Revised (WRMT-R),
for testing individuals from 5 through 75+ years of age
Reviewed by Katherine C. Schnepel, Ph.D.,
Educational Research and Measurement

Usefulness of the Test for Educators

Test Author's Purpose

The author states that the comprehensive nature of the WRMT-R tests and the wide age range of subjects for which it is appropriate make the WRMT-R suitable for a variety of purposes. These purposes include:

1. Clinical Assessment and Diagnosis—Within the school-age range, a primary application of the WRMT-R is with students having reading problems. For such students, the WRMT-R provides a comprehensive analysis from which to proceed with other diagnostic procedures, if needed, or with instructional planning.

2. Individual Program Planning—The WRMT-R may be used in setting instructional goals when developing an Individual Education Plan (IEP). The student's patterns of strengths and weaknesses among the tests can supply significant implications for remediation.

3. Selection and Placement—The WRMT-R can be used when placing new students in a school or other program to help ensure that they are assigned to the most appropriate level of instruction. The tests may also be used to group students for instruction within a reading class or to select students for special purposes. The WRMT-R can aid in occupational selection and placement, particularly when certain reading skills are necessary for successful job performance.

4. Guidance—The WRMT-R can aid teachers, counselors, social workers, and other personnel in understanding the nature of an individual's strengths and weaknesses in reading and the resultant implications for serving that individual.

5. Appraising Gains or Growth—The WRMT-R may be used to provide a record of individual growth over a relatively short time or across a wide time span.

6. Program Evaluation—The WRMT-R can be used to provide information about program effectiveness at the elementary and secondary levels, at the college level, and with adults.

7. Research (Examiner's Manual, p. 10).

Decision-Making Applications

The WRMT-R can be used effectively by teachers to identify deficiencies in reading skills and to serve as a basis for prescribing remedial instruction. The test can also be used effectively to place students in levels of instruction within a classroom. The test can be used to diagnose and prescribe for young children through adults. It can also be used with learning disabled or below-average students to pinpoint their deficiencies in reading and to guide remediation for those deficiencies.

Relevant Population

The WRMT-R is appropriate for students in grades K–16 or ages 5 through 75+.

Characteristics Described

Figure 1.1
Number of Items on Subtests by Form

	Number of Items	
Test or Subtest	Form G	Form H
Readiness Cluster (Form G only)		
Test 1: Visual-Auditory Learning	134	—
Test 2: Letter Identification	51	—
Supplementary Letter Checklist		
Capital Letters	27	—
Lowercase Letters	36	—
Basic Skills Cluster		
Test 3: Word Identification	106	106
Test 4: Word Attack	45	45
Reading Comprehension Cluster		
Test 5: Word Comprehension	146	146
Subtests		
Antonyms-Synonyms (combined)	67	67
Analogies	79	79
Vocabularies		
General Reading	30	30
Science-Mathematics	40	39
Social Studies	38	39
Humanities	38	38
Test 6: Passage Comprehension	68	68

Source: Examiner's Manual, Table 1.1, p. 5.

Test 1: Visual-Auditory Learning (Form G only)—The subject learns a vocabulary of unfamiliar visual symbols (rebuses) representing familiar words, and then translates sequences of rebuses that have been used to form sentences. Seven test stories are written with rebuses. Preceding each story is an introduction page that presents four new rebuses. All subjects begin the test with the first introduction. A vocabulary totaling 26 words and two word endings is presented throughout the seven introduction pages (Examiner's Manual, p. 4).

Test 2: Letter Identification (Form G only)—The term *identification* was used in the name of this test because the subject may be asked to respond to some letters in forms that he or she has never seen before. This is in contrast to the term *recognition*, which implies a response to a stimulus with which a person has had prior experience. The set of letter forms in this test includes roman, italic, and bold type; serif and sans serif type styles; cursive characters; and several special type styles (e.g., script and decorative type styles such as those appearing in advertisements). The examiner may accept either the name of the letter or its most common sound, whichever the subject chooses to provide (Examiner's Manual, p. 5).

Supplementary Letter Checklist (Form G only)—The Supplementary Letter Checklist presents letters only in a sans serif type style common in many beginning reading materials. The purpose of the two-part checklist (Capital Letters and Lowercase Letters) is to determine which letters the subject can name or identify by their sound. The examiner has the option of asking the subject to respond by giving the names or the sounds of the letters, or by giving both names and sounds in two separate administrations. There are 37 items in the Capital Letters section of the Supplementary Letter Checklist and 36 items in the Lowercase Letters section (Examiner's Manual, p. 5).

Test 3: Word Identification—This test requires the subject to identify isolated words that appear in large type on the subject pages in the test book. As subjects proceed through items, they encounter words that appear less and less frequently in written English. For an answer to be scored correct, the subject must produce a natural reading of the word within about five seconds (Examiner's Manual, p. 6).

Test 4: Word Attack—This test requires the subject to read either nonsense words (letter combinations that are not actual words) or words with a very low frequency of occurrence in the English language. The test measures the subject's ability to apply phonic and structural analysis skills in order to pronounce words with which he or she may be unfamiliar (Examiner's Manual, p. 6).

Test 5: Word Comprehension—This test comprises three subtests; antonyms, synonyms, and analogies. The antonyms subtest measures the subject's ability to read a word and then respond orally with a word opposite in meaning. The synonyms subtest requires the subject to read a word and then state another word similar in meaning to the presented word. The analogies subtest requires the subject to read a pair of words and ascertain the relationship between the words, then read the first word of a second pair of words and use the same relationship to supply a word from his or her oral vocabulary to complete the analogy appropriately (Examiner's Manual, p. 7).

Test 6: Passage Comprehension—This test measures the subject's ability to study a short passage, usually two to three sentences long, and to identify a key word missing from the passage. The items have been selected so that the subject will not be likely to provide an acceptable response based on reading just a few words on either side of the blank. Instead, to complete the item the subject must understand not only the sentence containing the blank but the other sentence(s) in the passage as well (Examiner's Manual, p. 8).

Test Scores Obtained

Eleven raw scores are obtained. They are Readiness Cluster (Visual-Auditory Learning, Letter Identification, Total), Basic Skills Cluster (Word Identification, Word Attack, Total), Reading Comprehension Cluster (Word Comprehension, Passage Comprehension, Total), Total Reading—Full Scale, and Total Reading—Short Scale, plus a Supplementary Letter Checklist. These raw scores can be converted into commonly understood derived scores: percentiles, standard scores, t-scores, normal-curve equivalents, and age and grade equivalents. Raw scores can also be converted to w-scores (a Rasch ability score) and to a Relative Performance Index (RPI), which is a ratio of the test taker's mastery of material to that mastered by 90% of the normative sample.

Technical Adequacy

Validity Confirmation

Evidence of *test item validity* is presented by showing that WRMT-R items were developed with contributions from outside experts, including experienced teachers and curriculum specialists. The items contained in each test were designed to be comprehensive in both content and difficulty. All items are open-ended, or free-response, in nature. An open-ended design most closely parallels the requirements of reading in real-life situations. This item design also virtually eliminates guessing as a confounding factor in scores (often a major problem with multiple-choice tests). Classical item selection techniques were used in the early stages of item development, and the Rasch model was used during later stages; both contributed to the stringent statistical criteria employed during the process of item selection in the WRMT-R.

As evidence of *test response validity*, data is presented showing correlations of the WRMT-R with the reading subtests of the Woodcock-Johnson Psychoeducational Battery. Correlations among subtests measuring similar behaviors are high (.60 to .90).

Reliability Confirmation

No data is given for stability reliability. Data is provided on the internal consistency reliability of the WRMT-R. Reliabilities were calculated using the split-half procedure, in which one-half of the items are correlated with the other half of the items. These reliabilities for the six tests exceed .80; most exceed .90.

Objectivity Confirmation

A scoring key is given for all of the subtests of the WRMT-R. Clear instructions for scoring are also given. However, there are no studies that show inter-rater objectivity. These probably should have been done, as the items are open-ended or free-response.

Statistical Confirmation

Statistical data for validity, reliability, and norms is presented in the Examiner's Manual.

Special Features

Acronym

WRMT-R.

Levels of the Test

Levels are determined by the use of basals and ceilings. The basal is determined by the six lowest-numbered consecutive correct responses that begin with the first item on a test page. The ceiling is the point at which the subject has failed the six highest-numbered consecutive items administered, provided that the last of these items is the final item on a test page.

Number of Test Forms

Two.

Norm-Referenced?

Yes. The norms for the WRMT-R are based on the performances of 3,184 students in grades 1 through 12 and 245 individuals between 18 and 22 years of age. Actual participants were selected from a pool of volunteers using stratified random-sampling techniques. At each grade, the sample appears representative in terms of sex, geographic region, parental education, race and ethnicity (that is, African-American, Hispanic, white, and other), and placement in special education programs for students with disabilities and for gifted students. However, only parts of the total sample were used to calibrate the items in each subtest. The numbers for each subtest range from 2,662 (Word Reading) to 721 (Word Comprehension).

Criterion-Referenced?

Yes. The WRMT-R is referenced to specific reading skills such as readiness (Visual-Auditory Learning, Letter Identification), Basic Skills (Word Identification, Word Attack), and Reading Comprehension (Word Comprehension, Passage Comprehension).

Other Features

A microcomputer scoring program, Automated System for Scoring and Interpreting Standardized Tests (ASSIST™), is a valuable aid for the examiner in computing scores for the WRMT-R. Another item available to aid in WRMT-R score reporting and record keeping is the Report to Parents.

Feasibility Considerations

Testing Time

Forty to 45 minutes for the entire battery; 15 minutes for the Short Scale.

For Testing Groups? Individuals?

Individuals.

Test Administration and Scoring

Clear and detailed instructions for administration and scoring are presented in the Examiner's Manual. Proper administration and scoring of the WRMT-R does not require formal training or an extensive background in test administration; the necessary procedures can be learned by a wide range of personnel. However, a clear distinction exists between the skills required to administer and score a test such as the WRMT-R and those required to evaluate the test results in order to make placement decisions or program plans (Examiner's Manual, p. 14).

Test Materials and Approximate Costs

Form G and Form H combined kit, including Form G and Form H test books, 25 each of test records, sample Form G and H summary record form, pronunciation guide cassette, sample report to parents, and Examiner's Manual (214 pages) plus ASSIST: $367.95.

Form G complete kit, including materials in combined kit for Form G only: $251.95.
Form H complete kit, including materials in combined kit for Form H only: $246.95.
Test records (25) (specify Form G or Form H): $41.95.
Form G and H summary record forms (25): $28.95.
Reports to parents (25): $20.95.
ASSIST scoring software (specify IBM PC/XT/AT, PS/2, and compatibles of Apple IIc, enhanced IIe, and IIGS): $199.95.
Examiner's Manual: $94.95.

Adequacy of Test Manuals

The Examiner's Manual is very clear and specific about administration of the WRMT-R and interpretation of the results. It provides an overview of the test and its development. The Examiner's Manual also very clearly presents the technical information (i.e., validity, reliability, objectivity, and norming data).

Excerpts from Other Test Reviews

The WRMT-R was reviewed by Crocker (2001), Murray-Ward (2001), and Salvia and Ysseldyke (2001). Crocker cautions that "The fact that validity and reliability data presented in the manual did not apply to the current norm sample should discourage use of this test when making individual decisions affecting examinee diagnosis or placement."

Murray-Ward states that "The WRMT-R should be used in conjunction with other measures of reading. Results should not be overinterpreted. The examiner should also be very cautious in using the test with a wide range of age groups. If these cautions are observed, the test may be useful in helping estimate reading achievement."

Salvia and Ysseldyke say that "The test is used to measure behaviors in ten subtests and clusters, and it is intended to be used for diagnostic and instructional planning purposes. The test is among the best-normed diagnostic reading tests, and there is good evidence for its reliability and validity."

Ordering Information

Publisher

American Guidance Service, Inc., 4201 Woodland Road, Circle Pines, MN 55014-1796; Phone: 800-328-2560; Fax: 800-471-8457; Web site: www.agsnet.com.

Author

Richard W. Woodcock.

Publication Date

1998.

Cautions and Comments

The WRMT-R is referenced to specific reading skills, so the examiner must be sure that he or she is using the test to measure the skills needed for the curriculum being used with his or her students. The skill assessment needed by the examiner might be addressed by one or more of the subtests or the entire WRMT-R. Thus, the examiner could use all or part of the test according to his or her needs.

References

Crocker, L. (2001). Review of the Woodcock Mastery Reading Test, Revised. In B. S. Plake & J. C. Impara (Eds.), *The Fourteenth Mental Measurements Yearbook* [Electronic version]. Retrieved February, 4, 2002 from Buros Institute's Test Reviews Online web site: http://www.unl.edu/buros.

Murray-Ward, M. (2001). Review of the Woodcock Mastery Reading Test, Revised. In B. S. Plake & J. C. Impara (Eds.), *The Fourteenth Mental Measurements Yearbook* [Electronic version]. Retrieved February, 4, 2002 from Buros Institute's Test Reviews Online web site: http://www.unl.edu/buros.

Salvia, J., & Ysseldyke, J. E. (2001). *Assessment* (8th ed.). Boston: Houghton Mifflin.

6

Mathematics Tests

KeyMath Revised: A Diagnostic Inventory of Essential Mathematics (KeyMath-R), for testing individuals from 6 through 22 years of age
Reviewed by Katherine C. Schnepel, Ph.D.,
Educational Research and Measurement

Usefulness of the Test for Educators

Test Author's Purpose

The author offers five uses or purposes of KeyMath-R: (1) assessment for general instruction, (2) assessment for remedial instruction, (3) contribution to global assessment (i.e., part of a comprehensive psychoeducational test battery), (4) pre-and post-testing, and (5) curriculum assessment.

Decision-Making Applications

It would be appropriate to use the KeyMath-R to make decisions about instructional prescription and/or intervention. The subtests of the KeyMath-R are designed to identify deficiencies in the many areas that make up the ability to understand and apply the concepts and skills of mathematics. However, the KeyMath-R would best be used as one of several tests given to determine the needs of individual students.

Relevant Population

This test is designed to assess understanding and applications of mathematics concepts and skills of students in ages 6–22, grades K–9. KeyMath-R was normed using students from kindergarten to adult.

Characteristics Described

KeyMath-R provides detailed information about a student's mathematical understanding and skill in three broad areas (Basic Concepts, Operations, and Applications), 13 general subareas called strands (Numeration, Rational Numbers, Geometry, Addition, Subtraction, Multiplication, Division, Mental Computation, Measurement, Time and Money, Estimation, Interpreting Data, and Problem Solving), and 43 very specific content domains in each of those strands (see Figure 1.1).

Figure 1.1
Content Specification of KeyMath-R: Areas, Strands, and Domains

BASIC CONCEPTS

Numeration
1. Numbers 0–9
2. Numbers 0–99
3. Numbers 0–999
4. Multidigit numbers and advanced numeration topics

Rational Numbers
1. Fractions
2. Decimals
3. Percents

Geometry
1. Spatial and attribute relations
2. Two-dimensional shapes and their relations
3. Coordinate and transformational geometry
4. Three-dimensional shapes and their relations

OPERATIONS

Addition
1. Models and basic facts
2. Algorithms to add whole numbers
3. Adding rational numbers

Subtraction
1. Models and basic facts
2. Algorithms to subtract whole numbers
3. Subtracting rational numbers

Multiplication
1. Models and basic facts
2. Algorithms to multiply whole numbers
3. Multiplying rational numbers

Division
1. Models and basic facts
2. Algorithms to divide whole numbers
3. Dividing rational numbers

Mental Computation
1. Computation chains
2. Whole numbers
3. Rational numbers

APPLICATIONS

Measurement
1. Comparisons
2. Using nonstandard units
3. Using standard units— length, area
4. Using standard units— weight, capacity

Time and Money
1. Identifying passage of time
2. Using clocks and clock units
3. Monetary amounts to $1
4. Monetary amounts to $100 and business transactions

Estimation
1. Whole and rational numbers
2. Measurement
3. Computation

Interpreting Data
1. Charts and tables
2. Graphs
3. Probability and statistics

Problem Solving
1. Solving routine problems
2. Understanding nonroutine problems
3. Solving nonroutine problems

Source: Manual, Table 2.1, p. 6. Reproduced with permission.

Students are asked to respond orally to pictures shown them and questions asked them by the examiner.

Test Scores Obtained

Basic Concepts	Raw	SS	%ile	Operations	Raw	SS	%ile	Applications	Raw	SS	%ile
Numeration	X	X	X	Addition	X	X	X	Measurement	X	X	X
Rational	X			Subtraction	X	X	X	Time and			
Numbers				Multiplication	X	X	X	Money	X	X	X
Geometry	X	X	X	Division	X	X	X	Estimation	X	X	X
				Mental				Interpreting			
				Comp.	X	X	X.	Data	X	X	X
								Problem			
								Solving	X	X	X
Basic				**Operations**	X	X	X	**Applications**	X	X	X
Concepts	X	X	X								

Grade/Age Equivalent	X		Grade/Age Equivalent	X		Grade/Age Equivalent	X
						(optional)	(optional)

Total	X	+	X	+	X	=	X	X	X	X	X	X	X
Test	1		2		3		Total	Std.	%ile	NCE	Stanine	Grade	Age
							Test raw	score	rank			equiv.	equiv.
							score						

Source: Manual, Figure 3.7, p. 19. Reproduced with permission.

The raw score for each subtest is recorded first, then these are added to get the three area raw scores. Then the three area raw scores are added to get the total test raw score. All other scores for the subtests and the areas and the total test are obtained by using the appropriate tables in the Examiner's Manual.

Technical Adequacy

Validity Confirmation

An extensive discussion of KeyMath-R *test item validity* is included in the Examiner's Manual. Apparently, KeyMath-R was developed in a thoughtful manner, with the help of many individuals with a substantial background in mathematics education. It seems that the domain structure and test blueprint used within KeyMath-R were designed to sample a wide variety of important mathematics concepts while maintaining a needed specificity in the domains sampled.

Test response validity is addressed by studies that investigated the relationships between scores from KeyMath-R and Comprehensive Test of Basic Skills (CTBS) scores and Iowa Tests of Basic Skills (ITBS) math scores. Total test correlations with the CTBS and ITBS math scores were .66 and .76, respectively. These correlations are not extremely high and might suggest that there are some differences in the aspects of mathematics being measured. The sample sizes used in the correlations are modest, but are probably adequate to suggest that the three instruments are measuring similar characteristics.

Reliability Confirmation

Reliability was investigated by retesting approximately 70% of the students in grades K, 2, 4, 6, and 8 who participated in the fall standardization program with the alternate form of KeyMath-R from two to four weeks after the initial testing. The order of administration was counterbalanced so that approximately half the students took Form A first, followed by Form B, and the other half took Form B first, followed by Form A. The correlations between the two forms range from the .50s to the .70s for the subtests, and fall in the low .80s for the areas, and average .90 for the total test. Therefore, the KeyMath-R seems to possess an acceptable degree of reliability.

Objectivity Confirmation

Scoring keys are provided to score all of the items of the subtests of KeyMath-R on the testing easels themselves. The test is designed to be given orally and the student is to respond orally. The examiner would note and score the response as it is given. Total test raw score is obtained by adding subtest raw scores and standard scores, and percentiles are obtained by using the tables provided in the Examiner's Manual.

Special Features

Acronym

KeyMath-R.

Levels of the Test

KeyMath-R is designed to be given to students ages 6–22 or grades K–9. Levels are determined by using basals and ceilings. On each subtest the basal consists of three consecutive correct responses prior to an error; on each subtest the ceiling consists of three consecutive errors or testing must have included every item that follows the basal.

Number of Test Forms

Two. Alternate test forms are provided, Form A and Form B.

Norm-Referenced?

Yes. This 1998 publication of the KeyMath-R was renormed. In fact, the normative update is the only difference from the earlier 1988 publication. The sample used to renorm the KeyMath-R was large. A total of 3,429 people (3,184 K–12 students and 245 young adults aged 18–22) participated in the norming effort. A total of 650 people received the entire KeyMath-R/NU (normative update) battery, with the rest of the sample receiving at least one KeyMath-R/NU subtest. Sample sizes were similar for each grade. Within each grade, the sample was carefully stratified to ensure that it was representative of the U.S. population.

Criterion-Referenced?

Yes. The KeyMath-R is not referenced to any specific criterion of curriculum or instruction. However, it is referenced to concepts and skills of mathematics, and there are several items that seem to measure each skill, so there are numerous opportunities for the student to make an error on the same skill. This allows the test to be used effectively for prescribing intervention or remediation of those skills. It also allows the test to be used to evaluate the student's progress in an already prescribed intervention.

Feasibility Considerations

Testing Time

KeyMath-R is a power test with open-ended items. Therefore, the administration time will fluctuate with the grade level, ability, and work habits of the student and by the skill and proficiency of the examiner. Students in the primary grades will usually complete the test in 30 to 40 minutes; older students may take 40 to 50 minutes.

For Testing Groups? Individuals?

Individuals.

Test Administration and Scoring

Instructions for administering the subtests of the KeyMath-R are given in the Examiner's Manual, and specific instructions for each item, along with the correct answer, are given with the item in the easels used to administer the tests. Four subtests in the Operations area (addition, subtraction, multiplication, and division) differ from the other subtests in that they include items that require written computation. These items are printed in the test record with space for computation. It is recommended that the testing be done with the examiner and the student seated at adjacent sides of a table so that the examiner can easily see both sides of the easel. Administrators of this test may include regular and special education teachers, classroom aides, and other paraprofessionals, as well as counselors, school psychologists, and others with special measurement training. Scoring should be done as the student responds. On the scoring pages of the test record, each item is followed by a box positioned in one of three or four columns designating the domain affiliation of the item. The examiner should note a 1 for correct and a 0 for incorrect in that box as the student responds. The scoring of the written computation subtests can be done after the test administration is completed. Reporting computer software for DOS, Windows, or Macintosh is available from the publisher.

Test Materials and Approximate Costs

Complete kit, including Form A and B test easels, Form A and B test records (25 each), sample report to parents, manual (1998, 255 pages), and carry bag: $478.95; Single form (A or B) kit including test easels, test records (25), sample reports to parents, and manual: $245.95; Test records (25) (select Form A or B): $54.95; Reports to parents (25): $21.95; Manual: $95.95; Complete ASSISTT™ reporting software: $199.95.

Adequacy of Test Manuals

The Examiner's Manual for the KeyMath-R provides an overview of the test and gives instructions for administering and scoring the subtests. The Examiner's Manual also gives directions for interpreting the results of each of the KeyMath-R subtests, and it includes all of the technical information about the test (i.e., validity, reliability, and objectivity evidence). Normative tables and tables for converting raw scores to standard scores, percentiles, and age and grade equivalents are provided. The technical information is given in detail, perhaps more detail than the average user requires and/or has the time to process. The Examiner's Manual is adequate but not as clear and easy to use as it could be. Too much of the manual is given to technical information and not enough to instructions about administration and interpretation.

Excerpts from Other Test Reviews

KeyMath-R has been reviewed by Kingsbury (2001) and Wollack (2001). Kingsbury says, "KeyMath-R seems to be a test that could be used in special settings to add information to a teacher's knowledge of a student's strengths and weaknesses in mathematics. It is a well-documented instrument with information about reliability, validity, and common performance in a national sample. On the other hand, KeyMath-R is somewhat dated in content, and somewhat more difficult to use with computer delivery or computer-based scoring. Finally, because KeyMath-R is designed to be used for students of many ages, it tends to lack content specificity that might make it more useful with students in any particular grade." Wollack says, "Overall, the KeyMath-R/NU remains one of the very best test batteries for assessing a student's knowledge and understanding of basic mathematics and providing useful diagnostic information to the teachers."

Ordering Information

Publisher

American Guidance Service, Inc., 4201 Woodland Road, Circle Pines, MN 55014-1796; Phone: 800-328-2560; Fax: 800-471-8457; Web site: www.agsnet.com.

Author

Austin J. Connolly.

Publication Date

1998.

Cautions and Comments

Use of the KeyMath-R for instructional prescription and assessment of the effectiveness of intervention and remediation seems to be warranted. It can only be used on an individual basis, but the test does seem to measure understanding and application of mathematics concepts and skills effectively. However, because KeyMath-R is designed to be used for students of many ages, it seems to lack content specificity for students in any particular grade. Therefore, it would probably best be used in conjunction with other measures to come up with a profile of a student's strengths and weaknesses in mathematics.

References

Kingsbury, G. G. (2001). Review of the KeyMath Revised: A Diagnostic Inventory of Essential Mathematics. In B. S. Plake & J. C. Impara (Eds.), *The Fourteenth Mental Measurements Yearbook* (pp. 638–640). Lincoln, NE: The Buros Institute of Mental Measurements.
Wollack, J. A. (2001). Review of the KeyMath Revised: A Diagnostic Inventory of Essential Mathematics. In B. S. Plake & J. C. Impara (Eds.), *The Fourteenth Mental Measurements Yearbook* (pp. 640–641). Lincoln, NE: The Buros Institute of Mental Measurements.

Stanford Diagnostic Mathematics Test, Fourth Edition (SDMT4),
for testing groups from grades 1.5 through 13
Reviewed by Katherine C. Schnepel, Ph.D.,
Educational Research and Measurement

Usefulness of the Test for Educators

Test Authors' Purpose

The authors state that the SDMT is intended to diagnose students' strengths and weaknesses in the major components of mathematics. They state that the results can be used to challenge students who are doing well and provide special help for others who lack some of the essential mathematics skills, and that results also can be used to identify trends in the mathematical ability of students in the district, provide information about the effectiveness of instructional programs, measure changes that have taken place over an instructional period, and keep the community and school board informed about students' overall progress in mathematics.

Decision-Making Applications

The SDMT4 can be used effectively to diagnose students' weaknesses and deficiencies in mathematics. However, it would not be appropriate to use the test to identify trends in the mathematics skills of students in a district or to measure changes that have taken place over an instructional period. The SDMT4 should not be used to monitor the effectiveness of instructional programs or to inform the community and/or school board about students' progress in mathematics. All of these purposes would be better served using an achievement instrument. Neither would it be appropriate to use the SDMT4 to challenge students who are doing well. Because of the nature of the test, it should be used only for below-average students who are suspected of having deficiencies in mathematics.

Relevant Population

Red Level—Grades 1.5–2.5; Orange Level—Grades 2.5–3.5; Green Level—Grades 3.5–4.5; Purple Level—Grades 4.5–6.5; Brown Level—Grades 6.5–8.9; Blue Level—Grades 9–13.

Characteristics Described

Table 1.1
Subtests and Objectives of the SDMT4

	Red Level	Orange Level	Green Level	Purple Level	Brown Level	Blue Level
Multiple Choice	1.5–2.5	2.5–3.5	3.5–4.5	4.5–6.5	6.5–8.9	9–12.9
Concepts and Applications	32	32	32	32	32	32
Number Systems and Numeration	12	12	12	10	10	10
Patterns and Functions	3	3	3			
Probability and Statistics				4	4	4
Graphs and Tables	3	3	3	4	4	4
Problem Solving	6	6	8	8	8	8
Geometry and Measurement	8	8	6	6	6	6
Computation	20	20	20	20	20	20
Addition of Whole Numbers	12	9				
Subtraction of Whole Numbers	8	11				

Table 1.1 (continued)

Multiple Choice	Red Level 1.5–2.5	Orange Level 2.5–3.5	Green Level 3.5–4.5	Purple Level 4.5–6.5	Brown Level 6.5–8.9	Blue Level 9–12.9
Addition and Subtraction of Whole Numbers			10	8	4	4
Multiplication of Whole Numbers			7	6	4	
Division of Whole Numbers			3	6	3	
Multiplication and Division of Whole Numbers						4
Operations with Fractions and Mixed Numbers					3	4
Equations					3	3

Free Response	Red Level 1.5–2.5	Orange Level 2.5–3.5	Green Level 3.5–4.5	Purple Level 4.5–6.5	Brown Level 6.5–8.9	Blue Level 9–12.9
Concepts and Applications	30	30	30	30	30	30
Number Systems and Numeration	8	8	8	8	8	8
Patterns and Functions	3	3	3	4	4	4
Probability and Statistics				3	3	3
Graphs and Tables	3	3	3	3	3	3
Problem Solving	6	6	6	6	6	6
Geometry and Measurement	10	10	10	6	6	6
Computation	20	20	20	20	20	20
Addition of Whole Numbers	12	9				
Subtraction of Whole Numbers	8	11				
Addition and Subtraction of Whole Numbers			10	8	4	4
Multiplication of Whole Numbers			7	6		
Division of Whole Numbers			3	6		

Table 1.1 (continued)

	Red Level	Orange Level	Green Level	Purple Level	Brown Level	Blue Level
Free Response	1.5–2.5	2.5–3.5	3.5–4.5	4.5–6.5	6.5–8.9	9–12.9
Multiplication and Division of Whole Numbers					7	4
Operations with Fractions and Mixed Numbers					3	4
Operations with Decimals and Percents					3	5
Equations					3	3

Source: Directions for Administering, Table 1, pp. 7–8.

Students are asked to write responses to Free Response items and to indicate their choice of responses to Multiple Choice items. Items are read to them by the Examiner.

Test Scores Obtained

Red Level—Yields 9 scores: Concepts and Applications (Number Systems and Numeration, Patterns and Functions, Graphs and Tables, Problem Solving, Geometry and Measurement, Total), Computation (Addition of Whole Numbers, Subtraction of Whole Numbers, Total).

Orange Level—Yields 9 scores: Same as for Red Level.

Green Level—Yields 10 scores: Concepts and Applications (Number Systems and Numeration, Patterns and Functions, Graphs and Tables, Problem Solving, Geometry and Measurement, Total), Computation (Addition and Subtraction of Whole Numbers, Multiplication of Whole Numbers, Division of Whole Numbers, Total).

Purple Level—Yields 11 scores: Concepts and Applications (Number Systems and Numeration, Patterns and Functions [free response only], Probability and Statistics, Graphs and Tables, Problem Solving, Geometry and Measurement, Total), Computation (Addition and Subtraction of Whole Numbers, Multiplication of Whole Numbers, Division of Whole Numbers, Total).

Brown Level—Yields 15 scores: Concepts and Applications (Number Systems and Numeration, Patterns and Functions [free response only], Probability and Statistics, Graphs and Tables, Problem Solving, Geometry and Measurement, Total), Computation (Addition and Subtraction of Whole Numbers, Multiplication of Whole Numbers [multiple choice only], Division of Whole Numbers [multiple choice only], Multiplication and Division of Whole Numbers [free response only], Operations with Fractions and Mixed Numbers, Operations with Decimals and Percents, Equations, Total).

Blue Level—Yields 11 scores: Concepts and Applications (Number Systems and Numeration, Patterns and Functions [free response only], Probability and Statistics,

Graphs and Tables, Problem Solving, Geometry and Measurement, Total), Computation (Operations with Whole Numbers, Operations with Fractions and Mixed Numbers, Operations with Decimals and Percents, Equations, Total).

Several types of scores can be obtained from the SDMT4. These scores can be grouped into three categories: content-referenced scores, scaled scores, and norm-referenced scores. Content-referenced scores provide information about students' performance on sets of specific test questions, while norm-referenced scores describe students' performance relative to that of other students. Scaled scores provide the basis for all of the norm-referenced scores. Content-referenced scores are most useful to teachers, who are primarily concerned with diagnosing students' strengths and weaknesses in specific areas. Since content-referenced scores deal with specific test content, their interpretation is restricted to the particular test taken.

Technical Adequacy

Validity Confirmation

Test item validity is supported by reporting that as test items were written, they were reviewed by content experts, who verified that the items were actually measuring the content objectives they were intended to measure. The manual contains an extensive list of the objectives measured by the items.

Support for *test response validity* is given by computing intercorrelations among the SDMT4 subtests and the Otis-Lennon School Ability Test, Sixth Edition. These correlations are high (almost all in the .60s and .70s), but this reviewer questions why a strong relationship between a student's relationship on a diagnostic test and on a general ability test substantiate test response validity. The authors also support test response validity by correlating students' performance on the SDMT3 and the SDMT4. This would be support for the validity of the SDMT4 if the validity of the SDMT3 had been substantiated. However, if this substantiation was available, it was not presented by the authors.

Reliability Confirmation

Reliability coefficients derived from alternate forms reliability on the subtests are all in the .70s and above except for the free-response computation subtest of the Brown Level (grades 6–8), where it is .51. No explanation is given for why this apparent anomaly occurred. The alternate forms reliabilities for this same subtest on the Purple and Blue levels are .78 and .81, respectively. Internal consistency reliability is reported in the form of correlations among the subtests. These correlations are very high (.70s, .80s, and .90s).

Objectivity Confirmation

Inter-rater objectivity correlations were given for the free-response assessments of the test. These were all .96 and above.

Statistical Confirmation

Statistical data on validity, reliability, objectivity, and norms can be obtained from the 1995 Multilevel Norms Book and Technical Information. However, these data could be summarized more effectively and could be made more clear for the classroom teacher who is not measurement trained.

Special Features

Acronym

SDMT4.

Levels of the Test

Six. Red Level: Grades 1.5–2.5; Orange Level: Grades 2.5–3.5; Green Level: Grades 3.5–4.5; Purple Level: Grades 4.5–6.5; Brown Level: Grades 6.5–8.9; Blue Level: Grades 9–13.

Number of Test Forms

One for Red, Orange, and Green levels; two for Purple, Brown, and Blue levels.

Norm-Referenced?

Yes. School districts for the SDMT4 standardization programs were selected through the use of a stratified random sampling technique. The sample was chosen to be representative of the national school population. The stratification variables were geographic region, socioeconomic status, urbanicity, and ethnicity. Type of school district (public versus nonpublic) was also a stratification variable. There was both a fall and spring standardization. The authors tell us that for the fall standardization 41,500 students from 425 school districts participated, and in the spring standardization 40,000 students participated.

Criterion-Referenced?

Yes. The manual for each level of the SDMT4 has an appendix that lists specific instructional objectives assessed by each level of the test.

Other Features

Practice tests, with their own administration booklets, are available for each level.

Feasibility Considerations

Testing Time

Red Level, Orange Level, and Green Level: 65 minutes for multiple choice; 90 minutes for free response.

Purple Level, Brown Level, and Blue Level: 65 minutes for multiple choice; 80 minutes for free response.

For Testing Groups? Individuals?

Groups.

Test Administration and Scoring

There is a separate administration booklet for each level. Clear and detailed directions for administering are given in the manuals. Both machine-scorable and hand-scorable answer forms are available. Instructions for preparing the answer forms for machine scoring as well as instructions for hand scoring are also in the manuals. The authors state that no specific training or certification is required for examiners or scorers.

Test Materials and Approximate Costs

Examination kit, including multiple-choice test booklet and free-response test booklet (specify level) and directions for administering for each, answer document, practice test and practice test directions for administering, and ruler/marker: $37.50.

Practice tests and directions (25) (specify level): $17.

Machine-scorable multiple-choice test booklets (25) (specify Red, Orange, or Green level): $112.

Hand-scorable multiple-choice test booklets (25) (specify Red, Orange, or Green level), directions for administering, and class record: $76.

Free-response test booklets (25) (specify Red, Orange, or Green level) and directions for administering: $76.

Hand-scorable multiple-choice/free-response combination kit including 25 hand-scorable multiple-choice test booklets and directions for administering, 25 free-response test booklets and directions for administering, and class record (specify Red, Orange, or Green level): $112.

Machine-scorable multiple-choice/free-response combination kit including 25 machine-scorable multiple-choice test booklets and directions for administering and 25 free-response test booklets and directions for administering (specify Red, Orange, or Green level): $139.

Reusable multiple-choice test booklets and directions for administering (25) (specify Purple, Brown, or Blue level and Form J or K): $76.

Free response test booklets and directions for administering (25) (specify Purple, Brown, or Blue level and Form J or K): $76.

Reusable multiple-choice/free-response test combination kit including 25 reusable multiple-choice test booklets and directions for administering and 25 free-response test booklets and directions for administering (specify Purple, Brown, or Blue level and Form J or K): $112.

Set of response keys for multiple-choice tests (specify level and form): $15.50.

Side-by-side keys for hand-scorable test booklets including blackline master of student record form (specify Red, Orange, or Green level): $16.

Scoring guide for free-response tests including blackline master of student record form (specify level and form): $15.50.

Stencil keys for hand-scorable answer documents (specify Purple, Brown, or Blue level and Form J or K): $22.

Hand-scorable answer documents with blackline master of student record form and class record (25) (specify Purple, Brown, or Blue level): $30.

Purple/Brown/Blue level machine-scorable answer documents, type I (25): $38.

Ruler/markers (25): $6.50.

Fall (1996, 166 pages) or Spring (1996, 166 pages) multilevel norms booklet: $52.

Teacher's manual for interpreting (specify Red/Orange level [1996, 61 pages], Green/Purple level [1996, 64 pages], or Brown/Blue level [1996, 63 pages]): $22.

Directions for administering (specify multiple-choice or free-response, and Red, Orange, Green, or Purple/Brown/Blue level): $10.

Practice test directions for administering (specify Red, Orange, Green, Purple, or Brown level): $6.50.

Class record (specify Red, Orange, Green, or Purple/Brown/Blue level): $6.50.

Price information for various scoring services is available from the publisher.

Adequacy of Test Manuals

There are eight different administration manuals (two for practice tests and one for each level of the test), three different interpretation manuals for the teacher, and two norms and technical information books. The administration and interpretation manuals are clearly written and easily understood by the teacher not trained in testing. However, the norms and technical manual is not easily understood by persons without a testing background. It would be helpful if the norms tables and the validity and reliability information could be summarized and presented more clearly.

Excerpts from Other Test Reviews

The SDMT4 was reviewed by Lehmann (1998), Nagy (1998), Poteat (1998), and Salvia and Ysseldyke (2001). Lehmann cautions that the SDMT4 "should not be used to assess the strengths and weaknesses of average or above-average pupils. Nor should it be used as a major criterion for grouping students into instructional groups. . . . It should not be used to test students with special needs." Lehmann also says that he feels that the validity "evidence presented poses a serious deficiency." Lehmann does say that SDMT4 users should "focus its use on the below-average student," be cognizant of the validity inadequacies, and "satisfy themselves that the content matches local instructional objectives."

Nagy says, "This test is best used to diagnose progress at the group (that is, the classroom) level. The best interpretations can be achieved by inspection of the actual items asked of the students. Because the test does not reflect a balanced curriculum appropriate for the wide range of students, normative uses should be avoided" (p. 937).

Poteat tells us that the SDMT4 is designed primarily to be a diagnostic test and he "does not recommend it for use if the goal is simply to obtain achievement test norms" (p. 938).

Salvia and Ysseldyke say that the SDMT4 "is reliable enough to be used in pinpointing math strengths and weaknesses." They do caution that "validity of the test should be judged relative to the content of local curricula" (p. 470).

Ordering Information

Publisher

Harcourt Educational Measurement, 19500 Bulverde Road, San Antonio, TX 78259-3701; Phone: 800-211-8378; Fax: 877-576-1816; Web site: www.hemweb.com.

Authors

Harcourt Educational Measurement.

Publication Date

1996.

Cautions and Comments

The SDMT4 is a diagnostic test, not an achievement test. Diagnostic tests place more emphasis on the lower achiever who is having problems. Thus, they contain more easy questions than do general mathematics achievement tests, which are intended to measure the broad range of ability of the entire student population. The authors say that the SDMT4 can also be used to "challenge students who are doing well" (Multilevel Norms Booklet, p. 7). This reviewer does not recommend this because it would seem that a good student might think that she or he knows more about those concepts measured than she or he really does. So, the SDMT4 should probably be used only with below-average students or with students who are suspected of having deficiencies. Also, using this test for program evaluation or to measure change might not be appropriate because the subtests are very specific in their coverage of instructional areas. A survey achievement test, which is broader in scope, would be more appropriate for these purposes. Also, because the subtests are so specific in focus, the test does not reflect a balanced curriculum. Thus, using the SDMT4 as a norm-referenced tool for comparison is probably not warranted.

References

Lehmann, I. J. (1998). Review of the Stanford Diagnostic Mathematics Test, Fourth Edition. In J. C. Impara & B. S. Plake (Eds.), *The Thirteenth Mental Measurements Yearbook* (pp. 932–936). Lincoln, NE: The Buros Institute of Mental Measurements.

Nagy, P. (1998). Review of the Stanford Diagnostic Mathematics Test, Fourth Edition. In J. C.

Impara & B. S. Plake (Eds.), *The Thirteenth Mental Measurements Yearbook* (pp. 936–937). Lincoln, NE: The Buros Institute of Mental Measurements.

Poteat, M. (1998). Review of the Stanford Diagnostic Mathematics Test, Fourth Edition. In J. C. Impara & B. S. Plake (Eds.), *The Thirteenth Mental Measurements Yearbook* (pp. 937–938). Lincoln, NE: The Buros Institute of Mental Measurements.

Salvia, J., & Ysseldyke, J. E. (2001). *Assessment* (8th ed.). Boston: Houghton Mifflin.

Test of Early Mathematics Ability-Second Edition (TEMA-2),
for testing individuals from 3 years through 8 years, 11 months of age
Reviewed by Katherine C. Schnepel, Ph.D.,
Educational Research and Measurement

Usefulness of the Test for Educators

Test Authors' Purpose

The authors state that the TEMA-2 has several important purposes: (1) identify those children who are significantly behind or ahead of their peers in the development of mathematical thinking; (2) identify specific strengths and weaknesses in mathematical thinking; (3) suggest instructional practices appropriate for individual children; (4) document children's progress in learning arithmetic; and (5) serve as a measure in research projects.

Decision-Making Applications

The TEMA-2 is appropriate for making diagnostic decisions to determine specific strengths and weaknesses about individual students. The test can be used to measure progress, evaluate programs, screen for readiness, discover the reasons for poor school performance, identify gifted pupils, and guide instruction and remediation.

Relevant Populations

The TEMA-2 is designed to measure the mathematics performance of children from 3 years through 8 years, 11 months of age. It can also be used with older children who have learning problems.

Characteristics Described

Informal and formal components of early mathematical thinking are measured by the TEMA-2. Three kinds of items were designed to measure the child's informal mathematics: (1) concepts of relative magnitude, (2) counting skills, and (3) calculation skills. Four kinds of items were designed to measure the child's formal mathematical skills: (1) knowledge of convention, (2) number facts, (3) calculation skills, and (4) base ten concepts. Students are asked to either say or write their response to the question asked or the stimulus given by the examiner.

Test Scores Obtained

The TEMA-2 yields three types of scores: Raw Score, Percentile, and Math Quotient. The Raw Score is the total number of items scored correct on the test. The Percentile represents a value that indicates the percent of the norming sample that is equal to or below a particular score. The Math Quotient provides the clearest indication of an examinee's performance on the TEMA-2. The Math Quotient is converted from raw scores using Table A in Appendix 1.

Guidelines for Interpreting Quotients

Quotient	Descriptor	*Percentages Included*
> 130	Very Superior	2.34
121–130	Superior	6.87
111–120	Above Average	16.12
90–110	Average	49.51
80–89	Below Average	16.12
70–79	Poor	6.87
< 70	Very Poor	2.34

Source: Examiner's Manual, p. 27.

Technical Adequacy

Validity Confirmation

The authors offer systematic and controlled item selection and analysis as support for *test item validity*. Evidence of *test response validity* is provided as a correlation of .93 between the original TEMA items and the TEMA-2 score. The authors suggest that this value allows the original TEMA's correlation of .40 and .59 with the Diagnostic Achievement Battery to also represent the test response validity of the TEMA-2. Johnson (1997) suggests that "This extension is questionable because the new questions in the TEMA-2 were considered easier than those on the TEMA and were clearly designed for a lower age level not measured previously." As further evidence of test response validity, using 35 6-year-olds, scores on a short form of the TEMA-2 were correlated with scores on the Math subtest of the Quick Score Achievement Test, with a resulting coefficient of .46. However, no information is provided regarding the composition of the short form and there are no lower-age children in this comparison, thus the value of this measure of test response validity also is suspect in its transfer to the TEMA-2. Gronlund (1985) suggests that "Validity is always specific to some particular use. No test is valid for all purposes. . . . Thus, when appraising or describing validity, it is necessary to consider the use to be made of the results. Evaluation results are never just valid; they have a different degree of validity for each particular interpretation to be made" (p. 57). As the name of this test, Test of Early Mathematics Ability, implies, its purpose is to assess mathematical ability in young children. However, it appears there are no statistical bases for this test as a measure of mathematical ability.

Reliability Confirmation

Test-retest reliability examines the extent to which a student's performance is constant over time. This gives a measure of stability reliability. The stability reliability of the original TEMA was studied using 71 4- and 5-year-old children who attended preschool day care centers in Austin, Texas. They were all given the TEMA twice, with one week between testings. A partial correlation procedure was used to account for the effects of age, and the resulting test-retest reliability coefficient was .94. No test-retest study was done for the TEMA-2. Apparently, the authors assumed that because the correlation between the TEMA and the TEMA-2 was so high (.93), the test-retest study using the original TEMA would suffice for the TEMA-2.

Objectivity Confirmation

Clear and specific scoring keys are given in the Examiner's Manual. The authors do suggest that examiners should have some formal training in assessment. If this is done, examiners should have little difficulty in scoring the TEMA-2 accurately.

Statistical Confirmation

Statistical information on validity, reliability, objectivity, and norms is given in the Examiner's Manual. However, this technical support for the test seems weak and poorly documented.

Special Features

Acronym

TEMA-2.

Levels of the Test

Six. Levels are determined by basals and ceilings. Basal (five consecutive correct items) is determined by beginning the testing with the item that corresponds to the child's age. The entry points for determining basals are shown below.

Child's Age	3	4	5	6	7	8
Begin Testing with Item	1	7	15	22	32	43

Source: Examiner's Manual, p. 7.

To determine the ceiling, the examiner begins testing at the entry level and tests until five consecutive items are missed or until the last item is administered.

Number of Test Forms

One.

Norm-Referenced?

Yes. The normative sample was composed of 896 children representing 27 states. The characteristics of the sample with regard to sex, residence, race, ethnicity, and geographic area were compared to the percentages reported in the *Statistical Abstract of the United States* (1985) for the general population. This comparison demonstrates that the sample is nationally representative.

Criterion-Referenced?

Yes. The TEMA-2 is referenced to seven mathematical skills: three informal skills and four formal skills. The informal skills measured are (1) concepts of relative magnitude, (2) counting skills, and (3) calculation skills. The formal skills are (1) knowledge of convention, (2) number facts, (3) calculation skills, and (4) base ten concepts. It is not referenced to specific curricular or instructional skills. The book of Assessment Probes and Instructional Activities provided by the authors addresses the skills measured by the test.

Other Features

The TEMA-2 now includes a book of remedial techniques for improving skills in the areas assessed on the test. In this book of Assessment Probes and Instructional Activities, numerous teaching tasks for skills covered by each item in the TEMA-2 have been assembled. Upon completion of the test administration, the examiner can use this book to help the student improve his or her mathematics skills and to provide useful strategies for problem solving.

Feasibility Considerations

Testing Time

The TEMA-2 is not a timed test. Therefore, no exact time limits are imposed on the children being tested. On average, children will be able to finish the relevant portion of the test in about 20 minutes.

For Testing Groups? Individuals?

Individuals.

Test Administration and Scoring

Both general administration guidelines and specific instructions for administration and scoring are given in the Examiner's Manual. These are easily followed. However, the authors do recommend that examiners who give and interpret the TEMA-2 should have some formal training in assessment. They suggest that this training should result in a basic understanding regarding testing statistics and general procedures governing test administration, scoring, and interpretation.

Test Materials and Approximate Costs

TEMA-2 complete kit, including Examiner's Manual, Picture Book, Profile/Examiner Record Forms (50), and Book of Assessment Probes and Instructional Activities: $169; Examiner's Manual: $46; Picture Book: $49; Profile/Examiner Record Forms (50): $39; Assessment Probes and Instructional Activities Book: $39.

Adequacy of Test Manuals

The Examiner's Manual is very clear and specific about administration of the TEMA-2 and interpretation of the results. It also provides an overview of the test and its development. The Examiner's Manual includes technical information (i.e., validity, reliability, and norming data).

Excerpts from Other Test Reviews

The TEMA-2 was reviewed by Johnson (1992) and McLarty (1992). Johnson suggests that "the TEMA-2 does meet an important need in its identification of strengths and weaknesses of a child's mathematical thinking . . . though . . . measures of reliability and validity raise numerous concerns. Additional research needs to be done in these areas. . . . There is an unjustified reliance on previous TEMA results and comparisons."

McLarty says, "The TEMA-2 delivers both less and more than it promises. Unfortunately, technical support for the test remains weak and poorly documented. There is no statistical basis for this test as a measure of mathematical ability; the validity evidence would be equally persuasive for its interpretation as a test of mathematical achievement. . . . Statistical . . . evidence supporting the separate interpretation scores on formal and informal mathematical items is also lacking."

Ordering Information

Publisher

PRO-ED, 8700 Shoal Creek Boulevard, Austin, TX 78757-6897; Telephone: 800-897-3202; Fax: 800-397-7633; Web site: http://www.proedinc.com.

Authors

Herbert P. Ginsburg and Arthur J. Baroody.

Publication Date

1990.

Cautions and Comments

The TEMA-2 is appropriate for identifying and exploring the mathematical skills and reasoning processes of younger children. The assessment probes are especially effective. The TEMA-2 should give valuable insights into the nature and extent of a child's mathematical difficulties and ways of addressing them. However, users should be careful not to overinterpret TEMA-2 scores, and they also should be aware of the weakness of the validity and reliability evidence for the test.

References

Gronlund, N. E. (1985). *Measurement and evaluation in teaching.* New York: Macmillan.
Johnson, J. (1992). Review of the Test of Early Mathematics Ability, Second Edition. In J. J. Kramer & J. C. Conoley (Eds.), *The Eleventh Mental Measurements Yearbook* [Electronic version]. Retrieved on September 25, 2001 from the Buros Institute's Test Reviews Online web site: http://www.unl.edu/buros.
McLarty, J. R. (1992). Review of the Test of Early Mathematics Ability, Second Edition. In J. J. Kramer & J. C. Conoley (Eds.), *The Eleventh Mental Measurements Yearbook* [Electronic version]. Retrieved on September 25, 2001 from Buros Institute's Test Reviews Online web site: http://www.unl.edu/buros.

Test of Mathematical Abilities, Second Edition (TOMA-2),
for testing groups and individuals from 8 through 18 years of age
Reviewed by Katherine C. Schnepel, Ph.D.,
Educational Research and Measurement

Usefulness of the Test for Educators

Test Authors' Purpose

The test authors state the following purposes for information from the test: (1) to identify students who are significantly below their peers in mathematics and who might profit from supplemental help, (2) to determine particular strengths and weaknesses among mathematics abilities, (3) to document progress that results from special interventions, and (4) to provide professionals who conduct research in the area of mathematics with a technically adequate measure.

Decision-Making Applications

It would be appropriate to use the TOMA-2 to make decisions about instructional prescription. The Math Quotient, which is the total score on the test, is designed to measure what most people mean when they say "math ability." Individuals who score well on this composite appear to demonstrate mastery of several integrated math abilities. They comprehend the meanings of words used in the area of math and are able to define them; they use basic math operations as well as advanced fractions, decimals, money, percentages, and other types of complex mathematical problems; they possess knowledge about the use of math in everyday situations; and they are mathematically competent for their age level. The interpretation of an individual's subtest performance will yield information about that person's strengths and weaknesses among these math abilities. Thus, the instruction needed to address the weaknesses and/or build on the strengths can be prescribed for that individual. Also, the results of the TOMA-2 might be used for placement of individual students. Based on the student's score, placement in remedial or accelerated classes might be considered for that student.

Relevant Population

The test is meant to measure mathematical ability in students from 8 through 18 years of age. It is normed on all of those ages. There is only one form of the test. So, in order for that one form to be administered to standards of all of those ages, the use of ceilings is employed. The ceiling for the Vocabulary, Computation, General Information, and Story Problems subtests is three consecutive incorrect items. In those subtests, testing always begins at the first item but stops after the student misses three in a row. There is no ceiling for the supplemental fifth subtest, Attitude Toward Math.

Characteristics Described

There are five subtests within the TOMA-2. Each of these is designed to measure a characteristic related to math. The subtests are designed to measure the following abilities:

1. Vocabulary: Measures the ability to understand words used in mathematical thinking.
2. Computation: Measures the ability to solve an array of arithmetical problems.
3. General Information: Measures knowledge of math as it is used in everyday situations.
4. Story Problems: Measures the student's ability to read and solve written problems.
5. Attitude Toward Math (supplemental): Measures a student's attitudes toward math and toward math instruction.

Students are asked to circle the response option they think is correct.

Test Scores Obtained

The raw score, number correct, can be converted into percentile, standard score, age equivalent, and grade equivalent using the normative tables provided in the Appendix of the Examiner's Manual. The Math Quotient can be found by summing the standard scores on the four subtests to find a value called "Sum of Standard Scores."

This summed value is converted into a quotient and a percentile for the quotient by using Table L in the Appendix of the Examiner's Manual. The Record of TOMA-2 Scores shown in Figure 1.1 below, along with a Profile of Test Scores in which the TOMA-2 scores are compared with the student's other test scores, is provided for each student as the cover page of the answer booklet. Very clear directions for interpreting the scores and for assigning the Descriptive Ratings based on the scores are given in Chapter 3 of the Examiner's Manual.

Figure 1.1
Individual Record of TOMA-2 Scores

Subtest	Raw Score	%ile	Std. Score	Σ of Std. Sc.	Descr. Rating	Age Equiv.	Grade Equiv.	Math Quotient
Vocabulary	X	X	X		X	X	X	
Computation	X	X	X		X	X	X	
General Information	X	X	X		X	X	X	
Story Problems	X	X	X		X	X	X	
				X				X
Test Scores Obtained	4	4	4	1	4	4	4	1

Source: Examiner's Manual, Section II, Figure 3.1, p. 16.

Technical Adequacy

Validity Confirmation

Test item validity was established for the test as follows. The authors provide a logical rationale and justification for the content and format of each subtest. They also identify at least one other test containing similar content for all subtests except General Information.

The authors attempted to establish *test response validity* by relating scores on the subtests and the math quotient or total score on the TOMA-2 to scores on similar tests. The TOMA-2 is presumed to measure math abilities. If it has validity, its scores should correlate well with other tests that are also known or presumed to measure that same ability, namely the KeyMath Diagnostic Arithmetic Test, the math subtest from the Peabody Individual Achievement Test, and the math subtest from the Wide Range Achievement Test. Correlations of the TOMA-2 with these other tests is weak (.29 to .51) and a little misleading. The authors say that because the correlation coefficients between the subtests of the TOMA (First Edition) and the TOMA-2 (Second Edition) are so high (greater than .85), they will use the acronym TOMA-2 to incorporate both the TOMA and the TOMA-2. This is misleading because these correlations among tests are based on the original TOMA and are labeled correlations of the TOMA-2 with the other tests. This correlation data is old, based on 38 students with learning disabilities aged 9 through 17. More recently, the scores of 290 students on the SRA Achievement Series are compared with the scores from the TOMA-2. These correlations are higher, ranging from .48 to .72.

Reliability Confirmation

Reliability was investigated by testing 198 students residing in New Orleans, Louisiana twice with a two-week period between testings. The correlations between the scores of the two testings were sufficiently high to confirm reliability. However, the reliability evidence is weakened because all ages targeted by the test were not tested and the exact same test was given to the same sample. Correlations between scores of the two testings were weak for the Attitude Toward Math subtest. Correlations among responses to different test items were also provided to further confirm reliability.

Objectivity Confirmation

Scoring keys are used to score all of the subtests of the TOMA-2. The items on the four main subtests are supply-type items (i.e., the student supplies the answer rather than selecting it as in multiple choice). The Attitude Toward Math subtest uses a rating scale format.

Statistical Confirmation

Statistical data on validity, reliability, and norms is available in the Examiner's Manual for the TOMA-2.

Special Features

Acronym

TOMA-2.

Levels of the Test

The TOMA-2 is designed to be given to students aged 8 through 18. Levels are determined by using a ceiling. Three consecutive incorrect answers determine the ceiling.

Number of Test Forms

One.

Norm-Referenced?

Yes. The test was nationally normed on 2,082 students who ranged in age from 8 years through 18 years, 11 months and who resided in 26 states (Arkansas, Alabama, Arizona, California, Colorado, Florida, Georgia, Idaho, Illinois, Kansas, Louisiana, Maryland, Minnesota, Mississippi, Missouri, Nebraska, Nevada, New Hampshire, New Mexico, Pennsylvania, Tennessee, Texas, Vermont, Virginia, Washington, and Wisconsin). Testing sites were identified in the four major census districts. The participating schools were selected because the demographic characteristics of the student body closely matched those of the region as a whole. The norming subsample for each year varies in size from 77 to 316 and is too small for some age groups (e.g., age 18). The administration was not standardized for all students. These two things raise issues about the utility of the norms.

Criterion-Referenced?

No.

Feasibility Considerations

Testing Time

This test has no time limits. The time required to give the test varies according to the abilities and ages of the students and whether it is given to individuals or to groups. Administration time for the test varies from one to two hours, the average time being about 1 hour and 15 minutes.

For Testing Groups? Individuals?

It is feasible to use the TOMA-2 for either groups or individuals. It is recommended by the authors that when testing groups, the test should be administered in two sessions. They suggest: first session—Vocabulary and Computation subtests; second session—General Information, Story Problems, and Attitude Toward Math subtests. When testing an individual, all of the subtests can usually be administered in one session.

Test Administration and Scoring

Explicit and easy-to-follow instructions for administering all of the subtests of the TOMA-2 are provided in the Examiner's Manual. The authors suggest that whoever administers and interprets the TOMA-2 should have some formal training in assessment. They suggest that this training should be obtained through college courses and/ or workshops sponsored by school personnel or private consultants.

Test Materials and Approximate Costs

Complete kit, including Profile/Record Forms/Answer Booklets (25) and Examiner's Manual: $89; Examiner's Manual: $47; Profile/Record Forms/Answer Booklets (25): $44.

Adequacy of Test Manuals

The Examiner's Manual is very clear and comprehensive. It provides an overview of the test and gives good instructions for administering and scoring the tests. The Examiner's Manual also gives clear directions for interpreting the results of the TOMA-2, and it includes all of the technical information about the test. Tables for converting raw scores to standard scores, percentiles, and age and grade equivalents are provided in the Appendix.

Excerpts from Other Test Reviews

The TOMA-2 has been reviewed by Davison (1985), Overton (1992), Sutton (1998), and Harnisch (1998). Davison gives the following criticism of the test: "Overall the standard scores and percentile ranks seem coarse . . . possibly because the test uses relatively few items per subtest to assess a wide range of abilities and ages . . . also [may] be due to the size of the norm group."

Overton offers this: "The research employed very small samples. . . . Modest-to-adequate correlations were found."

Harnisch expresses the following comments about the test: "The overall quality of the TOMA-2 has increased. . . . However, a concern that still remains is the scale range to qualify a wide range of abilities and ages. Davison (1985) described this as 'coarseness' and suggested that it may be due to the size of the norm group. Even with the revised normative sample, the 'coarseness' still remains but not to the same degree as noted by Davison."

Sutton expresses the following reservations about the TOMA-2: "Although some improvements have been made including a more representative norming sample, more discussion of validity evidence, and data on test bias, there are still serious issues associated with the standardization of the conditions in establishing norms and with the validity evidence presented. I recommend that, if possible, users select alternative instruments to measure mathematics achievement and attitudes towards mathematics."

Ordering Information

Publisher

PRO-ED, 8700 Shoal Creek Boulevard, Austin, TX 78757-6897; Phone: 800-897-3202; Fax: 800-397-7633; Web site: http://www.proedinc.com.

Authors

Virginia L. Brown, Mary E. Cronin, and Elizabeth McEntire.

Publication Dates

1984–1994.

Cautions and Comments

Care needs to be taken in using the scores on the TOMA-2 to make instructional prescription decisions for individual students. The number of items which would assess individual skills might not be large enough to represent the student's knowledge of that skill. This would be especially true for younger children and children who are suspected of performing below average. If the TOMA-2 is used for instructional prescription, it should be used in conjunction with at least one other math diagnostic measure. Also, the fact that the TOMA-2 is not criterion-referenced to specific curriculum or instruction may make it difficult to use it for instructional prescription. Some information about the TOMA-2 can be obtained on the publisher's web site, http://www.proedinc.com.

References

Davison, M. L. (1985). Review of the Test of Mathematical Abilities. In J. V. Mitchell, Jr. (Ed.), *The Ninth Mental Measurements Yearbook* (pp. 1578–1579). Lincoln, NE: The Buros Institute of Mental Measurements.

Harnisch, D. L. (1998). Review of the Test of Mathematical Abilities, Second Edition. In J. C. Impara & B. S. Plake (Eds.), *The Thirteenth Mental Measurements Yearbook* (pp. 1035–1038). Lincoln, NE: The Buros Institute of Mental Measurements.

Overton, T. (1992). *Assessment in special education: An applied approach.* New York: Merrill-Macmillan.

Sutton, R. (1998). Review of the Test of Mathematical Abilities, Second Edition. In J. C. Impara & B. S. Plake (Eds.), *The Thirteenth Mental Measurements Yearbook* (pp. 1038–1039). Lincoln, NE: The Buros Institute of Mental Measurements.

7

Spoken and Written Language Tests

Comprehensive Assessment of Spoken Language (CASL),
for testing individuals from preschool through adulthood
Reviewed by Katherine C. Schnepel, Ph.D.,
Educational Research and Measurement

Usefulness of the Test for Educators

Test Author's Purpose

The author states that the CASL was designed for assessing oral language knowledge, processes, and skills in examinees aged 3 to 21 years. The results of the CASL assessment provide information on oral language skills that children and adolescents need to become literate and to succeed in school and work environments.

Decision-Making Applications

The CASL is useful to the classroom teacher for determining the English language competence of students who are learning English as a second language. Also, the battery of tests in the CASL can help classroom teachers determine which specific aspects of oral language to emphasize in their classes. The CASL can also be helpful in prescribing instruction that will help remediate deficiencies in oral language skills. Because of the way the CASL is designed, the battery of tests is particularly valuable in the measurement of children who have delayed language development as well as those individuals who have oral language disorders, dyslexia, aphasia, impaired hearing, or mental retardation.

Relevant Population

The CASL is appropriate for use with children and young adults ages 3 through 21 years.

Characteristics Described

Figure 1.1
Oral Language Skills Measured by the CASL Tests

CASL Test	*Oral Language Skills Measured*
Comprehension of Basic Concepts	Auditory comprehension of words that refer to basic perceptual and conceptual relations
Antonyms	Word knowledge, retrieval, and oral expression in a linguistically decontextualized environment
Synonyms	Knowledge of the meaning of spoken words in a linguistically decontextualized environment
Sentence Completion	Word knowledge, retrieval, and oral expression in a linguistic context
Idiomatic Language	Knowledge, retrieval, and oral expression of idioms
Syntax Construction	Oral expression of words, phrases, and sentences using a variety of morphosyntactic rules
Paragraph Comprehension of Syntax	Auditory comprehension of syntax in spoken narratives
Grammatical Morphemes	Metalinguistic knowledge and use of the form and meaning of grammatical morphemes
Sentence Comprehension of Syntax	Auditory recognition of whether sentence pairs with different surface structures have the same or different meaning
Grammaticality Judgment	Judgment of and ability to correct the grammar of sentences
Nonliteral Language	Understanding of the meaning of spoken messages independent of the literal interpretation of the surface structure
Meaning from Context	Derivation of the meaning of words from their oral linguistic context
Inference	Use of previously acquired word knowledge to derive meaning from inferences in spoken language
Ambiguous Sentences	Auditory comprehension of words, phrases, and sentences that have more than one meaning
Pragmatic Judgment	Knowledge and use of pragmatic language rules and judgment of their appropriate application

Source: Test Manual, Table 1.2, p. 2. Reproduced with permission.

The examinee is asked to respond to a picture or a verbal stimulus or a question about the stimulus in some of the subtests. In other subtests an open-ended item format is used. Also, sentence completion is used in several of the subtests.

Figure 1.2
The CASL Tests by Language Category

Lexical/Semantic: Comprehension of Basic Concepts, Antonyms, Synonyms, Sentence Completion, Idiomatic Language

Syntactic: Syntax Construction, Paragraph Comprehension of Syntax, Grammatical Morphemes, Sentence Comprehension of Syntax, Grammaticality Judgment

Supralinguistic: Nonliteral Language, Meaning from Context, Inference, Ambiguous Sentences

Pragmatic: Pragmatic Judgment

Source: Test Manual, Table 1.1, p. 1. Reproduced with permission.

Figure 1.3
Core and Supplementary CASL Tests, by Age

CASL Test	*Age Band (in years and years/months)*					
	3 to 4/11	5 to 6/11	7 to 10/11	11 to 12/11	13 to 17/11	18 to 21/11
Basic Concepts	C	S				
Antonyms		C	C	C	S	S
Synonyms			S	S	C	C
Sentence Completion	S	S	S	S	S	S
Idiomatic Language				S	S	S
Syntax Construction	C	C	C	S	S	S
Paragraph Comprehension	S	C	C	S		
Grammatical Morphemes			S	C	S	S
Sentence Comprehension				C	S	S
Grammaticality Judgment			S	S	C	C
Nonliteral Language			C	C	C	C
Meaning from Context				S	C	C
Inference			S	S	S	
Ambiguous Sentences				S	S	S
Pragmatic Judgment	C	C	C	C	C	C

C = Core; S = Supplementary.

Source: Test Manual, Table 1.3, p. 3. Reproduced with permission.

Test Scores Obtained

A raw score is obtained for each of the 15 CASL tests. However, the number of scores obtained for an individual is dependent on the age of the individual. Examinees aged 3 to 4 can take up to five tests of the CASL, ages 5 to 6 can take up to six, ages 7 to 10 can take up to 10, ages 11 to 12 can take up to 14, ages 13 to 17 can take up to 13, and ages 18 to 21 can take up to 12. Each test raw score can then be converted to a standard score, which can be converted to a percentile, NCE (normal curve equivalent), stanine, and/or age equivalent by using the tables in the Norms Book. Also, scores from the age-appropriate Core tests may be combined to derive a CASL Core Composite score. In addition to the individual test scores and the Core Composite scores, six different Processing and Category Index scores can be reported at those ages where sufficient tests in each area of processing ability or language structure are administered.

Technical Adequacy

Validity Confirmation

Evidence of *test item validity* is given by the author in the form of an explanation as to how and why the items on the test were selected. The author states, "The task of each CASL test was selected on the basis of both theoretical design and previous research studies. The battery was designed to allow the nature and type of disordered language to be identified and the subsequent interventions to follow in a logical and progressive sequence. Items were developed that did not require reading and did not have an unnecessary memory requirement. Open-ended items were included to allow free responses, which provide important information on the examinee's use of language. Scoring criteria were developed based on actual responses obtained during tryouts and standardization" (Test Manual, p. 124).

As evidence of *test response validity*, the author correlated the CASL with five measures of language: the Test for Auditory Comprehension of Language-Revised (TACL-R), the Listening Comprehension (LC) and Oral Expression (OE) Scales of the Oral and Written Language Scales (OWLS), the Peabody Picture Vocabulary Test, Third Edition (PPVT-III), the Expressive Vocabulary Test (EVT), and the Kaufman Brief Intelligence Test (K-BIT). Each of the four measures of language chosen for the test response validity studies measures a different aspect of language ability. The TACL-R is a receptive measure of vocabulary and syntax, the OWLS LC and OE are measures of receptive and expressive language skills, the PPVT-III measures receptive vocabulary, and the EVT measures expressive vocabulary and word retrieval. The highest overall correlations for these studies are with the OWLS. Both the CASL and the OWLS measure the four categories of language structure (lexical/semantic, syntactic, supralinguistic, and pragmatic). The OWLS assessment has a wide-range approach, while the CASL allows for an in-depth study of specific skills. Correlations between the CASL and the OWLS range from .45 to .87, with most in the .70s and .80s.

Reliability Confirmation

In order to show evidence of stability reliability, the CASL was administered twice to 148 randomly selected examinees in three age groups: 5 years through 6 years, 11 months (41 cases), 8 years through 10 years, 11 months (38 cases), and 14 years through 16 years, 11 months (69 cases). The interval between tests ranged from 7 to

109 days, with 6 weeks being the median interval. Correlation coefficients for the 5 years–6 years, 11 months age groups ranged from .77 to .92; correlation coefficients for the 8 years–10 years, 11 months age groups ranged from .74 to .96, with only one below .81; and correlation coefficients for the 14 years–16 years, 11 months age groups ranged from .65 to .95, with only four below .81 (.65, .66, .74, .79). The results of these test-retest studies provides strong evidence of the stability of CASL scores. Internal consistency reliabilities for the CASL tests were computed using the split-half method. The items in each test were divided into comparable halves, with the odd-numbered items in one half and the even-numbered items in the other. The performance scores of the one half were correlated with the scores for the other half. The resulting correlation coefficients were generally high, ranging from .64 to .94, with most of them being in the .80s and .90s. This reliability data indicates a high degree of homogeneity among items in the tests.

Objectivity Confirmation

The correct responses to the multiple-choice items are given on the record forms or in the administration Test Books. Scoring of open-ended responses has been simplified by the listing of the most common correct and incorrect responses and by including scoring rubrics and criteria on the record forms or in the administration Test Books. Appendix C of the Norms Book provides additional responses for the examiner to use in making decisions about less-common examinee responses in certain tests. No statistical support for inter-rater objectivity is presented.

Statistical Confirmation

Statistical data for the validity and reliability of the CASL is given in the Test Manual. All of the standardization and norms data is given in the Norms Book.

Special Features

Acronym

CASL.

Levels of the Test

One. Levels of the test are determined by the use of basals and ceilings. The basal for each subtest is three consecutive correct items (except for Paragraph Comprehension, which is not more than one incorrect item in a paragraph set). The ceiling for each subtest is five consecutive incorrect items (except for Paragraph Comprehension, which is a total of zero or one correct item in a paragraph set).

Number of Test Forms

One.

Norm-Referenced?

Yes. To ensure representation of the national population, the CASL norm group was selected from public and private schools to match the U.S. Census data from the 1994 Current Population Survey. The sample was stratified within each age group by the following criteria: gender, race or ethnic group, geographic region, and socioeconomic status (mother's education level). Individuals were tested only if they could adequately speak and understand English. The total number of students in the norm group was 2,750. Special education status of school-aged children was monitored and tracked during the norming data collection.

Figure 1.4
Percentages of Special Education Categories Included in the CASL Standardization Sample

Special Education Category	CASL Sample	U.S. Population
Specific Learning Disabilities	3.4	4.3
Speech of Language Impairments	1.5	1.8
Mental Retardation	0.6	1.0
Emotional Disturbance	0.3	0.7
Other Impairments	0.4	0.6

Source: Test Manual, Table 7.15, p. 111. Reproduced with permission.

Criterion-Referenced?

Yes. The CASL is referenced to the following language processing skills.

Figure 1.5
Skills Referenced by the CASL

Category of Language Structure	Language Skills Assessed
Lexical/Semantic	Knowledge of the meaning of words
	Use of words in comprehension and expression of language
	Ability to recognize, retrieve, and elicit words that are similar or opposite in meaning
	Ability to derive word meaning from the linguistic context in which a word is embedded; ability to express word combinations in the form of idioms
Syntactic	Expressive knowledge of grammatical morphemes
	Ability to judge the grammaticality of syntax
	Comprehension and expression of syntactic structures
Supralinguistic	Ability to understand nonliteral spoken language such as indirect questions, figurative language, and sarcasm

Figure 1.5 (continued)

Category of
Language Structure   *Language Skills Assessed*

Ability to infer the meaning of an unknown word from the oral linguistic context

Ability to infer meaning using word knowledge when the information needed for responding is not available in the oral text provided

Ability to recognize ambiguity in spoken sentences and to verbalize the source of the ambiguity

Pragmatic   Knowledge and use of pragmatic rules of language

Source: Test Manual, pp. 33–66.

Feasibility Considerations

Testing Time

Testing time is approximately 30 minutes for children aged 3 to 5 years and approximately 45 minutes to one hour for older examinees.

For Testing Groups? Individuals?

Individuals.

Test Administration and Scoring

Instructions for administering each of the subtests of the CASL are provided in the Test Manual. The author indicates that the CASL may be administered, scored, and interpreted by individuals who are involved in language, educational, or psychological testing and who have graduate-level training in the use of individually administered assessment instruments. Individuals qualified to interpret CASL results include, but are not limited to, speech/language pathologists, school psychologists, clinical psychologists, neuropsychologists, and educational diagnosticians, as well as learning disability specialists, reading specialists, counselors, remedial reading teachers, resource room teachers, psychiatrists, and others within these and related fields who have had the special training described above. The examiner should become thoroughly familiar with the test materials and practice administering and scoring the test under the supervision of an experienced examiner before using the test as a standardized measure.

Test Materials and Approximate Costs

Complete kit, which includes Test Books (3), Record Forms 1 and 2 (12 each), Test Manual, and Norms Book: $299.95; complete kit (above) plus ASSIST scoring software: $398.95; ASSIST scoring software: $199.95; Record Form 1 (12) (ages 3–6): $20.95; Record Form 2 (12) (ages 7–21): $26.95; Overview video: $11.95.

Adequacy of Test Manuals

The Test Manual adequately explains administration procedures and scoring directions and provides validity and reliability information. Norms are provided in the separate Norms Book.

Excerpts from Other Test Reviews

No test reviews were found for the CASL.

Ordering Information

Publisher

American Guidance Service, Inc., 4201 Woodland Road, Circle Pines, MN 55014-1796; Phone: 800-328-2560; Fax: 800-471-8457; Web site: www.agsnet.com.

Author

Elizabeth Carrow-Woolfolk.

Publication Date

1999.

Cautions and Comments

The CASL is an effective assessment tool for the classroom teacher. It can be used with students with learning disabilities or speech disorders or hearing impairment. The CASL tests use oral instruction for administration and require either a verbal response or a nonverbal response, such as pointing. Examinees are not required to read or give written responses. Using the CASL in conjunction with tests of written language makes it possible for the teacher to differentiate between problems that relate to written and oral language and those related to oral language only.

Comprehensive Receptive and Expressive Vocabulary Test (CREVT),
for testing individuals from 4 years through 17 years, 11 months of age
Reviewed by Katherine C. Schnepel, Ph.D.,
Educational Research and Measurement

Usefulness of the Test for Educators

Test Authors' Purpose

The CREVT has four principal uses: (1) to identify students who are significantly below their peers in oral vocabulary proficiency, (2) to determine any discrepancy between receptive and expressive oral vocabulary skills, (3) to document progress in oral vocabulary development as a consequence of special intervention programs, and (4) to measure oral vocabulary in research studies.

Decision-Making Applications

The results of the CREVT are useful for identifying deficiencies in oral vocabulary development. Having determined that a student is deficient in oral vocabulary, the examiner may refer the student for more in-depth diagnostic assessment. The results of the CREVT will also help teachers determine if a student's problem is a general vocabulary deficit or if a deficiency exists in only the receptive or expressive modality. However, additional assessment will be necessary before making any definitive conclusion about an individual's oral vocabulary status.

Relevant Population

The CREVT Receptive Vocabulary subtest is appropriate for use with individuals between the ages of 4 years and 17 years, 11 months, while the CREVT Expressive Vocabulary subtest is appropriate for ages 5 years through 17 years, 11 months who can understand the directions of the subtests, who are able to formulate the necessary responses, and who can speak English.

Characteristics Described

The CREVT is meant to measure oral vocabulary. Subtest I assesses receptive vocabulary by using the "point-to-the-picture-of-the-word-I-say" technique. Subtest II assesses expressive vocabulary by asking the student to define words.

Test Scores Obtained

CREVT Scores	Raw Scores	Std. Scores	Sum of Std. Scores	%iles	Age Equiv.
Receptive Vocabulary	X	X		X	X
Expressive Vocabulary	X	X	X	X	X
General Vocabulary		X		X	X

Technical Adequacy

Validity Confirmation

Test item validity is demonstrated in three ways. First, a rationale for the subtest formats is presented. Second, a rationale for selecting test items is described. Third, the validity of the items is demonstrated statistically by the results of item analysis procedures that were used to choose items during the developmental stages of the test's construction (Examiner's Manual, p. 31).

Test response validity is shown by correlating the CREVT with several tests of oral vocabulary or spoken language including the Peabody Picture Vocabulary Test-Revised (PPVT-R) (Dunn & Dunn, 1981), the Expressive One-Word Picture Vocabulary Test-Revised (EOWPVT-R) (Gardner, 1990), the Clinical Evaluation of Language Fundamentals-Revised (CELF-R) (Semel & Wiig, 1987), and the Test of Language Development-Primary: Second Edition (TOLD-P:2) (Newcomer & Hammill, 1988). For the most part the coefficients are significant and of considerable magnitude. The coefficients between CREVT scores and the total scores of the PPVT-R range from .48 to .79; the coefficients between CREVT scores and the total scores of the TOLD-P:2 range from .79 to .89; the coefficients between CREVT scores and the total scores of the CELF-R range between .78 and .97; and coefficients between CREVT scores and the total scores of the EOWPVT-R range from .36 to .86.

Reliability Conformation

Stability reliability is supported in two ways; correlating alternate forms of the test and using the test-retest technique. The alternate forms technique shows that the correlation coefficients depicting the relationship between Forms A and B, with a single exception, exceed .80. This allows one to conclude that the CREVT evidences high reliability and possesses little content sampling error. The one exception mentioned above is the correlation coefficient for the two forms of the Expressive Vocabulary subtest for age level 6 years. That coefficient is .74. The test-retest technique produced coefficients consistently large enough to support strongly the idea that the CREVT has acceptable test-retest reliability. The test-retest was done using two different groups of students as subjects. Both forms of the CREVT were administered twice to both samples with two months intervening time with one sample and two weeks intervening time with the second sample. The first sample was comprised of 27 kindergarten children and the second was comprised of 28 twelfth graders. The coefficients of the subtests from both samples ranged from .79 to .94.

Objectivity Confirmation

Scorer objectivity was shown by having the two authors of the CREVT independently score a set of completed tests. Forty-two completed tests were drawn randomly from the students in the normative sample. The sample manifested a broad range of vocabulary ability, ranged in age from 4 to 14, and resided in six different states. The results of the scorings were correlated. The coefficients for Receptive Vocabulary were .99 for both Form A and Form B; coefficients for Expressive Vocabulary were also .99 for both forms of the tests. These coefficients provide strong evidence supporting the CREVT's scorer objectivity. Specific instructions for scoring and scoring criteria are given for each subtest. The CREVT can be administered by anyone who is reasonably competent in the administration of tests in education and language. The authors recommend that examiners should be thoroughly familiar with the Examiner's Manual and should practice giving the test several times before using it in a real situation.

Statistical Confirmation

Statistical confirmation for the validity, reliability, objectivity, and norms of the CREVT can be found in the Examiner's Manual.

Special Features

Acronym

CREVT.

Levels of the Test

The CREVT is designed to be given to students aged 4 years through 17 years, 11 months. Levels are determined by using a ceiling. The ceiling for the Receptive Vocabulary subtest occurs when the student misses two items in a row. The ceiling for the Expressive Vocabulary subtest occurs when the student misses three items in a row.

Number of Test Forms

Two.

Norm-Referenced?

Yes. The normative data for the CREVT are based on the test performance of 1,920 students residing in 33 different states. The sample's percentages demonstrate that, on the whole, the sample is nationally representative. The norming subsample for each age varies in size from 60 to 252 and seems too small for some age groups (e.g., ages 16 and 17).

Criterion-Referenced?

No.

Feasibility Considerations

Testing Time

This test has no time limits. The time required to give each subtest is rarely more than 10 to 15 minutes, thus making the time required for the entire test 20 to 30 minutes.

For Testing Groups? Individuals?

Individuals.

Test Administration and Scoring

Explicit and easy-to-follow instructions for administering the two subtests of the

CREVT are provided in the Examiner's Manual. The authors say that the CREVT can be administered by anyone who is reasonably competent in the administration of tests in education, language, or psychology. The authors also suggest that examiners should be thoroughly familiar with the Manual.

Test Materials and Approximate Costs

Complete kit, which includes Examiner's Manual, Photo Album Picture Book, Form A Profile/Record Forms (25), and Form B Profile/Record Forms (25): $184.00; Examiner's Manual: $49; Photo Album Picture Book: $61; Profile/Record Forms (25) (specify form): $39.

Adequacy of Test Manuals

The Examiner's Manual is clearly written, giving detailed administration procedures and scoring directions along with adequate technical information.

Excerpts from Other Test Reviews

The CREVT was reviewed by Kaufman and Kaufman (1998), McLellan (1998), and Salvia and Ysseldyke (2001). Kaufman and Kaufman say that "the Expressive Vocabulary section of the CREVT cannot be recommended for anything other than research use until its validity has been supported by additional studies." McLellan tells us that "the CREVT is easy to use and nicely packaged. The consumers of this product should be cautious of the low raw scores needed, in some cases, to support adequate language development. In addition, the Receptive Vocabulary measures provide limited evaluation of a child's ability to identify concrete representations as opposed to abstract representations of words." Salvia and Ysseldyke suggest that "Weaknesses include a lack of information on key psychometric parameters and a potential lack of sensitivity due to the relatively low number of items on the instrument (particularly on the Expressive subtest). Despite these weaknesses, the CREVT appears to be potentially useful as a quickly administered vocabulary screening instrument, to be followed up with more detailed vocabulary assessment, as needed."

Ordering Information

Publisher

PRO-ED, 8700 Shoal Creek Boulevard, Austin, TX 78757-6897; Phone: 800-897-3202; Fax: 800-397-7633; Web site: http://www.proedinc.com.

Authors

Donald D. Hammill and Gerald Wallace.

Publication Date

1994.

Cautions and Comments

The CREVT should be used primarily as a screening instrument to indicate whether a student's vocabulary weaknesses are expressive or receptive, thus indicating to the examiner which further diagnostic assessment is needed. The CREVT is only diagnostic in that it differentiates between expressive and receptive vocabulary skills. However, it is easily and quickly administered and would certainly be a useful starting place for assessment of a student's vocabulary skills.

References

Kaufman, A., & Kaufman, N. (1998). Review of the Comprehensive Receptive and Expressive Vocabulary Test. In J. C. Impara & B. S. Plake (Eds.), *The Thirteenth Mental Measurements Yearbook* (pp. 301–304). Lincoln, NE: The Buros Institute of Mental Measurements.

McLellan, M. (1998). Review of the Comprehensive Receptive and Expressive Vocabulary Test. In J. C. Impara & B. S. Plake (Eds.), *The Thirteenth Mental Measurements Yearbook* (pp. 304–305). Lincoln, NE: The Buros Institute of Mental Measurements.

Salvia, J., & Ysseldyke, J. E. (2001). *Assessment* (8th ed.) Boston: Houghton Mifflin.

Comprehensive Test of Phonological Processing (CTOPP),
for testing individuals from 5 years through 24 years, 11 months of age
Reviewed by Katherine C. Schnepel, Ph.D.,
Educational Research and Measurement

Usefulness of the Test for Educators

Test Authors' Purpose

The authors state that the CTOPP has four principal uses: (1) to identify individuals who are significantly below their peers in important phonological abilities, (2) to determine strengths and weaknesses among developed phonological processes, (3) to document individuals' progress in phonological processing as a consequence of special intervention programs, and (4) to serve as a measurement device in research studies investigating phonological processing.

Decision-Making Applications

If the CTOPP shows that a person does, in fact, have a deficit in one or more of the three kinds of phonological processing abilities that it assesses (phonological awareness, phonological memory, and rapid naming), then the examiner should investigate and recommend instructional activities that will enhance the person's phonological skills. It has been shown that a deficit in one or more of these kinds of phonological processing abilities is the most common cause of learning disabilities in general, and of reading disabilities in particular. The CTOPP was developed to identify these deficiencies in individuals from kindergarten through college. Instructional intervention to address phonological weaknesses can be effective at any age.

Relevant Population

The CTOPP is appropriate for use with individuals between the ages of 5 years and 24 years, 11 months who can understand the directions of the subtests, who are able to formulate the necessary responses, and especially who can pass the practice items (Examiner's Manual, p. 15).

Characteristics Described

The CTOPP is composed of 13 subtests in three areas of phonology: Phonological Awareness, Phonological Memory, and Rapid Naming (Salvia & Ysseldyke, 2001). The subtests are outlined below.

Phonological Awareness

Elision—measures the ability to delete sounds from spoken words in order to create new words. The student is asked to listen to a word and then repeat that word, and then to say the word without one of the sounds in the word.

Blending Words—measures the ability to synthesize sounds into words. The student listens to a series of audiocassette-recorded separate sounds and then is asked to put the separate sounds together to make a whole word.

Sound Matching—measures the ability to discriminate words with the same beginning or ending sounds. The student is asked to point to the picture that corresponds to the word that starts with the same sound as the first word the examiner said.

Blending Nonwords—measures the ability to synthesize sounds into units like words. The student listens to an audiocassette and then is asked to put separate sounds together to form a nonword.

Segmenting Nonwords—measures the ability to say the separate phoneme that make up a nonword. The student is asked to repeat each nonword, then to say it one sound at a time.

Phonological Memory

Memory for Digits—measures the ability to recall a sequence of numbers. After the student has listened to a series of audiocassette-recorded numbers, he or she is asked to repeat the numbers in the same order in which they were heard.

Nonword Repetition—measures the ability to recall nonwords. The student is asked to repeat a made-up word exactly as he or she heard it.

Rapid Naming

Rapid Color Naming—measures the ability to recall and fluently say the names of colors. The student is asked to name the colors in the Picture Book as quickly as possible.

Rapid Object Naming—measures the ability to recall and fluently say the names of familiar objects. The student names objects from left to right, right to left, and so on as rapidly as possible.

Rapid Digit Naming—measures the ability to recall and fluently say the names of numbers. The student is asked to name numbers as rapidly as possible.

Rapid Letter Naming—measures the ability to recall and fluently say the names of letters. The student is asked to name letters as rapidly as possible.

Additional Diagnostic Subtests

Phoneme Reversal—measures the ability to say phonemes in reverse order to create a meaningful word. The student is asked to say the same nonword backwards to form a real word.

Segmenting Words—measures the ability to separate the sounds in words. The student is asked to repeat a word, then to say it one sound at a time.

Test Scores Obtained

Figure 1.1
Test Scores Obtained

Subtests	Raw Score	Age Equivalent	Grade Equivalent	Percentile	Standard Score
Core					
1. Elision (EL)	X	X	X	X	X
2. Blending Words (BW)	X	X	X	X	X
3. Memory for Digits (MD)	X	X	X	X	X
4. Rapid Digit Naming (RD)	X	X	X	X	X
5. Nonword Repetition (NR)	X	X	X	X	X
6. Rapid Letter Naming (RL)	X	X	X	X	X
Supplemental					
7. Rapid Color Naming (RC)	X	X	X	X	X
8. Phoneme Reversal (PR)	X	X	X	X	X
9. Rapid Object Naming (RO)	X	X	X	X	X
10. Blending Nonwords (BN)	X	X	X	X	X
11. Segmenting Words (SW)	X	X	X	X	X
12. Segmenting Nonwords (SN)	X	X	X	X	X

Composites	EL	BW	MD	RD	NR	RL	Sum of SS	%ile	Comp. Score
Phonological Awareness	X	X					X	X	X

Figure 1.1 (continued)

Composites	EL	BW	MD	RD	NR	RL	Sum of SS	%ile	Comp. Score
Phonological Memory		X		X			X	X	X
Rapid Naming				X		X	X	X	X

Composites	RC	RO	BN	SN	Sum of SS	%ile	Comp. Score
Alternate Phonological Awareness			X	X	X	X	X
Alternate Rapid Naming	X	X			X	X	X

Source: Examiner's Manual, Section II, Figure 4.1, p. 38.

Technical Adequacy

Validity Confirmation

Test item validity for the CTOPP is shown by the authors in three ways. They present (1) a detailed discussion of the rationale that underlies the selection of items and the choice of CTOPP's subtest formats, (2) the results of conventional item analysis procedures and Item Response Theory (IRT) analyses used to choose items during the developmental stages of test construction, and (3) the results of differential item functioning analysis used to show the absence of bias in a test's items.

Several studies supporting the CTOPP's *test response validity* are described by the authors. Representative of these studies is one study that used the three composites to predict decoding scores on the Woodcock Reading Mastery Tests-Revised administered one year later. The correlations with decoding scores are impressive for kindergartners and first graders: .71 and .80 for Phonological Awareness, .66 and .70 for Rapid Naming, and .42 and .52 for Phonological Memory. Overall, there is considerable evidence of the CTOPP's test response validity. All of the study results are presented in very clear form in the Examiner's Manual.

Reliability Confirmation

Stability reliability was investigated using the test-retest method. Ninety-one persons were tested twice, with a two-week period between testings. Internal consistency reliability on the items of all of the CTOPP's subtests except the rapid naming subtests was investigated using Cronbach's coefficient alpha. The internal consistency reliability of the items on the rapid naming subtests was investigated using alternate-form reliability because other measures of internal consistency, such as Cronbach's coefficient alpha and split-half coefficients, are inappropriate for speeded tests. The resulting coefficients for internal consistency and test-retest reliability are presented in Figure 1.2.

Figure 1.2
Coefficients for Internal Consistency and Test-Retest Reliability

CTOPP Score	Internal Consistency	Test-Retest Reliability
Subtests		
Elision	.89	.82
Blending Words	.84	.73
Sound Matching	.85	.83
Memory for Digits	.77	.81
Nonword Repetition	.78	.70
Rapid Color Naming	.82	.87
Rapid Object Naming	.79	.85
Rapid Digit Naming	.87	.87
Rapid Letter Naming	.82	.92
Blending Nonwords	.81	.76
Phoneme Reversal	.89	.79
Segmenting Words	.89	.77
Segmenting Nonwords	.90	.81
Composites		
Ages 5–6 Years		
Phonological Awareness	.96	.79
Phonological Memory	.83	.92
Rapid Naming	.88	.70
Ages 7 Years and Older		
Phonological Awareness	.90	.78
Phonological Memory	.83	.84
Rapid Naming	.92	.86
Alternate Phonological Awareness	.90	.83
Alternate Rapid Naming	.88	.94

Source: Examiner's Manual, Table 6.5, p. 77.

Objectivity Confirmation

Inter-scorer error can be reduced considerably by the availability of clear administration procedures, detailed guidelines governing scoring, and opportunities to practice scoring. All of these are present with the CTOPP. Nevertheless, the test authors demonstrate inter-scorer objectivity statistically. Two staff persons in PRO-ED's research department independently scored a set of 30 completed protocols for 5- and 6-year-olds, and a set of 30 completed protocols for 7- through 24-year-olds, to make a total of 60 completed protocols. The two persons' scores were correlated and the resulting coefficients are shown in Figure 1.3.

Figure 1.3
Inter-scorer Coefficients

	5–6 Years	7 Years and Up
Subtests		
Elision	.96	.99
Blending Words	.96	.99
Sound Matching	.99	
Memory for Digits	.99	.95
Nonword Repetition	.95	.99
Rapid Color Naming	.99	.99
Rapid Object Naming	.98	.99
Rapid Digit Naming		.98
Rapid Letter Naming		.99
Blending Nonwords	.99	.99
Phoneme Reversal		.99
Segmenting Words		.99
Segmenting Nonwords		.99
Composites		
Phonological Awareness	.97	.99
Phonological Memory	.99	.98
Rapid Naming	.99	.99
Alternate Phonological Awareness		.99
Alternate Rapid Naming		.99

Source: Examiner's Manual, Table 6.5, p. 77.

Statistical Confirmation

Statistical data for validity, reliability, objectivity, and norms for the CTOPP is presented very clearly and succinctly in the Examiner's Manual.

Special Features

Acronym

CTOPP.

Levels of the Test

There are two levels of the CTOPP, one for use with children ages 5 and 6 and the other for those ages 7 and above. For each examinee, regardless of age, the examiner begins administering every subtest with the first item. Ceilings are uniform for all subtests (three items missed in succession) except the Sound Matching and Rapid Naming subtests (i.e., Rapid Color Naming, Rapid Object Naming, Rapid Digit Naming, and Rapid Letter Naming). The ceiling for the Sound Matching subtest is 4 out of

7 items incorrect to correct for guessing. The rapid naming subtests are timed and the score is determined by the amount of time required to complete the task.

Number of Test Forms

One, with two age-appropriate versions.

Norm-Referenced?

Yes. The CTOPP was normed on a sample of 1,656 persons in 30 states. The norming sites represented each of the four major U.S. geographic regions. The normative sample is representative of the current U.S. population except geographic representations of adults. All of the normative data is presented in the Examiner's Manual. However, the strategies used to locate the individuals in the sample are poorly described, and there is no explanation of the criteria used for categorization into urban-rural resident, ethnic group, or race. Also, the data presented do not correspond to the specific normative comparisons. Separate norm tables are provided for individuals in whole-year groups (that is, for individuals from 5 years through 5 years, 11 months and so on) except for persons aged 18 through 24. However, the data describing the norms is presented in two-year intervals, and no data is presented for the normative groups for individuals aged 18 through 24 years.

Criterion-Referenced?

Yes. The CTOPP is referenced to specific phonetic skills which may affect reading ability.

Other Features

Supplemental subtests are provided to allow the examiner to more carefully assess specific phonological strengths and weaknesses.

Feasibility Considerations

Testing Time

Approximately 30 minutes.

For Testing Groups? Individuals?

Individuals.

Test Administration and Scoring

Both general administration guidelines and specific instructions for administration and scoring of each of the subtests of the CTOPP are given in the Examiner's Manual. These are clearly written and easily followed. However, the authors do say that examiners who give and interpret the CTOPP should have extensive formal training in assessment. They say this training should result in a thorough understanding of test statistics; general procedures governing test administration, scoring, and interpretation; and specific information about phonological ability testing. The authors tell us that supervised practice in administering and interpreting phonological ability tests is also desirable (Examiner's Manual, p. 15).

Test Materials and Approximate Costs

Complete kit, which includes Examiner's Manual, Profile/Record Booklets for ages 5–6 (25), Profile/Record Booklets for ages 7–24 (25), Picture Book, and Audiocassette: $224; Examiner's Manual: $79; Profile/Record Booklets for ages 5–6 (25): $44; Profile/Record Booklets for ages 7–24 (25): $54; Picture Book: $34; Audiocassette: $19.

Adequacy of Test Manuals

The Examiner's Manual is very clear and specific about administration of the CTOPP and interpretation of the results. It also provides an overview of the test and its development. The Examiner's Manual also very clearly presents the technical information (i.e., validity, reliability, objectivity, and norming data).

Excerpts from Other Test Reviews

The CTOPP has been reviewed by Salvia and Ysseldyke (2001). They state that "questions about the representativeness of the sample remain because the sampling plan is poorly described and the data presented in the manual do not correspond to the actual normative comparisons. Except for Phonological Awareness, reliability estimates are generally too low for making decisions concerning individuals" (p. 457).

Ordering Information

Publisher

PRO-ED, 8700 Shoal Creek Boulevard, Austin, TX 78757-6897; Phone: 800-897-3202; Fax: 800-397-7633; Web site: http://www.proedinc.com.

Authors

Richard K. Wagner, Joseph K. Torgesen, and Carol A. Rashotte.

Publication Date

1999.

Cautions and Comments

The CTOPP should probably be administered by a trained specialist (i.e., speech pathologist or reading specialist) and then recommendations made by that specialist to the classroom teacher for areas to be addressed with instructional intervention. The purpose of instructional prescription tests such as the CTOPP is to diagnose weaknesses or deficiencies in skills in order to prescribe remedial instruction. The test is meant to be administered to individuals and prescription made for those individuals; thus, comparing the individual's scores to other scores does not seem necessary or even appropriate. This reviewer does not feel that the representativeness of the norming sample or the poorly described norming data should call into question making decisions based on results of the CTOPP.

Reference

Salvia, J., & Ysseldyke, J. E. (2001). *Assessment* (8th ed.). Boston: Houghton Mifflin.

Test for Auditory Comprehension of Language, Third Edition (TACL-3),
for testing individuals from 3 years through 9 years, 11 months of age
Reviewed by Katherine C. Schnepel, Ph.D.,
Educational Research and Measurement

Usefulness of the Test for Educators

Test Author's Purpose

The TACL-3 provides an inventory of grammatical forms for observing a child's auditory-comprehension behavior. The test helps to identify individuals having receptive language disorders.

Decision-Making Applications

The TACL-3 can be used effectively to assess auditory comprehension and to help the examiner pinpoint specific comprehension deficits and plan remedial instruction for those deficits. In addition, it can be useful for monitoring the progress of individuals who are involved in remedial instruction programs.

Relevant Population

The TACL-3 is appropriate for use with individuals between the ages of 3 years and 9 years, 11 months who can understand the directions of the subtests, who are able to formulate the necessary responses, who have some familiarity with printed pictures and forms, and especially who can pass the example items (Examiner's Manual, p. 13).

Characteristics Described

The TACL-3 consists of 139 items grouped into three subtests that assess a child's ability to understand the following categories of English language forms:

1. Vocabulary—the literal and most common meanings of word classes such as nouns, verbs, adjectives, and adverbs, and of words that represent basic precepts and concepts.

2. Grammatical Morphemes—the meaning of grammatical morphemes such as prepositions, noun number and case, verb number and tense, noun-verb agreement, derivational suffixes, and the meaning of pronouns, tested within the context of a simple sentence.

3. Elaborated Phrases and Sentences—the understanding of syntactically based word relations and elaborated phrase and sentence constructions, including the modalities of single and combined constructions (interrogative sentences, negative sentences, active and passive voice, direct and indirect object), embedded sentences, and partially and completely conjoined sentences.

Each item is composed of a word, phrase, or sentence, and a corresponding plate that has three drawings in color. One of the three pictures for each item illustrates the meaning of the word, morpheme, or syntactic structure being tested. The other two pictures illustrate either two semantic or grammatical contrasts of the stimulus or one contrast and one decoy. The examiner reads the stimulus aloud, and the subject is directed to point to the picture that he or she believes best represents the meaning of the word, phrase, or sentence spoken by the examiner. No oral response is required on the part of the subject.

Test Scores Obtained

Four. A raw score (number correct) is obtained for each of the three subtests and the total. These raw scores can be converted to standard scores and to age equivalents and percentiles, using the tables in Appendixes B and C in the Examiner's Manual.

Technical Information

Validity Conformation

Evidence of *test item validity* is given in five ways. First, a detailed discussion of the rationale that underlies the selection of items is presented. Second, the rationale for choosing the TACL-3's test formats is described. Third, the procedures used to develop and organize the TACL-3's pictures are described. Fourth, the validity of the items is ultimately supported by the results of "conventional" item analysis procedures used to choose items during the developmental stages of test construction. Fifth, the validity of the items is reinforced by the results of "differential item functioning analysis" used to show the absence of bias in a test's items (Examiner's Manual, p. 50).

The authors support *test response validity* by correlating the TACL-3 with the Comprehensive Receptive and Expressive Vocabulary Test (CREVT). The TACL-3 and the CREVT are both tests of spoken language. The CREVT has two subtests: one measures receptive vocabulary and the other measures expressive vocabulary. The results of the two subtests are combined to form a general vocabulary composite. Both tests (CREVT and TACL-3) were administered to 23 general-class students. In all cases, raw scores were converted to standard scores for the subtests and a quotient for the composite. These coefficients were correlated with the quotient scores of the CREVT. The coefficients are high enough to give support for the test response validity of the TACL-3 scores. The correlation coefficients are shown in Figure 1.1.

Figure 1.1
Correlations between the TACL-3 and the CREVT

	CREVT		
	Receptive	*Expressive*	*General*
TACL-3 Values	*Vocabulary*	*Vocabulary*	*Vocabulary*
Subtests			
Vocabulary	.65	.53	.65
Grammatical Morphemes	.65	.85	.80
Elaborated Phrases and Sentences	.62	.80	.74
TACL-3 Quotient	.78	.88	.86

Source: Examiner's Manual, Table 7.5, p. 65.

Reliability Confirmation

The TACL-3's stability reliability was investigated using the test-retest method. Twenty-nine children were tested twice, with a two-week period between testings. The examinees were in grades 2 and 3. Raw scores for the two testings were converted into standard scores and quotients in order to control for any effects of age in the sample. The values were then correlated, and the resulting coefficients were of sufficient magnitude to allow confidence in the test scores' stability reliability. Those coefficients are shown in Figure 1.2.

Figure 1.2
Correlations between the First and Second Testing of the TACL-3

TACL-3 Subtests	*Correlation between First and Second Testing*
Vocabulary	.96
Grammatical Morphemes	.86
Elaborated Phrases and Sentences	.88
TACL-3 Quotient	.97

Source: Examiner's Manual, Table 6.4, p. 46.

Internal consistency reliability, which is the degree of homogeneity among items, was investigated. Coefficients reported by age for TACL-3 subtests and the quotient range from .84 to .97, with just two coefficients below .90.

Objectivity Confirmation

Clear instructions for scoring are given in the Examiner's Manual. Also, inter-rater objectivity was shown by having two staff persons in the publisher's research department independently score a set of 30 completed protocols. The protocols were randomly selected from the normative sample. The sample ranged from preschool through grade 3. The raw scores were converted to standard scores, and then correlated and reported by age intervals. The resulting coefficients ranged from .86 to .97. The size of these coefficients provides convincing evidence of the test's inter-rater objectivity.

Statistical Confirmation

Statistical confirmation for the validity, reliability, objectivity, and norms of the TACL-3 can be found in the Examiner's Manual.

Special Features

Acronym

TACL-3.

Levels of the Test

Levels are determined by using ceilings. For each child, regardless of age, the examiner begins administering every subtest with the first item. The ceilings are the same for all subtests in that testing is ended when the child misses three items in a row. All items above the ceiling are scored as incorrect.

Number of Test Forms

One.

Norm-Referenced?

Yes. The normative data for the TACL-3 is based on the test performance of 1,102 persons ages 3 years through 9 years, 11 months in 24 states. The characteristics of the sample with regard to geographic region, gender, race, ethnicity, and disability are reported as percentages in the Examiner's Manual (Table 5.1, p. 37). These percentages are compared with those reported in the *Statistical Abstract of the United States* (U.S. Bureau of the Census, 1997) for the entire 1997 population, as well as the projected figures for the year 2000 (Table 5.1, p. 37). The comparison of those percentages demonstrates that the sample is representative.

Criterion-Referenced?

Yes. The TACL-3 is referenced to three categories of receptive spoken vocabulary: Vocabulary, Grammatical Morphemes, and Elaborated Phrases and Sentences.

Feasibility Considerations

Testing Time

Twenty to 30 minutes for the entire test. Usually the TACL-3 can be completed in one testing session. However, for some individuals, the testing may have to be conducted during several sessions.

For Testing Groups? Individuals?

Individuals.

Test Administration and Scoring

Specific and easy-to-follow instructions for administering and scoring the TACL-3 are provided in the Examiner's Manual. However, the author says that examiners who give and interpret the TACL-3 should have extensive formal training in assessment. This training should result in a thorough understanding of test statistics; general procedures governing test administration, scoring, and interpretation; and specific information about testing.

Test Materials and Approximate Costs

Complete kit, which includes Examiner's Manual, Picture Book, and Profile/Examiner Record Booklets (25): $254; Examiner's Manual: $79; Picture Book: $139; Profile/Examiner Record Booklets (25): $39.

Adequacy of Test Manuals

The Examiner's Manual is clearly written, giving detailed administration procedures and scoring directions and well-presented technical information.

Excerpts from Other Test Reviews

The TACL-3 was reviewed by Manikam (2001) and Novak (2001). Manikam says, "The test is well validated. . . . The test is highly recommended to address auditory comprehension and subsequent remedial planning." Novak expresses the opinion that "it appears to be a useful tool for identifying specific comprehension deficits in a wide range of children with sufficient reliability to allow progress monitoring."

Ordering Information

Publisher

PRO-ED, 8700 Shoal Creek Boulevard, Austin, TX 78757-6897; Phone: 800-897-3202; Fax: 800-397-7633; Web site: http://www.proedinc.com.

Author

Elizabeth Carrow-Woolfolk.

Publication Date

1999.

Cautions and Comments

This reviewer would caution teachers and other professionals using the TACL-3 to be sure that the test is administered and scored by a trained speech pathologist. The skills of the speech pathologist in encoding and decoding are essential for the valid, reliable, and objective administration and scoring of this test. Also, instructional planning based on the results of the TACL-3 must be limited to the areas referenced in the content (i.e., receptive spoken vocabulary, grammar, and syntax).

References

Manikam, R. (2001). Review of the Test for Auditory Comprehension of Language, Third Edition. In B. S. Plake & J. C. Impara (Eds.), *The Fourteenth Mental Measurements Yearbook* (pp. 1229–1230). Lincoln, NE: The Buros Institute of Mental Measurements.

Novak, C. (2001). Review of the Test for Auditory Comprehension of Language, Third Edition. In B. S. Plake & J. C. Impara (Eds.), *The Fourteenth Mental Measurements Yearbook* (pp. 1230–1231). Lincoln, NE: The Buros Institute of Mental Measurements.

Test of Adolescent and Adult Language-Third Edition (TOAL-3), for testing groups and individuals from 12 years through 24 years, 11 months of age
Reviewed by Katherine C. Schnepel, Ph.D.,
Educational Research and Measurement

Usefulness of the Test for Educators

Test Authors' Purpose

The results of the TOAL-3 may be used (1) to identify adolescents and adults whose scores are significantly below those of their peers and who might need interventions designed to improve language proficiency, (2) to determine areas of relative strength and weakness across language abilities, (3) to document overall progress in language development as a consequence of intervention programs, and (4) to serve as a measure for research efforts designed to investigate language characteristics of adolescents and adults.

Decision-Making Applications

The TOAL-3 can be used effectively to assess listening and speaking skills as well as reading and writing skills in relation to vocabulary and grammar in adolescents and adults. The results of the test can give the teacher information needed to prescribe instructional intervention or remediation of those skills. For prescriptive purposes the TOAL-3 would probably be best used in conjunction with other measures of these language skills. The TOAL-3 is probably not as effective in identifying students with language disorders or language deficiencies which may require more therapeutic intervention.

Relevant Population

The authors tell us that the TOAL-3 is appropriate for use with individuals between the ages of 12 years and 24 years, 11 months who can understand the directions of the subtests, who are able to formulate the necessary responses, and who can read and/or speak some English (Examiner's Manual, p. 9).

Characteristics Described

The TOAL-3 was designed to assess receptive and expressive spoken and written vocabulary (semantics) and grammar (morphology and syntax). Eight subtests are used to evaluate these skills. The eight subtests are meant to assess the following characteristics:

Listening/Vocabulary is measured by the picture-vocabulary subtest, in which the adolescent must select two pictures that relate to the stimulus word read by the examiner.

Listening/Grammar is measured in a 35-item subtest which contains three sentences that are read aloud to the adolescent, who must select the two sentences that have the same meaning.

Speaking/Vocabulary is measured by asking the adolescent to say a meaningful sentence that includes appropriate use of a stimulus word read by the examiner.

In the Speaking/Grammar subtest, the examiner reads a sentence to the adolescent, who must then repeat it.

In the Reading/Vocabulary subtest, each of up to 30 items has three stimulus words and a multiple-choice array containing four additional words. The adolescent is asked to select from the array two words that go with the stimulus words.

In the 25-item Reading/Grammar subtest, the adolescent must read five sentences and find the two that mean "about the same thing."

In the 30-item Writing/Vocabulary subtest, the adolescent must read a stimulus word and write a meaningful sentence using that word.

In the Writing/Grammar subtest, 30 items contain two to six sentences of varying complexity. The adolescent is asked to combine the sentences into one, prompting grammatically more complex constructions.

Test Scores Obtained

Figure 1.1
Subtest Scores Obtained

	Raw Scores	Percentiles	Standard Scores
Listening/Vocabulary (LV)	X	X	X
Listening/Grammar (LG)	X	X	X
Speaking/Vocabulary(SV)	X	X	X
Speaking/Grammar (SG)	X	X	X
Vocabulary (RV)	X	X	X
Reading/Grammar (RG)	X	X	X
Writing/Vocabulary (WV)	X	X	X
Writing/Grammar (WG)	X	X	X

Source: Examiner's Manual, Section II of Figure 4.1, p. 32.

Figure 1.2
Composite Scores, Percentiles, and Quotients Obtained

Standard Scores for Subtests

TOAL-3 Composites	LV	LG	SV	SG	RV	RG	WV	WG	Sums of SS	%iles	Quo.
General Language	X	X	X	X	X	X	X	X	X	X	X
Listening	X	X							X	X	X
Speaking			X	X					X	X	X
Reading					X	X			X	X	X
Writing							X	X	X	X	X
Spoken Language	X	X	X	X					X	X	X
Written Language					X	X	X	X	X	X	X
Vocabulary	X		X		X		X		X	X	X
Grammar		X		X		X		X	X	X	X
Receptive Language	X	X			X	X			X	X	X
Expressive Language			X	X			X	X	X	X	X

Source: Examiner's Manual, Section VII of Figure 4.1, p. 32.

Technical Adequacy

Validity Confirmation

Test authors usually support *test item validity* by showing that the abilities chosen to be measured are consistent with the current knowledge about a particular area and that their test items hold up statistically. The authors contend that they do this by describing the rationale for the subtests' contents and formats and by providing results of item analysis procedures that were used during the developmental stages of the test's construction to choose items. However, no empirical studies of test item validity are presented.

Evidence of *test response validity* for the first edition of the test is presented. Moderate correlations ranging from .37 to .73 are reported between the TOAL (1980) and the PPVT (Peabody Picture Vocabulary Test), a subtest of the DTLA (Detroit Tests of Learning Aptitude), the reading and language totals from the CTBS (California Test of Basic Skills) and the total score from the Test of Written Language and the Test of Language Competence. One subtest of the TOAL-3 correlated with the PPVT at .73; other than that the range is .37 to .69. Because the TOAL (1980), the TOAL-2 (1987), and the TOAL-3 (1994) are very highly correlated, the authors assume that these correlations with other tests are for TOAL-3 as well as for the TOAL and the TOAL-2. Also, the authors tell us that the TOAL (1980) correlated with intelligence measures and that students previously identified as mentally retarded or learning disabled attained lower scores. However, no data is provided to show that the TOAL-3 is sufficiently sensitive to monitor a student's progress, and no data is provided to show that the TOAL-3 identifies students who might profit from programs of language intervention.

Reliability Confirmation

Stability reliability is supported by the test-retest method. Two groups were given the TOAL twice. The first group consisted of 52 students in a parochial school. In 1980 they were given the TOAL twice with a two-week period between testings. The students ranged from 11 to 14 years of age. The second group was made up of 59 college students. They were given the TOAL-3 twice in 1993, with two weeks between testings. These students ranged in age from 19 to 24 years. The correlations between the raw scores on the subtests of the first and second testings of both groups averaged .80 to .87. Because these correlations are high, one may conclude that stability reliability is confirmed.

Objectivity Confirmation

Data to support objectivity of scoring is presented. Six different persons scored three TOAL subtests that use subjective scoring. The correlations among the scores obtained were high, ranging from .70 to .99. However, again, this data appears to have been gathered on an earlier version of the TOAL. Also, extensive and specific scoring criteria are given in the Examiner's Manual, though these criteria and directions for scoring are sometimes confusing and unclear.

Statistical Confirmation

Statistical data on validity, reliability, objectivity, and norms can be obtained in the Examiner's Manual.

Special Features

Acronym

TOAL-3.

Levels of the Test

There is just one level of the test, determined by the use of basals and ceiling. A basal for any subtest is established when the student correctly answers five items in a row. A ceiling is reached when three answers in any five items have been answered incorrectly by the student.

Number of Test Forms

One.

Norm-Referenced?

Yes. The TOAL-3 was normed on a total of 3,056 adolescents between 12 and 25 years of age, selected from 26 states. Of this total, 1,512 were from the original TOAL sample, 957 were added for the TOAL-2, and 587 were added for the TOAL-3. All of the subjects in the TOAL-3 group were from 18 to 24 years of age. The authors do not tell us where the normative testing was done, but the names of the school systems are found in the acknowledgments. Apparently, the majority of the normative sample was obtained from schools in Mobile, Alabama; Berthoud, Colorado; Hibbing, Minnesota; Kansas City, Missouri; Dover, Oklahoma; Moore, Oklahoma; Beaverton, Oregon; and Erie, Pennsylvania (Examiner's Manual, p. vii). This does not seem to be a cross-section of the United States and certainly seems to have little relevance to students in large-city school systems where a high concentration of students with language deficiencies is to be found.

Criterion-Referenced?

Yes. The subtests of the TOAL-3 are referenced to listening and speaking skills, in three aspects of language (semantics, morphology, and syntax). It is not referenced to any specific criteria of curriculum or instruction.

Feasibility Considerations

Testing Time

No time limits are imposed on the TOAL-3. The time required to give the entire test varies from one to three hours, the average time being about 1 hour and 45 minutes. The time ranges for giving the subtests are listed below:

Listening/Vocabulary	15–25 minutes
Listening/Grammar	10–30 minutes
Speaking/Vocabulary	5–15 minutes
Speaking/Grammar	5–20 minutes
Reading/Vocabulary	10–25 minutes
Reading/Grammar	10–25 minutes
Writing/Vocabulary	10–25 minutes
Writing/Grammar	15–35 minutes

For Testing Groups? Individuals?

Six of the eight subtests can be given in groups; the other two must be given individually. All of the subtests can be given individually.

Test Administration and Scoring

There is an IBM scoring system available from the publisher. However, three of the subtests are scored subjectively, so those might be problematic in a computer scoring system. The instructions for administering each subtest are given in the Examiner's Manual, but these are often vague and the methods for administering are not uniform among the subtests. The TOAL-3 can be administered by anyone who is reasonably competent in the administration of tests in education, language, and psychology. However, any further assessment based on TOAL-3 results should be completed only by those professionals who are experienced in normal language development and in language assessment (Examiner's Manual, p. 9).

Test Materials and Approximate Costs

Complete kit, which includes Examiner's Manual, Answer Booklets (50), Test Booklets (10), and Profile/Examiner Record Forms (50): $172; Examiner's Manual: $49; Answer Booklets (50): $54; Test Booklets (10): $34; Profile/Examiner Record Forms (50): $39; IBM Scoring System: $89.

Adequacy of Test Manuals

The Examiner's Manual gives an overview of the tests, describes how to prepare for testing, and describes how to administer and score the tests. A script is given for each subtest, though these instructions are sometimes vague and difficult to follow. All of the technical information (validity, reliability, objectivity, and norms) is provided in the Examiner's Manual.

Excerpts from Other Test Reviews

The TOAL-3 was reviewed by McDonald (1998), Richards (1998), and Salvia and Ysseldyke (2001). McDonald says, "The TOAL-3 has outdated norms, likely resulting in under identification of students with language disorders. The TOAL-3 is reliable, but what it measures is questionable. . . . It takes a long time to give for so little. A competent speech and language pathologist will get more useful information from informal conversation with the student."

Richards says, "The fuzziness of the theoretical underpinnings sets the tone for many other aspects of the test. . . . We can be reasonably confident that someone who does very well on the test has more highly developed language skills than someone who does poorly, but any conclusions beyond that would be problematic."

Salvia and Ysseldyke are a bit more positive about the TOAL-3 than the other two reviewers, although they do object to the norms and the normative sample. They say, "Despite the limitations noted, the TOAL-3 appears to be a useful instrument and is widely used."

Ordering Information

Publisher

PRO-ED, 8700 Shoal Creek Boulevard, Austin, TX 78757-6897; Phone: 800-897-3202; Fax: 800-397-7633; Web site: http://www.proedinc.com.

Authors

Donald D. Hammill, Virginia L. Brown, Stephen C. Larsen, and J. Lee Wiederholt.

Publication Date

1994.

Cautions and Comments

The TOAL-3 may be used to assess listening and speaking skills as well as reading and writing skills in adolescents and adults. However, care should be taken in using the results of this test to identify students with language disorders or deficiencies. Perhaps students who do not do well on some or all of the subtests of the TOAL-3 should be further tested on the skills that those subtests address before prescribing intervention or remediation of those skills.

References

McDonald, J. (1998). Review of the Test of Adolescent and Adult Language, Third Edition. In J. C. Impara & B. S. Plake (Eds.), *The Thirteenth Mental Measurements Yearbook* (pp. 1018–1019). Lincoln, NE: The Buros Institute of Mental Measurements.

Richards, R. A. (1998). Review of the Test of Adolescent and Adult Language, Third Edition. In J. C. Impara & B. S. Plake (Eds.), *The Thirteenth Mental Measurements Yearbook* (pp. 1019–1021). Lincoln, NE: The Buros Institute of Mental Measurements.

Salvia, J., & Ysseldyke, J. E. (2001). *Assessment* (8th ed.). Boston: Houghton Mifflin.

Test of Early Language Development, Third Edition (TELD-3),
for testing individuals from 2 years through 7 years, 11 months of age
Reviewed by Katherine C. Schnepel, Ph.D.,
Educational Research and Measurement

Usefulness of the Test for Educators

Test Authors' Purpose

The authors state that the TELD-3 has five purposes: (1) to identify those children who are significantly below their peers in early language development and thus may be candidates for early intervention, (2) to identify strengths and weaknesses of individual children, (3) to document children's progress as a consequence of early language intervention programs, (4) to serve as a measure in research studying language development in young children, and (5) to accompany other assessment techniques (Examiner's Manual, p. 7).

Decision-Making Applications

The TELD-3 can be used effectively for identifying young children who have language problems. The test can pinpoint these problems in both receptive and expressive language and can play a critical part in planning early intervention programs. This is particularly important because there is such a strong relationship between early language abilities and later school learning. The TELD-3 is helpful in targeting children who may be prone to later academic failure because of language deficiencies. The TELD-3 can be effective in monitoring the progress of children who have been placed in special early childhood or language programs. The TELD-3 may be especially helpful in identifying children with language difficulties that are masked by socially appropriate behavior (children who are well behaved, quiet, visually attentive, etc.) (Examiner's Manual, p. 8).

Relevant Population

The TELD-3 is for children between the ages of 2 years and 7 years, 11 months who can understand the directions for the items, can formulate the types of responses necessary for answering the questions, and can speak English.

Characteristics Described

The TELD-3 consists of two subtests: a Receptive Language subtest and an Expressive Language subtest. Each Receptive Language subtest contains 37 items. Form A has 24 semantic items and 13 syntax items; Form B has 25 semantic items and 12 syntax items. Sample items include whether the child answers when his or her name is called or whether the child responds to simple commands ("Come here," "Sit down," etc.). At a more advanced level, the child is shown several toys and asked to "Show me the car" or "Show me the ball." At another level, the child is asked to "Show me the boy under the table." Near the end of the test, the child is asked such questions as "Does lamp go with light or dark?" and "Are these the same or different: captive and prisoner?" Each Expressive Language subtest is composed of 39 items. Form A has 22 semantic items and 17 syntax items; Form B has 24 semantic items and 15 syntax items. Items at the lower end of this subtest allow the parent or caregiver to provide information. These items include whether the child uses exclamations such as "uh-oh" and whether the child has a vocabulary of at least 10 words. At the middle level, items include sentence repetition and responding to questions such as "What is the boy doing?" and "How old are you? Tell me how old you are." Near the end of the test, the child is asked such questions as "What does the word paddle mean?" and "Make a sentence using the words since and September" (Examiner's Manual, pp. 6–7).

Test Scores Obtained

	Total Raw Scores	Quotients (Std. Scores)	Age Equiv.	%iles	Rating
Receptive Language	X	X	X	X	X
Expressive Language	X	X	X	X	X
Sum of Quotients	X	X	X	X	X
Spoken Language Quotient	X	X	X	X	X

Source: Examiner's Manual, Section II, Figure 4.1, p. 56.

Technical Adequacy

Validity Confirmation

The authors state that they demonstrate *test item validity* in five ways. First, a detailed rationale for the items and testing formats of each subtest is presented. Second, the contents of the TELD-3 subtests are shown to measure areas that are usually included on other individually administered tests of early language ability. Third, the validity of the items is ultimately supported by the results of conventional item analysis procedures used to choose items during the developmental stages of test construction. Fourth, the validity of the items is reinforced by the results of "differential item functioning analysis" used to show the absence of bias in the test's items. Fifth, information is provided on the equivalence of the content for both Form A and Form B (Examiner's Manual, p. 89).

In order to support *test response validity*, the TELD-3 was correlated with several other language measures: the Communication Abilities Diagnostic Test, the Clinical Evaluation of Language Fundamentals-Preschool, the Expressive One-Word Picture Vocabulary Test, the Test of Early Language Development-2, the Test of Language Development-Primary-3, the Peabody Picture Vocabulary Test-Revised, the Preschool Language Scale-3, and the Receptive One-Word Picture Vocabulary Test. The correlation coefficients of the TELD-3 and the TELD-2 ranged from .84 to .92. The correlations with all of the subtests of the other tests ranged from .39 to .81, with only two subtest correlations below .40. The authors suggest that the validity information provided indicates that the TELD-3 is a valid measure.

Reliability Confirmation

Evidence of stability reliability is given using the test-retest method. Both forms of the test were administered twice to two different groups of children. One group was made up of 33 children (ages 2 to 4) and the second group of older children (ages 5 to 7) was a group of 50 children from one school and 33 children from another school. The two groups represented the age range targeted by the TELD-3. The intervening time between administration was approximately two weeks. After both testings the quotients were correlated for Form A and Form B at each testing. Internal consistency evidence is given using the Alternate Forms Method. In this method, both forms of the test are given during one testing session and the quotients of both forms are correlated. The resulting correlation coefficients are given in Figure 1.1.

Figure 1.1
Alternate Forms and Test-Retest Correlation Coefficients

TELD-3 Score	*Alternate Forms*	*Test-Retest*
Form A		
Receptive Language	.91	.86
Expressive Language	.92	.84
Spoken Language Quotient	.95	.94

Figure 1.1 (continued)

TELD-3 Score	Alternate Forms	Test-Retest
Form B		
Receptive Language	.91	.85
Expressive Language	.92	.92
Spoken Language Quotient	.95	.93

Source: Examiner's Manual, Table 6.5, p. 86.

The authors suggest that these coefficients are large enough to indicate that the TELD-3 possesses stability reliability as well as internal consistency reliability.

Objectivity Confirmation

Inter-rater objectivity for the TELD-3 is supported by the availability of clear administration procedures, detailed guidelines governing scoring, and opportunities to practice scoring. Statistical support for inter-rater objectivity is provided by having two advanced graduate students in special education independently score a set of 35 protocols. The protocols were drawn randomly from the children in the normative sample. The results of the scorings were correlated. The correlations of all subtests on both forms of the test were .99, presenting solid evidence of inter-rater objectivity.

Statistical Confirmation

Statistical confirmation for validity, reliability, objectivity, and norms of the TELD-3 is clearly presented in the Examiner's Manual.

Special Features

Acronym

TELD-3.

Levels of the Test

Levels of the test are determined by the use of entry points, basals, and ceilings. Entry points are based on the child's chronological age (see Figure 1.2).

Figure 1.2
Entry Points for TELD-3

Receptive Language Subtests	*Expressive Language Subtests*
Age 2: Start with item 5	Age 2: Start with item 10
Age 3: Start with item 10	Age 3: Start with item 15
Age 4: Start with item 15	Age 4: Start with item 20
Age 5: Start with item 20	Age 5: Start with item 25
Age 6: Start with item 25	Age 6: Start with item 30
Age 7: Start with item 28	Age 7: Start with item 33

Source: Examiner's Manual, p. 14.

The examiner is instructed to begin testing at the entry point. If the child does not answer three items in a row correctly, the examiner is instructed to test backwards until the child correctly completes three items. This is the basal. All items below this point are considered correct. The highest three correct items in a row are the basal. The examiner is then instructed to continue testing upwards until the child misses three items in a row. This is the ceiling.

Number of Test Forms

Two.

Norm-Referenced?

Yes. The TELD-3 was normed using 2,217 children residing in 35 states. The sample is representative of the nation as a whole. The characteristics of the sample with regard to geographic region, gender, race, residence, ethnicity, family income, educational attainment of parents, and disabling condition are reported as percentages and are based on the *Statistical Abstract of the United States* (U.S. Bureau of the Census, 1997). The percentages for these characteristics were compared to those projected for the U.S. population for the year 2000 by the U.S. Bureau of the Census. The comparison of the percentages demonstrates that the sample is representative. To further demonstrate the representativeness of the sample, the demographic information was stratified by age (Examiner's Manual, pp. 71–73).

Criterion-Referenced?

Yes. The TELD-3 is referenced to receptive and expressive language skills. The receptive and expressive language subtest scores combine to form the spoken language composite, which becomes a good indicator of general spoken language ability.

Other Features

Manipulatives that are required to give the test are provided.

Feasibility Considerations

Testing Time

Usually less than 30 minutes.

For Testing Groups? Individuals?

Individuals.

Test Administration and Scoring

Clear and specific directions for administration of each item on the subtests are provided. Directions for scoring appear directly after each item's instructions. Suggested prompts to children are listed where appropriate. The authors suggest that examiners have some formal training in assessment, which includes a basic understanding regarding test administration, scoring, and interpretation.

Test Materials and Approximate Costs

Complete kit, which includes Examiner's Manual, Picture Book, and Profile/Examiner Record Booklets (25) (specify forms): $264; Examiner's Manual: $74; Picture Book: $64; Profile/Examiner Record Booklets (25) (specify form): $39; Manipulatives: $54.

Adequacy of Test Manuals

The Examiner's Manual is very clearly written and provides all the information needed by the examiner.

Excerpts from Other Test Reviews

No test reviews were found for the TELD-3.

Ordering Information

Publisher

PRO-ED, 8700 Shoal Creek Boulevard, Austin, TX 78757-6897; Phone: 800-897-3202; Fax: 800-397-7633; Web site: http://www.proedinc.com.

Authors

Wayne P. Hresko, D. Kim Reid, and Donald D. Hammill.

Publication Date

1999.

Cautions and Comments

The TELD-3 is an effective tool which can be used to establish the presence of a language difficulty and to identify language areas in young children that may require more extensive clinical appraisal. The TELD-3 measures broad-based language abilities and takes a short time to administer. However, the TELD-3 is probably best used as a complement for rather than a replacement to a more systematic, extensive evaluation.

> **Test of Early Written Language, Second Edition (TEWL-2)**, for testing
> groups and individuals from 4 years through 10 years, 11 months of age
> Reviewed by Katherine C. Schnepel, Ph.D.,
> Educational Research and Measurement

Usefulness of the Test for Educators

Test Authors' Purpose

The authors state four purposes for the TEWL-2: (1) to identify those students who are significantly below their peers in the academic area of writing, (2) to determine writing strengths and weaknesses of individual students, (3) to document students' educational progress in written language as a consequence of special intervention programs, and (4) to provide a measurement device for research studies pertaining to the academic achievement of young children.

Decision-Making Applications

The TEWL-2 would be especially effective in identifying specific weaknesses in the writing skills of children who have already been shown to be beneath their peers in writing. It would be helpful in diagnosing these weaknesses for the purpose of prescribing instructional intervention. The TEWL-2 can also be used to assess change in a student's writing ability as a result of an instructional intervention.

Relevant Population

The TEWL-2 is appropriate for use with children between the ages of 4 years and 10 years, 11 months who can understand the directions of the subtests, who are able to formulate the necessary responses, and who can read and/or speak English.

Characteristics Described

The TEWL-2 is composed of two subtests: the Basic Writing Subtest, which is used to assess the mechanical aspects of writing, and the Contextual Writing Subtest, which is used to measure a student's ability to produce quality writing. Students are asked to write their response to a picture shown to them or a stimulus given to them by the examiner.

Test Scores Obtained

	Raw Score	Age Equiv.	NCE	%ile Rank	Quotient	Rating
Basic Subtest	X	X	X	X	X	X
Contextual Subtest	X	X	X	X	X	X
Global Score (Total)	X	X	X	X	X	X

Source: Examiner's Manual, Section II, Figure 4.1, p. 38.

Raw Score refers to the number correct. Age Equivalent refers to the age at which the student's writing would be appropriate. The NCE is a standard score based on the normal curve, which is used to compare the student's score to other students' scores. The Percentile Rank indicates the percentage of the normative sample that is equal to or below the student's score. The Quotient is also a standard score used to compare the student's score to other students' scores. The Rating is based on the NCE: > 92.12 = Very Superior, 78.09–92.12 = Superior, 64.05–78.08 = Above Average, 35.96–64.04 = Average, 21.92–35.95 = Below Average, 7.88–21.91 = Poor, < 7.88 = Very Poor.

Technical Adequacy

Validity Confirmation

In order to establish *test item validity*, the authors state that they reviewed the types of topics covered in research articles, published tests, assessment materials, and instructional materials. The selected items were developed directly from this research literature of what it means to write well.

The authors support the *test response validity* of the TEWL-2 by correlating it with several other tests. Among these are the subtests of the Comprehensive Scales of Student Abilities (CSSA), the Diagnostic Achievement Battery-Writing (DAB), the Peabody Individual Achievement Test-Revised-Written Language (PIAT-R), the Preschool Language Scale-Third Edition (PLS-3), the Test of Early Language Development-Second Edition (TELD-2), the Test of Early Reading Ability-Second Edition (TERA-2), the subtests of the Test of Language Development: Primary, Second Edition (TOLD-P:2), the Wide Range Achievement Test-Revised-Spelling (WRAT-R), the Wechsler Individual Achievement Test (WIAT), the Woodcock-Johnson Psycho-Educational Battery-Revised: Written Language (WJ WL), and the Woodcock-Johnson Psycho-Educational Battery-Revised: Dictation (WJ DIC).

The correlations of these tests with the TEWL-2 subtests are shown in Figure 1.1. The authors state that, as a whole, the correlations substantiate test response validity.

Figure 1.1
Correlations of the TEWL-2 and Other Tests

	Correlations			
Test	Basic Form A	Basic Form B	Contextual Form A	Contextual Form B
CSSA				
Verbal Thinking	.53	.50	.35	.36
Spelling	.49	.47	.39	.40
Reading	.62	.59	.55	.56
Writing	.67	.64	.58	.55
Handwriting	.64	.63	.42	.39
Mathematics	.61	.57	.43	.45

Figure 1.1 (continued)

	Correlations			
Test	*Basic Form A*	*Basic Form B*	*Contextual Form A*	*Contextual Form B*
General Facts	.58	.56	.41	.40
TERA-2	.43	.46	.40	.40
PIAT-R Written Language	.65	.65	.57	.56
PLS-3	.40	.47	.41	.40
TELD-2	.62	.77	.59	.60
TOLD-P:2				
Speaking	.34	.36	.33	.29
Listening	.28	.31	.48	.46
Syntax	.37	.38	.52	.48
Semantics	.46	.44	.90	.89
WRAT-R Spelling	.47	.49	.47	.48
DAB Writing	.56	.49	.49	.54
WIAT Total	.44	.42	.41	.41
WJWL	.59	.77	.62	.77
WJDIC	.48	.60	.49	.47

Source: Examiner's Manual, Table 7.3, p. 71.

Reliability Confirmation

Stability reliability was supported using the test-retest method. The coefficient that results from correlating the two sets of scores is a measure of stability over time. Several different samples were used to investigate test-retest reliability. The data was collected within a time period of 14 to 21 days between administrations. For the Basic Subtest Score, 6% of the correlations are between .80 and .84, 38% are between .85 and .89, and 56% meet or exceed .90. For the Contextual Subtest Score, 46% of the correlations are between .80 and .84 and 54% are between .85 and .88. For the Global Score, all reliabilities exceed .90.

Objectivity Confirmation

Inter-scorer objectivity refers to the amount of test error due to examiner variability in scoring. This type of objectivity is particularly important when the person doing the scoring is called on to make some degree of subjective judgment about a student's test performance, as is the case when scoring the TEWL-2 Contextual Writing Subtest.

Inter-scorer objectivity for the TEWL-2 Contextual Writing Subtest was estimated in the following way. Six scorers were selected to score a total of 25 TEWL-2 Contextual Writing Subtests each. The tests were drawn at random from the overall sample of children. All scorers scored the 25 tests. The scorings from the six scorers were correlated. The coefficients all exceeded .90.

Statistical Confirmation

Statistical confirmation of validity, reliability, objectivity, and norms is given clearly and completely in the Examiner's Manual.

Special Features

Acronym

TEWL-2.

Levels of the Test

One. Levels of the test are determined by the use of ceilings and basals. The ceiling is that point at which the examinee misses five consecutive items. The following entry points or basals are used:

Age	Entry Level
3 years through 3 years, 11 months	Item 1
4 years through 4 years, 11 months	Item 1
5 years through 5 years, 11 months	Item 10
6 years through 6 years, 11 months	Item 20
7 years through 7 years, 11 months	Item 30
8 years through 8 years, 11 months	Item 35
9 years through 9 years, 11 months	Item 40
10 years through 10 years, 11 months	Item 40

Source: Examiner's Manual p. 10.

Number of Test Forms

Two.

Norm-Referenced?

Yes. The TEWL-2 was standardized on a sample of 1,479 students residing in 41 states and British Columbia, Canada. The normative data were collected between September 1993 and February 1995. Tests were completed by students in both regular and special education classes and both public and private facilities. Demographic characteristics of the TEWL-2 Normative Sample are given in Figure 1.2.

Figure 1.2
Demographic Characteristics of the Normative Sample

Characteristics	% of Sample	N
Race		
White	80	1,183
Black	16	237
Other	4	59
Ethnicity		
Native American	1	15
African American	14	207

Figure 1.2 (continued)

Characteristics	% of Sample	N
Hispanic	12	177
Asian, Oriental, Pacific Islander	3	45
Other	70	1,036
Gender		
Male	50	739
Female	50	740
Residence		
Urban	78	1,154
Rural	22	325
Geographic Region		
Northeast	19	281
Midwest	25	370
West	18	266
South	38	562
Disability Status		
No disability	88	1,302
Learning disability	6	89
Speech/language disorder	4	59
Mental retardation	1	15
Other	1	15
Age		
3		103
4		155
5		213
6		246
7		255
8		233
9		169
10		105

Source: Examiner's Manual, Table 5.1, p. 52.

Criterion-Referenced?

No.

Feasibility Considerations

Testing Time

Depending on the child's age and ability, the TEWL-2 is administered in 50 minutes or less (when both the Basic and Contextual Writing Subtests are administered). The TEWL-2 is not a timed test; therefore, no precise time limits are imposed on the children being tested.

For Testing Groups? Individuals?

The TEWL-2 Basic Writing Subtest is to be administered individually, and basals and ceilings must be used. The Contextual Writing Subtest may be given to groups and does not require the use of basals and ceilings.

Test Administration and Scoring

Very clear instructions for administering and scoring the TEWL-2 are given in the Examiner's Manual. The authors suggest that the test can be administered by anyone who is reasonably competent in the administration of tests in education, language, literacy, and/or psychology.

Test Materials and Approximate Costs

Complete kit, which includes Examiner's Manual, Form A Student Workbooks (10), Form B Student Workbooks (10), Form A Profile/Record Booklets (10), Form B Profile/Record Booklets (10): $159; Examiner's Manual: $49; Form A Student Workbooks (10): $39; Form B Student Workbooks (10): $39; Form A Profile/Record Booklets (10): $19; Form B Profile/Record Booklets (10): $39.

Adequacy of Test Manuals

The Examiner's Manual is well written and organized for easy access. It includes all of the technical information, as well as administration and scoring procedures and the rationale and overview of the test.

Excerpts from Other Test Reviews

The TEWL-2 was reviewed by Hurford (2001) and Trevisan (2001). Hurford states: "The test was carefully constructed to assess the developmental status of written language in children between the ages of 3-0 and 10-11. The manual is well written and user friendly. Although developing a test that assesses written language skills is a formidable task, the TEWL-2 provides an excellent conceptual framework and content-appropriate items."

Trevisan "recommends the TEWL-2 without reservation." He says that "This measure has been developed with professional expertise. . . . Use of the TEWL-2 will surely aid personnel in the screening of writing skills of young children or those conducting research in this field."

Ordering Information

Publisher

PRO-ED, 8700 Shoal Creek Boulevard, Austin, TX 78757-6897; Phone: 800-897-3202; Fax: 800-397-7633; Web site: http://www.proedinc.com.

Authors

Wayne P. Hresko, Shelley R. Herron, and Pamela K. Peak.

Publication Date

1996.

Cautions and Comments

The TEWL-2 can be used effectively to measure the basic components of written language. However, it is not effective is assessing highly competent writers. It is best used and, in fact, was designed to identify children who could benefit from some type of intervention.

References

Hurford, D. P. (2001). Review of the Test of Early Written Language, Second Edition. In B. S. Plake & J. C. Impara (Eds.), *The Fourteenth Mental Measurements Yearbook* (pp. 1027–1030). Lincoln, NE: The Buros Institute of Mental Measurements.
Trevisan, M. S. (2001). Review of the Test of Early Written Language, Second Edition. In B. S. Plake & J. C. Impara (Eds.), *The Fourteenth Mental Measurements Yearbook* (pp. 1030–1031). Lincoln, NE: The Buros Institute of Mental Measurements.

Test of Handwriting Skills (THS), for testing groups
and individuals from 5 years through 10 years, 11 months of age
Reviewed by Katherine C. Schnepel, Ph.D.,
Educational Research and Measurement

Usefulness of the Test for Educators

Test Author's Purpose

The author states: "The purpose of the THS is to assess a child's neurosensory integration ability in handwriting in either manuscript or cursive and in upper and lower case forms, and to measure the speed with which a child handwrites" (Manual, p. 11).

Decision-Making Applications

The THS can be used effectively by the classroom teacher to diagnose the handwriting deficiencies and instructional needs of her students. The test can pinpoint weaknesses in handwriting, either manuscript or cursive, and can help the teacher plan instruction designed to address those weaknesses.

Relevant Population

Children from 5 years through 10 years, 11 months of age.

Characteristics Described

The THS was designed to measure 10 areas of handwriting skills. The 10 areas (i.e., subtests) are:

Subtest 1: AIRPLANE. Writing spontaneously from memory (in upper-case manuscript or cursive), the ability to write letters of the alphabet in alphabetical sequence, and speed of writing (i.e., number of letters produced in 20 seconds) are assessed.

Subtest 2: BUS. Writing spontaneously from memory (in lower-case manuscript or cursive), the ability to write letters of the alphabet in alphabetical sequence, and speed of writing (i.e., number of letters produced in 20 seconds), are assessed.

Subtest 3: BUTTERFLY. Writing from dictation in upper-case manuscript or cursive, all letters of the alphabet out of alphabetical sequence.

Subtest 4: FROG. Writing from dictation in lower-case manuscript or cursive, all letters of the alphabet out of alphabetical sequence.

Subtest 5: BICYCLE. Writing from dictation nine single numbers out of numerical order.

Subtest 6: TREE. Copying 12 upper-case manuscript or cursive, selected letters of the alphabet out of alphabetical sequence.

Subtest 7: HORSE. Copying 10 lower-case manuscript or cursive, selected letters of the alphabet out of alphabetical sequence.

Subtest 8: TRUCK. Copying six words (21 letters) lower-case and upper-case, manuscript or cursive.

Subtest 9: BOOK. Copying two sentences (six words, 29 letters) lower-case and upper-case, manuscript or cursive.

Subtest 10: LION. Writing from dictation six words (21 letters).

The THS Manuscript version (for children 5 years, 11 months) has other features besides the 206 scorable-language symbols, such as reversal of letters touching one another, speed of writing letters spontaneously from memory, and converting lower-case letters to upper-case letters and vice versa. The THS Cursive version (for children 8 years to 10 years, 11 months) has, in addition to the 206 scorable-language symbols, only one feature: speed of writing letters spontaneously from memory (Manual, pp. 14–15).

Test Scores Obtained

A raw score is obtained for each subtest, and from these raw scores the following scores can be derived using the tables given in the manual: Standard Scores, Scaled Scores, Percentile Ranks, and Stanines. Raw scores are obtained using the scoring criteria for Manuscript and for Cursive given in the Manual.

Technical Adequacy

Validity Confirmation

The test author gives evidence of *test item validity* by describing the development of the test items. He states that a total of 839 children participated in the development of the THS; 494 of these children were tested in manuscript handwriting and 345 were tested in cursive handwriting. Each child tested performed 206 items, along with performing some standardized and normed tests used for validation purposes. Selecting the items to use in the development of the THS was difficult, since it was necessary to select only those items that would be common and familiar to children ages 5 to 11 years. It was determined that the most common and familiar items to all school-age children would be the letters of the alphabet. Selecting the words to be used for dictation purposes was made by a group of 15 teachers (Manual, p. 13).

In order to show *test response validity*, the same children in the norming sample who were tested in manuscript handwriting were administered a number of other tests, including the Bender-Gestalt, the Test of Nonverbal Intelligence, Second Edition, the Test of Visual-Motor Skills-Revised, the Developmental Test of Visual-Motor Integration (VMI), the Wechsler Intelligence Scales for Child, Third Edition (WISC-III, Vocabulary subtest), and the Wide Range Achievement Test, Third Edition (Spelling subtest). Scores on these standardized and normed tests were correlated with scores on the THS Manuscript version. In general, scores on the subtests of the THS Manuscript version correlated positively with scores on the TVMS-R (−.05 to .45), indicating that the handwriting skills tested on the THS Manuscript version may include a visual-motor component. This is less true of the BICYCLE subtest (.05), which involves writing numbers rather than letters. All subtests (excluding the LION subtest) of the THS Manuscript version correlated in a moderately positive way with the WRAT-3 (Spelling subtest) (.08 to .42), indicating that the THS Manuscript version is measuring an area of academic function. Correlations with the Bender and VMI also tend to be moderately positive (−.02 to .63). Correlations with the WISC-III (Vocabulary subtest) are lower, often close to zero, indicating that the THS Manuscript version is not measuring general intellectual functioning, but is testing a specific skill (Manual, pp. 18–19). The evidence presented gives a weak picture of the overall validity of the THS.

Reliability Confirmation

Internal consistency reliability evidence is given for both the Manuscript version and the Cursive version of the THS. Internal consistency indicates the reliability or consistency of what the items are measuring. It is shown by correlating the items with each other and with the total test score. The correlation coefficients for the Manuscript version ranged from .51 to .78, and the coefficients for the Cursive version ranged from .29 to .89. Stability reliability is not supported for either version. Thus, it is difficult to come to any conclusion about the reliability of the THS.

Objectivity Confirmation

Statistical confirmation of inter-rater objectivity is not given for the THS. However, a very detailed scoring key with criteria is provided for each subtest, thus making objective scoring possible.

Statistical Confirmation

Statistical data for validity, reliability, and norms is provided in the THS Manual.

Special Features

Acronym

THS.

Levels of the Test

One.

Number of Test Forms

Two: Manuscript and Cursive.

Norm-Referenced?

Yes. The Manuscript version and the Cursive version of the THS were normed separately. The Manuscript version was normed on 494 children in various parts of the United States, ages 5 years through 8 years, 11 months, with a median age of 6 years, 11 months. The overall sample consisted of 235 males and 259 females; 406 of the children were right-handed and 61 were left-handed (Manual, p. 16). The distribution of age, gender, and handedness with the sample is shown in Table 2 of the Manual (p. 99). The Cursive version was normed on 345 children in various parts of the United States, ages 8 years through 10 years, 11 months, with a median age of 9 years, 8 months. The overall sample consisted of 172 males and 173 females; 309 of the children were right-handed and 36 were left-handed (Manual, p. 19). The distribution of age, gender, and handedness within the sample is shown in Table 2 of the Manual (p. 109).

Criterion-Referenced?

Yes. The THS is referenced to the specific handwriting skills measured by each of the subtests.

Feasibility Considerations

Testing Time

Fifteen to 20 minutes.

For Testing Groups? Individuals?

Groups and individuals.

Test Administration and Scoring

Clear and specific directions for administration are given in the Manual. The scoring keys and directions for scoring are also provided. The author suggests that the THS can be administered and scored by various professionals such as occupational therapists, teachers, psychologists, resource specialists, psychometrists, educational diagnosticians, learning specialists, optometrists, and other professionals (Manual, p. 15). The implication is that these professionals would have some training in assessment.

Test Materials and Approximate Costs

Complete kit, which includes Manual, Test Booklets and Individual Record Forms Cursive (15), and Test Booklets and Individual Record Forms Manuscript (15): $98; Manual: $39; Test Booklets and Individual Record Forms Cursive (15): $34; Test Booklets and Individual Record Forms Manuscript (15): $34.

Adequacy of Test Manuals

The one Manual provided for the THS provides all of the information needed by the examiner. It is clearly written and easily used.

Excerpts from Other Test Reviews

No test reviews were found for the THS.

Ordering Information

Publisher

Psychological and Educational Publications, Inc., P.O. Box 520, Hydesville, CA 95547-0520; Phone: 800-523-5775; Fax: 800-447-0907.

Author

Morrison F. Gardner.

Publication Date

1998.

Cautions and Comments

The THS seems to be an effective instrument for assessing handwriting skills in young children. However, this reviewer would caution the examiner that the low correlations of the THS with intelligence tests and with academic tests precludes drawing any conclusions from the results of the test about any academic skills (i.e., reading or general intelligence). Also, because of the weak evidence for validity and reliability, the THS should probably not be used as a norm-referenced instrument.

Test of Language Development-Intermediate, Third Edition (TOLD-I:3),
for testing individuals from 8 years through 12 years, 11 months of age
Reviewed by Katherine C. Schnepel, Ph.D.,
Educational Research and Measurement

Usefulness of the Test for Educators

Test Authors' Purpose

The authors state that the TOLD-I:3 has three principal purposes: (1) to identify children who are significantly below their peers in language proficiency, (2) to determine children's specific strengths and weaknesses in language skills, and (3) to measure language in research studies.

Decision-Making Applications

It would be appropriate to use the TOLD-I:3 to make decisions about instructional prescription and/or intervention. The subtests of the TOLD-I:3 are designed to identify deficiencies in the many language areas that make up the ability to communicate through speech. The test authors feel that the TOLD-I:3 has particular value for locating children whose language deficits may contribute to academic failure, students who have learning disabilities, children who require bilingual instruction, and children whose language problems or differences might be masked by other more easily observed behaviors. The results of the TOLD-I:3 seem to be useful for the diagnosis of strengths and weaknesses in specific skill areas. Thus, based on these diagnoses, the appropriate remedial or supplemental programs can be prescribed for individual students. Also, results of the TOLD-I:3 can be used to assess the effectiveness of interventions already in use for individual students.

Relevant Population

This test is designed to measure the language skills of most children between the ages of 8 years and 12 years, 11 months. It is normed on all of those ages. There is only one form of the test. So, in order for that one form to be administered to all of those ages, the use of ceilings is employed. The ceiling for the Sentence Combining, Word Ordering, Generals, and Malapropisms subtests is three consecutive incorrect items.

The ceiling for the Grammatic Comprehension subtest occurs when the student misses three of any five consecutive items. In all of these subtests, testing begins at the first item but stops when the ceiling is reached. For the Picture Vocabulary subtest, every student begins with item 1 of Picture Card 1 in the Picture Book and proceeds until he or she misses two items in a row (the ceiling).

Characteristics Described

The two-dimensional model of language structure shown in Figure 1.1 was used to generate the six subtests of the TOLD-I:3.

Figure 1.1
The Two-Dimensional Model of Language Structure Used to Generate the TOLD-I:3 Subtests

	Linguistic Systems	
Linguistic Features	*Listening*	*Speaking*
Semantics	Picture Vocabulary Malapropisms	Generals
Syntax	Grammatic Comprehension	Sentence Combining Word Ordering
Phonology	—	—

Source: Examiner's Manual, Table 1.1, p. 6.

The TOLD-I:3 is designed to assess overall spoken language, semantics, syntax, listening, and speaking. Six subtests are used to evaluate these skills. The Sentence Combining subtest measures the ability to combine two or more sentences into one complex or compound sentence while retaining all of the relevant information from the shorter sentences (e.g., I am big. I am tall. = I am big and tall.). Picture Vocabulary assesses the individual's ability to comprehend the meaning of two-word phrases by pointing to a picture depicting the phrase. Word Ordering measures the ability to combine randomly presented words into meaningful sentences (e.g., big-am-I = I am big or Am I big?). Generals measures the ability to identify the similarities among three words (e.g., Monday, Tuesday, Wednesday). Grammatic Comprehension requires the individual to identify the word that has been used in an ungrammatical way (e.g., Me play ball). Malapropisms measures the ability to realize that a similar sounding word has been incorrectly substituted for another (e.g., We should brush our feet every morning.). No subtest was developed to measure the phonology feature because it is thought that the components of phonology are so integrated into the semantic and syntactic abilities of children over the age of 6 or 7 that they are not easily measured distinctly.

Test Scores Obtained

Figure 1.2
Subtest Scores Obtained

Subtests	Raw Score	Age Equivalent	Percentile	Standard Score
Sentence Combining (SC)	X	X	X	X
Picture Vocabulary (PV)	X	X	X	X
Word Ordering (WO)	X	X	X	X
Generals (GL)	X	X	X	X
Grammatic Comprehension (GC)	X	X	X	X
Malapropisms (MP)	X	X	X	X

Source: Examiner's Manual, Section II, Figure 4.1, p. 24.

Figure 1.3
Composite Scores Obtained

Composites	SC	PV	WO	GL	GC	MP	Σ of SS	Quotient
Spoken Language (SLQ)	X	X	X	X	X	X	X	X
Listening (LIQ)		X			X	X	X	X
Speaking (SpQ)	X		X	X			X	X
Semantics (SeQ)		X		X		X	X	X
Syntax (SyQ)	X		X		X		X	X

Source: Examiner's Manual, Section II, Figure 4.1, p. 24.

The raw score for each subtest is recorded first (see Figure 1.2). Age equivalents that correspond to the raw scores are found in Appendix C of the Examiner's Manual and are recorded next. These are followed by the percentiles and standard scores, which are located in the normative tables in Appendix A of the Examiner's Manual. The standard scores for the subtests are then assigned to the constructs they represent in the model that was used to build the test (see Figure 1.1). This is done as shown in Figure 1.2. The standard scores that make up each composite are summed. This summed value is converted into a quotient (another type of standard score) using the table in Appendix B of the Examiner's Manual. The authors recommend that the composite scores or quotients be used to compare results of the TOLD-I:3 to the results of other tests.

Technical Adequacy

Validity Confirmation

Test item validity was established for the test as follows. First, a detailed rationale for the items and testing formats of each subtest is presented. Second, the opinions of experts are obtained relative to the test's model and subtests. Third, the validity of the items is ultimately supported by the results of "classical" item analysis procedures used to choose items during the developmental stages of test construction. Fourth, the validity of the items is reinforced by the results of differential functioning analysis used to show the absence of bias in a test's items. These are each described in detail in the Examiner's Manual. The TOLD-I:3 is presumed to measure spoken language ability. Therefore, it should correlate well with other tests that are also known or presumed to measure that same ability.

The authors attempt to establish *test response validity* by relating composite scores or quotients of the TOLD-I:3 to scores on the Test of Adolescent and Adult Language-Third Edition (TOAL-3). The TOAL-3 was designed to measure various aspects of spoken and written language in individuals ages 11 through 24. The authors argue that test response validity is supported by correlating TOLD-I:3 scores with composite scores from the TOAL-3 that measure spoken language and with the TOAL-3 scores that measure written language variables. The correlation of the TOLD-I:3 with the spoken language quotient of the TOAL-3 was extremely high (.85). The correlations with the other quotients (written language) all were above .65. The authors also attempt to support test response validity by showing correlations between age and performance of the students in the normative sample and by giving correlations between the TOLD-I:3 composite scores and school achievement scores as measured by the Comprehensive Scales of Student Abilities (CSSA). They state that it is reasonable to assume that spoken language abilities should relate to some degree to school performance (i.e., tests of school achievement).

Reliability Confirmation

Reliability was investigated by testing 55 children who attended regular classes in the Austin, Texas public schools. Twelve of the students were enrolled in grade 4, 28 were in grade 5, and 15 were in grade 6. The time lapse between the two testings was one week. The correlations between the two administrations of the subtests and the composite scores of the two administrations were all higher than .83, and most were higher than .90. Thus, the authors argue that the TOLD-I:3 possesses an acceptable degree of reliability.

Objectivity Confirmation

Scoring keys are provided to score all of the subtests of the TOLD-I:3. The test is designed to be given orally, and the student is to respond orally. The examiner would note and score the response as it is given. In order to confirm objectivity of scoring, two staff persons in the publisher's research department independently scored a set of 50 completed protocols randomly selected from the normative sample. The sample ranged in age from 8 years, 6 months through 12 years, 11 months. The results of the two scorings were correlated, and the coefficients were all .94 or above.

Statistical Confirmation

Statistical data on validity, reliability, objectivity, and norms is available in the Examiner's Manual.

Special Features

Acronym

TOLD-I:3.

Levels of the Test

The TOLD-I:3 is designed to be given to students aged 8 years through 12 years, 11 months. Levels are determined by using ceilings. Ceilings for the subtests (Sentence Combining, Word Ordering, Generals, and Malapropisms) occur when the student misses three items in a row. The ceiling for Grammatic Comprehension occurs when the student misses three of any five consecutive items. For the Picture Vocabulary subtest, every student begins with item 1 of Picture Card 1 in the Picture Book and proceeds until he or she misses two items in a row (the ceiling).

Number of Test Forms

One.

Norm-Referenced?

Yes. The test was normed on a sample of 779 persons in 23 states: Alabama, Arkansas, California, Connecticut, Florida, Illinois, Indiana, Kansas, Kentucky, Louisiana, Mississippi, Nebraska, New York, Ohio, Oklahoma, Pennsylvania, South Carolina, South Dakota, Tennessee, Texas, Virginia, Washington, and Wisconsin. The entire sample was tested in the spring of 1996. The characteristics of the sample with regard to geographic region, gender, race, residence, ethnicity, family income, educational attainment of parents, and disabling condition are reported in the Examiner's Manual. The percentages for these characteristics were compared with those reported in the *Statistical Abstract of the United States* (U.S. Bureau of the Census, 1997) for the general population. The comparison of the percentages demonstrates that the sample is representative.

Criterion-Referenced?

Yes. The TOLD-I:3 is not referenced to any specific criterion of curriculum or instruction. However, it is referenced to specific skills of language ability, and each subtest seems to be referenced to one skill, so there are numerous opportunities for the students to make the same error. This allows the test to be used effectively for prescribing intervention or remediation of that skill.

Feasibility Considerations

Testing Time

Administration of the entire test requires about one hour. The subtests are untimed. However, the authors recommend that the examiner encourage the student to progress fairly rapidly through the test and not to procrastinate unduly over specific items. Usually the test can be completed in one testing session. However, for immature or inattentive children, the test may be extended over several sessions.

For Testing Groups? Individuals?

Because the TOLD-I:3 is a measure of spoken language, it must be administered individually (i.e., to one student at a time). The subtests are administered orally and the student responds to the test items orally.

Test Administration and Scoring

Explicit and easy-to-follow instructions for administering all of the subtests of the TOLD-I:3 are provided in the Examiner's Manual. The authors suggest that whoever administers and interprets the TOLD-I:3 should have some formal training in assessment. This training should provide the examiner with a basic understanding of testing statistics; knowledge of general procedures governing test administration, scoring, and interpretation; and specific information about mental ability evaluation. Supervised practice in using mental ability tests is also desirable.

Test Materials and Approximate Costs

Complete kit, which includes Examiner's Manual, Picture Book, and Profile/Examiner Record Forms (25): $174; Examiner's Manual: $74; Picture Book: $64; Profile/Examiner Record Forms (25): $39.

Adequacy of Test Manuals

The Examiner's Manual for the TOLD-I:3 is very clear and comprehensive. It provides an overview of the test and gives excellent instructions for administering and scoring the subtests. The Examiner's Manual also gives clear directions for interpreting the results of the TOLD-I:3, and it includes all of the technical information about the test (i.e., validity, reliability, and objectivity evidence). Normative tables, tables for converting sums of standard scores to percentiles and quotients, and tables for converting raw scores to age equivalents are provided in the Appendixes.

Excerpts from Other Test Reviews

The TOLD-I:3 has been reviewed by Hurford (1998) and Mirenda (1998). Hurford comments that "Reliability and validity seem to be well established, although in some cases the sample sizes of the studies were quite small." Hurford also says, "The TOLD-I:3 provides information concerning listening, speaking, semantics, and syntax abilities as well as an overall measurement of spoken language ability. This information is useful for the diagnoses of weaknesses and the planning of interventions." Mirenda states, "The TOLD-I:3 is significantly improved from the previous versions, especially with regard to . . . evidence that scores from the test are valid and reliable when used with a wide variety of demographic subgroups as well as with the general population."

Ordering Information

Publisher

PRO-ED, 8700 Shoal Creek Boulevard, Austin, TX 78757-6897; Phone: 800-897-3202; Fax: 800-397-7633; Web site: http://www.proedinc.com.

Authors

Donald D. Hammill and Phyllis L. Newcomer.

Publication Date

1997.

Cautions and Comments

Use of the TOLD-I:3 for instructional prescription and assessment of the effectiveness of intervention and remediation seems to be warranted. It can only be used on an individual basis, but the test does seem to measure spoken language ability quite effectively. Care should be used, however, because as with most standardized tests the TOLD-I:3 is not criterion-referenced to any curricular or instructional criteria. Rather, the subtests of TOLD-I:3 are referenced to specific language skills. The user should be sure that the instruction or intervention prescribed addresses the same abilities assessed by the TOLD-I:3.

References

Hurford, D. P. (1998). Review of the Test of Language Development. In J. C. Impara & B. S. Plake (Eds.), *The Thirteenth Mental Measurements Yearbook* (pp. 1242–1245). Lincoln, NE: The Buros Institute of Mental Measurements.

Mirenda, P. (1998). Review of the Test of Language Development. In J. C. Impara & B. S. Plake (Eds.), *The Thirteenth Mental Measurements Yearbook* (pp. 1245–1246). Lincoln, NE: The Buros Institute of Mental Measurements.

Test of Language Development-Primary, Third Edition (TOLD-P:3),
for testing individuals from 4 years through 18 years, 11 months of age
Reviewed by Katherine C. Schnepel, Ph.D.,
Educational Research and Measurement

Usefulness of the Test for Educators

Test Authors' Purpose

The authors state that the TOLD-P:3 has four principal uses: (1) to identify children who are significantly below their peers in language proficiency, (2) to determine children's specific strengths and weaknesses in language skills, (3) to document children's progress in language as a consequence of special intervention programs, and (4) to measure language in research studies (Examiner's Manual).

Decision-Making Applications

The authors contend that the subtests of the TOLD-P:3 provide an objective and standard means of identifying deficiencies in the many language areas that make up the ability to communicate through speech. They claim that the test has particular value for identifying preschool children whose language deficits may contribute to later academic failure, students who have learning disabilities, children who require bilingual instruction, and children whose language problems or differences might be masked by other more easily observed behavior. Examiners may have to employ many types of assessment before they can reach a definitive conclusion about an individual's language proficiency. The TOLD-P:3 can contribute valuable quantitative information to the total diagnostic effort. Also, results of the TOLD-P:3 can be used to evaluate children's progress in prescribed remedial programs. Periodic assessment is desirable because it provides educators with evidence that the instructional program is appropriate to meet a child's needs.

Relevant Population

The TOLD-P:3 is designed to measure the spoken language skills of most children between the ages 4 years through 8 years, 11 months. It is normed on all of those ages. There is only one form of the test, so in order for that one form to be administered to all of those ages, the use of ceilings is employed. Any items mistakenly given above the ceiling are scored as incorrect. However, the examiner should administer all items on the three supplemental (phonological) subtests—Word Discrimination, Phonemic Analysis, and Word Articulation. The ceiling for the six core subtests (Picture Vocabulary, Relational Vocabulary, Oral Vocabulary, Grammatic Understanding, Sentence Imitation, and Grammatic Completion) is five consecutive incorrect answers.

Characteristics Described

The two-dimensional model of language structure shown in Figure 1.1 was used to generate the TOLD-P:3 Subtests.

Figure 1.1
The Two-Dimensional Model of Language Structure

Linguistic Systems

Linguistic Features	*Listening (Receptive Skills)*	*Organizing (Integrating-Mediating Skills)*	*Speaking (Expressive Skills)*
Semantics	Picture Vocabulary	Relational Vocabulary	Oral Vocabulary
Syntax	Grammatic Understanding	Sentence Imitation	Grammatic Completion
Phonology	Word Discrimination	Phonemic Analysis	Word Articulation

Source: Examiner's Manual, Table 1.1, p. 6.

The TOLD-P:3 is designed to assess overall spoken language, listening, organizing, speaking, semantics, and syntax. Nine subtests are used to evaluate these skills. The Picture Vocabulary (PV) subtest measures the extent to which a child understands the meanings associated with spoken English words. The Relational Vocabulary (RV) subtest is an associative task that measures a child's ability to understand and orally express the relationships between two words. The Oral Vocabulary (OV) subtest measures a child's ability to give oral definitions to common English words that are spoken by the examiner. The Grammatic Understanding (GU) subtest assesses the child's ability to comprehend the meaning of sentences. The Sentence Imitation (SI) subtest is designed to measure aspects of children's ability to produce correct English sentences. The Grammatic Completion (GC) subtest assesses children's ability to recognize, understand, and use common English morphological forms. The supplemental subtest, Word Discrimination (WD), assesses the child's ability to recognize the differences in significant speech sounds. The second supplemental subtest, Phonemic Analysis (PA), is an organizational task. It tests an aspect of auditory processing skill, specifically the ability to segment words into smaller phonemic units. The third supplemental subtest, Word Articulation (WA), measures the child's ability to utter important English speech sounds. In all of the subtests the child is asked to respond orally to the picture or stimulus presented by the examiner.

Test Scores Obtained

Figure 1.2
Subtest Scores Obtained

Subtests	Raw Score	Age Equivalent	Percentile	Standard Score
Core				
Picture Vocabulary (PV)	X	X	X	X
Relational Vocabulary (RV)	X	X	X	X
Oral Vocabulary (OV)	X	X	X	X
Grammatic Understanding (GU)	X	X	X	X
Sentence Imitation (SI)	X	X	X	X
Grammatic Completion GC)	X	X	X	X
Supplemental				
Word Discrimination (WD)	X	X	X	X
Phonemic Analysis (PA)	X	X	X	X
Word Articulation (WA)	X	X	X	X

Source: Examiner's Manual, Section II, Figure 4.1, p. 32.

Figure 1.3
Composite Scores Obtained

Composites	PV	RV	OV	GU	SI	GC	Sums of SS	Quotients
Spoken Language (SLQ)	X	X	X	X	X	X	X	X
Listening (LIQ)	X			X			X	X

Figure 1.3 (continued)

Composites	PV	RV	OV	GU	SI	GC	Sums of SS	Quotients
Organizing (OrQ)		X			X		X	X
Speaking (SpQ)			X			X	X	X
Semantics (SeQ)	X	X	X				X	X
Syntax (SyQ)				X	X	X	X	X

Source: Examiner's Manual, Section II, Figure 4.1, p. 32.

The raw score for each subtest is recorded first (see Figure 1.2). Age equivalents that correspond to the raw scores are found in Appendix C of the Examiner's Manual and are recorded next. These are followed by the percentiles and standard scores, which are located in the normative tables in Appendix A of the Examiner's Manual. The standard scores for the subtests are then assigned to the constructs they represent in the model that was used to build the test (see Figure 1.1). This is done as shown in Figure 1.2. The standard scores that make up each composite are summed. This summed value is converted into a quotient (another type of standard score) using the table in Appendix B of the Examiner's Manual. The composite scores or quotients should be used to compare the results of the TOLD-P:3 to the results of other tests.

Technical Adequacy

Validity Confirmation

Test item validity was established for the test as follows. First, a detailed rationale for the items and testing formats of each subtest is presented. Second, the validity of the items is supported by the results of "classical" item analysis procedures used to choose items during the developmental stages of test construction. Third, the validity of the items is reinforced by the results of differential functioning analyses used to show the absence of bias in the test's items. These are each described in detail in the Examiner's Manual. Generally, the results support a high degree of test item validity, although there is limited item difficulty at ages 4 and 5.

With respect to *test response validity*, the TOLD-P:3 is presumed to measure spoken language ability. Therefore, it should correlate well with other tests that are known or presumed to measure that same ability. The scores of the TOLD-P:3 were correlated with those of the Bankson Language Test-Second Edition (Bankson, 1990). The Bankson test offers scores for semantics, syntax, and overall language, as does the TOLD-P:3.

Figure 1.4
Correlations between TOLD-P:3 and the Bankson Language Test-Second Edition

	BLT-2 Values		
TOLD-P:3 Values	*Semantic Knowledge*	*Morphological/ Syntactic Rules*	*Overall Language Quotient*
Subtests			
Picture Vocabulary	.88	.69	.70
Relational Vocabulary	.78	.65	.67
Oral Vocabulary	.97	.81	.84
Grammatic Understanding	.79	.64	.67
Sentence Imitation	.87	.86	.84
Grammatic Completion	.86	.79	.80
Word Discrimination	.59	.69	.52
Phonemic Analysis	.78	.73	.70
Word Articulation	NS	.65	NS
Composites			
Listening	.89	.73	.75
Organizing	.89	.84	.84
Speaking	.93	.83	.86
Semantics	.90	.76	.79
Syntax	.95	.88	.91
Spoken Language	.96	.86	.89

NS = coefficients not significant (p > .05).

Source: Examiner's Manual, Table 7.4, p. 77.

The authors offer the coefficients in Figure 1.4 as strong evidence for the TOLD-P:3's test response validity. Also, because spoken language is developmental in nature, the authors argue that performance on the test should be strongly correlated with chronological age. The relationship of the subtest scores to age is shown to be strong (.50 to .62). This, they argue, is further evidence of test response validity. Tables showing the correlation coefficients with age are given in the Examiner's Manual.

Reliability Confirmation

Reliability was investigated by testing 33 children who attended regular classes in Austin, Texas. The students were enrolled in kindergarten and grades 1 and 2. The time lapse between the two testings was four months. The test-retest coefficients for the subtests were all greater than .80, and those for the composites rounded to or exceeded .90. The sizes of these coefficients indicate that the TOLD-P:3 possesses an acceptable degree of reliability to prescribe spoken language instruction for individual students.

Objectivity Confirmation

Scoring keys are provided to score all of the subtests of the TOLD-P:3. The test is designed to be given orally, and the student is to respond orally. The examiner would note and score the response as it is given. In order to confirm objectivity of scoring, two staff persons in the publisher's research department independently scored a set of 50 completed protocols randomly selected from the normative sample. The sample ranged in age from 4 years through 8 years, 11 months. The results of the scoring were correlated. The resulting coefficients for the subtests and composites were all .99. The size of these coefficients provides convincing evidence for scorer consistency or objectivity.

Statistical Confirmation

Statistical data on validity, reliability, objectivity, and norms is available in the Examiner's Manual.

Special Features

Acronym

TOLD-P:3

Levels of the Test

The TOLD-P:3 is designed to be given to children aged 4 years through 8 years, 11 months. Levels are determined by using ceilings. Ceilings for the core subtests (Picture Vocabulary, Relational Vocabulary, Oral Vocabulary, Grammatic Understanding, Sentence Imitation, and Grammatic Completion) occur when the child misses five items in a row. There are no ceilings for the supplemental subtests (Word Discrimination, Phonemic Analysis, and Word Articulation).

Number of Test Forms

One.

Norm-Referenced?

Yes. The test was normed on a sample of 1,000 persons in 28 states: Alabama, Arkansas, California, Connecticut, Florida, Illinois, Indiana, Kansas, Kentucky, Louisiana, Massachusetts, Mississippi, Nebraska, New Jersey, New Mexico, New York, North Carolina, Ohio, Oklahoma, Pennsylvania, South Carolina, South Dakota, Tennessee, Texas, Vermont, Virginia, Washington, and Wisconsin. The sample selection procedures, which are described in the Examiner's Manual, resulted in a normative sample that is representative of the nation as a whole. To further demonstrate the representativeness of the sample, the authors stratified the demographic information by age. This is shown in Table 5.2 in the Examiner's Manual. Data reported in this table show that the stratified variables conform to national expectations at each age covered by the test's norms.

Criterion-Referenced?

Yes. The TOLD-P:3 is not referenced to any specific criterion of curriculum or instruction. However, it is referenced to specific skills of language ability, and each subtest seems to be referenced to one or two skills, so there are numerous opportunities for the child to make an error on the same skill. This allows the test to be used effectively for prescribing instruction or remediation of those skills. It also allows the test to be used to evaluate the child's progress in an already prescribed intervention.

Feasibility Considerations

Testing Time

Because the subtests are untimed, the time required to administer the core subtests will vary from approximately 30 minutes to one hour. The supplemental subtests require about 30 minutes and should not be given at the same time the core subtests are administered. Usually the test can be completed in one testing session; however, for young, immature, or inattentive children, the test may be extended over several sessions.

For Testing Groups? Individuals?

Because the TOLD-P:3 is a measure of spoken language, it must be administered individually (i.e., to one student at a time). The subtests are administered orally and the student responds to the test items orally.

Test Administration and Scoring

Explicit and easy-to-follow instructions for administering all of the subtests of the TOLD-P:3 are provided in the Examiner's Manual. The authors suggest that whoever administers and interprets the TOLD-P:3 should have some formal training in assessment. This training should provide the examiner with a basic understanding of testing statistics and knowledge of general procedures governing test administration, scoring, and interpretation. Supervised practice in using mental ability tests is desirable though not necessary. The authors contend that examiners with such experience should have little difficulty in mastering the procedures necessary to give, score, and interpret the test properly. The authors also list some important points relating to motivation, testing situation, and so on, and suggest that the examiner consider them. Scoring instructions for each subtest are also given in the Examiner's Manual, and scoring criteria can be found in the Profile/Examiner Record Booklet. Also available from the test publisher is the TOLD-P:3 PRO-SCORE System for Windows or Macintosh computer operating systems.

Test Materials and Approximate Costs

Complete kit, which includes Examiner's Manual, Picture Book, and Profile/Examiner Record Forms (25): $239; Examiner's Manual: $79; Picture Book: $109;

Profile/Examiner Record Forms (25): $54; PRO-SCORE System for Windows or Macintosh: $98.

Adequacy of Test Manuals

The Examiner's Manual for the TOLD-P:3 is very clear and comprehensive. It provides an overview of the test and gives excellent instructions for administering and scoring the subtests. The Examiner's Manual also gives clear directions for interpreting the results of each of the TOLD-P:3 subtests, and it includes all of the technical information about the test (i.e., validity, reliability, and objectivity evidence). Normative tables, tables for converting sums of standard scores to percentiles and quotients, and tables for converting raw scores to age equivalents are provided in the Appendixes.

Excerpts from Other Test Reviews

The TOLD-P:3 has been reviewed by Madle (2001) and Stutman (2001). Madle says, "Although a few shortcomings are present, the TOLD-P:3 remains one of the best developed and . . . sound measures of children's language available today. Special care should be taken, however, when using it with children below the age of 5 1/2 due to its limited floors." In other words, Madle takes issue with the fact that the lowest possible Spoken Language Quotient at age 4 on this test is 85, only one standard deviation below the mean. Madle says, "They (the floors) do not meet Bracken's (1987) suggested criterion of at least two standard deviations below the mean until age 5 1/2. This substantially compromises the authors' stated purpose of identifying children who show significant delays in language proficiency at these ages."

Stutman comments that "Strengths of this test include objectivity of scoring, . . . relative freedom from bias, acceptable subtest reliability (except for the Word Discrimination subtest), and generally good evidence of validity. Its weaknesses include unnecessarily awkward test materials, . . . low ceilings on the phonemic measures, a high floor on the Relational Vocabulary subtest, and the lack of a table of test-retest coefficients that would enable the administrator to partial out practice effects when using the instrument to measure intervention effectiveness."

Ordering Information

Publisher

PRO-ED, 8700 Shoal Creek Boulevard, Austin, TX 78757-6897; Phone: 800-897-3202; Fax: 800-397-7633; Web site: http://www.proedinc.com.

Authors

Donald D. Hammill and Phyllis L. Newcomer.

Publication Date

1997.

Cautions and Comments

Use of the TOLD-P:3 for instructional prescription and identification of strengths and weaknesses, as well as assessment of the effectiveness of intervention and remediation, seems to be warranted. It can only be used on an individual basis, but the test does seem to measure spoken language ability effectively, although there may be some problem with assessing some of the specific abilities in children younger than 5 1/2 years of age. As other reviewers have noted, the problems seem to come with measuring very-low-performing and very-high-performing young children. Perhaps this could be helped by using another test designed only for very young children in conjunction with the TOLD-P:3. Care should be used because, as with most standardized tests, the TOLD-P:3 is not criterion-referenced to any curricular or instructional criteria. Rather, the subtests of TOLD-P:3 are referenced to specific language skills. The user should be sure that the instruction or intervention prescribed addresses the same abilities assessed by the TOLD-P:3.

References

Bankson, N. W. (1990). *Bankson Language Test* (2nd ed.). Austin, TX: PRO-ED.

Bracken, B. A. (1987). Limitations of preschool instruments and standards for minimal levels of technical adequacy. *Journal of Psychoeducational Assessment 4*, 313–326.

Madle, R. A. (2001). Review of the Test of Language Development. In B. S. Plake & J. C. Impara (Eds.), *The Fourteenth Mental Measurements Yearbook* (pp. 1247–1248). Lincoln, NE: The Buros Institute of Mental Measurements.

Stutman, G. (2001). Review of the Test of Language Development. In B. S. Plake & J. C. Impara (Eds.), *The Fourteenth Mental Measurements Yearbook* (pp. 1248–1250). Lincoln, NE: The Buros Institute of Mental Measurements.

Test of Written Language, Third Edition (TOWL-3), for testing groups and individuals from 7 years through 17 years, 11 months of age
Reviewed by Katherine C. Schnepel, Ph.D.,
Educational Research and Measurement

Usefulness of the Test for Educators

Test Authors' Purpose

The authors state that the TOWL-3 can be used (1) to identify students who perform significantly more poorly than their peers in writing and who as a result need special help, (2) to determine a student's particular strengths and weaknesses in various writing abilities, (3) to document a student's progress in a special writing program, and (4) to conduct research in writing (Examiner's Manual, p. 6).

Decision-Making Applications

The TOWL-3 can be used effectively to identify students who show deficiencies in writing and can help to pinpoint particular weaknesses in specific writing abilities. The TOWL-3 can also be helpful in prescribing instructional remediation for these weaknesses. However, its usefulness in documenting a student's progress in instructional programs is limited by the fact that the stability reliability or stability over time is low.

Relevant Population

The TOWL-3 is designed to be given to students between the ages of 7 years and 17 years, 11 months.

Characteristics Described

The TOWL-3 uses two writing formats (contrived and spontaneous) to evaluate written language. In the contrived format, students' linguistic options are purposely constrained to force the students to use specific words or conventions. The first five subtests elicit writing in contrived contexts and the last three subtests elicit more spontaneous, contextual writing by the student, in response to one of two pictures used as a story starter.

Subtest 1: Vocabulary. The student writes a sentence that incorporates a stimulus word. Example: For ran, a student writes, "I ran to the store."

Subtest 2: Spelling. The student writes sentences from dictation, taking particular care to make proper use of spelling rules.

Subtest 3: Style. The student writes a sentence from dictation, taking particular care to make proper use of punctuation and capitalization rules.

Subtest 4: Logical Sentences. The student edits an illogical sentence so that it makes better sense. Example: The student changes "John blinked his nose" to "John blinked his eyes."

Subtest 5: Sentence Combining. The student integrates the meaning of several short sentences into one grammatically correct written sentence. Example: The student combines "John drives fast" and "John has a red car" into the single sentence, "John drives his red car fast."

Subtest 6: Contextual Conventions. The student writes a story in response to a stimulus picture. Points are earned for satisfying specific requirements relative to capitalization, punctuation, spelling, and other arbitrary elements in writing (e.g., paragraph indents).

Subtest 7: Contextual Language. The student's story is evaluated relative to the quality of its vocabulary, sentence construction, and grammar.

Subtest 8: Story Construction. The student's story is evaluated relative to the quality of its plot, prose, development of characters, interest to the reader, and other compositional aspects (Examiner's Manual, pp. 5–6).

Test Scores Obtained

Figure 1.1
Test Scores Obtained from the TOWL-3

Subtest	Raw Score	Percentile	Standard Score
Vocabulary (VO)	X	X	X
Spelling (SP)	X	X	X
Style (ST)	X	X	X
Logical Sentences (LS)	X	X	X
Sentence Combining (SC)	X	X	X
Contextual Conventions (CC)	X	X	X
Contextual Language (CL)	X	X	X
Story Construction (StC)	X	X	X

Source: Examiner's Manual, Figure 4.1, p. 32.

Figure 1.2
Composite Scores Obtained from the TOWL-3

TOWL-3 Composites	Standard Scores								Sum of Std. Scores	Quo.
	VO	SP	ST	LS	SC	CC	CL	StC		
Contrived Writing	X	X	X	X	X				X	X
Spontaneous Writing						X	X	X	X	X
Overall Writing	X	X	X	X	X	X	X	X	X	X

Source: Examiner's Manual, Figure 4.1, p. 32.

Technical Adequacy

Validity Confirmation

The authors state that they support *test item validity* in three ways. First, they describe the rationale for each subtest's content and format. Second, the validity of the items is empirically demonstrated by the results of "classical" item analysis procedures that were used during the developmental stages of the test's construction to choose items. Third, the validity of items is reinforced by the results of differential item functioning analyses used to show the absence of bias in a test's items (Examiner's Manual, pp. 65–72).

Test response validity is supported by correlating the subtest scores and composite scores of both forms of the TOWL-3 with the Writing subscale of the Comprehensive Scales of Student Abilities (CSSA). These correlations range from .34 to .69, with just two correlations below .43. As further evidence of validity, the authors present results of correlating the subtest scores and composite scores of both forms of the TOWL-3 with the three academic subscales of the CSSA (Reading, Math, General

Facts) and with the Comprehensive Test of Nonverbal Intelligence. The correlation coefficients of the TOWL-3 with subscales of the CSSA range from .34 to .70, with only four coefficients below .40. The correlation coefficients of the TOWL-3 with the Comprehensive Test of Nonverbal Intelligence range from .30 to .60. All of these correlation coefficients are minimal, making the argument for test response validity weak. Plus, the reasons for correlating the TOWL-3 with the academic subscales of the CSSA are questionable. More studies with larger samples and with different criterion measures are needed.

Reliability Confirmation

Stability reliability is supported using the test-retest method. This type of reliability was investigated by administering both forms of the TOWL-3 twice to two different groups of students. These two groups represented the youngest and the oldest persons who should be given the TOWL-3—27 second grade students and 28 twelfth grade students. The intervening time between testings was two weeks. The raw scores of the subtests and the composite scores of both testings for both groups were correlated. The correlation coefficients for the second grade group ranged from .75 to .93; the correlation coefficients for the twelfth grade group ranged from .72 to .94. Internal consistency reliability—in other words, the extent to which test items correlate with each other—is supported by using the alternate forms method. This method entails giving the two forms of the test during the same testing session. The results of the testings are correlated. The correlations of the subtests of both forms by age range from .60 to .94, with just four correlations below .70.

The test-retest study was done only with the extremes in age (youngest and oldest) who would be given the TOWL-3. Thus, there is no substantiation of the stability reliability for all of the age groups in between. Also, the alternate forms study produced lower-than-desirable correlation coefficients, especially at the in-between ages, thus giving a weak argument for internal consistency reliability.

Objectivity Confirmation

Very clear directions for scoring, as well as scoring criteria, are given for all the subtests of the TOWL-3. Also, inter-rater objectivity is supported by having two members of the PRO-ED staff who were familiar with the test's scoring procedures independently score 38 complete TOWL-3 protocols drawn at random from the normative sample. The results of the two scorings were correlated for each of the TOWL-3 subtests. The coefficients for both forms ranged from .80 to .97. The indices reported are high enough to be accepted as evidence of TOWL-3 inter-rater objectivity (Examiner's Manual, p. 62).

Statistical Confirmation

Statistical data for validity, reliability, objectivity, and norms is clearly presented in the Examiner's Manual.

Special Features

Acronym

TOWL-3.

Levels of the Test

One. Ceilings are used with the five subtests that employ contrived formats (Vocabulary, Spelling, Style, Logical Sentences, and Sentence Combining). For all students, administration begins with item 1 and continues until a ceiling is achieved or until the final item is administered. The ceiling occurs when the student misses three consecutive items.

Number of Test Forms

Two.

Norm-Referenced?

Yes. The TOWL-3 was normed on a sample of 2,217 persons residing in 25 states. The percentages of the characteristics of the sample with regard to gender, residence, race, ethnicity, geographic area, family income, educational attainment of parents, and disabling condition were compared with those reported in the *Statistical Abstract of the United States* (1997) for the school-age population. The comparison of the percentages demonstrates that, on the whole, the sample is representative. To further demonstrate the representativeness of the sample, the demographic information was stratified by age group. Data shows that the stratified variables conform to national expectations at each age group covered by the test's norms.

Criterion-Referenced?

Yes. The TOWL-3 is referenced to the following writing skills; vocabulary, spelling, style, logical sentences, sentence combining, contextual conventions, contextual language, story construction.

Feasibility Considerations

Testing Time

With the exception of the 15 minutes allocated to story writing, the TOWL-3 has no set time limits. The entire test battery can be administered in approximately 1 1/2 hours (Examiner's Manual, p. 10).

For Testing Groups? Individuals?

The TOWL-3 was designed to be administered individually, but the authors provide a series of modifications to allow group administration, with minimal follow-up testing of individual students to assure valid testing.

Test Administration and Scoring

Clear and specific directions for administration of all of the subtests are provided. Scoring criteria and scoring directions are also clearly presented. The authors suggest that persons who administer, score, and interpret the test require training in these areas and in evaluation. They also say that examiners should be knowledgeable about the rules governing English language usage (Examiner's Manual, p. 9).

Test Materials and Approximate Costs

Complete kit, which includes Examiner's Manual, Student Response Booklets (25) (specify Form A or B), and Profile/Story Scoring Forms (50): $179; Examiner's Manual: $56; Student Response Booklets (25) (specify Form A or B): $44; Profile/Story Scoring Forms (50): $39; PRO-SCORE System (for IBM DOS, Windows, or Macintosh): $98.

Adequacy of Test Manuals

The Examiner's Manual is very clearly written and provides all the information needed by the examiner.

Excerpts from Other Test Reviews

The TOWL-3 was reviewed by Salvia and Ysseldyke (2001), Hansen (1998), and Bucy and Swerdlik (1998). Salvia and Ysseldyke state: "The content and structure of TOWL-3 appear appropriate, and the two forms of the test appear to be equivalent. ... The internal consistencies of composite and total scores are high enough for use in making individual decisions; the stabilities of subtest are incompletely reported and are lower. Although the test's content appears appropriate and well conceived, the validity of the inferences to be drawn from the scores is unclear. ... Given that TOWL-3 has only two forms and relatively low stability, its usefulness in evaluating pupil progress is also limited."

Hansen says that "The TOWL-3 is substantially improved from earlier versions. As a diagnostic and formative evaluation tool, it is most useful in identifying student writers who are performing substantially below their peers."

Bucy and Swerdlik state: "Studies support the reliability of this measure for diagnostic purposes, though interpretations at the subtest level are ill advised. Additional validity studies are needed. Notwithstanding these limitations, the TOWL-3 meets a need for a measure of written language for both diagnostic and research purposes."

Ordering Information

Publisher

PRO-ED, 8700 Shoal Creek Boulevard, Austin, TX 78757-6897; Phone: 800-897-3202; Fax: 800-397-7633; Web site: http://www.proedinc.com.

Authors

Donald D. Hammill and Stephen C. Larsen.

Publication Date

1996.

Cautions and Comments

The TOWL-3 appears to be an effective tool for measuring writing skills. However, the evidence provided to support the validity and reliability of the test is minimal, and the adequacy of the norms at certain age levels is questionable. Thus, the validity of the inferences to be drawn from the scores is unclear. Although the TOWL-3 is designed as a norm-referenced test, it is probably best used as a criterion-referenced tool for diagnostic and prescriptive purposes.

References

Bucy, J., & Swerdlik, M. (1998). Review of the Test of Written Language, Third Edition. In J. C. Impara & B. S. Plake (Eds.), *The Thirteenth Mental Measurements Yearbook* (pp. 1072–1074). Lincoln, NE: The Buros Institute of Mental Measurements.

Hansen, J. B. (1998). Review of the Test of Written Language, Third Edition. In J. C. Impara & B. S. Plake (Eds.), *The Thirteenth Mental Measurements Yearbook* (pp. 1070–1072). Lincoln, NE: The Buros Institute of Mental Measurements.

Salvia, J., & Ysseldyke, J. E. (2001). *Assessment* (8th ed.). Boston: Houghton Mifflin.

Test of Written Spelling, Fourth Edition (TWS-4), for testing groups and individuals from 6 years through 18 years, 11 months of age
Reviewed by Katherine C. Schnepel, Ph.D.,
Educational Research and Measurement

Usefulness of the Test for Educators

Test Authors' Purpose

The authors state that the test has three specific purposes: (1) to identify students whose spelling ability is deficient enough to call for direct instruction designed to improve their spelling, (2) to document overall improvement in spelling when it occurs as a consequence of intervention, and (3) to serve as a measure in research designed to measure spelling achievement in individuals with different types of learning disabilities.

Decision-Making Applications

The TWS-4 can be used to diagnose spelling difficulties and to prescribe instruction designed to improve spelling. It also might be helpful in discovering learning disabilities which involve listening and writing skills. It could be useful in determining the extent to which spelling difficulties interfere with reading ability.

Relevant Population

The TWS-4 is intended to assess the spelling ability of students ranging in age from 6 years through 18 years, 11 months or grades 1–12.

Characteristics Described

The TWS-4 describes the student's ability to spell both predictable and unpredictable words correctly by writing them. Predictable words are defined as words which conform to phonic rules; unpredictable words are defined as irregular words or words which do not conform to phonic rules.

Test Scores Obtained

Raw Score	X
Standard Score	X
Percentile	X
Spelling Age	X
Grade Equivalent	X

Source: Examiner's Manual, Section II, Summary/Response Form, p. 12.

Technical Adequacy

Validity Confirmation

Test item validity for the TWS-4 is offered in three ways. First, a detailed rationale for selection of test items is presented. Second, the validity of the items is supported by the results of "conventional" item analysis procedures used to choose items during the developmental stages of test construction. Third, the validity of the items is reinforced by the results of "differential item functioning analysis" used to show the absence of bias in a test's items (Examiner's Manual, pp. 33–34).

In order to support *test response validity*, the TWS-4 was correlated with several other tests of spelling ability: the Spelling subtests of the Durrell Analysis of Reading Difficulty (DARD), the Wide Range Achievement Test-Revised (WRAT-R), the California Achievement Test (CAT), the SRA Achievement Series (SRA), the Metropolitan Achievement Tests (MAT), and the Norm-Referenced Assessment Program for Texas (NAPT). Correlations are shown in Figures 1.1 and 1.2.

Figure 1.1
Correlations between TWS Total Words and Other Spelling Scores

Other Spelling Scores	TWS Total Words
DARD	.95
WRAT-R	.91
CAT (Spelling)	.97
SRA (Spelling)	.78

Source: Examiner's Manual, Table 7.4, p. 40.

Figure 1.2
Correlations between TWS-4 Scores and Other Spelling Measures

Other Spelling Measures	TWS-4 Form A	TWS-4 Form B
MAT Spelling	.59	.60
NAPT Spelling	.86	.85

Source: Examiner's Manual, Table 7.5, p. 41.

Reliability Confirmation

Two procedures are used to confirm the reliability of the TWS-4. First, both forms of the test are given during one testing session, and the scores of the two forms are correlated; this gives a measure of the reliability of the content. Second, the test-retest procedure is used to support reliability of the test over time. In this procedure both forms of the test were administered twice to the same sample; the intervening time was approximately two weeks. The scores from each testing for Form A and Form B were correlated. Salvia and Ysseldyke (2001) suggest that for those situations where test results are to be used to make educational decisions about a student, the minimum standard for test reliability should be .90. As shown in Figure 1.3, all of the alternate forms coefficients and the test-retest coefficients for the TWS-4 exceed their criteria.

Figure 1.3
Summary for TWS-4 Reliability to Two Sources of Test Error

	Source of Test Error	
TWS-4 Values	Alternate Forms	Test-Retest
Form A	.94	.95
Form B	.93	.96

Source: Examiner's Manual, Table 6.5, p. 31.

Objectivity Confirmation

Scoring criteria and scoring keys are given and explained clearly in the Examiner's Manual. To study inter-scorer objectivity, two members of the PRO-ED research staff independently scored the TWS-4 test protocols of 108 students in grades 1 through 8. The subjects were equally divided between boys and girls. Fifty-six percent of the subjects were Hispanic American and 44% were European American. The scorings of the two scorers were correlated. The coefficients for both Form A and Form B of the test were .99. The scorers were in almost perfect agreement, differing only on those few occasions where the student's handwriting was difficult to decipher.

Statistical Confirmation

Statistical confirmation of validity, reliability, objectivity, and norms is given clearly and completely in the Examiner's Manual.

Special Features

Acronym

TWS-4.

Levels of the Test

One. Levels of the test are determined by the use of ceilings and basals. The ceiling is that point at which the examinee misses five consecutive items. The following entry points or basals are used for both individual and group administration of the TWS-4:

Grade Level	*Entry Level*
Grades 1–3	Item 1
Grades 4–6	Item 10
Grades 7–9	Item 20
Grades 10–12	Item 30

(Examiner's Manual, p. 8)

If the examinee did not correctly answer five items in succession during the establishment of a ceiling, the examiner should return to the entry point and test downward until five items in a row are answered correctly or until item 1 has been administered.

Number of Test Forms

Two.

Norm-Referenced?

Yes. See Figure 1.4.

Figure 1.4
Demographic Characteristics of the Normative Sample

Characteristics	Percentage of Sample	Percentage of School-Age Population for 1997	Percentage of School-Age Population for 2000
Gender			
Male	48	51	51
Female	52	49	49
Residence			
Urban	75	75	75
Rural	25	25	25
Race			
White	82	79	79
Black	14	16	16
Other	4	5	5
Geographic Area			
Northeast	21	18	18
North Central	26	24	23
South	32	35	35
West	21	23	24
Ethnicity			
Native American	1	1	1
Hispanic	11	13	15
Asian	3	4	4
African American	12	15	15
Other	73	67	65

Age
  6 (N = 151)
  7 (N = 415)
  8 (N = 481)
  9 (N = 510)
  10 (N = 642)
  11 (N = 593)
  12 (N = 580)
  13 (N = 458)
  14 (N = 424)
  15 (N = 265)
  16 (N = 201)
  17 (N = 147)
  18 (N = 85)

Source: Examiner's Manual, Table 5.1, p. 25.

Criterion-Referenced?

No.

Feasibility Considerations

Testing Time

About 15 minutes.

For Testing Groups? Individuals?

The TWS-4 can be administered to groups or individuals.

Test Administration and Scoring

Very clear instructions for administering and scoring the TWS-4 are given in the Examiner's Manual. The authors do not suggest that any special training or certification is needed to give the test. However, they do suggest that the examiner should practice before giving it to students for diagnostic purposes.

Test Materials and Approximate Costs

Complete kit, which includes Examiner's Manual and Summary/Response Forms (50): $79; Examiner's Manual: $47; Summary/Response Forms (50): $34.

Adequacy of Test Manuals

The Examiner's Manual is well written and organized for easy access. It includes all the technical information as well as administration and scoring procedures and the rationale and overview for the test.

Excerpts from Other Test Reviews

The TWS-4 was reviewed by Salvia and Ysseldyke (2001), who say that "Changes to the fourth edition of this test include doing away with the format of having two different tests, one each for predictable and unpredictable words, and its replacement with two alternative forms. In addition, the authors conducted one reliability study, examined differential item functioning for different racial or ethnic groups, and examined the extent to which the words included in TWS-4 are still prominent in spelling basal series. No changes were made in items or in norms." Salvia and Ysseldyke also say that "the norms are more than 20 years old, and only one small new reliability and validity study was completed. Norms are dated, and while evidence for reliability and validity of the test is good, that evidence is based on a different format of the test. Users are cautioned against making norm-referenced comparisons using this test."

The Test of Written Spelling, Third Edition (TWS-3) was reviewed by Longo (1998) and Suen (1998). Longo asserts that "the test's continued reliance upon the examinee writing the correct spelling of a given word represents an authentic, true assessment of spelling ability, not an artificially contrived editing exercise." Suen says that "as the claimed purposes for using the TWS-3 lack supportive evidence, the usefulness of the TWS-3 remains unclear. In sum, the TWS-3 is a psychometrically excellent test in search of a useful, practical function." As the items were not changed when the Fourth Edition of TWS was made, the comments from Longo and Suen would apply to the TWS-4 as well.

Ordering Information

Publisher

PRO-ED, 8700 Shoal Creek Boulevard, Austin, TX 78757-6897; Phone: 800-897-3202; Fax: 800-397-7633; Web site: http://www.proedinc.com.

Authors

Stephen C. Larsen, Donald D. Hammill, and Louisa C. Moats.

Publication Date

1999.

Cautions and Comments

Using the TWS-4 to assess spelling skills across different types of words seems warranted. However, this reviewer shares the concerns of Salvia and Ysseldyke (2001) and Longo (1998) that the norms are outdated and that using the results of the TWS-4 to make norm-referenced comparisons would not be warranted. Also, in this day of spell checkers and an explosion of technical words, perhaps the ability to spell unspecified English words correctly may not be a high priority for many educators.

References

Longo, A. P. (1998). Review of the Test of Written Spelling, Third Edition. In J. C. Impara & B. S. Plake (Eds.), *The Thirteenth Mental Measurements Yearbook* [Electronic version]. Retrieved on December 10, 2001 from Buros Institute's Test Reviews Online web site: http://www.unl.edu/buros.

Salvia, J., & Ysseldyke, J. E. (2001). *Assessment* (8th ed.). Boston: Houghton Mifflin.

Suen, H. K. (1998). Review of the Test of Written Spelling, Third Edition. In J. C. Impara & B. S. Plake (Eds.), *The Thirteenth Mental Measurements Yearbook* [Electronic version]. Retrieved on December 10, 2001 from Buros Institute's Test Reviews Online web site: http://www.unl.edu/buros.

Written Language Assessment (WLA),
for testing groups and individuals from 8 through 18 years of age
Reviewed by Katherine C. Schnepel, Ph.D.,
Educational Research and Measurement

Usefulness of the Test for Educators

Test Authors' Purpose

The test authors state that the results of the WLA may be used with other data in making placement decisions about students in regular classrooms, as well as about students in various special education settings. They say that the test results may also be used for making instructional decisions (Manual, p. 9).

Decision-Making Applications

The WLA is probably best used by the classroom teacher for assessing writing composition skills of individual students or his or her students as a group. It would not be appropriate to use it as the only basis for placing students in instructional programs. Because of the weakness of the validity, reliability, and objectivity and the questionable norms, the WLA should not be used to compare students' composition skills with other students' composition skills or to diagnose deficiencies in student writing.

Relevant Population

The WLA is designed to be used with students ages 8 through 18 and above.

Characteristics Described

The WLA measures General Writing Ability, Productivity, Word Complexity, and Readability. In order to measure these characteristics, students are asked to do three separate writing tasks, each of which represents a different kind of written discourse. One task (write about HANDS) elicits expressive writing; a second task (write about how you would tell a child about the danger of FIRE) elicits instructive writing; and the third task (write a story about the CAT) elicits creative writing. In each of these three sessions they are given two combined verbal and visual prompts and one that is verbal alone. Students work without assistance from dictionaries or other sources. Examiners are told not to offer suggestions and to respond to questions only by saying that decisions must be made by students. Students write on lined paper on which the prompt appears.

Test Scores Obtained

Raw scores (number correct) are obtained for four components: General Writing Ability, Productivity, Word Complexity, and Readability. Each of these four raw scores is converted to a scaled score, and the resulting four scaled scores are summed to arrive at a composite Written Language Quotient. Percentile ranks are also derived from the scaled scores.

Technical Adequacy

Validity Confirmation

The authors say that there is support of *test item validity* because the content of the WLA (i.e., the tasks students are to perform) consists only of writing. In the WLA, writing is evaluated based exclusively on actual composition, just the way writing is evaluated in the world outside of school. The authors tell us that this is not a test with contrived tasks that isolate subskills of writing from composition.

Evidence of *test response validity* is given by correlating results of all subtests of the WLA with the three subtests of the Picture Story Language Test (PSLT), using number of words as the PSLT measure of productivity because it is directly comparable to the WLA Productivity score. The correlations are given in Figure 1.1.

Figure 1.1
WLA-PSLT Correlations (n = 158)

		WLA Scores		
PLST Scores	*GWA*	*Productivity*	*Word Complexity*	*Readability*
Words	.31	.77	.74	.42
Syntax Quotient	.16	.17	.17	.05
Abstract/Concrete Scale	.26	.50	.45	.33

Source: Manual, Table 9, p. 61.

Reliability Confirmation

No test-retest evidence for stability reliability is provided. Only internal consistency reliability support is given. Internal consistency reliability is a measure of how well a test or subtest measures one skill from beginning to end of the test or subtest (Manual, p. 54). Internal consistency correlation coefficients by age ranged from .53 to .91, with just four coefficients below .61. Those four coefficients were all in the Readability subtest.

Objectivity Confirmation

Detailed scoring criteria are not provided, nor are training requirements called for in the WLA Manual. Studies of inter-rater objectivity are presented and the results were given in percentages of exact and close agreements. The exact agreements ranged from 44% to 65%, and the close agreements ranged from 92% to 98%. However, the studies were conducted using as scorers graduate students identified as "trained in scoring the WLA and . . . experienced at the time of the studies" (Manual, p. 57). A more legitimate test of inter-rater objectivity would have been done with randomly selected teachers, school psychologists, and speech-language pathologists who were trained in scoring the WLA. Without training in the WLA or detailed scoring criteria, test users cannot be expected to provide more that unsupported judgment calls (Moran, 1992). Thus, inter-rater agreement is really meaningless.

Statistical Confirmation

Statistical data for validity, reliability, and norms is presented in the Manual.

Special Features

Acronym

WLA.

Levels of the Test

One.

Norm-Referenced?

Yes. The WLA was normed on 1,025 students in grades 3 through 12 who resided in upstate New York. The demographic characteristics considered in the sample were sex, race/ethnicity, residence, and school. The fact that 100% of the sample was from one geographic area and 94% of the sample was white indicates that the norming sample was not representative of the U.S. population of that age.

Criterion-Referenced?

The WLA seems to be referenced to writing skills, particularly composition.

Feasibility Considerations

Testing Time

Forty-five to 60 minutes.

For Testing Groups? Individuals?

Groups and individuals.

Test Administration and Scoring

Directions for administering the WLA are given clearly in the Manual, but no scoring criteria are provided and scoring instructions are minimal.

Test Materials and Approximate Costs

Complete kit, which includes Manual, 25 each of three Writing Record Forms, and

25 Scoring/Profile Forms: $80; Manual: $25; 25 each of three Writing Record Forms: $25; 25 Scoring/Profile Forms: $15; Hand counter: $15.

Adequacy of Test Manuals

The manual includes adequate administration instructions and minimal scoring instructions.

Excerpts from Other Test Reviews

The WLA was reviewed by Jurs (1992) and Moran (1992). Jurs says that "The Written Language Assessment is a new test that is limited by inadequate normative data and a lack of studies supporting its usefulness in a variety of applications. The WLA requires an actual written product, can be used comfortably in a classroom setting, and has straightforward scoring procedures. It has the potential to be an important component of a school testing program." Moran says that "the WLA represents a welcome effort to move writing evaluation in the direction of direct assessment of product, if not process. However, the attempt fails to yield a useful instrument because what is measured is not agreed by experts as representing important writing competencies, and the lack of specific criteria or anchor papers renders the scoring inappropriate even for experienced holistic raters, much less the untrained professional persons said to be the target users of the WLA."

Ordering Information

Publisher

Academic Therapy Publications, 20 Commercial Boulevard, Novato, CA 94949-6191; Phone: 800-422-7249; Fax: 888-287-9925; Web site: http://www.academic therapy.com.

Authors

J. Jeffrey Grill and Margaret M. Kirwin.

Publication Date

1989.

Cautions and Comments

The WLA would be useful for the classroom teacher to assess the writing composition skills of her students. However, because of the scoring limitations as well as weak validity, reliability, objectivity, and norming data, this reviewer would caution the user that its use as a standardized instrument for comparative purposes is severely limited.

References

Jurs, S. (1992). Review of the Written Language Assessment. In J. J. Kramer & J. C. Conoley (Eds.), *The Eleventh Mental Measurements Yearbook* [Electronic version]. Retrieved February 19, 2002 from Buros Institute's Test Reviews Online web site: http://www.unl. edu/buros.

Moran, M. (1992). Review of the Written Language Assessment. In J. J. Kramer & J. C. Conoley (Eds.), *The Eleventh Mental Measurements Yearbook* [Electronic version]. Retrieved February 19, 2002 from Buros Institute's Test Reviews Online web site: http://www.unl. edu/buros.

IV

Achievement Certification Testing and Decision-Making

INTRODUCTION

After instructional programs have been taught lesson by lesson, it is necessary to certify the achievement of the students in the program by administering achievement certification tests. Achievement certification tests summarize students' learning of the various lessons taught in one or more instructional programs. In that sense, achievement certification tests are comprehensive tests covering all of the knowledge and skills taught in the lessons of one or more instructional programs. Student performance on achievement certification tests is used to assign grades to students, promote them, or graduate them, as the case may be. Grade assignment decisions are made before promotion decisions, and promotion decisions are presumably based on assigned grades. Promotion decisions are made before graduation decisions, and graduations typically are conferred as a result of progressive promotions.

Achievement certification tests are also used to certify the effectiveness of schools, school administrators, and teachers in achieving the learning objectives they are responsible for achieving. Achievement certification tests are used in accountability testing to determine the rewards and sanctions to be issued as specified by outcome accountability regulations. It is no longer sufficient to judge administrators and teachers based only on the administrative and pedagogical practices they employ. They are also being held accountable for the achievement of the students in their charge.

Ideally, achievement certification tests are given after instructional programs are completed to assess the learning generated by the programs. And, ideally, the instructional programs provide all students with the instruction they need to pass the tests. However, this is seldom the case. There is no guarantee that the tests will not be given before teachers complete instructional programs. Time constraints are imposed. Grades are due at pre-set time intervals. Promotions occur at set times, as do graduations. This makes it possible for students to be given achievement certification tests before they complete the instructional programs the tests were designed to assess. Furthermore, although teachers may have completed instructional programs before corresponding achievement certification tests are given, there is no assurance that all students received all of the instruction they needed to pass the tests. It is not only possible, but also probable, that many students who fail achievement certification tests might have passed the tests if they had been given the extra instruction they needed during a grading period. So, time constraints and the amount of instruction teachers are able to provide during a grading period can affect students' performance on achievement certification tests. Too often achievement certification testing is considered separately from the instruction needed to pass the tests.

Achievement certification tests may be criterion-referenced, norm-referenced, or both. Criterion-referenced, or more precisely objective-referenced, achievement certification tests are used to certify the extent to which the objectives of instructional programs have been achieved. Norm-referenced achievement certification tests are used to certify the extent to which students are above or below average (when compared to peers who have taken the test). In either case, predetermined cutoff scores on a test are used to certify the extent to which students have learned the knowledge and skills in the instructional program(s) that have been taught in the past.

It is seldom made explicit that comparisons among students and groups of students can be made using objective-referenced tests as well as norm-referenced tests. Relative achievement of a learning objective can be assessed on an objective-referenced test using percentage of test items responded to correctly. It could then be said, when comparing students' performance on the test, that a student who answered 90% of the questions correctly achieved the learning objective to a greater extent than a student who answered 80% of the questions correctly, and so on. It is not an uncommon practice for test grades to be assigned on the basis of percentage of questions answered correctly. For example, "A" = 90% or more questions answered correctly, "B" = 80% to 89%, "C" = 70% to 79%, "D" = 60% to 69%, and "F" = below 60% of the test items answered correctly. In this case it can be said, for instance, that a school whose students earned on the average a "C" on the test achieved the learning objective pursued to a greater extent than a school whose students earned a "D," on the average. Since it is the purpose of schooling to engender the achievement of learning objectives, it would seem that objective-referenced tests are more appropriate than norm-referenced tests to assess and compare student achievement.

Most commercially available achievement certification tests to be reviewed are nationally standardized and norm-referenced. Some are also criterion-referenced. They attempt to sample and cover the objectives and subject matter common to the instructional programs in the United States. Before selecting a test, it is important to understand that it probably will not cover all of the objectives and subject matter included in the instructional programs of a local educational institution, as demonstrated in the User's Guide. Commercial tests may be sufficient to assess achievement of the learning objectives in an educational institution that correspond to the objectives assessed in the tests. For instance, it may be appropriate to compare performance of students in a school with students in other schools in the nation with respect to national common core curricula. However, the learning of other curricular offerings in a school will need to be assessed using other achievement certification tests.

Multi-Skill Academic Achievement Tests

Multi-skill academic achievement certification tests are designed to assess student achievement in several subject areas. Composite scores are used to certify overall level of achievement. Subtest scores may be derived for each subject area. They are used to profile levels of achievement in the various subject areas covered by the test, making it possible to show students' relative achievement in the subject areas (i.e., their highs and lows).

The multi-skill achievement tests reviewed in this part of the handbook are commercially developed and marketed. And it is profitable to expand the potential market by claiming that their tests have more rather than fewer advantages and applications. However, it is important to note that although claims may be made that their tests diagnose student weaknesses in subject areas, such claims must be qualified to be accurate. It may be true that most multi-skill tests' results can be used to profile relative highs and lows in students' achievement in the subjects covered by the test; it may also be acceptable to refer to the lows as weaknesses. However, it is an exaggeration to claim that the tests diagnose specific deficiencies as a basis for prescribing remedial instruction.

Diagnostic achievement tests include a number of test items to assess each skill and concept assessed by the tests so that error patterns can emerge and reveal deficiencies in learning the skills and concepts. Typically, commercial multi-skill achievement tests are designed to cover breadth of content and do not have a sufficient number of test items assessing specific skills and concepts to reliably reveal error patterns. As Salvia and Ysseldyke (2001) state in contrasting multi-skill achievement tests with diagnostic tests, "Diagnostic achievement tests have dense content. They have many more items to assess specific skills and concepts and allow finer analysis to pinpoint specific strengths and weaknesses in academic development. Tests with fewer items per skill allow comparisons to be made among test takers but do not have enough items to pinpoint students' strengths and weaknesses" (p. 384).

Instructional prescription tests are designed to diagnose academic deficiencies. Multi-skill achievement tests are not.

Some states develop their own achievement certification instruments. Commercially available tests can also be used instead of or in addition to state tests. Nationally normed commercial tests allow the performance in one state's schools to be compared to the performance of schools in other states. State-normed tests only allow comparisons to be made within a state.

Individual-Skill Academic Achievement Tests

Individual-skill academic achievement tests can probe in sufficient depth to enable the diagnosis of deficiencies in performing the skill and can also serve as achievement certification instruments. Tests or subtests that accurately yield age, grade, or mastery level of students' performance of a skill can be used to certify student level of achievement.

The following instructional prescription tests reviewed in Part III of the handbook can be considered for certifying level of achievement. Test reviews should be consulted before making a decision.

Multi-Skill Tests

Brigance Diagnostic Comprehensive Inventory of Basic Skills-Revised (CIBS-R)

Reading Tests

Early Reading Diagnostic Assessment (ERDA)

Gates-MacGinitie Reading Tests, Forms S & T (GMRT)

Gray Oral Reading Test, Fourth Edition (GORT-4)

Group Reading Assessment and Diagnostic Evaluation (GRADE)

Standardized Reading Inventory, Second Edition (SRI-2)

Stanford Diagnostic Reading Test, Fourth Edition (SDRT-4)

Test of Early Reading Ability, Third Edition (TERA-3)

Woodcock Reading Mastery Tests-Revised (WRMT-R)

Mathematics Tests

KeyMath Revised (KeyMath-R)

Stanford Diagnostic Mathematics Test, Fourth Edition (SDMT-4)

Tests of Early Mathematics Ability, Second Edition (TEMA-2)

Test of Mathematical Abilities, Second Edition (TOMA-2)

Spoken and Written Language Tests

Comprehensive Assessment of Spoken Language (CASL)

Comprehensive Receptive and Expressive Vocabulary Test (CREVT)

Comprehensive Test of Phonological Processing (CTOPP)

Test of Adolescent and Adult Language, Third Edition (TOAL-3)

Test for Auditory Comprehension of Language, Third Edition (TACL-3)

Test of Early Language Development, Third Edition (TELD-3)

Test of Early Written Language, Second Edition (TEWL-2)

Test of Handwriting Skills (THS)

Test of Language Development-Intermediate, Third Edition (TOLD-I:3)

Test of Language Development-Primary, Third Edition (TOLD-P:3)

Test of Written Language, Third Edition (TOWL-3)

Test of Written Spelling, Fourth Edition (TWS-4)

It is necessary to read the reviews of the instructional prescription tests to determine whether a test yields sufficient information for your purpose. If you are only interested in certifying achievement, then a test that provides age, grade, or mastery level of performance might serve your purpose. If all the diagnostic information you need to know is the extent to which students have mastered a skill, then any objective-referenced test that assesses the skill and indicates level of mastery may meet your needs. Keep in mind, however, that test results will only indicate the extent of students' deficiency in performing the skill, which in turn suggests the amount of re-teaching required. If you need additional diagnostic information, you will need to find a test that reveals deficiencies in subskill performance as well as deficiency in overall performance. With this information you will be able to provide corrective instruction to remediate each deficient subskill. Since tests that provide subskill scores as well as composite scores provide more diagnostic information, they are usually more useful.

Use the Characteristics Index and the Test Classification Index to identify tests that assess skills of interest to you. Then check the reviews to determine which tests provide the scores that enable you to make the decisions you need to make.

8

Multi-Skill Academic Achievement Tests

California Achievement Test, Fifth Edition (CAT/5),
for testing groups from kindergarten through grade 12
Reviewed by Myles I. Friedman, Ph.D., Educational Psychology

Usefulness of the Test for Educators

Test Authors' Purpose

The test battery is "designed to measure basic skills taught in schools throughout the nation" (Examiner's Manual).

Decision-Making Applications

The tests are most appropriate for making achievement certification decisions. They can also be used to obtain academic data to help make placement decisions. Scores are referenced to indicate degree of mastery of learning objectives in 12 subject areas. Low subtest scores reveal poor performance in a subject area. The test can be used as a screening device to locate relative strengths and weaknesses in subject areas. This academic data, along with other functional data, can be used to place students. However, the tests do not probe the subject areas in sufficient depth to diagnose specific learning difficulties that need to be remediated. Instructional prescription tests need to be used to identify error patterns. The kindergarten level of the test is considered to be a readiness rather than an achievement measure, so it may be useful in making grade school admission decisions.

Relevant Population

The tests cover grades K–12. There are 13 overlapping levels in the test battery: Level K, K.0–K.9; Level 10, K.6–1.6; Level 11, 1.6–2.2; Level 12, 1.6–3.2; Level 13, 2.6–4.2; Level 14, 3.6–5.2; Level 15, 4.6–6.2; Level 16, 5.6–7.2; Level 17, 6.6–8.2; Level 18, 7.6–9.2; Level 19, 8.6–10.2; Level 20, 9.6–11.2; Level 21/22, 10.6–12.9.

Characteristics Described

Following are the characteristics assessed by the subtests of the CAT/5 and the types of test items used in the assessments.

Visual recognition: Students are required to identify letters that are orally presented to distinguish upper and lower case forms of the letters, and to match letter groups.

Sound recognition: Students are required to recognize sounds in words spoken by the examiner. They must identify pictures of objects that have the same sounds as spoken words and that rhyme with spoken words.

Word analysis: Students are required to identify the meaning of unfamiliar words using structural clues.

Vocabulary: Students are required to exhibit their understanding of word meaning by identifying words that correspond to categories, synonyms, and antonyms. They also must use contextual clues to derive word meaning.

Comprehension: Students are required to derive meaning from written statements.

Spelling: Students must identify misspelled words in written sentences.

Language mechanics: Students are required to edit passages to exhibit their knowledge of punctuation and capitalization.

Language expression: Students exhibit skill in writing by showing that they can use parts of speech and form sentences correctly.

Mathematics computation: Students are required to solve addition, subtraction, multiplication, and division problems involving whole numbers, fractions, mixed numbers, decimals, and algebraic expressions.

Mathematics concepts and applications: Students are required to apply mathematical concepts pertaining to numeration, number sentences, number theory, problem solving, measurement, and geometry.

Supplementary Subject Areas

Study skills: Students are required to find and use information from books, libraries, dictionaries, and graphs.

Science: Students are required to show their understanding of scientific concepts and methods in various areas of science.

Social studies: Students are required to exhibit their understanding of geography, economics, history, political science, and sociology concepts.

Test Scores Obtained

Student achievement is described by the subtest scores of the CAT/5 in the following subject areas at each level of the test battery, as shown in Figure 1.1.

Figure 1.1
Subject Area Subtest Scores at Each Level of the CAT/5

Test	K	10	11	12	13	14	15	16	17	18	19	20	21/22
Visual Recognition	X												
Word Analysis (Sound Recognition at Level K)	X	X	X	X	X								
Vocabulary	X	X	X	X	X	X	X	X	X	X	X	X	X
Comprehension	X	X	X	X	X	X	X	X	X	X	X	X	X
Spelling			X	X	X	X	X	X	X	X	X	X	X
Language Mechanics			X	X	X	X	X	X	X	X	X	X	X
Language Expression			X	X	X	X	X	X	X	X	X	X	X
Mathematics Computation			X	X	X	X	X	X	X	X	X	X	X
Mathematics Concepts and Applications	X	X	X	X	X	X	X	X	X	X	X	X	X
Study Skills						X	X	X	X	X	X	X	X
Science			X	X	X	X	X	X	X	X	X	X	X
Social Studies			X	X	X	X	X	X	X	X	X	X	X
Test scores obtained	5	4	10	10	10	10	10	10	10	10	10	10	10 (119)

Source: Technical Bulletin 1. Reproduced with permission.

Technical Adequacy

Validity Confirmation

Both test item and test response validation procedures were used to validate the test battery. *Test item validity* was established for the tests as follows: Common curriculum subject matter and objectives were ascertained from an analysis of current curriculum guides, recently published textbooks, and instructional programs used in schools throughout the United States. Twice as many test items as would be needed were constructed to correspond to the objectives in each subject area at the required grade levels. Teachers and curriculum experts were used to approve the relevance of test items to the derived learning objectives. The original pool of test items was pilot tested, and test items that most closely matched item specifications were retained.

Test response validity was established by relating scores on the CAT/5 to scores on similar tests, such as the Comprehensive Test of Basic Skills (see Technical Bulletin 3 and the latest Technical Report.) In addition, scores on the tests were correlated with level of instruction and learning to see if there is a positive correlation, as hypothesized. Scores in each curriculum area covered by the tests increased with increased schooling.

Reliability Confirmation

Equivalent forms of the test, Batteries A and B, were given to students within a two-week interval. The correlations between the scores of the two forms were sufficiently high to confirm stability reliability. Total test score correlations of the two forms averaged .82. Other types of reliability confirmation are also provided.

Objectivity Confirmation

A scoring key is used to score the tests by hand or by machine. Most items are multiple choice, with at least four choice options. The performance assessment optional component uses a constructed response question format.

Statistical Confirmation

Statistical data on validity, reliability, and norms is available in the Technical Report for the CAT/5.

Special Features

Acronym

CAT/5.

Levels of the Test

Thirteen overlapping levels.

Number of Test Forms

Four: Forms A and B for both the complete and survey batteries.

Norm-Referenced?

Yes. The test battery was nationally normed and standardized. The national sample of schools was stratified as public, private, and Catholic. Public school samples were stratified on the basis of geographic region, community type (urban, rural, suburban), district size, and socioeconomic status. Approximately 100,000 scores from students in 360 schools were analyzed.

Criterion-Referenced?

Yes. The criteria used in the tests are learning objectives. School curricula were analyzed to derive learning objectives for each subject area to guide the construction of test items. To illustrate, the following objectives were derived for the visual recognition subject area.

Visual Recognition Objectives

1. Selecting upper and lower-case forms of letters presented orally
2. Matching upper-case and lower-case forms of letters
3. Matching letters in words
4. Matching identical letter groups

Three levels of mastery of each objective can be assessed in terms of test scores: (1) .00–.49, not mastered; (2) .50–.74, partially mastered; (3) .75–.99, mastered.

- Survey tests are available to obtain only norm-referenced information about students. They have fewer test items and take less time to administer than the complete battery. The survey tests are not to be used to make decisions about individual students.

- Locator tests are available to match students in the same grade with different levels of the test series.

- Thinking skill designations: Test items are developed in six categories to evoke thought processes of various types and complexity. The thinking skills categories are gathering information, organizing information, analyzing information, generating ideas, synthesizing elements, and evaluating outcomes.

- Practice tests are available for administration within two weeks of the administration of the complete test. They are recommended to help students develop their test-taking skills.

- Levels: 13 overlapping levels.

Feasibility Considerations

Testing Time (in minutes)

Level	K	10	11	12	13	14	15	16	17	18	19	20	21/22
Time	87	88	217	292	330	330	330	330	330	330	330	330	330

For Testing Groups? Individuals?

Groups.

Test Administration and Scoring

Tests can be machine scored. Testing directions are available for easy administration. No training or certification is needed to administer or score the tests.

Test Materials and Approximate Costs

Level	K	10	11	12	13	14 and above
30 practice tests	$8	$8	$8	$9	$9	$10
30 complete batteries	$50–85	$50–85	$60–95	$60–95	$60–95	$80
30 survey tests and scorable booklets	N/A	N/A	N/A	$85–95	$85–95	$80
Examiner's Manual (included with orders of 30 tests)	$9	$9	$9	$9	$9	$10

Adequacy of Test Manuals

The Examiner's Manuals are very helpful. They provide an overview of the tests and describe how to prepare for testing and how to administer and score the tests. A Class Management Guide, Administrator's Handbook, Test Coordinator's Handbook, and massive Technical Report are available for more detailed information.

Excerpts from Other Test Reviews

The CAT/5 has been reviewed by Salvia and Ysseldyke (2001), Nitko (1998), and McMorris (1998). Salvia and Ysseldyke express the following reservations about the test: "The information about standardization of the CAT/5 is incomplete. The complete battery appears to have sufficient reliability to support both educational decisions about groups of students and reports of data on group performance. The reliabilities of some subtests are too low for use in making decisions about individual students. Data on validity are very limited" (p. 391). Nitko concludes: "The CAT/5 continues the tradition of earlier editions of the California Achievement Tests by providing a technically solid achievement. . . . Educators should take the publishers' advice and not use the survey for serious decisions about individual students" (p.

155). McMorris states: "As Airasian (1989) observed in his review of the previous edition, the CAT has been a well respected test battery for over 50 years. The latest . . . represents an improvement on an already creditable test battery" (p. 156). "These supportive comments remain applicable with the CAT/5" (p. 160).

Ordering Information

Publisher

CTB/McGraw-Hill, 20 Ryan Ranch Road, Monterey, CA 93940-5703; Phone: 800-538-9547; Fax: 800-282-0266; Web site: www.ctb.com.

Authors

CTB/McGraw-Hill.

Publication Dates

1957–1993.

Cautions and Comments

Care needs to be taken in using scores on the CAT/5 to assess achievement of the learning objectives of a particular school. Since the CAT/5 is designed to assess learning objectives common to schools throughout the nation, it cannot be expected to assess achievement of all of the learning objectives of particular schools. Tests may need to be constructed to assess learning objectives established by particular schools and particular teachers. The tests are most appropriate for assessing basic skills achievement of students and comparing basic skills achievement among schools, school systems, and states. Other tests need to be used to assess achievement of other than basic skills objectives and to diagnose specific inadequacies in student achievement.

References

Airasian, P. W. (1989). Review of the California Achievement Tests, Forms E & F. In J. C. Conoley & J. J. Kramer (Eds.), *The Tenth Mental Measurements Yearbook* (pp. 126–128). Lincoln, NE: The Buros Institute of Mental Measurements.

McMorris, R. F. (1998). Review of the California Achievement Tests, Fifth Edition. In J. C. Impara & B. S. Plake (Eds.), *The Thirteenth Mental Measurements Yearbook* (pp. 156–160). Lincoln, NE: The Buros Institute of Mental Measurements.

Nitko, A. J. (1998). Review of the California Achievement Tests, Fifth Edition. In J. C. Impara & B. S. Plake (Eds.), *The Thirteenth Mental Measurements Yearbook* (pp. 153–156). Lincoln, NE: The Buros Institute of Mental Measurements.

Salvia, J., & Ysseldyke, J. E. (2001). *Assessment* (8th ed.). Boston: Houghton Mifflin.

General Educational Development Tests (GED), for testing groups
and individuals who are candidates for a high school equivalency diploma
Reviewed by Myles I. Friedman, Ph.D., Educational Psychology

Usefulness of the Test for Educators

Test Author's Purpose

"The GED tests are designed to provide an opportunity for adults who have not graduated from high school to earn a high school level diploma" (Technical Manual, p. 1).

Decision-Making Applications

The GED is designed primarily as an achievement certification test to certify that those who have passed the test have the equivalent of a high school education. It indirectly serves as an admission test as it opens the door to educational and employment opportunities that require a high school diploma. "The credential provided by passing the GED tests may be used in a manner identical to a high school diploma—to qualify for jobs and job promotions, for further education and training, and to enhance a candidate's personal satisfaction" (Technical Manual, p. 1). In addition, it can serve as an instructional prescription test. Test takers receive scores in five major subject areas. Should they fail the test and/or earn a low score in particular subject areas, they can plan to remediate their inadequacies. However, the scores provided do not reveal error patterns within a subject area. Diagnostic subject area tests must be administered for that purpose.

Relevant Population

Candidates for a high school equivalency diploma.

Characteristics Described

The GED assesses learning in five major subject areas:

Test 1: Writing skills, including capitalization, punctuation, spelling, possessives, contractions, sentence structure, word usage, and essay writing.

Test 2: Social Studies. Including history, geography, economics, political science, and behavioral science.

Test 3: Science, including biology, earth science, physics, and chemistry.

Test 4: Interpreting literature and the arts, including popular literature, classical literature, and commentary on the arts.

Test 5: Mathematics, entailing problem solving in arithmetic measurement, number relationships, data analysis, algebra, and geometry.

Test Scores Obtained

Test results for individuals are reported as standard scores for each of the five tests in the GED battery described above. In addition, percentile ranks are reported to examinees indicating the percent of high school seniors in the norming sample that scored below the examinee's standard score. Each state has its own minimum requirements for passing the test. Minimum score requirements may pertain to each test and/or the combined average of the five tests. The number of high school seniors able to meet minimum state requirements for the GED ranges from 51% to 75%.

Technical Adequacy

Validity Confirmation

Test item validity was achieved by first deriving test specifications. A Test Specifications Committee, consisting of recognized experts across educational disciplines, derived test specifications representing achievement of major high school learning objectives. Next, secondary school educators wrote and refined test items to meet the specifications. Items considered inappropriate by one or more reviewers were rewritten or discarded.

Test response validity was achieved by correlating GED standard scores in the five subject areas covered by the test and corresponding high school grades. The correlations ranged from .43 to .66. In addition, there was little difference in the performance of GED graduates and high school seniors on the GED tests, and ACT composite scores and average GED standard scores correlated .74. The ACT is a widely used college admission test. Finally, there was no significant difference in postsecondary educational achievement (e.g., GPA between GED and high school diploma recipients). Thus, performance on the GED tests appears to be related to several indicators of high school performance.

Reliability Confirmation

Reliability was confirmed by administering parallel forms of the test to the same individuals within a short span of time. The correlations ranged between .68 and .81 for the five subject area tests. When raw scores were correlated with each other in each of the five subject areas of the tests, the correlations (KR-20) ranged between .92 and .96, suggesting internal consistency among test items within tests.

Objectivity Confirmation

All but the essay tests are scored using a scoring key designating correct multiple-choice answers. They are scored by computer or by using a scoring stencil so there can be little inconsistency in scores obtained by different scorers. Performance on the essay portion of the writing skills test is scored using scoring criteria, which scorers must be trained to use. For scorers scoring the same set of essays, correlations in their scores ranged from .70 to .90.

Statistical Confirmation

Statistical confirmation of the validity and reliability of the GED tests is presented in the Technical Manual. Data on the norming sample is also provided in the manual.

Special Features

Acronym

GED.

Levels of the Test

One. The test is designed for adults who have not received a formal high school education.

Number of Test Forms

A U.S. English Anchor Form and two additional equated forms were developed initially in 1987. Since then other forms have been developed to be equivalent to the Anchor Form. Three other forms have been developed in addition to the U.S. forms: The English-Language Canadian GED, the French-Language Canadian GED, and the Spanish-Language GED tests.

Norm-Referenced?

Yes. The norm group for the 1987 sample of high schools was stratified as public and non-public schools and by geographic region and socioeconomic status to be representative of schools and students in the United States. The sample consisted of 557 schools. From 30 to 40 grade 12 students were sampled from each school.

Criterion-Referenced?

No. Although explicit criteria are not specified for the tests, the tests are designed to assess achievement of major high school learning objectives in five subject areas.

- The tests are designed to assess attainment of practical as well as academic skills. For instance, the mathematics tests require respondents to use math knowledge to solve practical problems. The interpreting of literature and the arts tests require respondents to comprehend and analyze literary selections and to apply interpretations to new contexts.
- Test items are developed to assess critical thinking at different cognitive levels: comprehension, application, analysis, synthesis, and evaluation.
- Study guides and preparation tests are available to help people pass the tests.
- Test-taking accommodations are made for disabled people and are available at

no extra charge. Special accommodations may be extended time, private testing, frequent breaks, and use of calculators.

- The GED tests are administered to more than 750,000 people each year at more than 27,000 sites across the United States. Testing sites and times are conveniently arranged.

- People interested in taking the GED can obtain a booklet orienting them to the test and application procedures.

- Local testing centers in cooperation with state agencies are responsible for administering the GED.

- Special editions of the GED are available, including Braille, audiocassette, and large print editions.

- Practice tests are available.

Feasibility Considerations

Testing Time

From 1 hour, 30 minutes to 1 hour, 50 minutes for each of the five tests in the GED battery. Typically, the battery is completed in a one-day session lasting from early morning until dinnertime, with a break for lunch. However, accommodations can be arranged for disabled examinees, and the entire battery does not need to be taken at one time.

For Testing Groups? Individuals?

Groups and individuals.

Test Administration and Scoring

The tests are scored by machine or by using a stencil, except for the essay portion of the writing skills test. Scorers of the essay test are trained to use specified scoring criteria to score the tests. An Examiner's Manual and Scoring Guide show how the tests are administered and scored. The GED Testing Service certifies scorers of the essay tests and centers where tests are scored. Scoring centers send official test results report forms to examinees. The Service also makes available a booklet describing GED Test Accommodations for Candidates with Specific Learning Disabilities (1992). Typically, there is no limit to the number of times the test can be taken.

Test Materials and Approximate Costs

Examinee's cost: Fees are approximately $40 per test administration, depending on the state or jurisdiction.

GED Preparation Guides that include sample test questions are available from several publishers ranging in cost from approximately $14 to $30. The names of some are "How to Prepare for the GED" (Barron's), "GED" (Kaplan), "GED Preparation Guide" (Arco), and "Cracking the GED" (Princeton).

Ordering Information

Publisher

General Education Development Testing Service of the American Council on Education.

Manuals and technical and general information are available from the General Education Development Testing Service, One Dupont Circle NW, Washington, DC 20036-1163; Phone: 202-939-9490; Fax: 202-775-8578; Web site: http://www.acenet.edu.

Adults interested in taking the test can obtain information pertaining to local testing sites and times as well as application procedures and fees from their state education agency.

Author

General Education Development Test Service.

Publication Dates

1944–1991.

Adequacy of Test Manuals

The test manuals are excellent. The Technical Manual provides validity, reliability, and norming data as well as information on the different forms of the GED. Standardized procedures for administering and scoring the test and interpreting test results are in the Examiner's Manual for the Tests of General Educational Development, GED Test Administration, Conducting Testing Sessions under Standard Conditions, and the GEDTS Scoring Guide.

Excerpts from Other Test Reviews

No reviews of the GED could be found subsequent to the publication of the First Edition of the GED Technical Manual in 1993. Reviewers of the GED prior to that time were not privy to all of the evidence in the Manual supporting the validity and reliability of the GED and noted the need for validation studies, for example, Michael S. Trevisan and Bruce G. Rogers (in Buros Test Reviews Online, http://frontiers.unl.educ/cgi-bin/buros-display.cgi).

Cautions and Comments

The GED testing program provides a valuable service by enabling adults without a formal high school education to obtain a high school diploma based on the education they have acquired informally. Many adults who for one reason or another did not finish high school can improve their job qualifications and earning power by passing the GED. It opens up opportunities for people who have fallen by the wayside and become social wards. The GED is technically sound. It assesses practical skills not always learned by attending high school classes that focus on academics. The test assesses higher-order thinking skills as well as practical problem solving. The GED is in need of updating. A new edition is scheduled for use early in 2003.

The Iowa Tests: Iowa Tests of Basic Skills (ITBS), for testing
groups from kindergarten through grade 9; **Iowa Tests of Educational
Development (ITED)**, for testing groups from grades 9 through 12
Reviewed by Myles I. Friedman, Ph.D., Educational Psychology

The nationally standardized achievement tests developed at the University of Iowa have changed formats over the years. The latest edition, published in 2001, is referred to as the Iowa Tests, consisting of the Iowa Tests of Basic Skills (ITBS), covering grades K–9, and the Iowa Tests of Educational Development (ITED), covering grades 9–12.

Usefulness of the Test for Educators

Test Authors' Purpose

The purpose of the ITBS is "to provide a comprehensive assessment of student progress in the basic skills." The purpose of the ITED is "to assess academic skills that represent the long-term goals of secondary education, particularly the critical thinking skills of analysis and evaluation" (Education Catalog 2001, Riverside Publishing Company).

Decision-Making Applications

The Iowa Tests are best suited for certifying achievement in several core subject areas (K–12). They are also suitable for profiling relative strengths and weaknesses in the subject areas. The tests do not probe particular subject areas in sufficient depth and breadth to diagnose inadequacies in need of remediation. Therefore, they are not suitable for making instructional prescription, placement, or referral decisions. After identifying poor performance areas, diagnostic tests need to be used to pinpoint shortcomings. Iowa Test data can be used to conduct research on achievement, for curriculum and administrative planning, and for reports to parents, school administrators, and school boards.

Relevant Population

The Iowa Tests are for elementary and secondary school students. The ITBS is for students in grades K–9 (test levels 5–15); the ITED is for students in grades 9–12 (test levels 15, 16, and 17/18).

Characteristics Described

The ITBS

Vocabulary: Students hear a word and are required to choose one of three pictorial options depicting the word.

Word analysis: Students are required to recognize letter and letter-sound relationships.

Listening: Students are required to show their understanding of short scenarios that are presented to them orally.

Language: Students are required to show their understanding of how language is used to express ideas. Skills measured include use of prepositions, singulars and plurals, and comparatives and superlatives.

Mathematics: Students are required to exhibit their understanding of numeration, geometry, measurement, and application of addition and subtraction in word problems.

Reading: Students are required to recognize words teachers read aloud, select printed words that describe a picture, and identify unfamiliar words using print, context, and picture clues.

Sample test items follow:

Vocabulary: The word is *skinny*. Fill in the circle under the picture of a cat that is skinny.

Word analysis: Fill the circle under the *a*.

Listening: After being read a story about dyeing eggs, students are required to "fill in the circle under Nina's favorite egg."

Language: The sandwiches are on the plate. Fill in the circle under the picture that shows the sandwiches are on the plate.

Mathematics: Count the watering cans. Fill in the circle under the number that tells how many watering cans there are.

Reading: The word is *rip*. Fill in the circle under the word rip.

(From Directions for Administration: Complete Battery)

The ITBS is available as a complete battery, a core battery (reading, language, and math tests only), and a survey battery, a shortened version of the core battery.

The ITED

Vocabulary: Students are asked to choose from among five words, phrases, or sentences the one closest in meaning to the tested word.

Reading comprehension: Students are required to demonstrate literal understanding and to make inferences, analyses, and generalizations about passages they read.

Language, revising written materials: Students are required to make revision choices pertaining to the focus, organization, clarity, sentence structure, usage, mechanics, and spelling of written material.

Spelling: Students are required to identify misspelled and correctly spelled words.

Mathematics concepts and problem-solving: Students are required to use basic arithmetic, measurement, data interpretation, logic, and thinking skills to solve practical problems.

Computation: Students are required to make computations pertaining to addition, subtraction, division, and multiplication of whole numbers, fractions, and percents. In addition, students are asked to manipulate variables and to evaluate expressions with exponents or square roots.

Analysis of social studies material: Students are required to answer questions in the fields of history, political science, psychology, sociology, anthropology, geography, and economics.

Analysis of science materials: Students are required to understand the scientific method and concepts in the fields of physics, chemistry, botany, zoology, health, medicine, and astronomy.

Sources of information: Students are required to understand and know how to use the resources of a well-equipped media center and supplemental sources of information, including private and public agencies.

The ITED is available in complete and shorter core battery forms. The core battery does not include the social studies, science, and sources of information subtests.

Sample questions follow:

Vocabulary:

Tepid water
a. Lukewarm
b. Impure
c. Foul-smelling
d. Stagnant
e. Sterile

Reading comprehension: After students read a passage describing how rings indicate the age of trees, they respond to the following test item.

Which rings represent a tree's most recent year's growth?
a. The widest rings
b. The narrowest rings
c. The outermost rings
d. The innermost rings

Language, revising written materials:

My friend is a terrible forgetful person. He managed to forget his algebra assignment three times last week.

My friend is *a terrible* forgetful person.

a. No change
b. An awful
c. A very
d. A real

Spelling: Circle the word that is misspelled or "No mistakes" if all words are spelled correctly.

a. Obay
b. Nickel
c. Loose
d. Deny
e. No mistakes

Mathematics concepts and problem solving:

A softball team won 16 of its first 28 games. Which of the following represents the number of games it lost?

a. 28 + 16
b. 28 – 16
c. 28 x 19
d. 28 divided by 16
e. 16 divided by 28

Computation:

32
+ 43

a. 11
b. 65
c. 75
d. 76
e. None of the above

Analysis of social studies materials:

A certain state is considering a sales tax on food items. From which of the following groups would this tax most likely create the greatest hardship?

a. Large families with low incomes
b. Large families with high incomes
c. Small families with low incomes
d. Small families with high incomes

Analysis of science materials: Students are shown a picture of a reading of 39.4° on a Celsius thermometer and asked to select the statement that indicates the correct reading.

a. 39.1° C
b. 39.2° C
c. 39.4° C
d. 39.6° C

Sources of information:

In which of the following sources could you most easily find the year in which Winston Churchill became the Prime Minister of England?

a. An encyclopedia
b. A news magazine
c. A periodical guide
d. A computerized card catalog

Source: Directions for Administration, ITED.

A different subtest is used to test for knowledge and skills in each of the above subject areas.

Test Scores Obtained

Raw scores, developmental standard scores, grade equivalents, national percentile ranks, normal curve equivalents, and national stanines can be obtained for the ITBS and the ITED. The tests can be hand scored or machine scored. Scoring keys are available for hand scoring the tests. The Interpretive Guide for Teachers and Counselors explains what the different types of scores mean, what the various student and class reports look like, how to interpret scores to others, and how to use the scores for instructional purposes. A Norms and Score Conversion Booklet contains norm tables for converting scores. Subject area subtest scores can be obtained for each level of the ITBS and the ITED.

Technical Adequacy

Data used to assess the validity and reliability of the Iowa Tests was collected in 2000.

Validity Confirmation

Test item validity is well supported by the procedures used to construct and select test items. Textbooks, standards of national curriculum groups, and recommendations of subject matter specialists were used to derive specifications for developing test items to be congruent with curricula commonly taught in American schools. Once potential test items were constructed, they were culled and refined based on analysis of tryout results and review by a diverse group for fairness and curriculum relevance. So, there is assurance that test items correspond to and assess the learning of common curriculum content of American schools.

Evidence of *test response validity* is lacking. No evidence was provided that Iowa Tests scores correlate with external criteria of achievement (e.g., student progress in school, student rank in class, or scores on validated nationally normed standardized achievement tests developed by other publishers). Nor was it established that test item responses represent curriculum constructs commonly taught in U.S. schools (i.e., construct validity).

Reliability Confirmation

The reliability of the Iowa Tests was estimated by correlating test items within tests with one another (KR-20) to assess internal consistency. Reliability correlations for raw scores on the ITBS Complete Battery subtests ranged from .65 to .92. Most reliability correlations are adequate. The tests at higher grade levels tend to have greater internal consistency. Some subject area subtest reliabilities below the third grade are weak (i.e., lower than .70)—for example, vocabulary and reading comprehension at the kindergarten level, listening at the first grade level, and social studies at the second grade level. These reliabilities are marginal at best for making decisions about individual students.

The reliabilities for the subtest raw scores of the ITED are all adequate, ranging from .85 to .92.

No reliability evidence is presented confirming the stability of test results over time for either the ITBS or the ITED. The tests were not administered more than once over time to assess test-retest reliability. Since only a Form A was developed for both tests, alternate form reliability could not be checked.

Objectivity Confirmation

Variations among scores assigned to the same responses by different scorers are highly unlikely. Scoring keys are used to score all test items by machine or by hand, and the test response format for all items is multiple choice.

Special Features

Acronym

The acronym for the Iowa Tests of Basic Skills is ITBS; the acronym for the Iowa Tests of Educational Development is ITED.

Levels of the Test

There are 14 levels of the Iowa Tests. There are 10 levels of the ITBS (5–14) and 4 levels of the ITED (15, 16, 17/18).

Number of Test Forms

One form of the ITBS, Form A and one form of the ITED, Form A. Form B is being developed.

Norm-Referenced?

Yes. The ITBS and the ITED were nationally normed and standardized in 2000. The norm sample was stratified by district size, region of the country, socioeconomic status, ethnicity, and type of school (public, Catholic, and private non-Catholic). The total sample seems adequate. Approximately 170,000 schools were sampled for the ITBS, 37,000 schools for the ITED.

Criterion-Referenced?

Yes. Although the ITBS and ITED tests are not constructed to assess achievement of specified learning objectives, they can be used as criterion-referenced tests if the criteria of interest is progress in subject areas covered by the tests. Test results can be used to measure progress.

- Practice tests are available.
- Braille editions are available.
- Interest Explorer is a companion instrument available to aid educational and career planning for students above grade 7.
- A Primary Reading Profile is available profiling developmental reading skill in grades K–3.
- An Iowa Early Learning Inventory is available for teachers to rate their students.
- Parents Summary Reports are available.
- Assessment Data Reporting Services are available for providing information on student performance.
- Scoring service is available.
- Thinking skills, such as analysis and evaluation, are tested.
- All test items are multiple choice.
- Reports are prepared comparing test performance with school district or state standards.

Feasibility Considerations

Testing Time

The ITED testing time for the complete battery is 260 minutes. The core battery testing time is 160 minutes. Subtest times range between 15 and 40 minutes.

The ITBS testing time for the complete battery is, on the average, less than three hours. The testing time for the survey battery is 90 minutes. Testing times for each test range from 20 to 30 minutes.

For Testing Groups? Individuals?

Groups.

Test Administration and Scoring

Tests can be hand or machine scored. Scoring keys and masks are available to facilitate hand scoring. Machine scoring services are provided by the publisher with an advertised turnaround time of five days. Directions for administering the tests are clear, detailed, and comprehensive. They include suggested accommodations and modifications for disabled and hard-to-test students. Some guidance and practice in administering the tests would be helpful but not necessary for educators who have test administration experience. Educators not familiar with interpreting results of standardized achievement tests and various reports that are designed for educators and parents would benefit from reading the Interpretive Guides and may need instruction. Extended training and certification are not needed to administer, score, and interpret the tests.

Test Materials and Approximate Costs

	ITBS	ITED
Practice test materials	$14.50–$21	$14.50–$21
Administration directions	$3.50–$13	$3.50–$13
Message to Parents (guide)	$22	$22
25 Test booklets: machine scored*	$104	$91–$101
25 Test booklets: reusable*	$91–$101	$91–$101
50 Answer forms*	$32.50–$40.50	$40.50
Scoring keys*	$25–$27.50	$25
Scoring masks*	$43.50–$51.50	$51.50
Record forms	$6–$10	$6–$10
Interpretive guides	$16.50–$26	$16.50–$26
Technical manuals**	$21.50–$26.50	$21.50–$26
Braille edition	$101–$121.50	$121.50
Large print edition	$43–$61.50	$61.50

* Core, survey, and complete battery prices differ.
** Technical data is in more than one manual.

Adequacy of Test Manuals

Manuals that contain directions for test administration, scoring, and interpretation are clear and complete. Directions for Administration booklets provide guidance for administering the tests. The Interpretive Guide for Teachers and Counselors and the Interpretive Guide for School Administrators provide guidelines for interpreting the data and reports. Technical data on norms, validity, reliability, and objectivity can be found in more than one manual: Interpretive Guides, Norms and Score Conversions Booklets, and Content Classifications with Spring Item Norms Booklets. Some technical data, usually presented in technical manuals, is absent, and discussions of data topics are fragmented and incomplete. Scoring Key Booklets clearly show scorers how to score tests and convert and record scores.

Excerpts from Other Test Reviews

Since the latest update of the Iowa Tests was published in 2001 and this review was written in 2001, other reviews of the tests were not published as yet. The previous renditions of the two tests were published in 1996. The following reviews pertain to the rendition published in 1996.

Salvia and Ysseldyke's (2001) review pertains, in general, to the ITBS, ITED, and Tests of Achievement and Proficiency (TAP), all products of the University of Iowa at that time. Since then the TAP has been discontinued. "Development and standardization of the tests appear exemplary. . . . There are no data on the long-term stability (test-retest reliability) of either the ITBS, the TAP, or the ITED. . . . There are no data on either the construct validity, or the criterion-related validity (in our terms, manifestations of test response validity) of the ITBS, TAP, or ITED" (p. 398). Mehrens (1998) states, in reviewing the ITED, "The ITED and related materials are an excellent integrated assessment system. The measures have high technical quality and the various user's guides are well done and should prove very useful to school personnel, parents, and students." Subkoviak (1998) concludes that "the ITED is one of the best alternatives available for testing high school achievement." Cross (1998), in reviewing the ITBS, stated, "No information was found in the review materials regarding the validity of the listening tests, the new integrated language tests, the writing assessments, or the constructed response tests in reading or mathematics. Moreover, evidence to support criterion-related validity was limited to a few older studies." Brookhart (1998) states, "The ITBS is one of the oldest and the best in the business . . . it is reliable enough to use for both individual and group judgments."

Ordering Information

Publisher

Riverside Publishing Company, 425 Spring Lake Drive, Itasca, IL 60143-2079; Phone: 800-323-9540; Fax: 630-467-7192; Web site: www.riverpub.com.

Authors

ITBS authors are H. D. Hoover, S. B. Dunbar, and D. A. Frisbie; ITED authors are R. A. Forsyth, T. N. Ansley, L. S. Feldt, and S. D. Alnot.

Publication Date

2001.

Cautions and Comments

Standardized achievement tests have been constructed by faculty at the University of Iowa since the early 1900s, incorporating many seminal contributions. They have been meticulous in norming their tests and ensuring that many standards of technical adequacy have been met. The Iowa Tests are technically adequate with respect to test item validity, which is essential for academic achievement tests. The test items cover the common curriculum content taught in the United States through high school. Their norming sample appears to be representative of U.S. students, and the internal consistency of test items supports that aspect of test reliability. However, support is lacking for other aspects of validity and reliability. Evidence showing that the tests are reliable over time is missing. Test-retest reliability evidence and equivalent form reliability evidence are absent. However, plans have been made to develop a second form of the Iowa Tests in the near future, after which equivalent form reliability can be checked. In addition, test response validation is lacking. Some evidence is provided showing that Iowa Tests scores correlate with scores of other tests of the publisher. But Iowa Tests scores were not correlated with scores of other publishers' validated nationally standardized multi-skill achievement tests. Also, correlations were not calculated between Iowa Tests scores and indices of advancement in school, nor with other external criteria of achievement, such as student grades or rank in class. The new Iowa Tests are to some extent a work in progress. New technical manuals are planned when the second forms of the tests are available. By that time, presumably evidence of validity and reliability presently lacking will be provided.

References

Brookhart, S. M. (1998). Review of the Iowa Tests of Basic Skills, Forms K, L, and M. In J. C. Impara & B. S. Plake (Eds.), *The Thirteenth Mental Measurements Yearbook* (pp. 539–542). Lincoln, NE: The Buros Institute of Mental Measurements.

Cross, L. H. (1998). Review of the Iowa Tests of Basic Skills, Forms K, L, and M. In J. C. Impara & B. S. Plake (Eds.), *The Thirteenth Mental Measurements Yearbook* (pp. 543–546). Lincoln, NE: The Buros Institute of Mental Measurements.

Mehrens, W. A. (1998). Review of the Iowa Tests of Educational Development, Forms K, L, and M. In J. C. Impara & B. S. Plake (Eds.), *The Thirteenth Mental Measurements Yearbook* (pp. 547–552). Lincoln, NE: The Buros Institute of Mental Measurements.

Salvia, J., & Ysseldyke, J. E. (2001). *Assessment* (8th ed.). Boston: Houghton Mifflin.

Subkoviak, M. J. (1998). Review of the Iowa Tests of Educational Development. In J. C. Impara & B. S. Plake (Eds.), *The Thirteenth Mental Measurements Yearbook* (pp. 550–552). Lincoln, NE: The Buros Institute of Mental Measurements.

Kaufman Test of Educational Achievement-Normative Update
(K-TEA-NU), for testing individuals from 6 through 22 years of age
Reviewed by Myles I. Friedman, Ph.D., Educational Psychology

The Kaufman Test of Educational Achievement (K-TEA) was first published in 1985. A normative update (K-TEA-NU) was published in 1998. There are comprehensive and brief forms of the test. Both will be reviewed.

Usefulness of the Test for Educators

Test Authors' Purpose

Although, in general, the purpose of both tests is to assess academic achievement in math, reading, and spelling, the purpose of the two tests differs. The purpose of the

Brief Form is the "screening of student achievement skills to determine the need for follow-up testing and evaluation" (Test Manual). The Comprehensive Form "provides an analysis of a child's strengths and weaknesses . . . to identify possible skill areas needing remediation or enrichment" (Test Manual).

Decision-Making Applications

The tests are most appropriate for assessing level of achievement in math, reading, and spelling. Although the Brief and Comprehensive forms of the test can be used to determine whether or not students need to be referred for further testing, the Brief Form serves the purpose more efficiently because it can be administered in half the time. The Comprehensive Form is more suitable for profiling strengths and weaknesses and making placement decisions. The Brief Form does not test the various types of errors a student can make in sufficient depth to diagnose the particular misconceptions that require remediation. The Comprehensive Form can diagnose some error patterns. However, diagnostic subject area tests are better suited for making instructional prescription decisions. Both tests can be used for research and program evaluation, depending on the purpose of the research or evaluation.

Relevant Population

Both forms of the K-TEA-NU are appropriate for assessing the academic achievement of students in grades 1 through 12 (ages 6–22).

Characteristics Described

Comprehensive Form

The Comprehensive Form of the test assesses five characteristics as follows:

1. Reading Decoding: Students are required to identify letters and then words.
2. Reading Comprehension: Students are required to respond appropriately to commands given in printed sentences. Students must also answer questions about passages they read.
3. Mathematics Applications: Students are required to use mathematical knowledge to solve mundane problems that are read to them.
4. Mathematics Computation: Students are required to solve problems involving basic operations, exponents, symbols, abbreviations, and algebraic equations.
5. Spelling: Students are required to spell words after the words are read to them and used in a sentence.

Brief Form

The Brief Form assesses the following three characteristics:

1. Reading: Test items are similar to the Reading Decoding and Reading Comprehension items in the Comprehensive Form, but there are fewer of them.

2. Mathematics: Test items are similar to the Mathematics Applications and Mathematics Computation items in the Comprehensive Form, but fewer in number.

3. Spelling: Test items are similar to the spelling items in the Comprehensive Form, but fewer in number.

The items in the Brief Form are not the same as the items in the Comprehensive Form. Test items in each unit are sequences from easy to difficult.

Test Scores Obtained

In addition to raw scores, standard scores, percentile ranks, stanines, normal-curve equivalents, age equivalents, and grade equivalents are derived. An error analysis can be conducted for each subtest of the Comprehensive Form. The number of errors made by a student can be compared to the number made by students in the norm sample.

Technical Adequacy

Validity Confirmation

Test item validity was established initially for the K-TEA by constructing test items to assess each of the characteristics that were defined. Expert judgment was used to ensure that the test items retained assess the characteristics they were constructed to assess. Textbooks were used to identify appropriate characteristics to assess and to guide the construction of test items to assess the characteristics.

Test response validity was established by correlating scores on the K-TEA with scores of other multi-skill achievement tests. Comprehensive Form scores were correlated with scores of both individually administered and group administered achievement tests. The results are as follows:

Standard Score Correlation Ranges for the Comprehensive Form and Other Achievement Tests at Various Ages

Individually Administered Tests	*K-TEA*
Wide-Range Achievement Test (WRAT)	.45–.86
Peabody Individual Achievement Test (PIAT)	.65–.86
Kaufman Assessment Battery for Children (K-ABC)	.28–.86
Peabody Picture Vocabulary Test-Revised (PPVT-R)	.47–.70
Group Administered Tests	
Stanford Achievement Test (SAT)	.77–.85
Metropolitan Achievement Test (MAT)	.67–.80
Comprehensive Tests of Basic Skills (CTBS)	.79–.90

Brief Form scores were correlated with scores of other individually administered achievement tests. The results are as follows:

Standard Score Correlation Ranges for the Brief Form and Other Individually Administered Achievement Tests

	K-TEA
WRAT	.35–.85
PIAT	.63–.84
K-ABC	.22–.90
PPVT-R	.35–.59

Reliability Confirmation

Each form was administered twice to the same populations with a short internal between testings. The test/retest reliability correlations for the Comprehensive Form ranged from .83 to .97. Test/retest correlations for the Brief Form ranged from .84 to .94. In addition, the Brief Form and Comprehensive Form were both administered to the same population with short intervals between administrations. Reliability correlations between scores of the two forms ranged from .87 to .97. Reliability was also estimated by correlating responses to half of the test items with responses to the other half of the test items. Reliability correlations for the Brief Form ranged, across grades, from .89 to .98. For the Comprehensive Form, reliability correlations ranged, across grades, from .83 to .97.

Objectivity Confirmation

Scoring keys are used to score all items of the test. The correct answer for each item is unambiguously specified on the examiner's side of the plates bound in an easel-kit used to test students, so agreement among the scores of different scorers scoring the same test responses should be consistent. Multiple answers to the same question can introduce ambiguity and scoring problems for the examiner. However, the Test Manual tells the examiners how to deal with multiple responses.

Statistical Confirmation

Statistical data on validity, reliability, and norms can be found in the Test Manual.

Special Features

Acronym

K-TEA-NU.

Levels of the Test

One for both the Brief Form and the Comprehensive Form.

Number of Test Forms

Two: the Brief Form and the Comprehensive Form.

Norm-Referenced?

Yes. The tests were normed in 1983–1985 and renormed in 1995–1996. Sampling was based on U.S. Census Bureau data. The sample was stratified by grade, sex, geographic region, parents' education level, and race or ethnicity. The size of the normative update sample was 3,184 students in grades K–12. However, the sample was used to norm other tests as well. Only one-fifth of the students took each test. The norm groups for the Brief and Comprehensive Forms were approximately 600 students, less than 100 students at certain grade levels.

Criterion-Referenced?

No. Although the tests are not designed to assess achievement of particular curriculum objectives, error analysis results on the Comprehensive Form can be used to identify weaknesses in the learning of skills. For example, errors on the Mathematical Computation subtest could suggest difficulty in learning how to add and/or subtract. At least it could indicate whether further in-depth diagnostic testing is needed in particular subject areas.

- Computer software packages are available to generate scores.
- Report to Parents Forms are available in English and Spanish.

Feasibility Considerations

Testing Time

Brief Form: 30 minutes; Comprehensive Form: 60–75 minutes.

For Testing Groups? Individuals?

Individuals.

Test Administration and Scoring

The authors claim that "with careful study of the test manual and test materials, an educator or paraprofessional should be able to master the information necessary to validly test subjects with the K-TEA" (Test Manual). Additionally, experience interpreting norm-referenced test scores (e.g., standard scores, grade equivalents, and stanines) is helpful. Since there is only one level of the test, examiners must learn how to identify starting points and stopping points for students. Starting points are designated for each level. Testing is stopped when students fail every item of a unit of a subtest. Items in units are sequenced from easy to difficult.

Test Materials and Approximate Costs

Brief Form: The cost of the complete special edition kit is $109.95. It includes 77 test plates on an easel, 25 record booklets, a sample Report to Parents form, wipeable test plates, carry bag, and a 269-page Test Manual. The regular edition costs $94.95. It includes all materials in the special edition except wipeable test plates. Separately, 25 record booklets cost $26.95. Twenty-five Report to Parents forms cost $19.95, and the Test Manual costs $31.95.

Comprehensive Form: The cost of the complete special edition kit is $184.95. It includes 133 test plates bound in an easel, 25 record booklets with error analysis formats, a sample Report to Parents form, wipeable test plates, a carry bag, and 569-page Test Manual. Regular edition kits cost $159.95, including all materials in the special edition except wipeable test plates. Separately, 25 record booklets cost $34.94; 25 Report to Parents forms cost $21.95; Test Manuals cost $52.95. An IBM or Macintosh software package costs $149.95. To run DOS/Windows on Macintosh, the software package costs $189.

Adequacy of Test Manuals

The Test Manual provides sufficient test adequacy data and clear instructions for administering and scoring the tests.

Excerpts from Other Test Reviews

Citations from reviews of the K-TEA-NU in 2001 offer the following assessments.

"Authors should have conducted a few validity and reliability studies on students in the late 1990's. All data on validity and reliability of the K-TEA-NU are for the original K-TEA. The performance of students on the two measures has changed" (Salvia & Ysseldyke, 2001).

"For users desiring an appraisal of student achievement in mathematics and reading it is difficult to imagine a context where the K-TEA can be recommended over more current assessment tools, even group achievement instruments" (Poggio, 2001).

"The development and psychometric characteristics of the Kaufman Test of Educational Achievement place the battery among the best available. However, the need for an individually administered achievement test, particularly at older ages (and grades) is not clear" (Schafer, 2001).

In *A Consumer's Guide to Tests in Print* (Hammill, Brown, & Bryant, 1992), the Comprehensive Form of the original K-TEA was rated "A" or "Highly Recommended" overall. On the other hand, the Brief Form is rated "F" or Unacceptable" overall, even though validity and reliability subratings were at the "A" and "B" level.

Ordering Information

Publisher

American Guidance Service, Inc., 4201 Woodland Road, Circle Pines, MN 55014-1796; Phone: 800-328-2560; Fax: 800-471-8457; e-mail: agsmail@agsnet; Web site: www.agsnet.com.

Authors

Alan S. Kaufman and Nadeen L. Kaufman.

Publication Dates

K-TEA, 1985; K-TEA-NU, 1992.

Cautions and Comments

In the Test Manual for the K-TEA-NU, the authors caution that about 12 years elapsed between the times data was collected for the K-TEA and the normative update. "Changes during that time in curriculum and educational practice, in population demographics, and in the general educational environment may have affected levels of academic achievement" (p. 257). In addition, the authors note the extent to which subtest scores vary in the 12 years. The variations indicate the need for more current validity and reliability data. Interpretations of results of multi-skill achievement tests that provide more recent validity and reliability confirmation would be more defensible, including multi-skill group achievement tests. Still, evidence confirming the validity and reliability of the original K-TEA is substantial and the normative update is helpful. Both forms are easy to administer and score. The Brief Form can be administered in 30 minutes to determine whether students need to be referred for further diagnostic testing. Analysis of subtest error patterns on the Comprehensive Form can be useful in identifying skill deficiencies in need of instructional remediation.

References

Hammill, D. D., Brown, L., & Bryant, B. R. (1992). *A consumer's guide to tests in print* (2nd ed). Austin, TX: PRO-ED.

Poggio, J. (2001). Review of the K-TEA-NU. In B. S. Plake & J. C. Impara (Eds.), *The Fourteenth Mental Measurements Yearbook* (pp. 629–630). Lincoln, NE: The Buros Institute of Mental Measurements.

Salvia, J., & Ysseldyke, J. E. (2001). *Assessment* (8th ed.). Boston: Houghton Mifflin.

Shafer, W. D. (2001). Review of the K-TEA-NU. In B. S. Plake and J. C. Impara (Eds.), *The Fourteenth Mental Measurements Yearbook* (pp. 630–632). Lincoln, NE: The Buros Institute of Mental Measurements.

Metropolitan Achievement Tests, 8th Edition (MAT-8),
for testing groups from kindergarten through grade 12
Reviewed by Myles I. Friedman, Ph.D., Educational Psychology

Usefulness of the Test for Educators

Test Authors' Purpose

"Metropolitan 8 is designed to assess the content areas of reading, language arts, mathematics, science, and social studies at every level where the content is appropriate. . . . The revised test configuration offers increased flexibility for designing school assessment programs" (Technical Manual, p. 7).

Decision-Making Applications

The MAT-8 is most appropriate for certifying achievement levels in reading, writing, spelling, math, science, and social studies and for profiling relative levels of achievement in those subject areas. It can also be used to help place students at the appropriate grade level. Some test scores are referenced to show degree of mastery of learning objectives. This data, along with other functional data, can be used in making placement decisions. However, the MAT-8 does not probe each subject area it covers in sufficient depth and breadth to pinpoint specific deficiencies in need of remediation. Instructional prescription tests need to be used to diagnose academic deficiencies. Referral tests need to be used to diagnose possible underlying causes of failure to learn.

Relevant Population

The battery covers grades K–12.

Characteristics Described

Reading

Emergent literacy: The test documents students' progress in phonemic awareness, concepts of print, letter recognition, word recognition, and sentence reading.

Reading comprehension: Students are required to identify detail, cause-effect, and main ideas in the passages they read as well as make inferences and analyze characters. Open-ended questions require students to convey their understanding of, indicate relationships in, and critically analyze reading passages.

Mathematics

Arithmetic operations: Students must select an appropriate operation and perform the computation indicated.

Concepts and problem solving: Students are required to apply mathematics concepts to solve problems in the following areas: (1) numbers and operations; (2)

patterns, relationships, and algebra; (3) geometry and measurement; and (4) data, statistics, and probability. Open-ended math questions assess students' ability to communicate, reason, and solve problems mathematically.

Language (Writing Process)

Prewriting skills: Students are tested on their ability to use resources, plan, and organize their writing.

Composing skills: Students are tested on their ability to write clear, concise, purposeful compositions.

Editing skills: Students are required to detect errors in language usage and mechanics in passages they read.

Spelling: Students are required to identify misspelled and correctly spelled words in sentences.

Writing

Students are required to compose written responses to picture prompts.

Science

Students are required to show understanding of basic concepts and processes in zoology, meteorology, physiology, biology, physical science, earth and space science, physics, and chemistry.

Social Studies

Students are required to show understanding of basic concepts and processes in political science, economics, history, geography, and sociology.

Test Scores Obtained

In addition to raw scores, the following derived scores may be obtained: scaled scores, percentile ranks, stanines, normal curve equivalents, grade equivalents, content cluster, category scores, p-values, performance indicators, and performance standards. Performance indicators are content-referenced scores that describe achievement on the open-ended assessments; performance standards are criterion-referenced scores that represent level of mastery based on the judgment of teachers. Four levels of mastery are distinguished: (1) below basic, (2) basic, (3) proficient, and (4) advanced. The MAT-8 may be hand scored or sent to the publisher to be machine scored.

Technical Adequacy

Validity Confirmation

Test item validity was established by developing test specifications to represent common curriculum content taught in schools in the United States. Textbooks, state curricula and educational objectives, and input from national professional organizations were used to derive test specifications. Then test items were constructed and selected to match the specifications. An advisory panel and statistical procedure were used to reduce bias in the selection of test items.

Test response validity was established by showing that achievement scores on the MAT-8 increase as students progress through school. Evidence is provided indicating that the tests are more difficult for students in lower grades and easier for students in higher grades, and that there is growth from year to year. No evidence is provided that MAT-8 scores correlate with scores on other multi-skill academic achievement tests. Evidence is offered that MAT-8 scores correlate with scores on the Otis-Lennon School Ability Test (OLSAT). However, the OLSAT is marketed as an ability test, not an achievement test.

Reliability Confirmation

Test item results were correlated with one another to ascertain the internal consistency of the test items. Derived reliability correlations obtained (on the spring standardization sample) for the full-length battery ranged (by grade) as follows: K: .77–.90; 1: .75–.97; 2: .72–.96; 3: .80–.95; 4: .83–.97; 5: .82–.97; 6: .81–.96; 7: .76–.97; 8: .79–.96; 9: .80–.97; 10: .80–.97; 11: .83–.97; 12: .84–.97.

No reliability evidence was provided showing stability of test scores over time.

Objectivity Confirmation

Consistency among scorers can be expected for the multiple-choice items on the tests because the scoring keys used eliminate the need for scorer judgment. On the other hand, open-ended questions requiring examinee-constructed responses do require scorers to judge the extent to which student responses meet scoring criteria. Scorer training is most often needed to achieve consistency among scorers before they are allowed to score open-ended test items, and correlations among scores of different scorers scoring the same test items are obtained to assess scorer consistency. No such correlations were provided.

Statistical Confirmation

Statistical data on validity, reliability, and norms is available in the MAT-8 Technical Manual and Norms Books.

Special Features

Acronym

MAT-8.

Levels of the Test

Thirteen: kindergarten through grade 12.

Number of Test Forms

Three: a full-length battery, a short form, and an online version that allows tests to be administered and scored by computer are available.

- Practice tests are available.

- Lexile measures can be used in reading to relate student reading level to appropriate reading material. The student Reading Pathfinder Report provides a book list appropriate to students' reading level.

- Achievement/ability comparisons can be made relating MAT-8 scores to scores on the Otis-Lennon School Ability Test (OLSAT).

- Pathway to Progress Reports are available in reading, math, language, and social studies to indicate tasks students can perform at various levels of achievement.

- Customized inclusion and organization of subtests is available.

- Reports are available on individual students and classes tailored for different audiences, such as administrators or parents.

- Compendium of Instructional Objectives describing MAT-8 instructional objectives is available.

- Understanding Test Results is published for parents and older students to help them interpret test performance.

- Guide for Classroom Planning is available to help teachers interpret and use test scores in their work.

- Guide for Organizational Planning is available for administrators.

- Strategies for Instruction is available to help teachers plan instruction.

- Various thinking skills are assessed in the MAT-8.

Norm-Referenced?

Yes. The MAT-8 was nationally normed and standardized using about 80,000 students from 151 school districts. A proportional random stratified sample was drawn based on data obtained from the *Census of Population and Housing* (1990, 1995) and the National Center for Education Statistics (1997–1998). The stratification variables included geographic region, socioeconomic status, urban-suburban-rural, ethnicity, type of disability, and Catholic and private non-public schools.

Criterion-Referenced?

Yes. Compendium of Instructional Objectives describes the instructional objectives the MAT-8 is structured to assess. Performance standards reported indicate one of four levels of mastery of objectives: (1) below basic, (2) basic, (3) proficient, and (4) advanced.

Feasibility Considerations

Testing Time

Estimated times are offered as guidelines rather than fixed times. Estimated times for the full battery range from 90 to 328 minutes, depending on grade level. Estimated times for the short form range from 30 to 50 minutes. Estimated times for individual subtests range from 20 to 50 minutes.

For Testing Groups? Individuals?

Groups.

Test Administration and Scoring

Tests can be hand or machine scored. No training is needed to administer or score the multiple-choice tests. Training is needed for scoring student-constructed response items because scorer judgment must be used to determine the correctness of responses. No evidence is provided that those scoring constructed responses for the publisher are trained and certified.

Test Materials and Approximate Costs

Response Key: $31.50; Norms books: $60–$86; Compendium of Instructional Objectives: $40; Understanding Test Results booklet: $25; Guide for Classroom Planning booklet: $25; Guide for Organizational Planning booklet: $34; Strategies for Instruction handbook: $25.90; Parent Guide: $24; Practice tests: $16; Directions for administering practice tests: $7; Machine-scorable booklets (25) (included are directions for administering tests): $104; Reusable test booklets (25): $83; Directions for administering reusable booklets: $11.50; 100 Machine-scorable answer documents: $69; Technical Manual: $60; "Pathways to Progress" booklet: $12.95–$24.95; Online Assessment (call for prices); Open-ended assessment kits: $10.50; Open-ended test booklets (25): $25.50; Directions for administering open-ended assessments: $8; Scoring guides for open-ended assessments: $25.

Adequacy of Test Manuals

Directions for administering and scoring tests are clear and comprehensive. Technical manuals and spring and fall norms books are adequate but would be easier to use if summary tables were provided for some of the data.

Excerpts from Other Test Reviews

The MAT-8 has recently been published. At present there are no other reviews of the MAT-8. Since the MAT-8 is sufficiently different from the MAT-7, reviews of the MAT-7 are not readily applicable.

Ordering Information

Publisher

Harcourt Educational Measurement, 19500 Bulverde Road, San Antonio, TX 78259-3701; Phone: 800-211-8378; Fax: 877-576-1816; Web site: www.hemweb.com.

Authors

Harcourt Educational Measurement.

Publication Date

2001.

Cautions and Comments

Since the MAT-8 is designed to assess achievement of learning objectives common to schools across the United States, it cannot be expected to assess idiosyncratic learning objectives of particular schools and programs. Each school system must determine which learning objectives assessed by the MAT-8 match the learning objectives of its curriculum before selecting the test. The MAT-8 is adequate for assessing and comparing basic skill levels of achievement, but is not appropriate for diagnosing specific skill deficiencies in particular subject areas. Although evidence of reliability and validity is provided, it is limited. No reliability evidence is provided showing that test scores are stable over time. No validity evidence is provided showing that MAT-8 test scores correlate with scores of other multi-skill achievement tests.

Mini-Battery of Achievement (MBA), for testing individuals
from ages 4 through adulthood
Reviewed by Myles I. Friedman, Ph.D., Educational Psychology

Usefulness of the Test for Educators

Test Authors' Purpose

"Provides a brief screening of achievement . . . the MBA is designed to give you more than you currently get from other brief achievement tests or screeners without increasing administration time. Educational uses include screening of new students and for special education referrals" (Riverside Publications, 2001 Assessment Catalog, p. 87).

Decision-Making Applications

The MBA is an academic achievement screening instrument that can be used to certify level of achievement in reading, writing, math, and acquiring basic academic knowledge. It can also be used to profile relative strengths and weaknesses in these four areas. In addition, it can be used in conjunction with other tests to place students in academic programs. However, test items do not probe in sufficient depth or breadth in any of the four areas to pinpoint specific deficiencies in need of remediation.

Relevant Population

Ages 4 through adulthood.

Characteristics Described

Four tests comprise the MBA, as follows:

Test 1, Reading. There are three parts to the reading test: (1) identification: students are required to identify letters and words they are shown; (2) vocabulary: students are required to state a word that is opposite in meaning to the word they are shown; (3) comprehension: students are required to identify missing words in short passages they read.

Test 2, Writing. There are two parts to the writing test: (1) dictation: students are required to write sentences to demonstrate their knowledge of letter forms, spelling, punctuation, capitalization, and word usage; (2) proofreading: students are required to identify mistakes in punctuation, capitalization, word usage, or spelling in passages they read.

Test 3, Mathematics. There are two parts to the mathematics test: (1) calculation: students are required to perform basic mathematics operations pertaining to arithmetic, geometry, trigonometry, logarithms, and calculus; (2) reasoning and concepts: students are required to decide the data and operations to use to solve math problems and then do the operations. In addition, students must exhibit knowledge of math concepts and vocabulary.

Test 4, Factual Knowledge. Students are required to exhibit knowledge of social studies, science, and humanities (art, music, and literature facts).

Test Scores Obtained

Raw scores, standard scores, grade equivalents, normal-curve equivalents, age equivalents, and percentile ranks can be obtained. Scores are obtained using the MBA Scoring and Reporting Program, a software program that is included as a part of the test. Reading, math, and writing scores are combined to obtain a basic skills cluster score.

Technical Adequacy

Validity Confirmation

Test item validity was established as follows. An effort was made to construct and select test items to cover a broad range of basic skills at varying levels of difficulty.

Expert opinion and test item validity studies were used in the selection process. However, no selection plan is detailed, and no evidence is provided that there is a match between test item coverage and school curriculum.

Test response validity was established by correlating MBA basic skills cluster scores with total or composite scores of other measures of achievement, including the Kaufman Tests of Educational Achievement (Brief), the Woodcock Johnson-Revised, the Peabody Individual Achievement Test-Revised, and the Wide Range Achievement Test-Revised. Correlations ranged from .77 to .88.

Reliability Confirmation

Scores obtained from administering one-half of the items on the test were correlated with the other half to assess internal consistency. Median reliability correlations ranged from .70 to .94. Reliability for the math subtest at age 5 was .70; all other reliabilities exceeded .90.

In addition, the entire test was administered to the same students twice, with a one-week interval between administrations to assess the stability of the test over time. Test-retest correlations ranged from .85 to .97. There were fewer than 60 students in the study. Overall, the reliabilities seem adequate.

Objectivity Confirmation

Criteria are provided for scoring test items as either correct or incorrect. Examples of correct and incorrect answers are provided for each item, so scorers must make judgments about the correctness of answers using the examples given. When scorers are unsure of the correctness of an answer, they are advised to ask follow-up questions of students and to seek the advice of colleagues. Although scoring test items is not difficult following the guidelines, it is advisable to train scorers to score the test and certify their competence. No correlations are provided showing degree of agreement of different scorers scoring the same tests.

Statistical Confirmation

The MBA Examiner's Manual provides adequate statistical validity, reliability, objectivity, and norms data.

Special Features

Acronym

MBA.

Levels of the Test

One.

Number of Test Forms

One.

Norm-Referenced?

Yes. Almost all of the test items of the MBA are from earlier Woodcock-Johnson Achievement Tests, and the MBA and the Woodcock-Johnson-Revised are standardized on the same norming sample of 6,026 subjects aged 4 to 95 years. The sample was randomly drawn from the following strata: census region, community size, gender, race, national origin, distribution of adult education, occupational status, and occupations in the community.

Criterion-Referenced?

No. Although the MBA is not referenced to any specific learning objectives, it implicitly can be used to assess general achievement in the subject areas of reading, writing, and math.

- Includes a computer scoring and reporting program that generates all scores and brief narrative. It comes in Windows and Macintosh versions.
- Each of the four subtests can be administered and scored independently.

Feasibility Considerations

Testing Time

Twenty to 30 minutes. Each subtest can be completed in 5 to 10 minutes.

For Testing Groups? Individuals?

Individuals.

Test Administration and Scoring

Directions for administering the test are clear and simple. Starting points are designated for different age groups and ceilings are specified. Examinees continue through the subtests until they fail four items in a row. Exceptions are noted. Scoring is made easy using the computer program included with the test. The program also produces a narrative report that facilitates interpretation.

Test Materials and Approximate Costs

The MBA complete test includes a test book and manual, 25 test records with examinee worksheets, and scoring and reporting program software.

MBA Windows version: $187; MBA Macintosh version: $187; Test records with subject worksheets (25): $28.50.

Adequacy of Test Manuals

The Examiner's Manual is clearly written and user-friendly. It describes how the test is administered, scored, and interpreted. It also describes test development and standardization procedures and provides summary tables to support test reliability and validity.

Excerpts from Other Test Reviews

The MBA was reviewed by Salvia and Ysseldyke (2001). They state: "The test is a good screening measure of academic achievement . . . more comprehensive than similar brief measures."

Ordering Information

Publisher

Riverside Publishing Company, 425 Spring Lake Drive, Itasca, IL 60143-2079; Phone: 800-323-9540; Fax: 630-467-7192; Web site: www.riverpub.com.

Authors

Richard W. Woodcock, Kevin S. McGrew, and Judy K. Werder.

Publication Date

1994.

Cautions and Comments

The MBA claims to be and is a multi-skill academic screening instrument that can be administered briefly in 20 to 30 minutes. Although it is by no means comprehensive, it does assess a broader range of skills than similar brief multi-skill academic achievement tests. Evidence of its technical adequacy is sufficient to warrant its use.

Reference

Salvia, J., & Ysseldyke, J. E. (2001). *Assessment* (8th ed.). Boston: Houghton Mifflin.

Peabody Individual Achievement Test-Revised-Normative Update (PIAT-R-NU), for testing individuals from 5 years through 18 years, 11 months of age
Reviewed by Myles I. Friedman, Ph.D., Educational Psychology

The original edition of the test (PIAT-R-NU) was published in 1970. The content of the test was updated in 1989 (PIAT-R). In the 1998 revision (PIAT-R-NU) a normative update was published. The content of the PIAT-R-NU is the same as the 1989 edition (PIAT-R).

Usefulness of the Test for Educators

Test Author's Purpose

"The Peabody Individual Achievement Test is an individually administered achievement test providing wide-range assessment" (Test Manual, p. 1).

Decision-Making Applications

The PIAT-R-NU is most appropriate for certifying achievement in the six subject areas it assesses. Strengths and weaknesses revealed in the six subject areas can be used, along with other data, to determine placement of students in special programs. The PIAT-R-NU is not designed to pinpoint specific misconceptions students may have in a subject area that requires particular instructional prescriptions to correct. Instructional prescription tests are better suited to diagnose student error patterns. Poor test performance on the PIAT-R-NU, when considered with other student data, may signal the need for referral testing.

Relevant Population

Students in grades K–12 (ages 5 years through 18 years, 11 months).

Characteristics Described

Mathematics: Knowledge and application of math concepts are assessed, ranging from students' ability to recognize and discriminate numbers to understanding advanced geometry and trigonometry concepts.

Reading Recognition: Students' ability to recognize letters in both upper and lower case, and words in isolation, are assessed.

Reading Comprehension: Students exhibit reading comprehension by reading sentences and indicating which of four pictures indicates the meaning of each sentence.

Spelling: Simpler test items require students to associate printed letters with spoken letters. More advanced items require students to choose the correct spelling of a spoken word from four printed words.

General Information: Students answer orally presented questions about social studies, science, sports, fine arts facts, and concepts.

Written Expression: Written expression skill is assessed at two levels. At Level 1 kindergarten and first grade students are required to copy and write letters, words, and sentences which are spoken to them; at Level 2 students write stories about pictures shown to them.

Test Scores Obtained

Responses to all but the written expression subtest items are scored pass or fail. Raw scores obtained are converted to age equivalents, grade equivalents, age-based standard scores, percentile ranks, normal-curve equivalents, and stanines. To score written expression free-response items, examiners use scoring criteria to rate student responses. Scores earned on the written expression items include grade-based stanines and developmental scaled scores.

Composite scores are obtained by combining total Reading, total test, and Written Language scores. The total Reading score is derived by combining Reading Recognition and Reading Comprehension scores. The total test score is obtained by combining General Information, Reading Recognition, Reading Comprehension, Mathematics, and Spelling scores. The Written Language score is obtained by combining the Spelling and Written Expression scores.

Technical Adequacy

The validity and reliability data for the Peabody Individual Achievement Test pertains to the 1970 and 1989 editions. It has not been updated along with the norming update for the 1998 edition.

Validity Confirmation

Test item validity was obtained by constructing test items to correspond to the content of school curriculum guides in the United States. Subject area specialists reviewed and refined subtest item pools to improve correspondence.

Test response validity was investigated by correlating the total scores on the PIAT (1970) with total scores on the PIAT-R (1989). Correlations ranged from .82 for 18-year-olds to .97 for 14-year-olds. Total PIAT scores were initially correlated with total scores on achievement tests including the Wide-Range Achievement Test, K-ABC, Woodcock-Johnson, CAT, Stanford, Metropolitan, and others. Correlations for normal and abnormal samples ranged from .67 to .86. Correlations between PIAT scores and mental ability test scores ranged from .42 to .72 for normal and abnormal samples. Performance of students on the PIAT-R (1989) and the PIAT-R-NU (1998) has changed, so generalizations from the validity of the PIAT-R to the validity of the PIAT-R-NU are questionable.

Reliability Confirmation

Total test score correlations obtained when the PIAT-R test was administered twice to the same sample over a span of two to four weeks were about .96. Correlations between subtest scores ranged from .84 to .98. Correlations when subtest item responses were correlated with one another ranged from .87 to .98.

Objectivity Confirmation

A scoring key is used to score most items on the test. Scoring criteria are used to score free response items on the Written Expression subtest. Although the manual for the PIAT-R-NU states that written expression test items that could not be scored consistently were deleted (p. 42), no correlation coefficients could be found indicating the degree of consistency among scorers ultimately achieved.

Statistical Confirmation

Statistical data on validity, reliability, and norms can be found in the PIAT-R-NU Test Manual. To obtain additional information on validity and reliability, see the PIAT-R Test Manual.

Special Features

Acronym

PIAT-R-NU.

Levels of the Test

There is one level of the test, except for the Written Expression subtest, which has two levels. Level 1 is for grades K–1; Level 2 is for grades 2–12.

Since there is only one test used for students in grades K–12, starting points are identified for students based on their prior achievement, and stopping points or ceilings are identified based on test performance.

Number of Test Forms

One.

Norm-Referenced?

Yes. The PIAT-R-NU was normed in the late 1990s and published in 1998. The norming sample included 3,184 students in grades K–12 and 245 young adults ages 18–22 from 129 sites throughout the United States. The sample was selected to be demographically representative of the U.S. population with respect to sex, ethnicity, parents' education, geographic location, and exceptionality of students. The sample seems to be an adequate representation of the intended population.

Criterion-Referenced?

No. The PIAT-R was not constructed to assess achievement of particular curricular or learning objectives, nor to assess in depth the acquisition of particular academic skills.

- The companion Assist Program is a computer program that is user-friendly. It converts raw scores to derived scores and generates various score reports. It greatly aids in reporting and interpreting test results.
- Training exercises to acquaint students with the type of test items in each subtest appear at the beginning of all subtests except for the Written Expression subtest.
- A pronunciation guide cassette is also available.

Feasibility Considerations

Testing Time

The PIAT-R-NU is an untimed power test. Although the time it takes to administer the test will vary, typically all six subtests can be administered in approximately 60 minutes.

For Testing Groups? Individuals?

Individuals.

Test Administration and Scoring

Administration of the test is not difficult but requires some preparation. Test items range widely in difficulty. For each student tested, administrators must identify a starting point for that student based primarily on the student's prior achievement. A stopping point or ceiling is determined for students based on the number of consecutive errors they make on the test.

Deriving scores is also not difficult if the Assist Program is used. Otherwise, sophistication is required to calculate and record scores, to convert them to derived scores, and to plot profiles. Once the procedure is learned it can be completed in about 15 minutes. Interpretation of scores requires an understanding of derived scores and test profiles. Educators with this knowledge should not need training to administer and score the test and to interpret the test results.

Test Materials and Approximate Costs

The complete kit costs $279.95, including 50 combined test record and written response booklets and a 261-page Test Manual. Separately, the cost is $69.95 for 50 combined test record and written response booklets, $79.95 for the Test Manual, $15.95 for a pronunciation guide cassette, and $199.95 for the Assist Program.

Adequacy of Test Manuals

The Test Manual is adequate in describing test administration, scoring, and interpretation procedures. However, to obtain a complete understanding of the validity and reliability of the PIAT-R-NU (1998), it is helpful to read the test manuals for the PIAT-R (1989) and the original PIAT (1970), as well as the manual for the PIAT-R-NU.

Excerpts from Other Test Reviews

PIAT-R-NU Normative Update Reviews

"Overall, the Normative Update provides users with critical information when administering the PIAT-R" (Fager, 2001, p. 907).

"The 1989 (PIAT-R) manual provides an elegant summary of reliability and validity evidence from studies conducted in the 1970's and 1980's, but the new manual has not been updated in this regard" (Cross, 2001).

Salvia and Ysseldyke (2001) indicate that a few reliability and validity studies should have been conducted in the late 1990s. "Generalizations from the PIAT-R to the PIAT-R-NU are suspect" (p. 414).

PIAT-R Reviews

Hammill, Brown, and Bryant (1992) rate the PIAT-R overall as "recommended." However, they rate the Written Language composite and Written Expression subtests as "not recommended." This seems partly due to the difficulty of obtaining valid and reliable test results of writing ability.

Other reviews of the PIAT-R state: "It is apparent that great effort was made to build upon the existing strength of the original PIAT and make it better . . . the PIAT-R (is) an excellent screening instrument for use in educational settings" (Benes 1994, p. 43); "Overall, the PIAT-R appears to be a useful instrument" (Rogers 1994, p. 46).

Ordering Information

Publisher

American Guidance Service, Inc., 4201 Woodland Road, Circle Pines, MN 55014-1796; Phone: 800-328-2560; Fax: 800-471-8457; e-mail: agsmail@agsnet; Web site: www.agsnet.com.

Author

Frederick C. Markwardt, Jr.

Publication Date

1998.

Cautions and Comments

The PIAT-R-NU is an adequate, individually administered achievement test for certifying students' academic achievement level in the subject areas it covers. Care should be taken to ensure that the content of the test corresponds to the content and objectives of the to-be-tested students' school. The test should not be used to diagnose student inadequacies.

References

Benes, K. M. (1994). Review of the PIAT-R Achievement Test. In J. C. Impara & L. L. Murphy (Eds.), *Psychological assessment in the schools* (pp. 40–43). Lincoln, NE: The Buros Institute of Mental Measurements.

Cross, L. H. (2001). Review of the PIAT-R-NU Achievement Test. In B. S. Plake & J. C.

Impara (Eds.), *The Fourteenth Mental Measurements Yearbook* (pp. 904–906). Lincoln, NE: The Buros Institute of Mental Measurements.

Fager, J. J. (2001). Review of the PIAT-R-NU Achievement Test. In B. S. Plake & J. C. Impara (Eds.), *The Fourteenth Mental Measurements Yearbook* (pp. 906–908). Lincoln, NE: The Buros Institute of Mental Measurements.

Hammill, D. D., Brown, L., & Bryant, B. R. (1992). *A consumer's guide to tests in print* (2nd ed.). Austin, TX: PRO-ED.

Rogers, B. G. (1994). Review of the PIAT-R Achievement Test. In J. C. Impara & L. L. Murphy (Eds.), *Psychological assessment in the schools* (pp. 43–46). Lincoln, NE: The Buros Institute of Mental Measurements.

Salvia, J., & Ysseldyke, J. E. (2001). *Assessment* (8th ed.). Boston: Houghton Mifflin.

Stanford Achievement Test Series, Ninth Edition (Stanford 9),
for testing groups from kindergarten through grade 12
Reviewed by Myles I. Friedman, Ph.D., Educational Psychology

The Stanford Achievement Test Series (Stanford 9) consists of the Stanford Early School Achievement Test (SESAT), to be used in kindergarten and grade 1, the Stanford Achievement Test (SAT), to be used in grades 1–9, and the Test of Academic Skills (TASK), to be used in grades 9–13. A basic abbreviated battery is available, as well as a complete battery.

Usefulness of the Test for Educators

Test Authors' Purpose

"The Stanford Achievement Test Series . . . measures students' school achievement in reading, language arts, mathematics and social science" (Technical Data Report, p. 7).

Decision-Making Applications

The tests are most suitable for making achievement certification decisions. Composite score indicates overall level of achievement. Scores on the subject area tests indicate level of achievement in the subject areas. In addition, comparisons of subject area scores can be profiled to indicate relative strengths and weaknesses in subject areas. Scores on the Stanford 9, along with other data in students' records, can be used to make some placement decisions. However, the tests are not adequate for making instructional prescription decisions. Test items in subject area tests are not of sufficient depth and breadth to diagnose specific error patterns in need of instructional remediation. Diagnostic subject area tests are needed for that purpose. The SESAT can be used as a grade school admissions test to reveal early academic capabilities, keeping in mind that preschoolers need social, self-help, and coordination skills as well to be ready to enter school.

Relevant Population

The Stanford 9 series covers grades K–13. The SESAT is used in grades K–1.5, the SAT in grades 1.5–9.9, and the TASK in grades 9–13.

Characteristics Described

Following are the characteristics assessed by the subtests of the Stanford 9 series and the requirements of items used in the assessments.

Sounds and Letters (used only in the SESAT, grades K–1.5): Students are required to match sounds in words and sounds and letters, and to recognize letters.

Word Study Skills (used only in the primary grade levels): Students are required to decode words and to identify relationships between sounds and letters.

Sentence Reading (used only in the SESAT Level 2): Students are required to identify pictures described by sentences they read.

Reading Vocabulary (used beyond grade level 2.5): Students are required to choose words that best correspond to definitions read by the examiner.

Reading Comprehension (used above grade level 1.5): After reading passages, students answer questions assessing their comprehension. Students are required to make inferences as well as literal interpretations.

Listening to Words and Stories (used only in the SESAT, grades K–1.5): In response to words and passages that are read to them, students are required to recall details, identify word meanings, follow instructions, identify cause-effect relations, and identify main ideas.

Listening (used in grade levels 1.5–9.9): Students are required to take notes on material that is read to them to show their ability to process information.

Language (assessed above grade level 1.5): Students are required to edit text to show knowledge of spelling, punctuation, and other mechanics as well as sentence structure and organization in written composition.

Study Skills (Assessed above grade level 4.5): Students are required to exhibit investigatory skills.

Spelling (Assessed above grade level 1.5): Students are required to identify the correct and incorrect spelling of words.

Mathematics (assessed at all grade levels): Students are required to meet standards of the NCTM for the Teaching of Mathematics at various grade levels. At lower grade levels students are required to identify numbers and number relationships and master basic computational skills. At higher levels students are required to solve problems in measurement, statistics, algebra, and geometry.

The following characteristics are not assessed in the basic battery:

Science (assessed above grade level 3.5): Students are required to answer questions pertaining to earth and space science, life science, physical science, and the scientific method.

Social Science (assessed above grade level 3.5): Students are required to address issues in geography, history, anthropology, sociology, political science, and economics.

Environment (assessed K–3.5): Science and social science questions are combined at K–3.5 levels to assess understanding of the social and natural environment.

Test Scores Obtained

The basic battery yields the following raw scores: Word Study Skills, Word Reading, Reading Vocabulary, Reading Comprehension, Mathematics, Mathematics Problem Solving, Mathematics Procedures, and Language.

The complete battery yields the same scores as the basic battery and, in addition, the following scores: Sounds and Letters, Spelling, Study Skills, Listening to Words and Stories, Listening, Environment, Science, and Social Science.

The following types of derived scores can be obtained for the series: scaled scores, individual percentile ranks and stanines, normal curve equivalents, grade equivalents, achievement/ability comparisons, group percentile ranks and stanines, content cluster performance categories, p-values, performance standards, and performance indicators.

The tests may be scored by hand or sent to the publisher's scoring service for machine scoring. The publisher scoring service can also provide analyses of test results in various formats including report forms for parents, individual student profiles, class profiles, and comparisons of individual students' achievement to criteria, such as learning objectives and personal capability.

Technical Adequacy

Validity Confirmation

Test item validity was obtained by first ascertaining common objectives of school curricula in the United States as specified in major textbooks, school district curricula, and by national professional organizations. Test items were then developed to assess achievement of the common curriculum objectives derived for the various grade levels. After test items were written they were critiqued by content, measurement, and language experts as well as classroom teachers. In addition, minority group educators reviewed test items for cultural bias. Test items were culled and refined based on the analyses of the critics.

Test response validity was obtained by showing a positive correlation between test performances and grades in school. In general, subtests are more difficult for students in lower grades and easier for students as they progress through school. Correlations between Stanford 9 test scores and Stanford 8 and Otis-Lennon School Ability Test scores are also offered as evidence of test response validity. Correlations between the Stanford 9 and 8 range between .58 and .93; correlations between the Stanford 9 and the Otis-Lennon range between .35 and .99.

Reliability Confirmation

Alternate forms of the test were given to the same students within a short span of time. The reliability correlations of the scores of the two tests ranged between .32 and .93. The lowest correlations are between scores on writing assessments. Internal consistency of test scores for items within subtests was also checked, yielding correlations (KR-20) ranging from .55 to .94. Lower correlations also tended to pertain to writing assessment. Most of the reliability correlations are sufficiently high to meet reliability standards.

Objectivity Confirmation

A scoring key is used to score multiple-choice items by hand or machine, so they are not subject to scorer variations. However, test items in the writing assessment program are hand scored using specified criteria and are subject to variations in scoring. Agreement among different scorers of the same writing tests was checked. Correlations ranged from .58 to .92.

Statistical Confirmation

Statistical data on validity, reliability, and test norms can be found in the companion Technical Data Report and Norm Books. However, procedures for obtaining and processing the validity and reliability data are not adequately described.

Special Features

Acronyms

Stanford 9 for the series, SESAT for the Stanford Early School Achievement Test, SAT for the Stanford Achievement Test, and TASK for the Test of Academic Skills.

Levels of the Test

Thirteen levels for the entire series: 2 for the SESAT, 3 for the TASK, and 8 for the SAT.

Number of Test Forms

Two equivalent forms: Form S and Form T.

Norm-Referenced?

Yes. The test series was nationally normed and standardized in 1995. The national sample of schools was stratified by state, socioeconomic status, urban/suburban/rural, and public/nonpublic schools. Both spring and fall norms were derived. 250,000 students from 1,000 school districts participated in the spring norming and standardization project, 200,000 in the fall project.

Criterion-Referenced?

Yes. Performance indicator scores have been established to describe levels of achievement on open-ended content area questions. Performance indicator scores range from 0 to 3. A score of 0 indicates essentially incorrect, 1 indicates marginally correct, 2 indicates partially correct, and 3 indicates essentially correct.

Performance standard scores have been established for multiple-choice items to indicate levels of content mastery. Four levels of performance have been established: Level 1, Below Basic (less than partial mastery), Level 2, Basic (partial mastery), Level 3, Proficient (solid academic performance), and Level 4, Advanced (superior performance).

A "Compendium of Instructional Objectives" booklet is available indicating objectives assessed in the series.

- Test items judged by minority group members to be culturally biased have been changed or removed.
- Test items have been constructed to assess various thinking skills as well as basic understanding.
- Large-print and Braille editions are available for visually impaired students.
- Screening tests are available in reading and math for hearing-impaired students to locate the level of the Stanford 9 to be administered.
- Special norms have been derived for the hearing impaired, students attending private schools or Catholic schools, students living in urban areas, and high-socioeconomic-status communities.
- Report forms are available for individual students, parents, and classes.
- Practice tests are available.

Feasibility Considerations

Testing Time

Administration of the basic abbreviated battery takes between 1 hour, 45 minutes and 4 hours, 35 minutes. Administration of the complete battery takes between 2 hours, 15 minutes and 5 hours, 25 minutes, depending on the number of tests administered.

For Testing Groups? Individuals?

Groups.

Test Administration and Scoring

Neither extended training nor certification are needed to score the tests. Test directions are available for easy administration. The publisher provides scoring, data analysis, and report form services. Administration, scoring, and interpretation are facilitated with training in assessment testing and practice.

Test Materials and Approximate Costs

Materials	SESAT Grades K–1.5	SAT Grades 1.5–9.9	TASK Grades 9–13
Exam Kits*	$24	$8–$32**	$8–$32**
25 Scorable Booklets/Forms	$12–$60	$20–$74**	$70
Keys for Hand Scorable Booklets	$25	$16–$92**	$16–$32**
Test Administration Directions	$9	$16–$24	$16–$24
Class Records	$3.50	$3.50	$3.50
Parents Preview Form	$15	$15	$15
25 Stanford Markers	$4	$4	$4
25 Practice Tests	$25	$12	$12
Norm Books	$50	$50	$50
Technical Data Reports	$45	$45	$45
Understanding Test Results booklet	$15	$15	$15
Compendium of Instructional Objectives booklet	$16	$16	$16
Strategies for Instruction booklet	$20	$20	$20
Guide for Organizational Planning	$24	$20	$20
Guide for Classroom Planning	$12	$12	$12

*Includes sample test booklet or form, practice test, and test administration directions.
**Separate charge for each subject area test.

Other services, such as scoring and report services, are available from the publisher at additional cost.

Adequacy of Test Manuals

Test manuals are adequate in their clarity of presentation and breadth of coverage. The Technical Data Report does not explain in detail the procedures used to collect and analyze data. Helpful guides for educators are the Compendium of Instructional Objectives, Understanding Test Results, Strategies for Instruction, the Guide for Organizational Planning, and the Guide for Classroom Planning.

Excerpts from Other Test Reviews

"Schools and school districts searching for an up-to-date achievement assessment series should give the Stanford 9 serious consideration. It builds on a long tradition of excellence" (Berk, 1998).

"Once again the Stanford series appears to be one of the best, most comprehensive standardized survey achievement tests available. A word of caution is offered about the open-ended tests. . . . In particular, reliability may be a problem" (Haladyna, 1998).

"The tests provide a comprehensive, continuous assessment of skill development in a variety of areas. Standardization, reliability, and validity are adequate for screening purposes" (Salvia & Ysseldyke, 2001).

Ordering Information

Publisher

Harcourt Educational Measurement, 19500 Bulverde Road, San Antonio, TX 78259-3701; Phone: 800-211-8378; Fax: 877-576-1816; Web site: www.hemweb.com.

Authors

Harcourt Educational Measurement.

Publication Date

1996.

Cautions and Comments

The Stanford 9 series is technically adequate. Test response validation would be improved if the test results were correlated with results of additional well-established achievement tests not developed by the publisher. Care needs to be taken in using Stanford 9 results to assess learning objectives of a particular school. Since the Stanford 9 is designed to assess achievement of learning objectives common to schools throughout the United States, it cannot be expected to assess achievement of all learning objectives of particular schools. The tests are most appropriate for assessing core skills, both level of achievement and profiling relative strengths and weaknesses in the subject areas covered. It is also suitable for comparing core skills achievement among schools, school systems, and states. Test items do not probe subject areas in sufficient depth and breadth to identify error patterns in need of instructional remediation. Diagnostic subject area tests are more appropriate for pinpointing learning difficulties in particular subject areas. In addition, other achievement tests are needed to assess achievement of local school learning objectives not covered by the Stanford 9.

References

Berk, R. A. (1998). Review of the Stanford Achievement Test, Ninth Edition. In J. C. Impara & B. S. Plake (Eds.), *The Thirteenth Mental Measurements Yearbook* (pp. 925–928). Lincoln, NE: The Buros Institute of Mental Measurements.

Haladyna, T. M. (1998). Review of the Stanford Achievement Test, Ninth Edition. In J. C.

Impara & B. S. Plake (Eds.), *The Thirteenth Mental Measurements Yearbook* (pp. 928–930) Lincoln, NE: The Buros Institute of Mental Measurements.

Salvia J., & Ysseldyke, J. E. (2001). *Assessment* (8th ed.) Boston: Houghton Mifflin.

TerraNova, for testing groups from kindergarten through grade 12
Reviewed by Myles I. Friedman, Ph.D., Educational Psychology

Usefulness of the Test for Educators

Test Authors' Purpose

"TerraNova is an assessment system designed to measure concepts, processes, and skills taught throughout the nation" (Technical Bulletin, p. 1).

Decision-Making Applications

TerraNova is best suited for making achievement certification decisions. Student achievement can be certified in all subject areas covered by the test. However, the test may not be appropriate for certifying achievement of uncommon learning objectives of many schools. TerraNova scores may also be used, along with other data, to make placement decisions. Profiles of strengths and weaknesses in subject areas covered by the test can be derived from test scores, which can be used to place high-scoring students in enrichment programs and low-scoring students in remedial programs. However, TerraNova does not test specific subject areas in sufficient depth to diagnose particular misconceptions that require particular instructional prescriptions to remediate. Subject area instructional prescription tests need to be used to pinpoint the type of errors a student is making. Test scores can be used to make decisions pertaining to instructional programs, school groups and, conditionally, individual students.

Relevant Population

The 12 overlapping levels of TerraNova relate to grade ranges as follows: Level 10: K.6–1.6; Level 11: 1.6–2.6; Level 12: 2.0–3.2; Level 13: 2.6–4.2; Level 14: 3.6–5.2; Level 15: 4.6–6.2; Level 16: 5.6–7.2; Level 17: 6.6–8.2; Level 18: 7.6–9.2; Level 19: 8.6–10.2; Level 20: 9.6–11.2; Levels 21/22: 10.6–12.9. The decimal number after the grade indicates the number of months that have elapsed in the school year. For example, K.6 refers to the sixth month (February) of kindergarten.

Characteristics Described

Following are the characteristics assessed by TerraNova.

Basic Characteristics

Reading/Language Arts: Skills assessed include listening comprehension, drawing conclusions, evaluation and editing, understanding of letters, words, signs, punctuation, capitalization, and prose writing.

Mathematics: Skills assessed include number recognition and relationships, computation, measurement, geometry, statistics, algebra, reasoning, and problem solving.

Science: Assessments include understanding the scientific method and concepts and principles of physical, life, earth, and space sciences. Understanding of the evolution and application of science to human advancement is also assessed.

Social Studies: Understanding of geography, culture, history, civics, and economics is assessed.

Supplemental Characteristics

Word Analysis: Recognition of consonants, blends, digraphs, sight words, vowels, contractions and compounds, and roots and affixes is assessed.

Vocabulary: Knowledge of word meaning and skill in deriving word meaning from contextual clues is assessed.

Language Mechanics: Knowledge of writing conventions, including punctuation and capitalization, is assessed.

Spelling: Ability to identify the correct spelling of words in written statements is assessed.

Mathematics Computation: Ability to add, subtract, multiply, and divide is assessed, as well as the use of decimals, fractions, and percentages. Understanding of algebraic operations is also assessed.

Test Scores Obtained

Both norm-referenced and criterion-referenced data are provided. Norm-referenced data includes national percentile ranks, normal curve equivalents, grade equivalents, and stanines. Criterion-referenced data pertain to the achievement of learning objectives. Two kinds of objective-referenced data are available. Degree of mastery of objectives is expressed as an estimated percentage of test items students can answer correctly: 0–49% indicates nonmastery, 50–74% indicates partial mastery, and 75–100% indicates mastery. Performance level is also derived on a scale from 1 to 5. Level 1 indicates starting out, Level 2 progressing, Level 3 nearing proficiency, Level 4 proficient, and Level 5 advanced. The above data is transformed into a number of different reports available for parents, teachers, administrators, and school board members. (See description of reports under "Special Features.")

Technical Adequacy

Validity Confirmation

Test item validity was established for the tests by ensuring that the content of the items constructed for the tests corresponded to the curriculum content commonly taught across the United States. Textbooks, state curriculum, and curriculum recommended by professional educational organizations were reviewed to identify the content to be covered by the test items. Test items were constructed accordingly and reviewed and refined by classroom teachers and experts in the subject areas tested. Test items were also constructed and reviewed to ensure that they covered a range of thinking skills.

Test response validity has not been established at this time. However, the publishers plan to correlate TerraNova scores with National Assessment of Educational Progress scores when available and with other test scores. TerraNova test scores were correlated with scores on the Test of Cognitive Skills-Second Edition (TCS/2), but the TCS/2 is a measure of cognition, not a broad measure of basic academic achievement, as TerraNova purports to be.

Reliability Confirmation

No effort was made to repeatedly administer the test or equivalent forms of the test over time to correlated scores of different administrations. Such reliability coefficients are not available. However, item responses of the test were correlated with one another to obtain reliability coefficients. The composite reliability coefficients were in the .80s and .90s. Reliability coefficients for subtests ranged from .72 to .97. Decisions about individual students should not be based entirely on scores of subtests with low reliability coefficients.

Objectivity Confirmation

A scoring key is used to score the multiple-choice test items by machine. Scoring criteria are used to score constructed-response items. The constructed-response items are scored by publisher employees. Studies were conducted at the third, sixth, and eighth grade levels to check scoring agreement between pairs of scorers who scored constructed-response test items. Correlations ranging from .85 to .97 indicated high scorer agreement.

Statistical Confirmation

Statistical data on validity, reliability, and norms can be found in the Technical Bulletins for TerraNova.

Special Features

Acronym

None.

Levels of the Test

Twelve overlapping levels (see "Relevant Population" for details).

Number of Test Forms

One form in English and one in Spanish, called the SUPERA. (This review does not pertain to the SUPERA, customized tests, or tests available to supplement TerraNova.)

Norm-Referenced?

Yes. TerraNova was normed in 1996. The norming sample totals about 180,000 students. Schools in the sample were selected to be demographically representative of schools in the United States.

Criterion-Referenced?

Yes. The criteria used are learning objectives. At least four test items are used to assess achievement of each learning objective; the sufficiency of four test items per objective can be challenged.

Reports on achievement of objectives are prepared at each test/grade level for the subjects tested. Reports include data on mastery level achieved and performance level achieved. The objectives specified for reading/language arts at the particular levels are shown in Figure 1.1.

TerraNova, the latest edition of the Comprehensive Test of Basic Skills (CTBS), is available in three formats: The CTBS Complete Battery, the CTBS Survey Battery, and the CTBS Multiple Assessment Battery. All three assess reading/language arts, mathematics, science, and social studies knowledge and skills. The Complete and Survey Batteries also assess "supplemental" skills described previously. The Survey Battery has fewer test items and can be administered in less time than the Complete Battery. The Complete Battery provides more accurate, criterion-referenced data than the Survey Battery. Custom-built tests can be ordered. Multiple-choice test items are used in the Complete and Survey Batteries. Both multiple-choice and constructed-response items are used in the Multiple Assessment Battery.

- Thinking Skill Variations: Test items are developed to evoke thought processes of various types and complexity.

- Reports Available: Reports on individual students are available for parents and teachers. They include Home reports, Individual Profile reports, and Student Performance Level reports. Group reports for teachers and administrators include Class Record Sheets, Group Performance Level reports, Objectives Performance reports, and Student Rank Order reports. Summary reports for instructional planning and policy making include Board reports, Class Summary reports, Evaluation Summary reports, Objective Performance summaries, and Performance Level Summary reports. The varieties of reports made available are noteworthy and appealing features of TerraNova.

- Performance assessment tasks can be custom ordered. Performance tasks move students through a series of activities culminating in a final outcome and a content area score.

Figure 1.1
Description of Objectives for Reading/Language Arts at the Various Levels of the Test

Objective and Description   *Level*

01 Oral Communication   10, 11
Demonstrate both literal and interpretive understanding of passages that are read aloud.
Use writing or other means to respond to literal and interpretive questions about passages that are read aloud.

02 Basic Understanding   10–21/22
Demonstrate understanding of the literal meaning of a passage through identifying stated information, indicating sequence of events, and defining grade-level vocabulary.
Write responses to questions requiring literal information from passages and documents.

03 Analyze Text   11–21/22
Demonstrate comprehension by drawing conclusions; inferring relationships such as cause and effect; and identifying theme and story elements such as plot, climax, character, and setting.
Write responses that show an understanding of the text that goes beyond surface meaning.

04 Evaluate and Extend Meaning 11–21/22
Demonstrate critical understanding by making predictions; distinguishing between fact and opinion, and reality and fantasy; transferring ideas to other situations; and judging author purpose, point of view, and effectiveness.
Write responses that make connections between texts based on common themes and concepts; evaluate author's purpose and effectiveness; and extend meaning to other contexts.

05 Identify Reading Strategies   11–21/22
Demonstrate awareness of techniques that enhance comprehension, such as using existing knowledge, summarizing content,

Objective and Description   *Level*

05 Identify Reading Strategies *(continued)*
comparing information across texts, using graphics and text structure, and formulating questions that deepen understanding.
Write responses that interpret and extend the use of information from documents and forms, and that demonstrate knowledge and use of strageies.

06 Introduction to Print   10–12
Demonstrate knowledge of sound/symbol and structural relationships in letters, words, and signs.
Write responses that show knowledge of letters and words.

07 Sentence Structure   11–21/22
Demonstrate an understanding of conventions for writing complete and effective sentences, including treatment of subject and verb, punctuation, and capitalization.
Demonstrate an understanding of conciseness and clarity of meaning in combining two sentences.

08 Writing Strategies   11–21/22
Demonstrate knowledge of information sources, outlines, and other pre-writing techniques.
Demonstrate an understanding of the use of topic sentences, concluding sentences, connective and transitional words and phrases, supporting statements, sequencing ideas, and relevant information in writing expository prose.

09 Editing Skills   11–21/22
Identify the appropriate use of capitalization, punctuation, nouns, pronouns, verbs, adjectives, and adverbs in existing text.
Demonstrate knowledge of writing conventions and sentence structure through identifying and correcting errors in existing text and in text written by the student.

Source: The Only One booklet. Reproduced with permission.

Feasibility Considerations

Testing Time (range in hours and minutes)

Complete Basic	3:30 at K to 4:10 at grades 9–12
Complete with Supplemental	3:30 at grade 1 to 5:15 at grades 9–12
Survey Basic	2:15 at grade 2 to 2:40 at grades 9–12
Survey with Supplemental	3:35 at grade 2 to 3:45 at grades 9–12
Multiple Assessment Basic	4:00 at grade 1 to 5:20 at grades 9–12

For Testing Groups? Individuals?

Groups.

Test Administration and Scoring

The publisher scores the test. A guide is available for interpreting scores. Any educator familiar with norm- and criterion-referenced scoring and test administration should have little difficulty following the directions provided for interpreting test scores or administering the test. Training and certification are not required to administer the test or to interpret the test scores and reports. School board members, parents, and educators with no test interpretation experience may need help.

- Practice activities are available.
- Locator tests are available to identify the most suitable level of the test for students.

Test Materials and Approximate Costs

	Test Booklets (All Levels)				Scoring
	Consumable For 30	Reusable For 30	Reflective For 50	Continuous For 1,250	Cost per Student
Complete Battery	$108.15	$83.75	$30.75	$770	$3.53
Complete and Supplemental Battery	$114.65	$90.25	$30.75	$770	$3.80
Survey Battery	$103	$81.25	$30.75	$770	$3.37
Survey and Supplemental Battery	$109.50	$87.75	$30.75	$770	$3.64
Multiple Assessment	$125			$9.80	
Practice Activities	$12.50; $2.70 for directions				
Teacher's Guide	$25				
Test Directions	$11.25				

Adequacy of Test Manuals

Several manuals are available with the test. A user-friendly Teacher Guide and a guide for interpreting test scores and report data are provided. Technical Bulletins provide details and statistics on the development and technical adequacy of the test.

Excerpts from Other Test Reviews

"The materials are well constructed, attractive and user-friendly. My only serious reservation is with the mastery classifications . . . the 'cut scores' are arbitrarily defined . . . I would caution teachers and schools to use the criterion-referenced scores carefully and devise their own mastery levels" (Monsaas, 2001).

"The TerraNova is a technically well-built achievement test. If the TerraNova's content and approach are a close fit to a school district's curriculum framework, it should be seriously considered for adoption. If this close match is not there, look elsewhere" (Nitko, 2001).

"There is less evidence for the technical adequacy of the TerraNova than for that of other comparable achievement batteries. . . . There is limited evidence for the validity of the TerraNova Batteries. . . . Reliabilities of some of the separate subtests are too low for use in making decisions about individuals. . . . There are no data on test-retest reliability or on alternate-form reliability" (Salvia & Ysseldyke 2001, p. 408).

Ordering Information

Publisher

CTB/McGraw-Hill, 20 Ryan Ranch Road, Monterey, CA 93940-5703; Phone: 800-538-9547; Fax: 800-282-0266; Web site: www.ctb.com.

Authors

CTB/McGraw-Hill.

Publication Date

1997.

Cautions and Comments

Reviews of TerraNova are inconsistent. The following strengths and limitations are mentioned to help readers decide whether to adopt the tests.

Strengths: The tests, guides, and manuals are user-friendly. Reports are well conceived and useful to teachers, parents, school administrators, school boards, and other policy makers. Both norm-referenced and criterion-referenced data are provided. Test item validity was established. Reliabilities obtained by correlating composite test item scores with one another to establish internal consistency were high. Much of the work done on the development of the TerraNova was innovative, useful, thorough, and well presented.

Limitations: Too few items are included to assess the achievement of some objectives. Reliability derived for some subtests is low. Test response validity was not established. Reliability was not confirmed by correlating scores of repeated test administrations of the same form or alternate forms of the test.

Many of the limitations can be overcome with extended effort. Further validation is planned.

References

Monsaas, J. A. (2001). Review of the TerraNova Achievement Tests. In B. S. Plake & J. C. Impara (Eds.), *The Fourteenth Mental Measurements Yearbook* (pp. 1223–1226). Lincoln, NE: The Buros Institute of Mental Measurements.

Nitko, A. J. (2001). Review of the TerraNova Achievement Tests. In B. S. Plake & J. C. Impara (Eds.), *The Fourteenth Mental Measurements Yearbook* (pp. 1226–1229). Lincoln, NE: The Buros Institute of Mental Measurements.

Salvia, J., & Ysseldyke, J. E. (2001). *Assessment* (8th ed.). Boston: Houghton Mifflin.

Wechsler Individual Achievement Test-Second Edition (WIAT-II),
for testing individuals from preschool through adulthood
Reviewed by Aileen C. Lau-Dickinson, Ed.D., Special Education Administration

---

Usefulness of the Test for Educators

Test Author's Purpose

The WIAT-II is a "comprehensive, individually administered test for assessing the achievement of children, adolescents, college students, and adults" (Examiner's Manual, p. 1).

Decision-Making Applications

When the results of the WIAT-II are linked with the results of the Wechsler Intelligence Scale for Children-Third Edition (WISC-III), an ability/achievement discrepancy score can be obtained. This discrepancy score can be useful for educators when making diagnostic and placement decisions for students with learning disabilities. In addition, the WIAT-II domains are consistent with areas specified by law when assessing students for learning disabilities, such as oral expression, listening comprehension, written expression, basic reading skill, reading comprehension, mathematics calculation, and mathematics reasoning. In addition, the WIAT-II assessment includes children as young as 4 years, allowing early identification of the young child who may be at risk for academic failure. College students and adults up to the age of 85 can also be assessed for academic skill levels using the WIAT-II Supplement for College Students and Adults.

Relevant Population

The WIAT-II can be used for children, adolescents, college students, and adults. The WIAT-II Supplement for College Students and Adults can be used for individuals up to 85 years of age.

Characteristics Described

WIAT-II Subtests

Word Reading: In this subtest, examinees are asked to identify letters, identify and generate rhyming words, identify beginning and ending sounds, and match sounds with visually presented letter blends, and beginning at grade 3 examinees read a list of words aloud. Skills assessed include: Letter identification, Phonological awareness, Letter-sound awareness, Accuracy of word recognition, and Automaticity of word recognition.

Reading Comprehension: In this subtest, the examinee reads sentences aloud and reads narratives including informative and functional passages. Skills assessed include: Literal comprehension, Inferential comprehension, Lexical comprehension, Reading rate, Oral reading accuracy, and Word recognition in context.

Pseudoword Decoding: The examinee is asked to pronounce unfamiliar words correctly while reading from a list of nonsense words that are phonetically correct. Skills assessed include Phonological decoding and Accuracy of word attack.

Spelling: The examinee must identify early spelling concepts through knowledge of sound/letter correspondence for vowels, consonants, and consonant blends. Skills assessed include Alphabet principle (sound-letter awareness), Written spelling of regular and irregular words, and Written spelling of homonyms (integration of spelling and lexical comprehension).

Written Expression: The examinee is asked to write the alphabet, develop a fluent writing sample, generate sentences in response to verbal and visual cues, and combine sentences. Also, examinees in grades 3–6 must compose a written paragraph, and older examinees must write a persuasive essay. Skills assessed include Timed alphabet writing, Word fluency (written), Sentence combining, Sentence generation, Paragraph writing, Descriptive writing, Essay writing, and Writing fluency (based on word count).

Numerical Operations: The examinee must demonstrate knowledge of early calculation skills such as number recognition and number counting and higher math calculation skills. Skills assessed include Counting, One-to-one correspondence, Numerical identification and writing, Calculation (addition, subtraction, multiplication and division), and Fractions, decimals, algebra.

Mathematics Reasoning: The examinee is asked to demonstrate knowledge of counting, concepts of quantity, and identification of geometric shapes. Additional items require knowledge of word problems, interpretation of graphs, telling time, money concepts, and usage of fractions, decimals, and percentages. Higher-level examinees must solve problems related to statistics and probability. Skills assessed include Quantitative concepts, Multi-step problem solving, Money, time, and measurement, Geometry, Reading and interpreting charts and graphs, Statistics and probability, Estimation, and Identifying patterns.

Listening Comprehension: The examinee must process incoming verbal information and demonstrate understanding by providing an appropriate verbal or motor response. The examinee must select a picture from a set of four that exactly matches a sentence that has been read aloud. Skills assessed include Receptive vocabulary, Sentence comprehension, and Expressive vocabulary.

Oral Expression: The examinee must generate nouns or verbs following a verbal prompt. Examinees in grades Pre-K–3 must repeat short sentences. Older examinees must develop stories based on cartoon-like passages and give verbal directions with and without visual cues. Skills assessed include Word fluency (oral), Auditory short-term recall for contextual information/Sentence repetition, Story generation/Visual passage retell, Giving directions, and Explaining steps in sequential tasks.

Source: Adapted from Examiner's Manual, Chapter 4, Administration and Scoring, Table 2.1, pp. 13–14.

Test Scores Obtained

Norm-referenced data includes standard scores, composite standard scores (Reading, Math, Written Language, Oral Language), percentiles, normal curve equivalents, and age and grade equivalents. Ability-Achievement Discrepancy Analysis using the WIAT-II and a Wechsler Intelligence Scale (WPPSI-R, WISC-R, WAIS-III) can also be calculated. There is a WIAT-II Scoring Assistant available. This software allows the user to enter raw scores, which are automatically converted to derived scores. A second software program, the WISC-III/WIAT-II Scoring Assistant, conducts the ability/achievement discrepancy analysis using the scores from the WISC-III. A third Scoring Assistant is available using the WAIS-III/WMS-III/WIAT-II.

Technical Adequacy

Validity Confirmation

Test item validity was established for the WIAT-II by ensuring that the content of the test items represented typical curriculum specifications across the United States. These specifications were influenced by current research findings outlined in the reports by the National Reading Panel, Principles and Standards for School Mathematics (National Council of Teachers of Mathematics, 2000), other research reports, and recommendations by advisory groups. In addition, the test items were reviewed by experts in the fields of reading, mathematics, and language. Pilot testing of test items and item analysis procedures were also conducted to identify the best test items.

Test response validity was established by comparing the WIAT-II with several other individually administered achievement tests, such as the Wechsler Individual Achievement Test (WIAT), the Peabody Picture Vocabulary Test-Third Edition (PPVT-III), the Wide Range Achievement Test-Third Edition (WRAT-3), the Differential Ability

Scales (DAS), and the Process Assessment of the Learner-Test Battery for Reading and Writing (PAL-RW). The Examiner's Manual reports correlation coefficients between individual subtests of the WIAT, PAL-RW, WRAT-3, DAS, and PPVT-III (only composite correlation coefficients are reported below for these tests).

Composite scores for the WIAT-II were correlated with the composite scores of the WIAT and the correlations were Reading .85, Math .86, Writing .66, and Language .66.

Composite scores for the WIAT-II were correlated with the WRAT-3 and the correlations were Reading .77, Math .68, and Spelling .73. Composite scores for the WIAT-II and the DAS were moderate with Reading .32, Math .64, and Spelling .47. Finally, correlation between the WIAT-II reading composite and the PPVT-III was .76.

Overall, correlations are moderate to high and consistent across various individually administered achievement tests. Other test response validity studies are reported for group-administered achievement tests, school grades, and special groups in the Examiner's Manual.

Reliability Confirmation

In test-retest studies, 297 subjects were tested twice. The sample consisted of three age groups (6–9, 10–12, and 13–19). Time between tests ranged from 7 to 45 days. For the children ages 6–9, the correlations for the subtests and composites ranged from .87 to .99. For the age group 10–12, the correlations for the subtests and composites ranged from .83 to .98. For the final group, ages 13–19, correlations for subtests and composites ranged from .86 to .98. Across age levels, subtests, and composites, the correlations were high between the first and second testing.

Objectivity Confirmation

There are three subtests in the WIAT-II that may require more independent judgment when scoring. These subtests are Reading Comprehension, Written Expression, and Oral Expression and may result in variations in examiner scoring. Two studies were conducted to evaluate subtest scoring agreement of these three subtests. A total of 2,180 protocols were scored independently by two scorers. The first study concentrated on scorer agreement with Reading Comprehension, and the second study analyzed scorer agreement in regard to Written Expression and Oral Expression. The reliability correlation coefficients between pairs of scorers on the first study ranged from .94 to .98. On the second study, correlation coefficients ranged from .71 to .94 for Written Expression and from .91 to .99 for Oral Expression across age groups. The test-retest correlation coefficients across age groups for composite scores ranged from .91 to .98. These results indicate that the WIAT-II can be scored consistently.

Statistical Confirmation

Statistical data on validity, reliability, and norms can be found in the Examiner's Manual.

Special Features

Acronym

WIAT-II.

Levels of the Test

One.

Number of Test Forms

One.

Norm-Referenced?

Yes. The WIAT-II was normed during the 1999–2000 and the 2000–2001 school years. The stratified random sampling plan was based on 1998 U.S. Census data. Stratification was based on the following variables: grade, age, sex, race/ethnicity, geographic region, and parent education. Eight to 10% of the standardized sample at each grade level consisted of students classified as those with special needs, and 3% of the sample were students in gifted and talented programs. The national sample consisted of 5,586 individuals: 199 children taken from the standardization sample were administered the WIAT-II and the WPPSI-R, 775 students were given the WIAT-II and the WISC-II, and 95 students ages 16–19 were given the WIAT-II and the WAIS-II. These linking samples consisted of 1,069 participants, and the demographic characteristics were stratified by race/ethnicity, parent/self education level, and geographic region. An additional normative sample for the adult standardization can be found in the WIAT-II Supplement for College Students and Adults.

Criterion-Referenced?

No.

Feasibility Considerations

Testing Time

For entire battery: grades Pre-K–K, 45 minutes; grades 1–6, 90 minutes; grades 7–16, 90–120 minutes. The entire test should be given in one setting. Breaks may be given, but individual subtests should be completed.

For Testing Groups? Individuals?

Individuals.

Test Administration and Scoring

Clearly stated directions are given for administering each individual subtest and are found in Chapter 4 of the Examiner's Manual. Starting Points and Discontinuation

Rules are clearly stated. Holistic scoring criteria for paragraphs are detailed clearly in the directions. The WIAT-II also has three different software scoring programs or WIAT-II Scoring Assistants: (1) WIAT-II Scoring Assistant; (2) WISC-III/WIAT-II Scoring Assistant; and (3) WAIS-III, WMS-III, WIAT-II Scoring Assistant. Reports are available for WAIS-III/WIAT-II and WAIS-III/WMS-III.

Only those individuals with professional training in educational or psychological assessment and who have had supervision in the administration of the WIAT-II should administer and interpret this assessment.

Test Materials and Approximate Costs

Complete Battery: $321; Examiner's Manual: $45; Record Forms (25): $100; Stimulus Books (each): $86; Response Booklets (25): $59.

Adequacy of Test Manuals

The WIAT-II has an Examiner's Manual and Scoring and Normative Supplement (Grades Pre-K–12). The Examiner's Manual is a comprehensive document. It is readable and includes information on the original WIAT scale and revisions to that scale, testing considerations, administration and scoring, development and standardization, and reliability, validity, and interpretation. The Interpretive chapter includes Eight Steps for Basic Interpretation of WIAT-II Performance. This information can be helpful to the educator when interpreting the overall results of the WIAT-II. The Scoring and Normative Supplement includes Conversion Tables and detailed information on scoring the Written Expression and Reading Comprehension and Oral Expression subtests. These manuals are user-friendly and readable for the educator. The Scoring and Normative Supplement is spiral bound for easy location and reading of conversion tables.

Excerpts from Other Test Reviews

No current reviews were found for the WIAT-II. Salvia and Ysseldyke (2001) reviewed the original WIAT (1992) and reported that "the test has an adequate standardization sample and appears to be very reliable and valid. . . . the subtests are designed to measure the seven areas of learning disability defined in Public Law 94-142" (p. 418).

Ordering Information

Publisher

The Psychological Corporation, 19500 Bulverde Road, San Antonio, TX 78259; Phone: 800-228-0752; Fax: 210-339-5873; Web site: www.psychcorp.com.

Authors

The Psychological Corporation.

Publication Date

2001.

Cautions and Comments

The WIAT-II is a fine addition for the assessment of learning disability and when linked to the WISC-III, an ability/achievement discrepancy score is available for the educator for determining eligibility for special services. The WIAT-II in combination with the WISC-III gives the professional an alternative to the Woodcock-Johnson Tests of Cognitive Ability and Tests of Achievement. The whole battery is user-friendly, and complete directions for administering the measure are located in the Stimulus Booklets, which saves the examiner time when administering the test. The WIAT-II has been modified to reflect changes in curriculum standards and classroom instructional demands. The link between assessment and instruction is included on the record form via Qualitative Observations checklists to aid the educator in planning an effective instructional plan.

Reference

Salvia, J., & Ysseldyke, J. E. (2001). *Assessment* (8th ed.). Boston: Houghton Mifflin.

Wide Range Achievement Test (WRAT-3),
for testing individuals from 5 through 75 years of age
Reviewed by Myles I. Friedman, Ph.D., Educational Psychology

Usefulness of the Test for Educators

Test Author's Purpose

The purpose of the WRAT-3 is to measure the codes that are needed to learn the basic skills of reading, spelling, and arithmetic (Administration Manual, p. 10).

Decision-Making Applications

The WRAT-3 is most appropriate for achievement certification. However, it is very limited in both scope and depth of subject matter assessment. The scope of school curriculum includes many more subjects than reading, spelling, and arithmetic; for example, social studies, science, literature, algebra, and geometry. And reading, spelling, and arithmetic skills can be assessed in greater depth; for example, the reading subtest does not assess reading comprehension, nor does the arithmetic test assess problem solving. Only reading, spelling, and arithmetic coding skills are assessed, and the ability to select the correct arithmetic computation operation. The test can also be used to profile relative strengths and weaknesses in arithmetic, spelling, and reading coding and to conduct research in those areas. However, it does not probe each of the three subject areas in sufficient depth and breadth to diagnose misconceptions in need of remediation. The WRAT-3 should be selected to assess achievement only if there is a limited interest in assessing achievement in reading, spelling, and arithmetic coding. Most schools teach more about reading, spelling, and arithmetic than coding and might well be interested in assessing those subjects in greater depth and breadth.

Relevant Population

Individuals from 5 through 75 years of age.

Characteristics Described

Three primary characteristics are assessed:

1. Reading: Recognizing and naming letters and pronouncing words out of context.
2. Spelling: Writing name and writing letters and words to dictation.
3. Arithmetic: Counting, reading number symbols, solving oral problems, and performing written computations (Administration Manual, p. 9).

The assessment of these characteristics is limited to determining whether students have learned language and math codes. Ability to comprehend or derive meaning is not assessed by the test.

The reading section consists of letter reading, which requires students to name letters of the alphabet, and word reading, which requires students to pronounce words. The spelling section requires students to write their name and letters of the alphabet, as well as to spell in writing words that are read to them. The arithmetic subtest consists of oral arithmetic, which requires students to respond to oral instructions to name numbers, count, add, and subtract by pointing to or saying the answer. It also consists of a written arithmetic section that requires students to solve arithmetic problems by selecting and executing the correct arithmetic computation operation and writing the answer.

Test Scores Obtained

Six scores are derived for the WRAT-3: raw, absolute, standard, grade equivalent, percentile, and normal-curve equivalent. A profile analysis form is used to compare WRAT-3 scores with intelligence test scores to indicate the degree of difficulty of the test items passed by the examinee.

Technical Adequacy

Validity Confirmation

Test item validity is questionable. Information was not provided showing that the test items correspond to common reading, spelling, and arithmetic coding curricula taught in the United States. However, the codes seem to be standard.

Test response validity was established by correlating WRAT-3 scores with scores of other achievement tests. Correlations with the California Test of Basic Skills range from .58 to .84, with the California Achievement Test from .41 to .77, and with the Stanford Achievement Test from .52 to .87. The author's claim that there is a positive correlation between WRAT-3 scores and age supports the tenet that the acquisition of basic academic skills increases with progress in school. Evidence is also provided that WRAT-3 scores correlate with intelligence test scores and discriminate between gifted, learning disabled, educable mentally handicapped, and normal groups.

Reliability Confirmation

Evidence is provided that the test results remain stable over time. Test-retest reliability was established by administering the same test to a sample of 142 individuals twice. The correlations ranged from .91 to .98. Alternate forms reliability was established by correlating the scores of the two forms of the test given to the same individuals. Correlations ranged from .82 to .99. Internal consistency reliability was established by correlating test items with one another. The correlations ranged from .85 to .95. The reliability of the WRAT-3 is adequate for making decisions pertaining to groups or individuals.

Objectivity Confirmation

Scoring keys are provided for the tests, and scoring procedures are clear and explicit, leaving little room for scorer judgment. Thus, variations among scorers are unlikely. However, evidence of agreement among different scorers scoring the same tests was not provided.

Statistical Confirmation

Statistical data on norm samples, validity, and reliability can be found in the Administration Manual.

Special Features

Acronym

WRAT-3.

Levels of the Test

One.

Number of Test Forms

Two equated alternate forms: blue and tan.

Norm-Referenced?

Yes. The WRAT-3 was nationally normed. A random stratified sample of 4,433 was drawn to be representative of the U.S. population, using 1990 U.S. Census data as criteria. The norm sample was stratified by region, gender, ethnicity, socioeconomic level, and age. However, the total number of states participating and rural/urban/suburban composition was not reported.

Criterion-Referenced?

No. The test does not assess achievement of specific learning objectives or learning of specific curricular content. However, a profile analysis form is provided which compares WRAT-3 scores with intelligence test scores, indicating the level of difficulty of examinees' achievement.

Feasibility Considerations

Testing Time

Fifteen to 30 minutes, depending on the age of the test taker.

For Testing Groups? Individuals?

According to the author, the spelling and arithmetic subtests can be administered to groups. However, very young children may need individual assistance.

Test Administration and Scoring

The directions for administering and scoring the test are simple and clear. Training and certification are not required.

Test Materials and Approximate Costs

Complete kit, which includes Examiner's Manual, blue test forms (25), tan test forms (25), profile analysis forms (25), and reading and spelling list on plastic cards: $139; Examiner's Manual: $44; blue test forms (25): $32; tan test forms (25): $32; profile analysis forms (25): $24; reading and spelling list on plastic cards: $18.

Adequacy of Test Manuals

The Administration Manual includes norm, validity, reliability, objectivity, and test development data. It also includes a description of the tests and administration and scoring directions. Everything provided is clearly presented.

Excerpts from Other Test Reviews

Salvia and Ysseldyke (2001) state: "The test is well standardized and has adequate reliability. The test's content validity is questionable" (p. 416). McLoughlin and Lewis (2001) state: "The WRAT-3 should not be used as the sole instrument for determining a student's current levels of academic achievement. It lacks coverage of some important skills. Reliability is adequate, but its relationship to other individual measures of academic achievement requires further study" (p. 188). Clark (1994) states: "This test seems to have potential as a research and clinical tool. . . . The test should not be used to assist in the diagnosis of learning disability, to help determine personality structure or check school achievement for vocational assessment, job placement and training" (p. 65). Harrison (1994) states: "Traditional internal consistency reliability coefficients are not available and test-retest reliability coefficients are questionable. Content validity reliability is not supported and information about construct and concurrent validity is limited. The general uses of the WRAT-R given in the test manual are not supported by the test's psychometric qualities. There is no supporting evidence that the WRAT-R can be used for placement of children into special education or for prescribing instruction" (p. 67).

Ordering Information

Publisher

Wide Range, Inc., P.O. Box 3410, 15 Ashley Place, Suite 1A, Wilmington, DE 19804; Phone: 800-221-9728; Fax: 302-652-1644; Web site: www.widerange.com.

Author

Gary S. Wilkinson.

Publication Dates

1940–1993.

Cautions and Comments

It may be tempting and not too difficult to find fault with an academic achievement test named Wide Range Achievement Test that is so limited in scope and can be completed by older students and adults in as little as 15 minutes. And as is evident by the test reviews cited above, reviewers do find fault with the test. After considering the limitations of the test, its tenable applications should be considered as well. The WRAT-3 only assesses learning of letter, word, and arithmetic codes, the most fundamental aspects of reading and math. It does not assess reading or math comprehension or anything else taught in school. However, there is little doubt that reading and arithmetic codes are taught in all schools in the United States. If your purpose is to test reading, spelling, and arithmetic coding achievement, the standardization, reliability, and validity of the test are adequate. Evidence of test-retest and alternate form reliability has been provided. Test item validity has been established by using experts to guide test item construction and selection. However, test items were not matched with school curriculum for congruity. Test response validity was established to some extent by correlating WRAT-3 test scores with progress in school and intelligence tests and other achievement test scores. If there is an interest in assessing achievement of reading and arithmetic coding, the test is adequate. Reading and arithmetic coding are fundamental but a very small percentage of school curricula.

References

Clark, E. (1994). Review of the Wide Range Achievement Test 3. In J. C. Impara & L. L. Murphy (Eds.), *Psychological assessment in the schools* (pp. 64–66). Lincoln, NE: The Buros Institute of Mental Measurements.

Harrison, P. L. (1994). Review of the Wide Range Achievement Test 3. In J. C. Impara & L. L. Murphy (Eds.), *Psychological assessment in the schools* (pp. 66–68). Lincoln, NE: The Buros Institute of Mental Measurements.

McLoughlin, J. A., & Lewis, R. B. (2001). *Assessing students with special needs*. Columbus, OH: Merrill/Prentice Hall.

Salvia, J., & Ysseldyke, J. E. (2001). *Assessment* (8th ed.). Boston: Houghton Mifflin.

9

Individual-Skill Academic Achievement Tests

Reading Tests

Nelson-Denny Reading Test, Forms G and H,
for testing groups from grades 9 through 16 and adults
Reviewed by Katherine C. Schnepel, Ph.D.,
Educational Research and Measurement

Usefulness of the Test for Educators

Test Authors' Purpose

The primary purpose of the Nelson-Denny Reading Test, Forms G and H, is to provide a trustworthy assessment of student ability in three areas of academic achievement: Vocabulary, Reading Comprehension, and Reading Rate.

Decision-Making Applications

The Nelson-Denny Reading Test can be of value in identifying high school students and adults who may need special help developing reading skills in order to take full advantage of their courses. The authors claim that the test is useful in predicting academic success and diagnosing students' reading problems. However, it would seem that these might not be decisions that should be based on the results of this test alone. It seems that it is basically a survey instrument and is best used for screening students with reading problems; alone it is probably not effective in pinpointing those problems and prescribing instructional remediation.

Relevant Population

Grades 9–16 and adults.

Characteristics Described

Vocabulary, Reading Comprehension, and Reading Rate are measured by the test. The Vocabulary test consists of 80 items, each with five answer choices. A sample vocabulary item would be: A chef works with (a) bricks, (b) music, (c) clothes, (d) food, (e) statues. The student is asked to choose the response he or she thinks is correct. The Reading Comprehension test contains seven reading passages and a total of 38 questions, each with five answer choices. In order to measure Reading Rate, the students are asked to begin reading the first passage at their normal rate. At the end of one minute, the examiner says, "mark." The student is then asked to stop on the line he or she is reading and to note the number at the right of that line and write that number in the place provided under the heading "Reading Rate." Then the students are asked to go on immediately with their reading and to answer the questions about each passage.

Test Scores Obtained

There are four raw scores: Vocabulary, Comprehension, Total, and Reading Rate. These raw scores (number correct) can then be converted to scale scores, grade equivalents, percentile rank, stanines, and normal curve equivalents using the tables in the Manual for Scoring and Interpretation (pp. 21–39).

Technical Adequacy

Validity Confirmation

There is limited evidence provided for *test item validity*. Limited information is provided on the sources of words and passages and the criteria for their selection. Passage readability and item passage dependence were not provided at all.

Test response validity is addressed by examining the test as a screening test. Several studies by education institutions are summarized in the Technical Report. In these studies, previous forms of the test have been used to support the use of cutoff scores from the test, and scores have been correlated with students' grades. Validity studies with Forms G and H are not reported.

Reliability Confirmation

Evidence for stability reliability was presented by using the alternate forms method. Alternate forms of the test were administered within a three-week period. Correlation coefficients ranged from .81 to .90 on the subtests and total and were .68 on the Reading Rate.

Objectivity Confirmation

A clear answer key is provided, so inter-rater objectivity should not be an issue. Directions for administration are clear and specific, so the test can be administered by persons not trained in assessment.

Statistical Confirmation

Statistical confirmation for validity, reliability, and norms of the Nelson-Denny Reading Test can be found in the Technical Report.

Special Features

Acronym

None.

Levels of the Test

One.

Number of Test Forms

Two.

Norm-Referenced?

Yes. Standardization of Forms G and H of the Nelson-Denny Reading Test was based on three samples: one from the population of students enrolled in grades 9 through 12 (high school), one from the two-year college population, and one from the four-year college/university population. Also, to obtain special norms for law enforcement academies, a sample was selected from the population of students enrolled in these institutions. Three stratifying variables were used to guide the selection of participants in the Nelson-Denny standardization; geographic region, district enrollment, and socioeconomic status of the community. The high school sample consisted of nearly 12,000 students, the two-year college sample consisted of nearly 5,000 students, and the four-year college sample totaled over 5,000 students. A volunteer sample of 531 students came from law enforcement academies.

Criterion-Referenced?

Yes. The Nelson-Denny Reading Test is referenced to three areas of ability in reading: Vocabulary, Reading Comprehension, and Reading Rate.

Other Features

Extended-time mode of administration is available, with a special set of norms. Populations especially likely to benefit from extended-time administration are students with English as a second language or as a foreign language. Also, situations where students are primarily returning adults may warrant using extended-time administration. Adult learners are often intimidated if they are rigidly timed while attempting to demonstrate academic proficiency. Extended-time administration should be done in two sessions. In the first session, students provide the information required on the answer sheets and take the Vocabulary Test. In the second session, students take the Comprehension Test (the Reading Rate measure is omitted). Times allotted for the two tests in this mode would be 24 minutes for the Vocabulary Test and 32 minutes for the Comprehension Test.

Feasibility Considerations

Testing Time

Forty-five minutes for the entire test.

For Testing Groups? Individuals?

Groups.

Test Administration and Scoring

Clear and specific directions for both standard administration and extended-time administration are given in the Directions for Administration. The scoring key and directions for scoring are provided in the Manual for Scoring and Interpretation. Two types of answer sheets, self-scorable and machine-scorable, are provided with the test. Quick and easy directions for the self-scorable answer sheets are given on the answer sheets themselves. A testing coordinator can easily give instructions about scoring machine-scorable answer sheets.

Test Materials and Approximate Costs

Test booklets (25) (specify form): $50.25; Directions for Administration (1993, 13 pages): $5.75; Manual for Scoring and Interpretation (1993, 53 pages): $17.75; Technical Report (1993, 58 pages): $12.25; Machine-scorable answer sheets (250): $214; Self-scorable answer sheets (250): $229.25; Class record sheets (25): $14.50; Students' personal records (50): $28; Examination kit: $13.50.

Adequacy of Test Manuals

The needed information for the examiner is given in the three manuals provided: the Directions for Administration, the Manual for Scoring and Interpretation, and the Technical Report. However, the manuals seem a bit disjointed and are not very user-friendly. The examiner must dig out information, especially about the validity and reliability of the Nelson-Denny.

Excerpts from Other Test Reviews

The Nelson-Denny Reading Test, Forms G and H was reviewed by Murray-Ward (1998) and Smith (1998). Murray-Ward states that "the Nelson-Denny is somewhat useful in testing the general reading skills of older students. It is a concise, practical assessment that is easy to score. However, examiners should not overinterpret the scores. Although the test does measure general reading, it does not measure performance on more current materials and varied reading tasks required of students. Furthermore, the validity evidence does not substantiate claims that the test can be used to diagnose specific reading problems. There is no author-generated evidence that the 1993 version is an accurate predictor of success in college." Smith says, "The most appropriate use of the Nelson-Denny Reading Test, Forms G and H, is for screening. It is an easily administered group measure of vocabulary and reading comprehension. As such it is useful in identifying high school students who may have difficulties in these areas. The authors provide a wealth of information regarding development of the instrument, bias analyses, and item difficulties. However, the norms are somewhat dated and unrepresentative of the U.S. population today. In addition, test-retest data and current validity studies are lacking."

Ordering Information

Publisher

Riverside Publishing Company, 425 Spring Lake Drive, Itasca, IL 60143-2079; Phone: 800-323-9540; Fax: 630-467-7192; Web site: www.riverpub.com.

Authors

James I. Brown, Vivian Vick Fishco, and Gerald Hanna.

Publication Date

1993.

Cautions and Comments

According to the authors, the vocabulary selected for the Nelson-Denny was taken from various texts. However, the selection procedures were not described, and this 1993 edition of the test uses the same means for measuring reading as the 1929 edition. The comprehension passages do not reflect current reading requirements involving use of pictures, charts, tables, and text. Thus, one wonders how useful this test is for diagnosing specific reading deficiencies that are relevant for today's adults.

References

Murray-Ward, M. (1998). Review of the Nelson-Denny Reading Test, Forms G and H. In J. C. Impara & B. S. Plake (Eds.), *The Thirteenth Mental Measurements Yearbook* [Electronic version]. Retrieved January 14, 2002 from Buros Institute's Test Reviews Online web site: http://www.unl.edu/buros.

Smith, D. K. (1998). Review of the Nelson-Denny Reading Test, Forms G and H. In J. C. Impara & B. S. Plake (Eds.), *The Thirteenth Mental Measurements Yearbook* [Electronic version]. Retrieved January 14, 2002 from Buros Institute's Test Reviews Online web site: http://www.unl.edu/buros.

Slosson Oral Reading Test-Revised (SORT-R),
for testing individuals from preschool through adulthood
Reviewed by Katherine C. Schnepel, Ph.D.,
Educational Research and Measurement

Usefulness of the Test for Educators

Test Authors' Purpose

The SORT-R is designed to provide a quick estimate of a person's oral word recognition or "word calling " level. The authors state that it is a "quick screening test to determine a student's reading level" (Examiner's Manual).

Decision-Making Applications

The SORT-R should be used primarily for initial screening or research purposes. It is not a diagnostic measure, nor does it measure all aspects of reading, such as word knowledge and comprehension. The authors say that the SORT-R can be used to assess a student's progress, to determine a student's grade level in reading, and to decide if a student is in need of further diagnostic assessment. Thus, it could be used for referral, but it would not be appropriate to use the SORT-R for instructional prescription.

Relevant Population

The test covers individuals from preschool through adulthood.

Characteristics Described

The SORT-R describes a student's "level of oral word recognition, word calling or reading level" (Examiner's Manual).

Test Scores Obtained

Scores obtained from the SORT-R are the raw score, the grade equivalent, age equivalent, and the standard score. The raw score is the number correct. From the raw score the grade equivalent and the age equivalent are determined by using Table D in the Examiner's Manual. Tables E and F are used to determine the standard score. Table G is used to convert SORT-R standard scores into other standard scores and percentiles.

Technical Adequacy

Validity Confirmation

Test item validity seems to be well supported. The words on the SORT-R word lists were drawn from word lists prepared by reading experts, reading lists in textbooks at selected grade levels, and other tests. All the words were reviewed by reading experts and textbook authors and were compared to various curriculum guides. The words were chosen to reflect a steady progress in reading difficulty from preschool to high school level.

Test response validity is supported by comparing the results of the SORT-R with the results of two tests of reading recognition: The Letter Word Identification subtest of the Woodcock-Johnson Test of Achievement and The Reading Recognition subtest of the Peabody Individual Achievement Test. The correlation of the SORT-R with each of these subtests was .90. The authors also compared the SORT-R with two other subtests: the Woodcock-Johnson Test of Achievement-Passage Comprehension and the Peabody Individual Achievement Test-Reading Comprehension. The correlations of the SORT-R with these two subtests were .68 and .83, respectively. However, that doesn't seem to support test response validity of the SORT-R for the purpose for which it was designed (i.e., word recognition).

Reliability Confirmation

Test-retest data was given as evidence of stability reliability. The test-retest results are on a portion of the standardization sample numbering 16 subjects. The retest was given one week after the initial test. The test-retest correlation was .98. No age or grade data for the sample was given.

Objectivity Confirmation

A very clear scoring key and scoring criteria are given in the Examiner's Manual. No special training or certification is needed for administering or scoring the test. Thus, objectivity of scoring does not seem to be a problem.

Statistical Confirmation

Extensive statistical data on reliability, validity, and norms is available in the Test Manual for the SORT-R.

Special Features

Acronym

SORT-R.

Levels of the Test

Ten levels. The levels from preschool through adult are determined by the word list used. There are 10 groups of 20 words, beginning with preschool. The last list covers grades 9–12 and are words which are most frequently encountered at the adult level. The examiner starts where he/she thinks the individual can pronounce all 20 words on one word list card correctly. If the student cannot pronounce all 20 words on that list, the examiner goes to the previous, less difficult list and continues to do that until the individual does pronounce all 20 words on the list correctly. That list then becomes the starting or basal card. The examiner continues (skipping over any word list card that the individual already completed but had to go to a previous word list card) until the stopping or ceiling card is reached. This card is reached when the individual is unable to pronounce any words on a list.

Number of Test Forms

One.

Norm-Referenced?

Yes. The SORT-R has been nationally normed on 1,331 individuals from preschool to adult across 30 states. It was co-normed with the Slosson Intelligence Test. The authors say that percentages of the sample reflect the gender and racial percentages of the total U.S. population.

Criterion-Referenced?

Yes. The SORT-R is referenced to one reading skill, oral word recognition, or "word calling" level. There are numerous opportunities for the student to make an error on that skill. This allows the test to be used effectively for referral for further diagnosis or remediation of that skill.

Other Features

A large-print edition is available for individuals with visual handicaps.

Feasibility Considerations

Testing Time

Three to five minutes.

For Testing Groups? Individuals?

Individuals.

Test Administration and Scoring

Scoring is based on total number of words read correctly. Words are considered to be read incorrectly if the student pronounces them incorrectly, takes longer than five seconds to read them, changes their form (e.g., rides/ride) or skips over them. Correct pronunciation of each word is given in the Examiner's Manual. No training or certification is needed to administer the test. However, it is recommended that examiners practice on several individuals before administering for record keeping.

Test Materials and Approximate Costs

Complete kit, which includes the Examiner's Manual, score sheets, and word lists: $60; Examiner's Manual: $40; Score sheets (25): $26; Word lists: $14; Large-print word lists: $7.

Adequacy of Test Manuals

The Examiner's Manual is adequate. It provides a brief overview of the test and describes how to prepare for testing and how to administer and score the test. It also includes extensive technical information including validity, reliability, objectivity, and normative data.

Excerpts from Other Test Reviews

The SORT-R was reviewed by Shaw and Swerdlik (1998) and Westby (1998). Shaw and Swerdlik express reservations about the sample used in norming the test: "Close inspection shows that large differences exist between sample and census data on geographic location and occupational status. There are also large differences in the number of subjects at different age levels. The authors say that subjects were included from 'special classes ranging from the retarded to gifted, learning disabled and regular' (p. 7). However, no data on these special populations were provided. The authors provide a list of school districts which were included in the sample, but don't give any demographic information about them or tell us how they were selected." Shaw and Swerdlik also question the relevance of the test to school-based instruction. They say that "the SORT-R fills a very small niche in reading assessment" and that "This niche may be filled better with teacher's judgment of a student's reading ability."

Westby seems to agree with Shaw and Swerdlik that the SORT-R is very limited in its usefulness for assessing reading ability, particularly to the classroom teacher.

Ordering Information

Publisher

Slosson Educational Publications, Inc., P.O. Box 280, East Aurora, NY 14052-0280; Phone: 888-756-7766; Fax: 800-655-3840; e-mail: slosson@slosson.com; Web site: http://www.slosson.com.

Authors

Richard L. Slosson and Charles L. Nicholson.

Publication Dates

1963 and 1990.

Cautions and Comments

The SORT-R can be used effectively as a screening test of reading ability. Its results can be used for referral to diagnostic assessment, which may lead to instructional intervention or remediation. However, the examiner needs to be aware that the SORT-R measures only two reading skills (i.e., word recognition and word calling or pronunciation). It does not measure other reading skills, such as word knowledge and comprehension. It is a quick screening measure to assess a student's reading level.

References

Shaw, S. R., & Swerdlik, M. E. (1998). Review of the Slosson Oral Reading Test, Revised. In J. C. Conoley & J. C. Impara (Eds.), *The Thirteenth Mental Measurements Yearbook* [Electronic version]. Retrieved October 12, 2001 from Buros Institute's Test Reviews Online web site: http://www.unl.edu/buros.

Westby, C. E. (1998). Review of the Slosson Oral Reading Test, Revised. In J. C. Conoley & J. C. Impara (Eds.), *The Thirteenth Mental Measurements Yearbook* [Electronic version]. Retrieved October 12, 2001 from Buros Institute's Test Reviews Online web site: http://www.unl.edu/buros.

STAR Reading Test, for testing individuals from grades 1 through 12
Reviewed by Katherine C. Schnepel, Ph.D.,
Educational Research and Measurement

Usefulness of the Test for Educators

Test Authors' Purpose

The test authors state that the STAR Reading Test serves three primary purposes. First, it provides teachers with quick and accurate estimates of students' instructional reading levels. Second, it offers sound estimates of students' reading levels relative to national norms. Third, because it can be administered multiple times within a school year, it can provide educators with a measure of growth in student reading ability during the year (Norms/Technical Manual, p. 2).

Decision-Making Applications

The STAR Reading Test can be used for screening and for determining reading level. However, the test does not indicate to the examiner which items are missed; it only indicates how many are missed (i.e., reading level). Thus, it cannot be used to pinpoint deficiencies in reading ability or to indicate instructional remediation needed. The test can be used for placement in groups which are determined by reading level.

Relevant Population

Individuals in grades 1 through 12.

Characteristics Described

The STAR Reading Test is a computerized test designed to measure instructional reading level. All of the items in the item pool of the test are in a vocabulary-in-context format that is similar to a cloze technique. Each item consists of a sentence with a missing word. The examinee must select the correct response for the missing word from three or four choices within a 60- or 45-second time limit, depending on grade level. All responses are made by the examinee on the computer.

Test Scores Obtained

The authors state that the STAR Reading Test provides two different types of test scores that measure student performance in different ways:

1. *Criterion-referenced scores* measure student performance by comparing it to a standard criterion. This criterion can come in any number of forms: common criterion foundations include material covered in a specific text, lecture, or course. It could also take the form of curriculum or district educational standards. These scores provide a measure of student achievement compared to a fixed criterion; they do not provide any measure of comparability to other students. The criterion-referenced score reported by STAR Reading software is the Instructional Reading Level, which compares a student's test performance to 1995 updated vocabulary lists that were based on the EDL Core Vocabulary.

2. *Norm-referenced scores* compare a student's test results to the results of other students who have taken the same test. In this case, scores provide a relative measure of student achievement compared to the performance of a group of students at a given time. Percentile ranks and grade equivalents are the two primary norm-referenced scores available in STAR Reading software. Both of these scores are based on a comparison of a student's test results to the data collected during the 1999 national norming program (Norms/Technical Manual, ch. 6, p. 2). Also available in STAR Reading software is the Normal Curve Equivalent (NCE), a scaled score similar to the percentile rank except that it is based on an equal interval scale. That is, the difference between two successive scores on the scale has the same meaning throughout the scale. Two additional scores can be obtained. They are the Zone of Proximal Development (ZPD) and Diagnostic Codes, both derived from the Grade Equivalent. The ZPD defines the reading range from which students should be selecting books to achieve optimal reading growth without experiencing frustration. The Diagnostic Code represents behavioral characteristics of readers at particular stages of development. However, these codes were not statistically validated.

Technical Adequacy

Validity Confirmation

Test item validity is supported by showing that the items were matched to the appropriate word-level placement information in Educational Development Laboratory's *A Revised Core Vocabulary* (1969). Text passages were created by identifying authentic texts, extracting appropriate passages, and creating cloze-type questions and answers (Norms/Technical Manual, ch. 2, p. 4). Each of the items in the resulting pool was then rated according to several criteria in order to determine which items were best suited for inclusion in the tryout and calibration. Three educators rated each item on the following criteria: (1) content material of the passage, (2) cohesiveness of the passage, (3) suitability of the passage for its grade level in terms of vocabulary, and (4) suitability of the passage for its grade level in terms of content density (Technical Manual, ch. 2, p. 5).

In order to give evidence of *test response validity*, more than 12,000 student test results from the STAR Reading Test were correlated with the same students' test results from the reading subtests of several other standardized instruments: the California Achievement Test (CAT), the Comprehensive Test of Basic Skills (CTBS), the Iowa Tests of Basic Skills (ITBS), the Metropolitan Achievement Test (MAT), the Stanford Achievement Test (SAT), and several state tests. These correlations were done across grade levels. The resulting correlation coefficients were .60 or higher.

Reliability Confirmation

Stability reliability is supported using a variation of the test-retest method. Normally, the test-retest method entails giving the same students the same test twice with a short time in between. In this case, the same students were given the STAR Reading Test twice, but different items from the item pool of the test were used in the two testings. The two tests were identical otherwise. Correlation coefficients from this test-retest study ranged from .79 to .94, with just the coefficient from grade 11 below .80. Evidence for the reliability of the STAR Reading Test was also given using the alternate forms method. Students in this study took a STAR Reading Test, release 1 and a STAR Reading Test, release 2. Some students took release 1 first and then release 2, and some took release 2 first and then release 1. The resulting correlations ranged from .82 to .95.

Objectivity Confirmation

Inter-rater objectivity is not an issue with the STAR Reading Test because each item is automatically scored using Adaptive Branching™, where the program weighs each answer provided by the student and presents the next question at an appropriate difficulty level. There is a time limit for answering each test question. Students in grades 1 and 2 have 60 seconds to answer each question; all other students have 45 seconds to answer each of the first 20 questions and 90 seconds to answer each of the last five questions. The program will notify the student that time has run out, and then the next question will appear. Any unanswered question will be counted as an incorrect answer.

Statistical Confirmation

Statistical confirmation for validity, reliability, and norms is provided the Norms/Technical Manual.

Special Features

Acronym

STAR Reading.

Levels of the Test

Thirteen. Levels of the test are determined by the grade level of the examinee. Levels 1 and 2 include only vocabulary items; levels 3 through 13 also include authentic text passage items.

Number of Test Forms

There is a large item pool. Thus, the same student may take the test several times in a year and never answer the exact same questions. In other words, many forms of the test can be constructed from this one test item pool.

Norm-Referenced?

Yes. School districts, schools, and individual students were selected to participate in the standardization study in order to obtain a sample as representative of the U.S. school population as possible. The three key variables used to identify this sample, in order of importance, were geographic region, school system and per-grade district enrollment, and socioeconomic status. The final norming sample included a nationally representative mix of approximately 30,000 students from 269 schools. These schools represented 47 states (Norms/Technical Manual, ch. 3, p. 3).

Criterion-Referenced?

Yes. The STAR Reading Test is referenced to 1995 updated vocabulary lists that were based on the Educational Development Laboratory's (EDL) Core Vocabulary.

Other Features

The software includes a management program, which enables the teacher to manage students, classes, and reports.

Feasibility Considerations

Testing Time

Approximately 10 minutes.

For Testing Groups? Individuals?

Individuals.

Test Administration and Scoring

Clear instructions for administering are given in the Administration Manual, including illustrations of what is shown on the computer screen. No specific training or certification is required of the examiner other than basic knowledge of the computer. Scoring is done within the program each time a student takes the test.

Test Materials and Approximate Costs

School license for up to 200 students, including Administrator's Manual (173 pages), teacher's guides (5), Norms/Technical Manual (94 pages), one-year Expert Support Plan, pre-test instruction kit, STAR Reading 2.2 Installation CD, STAR Reading 2.2 Software Manual, STAR Reading 2.2 Installation Guide, and STAR Reading Quick Reference Card: $1,499.

Single-computer license, including Administrator's Manual, QuickInstall card, one-year Expert Support Plan, and pretest instruction kit: $399.

Adequacy of Test Manuals

The Software Manual provides clear instructions for administering the test and managing test results.

Excerpts from Other Test Reviews

The STAR Reading Test was reviewed by Volpe-Johnstone (2001) and Ward (2001). Volpe-Johnstone states that "the STAR Reading was specifically developed to work well with Accelerated Reader. This is a shortcoming. If this program were not part of the curriculum, another type of organized reading program would need to be in place for this test to be useful. The results of the tests are based on grade placement and the ensuing reports are boilerplate—based on standard score and sequencing paradigms for the field of reading education that may not fit the profile of a student. Insufficient validity evidence is presented for 9th through 12th grades or for IRLs. This test has great potential but continued validation studies to support conclusions regarding the use of the STAR Reading for its entire intended purpose is needed."

Ward says, "A major concern regarding the use of the STAR Reading in establishing reading levels is its reliance on a single item type that represents an artificial reading task and depends heavily on vocabulary development. Consequently, this measure should be used as a screening device. Supplementary data on reading ability should be collected to support conclusions regarding reading level. The STAR Reading should not be used for the diagnosis of reading disabilities nor used for placement decisions."

Ordering Information

Publisher

Advantage Learning Systems, Inc., P.O. Box 8036, Wisconsin Rapids, WI 54495-8036; Phone: 800-338-4204; Fax: 715-424-4242; e-mail: answers@advlearn.com; Web site: www.advlearn.com.

Authors

Advantage Learning Systems, Inc.

Publication Date

1999.

Cautions and Comments

The STAR Reading Test is a way to obtain a cursory reading level quickly. However, it is based on a single item type (an artificial reading task), so it may not reflect reading ability. Also, it is heavily dependent on vocabulary development. STAR Reading only indicates how many items are missed, not which items are missed, so it cannot be used for diagnosis of reading deficiencies or for prescription of remedial instruction. It can be used for placement decisions which are based on reading level.

References

Volpe-Johnstone, T. (2001). Review of the STAR Reading Test. In B. S. Plake & J. C. Impara (Eds.), *The Fourteenth Mental Measurements Yearbook* (pp. 1175–1177). Lincoln, NE: The Buros Institute of Mental Measurements.

Ward, S. (2001). Review of the STAR Reading Test. In B. S. Plake & J. C. Impara (Eds.), *The Fourteenth Mental Measurements Yearbook* (pp. 1177–1179). Lincoln, NE: The Buros Institute of Mental Measurements.

Mathematics Test

STAR Math Test, for testing individuals from grades 3 through 12
Reviewed by Katherine C. Schnepel, Ph.D.,
Educational Research and Measurement

Usefulness of the Test for Educators

Test Authors' Purpose

The test authors state that the STAR Math Test serves two primary purposes. First, it provides teachers with quick and accurate estimates of students' mathematics achievement levels relative to national norms. Second, it provides the means for tracking growth in a consistent manner over long time periods for all students (Technical Manual, ch. 1, p. 2).

Decision-Making Applications

The STAR Math Test can be used effectively as a quick and easy-to-administer measure of students' mathematics achievement levels. It can also be used to decide at what level instruction should begin and is useful for tracking mathematics achievement over long periods of time. It is not useful for diagnosis of strengths and weaknesses of individual students in mathematics. This is so because the teacher does not know which items the student answers correctly or incorrectly, only the number of items answered correctly, so the teacher has no way of pinpointing deficiencies or strengths.

Relevant Population

The STAR Math Test is designed for use with students in grades 3 through 12.

Characteristics Described

The STAR Math Test is a computerized test designed to measure the following math skills: Numeration Concepts, Computation, Word Problems, Estimation, Statistics, Charts and Graphs, Geometry, Measurement, and Algebra (Technical Manual, ch. 2, pp. 2–6). The STAR Math Test is divided into two parts, each containing 12 questions. The first part of the test addresses the Numeration Concepts and Computation strands; all of the other strands are addressed in the second part (Technical Manual, ch. 1, p. 4). The questions include mathematical problems and concept questions in multiple-choice format. A list of four possible answers is shown below the question. The student selects an answer by pressing the <A>,<B>,<C>, or <D> key on the keyboard. A blue box will appear around the answer the student selected. The student can then change his or her answer if necessary by pressing a different key. When the student decides on an answer, he or she presses <Return> (Macintosh) or <Enter> (Windows) (Software Manual, ch. 8, p. 7). Adaptive Branching™ is used in the STAR Math Test; that is, if the student chooses an incorrect response to a question, the program gives an easier question next. If the student chooses the correct response to a question, the next question given is more difficult. Thus, the test difficulty matches each individual's performance level.

Test Scores Obtained

The STAR Test Math provides grade equivalents, percentile ranks, normal-curve equivalents, and scaled scores. The software is used to score the test and gives users immediate feedback on the student's performance. Raw score, the number correct, is also provided; however, there is no way for the teacher to see which questions a student answered correctly or incorrectly.

Technical Adequacy

Validity Confirmation

The authors support *test item validity* by providing the rules they used for writing items. The first rule was to have item content, wording, and format reflect the typical appearance of the content in curricular materials. Second, every effort was made to keep item content simple and to keep the required reading levels low. Third, efforts were made both in the item-writing and item-editing processes to minimize cultural loading, gender stereotyping, and ethnic bias in the items. Fourth, the items had to be written in such a way as to be presented in the computer-adaptive format. Finally, the items were all to be presented in a multiple-choice format (Technical Manual, ch. 2, pp. 6–7).

As evidence of *test response validity*, the STAR Math Test results of more than 9,000 students were correlated with the same students' test results from the math subtests of the California Achievement Test (CAT), the Comprehensive Test of Basic Skills (CTBS), the Iowa Test of Basic Skills (ITBS), the Metropolitan Achievement Test (MAT), the Stanford Achievement Test (SAT), and several state tests. The resulting correlation coefficients ranged from .63 to .88, with most higher than .70.

Reliability Confirmation

Stability reliability was supported using a variation of the test-retest method. Normally, the test-retest method involves giving the same students the same test twice with a short time in between. In this case, the same students were given the STAR Math Test twice, but different items from the item pool of the test were used in the two testings. The two tests were identical otherwise. Correlation coefficients from this test-retest study at grades 3 through 6 were in the high .70s, while in the higher grades they were in the .80s. Salvia and Ysseldyke (2001) say that "The test has sufficient reliability for use as a screening test, but not for making eligibility and placement decisions" (p. 473).

Objectivity Confirmation

Inter-rater objectivity is not an issue with the STAR Math Test because each item is automatically scored using Adaptive Branching™, where the program weighs each answer provided by the student and presents the next question at an appropriate difficulty level. There is a three-minute time limit for answering each test question. Thirty seconds before the time limit is up, the program flashes a picture of a clock in the top right corner of the question screen. Students should make their best guess based on the available solutions to the test item. If the student does not select an answer and press <Enter> or <Return> before time runs out, the screen will go blank, and the program will notify the student that time has run out. Then the next question will appear, and the unanswered question will be counted as an incorrect answer.

Statistical Confirmation

Statistical data for validity, reliability, and norms can be found in the Technical Manual.

Special Features

Acronym

STAR Math.

Levels of the Test

Ten. Levels of the test are determined by the grade level of the examinee.

Number of Test Forms

There is a large item pool. Thus, the same student may take the test several times in a year and never answer the exact same questions. In other words, many forms of the test can be constructed from this one test item pool.

Norm-Referenced?

Yes. School districts, schools, and individual students were selected to participate in the standardization study in order to obtain a sample as representative of the U.S. school population as possible. The three key variables used to identify this sample, in order of importance, were geographic region, school system and per-grade district enrollment, and socioeconomic status. The final norming sample included a nationally representative mix of approximately 25,800 students from 256 schools. These schools represented 42 states (Technical Manual, ch. 3, p. 3).

Criterion-Referenced?

Yes. The STAR Math Test is referenced to the objectives commonly taught in the mathematics curriculum of contemporary schools (primarily in the United States).

Other Features

The software includes a management program, which enables the teacher to manage students, classes, and reports.

Feasibility Considerations

Testing Time

Approximately 15 minutes.

For Testing Groups? Individuals?

Individuals.

Test Administration and Scoring

Clear instructions for administering are given in the Administration Manual, including illustrations of what is shown on the computer screen. No specific training or certification is required of the examiner other than basic knowledge of the computer. Scoring is done within the program each time a student takes the test.

Test Materials and Approximate Costs

Complete kit with school license for 200 students. The kit includes one-year support plan, Quick Reference Card, Administration Manual, 1.2 Installation CD, 1.2 Software Manual, 1.2 Installation Guide, and 1.2 Pre-Test Instructions: $1,499.

Adequacy of Test Manuals

The Software Manual provides clear instructions for administering the test and managing test results.

Excerpts from Other Test Reviews

The STAR Math Test was reviewed by Salvia and Ysseldyke (2001), who state: "It [STAR Math] provides teachers with immediate diagnostic profiles on student performance. Evidence for reliability is limited, but evidence for validity is good" (p. 473).

Ordering Information

Publisher

Advantage Learning Systems, Inc., P.O. Box 8036, Wisconsin Rapids, WI 54495-8036; Phone: 800-338-4204; Fax: 715-424-4242; e-mail: answers@advlearn.com; Web site: www.advlearn.com.

Authors

Advantage Learning Systems, Inc.

Publication Date

1999.

Cautions and Comments

The STAR Math Test is a quick and easy assessment of mathematics achievement. However, there are only 24 items on the test, so the sampling of skills is very small. Thus, perhaps it should only be used for screening or as a precursor of more in-depth diagnostic measures. It would not be appropriate to use the STAR Math as the only basis for placing a student in an instructional program. Also, the teacher has no way of knowing which items the student answers correctly or incorrectly, so it cannot be used to identify deficiencies or prescribe remediation.

Reference

Salvia, J., & Ysseldyke, J. E. (2001). *Assessment* (8th ed.). Boston: Houghton Mifflin.

Spoken and Written Language Tests

**Expressive One-Word Picture Vocabulary Test-Spanish Bilingual Edition
(EOWPVT-SBE)**, for testing individuals from 4 through 12 years of age
Reviewed by Katherine C. Schnepel, Ph.D.,
Educational Research and Measurement

Usefulness of the Test for Educators

Test Author's Purpose

The author states that the EOWPVT-SBE provides a measure which reflects the
extent of an individual's vocabulary that can be accessed and retrieved from memory
and used to produce meaningful speech in Spanish or English (Manual, p. 12). The
author says that the EOWPVT-SBE has the following specific uses: (1) Assessing the
Extent of Spoken Vocabulary, (2) Assessing Cognitive Ability, (3) Diagnosing Reading Difficulties, (4) Comparing Bilingual Language Acquisition to Monolingual Language Proficiency, (5) Diagnosing Expressive Aphasia, (6) Screening Preschool and
Kindergarten Children, (7) Monitoring Growth, and (8) Evaluating Program Effectiveness (Manual, pp. 12–13).

Decision-Making Applications

The EOWPVT-SBE can be used effectively to assess spoken vocabulary of Spanish bilingual students as well as English-only-speaking students. It can also be used
effectively as one means of assessing and comparing bilingual language acquisition to
monolingual language acquisition. However, the EOWPVT-SBE should not be used
as the sole basis for assessing cognitive ability or diagnosing reading difficulties, nor
should any vocabulary test be used as the sole basis for those purposes. The results of
the EOWPVT-SBE can prompt the user of the test to identify important questions
about the individual and then to pursue answers through further, more specific evaluation. The EOWPVT-SBE would be a practical, objective, and efficient first step in a
comprehensive evaluation of language skills.

Relevant Population

The EOWPVT-SBE is intended to be used with Spanish bilingual individuals from
4 through 12 years of age.

Characteristics Described

The EOWPVT-SBE measures an individual's bilingual speaking vocabulary. The
examiner presents a series of illustrations which depict an object, action, or concept.
The examinee is asked to name each illustration. Items become progressively more
difficult. When the examinee is unable to correctly name a number of consecutive

illustrations, testing is discontinued. Individuals may respond either in English or Spanish.

Test Scores Obtained

The only score obtained is the total raw score. This raw score can be converted to standard scores, percentile ranks, and age equivalents.

Technical Adequacy

Validity Confirmation

The author states that *test item validity* is built into the EOWPVT-SBE through its design specifications and through the procedures followed in item selection. A format for the test was selected which would elicit single English words of progressive difficulty in response to the presentation of a series of illustrations. Items were selected from a variety of sources to represent words that individuals at a given age level, regardless of their gender or cultural background, could be expected to know. The final items appearing on the EOWPVT-SBE were required to meet rigorous criteria of item discrimination and item bias studies. The final items were also selected to present difficulty levels appropriate for assessing a wide range of expressive vocabulary. Only items that could be illustrated were selected.

Evidence for *test response validity* is presented with correlations between the EOWPVT-SBE and the Receptive One-Word Vocabulary Test-Spanish Bilingual Edition (ROWPVT-SBE) and the vocabulary subtest of the Stanford Achievement Test, Ninth Edition (SAT-9). The ROWPVT-SBE is a receptive vocabulary test in which the examinee is asked to identify a picture from several alternatives that matches a word presented by the examiner; the SAT-9 is a multi-task, group-administered English vocabulary test. The correlations between the EOWPVT-SBE are .36 for the ROWPVT-SBE and .57 for the SAT-9, indicating a moderate relationship between these tests. Support for test response validity is also shown by correlating the EOWPVT-SBE with the Reading and Language composite scores of the SAT-9, which is a widely used achievement test that is group administered in English. The Reading and Language composite scores of this test survey a wide range of school-related skills. The Reading sections assess a range of vocabulary skills, such as word meanings, knowledge of synonyms and antonyms, multi-meaning words, and words in context as well as reading comprehension skills. The Language sections assess skills in usage and mechanics, such as grammar, spelling, and punctuation, as well as study skills. The correlation of the EOWPVT-SBE with the Reading composite score is .67 and with the Language composite score is .75. The magnitude of these correlations gives evidence that a considerable relationship exists between performance on the EOWPVT-SBE and Reading and Language as measured by these tests.

Reliability Confirmation

The test-retest technique was used to support stability reliability. Thirty-two examinees were each retested by the same examiner. The average time between the first and second testing was 20 days. The correlation coefficient was .91. Internal consistency reliability was assessed by using the split-half technique, in which performance scores on one-half of the items of the test were correlated with scores on the other half. The split-half correlations by age group ranged from .93 to .98.

Objectivity Confirmation

Scoring instructions and a scoring key are given and clearly described in the Manual. However, the authors state that the interpretation of the test results must be conducted by individuals who have formal training in testing and who have full knowledge of the use of derived scores and the limitations of test results.

Statistical Confirmation

Statistical data for validity, reliability, and norms can be found in the Manual.

Special Features

Acronym

EOWPVT-SBE.

Levels of the Test

One. Levels are determined by the use of basals and ceilings. The test plates are ordered in respect to difficulty; therefore, only those items within the individual's range of ability need to be administered. This is accomplished by establishing a basal of eight consecutive correct responses. From this point, continue presenting the test plates in ascending order until the examinee makes six consecutive errors or the last item of the test is administered. The ceiling will be the last item of the six consecutive items or the last item on the test if a ceiling is not otherwise reached.

Number of Test Forms

One.

Norm-Referenced?

Yes. Norms for the EOWPVT-SBE were derived from the same sample of 1,050 examinees that was used to derive the norms for the ROWPVT-SBE. The sample was comprised only of individuals who speak Spanish. Overall, the sample approximates the demographics of the U.S. Hispanic population. Over- and underrepresentation can be noted in some categories. Individuals from the Western region and those whose dialect is Mexican are overrepresented and, consequently, other categories of region and Hispanic origin are underrepresented.

Criterion-Referenced?

Yes. The EOWPVT-SBE is referenced to English-speaking vocabulary.

Feasibility Considerations

Testing Time

Ten to 15 minutes.

For Testing Groups? Individuals?

Individuals.

Test Administration and Scoring

Clear and detailed instructions for administration and scoring are presented in the Manual. These instructions are also summarized on the record form for reference. The EOWPVT-SBE is most often used to inform speech/language pathologists, psychologists, counselors, learning specialists, physicians, occupational therapists, and other educational, psychological, and medical professionals. In addition to these professionals, the test may be administered by those who do not have specific training in assessment. However, these individuals must be trained by and under the supervision of a professional familiar with the principles of educational and psychological assessment and interpretation. The examiner must be fluent in Spanish and English or should have an assistant present who is fluent in the language not spoken by the examiner. Prior to administration of the test, the examiner should become thoroughly familiar with the administration and scoring procedures presented and should conduct several trial administrations (Manual, p. 15).

Test Materials and Approximate Costs

Complete test kit, which includes Manual, Test Plates, and English Record Forms (25), in portfolio: $140; Manual: $40; Test Plates: $75; English Record Forms (25): $25.

Adequacy of Test Manuals

The Manual provided for the EOWPVT-SBE is clearly written and adequately provides all the information needed by the examiner.

Excerpts from Other Test Reviews

No test reviews were found for the EOWPVT-SBE. However, the items on the EOWPVT-SBE are the same as the items on the Expressive One Word Picture Vocabulary Test, Revised (EOWPVT-R), so the reviews of the EOWPVT-R are relevant to the EOWPVT-SBE. The EOWPVT-R was reviewed by Cizek (1995) and Grantham (1995) and by Salvia and Ysseldyke (2001). Cizek says, "The EOWPVT-R is best suited for use as a brief screening measure of a child's expressive vocabulary. It should not be used solely as an assessment of general verbal intelligence." Grantham states, "The EOWPVT-R appears to be strengthened as a screening instrument for expressive vocabulary. . . . There continues to be a need for more norming studies from wider geographical areas." Salvia and Ysseldyke conclude, "This instrument is useful in providing specific data from the expressive semantics language domain. Reliability and validity data are provided for application to English-speaking 4 to 11 year olds. Interpretations of results from 2 and 3 year olds and from Spanish-speaking children should be made with caution because of limited normative and validity data" (p. 499).

Ordering Information

Publisher

Academic Therapy Publications, 20 Commercial Boulevard, Novato, CA 94949-6191; Phone: 800-422-7249; Fax: 888-287-9925; Web site: www.academictherapy.com.

Author

Rick Brownell.

Publication Date

2001.

Cautions and Comments

The EOWPVT-SBE is not intended to measure Spanish or English proficiency; rather, it should be used to measure acquired expressive vocabulary without regard to whether the vocabulary is in the examinee's first or second language. However, there are several factors which can impact the results of the EOWPVT-SBE (i.e., hearing or visual problems), so the test results alone should not be used to confirm a learning problem. Neither the ROWPVT-SBE nor any other vocabulary test should be used as a total assessment of language ability.

References

Cizek, G. J. (1995). Review of the Expressive One-Word Picture Vocabulary Test-Revised. In J. C. Conoley & J. C. Impara (Eds.), *The Twelfth Mental Measurements Yearbook*. Lincoln, NE: The Buros Institute of Mental Measurements.

Grantham, L. B. (1995). Review of the Expressive One-Word Picture Vocabulary Test-Revised. In J. C. Conoley & J. C. Impara (Eds.), *The Twelfth Mental Measurements Yearbook*. Lincoln, NE: The Buros Institute of Mental Measurements.

Salvia, J., & and Ysseldyke, J. E. (2001). *Assessment* (8th ed.). Boston: Houghton Mifflin.

**Receptive One-Word Picture Vocabulary Test-Spanish Bilingual Edition
(ROWPVT-SBE)**, for testing individuals from 2 through 18 years of age
Reviewed by Katherine C. Schnepel, Ph.D.,
Educational Research and Measurement

Usefulness of the Test for Educators

Test Author's Purpose

The author states that the ROWPVT-SBE provides a measure of an individual's bilingual hearing vocabulary, which reflects the extent of that individual's understanding of single words presented in either Spanish or English. The author also states that the ROWPVT-SBE has the following specific uses: (1) Assessing the Extent of Hearing Vocabulary, (2) Assessing Cognitive Ability, (3) Diagnosing Reading Difficulties, (4) Comparing Bilingual Language Acquisition to Monolingual Language Proficiency, (5) Diagnosing Expressive Aphasia, (6) Screening Preschool and Kindergarten Children, (7) Assessing Vocabulary with a Nonverbal Response Requirement, (8) Monitoring Growth, and (9) Evaluating Program Effectiveness.

Decision-Making Applications

The ROWPVT-SBE can be used effectively to assess hearing vocabulary of Spanish bilingual students as well as English-only-speaking students. It can also be used effectively as one means of assessing and comparing bilingual language acquisition to monolingual language acquisition. However, the ROWPVT-SBE should not be used as the sole basis for assessing cognitive ability or diagnosing reading difficulties, nor should any vocabulary test be used as the sole basis for those purposes. The results of the ROWPVT-SBE can prompt the user of the test to identify important questions about the individual and then to pursue answers through further, more specific evaluation. The ROWPVT-SBE would be a practical, objective, and efficient first step in a comprehensive evaluation of language skills.

Relevant Population

The ROWPVT-SBE is appropriate for use with children ages 2 through 18.

Characteristics Described

The ROWPVT describes an individual's ability to identify the meaning of words that range from familiar to obscure by verbally identifying pictures of objects. The examiner presents a series of test plates that each show four illustrations. The examiner then orally presents a stimulus word, and the examinee must identify the illustration that depicts the meaning of the word. Items become progressively more difficult. When the examinee is unable to correctly identify the meaning of a specified number of items, testing is discontinued. The ROWPVT-SBE is meant to be used with Spanish bilingual individuals.

Test Scores Obtained

The only score obtained is the total raw score. This raw score can be converted to standard scores, percentile ranks, and age equivalents.

Technical Adequacy

Validity Confirmation

The authors say that *test item validity* is built into the ROWPVT-SBE through its design specifications and through the procedures followed in item selection. A format for the test was selected in which an examinee could demonstrate his or her understanding of single words by identifying illustrations that depict the meanings of words of progressive difficulty. Items were selected from a variety of sources to represent words that individuals at a given age level, regardless of their gender or cultural background, could be expected to have an equal likelihood of knowing. The final items appearing on the ROWPVT-SBE were required to meet rigorous criteria of item discrimination and item bias studies. The final items were also selected to present difficulty levels appropriate for assessing a wide range of receptive vocabulary. Items were eliminated that could not be translated accurately or consistently across Spanish dialects, that appeared to have different item difficulties in English and Spanish, that might be culturally biased, or that might otherwise prove to be problematic.

Evidence for *test response validity* is presented with correlations between the ROWPVT-SBE and the Expressive One-Word Picture Vocabulary Test-Spanish Bilingual Edition (EOWPVT-SBE) and the vocabulary subtest of the Stanford Achievement Test, Ninth Edition (SAT-9). The EOWPVT-SBE is an expressive vocabulary test in which the examinee is asked to name illustrations presented by the examiner; the SAT-9 is a multi-task, group-administered English vocabulary test. The correlations between the ROWPVT-SBE are .24 for the EOWPVT-SBE and .38 for the SAT-9, indicating a low to moderate relationship with these tests. Support for test response validity is also shown by correlating ROWPVT-SBE performance to Reading and Language achievement as measured by the Reading and Language subtests of the SAT-9. The correlation with Reading achievement is .46 and the correlation with Language achievement is .61.

Reliability Confirmation

The test-retest technique was used to support stability reliability. Thirty-two examinees were each retested by the same examiner. The average time between the first and second testing was 20 days. The correlation coefficient was .92. Internal consistency reliability was assessed by using the split-half technique, in which performance scores on one-half of the items of the test were correlated with scores on the other half. The split-half correlations by age group ranged from .97 to .99.

Objectivity Confirmation

Scoring instructions and a scoring key are given and clearly described in the Manual.

However, the authors state that the interpretation of the test results must be conducted by individuals who have formal training in testing and who have full knowledge of the use of derived scores and the limitations of test results.

Statistical Confirmation

Statistical data on validity, reliability, and norms can be found in the Manual.

Special Features

Acronym

ROWPVT-SBE.

Levels of the Test

One. Levels are determined by the use of basals and ceilings. The test plates are ordered in respect to difficulty; therefore, only those items within the individual's range of ability need to be administered. This is accomplished by establishing a basal of eight consecutive correct responses. From this point, testing is continued until a ceiling of four incorrect responses out of six consecutive items is obtained.

Number of Test Forms

One.

Norm-Referenced?

Yes. Norms for the ROWPVT-SBE were derived from a sample of 1,050 examinees comprised only of individuals who speak Spanish. Overall, the sample approximates the demographics of the U.S. Hispanic population. Over- and underrepresentation can be noted in some categories. Individuals from the Western region and those whose dialect is Mexican are overrepresented and, consequently, other categories of region and Hispanic origin are underrepresented.

Criterion-Referenced?

Yes. The ROWPVT-SBE is referenced to English hearing vocabulary.

Feasibility Considerations

Testing Time

Ten to 15 minutes.

For Testing Groups? Individuals?

Individuals.

Test Administration and Scoring

Clear and detailed instructions for administration and scoring are presented in the

Manual. These instructions are also summarized on the record form for reference. The ROWPVT-SBE is most often used to inform speech/language pathologists, psychologists, counselors, learning specialists, physicians, occupational therapists, and other educational, psychological, and medical professionals. In addition to these professionals, the test may be administered by those who do not have specific training in assessment. However, these individuals must be trained by and under the supervision of a professional familiar with the principles of educational and psychological assessment and interpretation. The examiner must be fluent in Spanish and English or should have an assistant present who is fluent in the language not spoken by the examiner. Prior to administration of the test, the examiner should become thoroughly familiar with the administration and scoring procedures presented and should conduct several trial administrations (Manual, p. 15).

Test Materials and Approximate Costs

Complete test kit, which includes Manual, Test Plates, and English Record Forms (25), in portfolio: $140; Manual: $40; Test Plates: $75; English Record Forms (25): $25.

Adequacy of Test Manuals

The Manual provided for the ROWPVT-SBE is clearly written and adequately provides all the information needed by the examiner.

Excerpts from Other Test Reviews

No test reviews were found for the ROWPVT-SBE. However, the English items on the ROWPVT-SBE are the same as the items on the original ROWPVT, which was only in English, so the reviews of the original ROWPVT are relevant to the ROWPVT-SBE. The ROWPVT was reviewed by Dole (1995) and Santogrossi (1995). Dole says, "The test is easy to administer, score, and interpret. . . . Inadequate information is provided to the examiner for understanding the test's usefulness in assessing potential language problems. Finally, reported reliabilities for this test are adequate, but insufficient evidence is provided in the manual to establish the validity of the test." Santogrossi states, "The ROWPVT is a quick, easy method for estimating a child's single-word receptive vocabulary. . . . Further research to establish the test-retest reliability and validity of the ROWPVT, more extensive normative studies, and improvement of the illustrations are needed before this reviewer would recommend use of the ROWPVT."

Ordering Information

Publisher

Academic Therapy Publications, 20 Commercial Boulevard, Novato, CA 94949-6191; Phone: 800-422-7249; Fax: 888-287-9925; Web site: www.academictherapy.com.

Author

Rick Brownell.

Publication Date

2001.

Cautions and Comments

The ROWPVT-SBE is not meant to assess Spanish or English proficiency; rather, it should be used to measure English hearing vocabulary of Spanish bilingual students. It is equivalent to the ROWPVT in that it can also be used to assess hearing vocabulary in English-speaking-only students. However, there are several factors which can impact the results of the ROWPVT-SBE (i.e., hearing or visual problems), so the test results alone should not be used to confirm a learning problem. Neither the ROWPVT-SBE nor any other vocabulary test should be used as a total assessment of language ability.

References

Dole, J. (1995). Review of the Receptive One-Word Picture Vocabulary Test. In J. C. Conoley & J. C. Impara (Eds.), *The Twelfth Mental Measurements Yearbook*. Lincoln, NE: The Buros Institute of Mental Measurements.

Santogrossi, J. (1995). Review of the Receptive One-Word Picture Vocabulary Test. In J. C. Conoley & J. C. Impara (Eds.), *The Twelfth Mental Measurements Yearbook*. Lincoln, NE: The Buros Institute of Mental Measurements.

Slosson Written Expression Test (SWET),
for testing groups and individuals from 8 through 17 years of age
Reviewed by Katherine C. Schnepel, Ph.D.,
Educational Research and Measurement

Usefulness of the Test for Educators

Test Authors' Purpose

The authors state that the SWET provides quick, meaningful information regarding children's writing skills. In general, it may be used (1) as a screening instrument for identification of at-risk children, remedial program determinations, or learning disabilities; (2) for screening children new to the school or agency; and (3) for curriculum evaluation by providing a norm- or criterion-referenced score for every student aged 8 through 17.

Decision-Making Applications

The SWET can be used to identify "at-risk" children and determine the need for remedial instruction. The test can also point to learning disabilities. It is a screening instrument and should not be used to diagnose weaknesses. It should be a means of identifying students who require further diagnostic assessment.

Relevant Population

The SWET was designed to provide information about the written expression skills of children aged 8 through 17 (grades 2–12).

Characteristics Described

The SWET describes two major constructs: Writing Maturity and Writing Mechanics. The test authors describe Writing Maturity by measuring Average Sentence Length and Vocabulary Density or Type-Token Ratio (number of different words [types] in the first 50 words [tokens] of a writing sample). The construct of Writing Mechanics is described by measuring spelling, capitalization, and punctuation. Students are asked to look at a picture and write a story about it. They are asked to capitalize and punctuate and spell as best they can.

Test Scores Obtained

Figure 1.1
Scores Obtained from the SWET

Subscale	Raw Score	Scaled Score Range	Percentile Rank Range	Interpretive Range
Type-Token Ratio (TTR)	X	X	X	X
Average Sentence Length (ASL)	X	X	X	X
Spelling	X	X	X	X
Capitalization	X	X	X	X
Punctuation	X	X	X	X

	Scaled Score Total	Standard Score Range	Percentile Rank Range	Interpretive Range
Writing Maturity Index Score	X	X	X	X
Writing Mechanics Index Score	X	X	X	X
Written Expression Total Standard Score (TSS)	X	X	X	X

Source: Manual, p. 74.

Technical Adequacy

Validity Confirmation

Test item validity was established by first identifying the major domains of written expression and then selecting the items for the five subscales which represent those domains.

Support *for test response validity* is given by correlating the SWET-Form A Subscales, the Woodcock-Johnson-Revised (WJ-R) Dictation and Writing Samples Subtests and Broad Written Language Domain, and the Test of Written Language, Second Edition (TOWL-2) Written Language Quotient (WLQ). The resulting coefficients which are significant at the $p < .05$ level range from .18 to .72, with most in the .30s and .40s.

Reliability Confirmation

The stability of the SWET subscales, index scores, and total score for Form A was derived by administering Form A to a sample of 150 students in grades 3–10, then readministering Form A after exactly two weeks.

The correlations ranged from .80 to .95. From these results it can be determined that the SWET subscales, index, and total scores display adequate stability for a screening test. The stability of the subscales, index, and total scores of the three alternate forms of the SWET was also derived by administering Forms A, B, and C to the students in the standardization sample. The correlations ranged from .73 to .95. From these results, it can be determined that the SWET subscales and the SWET total score are stable across forms.

Objectivity Confirmation

Inter-scorer objectivity was studied by having 13 graduate education students, most of whom were teachers, score a set of 10 Form A protocols. Eight of the teachers were novice scorers of the SWET and five were experienced scorers of the SWET. For the experienced scorers, correlations ranged from .77 to .95 for the total score with a median score of .91. For the novice group, correlations ranged from .60 to .94 for the total score with a median score of .81. Thus, it seems that experience in scoring the SWET substantially impacts scorer objectivity.

Statistical Confirmation

Statistical data on validity, reliability, objectivity, and norms is contained in the SWET Manual. All of the data is very clearly described and easily understood by the reader.

Special Features

Acronym

SWET.

Levels of the Test

One.

Number of Test Forms

Three.

Norm-Referenced?

Yes. The SWET was standardized on a sample of 1,913 students. Protocols were collected at each of 10 age levels, 8 through 17. The standardization sample was commensurate with recent U.S. population demographics in regard to sex, race, residential makeup, and socioeconomic status.

Criterion-Referenced?

Yes. The SWET is referenced to written expression skills common across curricula to which children may be exposed.

Other Features

Visual prompts for the three forms of the SWET—the dinosaur (Form A), space (Form B), and shipwreck (Form C)—are provided.

Feasibility Considerations

Testing Time

Less than 20 minutes.

For Testing Groups? Individuals?

Groups and individuals.

Test Administration and Scoring

The Manual contains very clear instructions for administrations and scoring of the SWET. Professionals and paraprofessionals can administer the SWET. No particular training or certification is required.

Test Materials and Approximate Costs

Complete kit, which includes Manual and student response forms A, B, and C: $95.

Adequacy of Test Manuals

The manual for the SWET is very well written and easily understood. It includes directions for administering, scoring, and interpreting the scores of the test.

Excerpts from Other Test Reviews

No test reviews were found for the SWET.

Ordering Information

Publisher

Slosson Educational Publications, Inc., P.O. Box 280, East Aurora, NY 14052-

0280; Phone: 888-756-7766; Fax: 800-655-3840; e-mail: slosson@slosson.com; Web site: www.slosson.com.

Authors

Donald B. Hofler, Bradley T. Erford, and William J. Amoriell.

Publication Date

2001.

Cautions and Comments

The SWET is a screening instrument intended for screening children for "at-risk" identification. It should not be used for diagnosis of learning problems; rather, children performing poorly on the SWET should be referred for diagnostic assessment.

STAR Early Literacy: Computer-Adaptive Diagnostic Assessment,
for testing individuals from pre-kindergarten through grade 3
Reviewed by Katherine C. Schnepel, Ph.D.,
Educational Research and Measurement

Usefulness of the Test for Educators

Test Authors' Purpose

The authors state that STAR Early Literacy (1) assesses the early literacy skills of pre-kindergarten through third grade students, (2) identifies literacy domains and skills within those domains where students need additional practice or instruction, (3) provides teachers with measurable information regarding individual and class literacy skills, (4) provides teachers with timely and accurate information that can be used to plan literacy instruction and intervention, (5) provides teachers with a tool that enables them to capture a comprehensive picture of student literacy skills in seven domains, and (6) helps teachers monitor student progress based on the specific literacy needs of each student (Technical Manual, p. 2).

Decision-Making Applications

The STAR Early Literacy test can be used effectively as a quick and easy-to-administer measure of students' early literacy achievement. It can also be used to decide at what level instruction should begin and is useful for tracking early literacy over periods of time. It is not useful for diagnosis of strengths and weaknesses of individual students. This is so because the teacher does not know which items the student answers correctly or incorrectly, only the number of items answered correctly, so the teacher has no way of pinpointing deficiencies or strengths.

Relevant Population

Pre-kindergarten through third grade students.

Characteristics Described

Extensive research into the pre-reading and reading skills necessary for later reading success revealed that STAR Early Literacy would need to cover the broad language arts areas of listening and reading. Item content is grouped into the following seven skill domains, each considered essential in reading development:

General Readiness (GR)—Understanding of written word length, position words, words versus letters, basic numeracy, word matching, word boundaries, shapes, and sequences.

Graphophonemic Knowledge (GK)—Understanding of letter names and sounds, alphabetic letter sequence, and alphabetical order.

Phonemic Awareness (PA)—Understanding of rhyming words, ability to blend word parts and phonemes, sound discrimination, oral word length, and ability to identify missing sounds.

Phonics (PH)—Understanding of long vowels, short vowels, beginning and ending consonants, consonant and vowel replacement, word families (onset and rime), consonant blends, clusters, and digraphs.

Comprehension (CO)—Ability to read and derive meaning from words, sentences, and paragraphs.

Structural Analysis (SA)—Ability to find words within other words, to build words, and to create compound words.

Vocabulary (VO)—Knowledge of high-frequency words, synonyms, and antonyms (Technical Manual, p. 9).

For each of the seven literacy domains listed above, several component skills were identified; in all, 146 component literacy skills were identified. These skills were organized into a total of 41 skill sets (Technical Manual, p. 10). All questions are in multiple-choice format, with three response alternatives. Students select their answers by pointing and clicking using a mouse (Technical Manual, p. 3). Adaptive Branching™ is used in the STAR Early Literacy test; that is, if the student chooses an incorrect response to a question, the program gives an easier question next. If the student chooses the correct response to a question, the next question given is more difficult. Thus, the test difficulty matches each individual's performance level.

Test Scores Obtained

STAR Early Literacy reports three different kinds of scores: Scaled Scores, Domain Scores, and Skill Scores. Scaled Scores provide a global measure of the student's current ability. They are derived directly from the updated ability estimate computed after the last test question. Domain Scores are separate estimates of the student's proficiency, expressed on a percent mastery scale, in each of the seven literacy domains. Like Domain Scores, Skill Scores are percent mastery estimates, but they are reported for each of the STAR Early Literacy skills (Technical Manual, p. 8).

Technical Adequacy

Validity Confirmation

Giving evidence of *test item validity* involves the content of the test items that make up the item bank of STAR Early Literacy. The original 2,929 STAR Early Literacy test items were designed explicitly to consist of indicators of seven specific literacy domains and the 41 sets of subordinate skills that comprise them. Almost 2,400 of those items have been retained for use in the 1.0 version of STAR Early Literacy. In every administration of STAR Early Literacy, items measuring each of the seven literacy domains are used. The content of the item bank, together with the content balancing specifications that govern the administration of each test, form the basis for STAR Early Literacy's test item validity (Technical Manual, p. 67).

All of the evidence presented in support of *test response validity* involves the relationship of STAR Early Literacy scores to external variables that are related to the development of literacy skills. Scores on the assessment should:

- Increase directly with test takers' ages;
- Increase with grade in school;
- Correlate with scores on related assessments, such as other tests of readiness and early literacy, early-grade reading tests, and teachers' ratings of students' mastery of literacy skills (Technical Manual, p. 67).

Pilot study data indicates that test-scaled scores show the expected pattern of relationship to age and grade level—scores increased systematically from pre-kindergarten through grade 3. Teachers completed skills ratings for 7,428 of the students in the pilot study. These skill ratings were then correlated with the students' scores on the STAR Early Literacy. The overall correlation was .69, indicating a substantial degree of relationship between the computer-adaptive STAR Early Literacy test and teachers' ratings of their students' literacy skills. The STAR Early Literacy test was correlated with several related assessments on each grade level: the Alabama Early Learning Inventory, the Brigance K & 1 Screen for Kindergarten and First Grade Children, the Canadian Achievement Test, the High/Scope Child Observation Record, the Dial-Developmental Indicators for the Assessment of Learning, the Developing Skills Checklist, the Florida Comprehensive Assessment Test, the Gates-MacGinitie Reading Test, the Indiana Statewide Testing for Educational Progress, the Iowa Tests of Basic Skills, the Kaufman Survey of Early Academic and Language Skills, the Metropolitan Early Childhood Assessment Program, the Metropolitan Readiness Test, the NWEA Levels

Test, the Stanford Achievement Test, the STAR Reading Test, the Stanford Test of Academic Skills, TerraNova, the Test of Phonological Awareness, and the Texas Primary Reading Inventory. The average correlations on each level were: K = .60, 1 = .64, 2 = .57, and 3 = .61.

Reliability Confirmation

Stability reliability is supported by using the test-retest method. This method involves administering the test twice to the same examinees. Next, a correlation coefficient is obtained by calculating the correlation between the two sets of test scores. The correlation coefficient was substantial: .87 overall.

Objectivity Confirmation

Objectivity is not an issue with the STAR Early Literacy test because each item is automatically scored using Adaptive Branching™, where the program weighs each answer provided by the student and presents the next question at an appropriate difficulty level. There is a time limit for answering each test question; the program will notify the student that time has run out, and then the next question will appear. Any unanswered question will be counted as an incorrect answer.

Statistical Confirmation

Statistical confirmation for validity and reliability is provided in the Technical Manual.

Special Features

Acronym

STAR Early Literacy.

Levels of the Test

Five. Levels of the test are determined by the grade level of the examinee.

Number of Test Forms

One. There is a large item pool. Thus, the same student may take the test several times in a year and never answer the exact same questions.

Norm-Referenced?

No.

Criterion-Referenced?

Yes. STAR Early Literacy items were written in accordance with pre-kindergarten through grade 3 curriculum standards to reflect emergent reading skills that are characteristic of those grade levels. Teachers can use STAR Early Literacy's criterion-referenced scores to estimate the student's proficiency in reading skills.

Other Features

The software includes a management program, which enables the teacher to manage students, classes, and reports.

Feasibility Considerations

Testing Time

Approximately 10 minutes.

For Testing Groups? Individuals?

Individuals.

Test Administration and Scoring

Clear instructions for administering are given in the Technical Manual, including illustrations of what is shown on the computer screen. No specific training or certification is required of the examiner other than basic knowledge of the computer. Scoring is done within the program each time a student takes the test.

Test Materials and Approximate Costs

Single-computer license kit (up to 40 students): $1,995; Schoolwide license kit (up to 200 students): $3,995.

Adequacy of Test Manuals

The Software Manual provides clear instructions for administering the test and managing test results.

Excerpts from Other Test Reviews

No test reviews were found for the STAR Early Literacy test.

Ordering Information

Publisher

Renaissance Learning, Inc., P.O. Box 8036, Wisconsin Rapids, WI 54495-8036; Phone: 800-338-4204; Fax: 715-424-4242; e-mail: answers@renlearn.com, support@renlearn.com; Web site: www.renlearn.com.

Authors

Advantage Learning Systems, Inc.

Publication Date

2001.

Cautions and Comments

STAR Early Literacy is a quick and easy assessment of early literacy skills. However, there are only 25 items on the test, so the sampling of skills is very small. Thus, perhaps it should be used only for screening or as a precursor of more in-depth diagnostic measures. It would not be appropriate to use STAR Early Literacy as the only basis for placing a student in an instructional program. Also, the teacher has no way of knowing which items the student answers correctly or incorrectly, so it cannot be used to identify deficiencies or prescribe remediation.

V

Referral Testing and Decision-Making

Amanda B. Nickerson, Ph.D., School Psychology

INTRODUCTION

A great many students need specialized services to succeed in school. In public school, about 75% of students referred for evaluation are declared eligible for special education services (Algozzine, Christenson, & Ysseldyke, 1982). The percentage would be even higher if students who needed medical and clinical services were added. Once students are referred for an in-depth evaluation, their need for special services is usually identified. Despite this, there are many students who may be in need of specialized services that are not referred by educators for further evaluation. Teachers have cited many barriers to the referral process, including inadequate training on behaviors that warrant a referral (Christenson, Ysseldyke, & Algozzine, 1982). As a result, underlying causes of students' academic failure may go undetected and untreated. To help their students succeed, educators need to become more involved in referral testing.

Teachers are in an excellent position to identify students who are having difficulty learning and who may need referrals to parents, school professionals, or outside agencies for further assessment. Estimates of children with learning problems in the United States range from 4 to 15% (Hammer, Shimada, & Hoffman, 1988), and procedures used to identify such children and youths have resulted in both under- and overidentification of students with disabilities (de La Paz & Graham, 1995). Many have called for improved methods for screening and referring children with such difficulties.

Many educators, even those who have taken a course in academic testing, are ambivalent about engaging in referral testing. On the one hand, they recognize the importance of identifying and treating underlying causes of student failure and want to help. On the other hand, they are keenly aware of their limitations in diagnosing and treating maladies such as vision, hearing, and psychological disorders that require the expertise of clinical specialists. Until educators learn how to conduct the simple screenings needed to make referrals, we cannot expect matters to improve.

It is important to recognize that most educators (with the exception of special education teachers, who specialize in teaching students with learning difficulties) do not have the time or need to be trained in the diagnosis of problems that underlie students' failure to learn. The diagnosis of many problems, such as visual impairment, requires years of specialized training and certification. What educators need is guidance in detecting manifestations of common disorders in students they routinely observe. Second, educators need tips on how to conduct simple, informal tests to help them obtain further evidence of disorders they suspect as a result of their observations. Third, they need knowledge of marketed tests they can obtain and use for further confirmation. These tests should be easy to administer and interpret by following simple companion test directions that will provide them with the data they need to make referrals with corroborating evidence and confidence. Fourth, educators need this information to be summarized, with key referral indicators highlighted. The purpose of this section is to provide educators with the help and resources they need to make referrals. More specifically, this section will describe:

1. *Observable manifestations and observational assessments* of common disorders that underlie students' failure to learn. For example, educators may suspect a hearing disorder when a student's name is called and he or she fails to respond on a number of occasions. Typically, poor student performance would initiate more probing observation of students' behavior.

2. *Informal testing procedures* of disorders suspected as a result of observation. For example, using a checklist that describes potential problems in the appearance of the eyes, behaviors (e.g., avoidance of reading), and complaints (e.g., blurred vision) may help the educator in deciding whether a child should be referred for a comprehensive eye examination. Informal testing procedures are used to collect data on variables to assist in diagnosis, but they are not held to the rigorous standards for reliability, validity, and objectivity that formal tests are.

3. *Formal testing procedures using published tests* that require no specialized training to administer and interpret can be used to further corroborate suspicions of a disorder. These tests, such as standardized behavior rating scales, compare an individual's scores to those of a large normative population, and have extensive research on reliability, validity, and objectivity.

4. *Key referral indicators* for each impairment. This section includes a practical summary of the most important behavioral indicators and rules of thumb for making referral decisions.

Under each of the aforementioned sections, six subject areas will be reviewed: (1) vision impairment referrals, (2) hearing impairment referrals, (3) perceptual-motor and motor impairment referrals, (4) adaptive deficiency referrals, (5) problem behavior referrals, and (6) vocational referrals. These areas are often the cause of concern for educators, for which referrals to parents, specialists, or other agencies may be indicated. Before exploring referral testing procedures in more depth, an overview of the referral process will be described.

THE REFERRAL PROCESS

When thinking of referrals, most educators probably think of making referrals for special education. Evidence suggests that, too often, referrals for special education are viewed as the primary resolution for students who deviate from expectations regarding classroom behavior or academic performance (Algozzine et al., 1982). To address this problem, there has been an increased use of prereferral intervention procedures, which include modifying instruction, implementing behavior modification plans, and consulting with a multidisciplinary team (e.g., student assistance team) for intervention ideas (Carter & Sugai, 1989). These alternatives to referrals for special education placement continue to be advocated for and enforced in recent legislation.

The definition of referrals used in this chapter is broader than the traditional definition. It refers to an educator making a recommendation to a third party that action be taken to assist a child who may be experiencing learning problems. This recommendation could be in the form of suggesting that the parent take a child for an eye examination if vision impairment is suspected. Alternatively, the teacher could be concerned about the behavior of a student, and may bring the matter to the prereferral assessment team or student assistance team for recommendations.

Typically, when a teacher is concerned about a child's learning difficulties, he or she may note the problem and intervene by modifying instruction or implementing an individualized behavior management plan. If the problems persist despite these interventions, teachers may choose to conduct observations or informal assessment procedures to determine whether or not the problem warrants a referral. Although many methods of assessment will be presented in this section, it should be noted that the first step in noticing these problems is a teacher or parent who is concerned about a child. There are many options to pursue from there, such as consulting with other professionals, who are often eager to further assess the problem and help teachers to intervene. Formal testing procedures will be reviewed, but educators should engage in ongoing dialogues with professionals from different disciplines within the school setting (e.g., school nurse, speech and language pathologist, school psychologist) to find out what referral procedures they have in place and what formal tests they use as part of an evaluation. Although teachers can use many of the tests reviewed in this section, professionals in different disciplines may use some of the formal tests routinely as part of their comprehensive assessment and may prefer to administer, score, and interpret them after the referral has been made.

10

Observable Manifestations
and Observational Assessments

In this chapter, the six aforementioned problems that may lead to referrals are described. The area of concern is introduced, with a brief definition of the problem and its possible impact on educational performance. Then, observable manifestations of the behavior are highlighted, followed by examples of observational assessments that educators can use.

VISION IMPAIRMENT REFERRALS

Much of learning occurs through the visual system, and unresolved visual problems can impact a student's ability to respond fully to educational instruction. It has been shown that students with learning problems have a higher incidence of vision disorders than children who do not have learning problems (Birnbaum, 1993; Hoffman, 1980; Optometric Extension Program Foundation, 1998).

The visual system involves both eyesight and vision. Eyesight is the ability to see, whereas vision is the ability to interpret and understand information that comes through the eyes. Schools typically screen for problems with students' eyesight with tools such as the Snellen Eye Chart. However, eye professionals caution that children assessed to have perfect (20/20) eyesight may still have vision problems that could interfere with learning (Hammer et al., 1988). In fact, many children with vision problems that affect learning actually have above-average visual acuity (Optometric Extension Program Foundation, 1998).

There are several types of vision, which will be briefly described below. Although educators need not be overly concerned about detecting distinctions between the various types of sight and vision, it is important to have some knowledge of the types of vision, in addition to the common signs and symptoms that may indicate a referral for more extensive vision assessment.

The first type of vision is ocular motility, or eye movement skills. These skills include the speed and control of visual inspection that are involved in tasks such as

scanning instructional materials. A second type of vision is binocularity, or eye teaming skills. This involves the two eyes working together, which is a skill that is acquired by children in the preschool years. Eye-hand coordination skills specifically
refer to the integration of the eye and hand as paired learning tools, and are involved
in tasks such as drawing and copying. Visual form perception is how people relate
experiences to the pictures and words seen on printed pages. Refractive status refers
to nearsightedness and farsightedness, and is the type of vision that educators may be
most familiar with (Optometric Extension Program Foundation, 1985).

Educators who are aware of some easily observable signs of these types of vision
problems may be instrumental in getting much-needed help for children. In fact, Hammer et al. (1988, p. 7) have stated that "The combined use of teacher observation of
signs and symptoms of learning-related visual problems and the proper referral of
these children may significantly reduce the number of children experiencing learning
difficulties."

The following descriptions of observable manifestations for each of these types of
vision were compiled from guidelines by Green (2000), Jose (1983), and the Optometric Extension Program Foundation (1985). Problems with eye movement skills would
most likely be observed when the student is reading or completing worksheets. Signs
to look for include slow, clumsy, or jumpy eye movements; shortened attention to
visually demanding materials; movement of the head back and forth when reading;
using the finger to underscore words when reading; and increased fatigue and/or rest-
lessness when involved in these activities.

Signs suggesting a problem with binocularity include general clumsiness, squinting or blinking, and little interest in visually demanding tasks, with a strong preference for listening activities. A student with this problem may report double vision,
which he or she may try to adapt to by resting his or her head while writing, sitting in
an awkward position when reading, or covering one eye when reading or writing.

Children with eye-hand coordination problems may produce paperwork that shows
a lack of coordination and illegibility. These children may be unable to stay within the
lines when coloring or be slow to copy information off the board. In addition, they
may appear to be clumsy in sports and other activities.

Students with problems in visual form perception are regarded as careless about
details. They often confuse similarities by reversing letter forms and letter sequences
in words. Other signs to look for include difficulty recognizing the same word in the
next sentence or page, or apparent lack of skill in drawing.

Lastly, the most obvious sign of problems with nearsightedness or farsightedness is
avoidance of specific tasks. For example, a child may avoid nearsighted tasks (e.g.,
desk activity and workbooks) or tasks that require seeing from a distance (e.g., copying from a chalkboard).

Useful information about a child's possible vision problems can be obtained by
listening to the child read. Birnbaum (1993) outlines reading habits that may indicate
vision problems, as compared to those that may suggest learning difficulties. For example, students with inadequate visual form perception may have poor sight recogni-

tion and show a tendency to read in a slow, laborious fashion. They may also have difficulty recognizing familiar words and confuse words that look alike. In contrast, students with poor phonic skills may recognize familiar words but be unable to decode unfamiliar or multisyllabic words.

Busby (1985) described informal procedures for assessing eye movement control and eye-hand coordination. For example, a teacher can assess for eye movement difficulties by timing students to see how long they can keep their eyes on a moving target (e.g., a pen light) held at a 12" distance for 30 seconds. The number of seconds that a child can follow the moving target indicates the level of eye movement control they have (0–6 seconds = absence, 7–12 seconds = poor, 13–18 seconds = fair, 19–24 seconds = good, 25–30 seconds = excellent). To assess eye-hand coordination, Busby suggests having the child put 2" round beads with 1/2" holes onto a string for 3 minutes, with the amount of beads the child puts on the string indicating various levels of eye-hand coordination (0–10 beads = absent, 11–20 beads = poor, 21–30 beads = fair, 31–40 beads = good, over 40 beads = excellent).

The most common test used to assess eyesight in schools is the Snellen Eye Chart, which is the standard for measuring distance vision. This chart consists of letters of varying sizes. The student being assessed stands 20 feet away from the chart and reads the letters, which decrease in size with each descending line. The vision expected at 20 feet is the numerator, and the number of the line of letters actually seen at 20 feet represents the denominator. Therefore, a distance vision of 20/20 indicates that a person sees at 20 feet what is expected to be seen at 20 feet. In contrast, a visual acuity of 20/100 means that someone sees at 20 feet what most people see at 100 feet.

The Snellen Eye Chart provides limited information about vision, as it only tests visual acuity. Therefore, it does not identify students with near-vision problems, problems with the internal structure of the eye, or difficulties with some of the previously identified types of vision. Because children with reading problems or very young children may not be able to read all the letters, the Snellen E Chart has been developed. This assesses vision by displaying the letter "E," faced in four different directions. The child is instructed to tell which direction the "E" is facing.

Although the Snellen Eye Chart seems to be the standard for comparison, other charts are used as well. Some of the more popular of these tests are the HOTV Test, which uses only the letters H, O, T, and V. The Landolt Ring Test uses a circle that has a blank area in one section of the circle (top, bottom, right, or left section). The Highthouse Test has symbols instead of letters, which preschool children and mentally retarded individuals respond to better than letters. Some of these tests can be administered at 10 feet rather than the Snellen's usual 20-foot distance.

HEARING IMPAIRMENT REFERRALS

Like vision, hearing is closely tied to learning. Undetected hearing loss in children can lead to delayed speech and language development and can contribute to academic as well as social and emotional problems (Gersten, 1997). Hearing problems fall under the broader area of communication disorders, including speech, language, and hearing disorders. Estimates suggest that approximately 5% of preschool and school-age children exhibit reduced hearing levels and related problems (Diefendorf & Leverett, 1988; Stewart, Hester, & Taylor, 1986).

Schools tend to screen for hearing problems with a portable screening audiometer. The American Speech, Language, and Hearing Association recommends that a trained professional use the following screening levels: 20 decibels at 1000, 2000, and 4000 hertz (Diefendorf & Leverett, 1988). It should be noted that hearing screenings are usually conducted by trained professionals in the schools, such as speech and language therapists or school nurses.

Related to hearing is central auditory processing, which is described as what an individual does with what he or she hears. These problems are not as easily detected by hearing screenings and may require more extensive evaluations by professionals such as speech and language pathologists. Because of the importance of hearing and auditory processing to learning, educators need to be aware of signs of these problems and to refer children who may need more extensive testing. As Gersten (1997, p. 3) reminds us, "little is lost by testing the normal child, but much is lost by not testing the hearing-impaired child."

Educators should be aware of observable signs that may indicate a problem with hearing or auditory processing. The following signs are adapted from Katz and Masters (2000) and Sanger (1986). First, children with hearing problems and auditory processing problems may exhibit behavioral signs, such as daydreaming, distractibility, irritability, or frustration. When one considers the vast amount of information in school that is presented verbally and required to be heard and understood through the auditory system, it is no surprise that children with difficulties in this area may become easily frustrated or exhibit behaviors often seen as incompatible with learning.

Second, individuals with hearing or auditory processing problems may appear to ignore a person who is speaking to them, or respond by saying "what?" or "huh?", or ask for the statement to be repeated. Their understanding may be enhanced when their attention is gained, through making eye contact or being in one-to-one situations. A rule of thumb offered by Adler (1988) is that any third grader who presents with poor selective attention and problems with retaining information should be referred to a speech and language clinician. Prior to this point distractibility is common, but third grade is generally the time when these problems decrease markedly for the typical child.

Third, children with these difficulties may have delayed responses or give inappropriate responses to questions asked. They may misunderstand what is being said and have trouble following multi-step tasks. Another possible manifestation of auditory processing problems is that these children may be slower at learning routines and may prefer to watch other children before doing things on their own.

Fourth, lack of interest in reading may be indicative of auditory processing problems. Children with these difficulties are often better at sight reading than in using phonics. These students may appear to lack motivation or to be fatigued by the end of a lesson.

PERCEPTUAL-MOTOR REFERRALS

Perceptual-motor skills typically involve an individual's ability to perceive information, usually through the visual system, and to respond to it with motor skills. For example, tasks involving copying symbols and taking notes involve perceptual-motor skills. Perceptual-motor skills are typically assessed for three purposes: (1) screening large groups of children, (2) assessing students with learning difficulties to determine if perceptual-motor deficits are interfering with learning, and (3) diagnosing brain injury (Salvia & Ysseldyke, 2001).

Direct systematic observation of perceptual-motor skills in the natural environment is the most useful way to assess these potential difficulties for children (Salvia & Ysseldyke, 2001; Witt, Elliott, Daly, Gresham, & Kramer, 1998). Because they involve visual perception and motor control, tasks such as writing and copying are good examples of these skills. Several indicators to look for in students' writing include (1) spacing between letters and words, (2) letter size, (3) alignment (proportion of parts of letters in relation to the different parts of the line), (4) quality of lines (consistency of pressure), (5) slant of letters, (6) formation of upper- and lower-case letters, and (7) style, such as cursive versus print. The teacher may notice that a child has large spaces between some letters and small spaces between others, or the child may switch between cursive writing and printing. As with any assessment, educators should consider typical performance depending on the child's age and the expectations in the classroom. For example, it is common for young children to reverse letters when first learning to write, and children whose teachers expect them to print should not be penalized for not having neat cursive writing.

In addition to the perceptual-motor difficulties mentioned above that focus specifically on fine motor skills, motor proficiency also involves gross motor skills. Gross motor behavior involves using the arms and legs for movement and coordination and includes such skills as walking, running, and climbing. Impairments in gross motor skills may indicate developmental delays, such as mental retardation.

Basic gross motor skills, such as walking and running, are typically assessed in young children, such as those in day care or preschool. Those who fail to meet developmental milestones, such as walking by 18 months, should be referred for further evaluation. Other more complex gross motor skills, such as catching and kicking, and weaving in and out of cones, can be assessed for older children. Possible indicators of gross motor impairment that may be noted by educators include taking extra time in moving from one place to another, clumsiness or poor coordination, and lack of strength compared to children of the same gender, age, and physical build.

ADAPTIVE BEHAVIOR REFERRALS

Adaptive behavior is defined as "the performance of the daily activities required for personal and social sufficiency" (Harrison, 1985, p. 6). Inherent in the definition, and important for assessment, is the degree to which the individual functions independently. Adaptive behavior is largely influenced by cultural norms and age-related expectations (Horn & Fuchs, 1987). Traditionally, adaptive behavior is assessed by having a trained professional, such as a psychologist, interview or gather information from people who know the child best, such as the parent and/or teacher. Therefore, teachers are critical to the reliable assessment of adaptive behavior.

Adaptive behavior is most often assessed when trying to determine if a person has mental retardation. Although many people think of mental retardation as being an intellectual deficiency, a diagnosis of mental retardation can only be made if there are also deficits in adaptive behavior. Adaptive difficulties for individuals with mental retardation are most evident in practical intelligence (i.e., the ability to maintain oneself as an independent person in the activities of daily living) and social intelligence, or the ability to conduct oneself appropriately in social situations (American Association on Mental Retardation, 1992).

The American Association on Mental Retardation (AAMR, 1992) has identified 10 areas of adaptive skills that are central to successful life functioning. These areas are communication, self-care, home living, social skills, community use, self-direction, health and safety, functional academics, leisure, and work. Communication skills are those that involve comprehending and expressing both verbal and nonverbal information. Self-care skills are involved in toileting, eating, dressing, and grooming oneself. Home living skills are those needed to function in a household, such as housekeeping and cooking. Social skills refer to the skills needed to interact with other individuals, such as recognizing emotions, sharing, and making choices. Community use skills involve using community resources, such as purchasing goods from stores and using public restrooms. Self-direction skills are those related to following a schedule, completing tasks, and resolving problems. Health and safety skills are related to maintaining one's health by eating, using basic first aid, and looking both ways before crossing the street. Functional academic skills are those skills that have a direct application to one's life, such as reading and using practical math concepts. Leisure skills are those activities that the individual engages in during free time, and includes skills such as choosing interests, playing socially with others, and behaving appropriately in recreational settings. Finally, work skills are those skills related to holding a job in the community, such as completing tasks, managing money, and interacting with coworkers.

Educators are in an excellent position to observe children's adaptive skills and compare them to the skills of same-aged peers. This is particularly important since adaptive behavior is so closely tied to the expectations of behavior for a certain age group. Teachers can use various observation techniques to assess the adaptive skills of students in the 10 areas outlined by the AAMR (1992).

One way to observe and record adaptive skills is through narrative recording. In this method, a teacher makes an anecdotal record of a student's behavior that does not meet the standards expected for his or her age. For example, a kindergarten teacher may be concerned about a child who does not seem to have average communication skills for this age (e.g., able to listen to a story, look at other children when talking, follow verbal instructions to end a task, and answer questions with relevant, complete sentences). She may decide to observe the child during free time every day for a week and keep a narrative of his or her communication. The narrative could read something like this:

> *When free time was announced, Johnny continued to sit in his chair while the other students went to the play centers in the room. After about a minute, he stood up and walked over to the puppet center and picked up a puppet. When his classmate asked him what his puppet's name was, Johnny did not make eye contact and put the puppet on the ground. He wandered over to the art center and when the teaching assistant asked him if he would like to color and held out a crayon, he took it. After watching another student draw on the paper, Johnny drew a line down the center of the page and made several scribble marks. When the teaching assistant guided the students in writing their names on the paper, Johnny appeared confused and wrote only the first letter of his name, and then looked at the assistant for help.*

In this example, the teacher provided useful information about the child's receptive, expressive, and written communication that suggests the child may be functioning at a level lower than his or her peers. Another method of recording observational data is event recording, or frequency recording. In this method of observation, a behavior could be identified (e.g., asks for help on a lesson). Each time the behavior occurs, the teacher could simply make a hash mark on a piece of paper within a specified time period. The teacher might record how many times a child asks for help within a 30-minute lesson, and compare this number to the amount of time an "average" child asks for help, to help provide information about how that child functions compared to other children in the class.

One final method of recording observational data that may be useful in the assessment of adaptive skills is duration recording. In this method, the amount of time it takes an individual to perform a task or engage in a behavior is recorded. For example, a teacher may notice that a child seems particularly slow in putting on his or her coat and mittens before going outside. The teacher may decide to actually time how long this takes, from the time when she gives the instruction to put coats and mittens on to when the child puts on his coat and mittens and goes to the door. Data that document teachers' observations may be very helpful when making a referral for concerns over a child's adaptive behavior.

PROBLEM BEHAVIOR REFERRALS

Problem behavior is a general term that can include a wide range of behaviors that interfere with a child's learning and development. Prevalence studies suggest that between 2 and 10% of the public school population is in need of services for behavior problems, although state surveys indicate that less than 1% of the school-age population is classified as emotionally disturbed and receive special education services (Walker et al., 1990). The large majority of the time, the classroom teacher is the first person to recognize a child's emotional and behavioral difficulties and initiate a referral.

A commonly accepted and well-researched way to categorize problem behaviors is to divide them into internalizing and externalizing behaviors. Internalizing refers to a class of behavior problems that are directed inwardly and often involve deficits in behaviors, such as lack of social skills, withdrawal, and isolation (Walker et al., 1990). If these problems are severe enough and interfere with the child's functioning, they may indicate depression or anxiety. Externalizing behaviors, which are often those referred in schools, are those that are directed outwardly and often involve behavioral excesses that tend to be disruptive, such as physical aggression, hyperactivity, and defiance or noncompliance (Walker et al., 1990).

Silverman and Serafini (1998) describe two classes of behaviors that can be observed when assessing internalizing problems: (1) verbal behavior (e.g., rate of speech, positive versus negative statements about the self) and (2) overt behavior (e.g., eye contact, solitary versus social play). Examples of verbal behavior that may indicate internalizing problems, such as depression or anxiety, include frequent complaints of physical pain, such as stomachaches and headaches, negative self-statements (e.g., "I hate myself," "I can't do anything right"), and screaming and/or crying. Overt behaviors that could be manifestations of internalizing problems include appearing tired or sleepy much of the time, eating either too little or too much, and avoidance of or withdrawal from activities.

The first step when observing behavior is to choose a target behavior and create a specific, observable definition of it. For example, if a teacher is concerned about a child being socially isolated, the target behavior may include solitary activity. This may be defined as the time the child spends alone, with a distance of five or more feet between him and the other children, engaging in activities such as reading or playing a game alone. This could be compared to group activity, which would involve the child interacting with at least one other child by talking, playing a game, or participating in a group activity.

The next step in observing behavior is to select the type of observational recording method that will be used. As mentioned above in the discussion of adaptive behavior, there are several methods of observation that can be used, such as narrative recording, event (or frequency) recording, and duration recording. A final type of recording that may be useful for the educator is interval recording. In this type of recording the observer selects a segment of time (e.g., 20 minutes) and breaks it into several intervals (e.g., 4 five-minute intervals or 10 two-minute intervals). At the end of each interval, the observer decides whether or not the behavior occurred during that period of time. A variation of interval recording is time sampling, where behaviors are recorded at a certain period of time at the end of an interval. For example, at the end of a five-minute interval, the teacher could look up for five seconds and determine whether the behavior is occurring within that five-second time period.

As an illustration, the teacher who is interested in finding out about a child's solitary behavior could decide to observe the behavior during a 20-minute free play period. The teacher may decide to break the period into 10 two-minute intervals and to record the child's behavior during the last five seconds of each interval. The recording sheet may look something like this:

1:55– 2:00	3:55– 4:00	5:55– 6:00	7:55– 8:00	9:55– 10:00	11:55– 12:00	13:55– 14:00	15:55– 16:00	17:55– 18:00	19:55– 20:00
S G	S G	S G	S G	S G	S G	S G	S G	S G	S G

For the last five seconds of each two-minute interval, the teacher would look up at the child and circle "S" if the child is engaged in a solitary activity and "G" is the child is involved in a group activity. After the observation period, the teacher can add up the number of intervals in which the child was engaged in solitary activity, divide this by the total number of intervals (e.g., 10 in this example) and multiply this by 100, which will give a percentage of time that the child was engaged in solitary play.

Externalizing behaviors also lend themselves well to observation, especially since the behaviors are outwardly directed. These problems are the ones that are usually recognized in schools, as educators tend to find these behavior problems disturbing and disruptive (Mooney & Algozzine, 1978; Safran & Safran, 1984). Observable manifestations of these difficulties may include calling out or being out of seat, being verbally aggressive (e.g., teasing, swearing, threatening), destroying property, being off task or easily distracted, and refusing to follow directions.

Frequency counts of these behaviors may be useful, especially for those that occur many times throughout the day. For example, a teacher may be concerned about a child's difficulty following directions. For one class period each day, the teacher may keep track of how many instructions she gives to the class and/or the individual student and record how many times the child follows the instructions and how many times the child does not follow the directions. To put this number in perspective, the teacher may also want to select another child in the class who is similar to the target child with regard to gender, age, and race, and record how many times that child follows directions and does not follow directions.

VOCATIONAL REFERRALS

Educators working with adolescents are very often involved in assisting students with decisions about employment both during and after the formal schooling years. Referrals of this nature are very important, as work plays an important role in life, and a person's choice of occupation has an impact on quality of life (Levinson, 1995). In addition, many individuals with disabilities are not gainfully employed, and legislation has mandated that schools assist these students in vocational and transitional planning.

Three types of evaluation procedures have typically been used for vocational evaluation: (1) aptitude matching, (2) work sampling, and (3) behavioral rating (Menchetti & Flynn, 1990). Aptitude matching involves measuring general traits and comparing them to performance on different occupations. For example, a person who does not like public speaking but who has good manual dexterity and eye-hand coordination may do well in a hands-on job, such as mechanical or electrical repair. The work sampling approach can be trait-oriented or work-oriented, and aims to measure specific traits (e.g., multi-level sorting) or work skills (e.g., bench assembly) that an individual has. Lastly, the behavior inventory approach assesses behaviors related to work, such as productivity, social skills, and self-help skills.

With regard to vocational planning, the aforementioned approaches can be used by educators to guide their observational assessments of students. Teachers are in an excellent position to assess students' strengths, weaknesses, and preferences, which can help guide vocational choices. For example, an English teacher may note that one student excels in writing and spends his or her free time writing poems, working on articles for the school newspaper, and reading novels. The teacher may work with the student on career options in writing and publishing, or refer him or her to the guidance counselor to obtain further information or vocational testing.

11

Informal Testing Procedures

VISION

There are several checklists available to teachers that can help detect vision problems that warrant a referral for further assessment. For example, the Optometric Extension Program Foundation (1985) has developed an Educator's Checklist that focuses on appearance of eyes, complaints that students may have when using eyes at his or her desk, and behavioral signs that may occur with each type of vision problem. Hritcko (1983) has also developed a checklist, called the ABCs of Visual Difficulties. This checklist also overviews the appearance of eyes, behavioral indicators, and complaints that may be associated with vision problems. These checklists are included here.

Educator's Checklist

Observable Clues to Classroom Vision Problems

Date: _____ Student's Name: _____ Age: _____

1. Appearance of Eyes:
_____ One eye turns in or out at any time
_____ Reddened eyes or lids
_____ Eyes tear excessively
_____ Encrusted eyelids
_____ Frequent sties on

2. Complaints When Using Eyes at Desk:
_____ Headaches in forehead or temples
_____ Burning or itching after reading or desk work
_____ Nausea or dizziness
_____ Print blurs after reading a short time

3. Behavioral Signs of Visual Problems:

A. Eye Movement Abilities (Ocular Motility):
_____ Head turns as reads across page

_____ Loses place often during reading
_____ Needs finger or marker to keep place
_____ Displays short attention span in reading or copying
_____ Too frequently omits words
_____ Repeatedly omits "small" words
_____ Writes up or down hill on paper
_____ Rereads or skips lines unknowingly
_____ Orients drawings poorly on page

B. Eye Teaming Abilities (Binocularity):
_____ Complaints of seeing double (diplopia)
_____ Repeats letters within words
_____ Omits letters, numbers or phrases
_____ Misaligns digits in number columns
_____ Squints, closes or covers one eye
_____ Tilts head extremely while working at desk
_____ Consistently shows gross postural deviations at all desk activities

C. Eye-Hand Coordination Abilities:
_____ Must feel things to assist in any interpretation required
_____ Eyes not used to "steer" hand movements (extreme lack of orientation, placement of words or drawings on page)
_____ Writes crookedly, poorly spaced; cannot stay on ruled lines
_____ Misaligns both horizontal and vertical series of numbers
_____ Uses his hands or fingers to keep his place on the page
_____ Uses other hand as "spacer" to control spacing and alignment on page
_____ Repeatedly confuses left-right directions

D. Visual Form Perception (Visual Comparison, Visual Imagery, Visualization):
_____ Mistakes words with same or similar beginnings
_____ Fails to recognize same word in next sentence
_____ Reverses letters and/or words in writing and copying
_____ Confuses likenesses and minor differences
_____ Confuses same word in same sentence
_____ Repeatedly confuses similar beginnings and endings of words
_____ Fails to visualize what is read either silently or orally
_____ Whispers to self for reinforcement while reading silently
_____ Returns to "drawing with fingers" to decide likes and differences

E. Refractive Status (Nearsightedness, Farsightedness, Focus Problems, etc.):
_____ Comprehension reduces as reading continues; loses interest too quickly
_____ Mispronounces similar words as continues reading
_____ Blinks excessively at desk tasks and/or reading; not elsewhere
_____ Holds book too closely; face too close to desk surface
_____ Avoids all possible near-centered tasks
_____ Complains of discomfort in tasks that demand visual interpretation
_____ Closes or covers one eye when reading or doing desk work
_____ Makes errors in copying from reference book to notebook
_____ Squints to see chalkboard, or requests to move nearer

_____ Rubs eyes during or after short periods of visual activity
_____ Fatigues easily; blinks to make chalkboard clear up after desk task

Observer's Suggestions:

_____
_____
_____

Signed _____
(encircle) Teacher, Nurse, Remedial Teacher, Psychologist, Vision Consultant, Other

Phone: _____
Address: _____

Teacher's Observation Checklist: The ABCs of Visual Difficulty (Hritcko, 1983)

Appearance of the Student's Eyes

1. Eyes crossed—turning in or out—at any time, or eyes do not appear straight, especially when the child is tired.
2. Reddened eyes or eyelids.
3. Watery eyes.
4. Encrusted eyelids.
5. Frequent sties.
6. Clouding of pupils or pupillary opening.
7. Eyes in constant motion.
8. Drooping eyelids.

Behavioral Indications of Possible Visual Difficulty

1. A rigid body when reading or viewing a distant object.
2. Thrusting the head forward or backward while looking at distant objects.
3. Avoiding close work.
4. A short attention span.
5. Turning the head to use one eye only.
6. Tilting the head to one side.
7. Placing the head close to a book or desk when reading or writing; holding reading material excessively close or too far away.
8. Frowning or scowling while reading or writing.
9. Excessive blinking.
10. Tendency to rub eyes.
11. Covering or closing one eye.
12. Dislike for reading or inattentiveness during reading.
13. Unusual fatigue after completing a vision task or a deterioration in reading after lengthy periods.
14. Losing the place while reading.
15. Using a finger or marker to guide the eyes.
16. Saying the words aloud or lip reading.

17. Moving the head rather than the eyes while reading.
18. General reading difficulties: the tendency to reverse letters and words or to confuse letters and numbers with similar shapes (e.g., a, c; f, t; e, c; m, n; and h, n, r), frequent omissions of words, or the attempts to guess words from quick recognition of a part of a word in easy reading material.
19. Stumbling over objects.
20. Poor spacing in writing and the inability to stay on or in a line. Reversal of letters or words.
21. Preference for reading versus play or motor activities or vice versa.

Complaints Associated with Using the Eyes

1. Headaches.
2. Nausea or dizziness.
3. Burning or itching eyes.
4. Blurred vision at any time.
5. Words or lines running together or grouped together.
6. Pains in the eyes.

Source: T. Hritcko, "Assessment of Children with Low Vision." In R. T. Jose (Ed.), *Understanding Low Vision* (pp. 105–137). New York: American Foundation for the Blind. © 1983. All rights reserved. Reprinted with permission from the publisher, the American Foundation for the Blind.

HEARING

There are several informal testing procedures that have been developed for the purpose of determining which students should be referred for testing. For example, Murdoch (1994) presents guidelines for conducting a functional hearing assessment to assess the extent to which students can distinguish relevant or irrelevant sounds and noises. He suggests that teachers present a range of sounds, under different conditions, and record the student's responses. Some things to note about the sounds or the conditions include: (1) How loud was the sound? (2) How far away from the sound was the person? (3) Which direction did the sound come from? (4) Was the sound high-pitched or low-pitched? (5) Was there a presence of background noise? (6) Was it a human voice, environmental sound, or music? (7) Was it a familiar or unfamiliar sound?

There are several aspects of the child's response to these noises and sounds that are useful to note, according to Murdoch (1994): (1) awareness of the sound (blinking, starting), (2) attention (staying still to listen), (3) localization (identifying where the sound comes from), (4) discrimination (differentiating between two sounds as the same or different, smiling at a familiar song), (5) recognition (knowing one's name, indicating that sound has meaning, and (6) comprehension (recognizing sounds and relating to their meanings). Educators can use this information to develop hypotheses about the child's impairment and can be given to the appropriate professional when making a referral.

An example of a checklist for potential hearing problems is the one created by the Royal National Institute for the Blind (n.d.), which provides information about appearance of ears, behaviors, and responses that educators should look for:

Appearance of Ears

- No ears at all
- Very small ears
- Closed or partially closed ears
- Unusually shaped ears
- Scarred ears or ears which appear damaged
- Discharging ears
- Ears with an unpleasant smell

Speech

- Does not speak at all
- Speaks very loudly or shouts
- Speaks very quietly or whispers
- Speaks in a monotonous voice—a dull single expressionless tone
- Speech which others find unintelligible or hard to understand
- Unusual pronunciation of certain words
- Poor communication skills
- Limited vocabulary

Behaviour

- Breathes through mouth—not nose
- Frequent catarrh—having a "blocked up" nose
- Frequent touching of ears—e.g., poking, banging or rubbing etc.
- Bangs or slaps side of face
- Puts objects (such as knitting needles or pencils) into ears
- Unusual head movements—cranes neck to hear
- Hears better on one side than the other
- Puts fingers (pointing upwards) under ear lobes
- "Ear-bending"—putting the ear lobes flat
- Cups hand behind ear to amplify sound
- Short attention span
- Poor self-care skills
- Poor balance
- Appears to be listening for sounds which no-one else can hear
- Puts hand over one ear, or a hand over each ear for no apparent reason

Changes in Behaviour

- Dramatic changes in behaviour—may have become "a different person"
- Seems confused
- Increasing lack of co-operation in a person who was previously co-operative
- Seems depressed for no apparent reason
- Responses to other people
- Hears people who speak close to them, or into one ear
- Watches people's faces very closely
- Has difficulty hearing people if their face and mouth cannot be seen
- Has difficulty recognizing voices—even people known well
- Needs to see people speaking to hear them or recognize their voice
- Ignores people who are not within sight

- Startled by people coming up close or touching them from behind or the side
- Does not respond when called by name
- Does not respond to verbal instructions
- Hears high pitched voices best—hears women and children better than men
- Hears deep voices best—hears men better than women and children
- Hears people some times, but not always

Understanding

- Seems to hear or understand certain people's voices—not others
- Misses parts of conversation
- Takes time to "tune in" and understand what is being said
- Understands people best who have expressive faces/body language
- Needs visual prompts—e.g. being shown a cup when offered a drink
- May have difficulty understanding when people change the subject in conversation
- Responses to sounds in the environment
- Obvious problems in hearing—e.g. distant sounds, or near sounds
- Needs to sit very close to television or music, or have it turned up loud
- Hears better in quiet areas, or without background noise
- Hears better in well-lit settings than in dark or poorly lit areas
- Hears high pitch sounds better
- Hears deep sounds better
- Does not recognise certain sounds or responds inappropriately
- Cannot identify where sounds come from
- Seems to hear sounds some times, but not always
- Avoids loud noise, or finds it painful, putting fingers into ears, or hands over ears
- Flinches or seems distressed by loud noise

In addition, Sanger (1986) developed the following nonstandardized checklist to help teachers observe communication relative to the speaker, listener, content, and context as signs of auditory processing problems.

Observational Profile of Classroom Communication
Project Director: Dixie D. Sanger
Barkley Memorial Center (1986), University of Nebraska–Lincoln

Instructions:

The teacher will observe the child for two weeks and report whether the following variables seem to affect the student's learning.

Scoring:

Check Yes is the statement appears to be in enough instances to affect the child's learning and No if it does not.

Name: _____   Name of Observer: _____

Birthdate: _____ CA: _____   Inclusive Dates of Observation: _____

Grade Level: _____   History of Hearing Loss: _____

Reason for Referral: _____

Background Information: _____

Signal and Presentation	**Yes**	**No**
1. The child displays difficulty using stress patterns to interpret speaker's intent.	☐	☐
2. The child is often confused by complex and embedded information.	☐	☐
3. The child has difficulty following multistage instructions.	☐	☐
4. The child misunderstands what is said, especially if the signal is presented at a fast rate.	☐	☐
5. The child displays more difficulty understanding the teacher when she moves around the room than when she is stationary.	☐	☐
6. The child frequently requires redundancy of auditory information.	☐	☐
7. The child appears to have trouble picking up new information and may require several repetitions in order to understand the material.	☐	☐
8. The child has difficulty understanding information presented at a normal level.	☐	☐
9. The child has difficulty understanding information which is academically challenging	☐	☐
10. The child often requires additional clues to understand information presented in class.	☐	☐
Is this true in contexts other than class?	☐	☐
11. The child frequently requires visual cues in addition to auditory information.	☐	☐

Comments: _____

_____

Environment	**Yes**	**No**
12. The child displays more difficulty learning when two or more speakers participate in the conversation.	☐	☐
13. The child appears inattentive or distracted, especially when significant background noise is present.	☐	☐
14. The child's learning seems to be affected by where he or she is seated in relation to the teacher.	☐	☐

    Explain _____

_____

	Yes	**No**
15. The child learns better in one-to-one situations than in small group or classroom situations.	☐	☐
16. The child tends to have difficulty learning in an environment with several visual distractions.	☐	☐

Comments: _____

_____

Response	**Yes**	**No**
17. The child often gives inappropriate or unrelated responses to questions or commands.	☐	☐
18. The child produces intermittent and inconsistent responses.	☐	☐
19. The child has difficulty recalling auditory information.	☐	☐

	Yes	No
Can the child recall auditory information if given special cues (e.g., a choice of words, association cues)?	☐	☐
20. The child displays difficulty recalling sequences of information such as telling a story or talking about an event.	☐	☐
21. The child displays difficulty formulating or generating expressive language.	☐	☐
22. The child displays language problems (evidenced in the usage of inappropriate "wh" questions, pronouns, word order, possessiveness, etc.).	☐	☐

Explain _____

_____

| 23. The child displays problems with articulation (phonology) consisting of substitutions, distortions, or omissions of sounds in words (especially when producing words which are similar auditorily). | ☐ | ☐ |

Explain _____

_____

| 24. Does the child often give inappropriate or delayed responses? | ☐ | ☐ |

Explain _____

_____

| 25. Does the child have difficulty in providing complex explanations to questions? | ☐ | ☐ |

Explain _____

_____

Comments: _____

_____

Strategies	Yes	No
26. The child does not tend to paraphrase information when having difficulty understanding information.	☐	☐
27. The child rarely rehearses information as a strategy for remembering it.	☐	☐
28. The child infrequently asks questions when uncertain of information.	☐	☐
29. The child is generally unaware of errors in processing information and does not attempt to get clarification of information.	☐	☐

Comments: _____

_____

Behaviors	Yes	No
30. The child displays some behavior problems (i.e., out-of-seat behavior, short attention span, day-dreaming).	☐	☐
31. The child appears unmotivated to learn (i.e., the child isn't persistent in trying to understand information he is having difficulty with; he is distracted quite easily).	☐	☐
32. The child shows irritability and hostility toward others, especially if he or she is having difficulty learning.	☐	☐

	Yes	No
33. The child becomes frustrated when trying to learn auditory information.	☐	☐

Comments: _____

PERCEPTUAL-MOTOR AND MOTOR PROFICIENCY

If an educator notices signs of possible perceptual-motor difficulties in a student, such as those described in Chapter 10, "Observable Manifestations and Observational Assessments," it may be worthwhile to follow up with some informal testing procedures. For example, if a teacher notices that a student seems to be having problems with the spacing or alignment of his/her letters, the teacher may ask the student to copy a variety of letters, numbers, and designs to note specific difficulties that the child may be having. After the child completes the task, the educator may ask the child to compare his/her work to the letters, numbers, and designs he/she was asked to copy. A child who does not recognize a difference between his/her drawing and the one he/she was asked to copy may have vision problems, whereas one who notices the problem may have more difficulty with motor control or the interaction between visual-motor skills.

Asking the child to do the same task again also provides helpful information. If the child makes the same errors, the problem may be more severe than a child who corrects his/her errors. In the latter case, the teacher may hypothesize that the initial failures may have been due to inattention, lack of interest in the task, or carelessness.

In addition, Sattler (2002, pp. 214–215) lists a number of questions that examiners can use to guide their observations of a child's performance on a perceptual-motor task:

1. How does the examinee hold the pencil?
2. In which hand does the examinee hold the pencil?
3. Are the examinee's drawings done with extreme care and deliberation, or are they done impulsively and haphazardly?
4. Does the examinee trace the design with a finger before he or she draws it?
5. Does the examinee count the dots, loops, or sides of figures before drawing a design?
6. Does the examinee glance at the design briefly and then draw it from memory?
7. Does the examinee rotate the card or paper (or both)?
8. Does the examinee make frequent erasures? If so, on what figures or parts of figures (e.g., curves, angulations, overlapping parts, or figures)?
9. What part of the design does the examinee draw first?
10. In what direction does the examinee copy the designs? For example, does the examinee draw the designs from top down or bottom up, from inside out or outside in? Does the examinee change direction of movement from design to design?

11. Does the examinee sketch the designs?

12. Does the examinee have particular difficulty drawing one or more designs? If so, which one or more?

13. How much space does the examinee use to draw the design? For example, is the drawing approximately the same size as the original or greatly reduced or greatly expanded?

14. How does the examinee arrange the designs on the paper? For example, are they laid out in an organized manner or in a random fashion? Is sufficient space allowed between the designs, or are they cramped?

15. How accurate are the examinee's drawings?

16. Do the examinee's drawings show any gross distortions?

17. Does the examinee spend approximately the same amount of time on each design? If not, how much time does he or she spend on different designs?

18. Does the examinee recognize his or her errors? If so, how does the examinee handle errors? What does she or he say about poorly executed drawings?

19. Does the examinee make comments about each design? If so, what are they?

20. Does the examinee show signs of fatigue? If so, what signs of fatigue does he or she show and when does he or she show them (e.g., at the beginning, middle, or end of the task)?

21. Does the examinee need encouragement to complete the drawings? If so, how does the examinee respond to encouragement?

22. How long does the examinee take to complete the task?

23. Is the amount of time taken by the examinee to draw the designs excessively long or unusually short?

24. What is the examiner's overall reaction to the task? For example, does the examinee express satisfaction or dissatisfaction with the end product?

25. Is there anything unusual or atypical about how the examinee responds to or carries out the task?

Although these questions were designed to be answered during the administration of some of the commonly used tests of visual-motor skills (reviewed in Chapter 12, "Formal Testing Procedures Using Published Tests"), answers to these questions during informal copying or drawing tasks may help the educator evaluate the child's skills, style of responding, and organizational ability. In addition, answers to these questions may provide information about factors that may influence the child's performance, such as motivation and reaction to frustration.

ADAPTIVE BEHAVIOR

Most measures of adaptive behavior follow the format of a clinical interview with parents or teachers, or standardized behavior rating scales. However, Sattler (2002, pp. 192–193) has developed an informal checklist of adaptive skill areas based on the American Association on Mental Retardation's (1992) definition of adaptive behavior.

Informal Checklist of the 10 AAMR Adaptive Behavior Skill Areas

Key:

Y (Yes) = Examinee can perform skill at a level appropriate for his or her age.
N (No) = Examinee cannot perform skill at a level appropriate for his or her age.
DK (Don't Know) = Don't know whether examinee can perform skill at a level appropriate for his or her age.
NR (Not Relevant) = This skill is not expected to be performed at the examinee's age level.

Communication (Ability to comprehend and express information through symbolic behaviors)

1. Knows how to comprehend or receive a request.	☐ Y	☐ N	☐ DK	☐ NR
2. Knows how to identify emotions.	☐ Y	☐ N	☐ DK	☐ NR
3. Knows how to write a letter.	☐ Y	☐ N	☐ DK	☐ NR
Other _____	☐ Y	☐ N	☐ DK	☐ NR

Self-Care (Ability to take care of oneself)

4. Uses utensils properly.	☐ Y	☐ N	☐ DK	☐ NR
5. Dresses self.	☐ Y	☐ N	☐ DK	☐ NR
6. Has adequate grooming.	☐ Y	☐ N	☐ DK	☐ NR
Other _____	☐ Y	☐ N	☐ DK	☐ NR

Home Living (Ability to take care of daily functioning within a home)

7. Helps with household tasks.	☐ Y	☐ N	☐ DK	☐ NR
8. Communicates needs and choices.	☐ Y	☐ N	☐ DK	☐ NR
9. Is aware of home safety precautions.	☐ Y	☐ N	☐ DK	☐ NR
Other _____	☐ Y	☐ N	☐ DK	☐ NR

Social Skills (Ability to engage in socially appropriate behavior)

10. Has friends.	☐ Y	☐ N	☐ DK	☐ NR
11. Takes turns in interactions.	☐ Y	☐ N	☐ DK	☐ NR
12. Demonstrates honesty, trustworthiness, and appropriate play.	☐ Y	☐ N	☐ DK	☐ NR
Other _____	☐ Y	☐ N	☐ DK	☐ NR

Community Use (Ability to make use of appropriate community resources)

13. Uses community facilities.	☐ Y	☐ N	☐ DK	☐ NR
14. Goes shopping.	☐ Y	☐ N	☐ DK	☐ NR
15. Uses public transportation.	☐ Y	☐ N	☐ DK	☐ NR
Other _____	☐ Y	☐ N	☐ DK	☐ NR

Self-Direction (Ability to make choices)

16. Knows how to follow a schedule.	☐ Y	☐ N	☐ DK	☐ NR
17. Initiates appropriate activities.	☐ Y	☐ N	☐ DK	☐ NR
18. Demonstrates appropriate assertiveness and self-advocacy.	☐ Y	☐ N	☐ DK	☐ NR
Other _____	☐ Y	☐ N	☐ DK	☐ NR

Health and Safety (Ability to maintain one's well-being)

19. Eats an appropriate diet.	□ Y	□ N	□ DK	□ NR
20. Identifies illnesses.	□ Y	□ N	□ DK	□ NR
21. Keeps physically fit.	□ Y	□ N	□ DK	□ NR
Other _____	□ Y	□ N	□ DK	□ NR

Functional Academics (Ability to learn at school)

22. Knows how to read.	□ Y	□ N	□ DK	□ NR
23. Knows how to write.	□ Y	□ N	□ DK	□ NR
24. Knows basic math.	□ Y	□ N	□ DK	□ NR
Other _____	□ Y	□ N	□ DK	□ NR

Leisure (Ability to pursue leisure and recreational activities related to personal preferences)

25. Chooses and initiates activities.	□ Y	□ N	□ DK	□ NR
26. Engages in and enjoys home and community leisure and recreational activities.	□ Y	□ N	□ DK	□ NR
27. Plays socially with others.	□ Y	□ N	□ DK	□ NR
Other _____	□ Y	□ N	□ DK	□ NR

Work (Ability to hold a part- or full-time job or participate in voluntary activity in the community)

28. Is competent on the job.	□ Y	□ N	□ DK	□ NR
29. Has appropriate work skills.	□ Y	□ N	□ DK	□ NR
30. Has appropriate skills related to working and going to work.	□ Y	□ N	□ DK	□ NR
Other _____	□ Y	□ N	□ DK	□ NR

PROBLEM BEHAVIOR

Generally speaking, the best informal methods for assessing problem behavior involve observing behaviors and the surrounding events. For example, once a target behavior, such as physical aggression, is established, educators may note what happens right before the behavior occurs (e.g., if the child was teased, if he was trying to gain an object that someone else had) and what consequences follow as a result of the physical aggression (e.g., if the child was verbally reprimanded, if he apologized). This information can be used to make hypotheses about the problem behavior and what can be done to intervene.

A useful framework for the informal assessment of problem behavior is a series of guiding questions posed by Sattler (2002, pp. 91–92). Answers to the following questions may provide helpful information on children's social and communication skills:

1. What are the child's facial expressions, gestures, and actions, as well as the body language and actions of others who communicate with the child?

2. How does the child communicate with others (e.g., rarely initiates verbal interactions, often initiates verbal interactions, uses gestures instead of speech)?

3. How do others respond to the child's communications (e.g., accept the communication, seem puzzled by the communications, withdraw from the child)?

4. Does the child use positive verbalizations such as please, thank you, and excuse me?

5. How does the child show interest in other children in the setting (e.g., plays with other children, stares at other children)?

6. How does the child make contact with other children (e.g., confidently, tentatively, aggressively)?

7. What is the quality of the child's behavior with other children (e.g., sharing, friendly, bullying, impatient, aggressive, withdrawn)?

8. How does the child respond when other children initiate interaction?

9. What is the quality of the child's relationship with adults in the setting? Note how frequently the child makes contact with adults and in which situations, and observe whether the child is matter-of-fact, warmhearted, reserved, open, whining, belligerent, clinging, or hostile.

10. How does the child gain attention from adults (e.g., politely or through excessive talking, tattling, sidling up and touching, or hanging on)?

11. Does the child comply with teacher and parent requests to share?

12. How does the child react to limits that are set by adults (e.g., accepts limits, defies them, slows but doesn't change present behavior)?

13. How does the child react to criticism from adults and from other children (e.g., accepts it, cries, pouts)?

14. What is the nature of the child's relationships with adults (e.g., dependent, respectful, disrespectful)?

VOCATIONAL AND EDUCATIONAL INTERESTS

Educators can do many informal things with students to help stimulate their thinking about vocational and educational plans. For instance, teachers can ask students to complete a questionnaire designed to think about their values, personality traits, interests, and skills and then follow up with a discussion about careers that may be a good match. Many informal checklists are based on the work of John Holland, who developed several categories of occupations that utilize different skills, interests, and abilities. These are: realistic, investigative, artistic, social, enterprising, and conventional. This example of a checklist was developed by the North Carolina State Occupational Information Coordinating Committee (2001):

Holland Occupational Themes

Based on the theory of John Holland, Ph.D., people with the same or similar interests are often found in the same work environments. To discover the work environments suited to your interests, abilities and personality, consider the following categories/themes.

Step 1: For each theme, check those items which describe you.

REALISTIC

R Total =

Are You:

☐ Practical
☐ Athletic
☐ Straightforward
☐ Mechanically inclined
☐ A nature lover

Can You

☐ Fix electrical things
☐ Solve mechanical problems
☐ Pitch a tent
☐ Play a sport
☐ Read a blueprint
☐ Operate tools and machinery

Like To:

☐ Tinker with mechanics
☐ Work outdoors
☐ Be physically active
☐ Use your hands
☐ Build things
☐ Work on cars

INVESTIGATIVE

I Total =

Are You:

☐ Inquisitive
☐ Analytical
☐ Scientific
☐ Observant
☐ Precise

Can You

☐ Think abstractly
☐ Solve math problems
☐ Understand physical theories
☐ Do complex calculations
☐ Use a microscope
☐ Operate tools and machinery
☐ Analyze data

Like To:

☐ Explore ideas
☐ Use computers
☐ Work independently
☐ Perform lab experiments
☐ Read scientific or technical magazines
☐ Work on cars

ARTISTIC

A Total =

Are You:

☐ Creative
☐ Intuitive
☐ Imaginative
☐ Innovative
☐ An individualist

Can You

☐ Sketch, draw, paint
☐ Play a musical instrument
☐ Write stories, poetry, music, sing, act, dance
☐ Design fashions or interiors

Like To:

☐ Attend concerts, theaters, art exhibits
☐ Read fiction, plays, poetry
☐ Work on crafts
☐ Take photographs
☐ Express yourself creatively

SOCIAL

S Total =

Are You:

☐ Friendly
☐ Helpful
☐ Idealistic

Can You

☐ Teach/train others
☐ Express yourself clearly
☐ Lead a group discussion

Like To:

☐ Work in groups
☐ Help people with problems

- [ ] Insightful
- [ ] Outgoing
- [ ] Understanding

- [ ] Mediate disputes
- [ ] Plan and supervise an activity
- [ ] Cooperate well with others

- [ ] Participate in meetings
- [ ] Do volunteer service
- [ ] Work with young people
- [ ] Play team sports

ENTERPRISING

E Total =

Are You:

- [ ] Self-confident
- [ ] Assertive
- [ ] Sociable
- [ ] Persuasive
- [ ] Enthusiastic
- [ ] Energetic

Can You

- [ ] Initiate projects
- [ ] Convince people to do things your way
- [ ] Sell things or promote ideas
- [ ] Give talks or speeches
- [ ] Organize activities and events
- [ ] Lead a group

Like To:

- [ ] Make decisions affecting others
- [ ] Be elected to office
- [ ] Win a leadership or sales award
- [ ] Start your own political campaign
- [ ] Meet important people

CONVENTIONAL

C Total =

Are You:

- [ ] Well groomed
- [ ] Accurate
- [ ] Numerically inclined
- [ ] Methodical
- [ ] Conscientious
- [ ] Efficient

Can You

- [ ] Work well within a system
- [ ] Do a lot of paperwork in a short time
- [ ] Keep accurate records
- [ ] Use a computer terminal
- [ ] Write effective business letters

Like To:

- [ ] Follow clearly defined procedures
- [ ] Use data processing equipment
- [ ] Work with numbers
- [ ] Type or take shorthand
- [ ] Be responsible for details

Step 2: Total the items checked for each theme/category. Identify the top 3 categories/themes which create the most accurate picture of you.

My top 3 categories/themes are: _____, _____, _____.

Step 3: How accurately do you believe your (3) top themes describe your personality and interests?

REALISTIC people are characterized by competitive/assertive behavior and by interest in activities that require motor coordination, skill, and physical strength. People oriented toward this role prefer situations involving "action solutions" rather than tasks involving verbal or interpersonal skills. They like to take a concrete approach to problem-solving rather than relying on abstract theory. They tend to be interested in scientific or mechanical rather than cultural and aesthetic areas.

INVESTIGATIVE people prefer to think rather than to act, to organize and understand rather than to persuade. They are not apt to be too "people oriented."

SOCIAL people seem to satisfy their needs in teaching or helping situations. In contrast to investigative and realistic people, social types are drawn more to seek close interpersonal relationships and are less apt to engage in intellectual or extensive physical activity.

CONVENTIONAL people don't mind rules and regulations and emphasize self-control. They prefer structure and order to ambiguity in work and interpersonal situations. They place value on prestige or status.

ENTERPRISING people are verbally skilled and use this skill in persuasion rather than support of others. They also value prestige and status and are more apt to pursue it than conventional people.

ARTISTIC people value self-expression and relations with others through artistic expression. They dislike structure, prefer tasks involving personal or physical skills, and are more prone to expression of emotion than others. They are like investigative people but are more interested in the cultural-aesthetic than the scientific.

Based on John L. Holland's *Making Vocational Choices: A Theory of Careers* (Englewood Cliffs, NJ: Prentice Hall, 1973). The formal validated assessment instrument using John Holland's theory is the "Self-Directed Search," available from PAR, Inc.

Step 4: Visit *Career Briefs* to view a sample of occupations which match your three Holland themes. (Look for your 3 letter code in all order configurations.)

Reprinted in part from "Career Choices in North Carolina," 2000–2001, Number 16, published by the North Carolina State Occupational Information Coordinating Committee.

Note: The checklist is in the process of being updated. For more information see their web site, http://www.soicc.state.nc.us/soicc/ or contact Judy Woodson Bruhn, Executive Director <judybruhn@ncmail.net>.

12

Formal Testing Procedures Using Published Tests

Vision Tests

Two criterion-referenced tests, created specifically to aid nonprofessionals in assessing visual problems in children, are reviewed. These are the Denver Eye Screening Test and the Visual Skills Appraisal.

Denver Eye Screening Test (DEST),
for testing individuals 6 months of age and older
Reviewed by Amanda B. Nickerson, Ph.D., School Psychology

Usefulness of the Test for Educators

Test Authors' Purpose

The Denver Eye Screening Test (DEST) was designed to aid the nonprofessional in screening for problems in visual acuity and non-straight eyes in children as young as 6 months old.

Decision-Making Applications

The DEST can be used to help educators identify children who are at risk for eye problems and diseases, and to make referral decisions about which children may need a complete eye examination by an eye specialist.

Relevant Population

The DEST can be administered to children 6 months of age and older.

Characteristics Described

The DEST assesses three different eye problems, and assesses each in the following ways:

Refractive error: The inability to see clearly due to a failure of the eye to focus correctly.

1. "E" test: This test, which is given to children 3 years and older, requires the examiner to stand 15 feet away from the child and to hold an "E" card in several different directions. The child indicates which direction the card is facing. This test is administered in three to five trials, and is stopped once the child gives three correct or three incorrect responses.

2. Picture card: This test is administered to children between the ages of 2 years, 6 months and 2 years, 11 months. Images of common objects are presented to the child and, from a distance of 15 feet, the child must identify the image. This test, like the "E" test, is administered in three to five trials, and is stopped once the child gives three correct or three incorrect responses.

3. Fixation: This test is given to children between the ages of 6 months and 2 years, 5 months. A penlight or a spinning toy is moved from the right to the left in front of the child, and the examiner records whether or not the child's eyes follow it.

4. Squinting: The examiner notes whether or not the child squints during these tasks.

Non-straight eyes: A condition where a person focuses on an object with only one eye, while the other eye turns up, out, or down.

Amblyopia: When a person develops impaired vision in one eye due to lack of use. This is sometimes called "lazy eye."

1. Question about eyes to parent: This involves asking the parent, "Do your child's eyes ever turn in or out, or are they ever not straight?"

2. Cover Test: In this test, a penlight or spinning toy is held about 1 1/2 feet from the child's face, while each of his or her eyes is covered, one at a time. The examiner records whether or not the eye definitely and consistently moves when it is uncovered.

3. Pupillary light reflex test: This test, also used to assess non-straight eyes, involves pointing the penlight into a child's eye from 1 1/2 feet away and recording where the light is reflected in the eye (i.e., in the middle of the pupil or more toward the nose side in one eye).

Test Scores Obtained

A score is obtained for each of the aforementioned items. The "E" test and picture cards are scored as either "3P" (child passed three trials) or "3F" (child failed three trials). The fixation test, cover test, and pupillary light reflex are scored as pass or fail, and the squinting and question to parent are scored as yes or no. In addition, any item can be scored "untestable." The following criteria determine whether a child receives a total rating of "Normal," " Abnormal," or "Untestable:"

Criteria	Total Test Rating
Passed vision test *and* no sign of squinting, *and* passes two of three tests for non-straight eyes	Normal
Abnormal on any vision test *or* squinting *or* fails two of three procedures for non-straight eyes.	Abnormal
Untestable on any vision tests *or* untestable on two of three tests for non-straight eyes.	Untestable

Technical Adequacy

Validity Confirmation

Test item validity: No specific information about the validity of the items is presented in the Manual. However, the test uses eye examination procedures (e.g., the "E" test) which are established and well regarded by eye care specialists.

Test response validity: No specific information about the validity of the test is presented in the Manual.

Reliability Confirmation

No specific information about the reliability of the test is presented in the Manual.

Objectivity Confirmation

To ensure the objectivity of the DEST, the Manual and accompanying video say that it is important to have good lighting, with the light falling directly on the test object. In addition, examiners should not let the child squint, as this can affect results. Finally, it is recommended that the examiner obtain cooperation from the child by using frequent praise.

Statistical Confirmation

More information about the test is available in the Manual. Because it is a criterion-referenced test, statistics for calculating reliability and validity are not included.

Special Features

Acronym

DEST.

Levels of the Test

There is one level of the test, although the examiner selects which of the three vision tests to administer, depending on the age of the child.

Number of Test Forms

One.

Norm-Referenced?

No.

Criterion-Referenced?

Yes.

Feasibility Considerations

Testing Time

No information is provided in the Manual, but it is likely that the test can be administered in 5 to 15 minutes.

For Testing Groups? Individuals?

Individuals.

Test Administration and Scoring

Because the DEST is designed for the nonprofessional, the Manual/Workbook and the accompanying videotape offer thorough instructions and practice on administration and scoring. It is recommended that the examiner go through four hours of classroom training, do practice tests on 12 children, and take a proficiency test before using the DEST.

Test Materials and Approximate Costs

The test kit, which includes the materials needed for administration (e.g., picture cards, spinning toy), costs $20. A package of 25 test forms costs $6, and the Manual/Workbook, with questions and answers, costs $20. The Reference Manual, which is the same as the other manual but does not include questions and answers, costs $17. The videotape costs $180 to buy and $50 to rent.

Adequacy of Test Manuals

The Manual/Workbook and videotape are comprehensive, and include practice tests, which is helpful. The scoring sheet is easy to use. Materials are somewhat dated, yet still relevant. The videotape is very useful in modeling the administration of the test and offering opportunities for practice.

Excerpts from Other Test Reviews

Although basic information about the DEST is cited in the Buros Institute's *Ninth Mental Measurements Yearbook*, there is no review of the test.

Ordering Information

Publisher

Denver Developmental Materials, Inc., P.O. Box 371075, Denver, CO 80237-5075; Phone: 800-419-4729; Fax: 303-344-5622.

Authors

William K. Frankenburg, Arnold D. Goldstein, and John Barker.

Publication Date

1973.

Cautions and Comments

The DEST is a useful way for educators to assess signs of eye problems that may indicate a need for further testing. The videotape and Manual are thorough and are especially helpful for the inexperienced examiner. Reference is made to obtaining four hours of classroom training, although it is unclear as to how educators can obtain this training.

The Manual offers helpful, clear criteria for when results are abnormal and when a referral is indicated, which is a great asset for educators. Therefore, if a child receives a score of "Abnormal" on any of the vision tests, or squints, or fails two of three procedures for non-straight eyes, he or she should be referred to a professional for further testing.

Reference

Frankenburg, W. K., Goldstein, A. D., & Barker, J. (1973). *Denver Eye Screening Test: Manual/ Workbook*. Denver, CO: Denver Developmental Materials.

Visual Skills Appraisal (VSA),
for testing individuals from kindergarten through grade 4
Reviewed by Amanda B. Nickerson, Ph.D., School Psychology

Usefulness of the Test for Educators

Test Authors' Purpose

The Visual Skills Appraisal (VSA) was developed to assist educators in the assessment of children's visual skills and difficulties related to classroom tasks.

Decision-Making Applications

The VSA can be used to help educators understand a child's visual abilities and difficulties. It can also be used to determine whether a student should be referred to a vision specialist for further evaluation.

Relevant Population

The VSA can be administered by a teacher, psychologist, occupational or physical therapist, optometrist, or other professional to children in kindergarten through grade 4. It can also be used with older children, following the assumption that if they score below the fourth grade level, they have visual difficulties.

Characteristics Described

The VSA is divided into two main categories, each of which includes several specific skills: (1) eye movement skills and (2) eye teaming skills.

Eye movement skills: Skills involved in locating and scanning the printed page and for aligning the eyes for inspecting details.

1. Pursuit movements: The ability to maintain visual attention on a moving object by moving eyes at the same speed as the object moves.
2. Scanning movements: Eye movements that help inspect the words on a page and read from one line to another without losing one's place.
3. Aligning: Turning in, or convergence, of both eyes to a specific letter or point in a smooth and even manner.
4. Locating movements: Visual saccades, or precise locating movements used when reading (i.e., jump from one fixation point to the next without pause).

Eye teaming skills: Skills involved in using both eyes in unison.

1. Eye-hand coordination: The ability of the eyes and hands to work together, which allows one to reproduce what he or she sees.
2. Fixation unity: The ability to obtain one clear interpretation from the two visual fields of the left and right eye.

Test Scores Obtained

A score is obtained for each subtest, which the examiner can add together for a total score. This total score can be converted to a percentage of accuracy. For each of the six subtests, a maximum score of 5 can be obtained. The author indicates that any student receiving a score lower than 4 on a subtest needs assistance in enhancing his or her visual skill efficiency. In addition, the following scores indicate the need for a referral to a qualified eye care professional:

Subtest	Score Indicating Need for Referral
1. Pursuits (Object Tracking)	0 or 1
2. Scanning (Trails)	0 or 1
3. Alignment (Push-ups)	0, 1, or 2

Subtest	Score Indicating Need for Referral
4. Locating (Numbers)	0 or 1
5. Eye-Hand (Design Completion)	0 or 1
6. Fixation Unity (Red/Green Trails)	0, 1, or 2

The test authors report that if a student receives a score of 2 or 3 on subtests 1, 2, 4, and 5, it is important to monitor the student's progress in individual vision training. A score of 3 on subtests 3 and 6 also indicates a critical need to monitor the student's progress and retest after a week or two. In addition, it is very important for a child with a score of 0, 1, or 2 on subtest 6 to be seen by a professional to determine the reason for the difficulty.

Technical Adequacy

Validity Confirmation

Test item validity: The test was developed through a process whereby professionals working with students in an educational therapy center noted the high frequency of vision problems and consulted with local optometrists. To meet the need of having a thorough assessment tool to inform educational planning for specific visual skills, an extensive test, called the Big Springs Visual Skills Test, was developed. This was refined, in consultation with a variety of optometrists, by identifying areas that are most important in appraising visual needs of children. This resulted in the VSA.

Test response validity: No specific information about the validity of the test is presented in the Manual.

Reliability Confirmation

No specific information about the reliability of the test is presented in the Manual.

Objectivity Confirmation

To ensure the objectivity of the VSA, specific guidelines for scoring each subtest are provided in the Manual.

Statistical Confirmation

More information about the test is available in the Manual.

Special Features

Acronym

VSA.

Levels of the Test

One.

Number of Test Forms

In addition to the VSA Score Sheet, there are stimulus cards, Design Completion Forms, Red/Green Trail Forms, and Red/Green glasses.

Norm-Referenced?

No.

Criterion-Referenced?

Yes. Two hundred children in the top one-third of their class in school were administered the test to determine the scores considered "Criteria for Success."

Feasibility Considerations

Testing Time

Ten to 15 minutes.

For Testing Groups? Individuals?

Individuals.

Test Administration and Scoring

The administration and scoring of the VSA can be complicated, and some practice and judgment is required. Extensive information on administration and scoring is provided in the Manual to assist examiners.

Test Materials and Approximate Costs

The complete test kit, which includes the Manual and all accompanying materials, costs $85. The Manual costs $27. In addition, components can be purchased separately. The Red-Green Trail Forms, Score Sheets, and Design Complete Forms can each be purchased in sets of 25 for $12. The stimulus cards cost $12, and the Red-Green glasses cost $8.

Adequacy of Test Manuals

The Manual is comprehensive, and provides information on the test development, administration, and scoring, as well as case studies and techniques used to enhance visual skill development.

Excerpts from Other Test Reviews

Although basic information about the VSA is cited in the Buros Institute's *Eleventh Mental Measurements Yearbook*, no review is included.

Ordering Information

Publisher

Academic Therapy Publications, 20 Commercial Boulevard, Novato, CA 94949-6191; Phone: 800-422-7249; Fax: 888-287-9975; Web site: www.academictherapy.com.

Authors

Regina G. Richards and Gary Oppenheim, in consultation with G. N. Getman.

Publication Date

1984.

Cautions and Comments

The VSA is a useful test for educators, especially since it provides clear guidelines for scores that indicate the need for a referral to an eye care specialist. The test was developed through the collaborative effort of educators and optometrists. The authors give clear advice about what scores necessitate a referral to a qualified eye care professional (score of 0 or 1 on subtests 1, 2, 4, 5, or score of 0, 1, or 2 on subtests 3 or 6). The authors specifically caution about the inadvisability of nonprofessionals to attempt to interpret scores from the Fixation Unity subtest, and underscore the importance of a child receiving a score of 0, 1, or 2 to be seen by a professional clinician.

Reference

Richards, R. A. (1984). *Visual Skills Appraisal Manual*. Novato, CA: Academic Therapy Publications.

STEREOSCOPIC VISION SCREENING INSTRUMENTS

Many schools use stereoscopic vision screening instruments because they do not require a large room in which to measure visual acuity as the traditional Snellen Test does. Also, illumination is controlled and supplemental tests, such as eye-muscle balance, stereo vision (depth perception), and color discrimination are included. These instruments use an optical system to adjust to the shorter distance for administration. Two of the more popular models are the Titmus Vision Tester from Titmus Optical Company and the Optec 2000 Vision Tester from Stereo Optical Company.

Hearing Test

Most formal hearing tests require the aid of equipment and are administered by professionals. However, there are several published tests of auditory and language skills, such as the Clinical Evaluation of Language Fundamentals (reviewed elsewhere in this handbook) that can be used by educators. One such test is The Test of Auditory-Perceptual Skills-Revised, which is reviewed here due to its assessment of a broad range of skills related to auditory-perception, and its ease of use for educators.

Test of Auditory-Perceptual Skills-Revised (TAPS-R),
for testing individuals from 4 years through 12 years, 11 months of age
Reviewed by Amanda B. Nickerson, Ph.D., School Psychology

Usefulness of the Test for Educators

Test Author's Purpose

The Test of Auditory-Perceptual Skills-Revised (TAPS-R) was developed to give professionals one test that would assess various areas of auditory-perceptual skills. It was designed to help a wide variety of professionals to understand more about what the child does with what he or she hears.

Decision-Making Applications

The test can be used to assess children's strengths and weaknesses in several areas of auditory-perceptual skills. Poor performance on the TAPS-R also suggests the need for a hearing evaluation. Results of the TAPS-R should be evaluated by the test administrators and relevant specialists to determine the need for remediation.

Relevant Population

The TAPS-R can be administered to children between the ages of 4 years and 12 years, 11 months.

Characteristics Described

The TAPS-R yields an Auditory-Perceptual Quotient (sum of the seven scaled subtest scores), as well as seven subtests:

1. Auditory Number Memory—Forward: This subtest measures a student's immediate recall of rote nonsensical auditory information, which may give an estimate of a child's ability to learn academic and nonacademic information through rote sequential memory.

2. Auditory Number Memory—Reversed: This subtest requires the child to be attentive to rote, sequential, non-meaningful auditory matter and to recall the numbers, reorganize and remanipulate the number structure, and repeat the digits correctly in reverse sequence. This task requires concentration and mental control.

3. Auditory Sentence Memory: The child recalls rote auditory information on this subtest, providing the examiner some diagnostic clues by noting if the subject omits words, substitutes words, or changes the sequence of words.

4. Auditory Word Memory: This subtest requires the student to recall a series of single words that become progressively more difficult. This can aid examiners in assessing speech distortions or articulation problems, depending on how a subject perceives a word.

5. Auditory Interpretation of Directions: This subtest, which involves both auditory memory and sequencing, assesses the child's ability to understand and interpret meaningful auditory information.

6. Auditory Word Discrimination: The student's ability to discriminate between paired words with phonemically similar consonants, cognates, and vowel differences is assessed by this subtest.

7. Auditory Processing (Thinking and Reasoning): This subtest consists of thought-provoking items that tap a child's ability to use common sense and insight to solve common thought problems.

In addition, the TAPS-R includes a Hyperactivity Index Scale, or Parent's Questionnaire. This scale is the only one that is not administered to the child. The questionnaire, administered to the parent, is used primarily to provide information about the child's hyperactive, social, and emotional behavior in an effort to assess how the student's behavior may affect test results.

Test Scores Obtained

Raw scores are calculated for each subtest, and four types of derived scores are obtained for subtests and for the Auditory-Perceptual Quotient:

1. Standard scores (mean of 100 and standard deviation of 15), scaled scores (mean of 10 and standard deviation of 3), and T-scores (mean of 50 and standard deviation of 10)

2. Percentile ranks, stanines

3. Auditory-perceptual ages

The test author does not include classification information to help determine cutoff criteria for determining if there is a problem, except for the Hyperactivity Scale. For this scale, two standard deviations above the mean (e.g., T-score of 70) suggests that the subject is hyperactive, and his or her scores may be affected by this.

Technical Adequacy

Validity Confirmation

Test item validity: Several procedures were used to ensure that the test items developed and selected for the revised version of the instrument were valid. First, items selected were not biased according to gender, education, ethnicity, or language, and could be used for subjects from different geographic regions and between the ages of

4 years and 12 years, 11 months. Any items that were related to the aforementioned variables (e.g., gender, ethnicity) were eliminated from the final form of the test. To be included in the final form of the TAPS-R, each item had to meet several pre-established criteria. First, the items on the test had to represent a wide range of difficulty. Second, items needed to be reliable. Third, any item with a correlation with gender that was higher than .15 was eliminated. Fourth, items were correlated with chronological age and grade to ensure that the auditory-perceptual items became more sophisticated with age.

Test response validity: Children's responses to the test were validated in several ways. First, as part of the standardization procedure, subtests from several other standardized tests were administered along with the TAPS-R to assess the extent to which the TAPS-R assessed specific auditory-perceptual skills. This table shows the correlation between different tests and the Auditory-Perceptual Quotients of the TAPS-R:

Test and/or Subtest	Number of Students	Correlation with Auditory-Perceptual Quotient of TAPS
TONI-2	115	.44
TAAS (Spelling)	192	.54
TAAS (Arithmetic)	103	.35
TAAS (Reading)	192	.42
WRAT-3 (Reading-Blue)	96	.33
WRAT-3 (Reading-Tan)	95	.57
WRAT-3 (Spelling-Tan)	132	.49
DTLA-3 (Basic Information)	61	.53
DTLA-3 (Sentence Imitation)	61	.62
DTLA-3 (Word Opposites)	51	.48
DTLA-3 (Word Sequence)	61	.47
WISC-III (Digit Span)	34	.37
WISC-III (Vocabulary)	446	.19
WPPSI-R (Vocabulary)	240	.59
TVPS-R	750	.26

The test author interprets these correlations, along with the correlations between these tests and the various subtests of the TAPS-R, to indicate that the TAPS-R assesses specific auditory-perceptual skills as opposed to aspects of overall intellectual functioning. In addition, the TAPS-R was administered to 42 learning-disabled students, who scored significantly lower than their average peers in all subtests.

Reliability Confirmation

The only type of reliability that was reported in the Examiner's Manual was split-half reliability. This involves splitting the test items into two halves and correlating the items. The reliability coefficients for the total scale ranged from .85 to .90. Reliabilities for individual subtests ranges from .35 to .92.

Objectivity Confirmation

Extensive information about scoring each subtest, to ensure that scoring is as objective as possible, is provided in the Examiner's Manual. No studies were reported where the TAPS-R was administered and scored by more than one person.

Statistical Confirmation

More information about reliability and validity are reported in the TAPS-R Examiner's Manual.

Special Features

Acronym

TAPS-R.

Levels of the Test

One.

Number of Test Forms

One.

Norm-Referenced?

Yes. 1,038 subjects participated in the development of the TAPS-R. All subjects were enrolled in an educational program through public, private, or parochial school. Subjects with language disorders, hearing impairment, mental retardation, severe learning problems, or emotional disturbance were excluded. Most of the subjects lived in the San Francisco Bay area, although some came from other states, with a total of 19 states included. There were an equal number of males and females, and the racial and ethnic background of subjects was reasonably representative of the 1990 U.S. Census.

Criterion-Referenced?

No.

Feasibility Considerations

Testing Time

Fifteen to 25 minutes.

For Testing Groups? Individuals?

Individuals.

Test Administration and Scoring

The TAPS-R is relatively straightforward to administer and score, although examiners should read the Examiner's Manual carefully, as extensive instructions are provided.

Test Materials and Approximate Costs

The TAPS-R Complete Kit, which includes the Examiner's Manual, 25 Test Booklets, and a sturdy storage box, costs $89. The Examiner's Manual costs $39 and a package of 25 Test Booklets costs $69.

Adequacy of Test Manuals

The Examiner's Manual is informative, and the test form is clear and easy to use.

Excerpts from Other Test Reviews

Cohen (1998) reviewed the original edition of the TAPS, noting that the test was short, easy to administer, and provided an overview of performance on several auditory perceptual skills. Criticisms of the TAPS included the fact that it was not clear how auditory perceptual skills were defined, and the reliance on writing children's responses verbatim could be problematic, depending on the examiner's short-term memory skills. She also commented that the test could be improved and updated, but it should be noted that these comments pertained to the original TAPS, not the revised version. Kessler and Spitzer (1998) also reviewed the original TAPS, stating that it was a useful, easy-to-use test. However, they noted that a major drawback of the TAPS is that it is presented orally, so scores are highly influenced by the child's receptive language skills. Both of the aforementioned reviews also pointed out that standardization of the test is problematic, because there are differences in the way examiners present oral information, which could affect the results.

Ordering Information

Publisher

Psychological and Educational Publications, Inc., P.O. Box 520, Hydesville, CA 95547-0520; Phone: 800-523-5775; Fax: 800-447-0907.

Author

Morrison F. Gardner.

Publication Date

1996.

Cautions and Comments

The TAPS-R is a useful screening tool for auditory processing problems. It should be noted that it only assesses a person's ability to perceive and process auditory information, so it is not a test of physical hearing. One caution that has been noted by reviewers is the lack of standardization in administration, since each administrator has a different way of presenting oral information, which could affect the child's performance. Therefore, it is important that educators administering the TAPS-R pronounce words correctly and succinctly.

No specific cutoff scores are provided, but a good rule of thumb is that an Auditory-Perceptual Quotient that is one standard deviation or more below the mean (i.e., score of 85 or below) indicates the need for a professional, such as a Speech and Language Pathologist, to do a more comprehensive assessment of the child. The author cautions that no claim is made that low performance on any of the subtests suggests that the child will have an academic disorder, and that results should be considered along with the results of other evaluative instruments.

References

Cohen, A. J. (1998). Review of the Test of Auditory-Perceptual Skills. In J. C. Impara & B. S. Plake (Eds.), *The Thirteenth Mental Measurements Yearbook* (pp. 1021–1025). Lincoln, NE: The Buros Institute of Mental Measurements.

Gardner, M. F. (1996). *TAPS-R: Test of Auditory-Perceptual Skills-Revised Manual*. Hydesville, CA: Psychological and Educational Publications.

Kessler, A. R., & Spitzer, J. B. (1998). Review of the Test of Auditory-Perceptual Skills. In J. C. Impara & B. S. Plake (Eds.), *The Thirteenth Mental Measurements Yearbook* (pp. 1025–1026). Lincoln, NE: The Buros Institute of Mental Measurements.

Perceptual-Motor and Motor Proficiency Tests

This section reviews two kinds of standardized tests of motor skills: (1) visual-motor skills and (2) fine and gross motor skills. It should be noted that the Bender Visual Motor Gestalt Test is another commonly used test of visual-motor skills. However, due to its long history of use by professionals to assess emotional indicators and other characteristics, it was felt that more useful screening tests for educators would be the Developmental Test of Visual-Motor Integration (Fourth Edition, Revised) and the Test of Visual-Motor Integration. Also reviewed are two tests of motor proficiency, the Bruininks-Oseretsky Test of Motor Proficiency and the Test of Gross Motor Development: Second Edition.

Bruininks-Oseretsky Test of Motor Proficiency, for testing
individuals from 4 years, 6 months through 14 years, 6 months of age
Reviewed by Amanda B. Nickerson, Ph.D., School Psychology

Usefulness of the Test for Educators

Test Author's Purpose

The Bruininks-Oseretsky Test of Motor Proficiency was developed to provide educators, clinicians, and researchers with useful information in the assessment of motor skills in children, the development of motor training programs, and the assessment of motor dysfunction or developmental handicaps in children.

Decision-Making Applications

There are several uses of the Bruininks-Oseretsky Test of Motor Proficiency. First, it can be used to make educational placement decisions. For example, results can be used to decide which physical education program is most appropriate for an individual, or which corrective motor training program may be needed. The Bruininks-Oseretsky Test of Motor Proficiency can also be used to assess fine and gross motor skills, which is helpful for physical education teachers, physical therapists, and occupational therapists. The test can also be used to develop and evaluate motor training programs. Lastly, the Bruininks-Oseretsky Test of Motor Proficiency can be used to screen children for possible developmental problems.

Relevant Population

The Bruininks-Oseretsky Test of Motor Proficiency was developed to be administered to children between the ages of 4 years, 6 months and and 14 years, 6 months.

Characteristics Described

The Bruininks-Oseretsky Test of Motor Proficiency assesses both gross and fine motor skills through eight subtests:

1. Running speed and agility: This subtest measures a child's running speed by requiring him or her to run for a specified distance, pick up a block, and run back.
2. Balance: Items on this subtest require the child to maintain balance while standing on one leg and to maintain balance while walking.
3. Bilateral coordination: This subtest assesses the child's sequential and simultaneous coordination of upper and lower limbs.
4. Strength: This subtest measures the strength of the child's arms, shoulder, abdomen, and legs.

5. Upper-limb coordination: These items assess the coordination of visual tracking with arm and hand movements, as well as the precise movements of arms, hands, or fingers.

6. Response speed: This subtest assesses the ability to respond quickly to a moving stimulus.

7. Visual-motor control: This subtest assesses the ability to coordinate precise hand and visual movements.

8. Upper-limb speed and dexterity: This subtest assesses hand and finger dexterity, as well as hand and arm speed.

The Complete Battery of the Bruininks-Oseretsky Test of Motor Proficiency yields a Gross Motor Composite, which summarizes performance on subtests 1–4. This is a measure of the child's ability to use large muscles effectively. A Fine Motor Composite, summarizing performance on subtests 5–8, is also derived. This describes the child's ability to use small muscles of the lower arm and hand effectively. The Battery Composite summarizes performance on all eight subtests.

Test Scores Obtained

Several scores are obtained from the Bruininks-Oseretsky Test of Motor Proficiency, such as standard scores for each age group, percentile ranks, stanines, and age equivalents. The Composite Standard Scores have a mean of 50 and a standard deviation of 10. Subtests have a mean of 15 and a standard deviation of 5, with the following descriptions of performance:

Subtest Standard Score	Percent of Norm Group	Description of Performance
Above 23	4	High
19–23	19	Above Average
12–18	54	Average
6–11	19	Below Average
Below 6	4	Low

Technical Adequacy

Validity Confirmation

Test item validity: The test author conducted a comprehensive review of studies of motor development of children and adults, which led to the development of the test content. Items from the original Oseretsky Tests of Motor Proficiency were evaluated according to several criteria, such as: "includes broad sampling of motor behavior," "requires minimal verbal comprehension," "easy to administer," and "ability to be scored objectively." Half of the original 60 items met the criteria, and 70 more items were constructed for the experimental version of the tests. This was administered to 75 children to determine the clarity and adequacy of items. Another more intensive item analysis program was then conducted with 250 students, and statistics were used to determine item difficulty and discrimination. In addition, studies of test-retest reliability, intercorrelations among items, and inter-rater agreement were conducted. The final version contains 46 items. A short form was also constructed from data analyses of the standardization sample.

Test response validity: Responses on the Bruininks-Oseretsky Test of Motor Proficiency were validated in several ways. First, subtest scores and chronological age were compared for children in the standardization sample, since motor ability is hypothesized to be developmental in nature. Correlations between subtest scores and chronological age range from .57 to .86, with a median correlation of .78, indicating a close relationship between scores and age. In addition, items were correlated with subtests and with the total test scores, yielding higher correlations of items within their subtest than within the total test. This suggests that the subtests are more homogeneous than the total test, as would be expected. A statistical procedure called factor analysis was also conducted on the standardization sample, and results from this confirmed the construction of the test into the eight subtests. There were also three studies reported in the manual that compared the performance of children with different disabilities (those with mild mental retardation, moderate to severe mental retardation, and learning disabilities) to normal samples. In each of these studies, children with disabilities scored significantly lower on the Bruininks-Oseretsky Test of Motor Proficiency than children without disabilities.

Reliability Confirmation

The Bruininks-Oseretsky Test of Motor Proficiency was administered twice to 63 second graders and 63 sixth graders, with a 7- to 12-day interval between administrations. The test-retest correlations were .89 and .86 for the Battery Composite, and subtest correlations ranged from .58 to .89 for second graders and from .29 to .89 for sixth graders. The author noted that caution should be interpreted with the low correlations, as this was reflective of students who mastered specific motor skills between administrations.

Objectivity Confirmation

Two inter-rater agreement studies were conducted on the scores for the eight items on the visual-motor control subtest, as scoring of these items requires more judgment than do the others. In the first study, five raters with no training in psychological testing were given a brief orientation to the Bruininks-Oseretsky Test of Motor Proficiency and scoring of the subtest. They practiced scoring on five protocols, then scored 74 randomly selected protocols from the standardization sample, resulting in a mean inter-rater agreement correlation of .98. In the second study, three students in training for their master's degree in special education independently scored 30 protocols from the standardization sample. Their mean inter-rater agreement correlation was .90.

Statistical Confirmation

Extensive information on the test development, normative sample, reliability, and validity are in the Manual.

Special Features

Acronym

None.

Levels of the Test

One.

Number of Test Forms

The Bruininks-Oseretsky Test of Motor Proficiency includes three forms: (1) Individual Record Form: Complete Battery and Short Form, (2) Individual Record Form: Short Form, and (3) Student Booklet.

Norm-Referenced?

Yes. The standardization sample consisted of 765 subjects stratified according to 1970 U.S. Census data by age, sex, race, community size, and geographic region.

Criterion-Referenced?

No.

Feasibility Considerations

Testing Time

Forty-five to 60 minutes for Complete Battery, 15 to 20 minutes for Short Form.

For Testing Groups? Individuals?

Individuals.

Test Administration and Scoring

Administration of the Bruininks-Oseretsky Test of Motor Proficiency is relatively straightforward, and most physical education teachers and educators familiar with motor development should be familiar with the test procedures. Specific directions are given in the Manual, and no special training is needed. It should be noted that the Bruininks-Oseretsky Test of Motor Proficiency requires a large physical space (e.g., a gymnasium or large field), and there is some set-up involved. Scoring is fairly straightforward, although some judgment is required to determine whether or not the individual performs the skill correctly.

Test Materials and Approximate Costs

The test kit, which includes the Manual, 25 Student Booklets, 25 Individual Record Forms for Complete Battery/Short Form (plus sample of alternate Short Form), Testing Equipment, and a canvas carry bag, costs $524.95. A package of 25 Individual Record Forms, which can be used for the Complete Battery or Short Form, costs $30.95, and a package of the Short Form costs $16.95. A package of 25 Student Booklets costs $30.95. The Manual costs $93.95. In addition, items from the test equipment (e.g., balance beam, ball, and stream) can be purchased separately.

Adequacy of Test Manuals

The Manual is comprehensive and easy to read. Record forms are also well laid out, and the kit is accompanied by all of the materials needed to administer the test.

Excerpts from Other Test Reviews

Sattler (2002) describes the Bruininks-Oseretsky Test of Motor Proficiency as a useful tool in the screening and evaluation of motor skills. He notes that the Manual and materials are attractive and well designed. Sattler cautions that the factor analysis did not adequately support the structure of the test, particularly since many of the subtests of fine motor skills did not cluster together the way they should. He also cautioned about the low test-retest reliabilities, and outlined research indicating that the short form may not be reliable for young children.

Ordering Information

Publisher

American Guidance Service, Inc., 4201 Woodland Road, Circle Pines, MN 55014-1796; Phone: 800-328-2560; Fax: 800-471-8457; Web site: www.agsnet.com.

Author

Robert H. Bruininks.

Publication Date

1978.

Cautions and Comments

This test can be a helpful tool for assessing the motor skills of children. It should be noted that scores are highly influenced by teaching and practice effects (e.g., a child could master a skill and go from receiving a very low score to a very high score on a given subtest). A child who obtained a standard score of 40 or below on the Battery Composite may benefit from motor training or a referral to a specialist, such as a physical or occupational therapist, for further evaluation. Caution should be used when interpreting the Fine Motor Composite, as factor analysis has not supported that the subtests of this composite relate to each other enough to form this composite.

References

Bruininks, R. H. (1978). *Bruininks-Oseretsky Test of Motor Proficiency Manual.* Circle Pines, MN: American Guidance Service.

Sattler, J. M. (2002). *Assessment of children: Behavioral and clinical applications* (4th ed.). San Diego: Author.

Developmental Test of Visual-Motor Integration, 4th Edition, Revised (VMI), for testing groups and individuals from 3 through 17 years of age
Reviewed by Amanda B. Nickerson, Ph.D., School Psychology

Usefulness of the Test for Educators

Test Author's Purpose

The primary purpose of the Developmental Test of Visual-Motor Integration (VMI) is to "help identify, through early screening, significant difficulties that some children have in integrating, or coordinating, their visual perceptual and motor (finger and hand movement) abilities" (Beery, 1997).

Decision-Making Applications

The VMI can be used to identify children with visual-motor integration problems and aid in the prevention of further difficulties or remediation by educational, medical, or other interventions. If the child performs poorly on the VMI, it could indicate a problem with visual skills, motor skills, or the integration of the two skills. Therefore, supplemental follow-up tests to assess Visual Perception and Motor Coordination are also included with the VMI. The identification of visual-motor difficulties may lead to identifying children who are at-risk for other problems and who may be in need of a wide variety of services. The VMI can also be used to evaluate the effectiveness of education, psychological, and medical interventions, and can be used in research studies.

Relevant Population

The VMI is intended for children between the ages of 3 and 17. Research has indicated that the VMI is virtually culture free, largely due to its reliance on copying geometric forms instead of letters and numbers.

Characteristics Described

The VMI describes a child's ability to integrate, or coordinate, their visual perception and motor abilities. In addition, two supplemental tests (Visual Perception and Motor Coordination) are included. Visual Perception describes the child's ability to perceive objects visually without the motor requirements of the task. Motor Coordination describes the ability to control finger and hand movements with the aid of strong visual guides to greatly reduce the visual perceptual demands.

Test Scores Obtained

Raw scores, standard scores, scaled scores, stanines, normal curve equivalents, percentiles, and age and grade equivalents are provided for the VMI score, the Visual Perception score, and the Motor Coordination score. Beery (1997, p. 94) provides a table to interpret the standard scores, which have a mean of 100 and a standard deviation of 15:

Standard Score	Performance	Percent of Age Group
133–160	Very High	2
118–132	High	14
83–117	Average	68
68–82	Low	14
40–67	Very Low	2

Technical Adequacy

Validity Confirmation

Test item validity: Several procedures were used to ensure that the test items developed and selected for the instrument were valid. Based on an extensive review of literature and clinical experience, 72 geometric forms were selected initially. Approximately 600 children between the ages of 2 and 15 copied the forms, and item analyses resulted in the selection of 30 forms, which were administered to another 600 children. Item analyses resulted in 24 forms which met criteria, including clear-cut chronological sequences in the ability of children to copy the forms. Variables that may affect performance, such as glare of paper and rotation of forms, were studied and addressed.

Test response validity: Students' responses to the test were validated in several ways. First, the VMI, the Copying subtest of the Developmental Test of Visual Perception, and the Drawing subtest of the Wide Range Assessment of Visual Motor Abilities were administered to 122 students from kindergarten through grade 5. Correlations ranged from .52 to .75. In addition, past versions of the VMI have been correlated with the Bender-Gestalt Test, yielding correlations ranging from .29 to .93. The VMI has also been moderately correlated with measures of intelligence, with a range from .38 to .70. The relationship between the VMI and tests of academic achievement are also moderate, with a correlation of .63 found between the VMI and the Comprehensive Test of Basic Skills Total Score. Research has also indicated that the VMI measures developmental abilities, as correlations between chronological age and the VMI, Visual Perception, and Motor Coordination were .83, .75, and .74, respectively.

The abilities measured by the VMI are sensitive to different disabling conditions. For example, students with brain injury, educable mental retardation, and vision impairments have done less well on the VMI than their peers, although there is no difference between children with delayed language and those with normal language development. Significantly lowered VMI scores have been found for low birth weight children and those with spina bifida. The VMI, when used with other instruments, has successfully predicted school performance, especially for children in kindergarten and first grade.

Reliability Confirmation

The VMI was administered twice to 122 children between the ages of 6 and 10 in public school classrooms, with an average of a three-week interval between the administrations. The test-retest correlations were .87 for the VMI, .84 for Visual Perception, and .83 for Motor Coordination. Studies on previous versions of the VMI have yielded test-retest correlations of .59–.92. In addition, one-half of the test items were correlated with the other half of the test items for 750 children, yielding a correlation of .88. In addition, items were split and correlated in every way possible to measure how homogeneous the items were. This procedure resulted in a correlation of .82.

Objectivity Confirmation

To ensure accurate scoring, each form is rated as "Score" or "No Score." Clear scoring criteria and examples, based on thousands of children's reproductions, are provided in the VMI Manual. To study the objectivity of scoring procedures, two individuals independently scored 100 VMI, Visual Perception, and Motor Coordination tests of a random sample from the normative group. Correlations between the two raters were .94 for the VMI, .98 for Visual Perception, and .95 for Motor Coordination. Studies on previous versions of the VMI yielded correlations ranging from .73 to .99. Studies have suggested that two-hour trainings in the administration and scoring of the VMI improve objectivity. For example, the inter-scorer correlation prior to training was .73, but this correlation increased to .98 after a follow-up workshop.

Statistical Confirmation

Extensive information on the reliability, validity, and norms are in the VMI Manual.

Special Features

Acronym

VMI.

Levels of the Test

There are two levels of the VMI: a 19-item short version for 3- to 7-year-old children and the full, 27-item VMI.

Number of Test Forms

In addition to the VMI, there are two supplemental tests: (1) Visual Perception and (2) Motor Coordination.

Norm-Referenced?

Yes. The original norm group consisted of 1,030 students from Illinois. It was cross-validated in 1981 with 2,060 children from California and in 1989 with 2,734 children from a national sample. The VMI, the Visual Perception, and the Motor Coordination tests were normed in 1996 on 2,614 children between the ages of 3 and 18. The normative samples were representative of the U.S population with regard to gender, ethnicity, residence in rural, urban, or suburban settings, geographic region, and socioeconomic status.

Criterion-Referenced?

No.

Feasibility Considerations

Testing Time

Ten to 15 minutes.

For Testing Groups? Individuals?

It is advised that preschool children be tested individually. According to the test author, it is best to test kindergartners in small groups of about six children. Children in grades 1 or above can be tested as an entire class.

Test Administration and Scoring

Administration is straightforward, with clear directions on the test forms. The VMI Manual provides clear criteria and several examples to aid in scoring. Despite the attempts to standardize scoring, some subjective scoring judgments are required, and Sattler (2002) advises that a protractor be used for accurate scoring. Scorer training is advised and increases objectivity.

Test Materials and Approximate Costs

The Revised VMI tests are available in packages of 25 or packages of 100. The Short-Form costs $57.50 for a package of 25 and $210.50 for a package of 100. The Full-Form costs $77.95 for a package of 25 and $295.50 for a package of 100. The Visual Perception and Motor Coordination Tests each cost $12.95 for a package of 25 and $50.50 for a package of 100. The VMI Manual, 4th Edition costs $46.95.

Adequacy of Test Manuals

The test forms are easy to use, and the VMI Manual is well written and comprehensive.

Excerpts from Other Test Reviews

Sattler (2002) characterizes the VMI as a useful measure of visual-motor ability, but cautions that care needs to be taken in scoring. In addition, standard scores are restricted dramatically at age 12 (only two standard deviations or less above the mean), so comparing scores on a child who has been tested before and after age 12 can be problematic. Salvia and Ysseldyke (2001) note that the VMI has relatively high reliability and validity when compared to other measures of perceptual-motor skills. Visser (2001) also concludes that the psychometric properties of the VMI make it a valuable screening instrument, but cautions that using the VMI for remediation of academic problems is highly questionable, given the lack of evidence that this is an appropriate or effective practice. Wiese (2001) notes the standardized administration procedure and sound normative sample that make the VMI a good choice for measuring visual-motor skills.

Ordering Information

Publisher

Modern Curriculum Press (an imprint of Pearson Learning), 299 Jefferson Road, P.O. Box 480, Parsippany, NJ 07054-0480; Phone: 800-321-3106; Fax: 800-393-3156; Web site: www.pearsonlearning.com.

Author

Keith E. Beery.

Publication Date

1997.

Cautions and Comments

The VMI is intended to be used as a screening tool, so that children who may need extra help in their education will be identified and referred to appropriate professionals. Generally, standard scores on the VMI of 82 or below are considered "low" or "very low" and indicate that a child may need further evaluation by a professional. If the examiner suspects a problem with visual acuity or other special problems, a referral to a school nurse, an ophthalmologist, or another professional may be indicated.

Although the VMI can be administered and scored by any intelligent adult who is familiar with the test materials, objectivity is optimal when the individual is trained to use the instrument. Any interpretation of the test results, beyond using the VMI as a screening tool, should be done by experienced specialists in psychology, learning disabilities, or related fields.

An important caution for users of any test of perceptual-motor skills is that intervention to improve these skills has not been shown to relate to improved academic performance. Therefore, it is important that educators not implement a remediation plan (e.g., requiring the child to copy figures repeatedly) without a careful consideration of the impact of these skill deficits on academic performance and a more comprehensive understanding of the child's difficulties.

References

Beery, K. E. (1997). *The Beery-Buktenica Developmental Test of Visual-Motor Integration* (4th ed.) Parsippany, NJ: Modern Curriculum Press.
Salvia, J., & Ysseldyke, J. E. (2001). *Assessment* (8th ed.). Boston: Houghton Mifflin.
Sattler, J. M. (2002). *Assessment of children: Behavioral and clinical applications* (4th ed.). San Diego: Author.
Visser, J. (2001). Review of the Developmental Test of Visual-Motor Integration, 4th Edition, Revised. In B. S. Plake & J. C. Impara (Eds.), *The Fourteenth Mental Measurements Yearbook* (pp. 405–407). Lincoln, NE: The Buros Institute of Mental Measurements.
Wiese, M. J. (2001). Review of the Developmental Test of Visual-Motor Integration, 4th Edition, Revised. In B. S. Plake & J. C. Impara (Eds.), *The Fourteenth Mental Measurements Yearbook* (pp. 407–408). Lincoln, NE: The Buros Institute of Mental Measurements.

Test of Gross Motor Development: Second Edition (TGMD-2),
for testing groups and individuals from 3 through 10 years of age
Reviewed by Amanda B. Nickerson, Ph.D., School Psychology

Usefulness of the Test for Educators

Test Author's Purpose

The original Test of Gross Motor Development (TGMD), published in 1985, was designed to be a brief, standardized assessment tool for the motor behavior of children. The TGMD was recently revised to improve the normative sample, update the pictures on the test, and conduct new reliability and validity studies.

Decision-Making Applications

There are several uses of the TGMD-2. First, it can be used to identify children with delayed motor development. Second, results can be used in the instructional planning for motor skill development. Third, the TGM-2 can be administered several times on the same child to assess progress in motor skill development. Fourth, the test can be used to evaluate the success of programs. Fifth, it can be used for research purposes.

Relevant Population

The TGMD-2 is designed to be used by occupational therapists, physical therapists, diagnosticians, physical education teachers, and others to assess children between the ages of 3 and 10.

Characteristics Described

The test assesses two main areas of motor skills:

1. Locomotor: This subtest measures skills involved in moving the center of gravity from one point to another (e.g., running, hopping).
2. Object Control: This subtest assesses skills involved in projecting and receiving objects (e.g., kicking, catching).

The test also yields a Gross Motor Quotient, which is the total test score.

Test Scores Obtained

Several scores are obtained from the TGMD-2, such as raw scores, percentiles, standard scores (with a mean of 100 and a standard deviation of 15), and age equivalents (for subtests).

The test author provides the following descriptive ratings for standard scores:

Subtest Standard Score	Gross Motor Quotient	Descriptive Rating
17–20	> 130	Very Superior
15–16	121–130	Superior
13–14	111–120	Above Average
8–12	90–110	Average
6–7	80–89	Below Average
4–5	70–79	Poor
1–3	< 70	Very Poor

Technical Adequacy

Validity Confirmation

Test item validity: The skills selected for the TGMD-2 were judged by three content experts who had graduate degrees and experience in teaching physical education and observing and evaluating children's motor development. Each expert independently judged that the skills measured by the TGMD-2 were representative of gross motor domains for the age group. In addition, the author conducted statistics on the items to assess the item discrimination and difficulty levels, both of which were satisfactory.

Test response validity: Students' responses to the test were validated in several ways. Forty-one children were administered the TGMD-2 and then the Basic Motor Generalizations subtests of the Comprehensive Scales of Student Abilities (CSSA). Partial correlation coefficients, controlling for age, between the TGMD-2 subtests and the CSSA subtests were .63 for Locomotor, .41 for Object Control, and .63 for Gross Motor Quotient. The TGMD-2 was hypothesized to be correlated with age, due to the developmental nature of motor skills, and this was validated by correlations showing that the relationship between test scores and age increases for older children. In addition, the subtests of the TGMD-2 are moderately correlated with each other.

The TGMD-2 was administered to several different groups (males, females, European Americans, African Americans, Hispanic Americans, and individuals with Down Syndrome). Each of the gender and ethnic groups scored in the "average" range, whereas those in the Down Syndrome group scored in the "very poor" range, providing support that the test is nonbiased and assesses what it is supposed to measure. Statistical procedures called exploratory and confirmatory factor analysis were used to validate the organization of the TGMD-2 into its respective subtests. Results of the factor analyses did support the test's structure.

Reliability Confirmation

The TGMD-2 was administered twice to 75 children in Illinois, with a two-week interval between administrations. The test-retest reliability coefficients were as follows: .88 for Locomotor, .93 for Object Control, and .93 for Gross Motor Quotient. In addition, one-half of the items of the test were compared to the other half of the items for the entire norm sample. The average internal consistency coefficients were as follows: .85 for Locomotor, .88 for Object Control, and .91 for Gross Motor Quotient.

Objectivity Confirmation

Several procedures were used to ensure that the administration and scoring of the TGMD-2 was as objective as possible. For example, examiners are advised to study the Manual carefully, to thoroughly practice giving and scoring the test to three persons before giving it in a real situation, and to praise examinees on their effort but not their ability. To aid in the objectivity of scoring, each skill is broken down into observable behavioral components, which the examiner scores as "0" (does not perform behavioral component correctly) or "1" (does perform the behavioral component correctly). Two individuals independently scored 30 protocols from the normative sample, yielding correlations of .98 or higher for both subtests and the Gross Motor Quotient.

Statistical Confirmation

Extensive information on the test development, normative sample, reliability, and validity are in the TGMD-2 Manual.

Special Features

Acronym

TGMD-2.

Levels of the Test

One.

Number of Test Forms

One.

Norm-Referenced?

Yes. 1,208 persons in 10 states representing each of the four major geographic regions of the United States served as the normative sample. The sample was almost entirely representative of a national sample with regard to geographic region, gender, race, rural/urban residence, parental education, disability, and age.

Criterion-Referenced?

No.

Feasibility Considerations

Testing Time

Fifteen to 20 minutes.

For Testing Groups? Individuals?

The Manual states that two or three students can be tested at a time, and that while one child is tested on an item, the other children can watch and rest. It is recommended that children take turns being tested first on different items.

Test Administration and Scoring

The test author states that the administration is "rather easy because most examiners and examinees are familiar with the skills being tested" (Ulrich, 2000, p. 8). In addition, explicit directions for the administration and scoring are provided in the Manual and on the test forms. It should be noted, however, that several materials are needed to administer the TGMD-2, including six types of balls (e.g., softball, playground ball, soccer ball), a 4- or 5-inch-square beanbag, tape, two cones, a bat, and a batting tee. Scoring is fairly straightforward, although some judgment is required to determine whether or not the individual performs the skill correctly.

Test Materials and Approximate Costs

The complete kit costs $96. The TGMD-2 Manual costs $49, and a package of 50 TGMD-2 Profile/Examiner Record Booklets costs $49.

Adequacy of Test Manuals

The Manual is comprehensive and easy to read. Record forms are also comprehensive, with materials needed, directions, and performance criteria listed for each skill.

Excerpts from Other Test Reviews

Bunker (1989) reviewed the original Test of Gross Motor Development (TGMD), summarizing it as an exceptionally good screening instrument that can be used by classroom teachers. She also noted that a more comprehensive understanding of motor development could be gained by combining the use of the TGMD with a more thorough, criterion-referenced test to aid in educational planning. Edwards (1989) also reviewed the original TGMD, and assessed it to be a well-constructed test of motor skills. He commented on the exceptionally well-written manual that could be easily understood by both inexperienced and sophisticated examiners. Edwards did note that additional reliability information for larger samples of children should be collected, although these comments referred to the original TGMD, not the second edition. Another review of the original TGMD was conducted by Weeks (1992). This review characterized the TGMD as a useful tool for educators and researchers, and noted that it generally delivers accurate scores about general motor functioning. He did caution that performance on the TGMD is heavily influenced by prior instructional experiences, and that precision of the test could be improved by rating performance criteria on a scale from 0 to 3 rather than a dichotomous scale.

Ordering Information

Publisher

PRO-ED, 8700 Shoal Creek Boulevard, Austin, TX 78757-6897; Phone: 800-897-3202; Fax: 800-397-7633; Web site: http://www.proedinc.com.

Author

Dale A. Ulrich.

Publication Date

2000.

Cautions and Comments

Overall, the TGMD-2 is a very useful test for educators concerned with the motor skills of students. One of the strengths noted is its ease of use by both professionals and nonprofessionals. In addition, the manual is extensive and well written. One drawback of the TGMD-2 is that it requires many materials, such as various types of balls that are needed for administration, that are not provided in the test kit. In addition, it should be cautioned that the skills assessed by the TGMD-2 are largely influenced by practice, and the dichotomous scoring of the skills does not lend itself to really differentiating between skill levels of children.

Despite its limitations, the TGMD-2 is a useful screening measure for educators. A good rule of thumb is that scores of 89 or below, which are classified as "Below Average," "Poor," or "Very Poor" on the Gross Motor Quotient, indicate the need for motor training or referral for further evaluation.

References

Bunker, L. K. (1989). Review of the Test of Gross Motor Development. In J. C. Conoley & J. J. Kramer (Eds.), *The Tenth Mental Measurements Yearbook* (pp. 843–845). Lincoln, NE: The Buros Institute of Mental Measurements.

Edwards, R. (1989). Review of the Test of Gross Motor Development. In J. C. Conoley & J. J. Kramer (Eds.), *The Tenth Mental Measurements Yearbook* (pp. 846–847). Lincoln, NE: The Buros Institute of Mental Measurements.

Ulrich, D. A. (2000). *Test of Gross Motor Development: Second Edition: Examiner's Manual.* Austin, TX: PRO-ED.

Weeks, D. L. (1992). Test of Gross Motor Development. In D. J. Keyser & R. C. Sweetland (Eds.), *Test critiques* (vol. 9). Austin, TX: PRO-ED.

Test of Visual-Motor Integration (TVMI), for testing groups
and individuals from 4 years through 17 years, 11 months of age
Reviewed by Amanda B. Nickerson, Ph.D., School Psychology

Usefulness of the Test for Educators

Test Authors' Purpose

The Test of Visual-Motor Integration (TVMI) is "a standardized test of visual-motor integration that uses a copying format" (Hammill, Pearson, & Voress, 1996, p. 3).

Decision-Making Applications

The four principal uses of the TVMI, as highlighted by the test authors, are (1) to document the presence of visual-motor integration deficits in children and adolescents, (2) to identify children that may need to be referred to other professionals or agencies for further diagnostic work (e.g., the child may need to be examined by an optometrist or ophthalmologist to rule out visual problems or to physicians, psychiatrists, and other specialists in case of brain injury or organic problems), (3) to assess the effectiveness of training programs to correct visual-motor problems, and (4) to conduct research.

Relevant Population

The TVMI is designed to be administered to children between 4 years and 17 years, 11 months of age.

Characteristics Described

The TVMI yields only a total test score that measures overall visual-motor integration. This is defined as "the ability to relate visual stimuli to motor responses in an accurate, appropriate manner" (Hammill et al., 1996, p. 1).

Test Scores Obtained

The raw score on the TVMI yields a standard score, age equivalent, and percentile. The classification of standard scores, which have a mean of 100 and a standard deviation of 15, are as follows:

Standard Score	Descriptive Rating
> 130	Very Superior
121–130	Superior
111–120	Above Average
90–110	Average
80–89	Below Average
70–79	Poor
< 70	Very Poor

Technical Adequacy

Validity Confirmation

Test item validity: The TVMI was developed by using ideas about content and format from the existing research literature on the measurement of visual-motor integration, and the majority of actual designs used have appeared in other tests where test developers provided evidence regarding the validity of items. An experimental version of the test was formulated, and an item analysis was conducted. Items that did not meet the established criteria (correlating .30 or higher with the total test score) were eliminated. A final item analysis was conducted for the entire norm group, and median discrimination powers for the different age groups ranged from .46 to .76. To ensure that items were not biased, the TVMI was administered to three different dichotomous groups (male/female, white/non-white, and Hispanic/non-Hispanic). Correlation coefficients were very high, ranging from .96 to .99, which suggested little or no test bias.

Test response validity: Students' responses to the test were validated in several ways. First, the TVMI was administered to 49 students with neurological impairments, along with the Developmental Test of Visual-Motor Integration (VMI) and the Motor-Free Visual Perception Test (MVPT). The TVMI's correlation with the VMI was .95 and the correlation with the MVPT was .67, which indicated that it is, indeed, measuring visual-motor integration. TVMI scores also correlated with age, with older subjects obtaining higher scores than younger ones, although this trend leveled off at age 12. It was hypothesized that the TVMI would not correlate highly with school achievement, as it does not involve reasoning or academic ability, but that it would correlate moderately with intelligence tests, as most include some measures of visual-motor ability. To test these hypotheses, the TVMI and the Comprehensive Scales of Student Abilities (CSSA), a teacher-completed checklist assessing achievement of students, were administered on 411 children. The median correlation between the CSSA and the TVMI was .20. The TVMI and the WISC-R were also administered to 24 students, and moderate-to-high correlations of .45 for Verbal IQ, .93 for Performance IQ, and .90 for Full Scale IQ were obtained.

Reliability Confirmation

The TVMI was administered twice to 88 students between the ages of 4 and 10, with a two-week interval between administrations. The test-retest correlation was .80. In addition, one-half of the test items were correlated with the other half of the test items for 49 organically disordered children between 5 and 12 years of age, yielding a correlation of .94.

Objectivity Confirmation

To make the scoring as objective as possible, each item is scored with a 0, 1, 2, or 3, with scoring examples provided in the Examiner's Manual. In addition, the authors provide recommendations for the objective administration of the test, including using the Examiner's Manual, practicing administering the test three times, tests in an adequate environment, establishing rapport with the student, being alert to signs of fatigue in the student, and consistently praising the student. In addition, two individuals independently scored 40 completed TVMI protocols, which yielded an inter-rater reliability coefficient of .96.

Statistical Confirmation

Extensive information on the reliability, validity, and norms are in the Examiner's Manual.

Special Features

Acronym

TVMI.

Levels of the Test

One.

Number of Test Forms

One.

Norm-Referenced?

Yes. The normative sample consisted of 2,478 children from 13 states. The sample, as a whole, was representative of a national sample in terms of gender, residence, race, geographic region, ethnicity, family income, educational level of parents, and age.

Criterion-Referenced?

No.

Feasibility Considerations

Testing Time

Fifteen to 30 minutes.

For Testing Groups? Individuals?

Groups and individuals.

Test Administration and Scoring

Administration of the TVMI is straightforward, although scoring can be challenging, as the examiner scores each of the designs on a 4-point scale. Scoring is aided by numerous examples provided in the Examiner's Manual, and it is recommended that educators administering the TVMI be thoroughly familiar with scoring procedures and practice scoring to increase objectivity.

Test Materials and Approximate Costs

The TVMI complete kit costs $116. Fifty TVMI Summary/Response Forms cost $69, and the Examiner's Manual costs $49.

Adequacy of Test Manuals

The test forms are clear, and the Examiner's Manual is comprehensive and easy to read.

Excerpts from Other Test Reviews

Salvia and Ysseldyke (2001) state that the evidence of reliability and validity for the TVMI is limited. Erickson (2001, p. 1268) asserts that the TVMI is a valuable tool that "can be used with confidence to screen for children with visual-motor integration problems." Erickson does caution that the TVMI results, as with any test of visual-motor integration, are difficult to interpret because problems could be due to motoric issues, sensory acuity problems, or cognitive processing deficits.

Ordering Information

Publisher

PRO-ED, 8700 Shoal Creek Boulevard, Austin, TX 78757-6897; Phone: 800-897-3202; Fax: 800-397-7633; Web site: http://www.proedinc.com.

Authors

Donald D. Hammill, Nils A. Pearson, and Judith K. Voress.

Publication Date

1996.

Cautions and Comments

The TVMI is well suited for screening children who may have visual-motor impairments in need of follow-up by professionals. It is recommended that examiners thoroughly familiarize themselves with scoring criteria and practice administering and scoring the TVMI with three children before using it in practice. Children scoring 89 or below, with a classification in the "Below Average," "Poor," or "Very Poor" range, should be referred for further testing.

As with any test of visual-motor integration, it is wise for the examiner to approach the TVMI with caution. As many leaders in the field of assessment (e.g., Salvia & Ysseldyke, 2001; Sattler, 2002) have asserted, assessment of visual-motor integration is problematic, as there is no demonstrated relationship between visual-motor problems and academic achievement, and training of visual-motor skills has not shown to result in meaningful change.

References

Erickson, D. (2001). Review of the Test of Visual-Motor Integration. In B. S. Plake & J. C. Impara (Eds.), *The Fourteenth Mental Measurements Yearbook* (pp. 1267–1268). Lincoln, NE: The Buros Institute of Mental Measurements.

Hammill, D. D., Pearson, N. A., & Voress, J. K. (1996). *Test of Visual-Motor Integration: Examiner's Manual*. Austin, TX: PRO-ED.

Salvia, J., & Ysseldyke, J. E. (2001). *Assessment* (8th ed.). Boston: Houghton Mifflin.

Sattler, J. M. (2002). *Assessment of children: Behavioral and clinical applications* (4th ed.). San Diego: Author.

Adaptive Behavior Tests

There are far too many tests of adaptive behavior to provide a comprehensive review of each of them. The tests selected for review are those that are commonly used and that assess a broad range of adaptive behaviors. These tests are the Adaptive Behavior Assessment System, The Adaptive Behavior Scale-School: Second Edition, and the Vineland Adaptive Behavior Scales: Classroom Edition.

Adaptive Behavior Assessment System: Teacher Form (ABAS),
for testing individuals from 5 through 21 years of age
Reviewed by Amanda B. Nickerson, Ph.D., School Psychology

Usefulness of the Test for Educators

Test Authors' Purpose

"A primary purpose of the ABAS is in the comprehensive, diagnostic assessment of individuals having difficulties with the daily adaptive skills necessary to function effectively in their environments, given the typical demands placed on individuals the same age" (Harrison & Oakland, 2000, p. 1). It allows assessment with multiple informants and across settings.

Decision-Making Applications

The ABAS can be used to help determine if an individual has mental retardation, as the assessment of adaptive behavior is required by federal regulations before this classification is made. It can also be used to assess emotional disabilities, autism, and other health impairments. The ABAS is also helpful in identifying individual strengths and weaknesses in adaptive skills, and identifying service needs with regard to intervention and training. It can also be used to monitor progress, and can be used for research and evaluation purposes.

Relevant Population

The ABAS is designed to be completed by teachers, teacher's aides, or other school informants for children between the ages of 5 and 21.

Characteristics Described

The ABAS assesses 10 Adaptive Skill Areas: Communication, Community Use, Functional Academics, Home/School Living, Health and Safety, Leisure, Self-Care, Self-Direction, Social, and Work. These 10 areas are added and a General Adaptive Composite (GAC) is obtained. The following is a description of the 10 Adaptive Skill Areas:

1. Communication: This area assesses the speech, language, and listening skills needed for communication. Items include ending conversations appropriately and using up-to-date information to discuss current events.

2. Community Use: The items in this area measure an individual's functioning in the community. Community functioning includes using pay phones, shopping, and ordering meals in restaurants.

3. Functional Academics: This area assesses basic reading, writing, math, and other academic skills necessary for independent functioning. Items include

reading one's own name, making lists, and locating a telephone number in the phone book.

4. Home/School Living: This section pertains to skills needed for basic care of the classroom setting, such as cleaning, straightening, wiping up spills, and keeping belongings neat and clean.

5. Health and Safety: Skills that are needed for protection of health, such as following safety rules and using caution, are assessed in this area.

6. Leisure: This area assesses the skills needed for planning leisure and recreational activities, such as following rules in games and trying new activities.

7. Self-Care: The items in this area assess personal care skills, such as eating, toileting, grooming, and hygiene.

8. Self-Direction: These are skills needed for independence and responsibility, such as keeping a schedule, following directions, controlling one's temper during disagreements, and completing projects on time.

9. Social: This area assesses skills needed to interact socially, such as laughing in response to jokes, listening when people try to talk, and using manners.

10. Work: Items in this area assess skills needed to function successfully in a work setting, such as completing tasks, following a work schedule, and showing a positive attitude towards jobs.

Test Scores Obtained

Raw scores are obtained for each Adaptive Skill Area. In addition, scaled scores are derived for Adaptive Skill areas (mean of 10 and standard deviation of 3) and for the GAC scores (mean of 100 and standard deviation of 15). Percentile ranks and test-age equivalents are also derived. The descriptive classification system is as follows:

Classification for GAC Scaled Scores

GAC Scores	Classification
120 or more	Superior
110–119	Above Average
90–109	Average
80–89	Below Average
71–79	Borderline
70 or less	Extremely Low

Classification for Adaptive Skill Area Scaled Scores

Adaptive Scores	Classification
15 or more	Superior

Adaptive Scores	*Classification*
13–14	Above Average
8–12	Average
6–7	Below Average
4–5	Borderline
3 or less	Extremely Low

Technical Adequacy

Validity Confirmation

Test item validity: Several procedures were used to ensure that the test items developed and selected for the instrument were valid. Items were first selected based on a comprehensive review of research related to developmental skills in children, youth, and adults; functional skills necessary for home, school, community, work, and other settings; and developmental disabilities. The initial item pool, which consisted of more than 1,000 items, was reviewed by experts in psychology, education, and mental retardation, and narrowed to 789 items. These items were field tested with 428 individuals. Data was analyzed, and 980 teachers completed ratings during the field trial. The items selected for the final version met several criteria, including measuring skills that are relevant to applied practice, having a sufficient number of items to comprise a comprehensive measure, and assessing qualities that are readily observable.

Test response validity: Teachers' responses to the test were validated in several ways. First, to test the hypothesis that the adaptive skills measured by the ABAS were age related, older subjects' scores were compared to those of younger subjects, which showed that older subjects displayed the behavior more frequently than younger subjects. The Adaptive Scales were then correlated with each other and with the GAC. All scales correlated highly (< .80) with the GAC, and were only moderately correlated with each other, suggesting that the scales measured the same overall concept, yet were relatively independent from each other. In addition, a factor analysis was conducted, which supported the GAC. Teachers also completed the ABAS and the Vineland Adaptive Behavior Scales: Classroom Edition for 57 students between the ages of 5 and 12. Correlations between the GAC and each of the domains measured by the Vineland Classroom Edition ranged from .66 to .82. The ABAS was also compared to intelligence test scores, yielding moderate correlations (e.g., .44 to .55 for Wechsler Intelligence Scale for Children scores and .50 for Stanford-Binet scores). The GAC of the ABAS was also correlated with subtests of the Wechsler Individual Achievement Test, with correlations ranging from .56 to .79. The ABAS was also administered to several clinical groups (e.g., mental retardation, emotional disabilities, learning disabilities, Attention Deficit Hyperactivity Disorder), who scored significantly lower than the matched control sample. In addition, the ABAS discriminated between clinical groups. For example, individuals with mild mental retardation scored higher than those with moderate mental retardation.

Reliability Confirmation

Teachers of 143 students completed the ABAS two times, with an average of 11 days between administrations. Across ages, the GAC test-retest correlations ranged from .91 to .99, and Adaptive Skill Area correlations ranged from .71 to .98. In addition, half of the items of the ABAS were compared to the other half of the items for the standardization groups. The internal consistency coefficients ranged from .98 to .99 for the GAC across age groups, and from .83 to .97 for Adaptive Skill Areas across age groups.

Objectivity Confirmation

To ensure objective ratings, the authors suggest that informants be familiar with the child they are rating in school settings by having frequent contact (almost daily), contacts of long duration (several hours), contact in the recent past (one to two months), and ample opportunity to observe the skills measured by the ABAS. Ratings are made on a 4-point scale, with 0 = is not able, 1 = never or almost never when needed, 2 = sometimes when needed, 3 = always or almost always when needed. The informant is also supposed to indicate when he or she has guessed on an item, and if the person makes three or more guesses within a skill area, the administrator of the scale is supposed to interview the respondent. To assess how objective the ratings are, 84 children between the ages of 5 and 18 were rated independently by two of their teachers. The mean correlation coefficient for the GAC for all ages was .89, and the range for Adaptive Skill Areas was .59 to .83. In addition, teachers and parents completed the ABAS for 30 children, yielding a mean GAC correlation of .70 and a range of Adaptive Skill Area correlations from .31 to .78.

Statistical Confirmation

Extensive information on reliability, validity, scale development, and standardization is available in the Test Manual.

Special Features

Acronym

ABAS.

Levels of the Test

There is an ABAS Infant and Preschool Form (published in 2002), with a Teacher/Day Care Provider Form and Parent Form (ages 2 years to 5 years, 11 months). There is also a Child Form (ages 5 to 21), with a Parent Form and a Teacher Form. The Adult Form is for individuals between the ages of 16 and 89.

Number of Test Forms

There are five different forms: (1) Teacher Form (Infant and Preschool), (2) Teacher

Form (Child), (3) Parent Form (Infant and Preschool), (4) Parent Form (Child), and (5) Adult Form.

Norm-Referenced?

Yes. The ABAS Teacher Form was standardized on 1,690 individuals between the ages of 5 and 21. The sample was stratified by sex, race/ethnicity, and educational levels according to the 1999 U.S. Census data.

Criterion-Referenced?

No.

Feasibility Considerations

Testing Time

Fifteen to 20 minutes.

For Testing Groups? Individuals?

Individuals.

Test Administration and Scoring

The directions for the ABAS are very clear, and scoring is straightforward. Although no specialized training is needed, the authors state that professional users of the ABAS should supervise others in administering and scoring the scale. In addition, individuals completing the ABAS should know when to consult professionals for guidance, therefore adhering to guidelines for ethical testing.

Test Materials and Approximate Costs

The ABAS School Kit, consisting of the Manual, 25 Teacher Forms, and 25 Parent Forms, costs $150. The Manual itself (for school and adult) costs $75. A package of 25 Teacher Forms costs $43, and a package of 100 Teacher Forms costs $155.

Adequacy of Test Manuals

The ABAS is well organized and easy to complete. The Manual provides extensive information in an organized format.

Excerpts from Other Test Reviews

Sattler (2002) notes that the ABAS is a reliable and valid instrument for assessing adaptive behavior. He cautions that the scale does require a seventh grade reading level, and that some of the items may be difficult for parents to understand. As with other adaptive behavior scales, the ABAS does not have normally distributed standard scores, so the scales differ for children of different ages (e.g., the highest GAC score for a 7-year-old is 130, but the highest possible GAC score for an 8-year-old is 120). Age-equivalent scores also vary dramatically for the Teacher Form, so caution should be used. Lastly, Sattler points out that the ABAS only has one factor (the GAC), so support for the 10 skill areas was not gathered through factor analysis.

Ordering Information

Publisher

The Psychological Corporation, 19500 Bulverde Road, San Antonio, TX 78259; Phone: 800-228-0752; Fax: 210-339-5873; Web site: www.psychcorp.com.

Authors

Patti L. Harrison and Thomas Oakland.

Publication Date

2000.

Cautions and Comments

The ABAS is a promising new instrument that assesses adaptive behavior within the framework suggested by the American Association on Mental Retardation (1992). Preliminary information about the reliability and validity of the ABAS is good, but more research is needed, particularly in comparing it to other adaptive behavior scales for clinical groups. As with any test, caution should be used in making any determination about a child's level of functioning based on one measure.

Because of the variability in the scaled scores and age-equivalent scores across domains, caution should be used in making direct comparisons. Instead, educators should first look at the GAC to determine if it is 89 or below, which is classified as "Below Average," "Borderline," or "Extremely Low." The same can also be done for each domain, where a score of 7 or below signifies "Below Average" or lower classification. If a child receives a score of 7 or below in two or more domains, further assessment is warranted. Educators can also look specifically at problem areas for the child and target these for intervention and skills training.

References

Harrison, P. L., & Oakland, T. (2000). *Adaptive Behavior Assessment System Manual*. San Antonio, TX: The Psychological Corporation.

Sattler, J. M. (2002). *Assessment of children: Behavioral and clinical applications* (4th ed.). San Diego: Author.

Adaptive Behavior Scale-School: Second Edition (ABS-S:2),
for testing individuals from 3 through 18 years of age
Reviewed by Amanda B. Nickerson, Ph. D., School Psychology

Usefulness of the Test for Educators

Test Authors' Purpose

"The ABS-S:2 was developed to assess school age children's personal and community independence, as well as aspects of personal and social performance and adjustment—characteristics that are associated with the construct of adaptive behavior" (Lambert, Nihira, & Leland, 1993, pp. 2–3).

Decision-Making Applications

The ABS-S:2 has several applications. It is most commonly used in the comprehensive assessment of mental retardation, as adaptive behavior is a required component to be assessed when classifying an individual as mentally retarded. The scale can also be used to help professionals create individualized education and treatment plans for people with disabilities, and to document the progress of these plans. In addition, individual strengths and weaknesses can be detected by the ABS-S:2. The scale can also be used for research purposes.

Relevant Population

The ABS-S:2 was designed to be administered by psychologists, speech/language pathologists, residential aides and nurses, parents, teachers, vocational trainers, and other professional or paraprofessional staff for children between the ages of 3 and 18.

Characteristics Described

Teachers, parents, or others familiar with the student rate the child's level of performance in several skill areas. The ABS-S:2 consists of 16 domain scores, broken into two parts, and five factor scores. Each of these is listed and briefly described below:

Part One Domain Scores

Independent Functioning: The items of this domain assess an individual's eating, toileting, and self-care skills. Items also include those related to use of public transportation and facilities.

Physical Development: This domain assesses a child's sensory and motor abilities, including sight, hearing, and fine and gross motor skills.

Economic Activity: This relates to a person's ability to handle money, use banks, maintain a budget, and purchase goods.

Language Development: This domain assesses receptive and expressive communication and a person's ability to use these skills to function.

Numbers and Time: This domain assesses basic mathematical competencies, with an emphasis on those skills that involve daily functioning (e.g., telling time).

Prevocational/Vocational Activity: Items in this domain measure behaviors such as tardiness, habitual absences, carelessness, and other skills related to job performance.

Self-Direction: Items in this domain assess the extent to which an individual maintains an active or passive lifestyle.

Responsibility: This domain assesses dependability, such as taking care of one's possessions, carrying out assigned tasks, and maintaining self-control.

Socialization: This domain measures a person's ability to interact with others by assessing behaviors such as cooperation and consideration.

Part Two Domain Scores

Social Behavior: This domain pertains to behaviors that are physically and emotionally abusive, such as threatening others and losing control of one's temper.

Conformity: This domain assesses several aspects of rebelliousness, such as tardiness and misbehavior.

Trustworthiness: Items in this domain relate to stealing, lying, cheating, and disrespect for property.

Stereotyped and Hyperactive Behavior: Behaviors that are upsetting to others are included in this domain. These include being overly active or making inappropriate physical contact.

Self-Abusive Behavior: This domain assesses behaviors that cause harm to oneself.

Social Engagement: This domain assesses the extent to which a person withdraws from activities or fails to respond to others.

Disturbing Interpersonal Behavior: This domain assesses annoying behaviors such as feeling persecuted or reacting poorly to criticism.

Factor Scores

Personal Self-Sufficiency (consists of items from Independent Functioning and Physical Development Domains): This factor relates to caring for oneself, reflecting the ability to live alone.

Community Self-Sufficiency (consists of items from Independent Functioning, Economic Activity, Language Development, Numbers and Time, and Prevocational/Vocational Activity Domains): This factor includes many abilities needed for a person to fully function in mainstream society.

Personal-Social Responsibility (consists of items from Prevocational/Vocational Activity, Self-Direction, Responsibility, and Socialization Domains): This factor includes behaviors related to social competency that are necessary to maintain interpersonal relationships and hold down a job.

Social Adjustment (includes items from Social Behavior, Conformity, and Trustworthiness Domains): This factor includes aggressive, antisocial behaviors and inappropriate interpersonal relationships.

Personal Adjustment (includes items from Stereotyped and Hyperactive Behavior and Self-Abusive Domains): This factor includes inappropriate interpersonal behaviors that are not aggressive or antisocial, such as excessive hugging, touching, or hyperactive behaviors.

Test Scores Obtained

Raw scores for each domain can be converted into standard scores (mean of 10 and standard deviation of 3), percentiles, and age equivalents (for Part One only). The same scores are obtained for factor scores, except the standard scores have a mean of 100 and a standard deviation of 15. The following classification systems are used:

Classification System for Domain Scores

Standard Scores	Descriptive Ratings
17–20	Very Superior
15–16	Superior
13–14	Above Average
8–12	Average
6–7	Below Average
4–5	Poor
1–3	Very Poor

Classification System for Factor Scores

Standard Scores	Descriptive Ratings
> 130	Very Superior
121–130	Superior
111–120	Above Average
90–110	Average
80–89	Below Average
70–79	Poor
< 70	Very Poor

Technical Adequacy

Validity Confirmation

Test item validity: Several procedures were used to ensure that the test items developed and selected for the instrument were valid. The first edition of the Adaptive

Behavior Scale was developed based on a comprehensive review of literature and rating scales, and several item analysis and validity studies. The school version was specifically geared toward items that could be answered by classroom teachers. To examine the validity of items in the ABS-S:2, an item analysis was conducted, which determined the extent to which each item related to the total test score.

Test response validity: Responses to the test were validated in several ways. First, 63 individuals were administered the ABS-S:2 and the Vineland Adaptive Behavior Scales, with correlations between Part One domain scores and Vineland scores ranging from nonsignificant correlations to .65. In another study, 30 students with mental retardation were rated on the ABS-S:2 and the Adaptive Behavior Inventory (ABI), with Part One domain scores from the ABS-S:2 correlating with the ABI from .37 to .64. Scores from the ABS-S:2 Part Two domains were not significantly correlated with these other adaptive behavior scales, which was not surprising since these domain scores assess maladaptive behavior, whereas comparison scales only focus on adaptive behavior. Individuals in the standardization sample were also given various tests of mental ability, and moderate correlations were obtained between these tests and the Part One domains of the ABS-S:2. For example, correlations between the domains and scores on the WISC-R ranged from .28 to .61, and the correlation for domains with scores on the Stanford-Binet ranged from .47 to .71. The ABS-S:2 also discriminates between individuals with mental retardation and those without mental retardation, evidenced by the scores of people with developmental disabilities being significantly below the average for the norm group. In addition, a procedure called confirmatory factor analysis was conducted to determine how well the items in a domain grouped together, and how well the domains were differentiated from each other. This analysis supported the domains of the ABS-S:2.

Reliability Confirmation

The ABS-S:2 was administered twice to the employers of 45 individuals with mental retardation with a two-week interval between the administrations. The test-retest reliability correlations ranged from .88 to .99 for the domains and from .85 to .98 for the factor scores. A similar study was conducted with teachers of students with emotional disturbance. Correlations between scores for the two-week administrations ranged from .75 to .98 for domain scores and from .72 to .94 for factor scores. In addition, one-half of the test item responses were correlated with the other half of the items for the standardization samples. For the sample with mental retardation, the average internal consistency reliability for domain scores ranged from .82 to .98, and the average factor scores ranged from .93 to .98. For the non–mental retardation sample, average correlations ranged from .82 to .97 for domain scores and from .96 to .99 for factor scores.

Objectivity Confirmation

The authors assessed the extent to which different professionals scoring the ABS-S:2 would agree as to the scoring. Two professionals trained in the scoring were provided with 15 ABS-S:2 protocols that had been completed by high school teachers for students with emotional disturbance. A very high rate of scoring agreement was found, with correlations ranging from .95 to .99 for domain scores, and from .96 to .99 for factor scores. To assess how objective the ABS-S:2 is with different raters, teachers and teacher's aides completed the scale for 30 students with emotional disabilities. Correlations for Part One domain scores ranged from .51 to .92, and Part One factor correlations ranged from .66 to .80. Similar results were found for Part Two domains, with correlations ranging from .55 to .88 and Part Two factors ranging from .53 to .61.

Statistical Confirmation

Extensive information on the reliability, validity, and standardization procedures is available in the Examiner's Manual.

Special Features

Acronym

ABS-S:2.

Levels of the Test

One.

Number of Test Forms

One Examination Booklet and one Profile/Summary Sheet.

Norm-Referenced?

Yes. The ABS-S:2 was standardized on both a mental retardation and a non–mental retardation population. The MR sample consisted of 2,074 students that were representative of the national population of persons with mental retardation. The non–mental retardation group consisted of 1,254 students. This sample was stratified according to variables of race, ethnicity, gender, residence in rural or urban areas, geographic region, and age.

Criterion-Referenced?

No.

Feasibility Considerations

Testing Time

Fifteen to 30 minutes.

For Testing Groups? Individuals?

Individuals.

Test Administration and Scoring

Clear directions for completing the ABS-S:2 are provided, although there are two types of ratings. One involves rating the highest level of the individual's performance, and the other involves answering "yes" and "no" questions. Scoring of the domains is straightforward, although the scoring of factors is tedious, as each item score comprising the factor needs to be transferred to the Profile/Summary Form. Kamphaus and Frick (1996, p. 308) note that the ABS-S:2 "has relatively complicated scoring procedures that may invite clerical errors." However, the ABS-S:2 Software Scoring and Report System, available for Apple II, Macintosh, and IBM-PCs, makes this easier. Although no specific training is needed, it is advisable for individuals to become thoroughly familiar with the instructions for completing and scoring the ABS-S:2 and to consult with professionals knowledgeable about the test if questions arise.

Test Materials and Approximate Costs

The complete kit, which includes 25 Examination Booklets, 25 Profile/Summary Forms, and one Examiner's Manual, costs $149.50. The Examiner's Manual alone costs $55. Examination Booklets are available in packages of 10, with one package costing $32.50. If 2 to 9 packages are ordered, the cost is $29 per package, and if 10 or more packages are ordered, the cost is $27 per package. Profile/Scoring Forms also come in packages of 10 and cost $13.50 per package. If 2 to 9 packages are ordered, the cost is $12 per package, and 10 or more packages cost $9.95 per package.

Adequacy of Test Manuals

The Examination Booklet provides excellent directions, although it is lengthy and items are closely spaced together. The Profile/Summary Form provides useful information and a graph for plotting scores. The Examiner's Manual is also comprehensive, including an impressive number of tables to display relevant reliability and validity studies.

Excerpts from Other Test Reviews

Sattler (2002) comments that the ABS-S:2 is a reliable, valid measure of an individual's adaptive behavior. Some notable cautions in using the ABS-S:2 include the lack of uniformity in standard scores across the domains. For example, the Socialization domain ranges from scaled scores of 1 to 16 for 3-year-olds, whereas Numbers and Time scale scores range from 7 to 17. Therefore, making direct comparisons across domains is difficult. In addition, converting raw scores to age equivalents varies greatly across grade levels, so caution must be used in interpreting these. Another point about the ABS-S:2 is that it does not provide a good match with the American Association on Mental Retardation's domains of adaptive behavior, so results may need to be supplemented by other measures. Kamphaus and Frick (1996) point out similar issues, such as the good reliability of the ABS-S:2, but the lack of broad sampling of adaptive behavior. Salvia and Ysseldyke (2001) further point out that domain and factor scores are not stable enough on their own to be used to make important educational decisions.

Ordering Information

Publisher

Western Psychological Services, 12031 Wilshire Boulevard, Los Angeles, CA 90025-1251; Phone: 310-478-2061; Fax: 310-478-7838; Web site: http://www.wps publish.com.

Authors

Nadine Lambert, Kzuo Nihira, and Henry Leland.

Publication Date

1993.

Cautions and Comments

The ABS-S:2 is a comprehensive assessment of both adaptive and maladaptive behavior that enjoys good reliability and validity. Some cautions about the ABS-S:2 are that the age equivalent scores are highly variable across domains and that the domains are not consistent with the 10 adaptive behavior areas specified by the American Association on Mental Retardation. In addition, caution should be used when scoring the factors on the ABS-S:2, as it is a tedious process in which errors can easily be made.

As with any test, it should not be used alone to make important educational decisions, but it can be used by educators to decide if further intervention or referrals are needed. It is recommended that educators look at the classification system described above, and if a child receives a GAC of 89 or below (classification of "Below Average," "Poor," or "Very Poor"), he or she should be referred for further assessment. Also, a score of 7 or below on two or more domains warrants further assessment.

References

Kamphaus, R. W., & Frick, P. J. (1996). *Clinical assessment of child and adolescent personality and behavior*. Boston: Allyn and Bacon.

Lambert, N., Nihira, K., & Leland, H. (1993). *Adaptive Behavior Scale-School: Second Edition: Examiner's Manual*. Los Angeles: Western Psychological Services.

Salvia, J., & Ysseldyke, J. E. (2001). *Assessment* (8th ed.). Boston: Houghton Mifflin.

Sattler, J. M. (2002). *Assessment of children: Behavioral and clinical applications* (4th ed.). San Diego: Author.

<hr>

Vineland Adaptive Behavior Scales: Classroom Edition (The Vineland),
for testing individuals from 3 years through 12 years, 11 months of age
Reviewed by Amanda B. Nickerson, Ph.D., School Psychology

<hr>

Usefulness of the Test for Educators

Test Authors' Purpose

The Vineland Adaptive Behavior Scales: Classroom Edition is an assessment of adaptive behavior in the classroom.

Decision-Making Applications

The Vineland can be used whenever an assessment of an individual's daily functioning is required. For example, a diagnosis of mental retardation can only be made if an individual's adaptive behavior, in addition to his or her intellectual ability, is found to be deficient. The Vineland can also be used to provide a comprehensive picture of the daily functioning abilities of handicapped and nonhandicapped students. Scores on the Classroom Edition can be compared to scores on the Survey Edition, which is administered to the parent in a semistructured interview format by a trained professional to gather information about children's functioning across settings. In addition, the Vineland can identify an individual's strengths and areas to be improved on for individualized programs. The Classroom Edition can also be used to determine the need for further assessment.

Relevant Population

The Vineland is intended to be completed by teachers of children between the ages of 3 years and 12 years, 11 months.

Characteristics Described

The Vineland Classroom Edition has an Adaptive Behavior Composite and four domains: (1) Communication, (2) Daily Living Skills, (3) Socialization, and (4) Motor Skills. Each of the domains is further broken down into subdomains. A description of the content of these characteristics is provided below:

Communication

- Receptive: This subdomain assesses what the individual understands.
- Expressive: The individual's verbal communication patterns are assessed in this subdomain.
- Written: This subdomain includes items assessing what the student reads and writes.

Daily Living Skills

- Personal: This subdomain includes items assessing the individual's eating, dressing, and personal hygiene habits.

- Domestic: Assesses household chores and tasks performed by the person.

- Community: Items include how the student uses times, money, communication devices (e.g., telephone), and vocational skills.

Socialization

- Interpersonal Relationships: Assesses how the individual interacts with others.

- Play and Leisure Time: Items include the child's play skills and use of free time.

- Coping Skills: This subdomain assesses the way the student demonstrates responsibility and sensitivity to others.

Motor Skills

- Gross: Items relate to the individual's use of arms and legs for movement and coordination.

- Fine: This subdomain assesses the student's use of hands and fingers for object manipulation.

Test Scores Obtained

For each of the four adaptive behavior domains and the Adaptive Behavior Composite, standard scores (mean of 100 and standard deviation of 15), percentile ranks, stanines, adaptive levels, and age equivalents are given. Adaptive levels are as follows:

Adaptive Level	Standard Deviation from Mean	Standard Score Range	Percentile Rank Range
High	Above 2.0	131–above 160	98 and above
Moderately High	1.0–2.0	116–130	85–97
Adequate	−1.0 to 1.0	85–115	16–84
Moderately Low	−2.0 to −1.0	70–84	3–15
Low	Below −2.0	Below 70	2 and below

Technical Adequacy

Validity Confirmation

Test item validity: Several procedures were used to ensure that the test items developed and selected for the Vineland were valid. The authors conducted an intensive review of the child development literature and of other adaptive behavior rating scales to determine the four domains of Communication, Daily Living Skills, Socialization, and Motor Skills. Three thousand items were originally developed and subjected to criteria for inclusion, such as "representing self-sufficiency," "having the potential for lasting relevance," "being easily understood by people from different backgrounds," "amenability to objective scoring," and "translatable to educational and treatment goal objectives." The number of items was reduced to 800, and these items were pilot tested on 50 children, after which time 529 were included for a tryout with 875 students. Because many teachers in the tryout testing answered "Don't know" for items for junior and senior high school students, the Classroom Edition was limited to preschool and elementary school.

Test response validity: In the development and standardization of the Vineland, several procedures were used to assess how well the test measured what it was supposed to measure. Scores for adaptive behavior increased with age, supporting the hypothesis that it is age-related. A statistical procedure called factor analysis was used to support the validity of the Adaptive Behavior Composite and the four domains. The Classroom Edition was also compared with the Interview Edition of the Vineland, yielding modest correlations, ranging from .31 to .54. A few studies compared the Vineland Classroom Edition to other adaptive rating scales, finding a wide range of correlations (.18 to .51 in one study, .62 to .92 in another). The Vineland Classroom Edition was also moderately correlated with measures of intelligence. For example, correlations between the Adaptive Behavior Composite and subtests of the K-ABC ranged from .42 to .50. Correlations between the Adaptive Behavior Composite and Full Scale IQ scores were also moderate (.59 with WISC and .49 with Stanford-Binet).

Reliability Confirmation

Reliability of the Vineland was assessed by splitting the test in half, and correlating one-half of the items with the other half of the items for 479 students. The median reliability coefficients for all age groups were as follows: .98 for Adaptive Behavior Composite, .93 for Communication, .95 for Daily Living Skills, .94 for Socialization, and .80 for Motor Skills.

Objectivity Confirmation

To ensure that ratings on the Vineland are as objective as possible, the Manual states that the person completing the rating should be a teacher who is familiar with the behavior of the child. In addition, the directions on the Classroom Edition instruct the teacher to make a determination about how familiar they are with each aspect of the child's adaptive behavior, and to complete ratings under "Observed Performance" if they are very familiar or "Estimated Performance" if they are less familiar. The directions are also explicit that the ratings of the behavior should be based on what the child *does*, not what he or she *can do*. The ratings are on a 3-point scale: 0 = never performs the activity, 1 = sometimes performs the activity or performs the activity with partial success, and 2 = usually/habitually performs the activity. There are no reports of inter-rater agreement studies for the Vineland.

Statistical Confirmation

Extensive information on the reliability, validity, and standardization of the Vineland can be found in the Manual.

Special Features

Acronym

None.

Levels of the Test

There is only one level of the Classroom Edition, but there is also a separate Preschool Edition for younger children.

Number of Test Forms

The Vineland Adaptive Behavior Scales includes four forms: Survey, Expanded, Classroom, and Preschool. Only the Classroom and Preschool forms can be completed by teachers in the form of a checklist. The others need to be conducted through an interview.

Norm-Referenced?

Yes. The norm group consisted of 2,984 students between the ages of 3 years and 12 years, 11 months. The sample was stratified to adequately represent the U.S. population according to variables of sex, race/ethnicity, community size, geographic region, and parents' level of education.

Criterion-Referenced?

No.

Feasibility Considerations

Testing Time

Twenty minutes.

For Testing Groups? Individuals?

Individuals.

Test Administration and Scoring

Extensive directions are provided. Although no specific training is needed, the Manual says that the person administering the Vineland to the teacher should explain that items must be completed according to what the child *does* rather than what he or she *can do*. In addition, an emphasis is placed on whether a given activity is usually or habitually performed. The scoring is fairly straightforward.

Test Materials and Approximate Costs

The Classroom Edition Starter Set, which includes 10 questionnaire booklets, the Manual, and one Report to Parents, costs $54.95. The starter set is also available with a nylon briefcase for $87.95. A package of 25 Classroom Edition questionnaires costs $46.95, and a package of 25 Classroom Edition Report to Parents, available in Spanish or English, costs $19.95 The Manual alone costs $44.95.

Adequacy of Test Manuals

The Classroom Edition questionnaires are easy to read and complete. The manual is extensive, although it lacks some important information on the test-retest reliability and inter-rater agreement among test scores.

Excerpts from Other Test Reviews

Sattler (2002) characterizes the Vineland Adaptive Behavior Scales, including the Classroom Edition, as useful tools for assessing adaptive behavior. He cautions, however, that the standardization procedures include an underrepresentation of Hispanic students, children from rural areas, and students with parents with low educational attainment. He also notes that the manual does not report test-retest reliability and inter-rater agreement information, which are important aspects of reliability and objectivity. In addition, standard scores and age equivalents are not uniform across ages and domains, so one needs to be cautious when interpreting this information. Sattler also points out that the Vineland only assesses three of the 10 adaptive behavior skills deemed important by the American Association of Mental Retardation. Kamphaus and Frick (1996) point out that the Vineland has a large national normative sample and multiple components that make it useful for diagnostic and planning purposes. They do caution that the age-equivalent scores are problematic. Salvia and Ysseldyke (2001) agree that the norming of the Vineland is good, yet they caution that the reliability varies across domains, which means that people should be cautious when interpreting the domain scores to make important individual decisions.

Ordering Information

Publisher

American Guidance Service, Inc., 4201 Woodland Road, Circle Pines, MN 55014-1796; Phone: 800-328-2560; Fax: 800-471-8457; Web site: www.agsnet.com.

Authors

Sara S. Sparrow, David A. Balla, and Dominic V. Cicchetti.

Publication Date

1985.

Cautions and Comments

The Vineland enjoys a long history of use in the assessment of adaptive behavior. Test reviewers have asserted caution about some aspects of reliability and objectivity (i.e., test-retest reliability and inter-rater agreement), as no information is provided about these in the Manual. A critical part of accurately completing the Vineland is to focus on what a child *does* as opposed to what a child *can do*. This point is emphasized to professionals who administer the Survey Edition of the Vineland in an interview format, and it is important that it be understood by those completing the rating scales.

The authors state that a trained examiner is not required to complete the Vineland Classroom Edition, but that the interpretation of scores should be done by a professional (e.g., psychologist, social worker) with a graduate degree and training/experience in assessment and interpretation. Therefore, teachers and other educators should restrict interpretation to making decisions about referrals. A good rule of thumb is that if the Adaptive Behavior Composite, or the scores in two or more domains, equals 84 or below ("Moderately Low" or "Low") compared to the normative population, further assessment is indicated.

References

Kamphaus, R. W., & Frick, P. J. (1996). *Clinical assessment of child and adolescent personality and behavior*. Boston: Allyn and Bacon.

Harrison, P. L. (1985). *Vineland Adaptive Behavior Rating Scales: Classroom Edition Manual.* Circle Pines, MN: American Guidance Service.

Salvia, J., & Ysseldyke, J. E. (2001). *Assessment* (8th ed.). Boston: Houghton Mifflin.

Sattler, J. M. (2002). *Assessment of children: Behavioral and clinical applications* (4th ed.). San Diego: Author.

Problem Behavior Tests

Many standardized behavior rating scales exist for assessing problem behavior in children and adolescents. These scales range from comprehensive scales that measure multiple domains of psychopathology to tests that are designed to measure specific kinds of problems, such as attention and hyperactivity, self-esteem, or depression. The scales selected for review in this section are those that measure a broad range of behaviors, as well as those that assess behaviors of interest to educators, for their potential impact on the child's learning.

Behavior Assessment System for Children-Teacher Rating Scale (BASC-TRS), for testing individuals from 2 years, 6 months through 18 years of age
Reviewed by Amanda B. Nickerson, Ph.D., School Psychology

Usefulness of the Test for Educators

Test Authors' Purpose

"The Teacher Rating Scale (TRS) is a comprehensive measure of both adaptive and problem behaviors in the school setting" (Reynolds & Kamphaus, 1992, p. 2). It was designed to aid in the identification of emotional and behavioral disorders in children and adolescents.

Decision-Making Applications

The BASC is intended to facilitate the differential diagnosis and educational classification of a variety of children's emotional and behavioral disorders. It can also link diagnosis to intervention and aid in treatment planning. Repeated administration of the TRS can be used to evaluate the effectiveness of programs.

Relevant Population

The TRS is intended to be completed by teachers or others who fill a similar role (e.g., teacher aides or preschool caregivers) for children from 2 years, 6 months through 18 years of age.

Characteristics Described

Teachers complete the BASC-TRS by reading each item, which consists of a brief description of behavior, and rating how often the behavior occurs for the child on a 4-point scale from "Never" to "Almost Always." The following is a list of the composites and their respective subscales:

Externalizing Problems

- Aggression
- Hyperactivity
- Conduct Problems

Internalizing Problems

- Anxiety
- Depression
- Somatization

School Problems

- Attention Problems
- Learning Problems

Other Problems
- Atypicality
- Withdrawal

Adaptive Skills
- Adaptability
- Leadership
- Social Skills
- Study Skills

In addition, there is a Behavioral Symptoms Index, which is a combination of the clinical scales and provides an index of the overall level of problem behavior.

Another feature of the TRS is the inclusion of a fake bad index (F), which helps to assess the possibility that the teacher rated a child in an overly negative pattern.

Test Scores Obtained

Raw scores, standard T-scores (mean of 50 and standard deviation of 10), and percentiles are derived for each scale.

Classification for the Adaptive and Clinical Scale Standard Scores

Adaptive Scales	Clinical Scales	T-Score Range
Very High	Clinically Significant	70 and above
High	At-Risk	60–69
Average	Average	41–59
At-Risk	Low	31–40
Clinically Significant	Very Low	30 and below

Technical Adequacy

Validity Confirmation

Test item validity: Several procedures were used to ensure that the test items developed and selected for the TRS were valid. Based on reviews of more than 20 behavior rating scales, positive as well as pathological behavioral and personality traits were identified. The test authors then identified constructs with explicit definitions, which were reviewed by several clinicians and doctoral students. Items were written that conformed to these definitions and were consistent with the literature. In addition, over 20 teachers completed questionnaires asking them to describe the five most obnoxious, disturbing, or disruptive behaviors and the five most positive behaviors they have seen in the classroom. More than 500 public school students completed similar surveys about behaviors of classmates that they have seen. The test items were then sorted into subscales and reviewed by a reading specialist, public school administrators, research assistants, the publisher, and the authors. For the initial item tryout, 600 teachers completed the test. A statistical technique called factor analysis was then conducted on the items, and over 2,000 teachers completed the second tryout of items. The resulting items were based on these methods, in addition to several different statistical analyses that were conducted on the data.

Test response validity: Teachers' responses to the test were validated in several ways. To determine how closely the TRS relates to similar tests, several studies were conducted where teachers were asked to complete the TRS and other popular rating scales. The following is a summary table of these studies:

Rating Scale	Sample Size	Age	Total Scale Correlation	Comparable Scale Correlations
Teacher's Report Form	50	6–11	.92	.71–.86
Teacher's Report Form	38	12–17	.90	.66–.93
Revised Behavior Problem Checklist	43	12–17	N/A	.38–.69
Conner's Teacher Rating Scales	92	3–5	.66	.38–.69
Burk's Behavior Rating Scales	27	6–11	N/A	Most > .80
Behavior Rating Profile (Note: all positive scales)	37	6–11	N/A	–.60 to –.25 (problem scales) .25–.41 (adaptive)

In addition to the aforementioned studies, the authors also tested several groups of children with the TRS that had been classified with different diagnostic labels (e.g., Depressed, Conduct Disorder, Emotionally Disturbed, Attention Deficit Hyperactivity Disorder, Learning Disabled, Mental Retardation, and Autism). The groups were differentiated from one another by their scores on the TRS. For example, the depressed individuals scored highest on Depression, whereas those classified with Conduct Disorder scored highest on the Externalizing Composite and Conduct Problems scale.

Reliability Confirmation

The TRS was administered twice to teachers, with an interval of two to eight weeks between the administrations. The test-retest median reliability correlations were as follows: .89 for preschool form, .91 for child form, and .82 for adolescent form. To determine how stable the TRS test scores were over a longer period of time, teachers of 55 children between 6 and 11 years of age rated the students' behavior twice, with a seven-month interval between ratings. This resulted in a median scale correlation of .69. In addition, one-half of the test item responses were correlated with the other half of the items for the 2,401 students in the general sample. The median internal reliability coefficients were .82 (ages 4–5), .84 (ages 6–7), .88 (ages 8–11), .90 (ages 12–14), and .89 (ages 15–18).

Objectivity Confirmation

To ensure accurate ratings, teachers do not complete the TRS unless they have spent a considerable amount of time with the child. The authors advise that a month of daily contact or six to eight weeks of almost daily contact should be sufficient. Items are written in descriptive behavioral terms, and raters are to score each item on a 4-point scale indicating how often the behavior has been observed by the teacher (0 = Never, 1 = Sometimes, 2 = Often, 3 = Always). Scales are not to be scored if three or more items are omitted. In addition, the TRS contains an F index, which consists of items designed to detect excessively negative responses made by the teacher. If the F index falls into the "Caution" or "Extreme Caution" range, the rating may be invalid.

Two different studies were conducted to further confirm the objectivity of ratings on the TRS. First, four pairs of preschool teachers each rated 8 to 20 students, resulting in a median scale inter-rater agreement correlation of .83. Second, many different pairs of teachers each rated 1 to 2 children. Median scale inter-rater agreement correlations were .63 for the preschool sample and .71 for the child sample.

Statistical Confirmation

Extensive information on the reliability, validity, and norms can be found in the Behavior Assessment System for Children Manual.

Special Features

Acronym

BASC-TRS.

Levels of the Test

There are three levels of the TRS for different age groups: (1) preschool (ages 2 years, 6 months–5), (2) child (ages 6–11), and (3) adolescent (ages 12–18).

Number of Test Forms

There are three formats: (1) hand-scored (printed in self-scoring format), (2) scannable, and (3) computer-scored (one-part forms).

Norm-Referenced?

Yes. The normative sample included 2,401 students. There are actually four norm samples in the TRS Manual: (1) General Norms (representative of the U.S. population based on sex, race/ethnicity, and clinical or special education classification), (2) Female Norms (subset of General Norms), (3) Male Norms (subset of General Norms), and (4) Clinical Norms (used for differential diagnoses of individual behavior problems). The 1998 version expanded the norm group to include norms for ages 2 years, 6 months through 3 years, 11 months.

Criterion-Referenced?

No.

Feasibility Considerations

Testing Time

Ten to 20 minutes.

For Testing Groups? Individuals?

Individuals.

Test Administration and Scoring

Administration of the TRS is clear and straightforward, with instructions provided for teachers on the forms. Scoring is relatively easy, with the two-part carbonless forms that do not require the use of a template. Scoring can be tedious, however, and one must be careful to add the numbers carefully. The scannable and computer-scored forms are much simpler. No special training is needed to administer and score the TRS.

Test Materials and Approximate Costs

The BASC Manual costs $73.95, and Teacher Rating Scales-Hand-Scored Formats cost $27.95 for a package of 25. The Scannable Formats cost $38.95 for a package of 25. The BASC Plus Scannable Windows Kit, which includes 3.5" program diskettes and the software manual, costs $259.95, and the BASC Enhanced ASSIST Scannable Windows Kit, which includes the program on CD-ROM and the ASSIST software manual, costs $524.95. Teacher Rating Scales in the computer-entry format (for use with either the BASC Plus or ASSIST software) cost $18.95 for a package of 25.

Adequacy of Test Manuals

The Manual is comprehensive and well written, and the rating scales are clear and easy to use. In addition to the Teacher Rating Scale, the BASC has a parent rating scale, a self-report instrument, and a classroom observation system.

Excerpts from Other Test Reviews

DiPerna (2001) reviewed the BASC, with a particular emphasis on the preschool version, and cautioned that practitioners should not use the BASC to diagnose emotional and behavioral disorders in preschoolers. He noted that using the scores for treatment planning is more appropriate for a preschool population. DiPerna also highlighted the lack of evidence for reliability and validity for children ages 2 years, 6 months through 3 years, 11 months. Similarly, Spies and Jones (2001) also caution about the dangers inherent in diagnosing emotional and behavioral disorders in preschool populations. Despite these cautions, these authors view the BASC for older children and adolescents as a notable advance in behavioral assessment. Sattler (2002) highlights the BASC's strength as an integrative assessment tool, especially for evaluating externalizing behaviors. However, he also notes the limited validity of using it with a preschool population. Salvia and Ysseldyke (2001) concur that the BASC appears better able to differentiate externalizing problems than internalizing problems of emotional disturbance. They further comment that the BASC is one of the most comprehensive assessment tools on the market and that it is supported for content, criterion-related, and construct validity.

Ordering Information

Publisher

American Guidance Service, Inc., 4201 Woodland Road, Circle Pines, MN 55014-1796; Phone: 800-328-2560; Fax: 800-471-8457; Web site: www.agsnet.com.

Authors

Cecil R. Reynolds and Randy W. Kamphaus.

Publication Date

1998.

Cautions and Comments

One of the best features of the BASC is that it can be used in the comprehensive assessment of emotional and behavioral problems. In addition to the TRS reviewed here, the BASC system includes a parent rating scale, a self-report scale, and a classroom observation form. The TRS enjoys good reliability, validity, and objectivity for children and adolescents, and the inclusion of the F index to detect if a teacher's ratings are biased toward the negative is helpful. The assessment of social and emotional functioning in preschoolers needs to be done with extreme caution, and it is recommended that scores be used for intervention purposes, as opposed to classification purposes.

According to information on the BASC web site, users of the BASC are expected to have had formal training in the administration, scoring, and interpretation of behavior rating scales. Although clerical staff, with appropriate training, may administer and score various BASC components, it is required that interpretation of the results be done by persons with a graduate level of education in psychology. Therefore, educators who use the BASC-TRS should only interpret scores to the extent that they signify a need for intervention or referral. Using the classification system can aid educators in determining where the child's scores fall relative to a normal population. If a child receives a score of 60 or above ("At-Risk" or "Clinically Significant" range) on the Behavioral Symptoms Index or on one of the Clinical Scales, a referral for further evaluation or intervention is indicated. Similarly, if a child receives a score of 40 or below ("At-Risk" or "Clinically Significant" range) on one or more adaptive scales, further attention is needed. It should be noted that a "Clinically Significant" score on a scale (e.g., Depression) does not necessarily mean that a child has a mental disorder in that area, as multiple sources of information are needed to make that determination.

References

DiPerna, J. C. (2001). Review of the Behavior Assessment System for Children, Revised. In B. S. Plake & J. C. Impara (Eds.), *The Fourteenth Mental Measurements Yearbook* (pp. 134–137). Lincoln, NE: The Buros Institute of Mental Measurements.

Reynolds, C. R., & Kamphaus, R. W. (1992). *Behavior Assessment System for Children Manual.* Circle Pines, MN: American Guidance Service.

Salvia, J., & Ysseldyke, J. E. (2001). *Assessment* (8th ed.). Boston: Houghton Mifflin.

Sattler, J. M. (2002). *Assessment of children: Behavioral and clinical applications* (4th ed.). San Diego: Author.

Spies, R., & Jones, C. F. (2001). Review of the Behavior Assessment System for Children, Revised. In B. S. Plake & J. C. Impara (Eds.), *The Fourteenth Mental Measurements Yearbook* (pp. 137–139). Lincoln, NE: The Buros Institute of Mental Measurements.

Devereux Behavior Rating Scale-School Form (DBRS-SF),
for testing individuals from 5 through 18 years of age
Reviewed by Amanda B. Nickerson, Ph.D., School Psychology

Usefulness of the Test for Educators

Test Authors' Purpose

The Devereux Behavior Rating Scale-School Form (DBRS-SF) was developed as a method of evaluating behaviors typical of children and adolescents with emotional disturbance.

Decision-Making Applications

The DBRS-SF can be used in many ways. First, results from the scale can be used to identify children and adolescents who are in need of a more in-depth evaluation. Second, scores on the different subscales can be compared to decide which of the child's behaviors are more problematic, or atypical, than others. Third, individual items can be analyzed to determine specific behavioral difficulties that may require intervention. Fourth, the DBRS-SF can be used to monitor and evaluate changes in behavior over time.

Relevant Population

The DBRS-SF is intended to be completed by a person fulfilling the role of a parent or a teacher (e.g., regular or special education teacher, teacher's aide) on children ages 5 through 18. The individual should have sufficient opportunity to observe the child's behavior for four weeks prior to completing the rating.

Characteristics Described

The 40-item scale is organized into four subscales of 10 items each that reflect emotional and behavioral criteria in the federal definition of emotional disturbance: Interpersonal Problems, Inappropriate Behaviors/Feelings, Depression, and Physical Symptoms/Fears. In addition, a Total Scale Score is obtained. A further description of the subscales is as follows:

1. Interpersonal Problems: This subscale assesses problems in developing and maintaining satisfactory relationships with peers and teachers. Typical problems include avoiding interactions with peers, being bossy, or appearing anxious around others.

2. Inappropriate Behaviors/Feelings: Items on this subscale assess a variety of inappropriate behaviors and feelings under normal circumstances, such as failing to control anger, refusing to speak, and hitting, biting, or injuring oneself.

3. Depression: This subscale measures signs of depression or a general and pervasive mood of unhappiness. Behaviors assessed include not showing joy at a happy occasion, stating that he or she is worthless, and threatening suicide.

4. Physical Symptoms/Fears: These items assess physical symptoms or fears associated with personal or school problems, such as overreacting to minor pain, showing an exaggerated fear of getting hurt, or refusing to go to school.

Test Scores Obtained

The DBRS-SF provides raw scores and standard scores for each subscale and the total score. Subscales yield a standard score with a mean of 10 and a standard deviation of 3. The total test standard score has a mean of 100 and a standard deviation of 15. Scores are classified as follows:

Total Scale Standard Score	Classification	Subscale Standard Score
109 and below	Normal	11 and below
110–114	Borderline	12
115–124	Significant	13–14
125 and above	Very Significant	15 and above

Technical Adequacy

Validity Confirmation

Test item validity: Several procedures were used to develop appropriate items for the DBRS-SF. First, items from the original Devereux Child Behavior Rating Scale and the Devereux Adolescent Behavior Rating Scale were reviewed. These items were simplified, outdated terms were eliminated, and psychological jargon was minimized. The selection of items and the development of new items were guided by a thorough review of the fourth edition of the *Diagnostic and Statistical Manual of Mental Disorders* (American Psychiatric Association, 1994), comparisons to items in other behavior rating scales, and relevant literature on behavior problems. Items were also changed to be consistent with a sixth-grade reading level. In addition, noted experts in the field reviewed items for possible cultural, racial, and gender bias.

Test response validity: Several studies have been conducted to validate the ratings on the DBRS-SF. Six studies are reported in the Manual, with samples including students from regular and special education programs, approved private schools, residential centers, and inpatient units for the treatment of severe emotional disturbances. Overall, the cutoff scores used by the DBRS-SF accurately classified 75% of the 5- to 12-year-old sample as emotionally disturbed or not emotionally disturbed, and the DBRS-SF accurately classified 78% of the 13- to 18-year-old sample. In a separate study, the DBRS-SF was found to accurately classify 77% of the 5- to 12-year-old sample and 74% of the 13- to 18-year-old sample (Naglieri, Bardos, & LeBuffe, 1995).

Reliability Confirmation

The DBRS-SF was administered twice to the same teachers for 5- to 12-year-old children in regular education. Correlations ranged from .80 to .84 for the subscale scores and .85 for the total scale. The reliability coefficients for the adolescent (13–18) regular education sample were slightly lower, ranging from .53 to .82 for the subscales and .69 for the total scale. In addition, the DBRS-SF was administered to teachers for a clinical sample, yielding correlations of .75 over 24 hours, .65 for two weeks, and .52 for four weeks.

In addition, one-half of the test item responses were correlated with the other half. Internal reliability correlations for the total scale ranged from .92 to .97. The median internal reliability coefficients for the subscales across rater, sex, and age were .85 (Interpersonal Problems), .84 (Inappropriate Behaviors/Feelings), .84 (Depression), and .82 (Physical Symptoms/Fears).

Objectivity Confirmation

To ensure accurate ratings, teachers need to be sufficiently familiar with the child's behavior for four weeks prior to completing the DBRS-SF. Each item is rated on a 5-point scale: Never (0), Rarely (1), Occasionally (2), Frequently (3), and Very Frequently (4).

Two inter-rater agreement studies were presented in the manual for the DBRS-SF.

For the first study, teachers and residential counselors rated the same children in a residential treatment center for children with emotional disturbance. Correlations for the subscales ranged from .36 to .45, with a total scale correlation of .40. The second study compared teacher and teacher aide ratings for 45 children residing in the inpatient unit of a psychiatric hospital. Correlations ranged from .40 to .60 for the subscales, with a total scale coefficient of .53.

Statistical Confirmation

Comprehensive information regarding the normative sample and the reliability and validity of the DBRS-SF is available in the Manual.

Special Features

Acronym

DBRS-SF.

Levels of the Test

Two levels, one for children from 5 through 12 years of age and one for adolescents from 13 through 18 years of age.

Number of Test Forms

One form, that can be completed by a parent or teacher.

Norm-Referenced?

Yes. The standardization sample consisted of 3,153 children and adolescents between the ages of 5 and 18. The sample was representative of the U.S. population in terms of age, gender, socioeconomic status, race/ethnicity, geographic region, community size, and educational placement.

Criterion-Referenced?

No.

Feasibility Considerations

Testing Time

Ten minutes.

For Testing Groups? Individuals?

Individuals.

Test Administration and Scoring

The administration of the DBRS-SF is straightforward, with instructions provided on the forms. Scoring is also easy, as the ratings made by teachers are transferred through the carbon paper.

Test Materials and Approximate Costs

The complete kit, which consists of the Manual, a package of 25 Child Forms, and a package of 25 Adolescent Forms, costs $149. The Manual costs $80. A package of 25 Child Forms costs $36, and a package of 25 Adolescent Forms costs $36.

Adequacy of Test Manuals

The Manual is comprehensive and well written, and the test forms are clearly laid out and easy to complete. Since carbon paper is used, teachers must press hard to ensure that the marks transfer to the scoring page.

Excerpts from Other Test Reviews

Kamphaus and Frick (1996) describe the DBRS-SF as a relatively brief rating scale with acceptable reliability and an excellent normative base. Although they say that the scale does a good job in discriminating emotionally disturbed children from non-disturbed children, it is limited in the behavioral domains assessed, making it limited in its ability to differentially diagnose children. These reviewers also note that further evidence is needed about the scale's validity.

Ordering Information

Publisher

The Psychological Corporation, 19500 Bulverde Road, San Antonio, TX 78259; Phone: 800-228-0752; Fax: 210-339-5873; Web site: www.psychcorp.com.

Authors

Jack A. Naglieri, Paul A. LeBuffe, and Steven I. Pfeiffer.

Publication Date

1993.

Cautions and Comments

The DBRS-SF is a brief scale that is very useful in the screening of children for emotional disturbance in schools. It is the only scale that was developed specifically according to the federal definition of emotional disturbance, and it has consistently been shown to differentiate between children with emotional disturbance and children without disabilities. A good rule of thumb is that a total score of 110 or above ("Borderline," "Significant," or "Very Significant" ranges) should signify the need for further evaluation. In addition, if one or more subscale scores is 13 or higher ("Significant" or "Very Significant" range), it is advisable for educators to refer the child to a professional to further investigate the emotional or behavioral concern. This said, caution should be used when using the test for making more specific diagnostic decisions. For example, a "Significant" rating of depression does not mean that the child should be diagnosed as clinically depressed. Rather, this information should be integrated with information from other methods and sources by a qualified professional to make this determination.

References

Kamphaus, R. W., & Frick, P. J. (1996). *Clinical assessment of child and adolescent personality and behavior*. Boston: Allyn and Bacon.

Naglieri, J. A., Bardos, A. N., & LeBuffe, P. A. (1995). Discriminant validity of the Devereux Behavior Rating Scale-School Form for students with serious emotional disturbance. *School Psychology Review 24*(1), 104–111.

Naglieri, J. A., LeBuffe, P. A., & Pfeiffer, S. I. (1993). *Devereux Behavior Rating Scale-School Form*. San Antonio, TX: The Psychological Corporation.

Systematic Screening for Behavior Disorders, Second Edition (SSBD),
for testing groups and individuals from grades 1 through 6
Reviewed by Amanda B. Nickerson, Ph.D., School Psychology

Usefulness of the Test for Educators

Test Authors' Purpose

The Systematic Screening for Behavior Disorders, Second Edition (SSBD) is a three-stage procedure for identifying at-risk students in the elementary age. The SSBD identifies students who have problems of either an externalizing (behavior directed outward) or internalizing (behavior directed inward) nature.

Decision-Making Applications

The SSDB is a mass screening procedure designed to identify children who may need referrals to a child study team for further evaluation or who may need school-based interventions. It can also be used as one piece of information for a comprehensive evaluation by child study teams. Another use of the SSBD is for program evaluation and research purposes.

Relevant Population

A teacher completes Stages One and Two of the SSBD for children in elementary school (grades 1 through 6) and another professional (e.g., school psychologist, counselor, special education teacher) completes Stage Three.

Characteristics Described

The SSBD is a three-stage process. Stage One involves having teachers list 10 children in their class with externalizing behavior and 10 children with internalizing behavior. Next, teachers rank order both the externalizing and internalizing students according to severity. The top three children ranked in each category are those who are rated in Stage Two. In Stage Two, teachers complete two forms, a Critical Events Index and a Combined Frequency Index for Adaptive and Maladaptive Behavior. Students who meet criteria then go through Stage Three, where a professional other than the teacher conducts two 15-minute structured observations, one assessing Academic Engaged Time (AET) and the other measuring Peer Social Behavior (PSB). The following is a description of characteristics described in each of the stages:

Stage One

1. Externalizing Behavior: Behaviors that are directed outward, toward the social environment. These usually involve an excess in inappropriate behaviors, such as aggression, arguing, and noncompliance.

2. Internalizing Behavior: These behavior problems are directed inwardly, and represent problems with the self, such as social avoidance, withdrawal, acting afraid, and not standing up for oneself.

Stage Two

1. Critical Events: This index measures 33 internalizing and externalizing behavior problems that are considered critical, such as physical aggression, temper tantrums, and evidence of physical or sexual abuse.

2. Adaptive Behavior: These positive behaviors can be teacher or peer directed, and include things such as cooperating with others, following classroom rules, and expressing anger appropriately.

3. Maladaptive Behavior: These behaviors include socially inappropriate behaviors such as creating disturbances in class, manipulating others to get his or her way, and pouting or sulking.

Stage Three

1. Academic Engaged Time: The time in which the student is appropriately engaged in working on assigned academic material that is geared toward his or her ability and skill levels.

2. Peer Social Behavior: Several different types of peer social behavior are assessed, including:

   a. Social Engagement: An exchange of social signals between two or more children that involves verbal or nonverbal interaction.

   b. Participation in structured games or activities: The child is participating in a game or activity with others that has agreed-upon rules.

c. Parallel play: When a child is within five feet of another child and is engaged in the same activity but is not interacting.

d. Alone: When the child is not within five feet of another child and is not socially engaged.

e. No code: When a child's behavior does not fit one of the other play categories.

f. Positive behavior: For social engagement and participation, behavior is coded as positive if the child is playing appropriately or displaying prosocial behavior (e.g., sharing, cooperating).

g. Negative Behavior: This is coded for social engagement and participation if the child is negative, aggressive, or inappropriate in any way, including teasing, pushing, or refusing to play by rules.

Test Scores Obtained

The Critical Events Index has a range of raw scores from 0 to 35, the Adaptive Behavior Index has a range of scores from 12 to 60, and the Maladaptive Behavior scores has a range of scores from 11 to 55. Each of these scores can be converted into standard T-scores (mean of 50 and standard deviation of 10) and percentiles based on norms for internalizers, externalizers, and nonidentified students. The AET yields a percentage, ranging from 0 to 100%, and the PSB yields several percentages for each of the types of behaviors described above.

The following criteria have been established by the test authors to determine which students pass to the next stage of the SSBD:

SSBD Stage   *Criteria to Pass to Next Stage*

Stage One   The top three internalizing students and the top three externalizing students

Stage Two   *Externalizers*

≤ 5 on Critical Events Index *or*

1–5 on Critical Events and ≤ 30 on Adaptive Behavior and ≥ 35 for Maladaptive Behavior

Internalizers

> 4 on Critical Events *or*

1–3 on Critical Events and ≤ 41 on Adaptive Behavior and ≥ 19 on Maladaptive Behavior

Stage Three   *Externalizers*

Academic Engaged Time $\leq 35\%$ *or*

Total Negative Behavior on Peer Social Behavior $\geq 12\%$

SSBD Stage   Criteria to Pass to Next Stage

Stage Three   *Internalizers*

Academic Engaged Time $\leq 45\%$ *or*

Time Spent Alone + Parallel Play $\geq 40\%$ (grades 1–3) *or* $\geq 35\%$ (grades 4–6)

Technical Adequacy

Validity Confirmation

Test item validity: Three separate versions of the SSBD Stage One definition and rating forms were investigated and evaluated before selecting the final forms. These versions were given to teachers and teacher's aides, for which inter-rater objectivity, test-retest reliability, and the ability of the ratings to discriminate children with previously identified problems from a normal sample. Stage Two instruments were adapted from item lists developed by Walker and colleagues and from an existing reliable and valid rating scale, both of which had been trial tested. Stage Three instruments included a coding system previously developed and field tested by Walker and colleagues. Extensive study, including factor analysis, was done on all instruments during the development to ensure that they were valid.

Test response validity: Many procedures were conducted to demonstrate the validity of the instruments used in all stages of the SSBD. Three groups of students (internalizers, externalizers, and controls) were shown to differ significantly on the instruments in all three stages. The controls, internalizers, and externalizers were rated in order as most adaptive and least maladaptive, respectively. In addition, 89% of students were classified into their correct groups through Stage Two and Three procedures. The Adaptive and Maladaptive rating scales and the observational measures were compared to the Achenbach Child Behavior Checklist externalizing and internalizing subtests, yielding correlations of –.63 to –.68 for Adaptive Behavior and Externalizing Behavior. The observational measures were significantly correlated with the Externalizing subtest, with Academic Engaged Time –.42, Negative Social Interaction .29, and Positive Social Interaction –.35. There are several other validation studies cited in the Manual, which demonstrate that the SSBD discriminates between previously identified and nonidentified students.

Reliability Confirmation

Forty teachers were administered the measures with 31 days between administrations. The mean test-retest reliability of the rank ordering of externalizing and internalizing students were .79 and .72, respectively. The test-retest reliability was .81 for Critical Events, .90 for Adaptive Behavior, and .87 for Maladaptive Behavior. In another study, 18 teachers completed the SSBD Stages One and Two on two occasions, with 31 days between administrations. Seventy percent of the individuals classified by teachers as externalizers at time 1 were classified as externalizers again at time 2, and 80% of internalizers were classified as such at both time 1 and time 2. The test-retest reliability coefficients for the rank ordering of students ranged from .33 to .96 for externalizing behaviors and .37 to .94 for internalizing behaviors. The mean test-retest reliabilities were .88 for the Adaptive Index and .83 for the Maladaptive Index. In addition, half of the items of the Adaptive and Maladaptive Indexes were compared to the other half of the items for the entire standardization sample. Mean internal consistencies were .94 for Adaptive Behavior and .92 for Maladaptive Behavior.

Objectivity Confirmation

To ensure the objectivity of the Stage Three ratings, extensive instructions and training procedures are provided in the Manual and the corresponding training tapes. Nineteen reliability checks were conducted, where two observers independently rated students' academic engaged time and peer social behavior. Inter-rater reliability agreement correlations ranged from .86 to 1.00, with a mean of .96, for AET and from .65 to 1.00, with a mean of .84, for PSB. Other studies have shown agreements of 95% for AET and 85% for PSB.

Statistical Confirmation

Extensive information on the reliability, validity, and development of the SSBD can be found in the Manual.

Special Features

Acronym

SSBD.

Levels of the Test

One.

Number of Test Forms

The SSBD includes several test forms: (1) Rank ordering of externalizing and internalizing students, (2) Critical Events Index and Combined Frequency Index for Adaptive and Maladaptive Behavior for Internalizers, (3) Critical Events Index and Combined Frequency Index for Adaptive and Maladaptive Behavior for Externalizers, (4) Academic Engaged Time Recording Form, (5) Peer Social Behavior Recording Form, and (6) Peer Social Behavior Summary Form.

Norm-Referenced?

Yes. The standardization sample for Stage Two measures consisted of approximately 4,500 students and the standardization sample for Stage Three measures included 1,300 students. All students came from 18 school districts in 8 different states Information is provided on demographics of the samples, but it is not compared to census data for the United States.

Criterion-Referenced?

Yes. Criteria are established at each stage of the SSDB to determine if the child should pass to the next stage and, at Stage Three, to decide if a referral to a child study team is needed.

Feasibility Considerations

Testing Time

One and one-half hours for Stages One and Two, 30 minutes for Stage Three.

For Testing Groups? Individuals?

Some phases (i.e., Stage One) of the SSBD are designed to assess entire groups, whereas the other stages are more individually focused.

Test Administration and Scoring

Stages One and Two are fairly straightforward and do not require specialized training. Stage Three, completed by someone other than the teacher, requires that the individual read the Administration Manual, take quizzes on the information, then practice coding videotaped interactions. It is also suggested that the individual do a live observation with another person and compare ratings to ensure objectivity. Scoring needs to be done carefully, with attention to the established criteria to pass to the next level.

Test Materials and Approximate Costs

The program kit, which contains three manuals (User's Guide and Administration Manual, Observer Training Manual, and Technical Manual), an 80-minute training video, an audiotape to prompt observation, and forms for screening in 25 classrooms costs $95. Twenty-five forms cost $10.

Adequacy of Test Manuals

The SSBD manuals and accompanying forms are clear, comprehensive, and include an impressive amount of research.

Excerpts from Other Test Reviews

Salvia and Ysseldyke (2001, p. 573) characterize the SSBD as "a well-conceived and well-researched instrument for screening and identifying children in need of further assessment for behavior disorders." They particularly note its strength in differentiating between internalizing, externalizing, and well-adjusted students. They also note that the SSBD was cited by the U.S. Department of Education's Program Effectiveness Panel as an effective instrument. Salvia and Ysseldyke do point out that there is limited descriptive information about the normative sample, and there are some gaps in the research, such as lack of information on inter-rater reliability.

Ordering Information

Publisher

Sopris West, 4093 Specialty Place, Longmont, CO 80504; Phone: 800-547-6747; Fax: 888-819-7767; Web site: www.sopriswest.com.

Authors

Hill M. Walker and Herbert H. Severson.

Publication Date

1992.

Cautions and Comments

The SSBD has received rave reviews for its potential for use in the screening of children for behavior problems. It has excellent reliability and validity, and clearly defined criteria for what scores constitute a need for referral. Educators should follow the defined criteria as described under "Test Scores Obtained" to determine if a child should pass through the next stage of assessment and, after Stage Three of assessment, if the child should be referred. It should be cautioned that, to date, the SSBD has been used for research purposes, not as much for educational or clinical use, although it shows great promise for these applications.

References

Salvia, J., & Ysseldyke, J. E. (2001). *Assessment* (8th ed.). Boston: Houghton Mifflin.
Walker, H. M., & Severson, H. H. (1992). *Systematic Screening for Behavior Disorders* (2nd ed.). Longmont, CO: Sopris West.

Teacher's Report Form (TRF),
for testing individuals from 6 through 18 years of age
Reviewed by Amanda B. Nickerson, Ph.D., School Psychology

Usefulness of the Test for Educators

Test Authors' Purpose

The purpose of the Teacher's Report Form (TRF) is to obtain teachers' reports of students' academic performance, adaptive functioning, and behavioral/emotional problems in a standardized format by comparing a child's functioning in school to a national sample of same-aged peers.

Decision-Making Applications

The TRF can be used for a variety of purposes, as it compares student functioning to a normative sample of peers. It can be used routinely in virtually all school settings in the referrals of emotional and behavioral problems. This test can be used when teachers become concerned about a student's behavior that has persisted despite the use of interventions (e.g., contacting parents, individual behavior program). The TRF can help determine whether or not the concerns are, indeed, deviant compared to other students of the same age and sex. In addition, the TRF can be used to guide interventions by giving information about which specific areas the child may be having difficulty with. To evaluate the effectiveness of interventions, the TRF can be readministered to assess change as a result of the intervention. Several teachers can complete the TRF on the same child to see if the behavior differs, which provides information about differences in functioning in different settings or possible differences in teachers' standards of judging behavior. Because the TRF has a counterpart test that can be completed by parents (The Child Behavior Checklist), comparisons can be made between parent and teacher ratings to provide information about the child's functioning in these different settings. The TRF can also provide professionals with information that may indicate the need for further evaluation (e.g., the endorsement of many Somatic Complaint items may lead to a medical evaluation).

In addition to its use in schools, the TRF can be used in mental health settings to help determine what kind of services may be most appropriate for a child. It can also be used on a programmatic level, to determine the emotional and behavioral needs of large numbers of students, and to evaluate the effectiveness of such programs.

Relevant Population

The TRF has been designed primarily for teachers to complete on school-age children between the ages of 6 and 18. School personnel, such as guidance counselors, administrators, and special educators who are familiar with the student, can also complete the TRF.

Characteristics Described

The TRF assesses teachers' perceptions of Academic Performance, Adaptive Functioning, and Problem Scales (eight Syndrome Scales, six DSM-criteria scales, Internalizing and Externalizing, and Total Problem Scale).

Academic Performance: Teachers' ratings of the student's grade-level functioning are assessed on a 5-point scale from 1 (far below grade level) to 5 (far above grade level) for all subjects.

Adaptive Functioning: Assesses the student's adaptive behaviors in the areas of working hard, behaving appropriately, learning, and happiness by comparing student behavior in these areas to other students of the same age.

Problem Scales: There are eight syndromes identified by the TRF: Withdrawn/Depressed, Somatic Complaints, Anxious/Depressed, Social Problems, Thought Problems, Attention Problems, Rule-Breaking Behavior, and Aggressive Behavior.

1. Withdrawn/Depressed: This syndrome samples behaviors and qualities relating to isolation, shyness, and lack of participation.
2. Somatic Complaints: Items comprising this syndrome include complaints of physical problems, such as dizziness, aches, and problems with eyes or skin.
3. Anxious/Depressed: This syndrome samples behavioral and emotional responses such as crying, feelings of worthlessness, and worrying.
4. Social Problems: This assesses problems in social relationships, such as being teased, clinging to adults, and acting younger than one's age.
5. Thought Problems: This syndrome samples a variety of strange thoughts and behaviors.
6. Attention Problems: Items comprising this syndrome include difficulties with concentration, fidgeting, and underachieving.
7. Rule-Breaking Behavior: This syndrome assesses conduct problems, such as lying, stealing, and using drugs and alcohol.
8. Aggressive Behavior: These behaviors include verbal and physical aggression, in addition to destroying property.

Three of the syndromes (Withdrawn/Depressed, Somatic Complaints, and Anxious/Depressed) are grouped as Internalizing Problems, as they are more reflective of internal emotional difficulties. Rule-Breaking Behavior and Aggressive Behavior are grouped together as Externalizing Problems, which are more reflective of acting-out, conduct-related difficulties.

In addition, the TRF also includes six scales that reflect categories of mental disorders in the *Diagnostic and Statistical Manual of Mental Disorders*, Fourth Edition (DSM-IV; American Psychiatric Association, 1994). The six DSM-Oriented Scales are Affective Problems, Anxiety Problems, Somatic Problems, Attention Deficit/Hyperactivity Problems (separate scores for Inattention and Hyperactivity-Impulsivity), Oppositional Defiant Problems, and Conduct Problems.

Test Scores Obtained

The TRF provides raw scores, standard T-scores (mean of 50 and standard deviation of 10), and percentiles for Academic Performance, Total Adaptive Functioning, the eight syndrome scales, and the Total Scale. There are separate scores for Inattention and Hyperactivity-Impulsivity subscales of the Attention Problems Scale, and the six DSM-Oriented Scales. Scoring is classified as follows:

Classification for Academic Performance and Adaptive Functioning Scales

Standard T Score	*Classification*
> 40	Normal
37–40	Borderline Clinical
< 37	Clinical

Classification for Syndrome Scales

Standard T-Score	*Classification*
< 65	Normal
65–69	Borderline Clinical
> 69	Clinical

Classification for Total Problems Scores and Internalizing/Externalizing Scores

Standard T Score	*Classification*
< 60	Normal
60–63	Borderline Clinical
> 63	Clinical

Technical Adequacy

Validity Confirmation

Test item validity: Several procedures were used to ensure that the test items developed and selected for the instrument were valid. Items were first selected based on extensive literature searches, collaboration with mental health professionals and special educators, and pilot testing with teachers. The authors of the 2001 revision of the TRF omitted problem items (i.e., those that did not discriminate between referred and nonreferred children) from the previous version of the test (Achenbach, 1991) and replaced them with new items. A statistical technique called factor analysis was used to analyze data from 4,437 students who received high scores on the TRF to create the scales. In addition, the DSM-oriented scales were constructed by having 22 experienced child psychiatrists and psychologists from 16 cultures rate the consistency of the items with DSM-IV categories of mental disorders. Items that were rated "very consistent" by at least 14 of the 22 raters were included in the DSM-oriented scales.

Test response validity: Teachers' responses to the test were validated in several ways. First, the authors compared teachers' ratings on the TRF for 1,543 children who had been referred for mental health or special education services in the past 12 months to teachers' ratings on the TRF for 1,543 children who had not been referred for such services. All of the items of the TRF discriminated significantly between the referred and nonreferred groups of students. Second, the TRF cutpoint scores (e.g., T-score > 69 = Clinical range for Syndrome Scales) were used to determine how accurate these scores were in discriminating referred from nonreferred students. The TRF correctly classified 85% of students as referred or nonreferred based on these clinical cut points. Third, teachers rated children on the TRF and on similar rating scales. Teachers completed the TRF and Conner's Rating Scales for 46 children, yielding correlation coefficients ranging from .77 to .89 between the relevant TRF Syndrome and DSM-Oriented Scales and Conner's subscales. In addition, teachers completed the TRF and the Behavior Assessment System for Children (BASC) for 51 children, and correlations were also moderate to high (ranging from .40 to .87) for comparable subscales.

Reliability Confirmation

The TRF was administered twice to the teachers of 44 students with an average of a 16-day interval between the administrations. The test-retest mean reliability correlations were as follows: .90 for Adaptive Scales, .90 for Syndrome Scales, and .85 for DSM-Oriented Scales. The mean for the Total Problem Scale was .95. To determine how stable the TRF test scores were over a longer period of time, teachers of 22 students receiving special education services for emotional and behavioral problems completed the test over two- and four-month intervals. Over two and four months, respectively, the mean correlations were .70 and .60 on the Syndrome Scales and .62 and .59 on the DSM-Oriented Scales. In addition, one-half of the test item responses were correlated with the other half of the items for 3,086 students, resulting in internal reliability coefficients of .90 for Adaptive Scales, .97 for the Total Problems Scale, and coefficients ranging from .73 to .94 for DSM-Oriented Scales.

Objectivity Confirmation

To ensure accurate ratings, teachers do not complete the TRF unless they have had the child in class for at least two months. For the Adaptive Scales, teachers compare students to typical students of the same age. For the Problem Scales, teachers rate behaviors on a 3-point scale (0 = Not True, 1 = Somewhat or Sometimes True, 2 = Very True or Often True). If a respondent circles more than one number (e.g., 1 and 2), the Manual specifies that the lower number should be scored. If any of the questions on the Adaptive Scales are omitted, a total score should not be calculated. If more than eight items on the rating form itself are left blank, the Syndrome Scales and Total Scale should not be calculated.

In addition, two different teachers rated 88 children referred for mental health and special education services. There was a mean agreement between pairs of teachers of .49 for the Academic and Adaptive Scales, .60 for the Syndrome Scales, and .58 for the DSM-Oriented Scales. Achenbach (1991) also reported on a study using the 1991 version of the TRF where teachers and teacher's aides rated 635 special education students, resulting in mean inter-rater reliability correlations of .60 for Adaptive Scales, .55 for Syndrome Scales, and .57 for Total Problems.

Statistical Confirmation

Extensive information on the reliability, validity, and norms is in the Manual for the Teacher's Report Form and Profile for ages 6 through 18.

Special Features

Acronym

TRF.

Levels of the Test

One.

Number of Test Forms

There is one test form, but there are separate scoring profiles for boys and girls.

Norm-Referenced?

Yes. The TRF was normed on a sample of 2,319 non-referred students. This sample was comprised of all the children from the norm group of the previous version of the TRF (Achenbach, 1991) in addition to 976 students whose teacher ratings were obtained in 1999. The sample was stratified to be representative of a national sample of children in terms of gender, socioeconomic status, ethnicity, and geographic region.

Criterion-Referenced?

No.

Feasibility Considerations

Testing Time

Fifteen to 20 minutes.

For Testing Groups? Individuals?

Individuals.

Test Administration and Scoring

Administration of the TRF is straightforward, with clear instructions provided for teachers on the forms. No training and certification are needed to complete and score the test. Kamphaus and Frick (1996) note that hand scoring can be tedious due to the need to transfer item scores to the separate profile sheet. However, the computer-scoring kit that is now available makes scoring much simpler.

Test Materials and Approximate Costs

The complete starter kit which is used for the TRF, as well as its parent rating counterpart (Child Behavior Checklist, or CBCL) and the self-rating forms (Youth Self-Report, or YSR), costs $325. The kit includes 50 CBCL forms, 50 TRF forms, 50 YSR forms, the Manual for the Achenbach System of Empirically Based Assessment (ASEBA) School-Age Forms and Profiles, and the computer scoring module.

Classic TRF forms for students aged 6–18 cost $25 for 50. Profiles for hand scoring the TRF cost $25 for 50, but these need to be purchased separately for boys and girls. The reusable templates for hand scoring the profiles (same for both genders) are $7, and the TRF DSM-criteria profile (same for both genders) costs $25 for 50. The Manual for the ASEBA School-Age Forms and Profiles costs $35.

Adequacy of Test Manuals

The Manual is comprehensive and well written, and the accompanying forms are easy to use.

Excerpts from Other Test Reviews

Because the newest version of the TRF has only been made available recently, there are no reviews available. However, Elliott and Busse (1992) reviewed the previous version (the CBCL) in *The Eleventh Mental Measurements Yearbook*. They concluded that the TRF is a useful, psychometrically sound instrument for assessing the behavioral functioning of school-aged children. Elliott and Busse also note that the Adaptive Functioning Scale is conceptually weak and that hand scoring can be tedious. Despite these limitations, its psychometric qualities and superior research base make it one of the best teacher rating scales available. Kamphaus and Frick (1996) also note that the TRF is supported by many research studies showing strong associations between the scales and important clinical criteria. They critiqued the norming sample of the 1991 version due to its size and lack of representation, although it should be noted that the 2001 version has a new norm sample, so these criticisms may not apply. Also referring to the previous version of the TRF, Salvia and Ysseldyke (2001, p. 546) describe it as "a well-researched instrument that appears to measure what it is supposed to measure—the overall emotional/behavioral status of children and youth."

Ordering Information

Publisher

Thomas M. Achenbach, Ph.D., Child Behavior Checklist, University Medical Education Associates, 1 South Prospect Street, Room 6434, Burlington, VT 05401-3456; Phone: 802-656-8313; Fax: 802-656-2602; Web site: checklist.uvm.edu.

Authors

Thomas M. Achenbach and Leslie A. Rescorla.

Publication Date

2001.

Cautions and Comments

The TRF is useful in obtaining a differentiated, comprehensive picture of student behavior. It is not intended to be interpreted on its own as a means of inferring children's internal functioning, nor should high scores on certain syndromes suggest that a child should be diagnosed with a disorder based on that information alone. Rather, a qualified professional should integrate the information obtained from the TRF with other sources of data about the student. The authors suggest that the forms be interpreted by persons with knowledge of the theory and methodology of standardized assessment and supervised training in working with the relevant kinds of clients, with graduate training of at least the master's degree level expected. It should be noted that, although the TRF can be used as a stand-alone instrument, the authors promote assessment from multiple sources, such as teachers, parents, and students. The 2001 Manual, which contains information on not only the TRF, but also on the CBCL and the YSR, reflects this and includes methods for comparing results from these different instruments.

These cautions aside, the TRF is an excellent tool to be used by teachers in deciding if students' behaviors warrant a referral. By completing and scoring the TRF, teachers can use the classification system described previously to decide whether a student's behavior differs significantly from that of a normal sample. If the scores for the Academic Performance and Adaptive Functioning, the Syndrome Scales, or the Total Scores fall in "Borderline Clinical" or "Clinical" range (see "Test Scores Obtained" for specific scores), a referral for further testing and/or intervention is indicated.

References

Achenbach, T. M. (1991). *Manual for the Teacher's Report Form and 1991 Profile*. Burlington: University of Vermont Department of Psychiatry.

Achenbach, T. M., & Rescorla, L. A. (2001). *Manual for the ASEBA School-Age Forms and Profiles*. Burlington: University of Vermont, Research Center for Children, Youth, & Families.

American Psychiatric Association. (1994). *Diagnostic and statistical manual of mental disorders* (4th ed.). Washington, DC: Author.

Elliott, S. N., & Busse, R. T. (1992). Review of the Child Behavior Checklist. In J. J. Kramer & J. C. Conoley (Eds.), *The Eleventh Mental Measurements Yearbook* (pp. 166–169). Lincoln, NE: The Buros Institute of Mental Measurements.

Kamphaus, R. W., & Frick, P. J. (1996). *Clinical assessment of child and adolescent personality and behavior*. Boston: Allyn and Bacon.

Salvia, J., & Ysseldyke, J. E. (2001). *Assessment* (8th ed.). Boston: Houghton Mifflin.

Vocational and Educational Interest Tests

Many vocational assessments exist that measure a broad range of constructs. Some assess aptitudes or abilities, others measure personality traits related to different occupations, and still others focus on career maturity, or readiness. The two tests reviewed in this section include the most widely used and well-researched vocational tools that can be used by educators making referrals. These are the Harrington–O'Shea Career Decision-Making System-Revised and the Strong Interest Inventory.

Harrington–O'Shea Career Decision-Making System-Revised (CDM-R),
for testing groups and individuals from middle school age through adulthood
Reviewed by Amanda B. Nickerson, Ph.D., School Psychology

Usefulness of the Test for Educators

Test Authors' Purpose

The CDM-R is a reliable, valid interest inventory that assesses career interests. The comprehensive system surveys interests, stated career choices, school subjects, work values, abilities, and future training plans.

Decision-Making Applications

The CDM-R can be used to help high school students see the need for career exploration and planning and to help them make educational course choices. Another use of the CDM-R is to give basic occupational information. The CDM-R also introduces students to concepts such as work values, interests, and abilities. An additional use is to organize thinking about these various aspects of educational and vocational selection. For more mature students (e.g., grade 11 through college), the CDM-R can be helpful in making choices about college majors, career training, and occupations. It can also be useful for adults who are facing decisions related to career change or those reentering the work worlds after years of absence. The CDM-R can also be used for a variety of research purposes.

Relevant Population

The CDM-R can be used with students between grades 7 and 12. It can also be used for college students and adults. The Level 1 booklet, intended for students in grades 7 through 10, is written at the fourth grade reading level. The Level 2 booklet, intended for eleventh and twelfth grade high school students, college students, and adults, is written at the seventh grade reading level. There is also a Spanish version of the CDM-R.

Characteristics Described

Individuals completing the CDM-R Level 1 booklet are asked to circle "Like," "Not Sure," or "Dislike" in response to 96 items representing six personality types, described in terms of career interests:

Crafts (Realistic): Craftspersons have an interest in mechanical activities, often involving building things. They like to work with tools rather than people, and they are often practical, strong, and reserved. Occupations in this area include auto technician, carpenter, electrician, and cook.

Scientific (Investigative): Scientific persons value mathematics and science, and they tend to be theoretical, studious, and to show a preference for working alone. Occupations include biologist, physician, and architect.

The Arts (Artistic): Persons with high interest in the arts tend to like creative activities, such as music, entertainment, and art. They tend to be independent, sensitive, and expressive. Occupations include musician, writer, artist, and photographer.

Social (Social): Social persons are concerned with the well-being of others. They tend to have strong verbal skills and are often popular and sociable. Careers that suit this type of person include counselor, nurse, teacher, and psychologist.

Business (Enterprising): Businesspersons are often self-confident, verbally persuasive, enthusiastic, and aggressive. They tend to be attracted to careers that allow them to lead others or convince others. Occupations include banker, salesperson, financial planner, and lawyer.

Office Operations (Conventional): Office Operations persons enjoy organized tasks that are clearly defined. They tend to be systematic and dependable, and often place a high value on financial success. Occupations include bank teller, secretary, accountant, and budget analyst.

Individuals completing the CDM-R Level 2 booklet first study 18 career clusters (Manual, Skilled Crafts, Technical, Math-Science, Medical-Dental, Literary, Art, Music, Entertainment, Customer Service, Personal Service, Social Service, Education, Sales, Management, Legal, Clerical, and Data Analysis) and select two that include their current preferences for career choices. They then select from 15 school subject areas the four they prefer most. Next, individuals select the four work values most important to them and their four strongest abilities. They also choose one education or training option that best reflects their future plans. Finally, they complete a 120-item interest inventory of jobs and job-related activities.

Test Scores Obtained

Each of the six career interests yields a raw score ranging from 0 to 32 for Level 1 and from 0 to 40 for Level 2. These raw scores also correspond to percentile ranks, which are divided by gender, type of interest, and level of the test (Level 1 or Level 2). Individuals also rank their school subjects, work values, and education/training plans. Individuals hand score the CDM-R, and the two highest scores obtained on the six career interests are identified as the two highest areas of interest. The CDM-R includes job charts, which are organized according to the six career interest areas. They are further broken down into the 18 career clusters, and information is provided about specific jobs and the school subjects they correspond to, as well as the work values, abilities, and education/training needed (apprenticeship or on-the-job training, vocational or technical programs, four-year college degree, or more). Information is also provided about the job opportunities (excellent, good, fair, poor, or estimate not available).

Technical Adequacy

Validity Confirmation

Test item validity: The CDM-R is based on Holland's theory of vocational development and other research. Therefore, the career interests are based on Holland's six basic personality types: realistic, investigative, artistic, social, enterprising, and conventional. The original CDM and the revised CDM were given to over 2,000 individuals and compared with the results of Holland's Vocational Preference Inventory (VPI), which was administered to 759 individuals. The six scales were correlated with each other, and results were consistent for both the CDM and the VPI. In fact, correlations between the scales were lower for the CDM, suggesting that the scales are unique from each other.

Test response validity: Several studies have been done on the CDM-R and the original CDM to support its usefulness in differentiating between people in different occupations. As mentioned in "test item validity" above, the extent to which the CDM-R reflected Holland's theory, upon which the test was based, was assessed. This was confirmed, evidenced by the relationships of the scales being consistent with Holland's theory and the VPI. Similar results were obtained for a group of 267 Spanish-speaking high school and college students. The CDM and the California Psychological Inventory (CPI) were administered to a group of college females. The CDM scales corresponded to the relevant CPI scales. For example, women in the Investigative group scored higher than women in the Enterprising group on the CPI's scales of Responsibility, Self-Control, Achievement, and Intellectual Efficiency. The Enterprising group scored higher than the Investigative group on Dominance, Social Presence, and Self-Acceptance on the CPI.

Several studies were conducted which involved administering the CDM-R to people in different occupational groups and educational majors. The CDM-R scores of these individuals were highly consistent with other sources of occupational groups and educational majors, such as the Dictionary of Holland Occupational Code and College Major Finders. A three-year follow-up study of 164 individuals who had completed the CDM in ninth grade revealed that two-thirds of the occupational choices were highly congruent with CDM codes and one-third were intermediately congruent. Similarly, college major was highly consistent with CDM-R codes for 73% of the sample. Another follow-up study found that one-third of individuals who had completed the CDM were in predicted occupations five years later, which is comparable to findings with the Strong Vocational Interest Inventory. Finally, the cross-cultural validity of the CDM was assessed by administering the inventory to students from culturally diverse backgrounds. It was found that results of different cultural groups were more alike than different, lending support to the applicability of the CDM-R across diverse groups.

Reliability Confirmation

The Level 1 CDM-R was administered twice to 45 unemployed adults, with a one-month interval between administrations. Test-retest reliability correlations ranged from .74 to .97 for the six interest scales, with a median correlation of .79. The original CDM was administered to 186 individuals, with 30-day intervals between administrations. Median test-retest reliability correlations ranged from .80 to .91. To assess the stability of the CDM over a longer period of time, the CDM was administered twice to 66 college freshmen and 106 high school seniors with five months between administrations. The median test-retest correlations ranged from .75 to .82. In addition, one-half of the items on the CDM-R were compared to the other half of the items for the 1991 standardization sample, yielding a median internal consistency coefficient of .90 for Level 1 subjects and .93 for Level 2 subjects. These results are similar to the median .92 and .94 for the Level 1 and Level 2 of the original CDM. In addition, 267 high school and college students were administered the Spanish CDM, with a median of .87.

Objectivity Confirmation

Studies have been conducted to ensure the accurate scoring of the CMD-R hand-scored versions. The CDM-R Levels 1 and 2 were administered to 230 tenth-grade students in a lower-middle-class high school. Ninety-four percent of the sample arrived at the correct code. In addition, correlations between 536 student-scored tests and author-scored versions of the CDM-R were calculated, yielding median correlations ranging from .98 to .99.

Statistical Confirmation

The Manual provides more information on the reliability and validity of the CDM-R.

Special Features

Acronym

CDM-R.

Levels of the Test

There are two levels of the test. Level 1 is intended for younger students (i.e., grades 7 through 10) and Level 2 is intended for individuals from grade 11 through college.

Number of Test Forms

There are Spanish and English versions of the CDM-R Level 1 and Level 2. In addition, there are hand-scoring booklets and computer-scored versions.

Norm-Referenced?

Yes. The standardization sample for the CDM-R Level 1 consisted of 965 subjects, and the sample for the CDM-R Level 2 consisted of 996 subjects. Samples approximated the 1990 U.S. Census for gender and race. Efforts were made to approximate U.S Census data in terms of geographic region, although there was less representation from the south in the standardization sample for Level 1.

Criterion-Referenced?

No.

Feasibility Considerations

Testing Time

Twenty minutes for Level 1, 30 to 45 minutes for Level 2. It should be noted that these times are the amount of time to complete the CDM-R, but hand scoring and interpretation can take up to two hours.

For Testing Groups? Individuals?

Groups and individuals.

Test Administration and Scoring

The administration of the CDM-R is straightforward, and instructions are clear. The hand scoring of the CDM-R is relatively easy, although "administrators are encouraged to guide clients through the survey and help them score it to ensure accuracy" (Harrington & O'Shea, 2000, p. 8). Individuals with reading or learning difficulties might find the scoring confusing. There is also a computer-scored edition for the Level 2 booklet, which simplifies scoring.

Test Materials and Approximate Costs

The CDM-R is available in classroom sets, which include CDM Booklets and Instruction Folders (25); CES Workbooks (25); Teacher's Guide; and "Tour of Your Tomorrow" Video Series for $399.95 (specify Level 1 or Level 2). A package of 25 Level 1 hand-scored booklets, in English or Spanish, costs $52.95. A package of 25 Level 1 booklets and 25 Interpretive Folders/Directions, in English or Spanish, costs $52.95. The "Tour of Your Tomorrow" Career Videos (set of 6) costs $199.95. The software package, which includes a CD-ROM, Test Manual, and 50 administrations of the CDM-R, for Windows or Macintosh, costs $199.95. A package of 25 Scannable Level 2 forms and 25 Level 2 Interpretive Folders costs $52.95, and the CDM 2000 Manual costs $29.95.

Adequacy of Test Manuals

The Test Manual is thorough and well written. The test booklets are easy to use, and information on interpretation is provided in the booklets. The extensive information provided in the test booklet is one of the strengths of the test. In addition, there is a series of videotapes called "Tour of Your Tomorrow," which includes views of workers in traditional and nontraditional roles in the six career interest areas.

Excerpts from Other Test Reviews

Neubert (1995) reviewed the CDM-R and found the test materials to be comprehensive, with step-by-step, easy-to-follow instructions. She did note, however, that individuals with reading and learning difficulties may need assistance, as the job chart section can be overwhelming. Neubert also cautions that the large majority of the reliability and validity studies were conducted with the original CDM. Schaffer (1995) also found the Manual to be excellent, and characterized the CDM-R as a well-researched instrument with a good theoretical foundation. Although Schaffer reports that the videotaped series was useful, she found it confusing that it tended to jump from one job description to another.

Ordering Information

Publisher

American Guidance Service, Inc.,4201 Woodland Road, Circle Pines, MN 55014-1796; Phone: 800-328-2560; Fax: 800-471-8457; Web site: www.agsnet.com.

Authors

Thomas F. Harrington and Arthur J. O'Shea.

Publication Date

2000.

Cautions and Comments

The CDM-R is a comprehensive instrument to help both adolescents and adults with planning for careers or career changes. The materials are thorough and well-written, and the accompanying interpretation includes job charts, which specify relevant information about different jobs, such as education, personality characteristics, work values, and job opportunities. In addition, a series of videotapes introduces people to the perspectives of workers in different careers. The instrument has a wealth of research that supports its theoretical foundation, reliability, and validity. A unique and desirable feature of the CDM-R is its research on the applicability across diverse cultural groups.

It should be noted that most of the research conducted on the instrument was done with the original version, as opposed to the revised version. Although the versions are very similar, more research needs to be done on the CDM-R. Another potential limitation of the CDM-R is the tendency for the scoring and interpretation to be somewhat confusing for individuals with learning or reading problems. In these cases, it is advised that a career counselor or someone familiar with the CDM-R assist these individuals in scoring and interpretation.

References

Harrington, T. F., & O'Shea, A. J. (2000). *The Harrington–O'Shea Career-Decision Making System Revised Manual.* Circle Pines, MN: American Guidance Service.

Neubert, D. (1995). Review of the Harrington–O'Shea Career Decision-Making System Revised. In J. C. Conoley & J. C. Impara (Eds.), *The Twelfth Mental Measurements Yearbook* (pp. 456–457). Lincoln, NE: The Buros Institute of Mental Measurements.

Schaffer, M. B. (1995). Review of the Harrington–O'Shea Career Decision-Making System Revised. In J. C. Conoley & J. C. Impara (Eds.), *The Twelfth Mental Measurements Yearbook* (p. 457). Lincoln, NE: The Buros Institute of Mental Measurements.

Strong Interest Inventory, Fourth Edition (The Strong),
for testing groups and individuals from 14 years of age through adulthood
Reviewed by Amanda B. Nickerson, Ph.D., School Psychology

Usefulness of the Test for Educators

Test Authors' Purpose

The Strong Inventory is a carefully constructed questionnaire that asks about a person's level of interest on a wide variety of items. These responses are compared to the patterns of responses of people in different occupations. The information obtained can be used to help make assumptions about whether a person is likely to be satisfied in a given occupation.

Decision-Making Applications

The Strong can be used for several different purposes. First, results can aid people in making educational and occupational decisions. Second, the Strong can be used to help people identify preferences for nonwork activities, such as recreational activities. Third, results can guide choices, such as which courses to take to help prepare a student for a given career. Fourth, the inventory can be used to help people who are dissatisfied with their current career to understand the reasons for this dissatisfaction. Fifth, the Strong can be used for research purposes.

Relevant Population

The Strong can be used with a variety of age groups, such as high school students, college students, and adults. It should be administered by a qualified psychologist, counselor, or personnel worker. Respondents should have a grade 8 or 9 reading level and be at least 14 years of age.

Characteristics Described

Individuals completing the Strong are asked to respond by saying "Like," "Indifferent," or "Dislike" to 131 occupations, 36 school subjects, 90 activities, and 24 types of people. They are also given 30 paired activities/occupations and are asked to indicate which one they prefer. In addition, respondents rate how well each of 14 characteristics describe them.

Five types of information are obtained from the Strong Interest Inventory:

1. Occupational Themes: These themes reflect a person's orientation toward work.
2. Basic Interest Scale: This scale measures the consistency of a person's interests or aversions across 25 areas.
3. Occupational Scales: These scales compare the similarities of the respondent's interests to the interests of people in 109 occupations.
4. Personal Style Scales: These scales assess the aspects with which an individual likes to learn.
5. Administrative Indexes: These identify unusual profiles of responses that may deserve special attention.

Test Scores Obtained

The Strong is computer scored and yields an extensive profile for each individual. The profile contains the following information:

Snapshot: There is a one-page snapshot, which is broken down into General Occupational Themes, Basic Interest Scales, and Occupational Scales. Each of these is further broken down (see descriptions under "Characteristics Described").

The profile gives the following ratings for the General Occupational Themes and Basic Interest Scales: Very Little Interest, Little Interest, Average Interest, High Interest, or Very High Interest. The profile for the Occupational Scales yields these ratings: Very Dissimilar, Dissimilar, Mid-range, Similar, Very Similar.

General Occupational Themes and Basic Interest Scales also yield standard T-scores, with a mean of 50 and a standard deviation of 10. Each score is also classified in terms of amount of interest, ranging from Very Little Interest to Very High Interest.

Raw Scores on the Occupational Scales are given and compared to both males and females in each of the occupations. Next, the person's same-gender score is plotted and is on a range from Dissimilar Interests to Similar Interests. Raw scores signify the following:

Score	*Interpretation*
40 and above	Person shares the likes and dislikes of people in that occupation; would probably enjoy this work.
30–39	Person shares some of the likes and/or dislikes of people in that occupation; would enjoy some of this work.
29 and below	Person has few likes and dislikes in common with people in that occupation; would probably not enjoy this work.

Personal Style Scales yield standard T-scores with a mean of 50 and a standard deviation of 10. The higher the score on each personal style, the stronger the person's personal preference for that style.

In addition, the Strong has Administrative Indexes, which yield percentages of "Like," "Indifferent," and "Dislike" scores on several dimensions.

Technical Adequacy

Validity Confirmation

Test item validity: For the 1994 revision of the Strong, a research version of the test (containing all 325 items from the 1985 Strong Interest Inventory plus an additional 54 items) was administered to 55,000 people. The items were analyzed in several ways to decide which should be included and which should be omitted. Any item that was extremely popular or extremely unpopular was omitted, as it would not differentiate well between different occupational groups. Responses of likes and dislikes for old and new items were also compared to determine if the updated wording affected the responses. Items that appeared to contribute to fewer than five scales were also deleted. All items that were considered for deletion were verified with the scales to ensure that the reliability and validity of the scales would not be affected if they were removed. This process resulted in 317 items, which were included in this version of the inventory.

Test response validity: Several studies have been done on this and previous versions of the Strong to support its usefulness in differentiating between people in different occupations. These studies have shown that people in different occupations and with different college majors score differently on the Strong subtests. In addition, the ability of the Strong to predict future careers has been studied, with results indicating that about 59% of both males and females enter careers related to their results on the Strong within a three-year time span.

Reliability Confirmation

Four different samples of people (one sample of employed adults and three samples of college students), with over 400 individuals in total, were administered the Strong two times. The time between administrations ranged from three to six months for the employed adults and one to three months for the college students. Test-retest reliability coefficients ranged from .74 to .92 for Occupational Themes, from .66 to .93 for Basic Interest Scales, from .66 to .93 for Occupational Scales, and from .81 to .92 for Personal Style Scales. In addition, one-half of the items of the Personal Styles Scale were compared to the other half of the items for the general reference sample, yielding internal consistency coefficients ranging from .78 to .91.

Objectivity Confirmation

Because the Strong is based on people's personal preferences, objectivity confirmation is not that relevant. The Strong does compare each person's response to those of both males and females, and the Manual provides extensive information on interpreting unusual results, such as people who have "flat profiles" (i.e., very few "likes") and those who have "elevated profiles" (i.e., many "likes"). In addition, the Strong provides information about how many responses the individual gives that are unusual to aid in interpretation.

Statistical Confirmation

The Manual provides extensive coverage of the development of the Strong Interest Inventory and its reliability, validity, and general reference sample.

Special Features

Acronym

None.

Levels of the Test

One.

Number of Test Forms

The Strong includes (1) an Item Booklet/Answer Sheet, (2) the Strong Profile, and (3) two narrative reports that interpret results.

Norm-Referenced?

Yes. The General Reference Sample consists of 9,484 males and 9,467 females with a mean age of 40 for females and 44 for males. The inventories were sent to people in a variety of occupations, but the sample depended on response rates of these individuals. Therefore, the sample was not stratified.

Criterion-Referenced?

No.

Feasibility Considerations

Testing Time

Thirty-five to 40 minutes.

For Testing Groups? Individuals?

Groups and individuals.

Test Administration and Scoring

The administration of the Strong is fairly straightforward, and the respondent needs a number 2 pencil to complete the scannable sheet. All response sheets are sent away to the publisher's scoring center to be scored. No specialized training is needed, although the Strong should be administered by a qualified psychologist, counselor, or personnel worker.

Test Materials and Approximate Costs

The Strong Application and Technical Guide costs $72, and the prepaid Strong Profiles, which include combined Item Booklet/Answer Sheets for mail-in scoring, cost $75 for a package of 10.

Adequacy of Test Manuals

The test materials are thorough and well organized. The profile provides useful information in numeric, graphical, and narrative formats. The Manual and User's Guide are recognized as being outstanding.

Excerpts from Other Test Reviews

Busch (1995) notes that the Strong has been used for over 60 years and that it has gone through continual evaluation and revision during that time period. There is a considerable research base to support its use, and Busch states that the Strong "more than satisfies the standards for tests . . . that have been set by the profession" (p. 998). He particularly calls attention to the ability of the profile to provide information to clients in a clear and understandable format. Worthen and Sailor (1995, p. 1002) describe the Strong as "by far the best available interest inventory." They point out that the Manual and User's Guide are excellent. However, all of the aforementioned reviewers point out the limitations of the normative sample, which was subject to volunteer bias. Because individuals in various occupational groups were sent the Strong, the sample was based on the data from those who returned it, making it a nonrepresentative sample. It is also important to note that women and men differ considerably in their responses to about one-third of the items, making it very important to use separate scales and norms for each sex.

Ordering Information

Publisher

Consulting Psychologists Press, 3803 East Bayshore Road, Palo Alto, CA 94303; Phone: 800-624-1765; Fax: 650-969-8608; Web site: www.cpp-db.com.

Authors

Lenore W. Harmon, Jo-Ida C. Hansen, Fred H. Borgen, and Allen L. Hammer.

Publication Date

1994.

Cautions and Comments

The Strong is regarded as the best choice of instrument to assess an individual's interests and preferences, which can be helpful in making career choices. The instrument has a long history of use and has been revised and updated several times. The Strong also has a comprehensive and impressive research base, which supports its reliability and validity.

Although students can complete the Strong, it may be difficult for individuals with learning or other problems to complete, as an eighth to ninth grade reading level is required. The scored profile conveys the information in a clear and understandable format, although a qualified psychologist, counselor, or personnel worker should guide students through the results to help them make decisions about future educational and vocational planning.

References

Busch, J. C. (1995). Review of the Strong Interest Inventory (4th ed.). In J. C. Conoley & J. C. Impara (Eds.), *The Twelfth Mental Measurements Yearbook* (pp. 997–999). Lincoln, NE: The Buros Institute of Mental Measurements.

Harmon, L. W., Hansen, J. C., Borgen, F. H., & Hammer, A. L. (1994). *Strong Interest Inventory: Applications and Technical Guide*. Palo Alto, CA: Consulting Psychologists Press.

Worthen, B. R., & Sailor, P. (1995). Review of the Strong Interest Inventory (4th ed.). In J. C. Conoley & J. C. Impara (Eds.), *The Twelfth Mental Measurements Yearbook* (pp. 999–1002). Lincoln, NE: The Buros Institute of Mental Measurements.

KEY REFERRAL INDICATORS

This section summarizes the preceding sections by highlighting some of the most important indicators for referrals. Indicators include important observable signs of the various types of problems and rules of thumb to use in interpreting informal and formal testing procedures for the purposes of making a referral.

Vision Impairment

Persistent abnormalities in the appearance of a student's eye or eyes, such as crossed eyes or red, watery eyes, are signs that a child should be referred for follow-up. In addition, consistent problems associated with particular vision-related tasks (e.g., paperwork, copying from the blackboard) may indicate the need for a referral. Examples of these problems may include complaints of headaches or blurred vision, or behaviors, such as covering one eye or squinting when engaging in these activities.

The educator who wishes to further substantiate his or her suspicions about a child's vision problems can administer the Denver Eye Screening Test or the Visual Skills Appraisal. Each of these instruments clearly states the scoring criteria that indicate the need for a referral. This information can be found under "Test Scores Obtained" and also is summarized under the "Cautions and Comments" section of these test reviews.

Hearing Impairment

Key indicators of hearing or auditory problems include a student's consistent lack of response or inappropriate response to someone else who is speaking. Another clue to a hearing problem is a child who appears to hear certain kinds of voices better than others and appears to understand more when the teacher stands close to him or her, as opposed to standing across the classroom.

The educator can also complete an informal checklist, such as the Observational Profile of Classroom Communication, to gather further data about the child's auditory response to classroom stimuli. Although many formal tests of hearing and auditory processing are typically administered by school nurses and/or speech and language clinicians, the educator can use a test such as the Test of Auditory-Perceptual Skills-Revised to assess a child's auditory processing. If the student receives a score one or more standard deviations below the mean (e.g., < 85), the teacher should make a referral for further evaluation.

Perceptual-Motor or Motor Impairment

For educators working with children prior to the formal schooling years, failure of a child to meet age-appropriate developmental milestones for motor skills may indicate the need for follow-up. For example, an 18-month-old child who is not yet walking should be referred for further evaluation. For older children, persistent motor coordination difficulties, such as taking much longer than the average child of the same age to perform motor tasks (e.g., copying from the board, buttoning a coat), may indicate the need for a referral. In addition, a student who makes persistent errors when copying or writing (e.g., spacing problems, rotated letters), especially if he or she does not recognize the errors or improve them when attention is called to them, may need special attention to better understand the nature of the problem.

Educators who are familiar with motor skills, such as physical education teachers, are in an excellent position to use standardized tests such as the Bruininks-Oseretsky Test of Motor Proficiency and the Test of Gross Motor Development: Second Edition to assess the child's fine and gross motor skills as compared to average children of the same age. The educator who is concerned about the child's perceptual-motor skills, such as copying and writing, may administer standardized tests such as the Developmental Test of Visual-Motor Integration (4th Edition, Revised) and the Test of Visual-Motor Integration. Guidelines for making referrals are provided in the "Cautions and Comments" section of each review.

Adaptive Behavior Deficits

Because adaptive behavior is so closely tied to child development and age-related expectations for performance, the most useful way for educators to assess a student's adaptive behavior is by observing the child's skills in relation to same-aged peers. A child who is consistently delayed in two or more areas, as evidenced by doing things much slower, less frequently, or in a less competent way than peers, should be referred for further evaluation.

The 10 areas of adaptive skills that are recognized by the American Association on Mental Retardation (1992) are communication, self-care, home living, social skills, community use, self-direction, health and safety, functional academics, leisure, and work. A teacher interested in gathering more information on these areas could use Sattler's (2002) informal checklist for adaptive behavior. If an educator desires further corroboration for the existence of adaptive behavior deficits, he or she could complete one of the standardized rating scales of adaptive behavior reviewed in this chapter. A good rule of thumb is that a child who scores "Below Average" or lower on two or more areas of adaptive behavior should be assessed further.

Problem Behavior

Pervasive problems that interfere with a child's learning, either of an internalizing (directed inward) or externalizing (directed outward) nature that go beyond the typical problems of the average child, may be cause for a referral. Signs of internalizing problems that are noteworthy include a child's avoidance of or withdrawal from academic and social activities that goes beyond personality characteristics, such as shyness. In addition, a child who cries often or frequently complains of physical problems, such as headaches or stomachaches, may need further attention. Externalizing behaviors, which are often very easy to detect given their disruptive nature, include persistent defiance or refusal to follow directions, destruction of property, and verbal and physical aggression.

An educator's careful observation and accurate recording of these behaviors can be very useful to professionals who evaluate for the presence of possible emotional and behavioral problems. Examples of observational methods to use, such as narrative recording and frequency recording, are contained in Chapter 10, "Observable Manifestations and Observational Assessments." In addition, using standardized behavior rating scales, such as those described in this chapter, can be helpful in determining which problems occur more frequently than would be expected in an average child of the same age and gender. Educators should refer to the "Cautions and Comments" section of each test review to determine which scores on these instruments indicate the need for a referral for further evaluation.

Vocational Referrals

Making referrals for further educational and/or vocational planning typically occurs in high school, although planning can certainly be done for students in earlier grades. Students with documented disabilities, such as those receiving special education services, are required by federal law to have a transition plan, including vocational planning, at least by the age of 16. An obvious implication of this is that educators working as part of the multidisciplinary team for students with disabilities should be aware of this requirement and help the student plan accordingly.

Educators can help students with these plans by informally or formally assessing the student's interests, personality traits, skills and aptitudes, and preferences for certain types of careers. There are several informal tests available on the Web, in addition to formal published tests, such as the Strong Interest Inventory and the Harrington–O'Shea Career Decision-Making System Revised, which can be administered to students. Results will be helpful to the student, his or her parents, guidance counselors, transition coordinators, and others who can be of further assistance in planning for the child's future.

REFERENCES

Adler, S. (1988). An introduction to communicative behavior. In S. Adler (Ed.), *Oral communication problems in children and adolescents* (pp. 3–7). Philadelphia: Grune and Stratton.

Algozzine, B., Christenson, S., & Ysseldyke, J. (1982). Probabilities associated with the referral to placement process. *Teacher Education and Special Education 5*(3), 19–23.

American Association on Mental Retardation. (1992). *Mental retardation: Definition, classification, and system of supports* (9th ed.). Washington, DC: Author.

Birnbaum, M. H. (1993). Vision disorders frequently interfere with reading and learning: They should be diagnosed and treated. *Journal of Behavioral Optometry 4*(3), 66–71.

Busby, R. A. (1985). Vision development in the classroom. *Journal of Learning Disabilities 18*, 266–272.

Carter, J., & Sugai, G. (1989). Survey on prereferral practices: Responses from state departments of education. *Exceptional Children 55*(4), 298–302.

Christenson, S., Ysseldyke, J., & Algozzine, B. (1982). Institutional constraints and external pressures influencing referral decisions. *Psychology in the Schools 19*, 341–345.

de La Paz, S., & Graham, S. (1995). Screening for special diagnoses. In ERIC Digest [online]. Available: http://ericae.net/edo/ed389965.htm.

Diefendorf, A. O., & Leverett, R. G. (1988). Hearing impairment in children: Causation, assessment, and treatment. In S. Adler (Ed.), *Oral communication problems in children and adolescents* (pp. 127–149). Philadelphia: Grune and Stratton.

Gersten, C. R. (1997). Detecting potential hearing problems in young children. *Healthy Child Care America 1*(3), 3–4.

Green, N. S. (2000). The vision connection to learning charts [online]. Available: http://www.kidcite.net/vision_connect.htm.

Hammer, L. R., Shimada, L. M., & Hoffman, L. G. (1988). Teacher awareness of the role of vision therapy in the child with learning problems. *Journal of Optometric Vision Development 19*(3), 6–12.

Harrison, P. L. (1985). *Vineland Adaptive Behavior Rating Scales: Classroom Edition Manual.* Circle Pines, MN: American Guidance Service.

Hoffman, L. G. (1980). Incidence of vision difficulties in children with learning disabilities. *Journal of the American Optometric Association 51*(5), 447–451.

Horn, E., & Fuchs, D. (1987). Using adaptive behavior in assessment and intervention: An overview. *The Journal of Special Education 21*(1), 11–26.

Hritchko, T. (1983). Assessment of children with low vision. In R. T. Jose (Ed.), *Understanding low vision* (pp. 105–137). New York: American Foundation for the Blind.

Jose, R. T. (1983). Minimum assessment sequence: The optometrist's viewpoint. In R. T. Jose (Ed.), *Understanding low vision* (pp. 75–83). New York: American Foundation for the Blind.

Katz, J., & Masters, M. G. (2000, October). *Central auditory processing: A coherent approach.* Workshop presented at the United Cerebral Palsy of Philadelphia and Vicinity, Philadelphia, PA.

Levinson, E. M. (1995). Best practices in vocational assessment in the schools. In A. Thomas & J. Grimes (Eds.), *Best practices in school psychology—III* (pp. 741–751). Washington, DC: National Association of School Psychologists.

Menchetti, B. M., & Flynn, C. C. (1990). Vocational evaluation. In F. R. Rusch (Ed.), *Supported employment: Models, methods, and issues* (pp. 111–130). Sycamore, IL: Sycamore Publishing.

Mooney, C., & Algozzine, B. (1978). A comparison of the disturbingness of behaviors related to learning disability and emotional disturbance. *Journal of Abnormal Child Psychology 6*(3), 401–406.

Murdoch, H. (1994). "He can hear when he wants to!" Assessment of hearing function for people with learning difficulties. *British Journal of Learning Disabilities 22*, 85–89.

North Carolina State Occupational Information Coordinating Committee. (2001). Holland Occupational Themes [online]. Available: http://jobs.esc.state.nc.us/soicc/planning/c1a.htm.

Optometric Extension Program Foundation. (1985). Educator's guide to classroom vision problems [online]. Available: http://www.healthy.net/oep/educate.htm.

Optometric Extension Program Foundation. (1998). *When a bright child has trouble reading.* Santa Ana, CA: Author.

Royal National Institute for the Blind. (n.d.). Looking for hearing problems in people with learning difficulties: What to look for [online]. Available: http://www.rnib.org.uk/multdis/hearing.htm.

Safran, S. P., & Safran, J. S. (1984). Elementary teachers' tolerance of problem behaviors. *Elementary School Journal 85*(2), 237–243.

Salvia, J., & Ysseldyke, J. E. (2001). *Assessment* (8th ed.). Boston: Houghton Mifflin.

Sanger, D. D. (1986). *Observational profile of classroom communication.* Lincoln: University of Nebraska.

Sattler, J. M. (2002). *Assessment of children: Behavioral and clinical applications* (4th ed.). San Diego: Author.

Silverman, W. K., & Serafini, L. T. (1998). Assessment of child behavior problems: Internalizing disorders. In A. S. Bellack & M. Hersen (Eds.), *Behavioral assessment: A practical handbook* (4th ed., pp. 342–360). Boston: Allyn and Bacon.

Stewart, J. M., Hester, E. J., & Taylor, O. L. (1986). Prevalence of language, speech, and hearing disorders in an urban preschool black population. *Journal of Childhood Communication Disorders 9*(2), 107–123.

Walker, H. M., Severson, H. H., Todis, B. J., Block-Pedego, A. E., Williams, G. J., Haring, N. G., & Barckley, M. (1990). Systematic screening for behavior disorders (SSBD): Further validation, replication, and normative data. *Remedial and Special Education 11*(2), 32–46.

Witt, J. C., Elliott, S. N., Daly, E. J., Gresham, F. M., & Kramer, J. J. (1998). *Assessment of at-risk and special needs children* (2nd ed.). Boston: McGraw-Hill.

VI

Criteria for Evaluating Educational Practices

Jacqueline E. Jacobs, Ph.D.,
Special Education and Higher Education Administration

INTRODUCTION

Noted educator Phillip Schlechty says, "We're the best we've ever been, at doing what we've always done." This statement speaks as much to where we have been in education as to where we are going. Much of what drives student achievement is based in the people who teach and the programs they use. Yet, the use of evaluation to measure student achievement, teacher performance, and program effectiveness continues to generate much debate and discussion. There are many fine textbooks written on both personnel and program evaluation, and most higher education school administration programs require a course that involves personnel and program evaluation.

So, why does evaluation continue to be an area that is left to chance, developed by people who are overloaded with other responsibilities, or created by a committee with little or no background or expertise in evaluation? Perhaps it is because there is little interest on the part of administrators in the evaluation process (Wiles & Bondi, 2000), except, perhaps, when needed to support personnel dismissal or when required to defend a program that some educators, parents, or politicians support and like (or want to eliminate). Or, more likely, it is because the human resources are so stretched in most school districts that evaluation is viewed as a luxury that cannot be supported by time or finances. It is the purpose of this part of the handbook to address the importance of evaluation to teaching and learning, to address the important components of an evaluation procedure or instruments, to address the sources and derivations of evaluation criteria, and to provide a framework for standards and criteria in personnel and program evaluation which should be considered in the development of an evaluation plan.

THE IMPORTANCE OF EVALUATION TO TEACHING AND LEARNING

Student achievement should be the goal of every educator, faculty group, school district administrative group, and school board. It is certainly the expectation of parents, community members, and politicians. Student achievement is generally addressed, albeit with much controversy, by some standardized test performance. This may include state-normed achievement tests, nationally normed achievement tests, and nationally normed entrance exams. Clearly, student performance on an achievement test is the action and responsibility of the student. However, unless it is assumed that what the student knows, as measured on an achievement test, is solely the responsibility of the student, it is unrealistic that evaluation of student achievement continues to be measured by the student's performance on an achievement test alone. There are any number of evaluations that can and should contribute to the determination of what constitutes student achievement and even accountability. Currently, in many states, accountability legislation is based on state or national achievement tests. However, there is no clear evidence that *personal characteristics* of teachers make a difference in student achievement (Fox & Peck, 1978), so quality measures of effective teacher *performance* must be used. There is research evidence that certain teaching behaviors positively affect student learning (Friedman, 2000), thus making clear that it is important to have measures of teachers that measure those behaviors.

The development of standards for teacher performance, such as the National Board of Professional Teacher Standards (NBPTS), provides the possibility, for example, to compare teacher performance to student test scores. Likewise, the substantive work of Friedman (2000) presents extensive research evidence identifying 15 effective teaching strategies. Each of these can be used to develop an evaluation system that compares the performance of teachers to student achievement, which administrators could use to assess the teaching/learning process, particularly through observation by self and peers. Yet administrators spend very little time in classrooms, often only observe teachers teach once a year, and rarely create and support a collegial environment that fosters an inquiry approach to instruction.

The importance of an inquiry approach to instruction rests in the need to continually evaluate lessons, curriculum, programs, and instructional strategies. There are many ways in which evaluation can and does occur in schools, but little of it is systematic and in the majority of schools the people who could foster and develop such a view of evaluation are not available or do not have time, given the limited human resources most schools have. When the focus of a school or district is on inquiry, the stress of being "right" is lessened because the inquiry perspective means that all matters are open to question and subject to objective observation and constructive feedback.

In an atmosphere of inquiry, evaluation can become a systematic way of providing support for teachers in the instructional process and a valid and reliable measure of the usefulness of programs in meeting the learning needs of students. The design of the evaluation procedure or instrument is important to the usefulness of the information or data gathered. The objectivity of the evaluator and the use(s) to which the evaluation is put are also important.

Whether considering evaluation of educational personnel or programs, the purpose of evaluation should be to improve student achievement through the use of appropriate instructional strategies and programs. The components of an evaluation process will determine the usefulness of the information gathered.

IMPORTANT COMPONENTS OF AN EVALUATION PROCEDURE OR INSTRUMENTS

The most important part of any evaluation procedure is the development and application of an evaluation plan. The plan may be as simple as analyzing data on a specific issue or topic, such as student discipline referrals to the office, or as complex as a longitudinal study of the impact of a specific program on student achievement as measured by a standardized test. If we consider the first example, it may arise from the frustration of a principal in seeing so many students for discipline referrals. Given the frustration level, having the actual data may or may not lead to a solution. However, failure to examine the data may certainly lead to mistakes in addressing the issue. The second example, while perhaps more complex to develop and conduct, may have equally grave considerations for decisions regarding personnel, costs, cost-benefit, public opinion, and so forth. In either case, objective consideration regarding what and how to evaluate the issue is paramount to the successful outcome of the use of the information acquired.

Evaluation plans can be reasoned by the people involved or can follow specific guidelines that may be found in a number of evaluation texts. The Joint Committee on Standards for Educational Evaluation (JCSEE) provides a framework for evaluating both personnel and program evaluation. According to the JCSEE, every evaluation plan should address the criteria of *propriety*, *utility*, *feasibility*, and *accuracy*.

The development of an evaluation plan will need to be based on specific criteria. These criteria may be taken from the standards established by various professional groups and organizations and/or based on evidence available from research. The standards may subsume state or district criteria, such as a district's curriculum for science that is built on the national standards for science education, or such as the research-based effective teaching strategies mentioned earlier. The evaluation itself, however, may be conducted in any of a number of formats.

The evaluations that yield quantitative data will generally use some sort of scale (e.g., a rating scale, Likert or Likert-like scale, or checklist). These scales provide a numerical value that is then analyzed and data is reported based on the value given in the scale. In quantitative analysis there is generally not an interpretation given to the data. That is, the evaluator will report the information based on statistical analyses, but will generally not speculate as to *why* the results were as obtained.

In qualitative analyses, information is gathered through such things as observation notes, interviews, and focus groups. The reporting of this information may be in any number of formats. For example, there may be a listing of responses, a reporting of patterns of responses, a narrative explanation based on the responses, and so forth. One of the purposes of qualitative analysis is to allow the evaluator to gather evidence to try and explain what is happening, in this case in the learning environment.

While an evaluation may involve a combination of quantitative and qualitative methods, the decision of what form of analysis to use should be made during the design phase of the evaluation plan or in the design of the evaluation procedure or instrument.

SOURCES AND DERIVATIONS OF EVALUATION CRITERIA

A professional group or organization, as mentioned earlier, frequently establishes standards on which other groups (e.g., state departments of education or school districts) base both personnel and program evaluations. Curricula are often developed from these standards and frequently provide a basis for the development of evaluation instruments and/or evaluation plans.

An important consideration for the curriculum or evaluation developer is to consider the techniques used to develop the standards. In the 1990s there was a national movement to establish standards in curriculum, teaching, and administration. The major professional groups with interests in each of these areas joined, or in some cases led, the movement, and as a result there are now standards for teaching (e.g., the National Board of Professional Teaching Standards—NBPTS), for curriculum (e.g., the National Council of Teachers of Mathematics—NCTM), and for administration (e.g., the Interstate School Leaders Licensure Consortium—ISLLC). The way in which these standards have been developed differs by group or organization.

A common practice for the development of standards, whether by professional organizations or policy groups, is the use of expert opinion. In general, the organization will call on specific respected individuals or solicit volunteers from school-level and university-level faculty and administrators to serve on a committee. In most instances, these individuals will serve as the steering committee and may, in fact, be personally involved in some writing for the standards. Sometimes there will be subcommittees, depending on the breadth of the standards and the supporting materials (e.g., the NCTM provides supporting principles for each of the mathematics standards). Once standards have been drafted, most professional organizations broadly disseminate the standards in draft form and solicit feedback from their membership and perhaps others who have an interest in the standards for that group. This input is considered, revisions are made as needed, and the final draft of the standards is generally taken before the general meeting of the organization for approval. In some cases, the Board of the organization may have final approval. The organization then usually takes responsibility for disseminating the standards to state departments of education, school districts, and their organizational members.

One of the considerations regarding the use of organizational standards in the evaluation process is that the standards are often broad, sometimes contain multiple concepts or ideas, and may not have discrete elements that are identifiable or measurable. It is important for the evaluator to consider the role of the standards in the particular evaluation being undertaken and to discuss with those for whom the evaluation is being conducted their goal in the evaluation process. It is worth noting that while standards development through this organizational process is generally thorough and based on the best knowledge available from those who participate, it is not always based on research evidence.

The role of research in the development of standards in the last decade has been mixed, and more often than not rests in the knowledge base of those contributing to the standards rather than specifically driving the development and wording of the standards. This serves as a caution in the interpretation of standards and any evaluation based on them because the techniques, which are available for determining the usefulness and applicability of the knowledge from research, may not have been employed in the development of the standards.

The nature of research in education is that it is often narrow in focus as the researcher tries to determine the impact of some phenomenon or to explain the effects of some condition. Therefore, having one specific piece of research that can be used to create standards for the range of education in even one specific curriculum area, for example, is impossible. Later in Part VI a number of topical issues in education are presented, with evidence from research on which evaluations can be planned. Derivation of the evidence, the evidence, and cautions and comments are provided.

There are several techniques that can be employed to determine if the available research evidence supports a practice, or outcome, that may be a part of any given set of standards. Through a technique known as meta-analysis, it is possible to consider various research studies and their applicability to the standard being developed or the evaluation technique being used.

In meta-analysis, multiple studies on a topic that appear to support the same position may be analyzed through either a statistical analysis or comparative review to confirm the efficacy of the position. For example, in the work done by Friedman and Fisher (1998), meta-analysis was used to determine the 15 effective instructional practices presented. Each of the instructional practices was described from a meta-analysis of 50 to 200 research studies that support the efficacy of the practice.

When determining which strategies have been used to develop standards, if there is no evidence of a meta-analysis, another technique that may be used to compromise between the challenge of the lack of a specific piece of research being available to drive the development of standards and the use of a committee-of-experts process is the Delphi Technique.

The Delphi Technique, based on a three-step process of thesis, antithesis, and synthesis, has been used to gather the opinions of experts and ultimately lead to the development of an evaluation process or product. One example of this technique is illustrated by the work of Lempesis (1984) to determine the important competencies for effective department leaders in secondary schools. After a comprehensive review of the literature to determine what research showed about the competencies described as being important for department leaders in secondary schools, an opinionnaire was sent to principals to rate each of the competencies (thesis) on a 1-to-5 interval scale. This information was analyzed, and then a second round asked the principals who had returned the first opinionnaire to consider their response and the most common response from all responders. In this round (antithesis) the principals were asked to comment if they chose to remain with their original response or chose to select yet a different one than their original or the group response. In the final round (synthesis), the principals were provided second round anonymous comments and their response, along with the most common response. The principals were asked to consider all of this and to indicate their final response for each competency. This technique combined the use of research in the identification of the original competencies and the assessment and analysis of these competencies by experts in the field. And while this particular study was designed to determine what experts viewed as being the most important competencies for a department leader in a secondary school, it would be possible to then take this information and conduct an evaluation (for example, to determine whether department leaders in a given school district demonstrate those competencies).

Thus, it is evident that the evaluator will need to be well informed of the basis for the development of the standards and may need to determine what research has been done relative to the standards and their impact. Whether developing standards by a committee of experts, from reviewing the literature, from a meta-analysis, or through a method such as the Delphi Technique, it is important in the evaluation process to remember that understanding the derivation of the standards used is critical to the development of a good, objective evaluation plan.

A FRAMEWORK FOR STANDARDS AND CRITERIA IN PERSONNEL AND PROGRAM EVALUATION

Objectivity is one of the most important considerations in any evaluation plan. Objectivity is assured in a number of ways. First, the credibility of the evaluator is paramount in this assurance and should be determined by anyone using the information from an evaluation. Frequently educators rely on limited information, often provided by those supporting or opposing the program, or observation of a limited aspect of a person's job in evaluating programs and personnel. An assistant superintendent for business and finance recently commented, "It is amazing to me that we continue to pay large sums of money for programs without any consideration for whether they are contributing to the academic achievement of *our* students."

The procedures for determining that there is objectivity in an evaluator will differ based on the type of evaluation (i.e., program or personnel) being conducted. In program evaluation, one will generally determine that the evaluator has the academic and work credentials to conduct evaluations and will check references to determine the value of the evaluations conducted for others. In some larger districts, program evaluators may be part of the district staff. These people are usually hired with credentials that support their knowledge and ability to do research and evaluation. While these individuals may assist in personnel evaluation, they will usually assist in the development of instrumentation and address issues of reliability and validity. In personnel evaluation or assessment of implementation of standards, a number of practices need to be in place to ensure objectivity. First, one cannot assume that everyone who conducts evaluations is objective. As presented earlier, without frequent visits to a classroom on the part of administrators, and without the use of an evaluation instrument that has agreement among evaluators showing that the same practices are being measured, it is difficult to ensure objectivity. Frequently judgments are required in the observations and documentation that lead to an evaluation of personnel (e.g., teachers). Training and certification that the evaluators are looking for the same behaviors, or evidence, when judging practice is critical. The training should include knowledge of how to observe and record or document the effective practice; it should also provide opportunities for those who will serve as evaluators to compare the effective practice to criteria in order to judge conformity to the criteria. The technique most frequently employed to assess the degree to which evaluators agree is inter-observer agreement. That is, do multiple observers record the same information based on the observation or demonstration of a specific practice? The more closely aligned inter-observer agreement is, the more likely the criterion for the observed behavior is adequately defined.

Whether it is the evaluation of an individual's performance (e.g., a teacher's evaluation) or the evaluation of a program (e.g., a specialized reading program), the credibility of the evaluator will contribute greatly to the reliability of the information obtained.

Second, the standards and criteria used to develop the evaluation instrument or process must provide for objectivity. Part VI provides a listing of standards for personnel and program evaluation that are currently available and addresses the derivation of the criteria, as well as the criteria or standards themselves, and provides some cautions and comments. A state department of education, district, or school, in order to develop curricula from which to teach, may have used these standards. The standards would then be part of the framework for developing an evaluation plan for curriculum and instruction in that district. As cautioned earlier, the multiple concepts covered in some standards will require the evaluator to ensure which aspects are to be evaluated in order to develop a useful evaluation plan. Additionally, because many of the criteria are not defined in terms of observable behaviors, it will be important for evaluators to determine if the organization which developed the standards has elaborated on the criteria to provide observable behaviors, or whether they will need to be developed. Without clear understanding of the expected behaviors, it is unlikely that evaluators will be able to give feedback to a teacher (for example, on what he/she needs to do to demonstrate that the known effective practices are leading to the desired standards of learning and teaching). The more precise a personnel evaluator can be in providing feedback and the greater reliability there is that any evaluator in a system (e.g., principals) will look for the same observable behaviors to ensure best practice, the more confidence there will be in the objectivity of the evaluation and the greater the likelihood that the evaluation system will lead to improved student achievement through teaching with best practices.

Finally, giving consideration to the criteria set forth by the JCSEE in assessing the quality of an evaluation instrument or procedure will contribute to the objectivity brought to the evaluation process. Evaluators, whether evaluating programs or personnel, must have clearly defined observable criteria in order to ensure objectivity so that they can determine that the program or teacher practice conforms to the specified criterion.

CONSIDERATIONS IN ESTABLISHING AND EVALUATING EVIDENCE-BASED CRITERIA IN PERSONNEL EVALUATION

Blumberg (1987) addressed a major issue in the evaluation of personnel in public schools, stating that schools are "institutions premised on having mature, competent adults as employees, yet treating these same adults as children when it comes to deciding and operationalizing their work." In determining the process and purpose of evaluation of school personnel, it is important to consider the large number of research studies contributing to the knowledge base of what constitutes effective personnel performance in schools, particularly by administrators and teachers. These studies provide a sound basis for consideration in the development and use of personnel evaluation. For example, the most important role of a principal is generally considered to be that of instructional leader (Edmonds, 1979; Good & Brophy, 1985), and there are studies which show that administrators have an effect on student achievement (Hart & Ogawa, 1987). Since there appears to be no uniform agreement on the definition of the word *instruction* (Council of Professors of Instructional Supervision, 1988), what can be defined as effective teaching and instructional improvement must be done within the context of particular instructional goals (Glickman, Gordon, & Ross-Gordon, 2001). So, if the role of principal is to be evaluated relative to instructional impact, it is important that what the principal actually *does* related to instruction be measured as part of any evaluation system. This may be done in a number of ways, but examples include surveys of teachers and/or observation of actual performance. In the use of observation for evaluation, it is important to use specific behaviors from research (e.g., the principal sets and monitors high expectations for student achievement) (Edmonds, 1979) with identifiable evidence of behaviors (e.g., the principal discusses high expectations with faculty) or artifacts (e.g., faculty newsletters show evidence of the principal's attention to high expectations through quotes from experts to remind teachers of this vision). Likewise, teacher evaluation can be developed through evidence of performance. Joyce, Showers, and Rolheiser-Bennett (1987) did an extensive review of research based on experimentally tested instructional strategies and programs and identified those that had the highest likelihood of impact on student achievement (e.g., cooperative learning). In the synthesis provided of research on 15 effective instructional practices (Friedman & Fisher, 1998), the practices are identified, along with tactics that, if present in a teacher's performance, provide evidence the teacher is using those practices that are most likely to have a positive impact on student achievement. Through the development of teacher evaluation systems using research-based evidence, it is possible both to assess whether teachers are using the best practices (e.g., through observation of behaviors and artifacts) and to create staff development programs to ensure that teachers are trained in those practices that do work.

Cautions that apply in the assessment strategies mentioned include such things as the need to provide anonymity for the survey completers so that their responses have a higher probability of being honest (for example, the teacher is not concerned that his/her *own* evaluation will be affected by how he/she completes the survey). Additionally, as administrators create change in an environment, the perceptions of them by teachers are likely to be affected by fear of the unknown. Thus, surveys over several years will provide the evaluator with a more reliable assessment of the administrator's impact on the instructional process as perceived by teachers. When observation is used in personnel evaluation, it is necessary to ensure that there are multiple observers (e.g., an administrator and a peer) to provide for inter-observer agreement considerations, and multiple observations to provide a more reliable assessment of the behavior.

The use of specific evidence (as identified in the research as providing effective instruction and leadership) in the evaluation of school personnel should lead to more meaningful evaluation of teachers and principals. And, more important, when teachers and administrators know what is expected of them and that the practices identified will make them more successful, they will be much more likely to seek ways to learn and use the practices.

CONSIDERATIONS IN ESTABLISHING AND EVALUATING EVIDENCE-BASED CRITERIA REGARDING SEXISM AND RACISM

An issue of longstanding concern in education is that of sexism and racism with respect to curricular programs, student achievement, and hiring and retention practices of school personnel. Because much of the research in education has been done on white males (Shakeshaft, Campbell, & Karp, 1992), concerns have been raised that the ability to generalize the findings to girls/women and people of color and different ethnic groups limits our ability to determine whether the effects would be the same on these other groups.

This evidence supports the need for ensuring that evaluations of programs and personnel in schools do not allow the limitation of sampling only one group, unless the evaluation is to determine the effects *only* on that group. For example, in program evaluation, studies have been done on the academic achievement of girls of African-American heritage in middle school science achievement. This level of specificity lets the reader know that while it may be possible to generalize the results to girls of African-American heritage in middle school science in other places than where the research was conducted, it may not be representative of boys of African-American heritage in middle school science achievement. If, on the other hand, a meta-analysis (explained in the introduction) has been done on numerous studies of middle-school science achievement and results are similar regardless of race or sex, then the results can be generalized to all middle school students in science.

In personnel evaluation it is important to ensure the development of evaluation instruments that represent the range of personnel, not just a predominant group. For example, women are the predominant group as teachers and administrators in elementary schools. So, in addition to assessing the behaviors that support student achievement as indicated by research evidence, to include the assessment of "being a caring and nurturing person" (a characteristic most often associated with women) in assessing elementary principals when there is no research evidence to support the impact of that behavior on student achievement may provide a bias that works against male elementary teachers or principals. Thus, in personnel evaluation, it will be much easier to assess and develop those behaviors that are clearly shown through research evidence to be associated with whatever characteristic or behavior is identified, without the use of clearly questionable bias in sex or race.

CONSIDERATIONS IN ESTABLISHING AND EVALUATING EVIDENCE-BASED CRITERIA REGARDING CURRICULUM ISSUES AND PROGRAM EVALUATION

The curriculum which students are offered is based both in history and the current views of educators, politicians, and employers. While standards now exist in the overwhelming majority of curricular areas, the ability exists to assess various curricula through evidence-based evaluation. In general, the area of curricular evaluation will be found in the research on program evaluation. That is, a specific program or curriculum directed at student learning on a specific area or topic has been evaluated. A large number of studies address curriculum organization. One of the early works (Tyler, 1950) presented the importance of the use of what today is known as scope and sequence of courses of study within the concept of a curriculum element (concept, generalization, skill, value, and procedure). In an extensive review on sequence and synthesis (Van Patten, Chao, & Reigeluth, 1986), there is evidence that when considering the macro level (programs and courses) and the micro level (single lessons) of curriculum, there is support for the greater importance of micro sequences (generality, example, and practice) than macro sequences (which courses are taken in what order). These studies on organization reflect the difficulty for educators in curricular evaluation when trying to determine whether a specific program, sequence of courses, or in fact the actual instruction has the most impact on student achievement.

When considering specific curricular impact, the research is either subject specific (e.g., math) or program specific (e.g., Success for All) (Slavin & Madden, 1999). The advantages to schools and school districts when considering adopting programs that have already been developed is that they can and should assess the available evidence as provided by research to determine under what conditions the program reports effectiveness.

The adoption of a specific curriculum or curricular organization is only one step in the process. It is important, even when research evidence has been used in the adoption, to assess the impact of the organizational structure, curriculum, or curricular program on students in your district. A caution that is necessary in the evaluation of curricular areas from an evidence base is the need to ensure that the specificity of *what* is to be evaluated is consistent with both the defined student achievement goals and the prevailing research so that appropriate comparisons can be made relative to impact. For example, a specific program may report research based on post-test assessment using a test designed on the program's materials. If an evaluation is based on student achievement as measured by a nationally normed achievement test, the results could not be compared to the study that used the programs post-test to indicate whether the results were the same or not. However, if the evaluator defined student achievement as being based on a nationally normed achievement test, then the program could be evaluated in that context.

It is important to know that there are extensive research studies on many aspects of curriculum organization, structure, and programs. Those seeking to implement certain curricula or to evaluate existing curricula need to ensure, either through the evaluator's knowledge of the research evidence or through review of the evidence available in the research, that decisions are based in evidence, not just in "reporting" from those who like the program or publishers' hype. The impact on student achievement may rest in the balance.

SUMMARY

The following chapters provide information, in one place, on the majority of the national standards currently available, as well as research-based evidence on a number of topical issues. The topical issues are presented with the derivation of the evidence and the specific evidence-based criteria, followed by cautions and comments. For the standards, the format allows the reader to view the standards, their derivation, and considerations for evaluation. Many web sites are now posting research related to their standards as it becomes available. Addresses, phone numbers, and web sites (where available) for the organizations involved with each of the standards is provided and direct contact is encouraged to ensure that you have the needed information for using the standards to develop curricula or evaluation. Additionally, the reader is encouraged to review the research cited for the evidence-based criteria prior to embarking on evaluation utilizing the criteria.

Consider the words of Williams Jennings Bryan: "Destiny is not a matter of chance, it is a matter of choice; it is not a thing to be waited for, it is a thing to be achieved." So, too, it is with the value of education, if we are to truly impact student achievement. In order to achieve the level of student competence that is professed in this country, it is absolutely imperative that we take a collective view of open inquiry, establish a willingness to evaluate the performance of educators and students alike, and determine which aspects of the instructional programs employed do, in fact, make a difference and then use them.

There is some debate that not all programs work for all students, and this position would not take much effort to support from the literature. However, the real strength in this perspective is not in the condemnation of "one size does not fit all," but rather that every educator and school board member must take personal responsibility for encouraging, developing, and learning from quality evaluation programs in all aspects of teaching and learning.

The following descriptions of standards are an attempt to provide, in one place, basic information that can be used for determining which standards are available, their derivation, and considerations for evaluation.

13

Evidence-Based Criteria by Area

This chapter provides evidence-based criteria from research that address a number of topical issues. The criteria provide a framework from which evaluations can be developed and for issues which should be addressed in either personnel or program evaluation. Each topical issue is presented as an area with derivation of the criteria, the criteria, and cautions and comments.

Correctional Education

Derivation of Criteria

A number of students are served in most communities in correctional facilities, either through juvenile or adult programs. During the 1990s there was an increased involvement in this educational process by the U.S. Department of Education, to a large extent driven by the high percentage of students who were eligible for federally mandated special education services. Historically, the attempts at research on education in these settings were an attempt to assess the effects of education, while incarcerated, on the reassimilation when returned to communities or the recidivism rate (MacCormick, 1976).

Criteria

Although there are not specific criteria for correctional education as such, several studies present evidence that one specific criterion is worth consideration in assessing the impact of correctional education on the students served. That criterion is the effect of mandatory participation in a functional literacy program. Results suggest significant gains in participation, an indication that when inmates are required to participate in educational programs, more do.

Cautions and Comments

It is clear that correctional education during the 1990s increased in educational services. The resulting need to evaluate programs is evident and will likely be available in the literature in the coming years. Since most juveniles who are incarcerated leave that system prior to or at age 21, they will return to compete for jobs in a society with others who have been educated in a more traditional environment. Therefore, for a district that serves these students, it is critical to understand the need for assessing which strategies work with incarcerated students and the impact of teaching on rehabilitation and recidivism.

Discipline Issues

Derivation of Criteria

The criteria for evaluating student discipline issues arise from the need to provide a safe and orderly environment. There are many studies which show that students who misbehave in school are less likely to achieve academically and are at greater risk for failure, dropping out, and committing acts of violence. In addition, students who themselves behave are at greater risk when there is a high incidence of misconduct in a class or school.

Criteria

There are criteria based in research evidence relating to specific student behavior, teacher behavior, and organizational behavior that impact student discipline. Clearly defining expectations for student behavior (e.g., fighting) and consequences for misbehavior, as well as ensuring that students know both expectations and consequences, has been shown to have a positive impact on student behavior (Friedman, 2000; Gottfredson, 1987). For teachers, their behaviors (Rhodes & Jason, 1988) directed at improving management of student behavior (e.g., stopping misconduct immediately, clarifying rules) have been shown to have a positive impact on student behavior. Teacher behavior also includes prompting students to maintain appropriate behavior, providing consequences for violations of rules promptly and briefly so as not to disrupt instruction, and keeping rules to a minimum (about five) (Friedman, 2000).

Additionally, there is evidence that classroom reward structures and level of participation in classroom activities (Epstein, 1983; Hallinan & Tuma, 1978) influence student behavior. Clearly, students who are actively engaged in appropriate classroom activities cannot be engaged in inappropriate behavior at the same time.

Cautions and Comments

There are numerous programs that may be implemented to address the issue of appropriate student behavior (e.g., Character Education Partnership, 2002), but the cautions about program implementation (i.e., that the evidence that a specific program addresses the behaviors desired must be examined) remain. The level to which personnel, teachers, and administrators must be involved in the program should be considered as well. The most important first step is to determine acceptable standards of behavior. This is a case where the use of the Delphi Technique would be beneficial. Given a list of acceptable behaviors generated from the criteria that are supported by research and by all teachers and administrators in a school or district, including parents if possible, the evaluator could then assist in the development of a list of acceptable behaviors through the Delphi Technique. A discipline plan is more likely to be effective if designed for the student population in a given school, using the criteria shown through research, and placing the emphasis on those behaviors that are of greatest concern in that school. It is important to note the evidence that the reward structure, as mentioned earlier, is as important as the consequences for inappropriate behavior.

Dynamic Assessment of Learners

Derivation of Criteria

Much of the assessment that is done in schools is based on the outcomes of learning (e.g., grades) or what is perceived to be the accumulation of knowledge (e.g., achievement tests), but an important type of assessment is that of determining a student's needs in the learning environment. This type of assessment is predictive in nature and is referred to as dynamic assessment (Palinscar & Winn, 1992). There are a number of research studies that have addressed the issues of cognitive development as measured through dynamic assessment. While there is some controversy about how cognitive functioning is defined, there is a growing interest, particularly in the areas of reading and mathematics, in determining how students construct meaning (e.g., Reynolds & Wheatley, 1996; Wixson & Lipson, 1986).

Criteria

The criteria for dynamic assessment include such factors as determining motivation and strategy use (Carlson & Wiedl, 1978), facility with which students learn from others (Brown & Ferrara, 1985; Campione & Brown, 1984), and discussions between teachers and students regarding the meanings of text by generating questions, summarizing, predicting upcoming content, and clarifying ambiguities (Palincsar & Brown, 1989).

Cautions and Comments

The importance of dynamic assessment in the evaluation process of programs and of educational personnel is how the program uses dynamic assessment in the learning model, or how teachers apply dynamic assessment in building instructional lessons. The research supports the importance of dynamic assessment in learning but raises questions about the ability to actually measure some aspects of cognitive development. Any evaluation of teachers or programs will need to ensure that the uses of the criteria of dynamic assessment are clearly understood.

Homework

Derivation of Criteria

Homework has long been considered an integral part of schooling, particularly as students move through the grades. The issues of purpose and results related to homework, for teachers and administrators, are often based on student responsibility for completing and turning in such work. However, a greater consideration, particularly from a program evaluation perspective, should be the impact of homework on knowledge and/or classroom performance. The evidence from research is mixed on the issue of homework, but provides some criteria for creating an evaluation of the effects of homework in a school or district. Cooper (1989) conducted a meta-analysis of the available research on homework and provides the most extensive basis for criteria related to evidence on the effects of homework.

Criteria

In an exhaustive study of the available research on homework (Cooper, 1989), the evidence is clear that students who do some or more homework are more likely to perform better in school than those students who do none. This is particularly true for high school students and less true for middle school students, with negligible effect for elementary school students. A second criterion appears in the amount of time spent on homework. For high school students, the time per week, which affects achievement, appears to be up to 10 hours, and for middle school students 5 to 10. While students who spend more time learning outside of class tend to do better, there is no evidence to support that spending more time than previously indicated makes a difference. A third criterion addresses a frequent concern on the part of teachers, that of marking homework. Cooper reports that there is no available evidence to show that there is any effect on achievement from teacher feedback on homework. Parental involvement (addressed specifically in this chapter) is also a consideration in homework effect. While parental contact with the school appears to have an effect, there is no evidence that a parent being involved in homework completion has an effect. Lastly, there is evidence (Becker & Epstein, 1982) that school and districtwide homework policies positively affect achievement. According to Cooper's research, these policies should include the following criteria: homework is expected of all students; time expectations are made clear, as previously mentioned; expectations are communicated to parents and monitored by administrators; there are both mandatory and voluntary assignments; homework focuses on simple rather than complex skills; parents are not required to be instructors in the process; and not all assignments will be evaluated.

Cautions and Comments

Teachers and school administrators, whose primary concern is student achievement, have generally assumed that homework makes a difference in that achievement. Since there is evidence that high school students in more advanced courses have been assigned more homework than those, say, in vocational courses, it may be difficult to say that the evidence on homework's effect for all students is clear. That is, there is no evidence that students in lower-level classes will attain the level of achievement of students in higher-level classes from doing homework. What appears to be clear is that, regardless of the level of high school student course level assignment (e.g., advanced placement or vocational), those students who do some or all homework achieve more in classroom performance and on standardized achievement tests.

Perhaps the consideration for elementary school students should rest in the development of behaviors outside of school that are focused on the development of lifelong learning habits, rather than *homework* per se. There is no evidence that having homework in elementary school affects achievement, but given that there is evidence that those in high school doing homework do better, it may be important to know if those who do attempt or complete homework were more likely to have had homework in earlier grades.

Student achievement, addressed under "Knowledge Acquisition and Comprehension," is a composite of a number of variables, and it is important to consider the impact of each as shown by the available research evidence.

Knowledge Acquisition and Comprehension

Derivation of Criteria

The ability to acquire knowledge is defined as the learning of organized information, and comprehension is learning with understanding (Wittrock, 1992). The longstanding consideration of these concepts is worthy of consideration in many aspects of the evaluation of programs, personnel, and standards.

Criteria

Several criteria are applicable when considering knowledge acquisition and comprehension. One such criterion is the interaction of reception through the senses, short-term memory and long-term memory (Shiffrin & Atkinson, 1969). Another criterion is the organization of memory, on which there is extensive research and considerable evidence, including the recent constructivist theories that should be considered in evaluating the impact of specific programs or texts on learning. And a third criterion that is worth noting is metacognition. Metacognition is the students' awareness of their own thought processes in the learning environment.

Cautions and Comments

As specific criteria, these are more likely areas for research than they are for evaluation of impact in the classroom on learning. However, since they are at the core of individual learning, it is important to be aware of them and to try and determine in the development of an educational program or educational evaluation of a program if these criteria account for any of the variance, if possible, in the impact of the program.

Although these criteria will be difficult to assess in the classroom, as more is learned about brain functioning through medical research it will certainly have implications for assessment and program development for learning as we currently know it.

Parents

Derivation of Criteria

Educating and involving parents in the education of children in our society is of concern to educators as they try to support academic achievement among children and contribute to the social and democratic well-being of the society. While there is great historical precedence for parental responsibilities in such basic child development as building character, instilling obedience to societal rules, and rearing an emotionally healthy child, the development of specific criteria for effective parent and community involvement in the schools has been predominantly focused on parent education programs. Most parent education programs are conducted and perceived to be effective, but few are based on specific evaluation of the impact of the programs on achievement.

Criteria

The programs with the most extensive research are parent education programs, which focus on behavioral management. There is evidence which shows that teaching parents behavioral management techniques can lead to changes in children's behavior. Additionally, programs that focus on cognitive interventions (Goodson & Hess, 1976) improve language and academic readiness for school.

There is some strong evidence, based on extensive research reviews by Ziegler (1987), that parents affect long-term gains in achievement when contact and relationships with schools are established early. Additionally, the act of parents signing homework assignments appears to enhance motivation to do the work on the part of the student. (The effects of attempting and completing homework are addressed under the heading of "Homework.") Additionally, Baker and Soden (1998) report the following criteria as being effective: parents' providing stimulating literacy and materials; appropriate monitoring of television viewing and homework completion; participation in joint learning activities at home; and emphasis on effort over ability and high expectations and moderate levels of parent support and supervision.

Cautions and Comments

At this point there are some specific criteria for what will support and encourage parent involvement in the education of their children. Several authors (Baker & Soden, 1998; Dembo, Sweitzer, & Lauritzen, 1985) discuss the many issues that exist in the design and implementation of current program evaluation in parent education and involvement. There is also a concern that teaching parents such things as behavioral management and cognitive strategies will make them feel that their roles are being managed by the professionals or that they must rely on professionals to know what to do. It should also be noted that the research to date does not address the role and effect of parent participation on school planning teams that now exist in most states under accountability legislation.

Clearly, with the added emphasis in most school districts and states on parent involvement, there is a need to design and evaluate programs that involve parents. Whether the programs are specific instructional delivery of skills (e.g., behavior management) or plans that have parents doing specific tasks with their child at school or home, personnel in schools and districts should remember that involving parents is another aspect of schools that requires time and effort on the part of professional staff and should therefore be well thought out and evaluated for making the best use of parents' time and interests and the best use of school resources.

Rural Schools

Derivation of Criteria

Although much of the focus on educational research in the United States during the 1980s and 1990s involved urban and suburban schools, rural schools comprise 30% of the schools in America, serving 20% of the school-age population (U.S. Department of Education, 2001). Rural schools are extremely diverse in geographic location by state, distance from an urban center, economic conditions, students served, and so forth. Most federal agencies have no uniform definition of rural schools and generally do not collect data differentiating rural schools from others. Major issues that appear in the literature related to education in rural schools focus on quality and equity, successful and/or effective rural schools, and telecommunications.

Criteria

The criterion of quality rural schools has been defined, as in most schools under the standards movement, as performance on standards. Operationalizing these standards in rural schools is often difficult due to low numbers and difficulties in attracting teachers with needed skills in critical shortage areas (e.g., math, science). However, while districts may have to consider consolidation with larger schools in neighboring districts, many are beginning to rely on the availability of technology (see "Distance Education Standards" in Chapter 14) to provide needed courses. The financial resources needed to address technology, for example, may well lie in issues related to equity. In many states there are lawsuits charging legislatures with inequitably providing resources for the mandated programs and for schools that are in poor economic regions of the various states.

In looking for evidence of successful or effective rural schools, Carlson (1989) defines successful schools as those that address continuous improvement.

Cautions and Comments

Based on the issues raised in the literature as identified above, assessing the ability of rural schools to meet standards (and, if utilized, the impact of technology in doing so) will be important. Since the demographic concerns that affect rural schools are different than those for urban and suburban schools, it will be important in program evaluation to ensure that the design of the evaluation is clear and well defined.

As a specific criterion, the concept of continuous improvement would need to be defined as part of an evaluation plan. This is a place where the use of the Delphi Technique (in determining, for the specific evaluation, what constitutes continuous improvement) would be appropriate. A concern that needs to be addressed is whether there *are* advantages to students in continuous improvement, or if the skills of problem solving are no different for rural schools than for suburban or urban schools.

Teaching Evaluation

Derivation of Criteria

In the *Handbook on Effective Instructional Strategies: Evidence for Decision-Making* (1998), Friedman and Fisher report 15 techniques that research shows increase student achievement. These criteria have been researched by various researchers and are supported by 50 to 200 research studies.

Criteria

The criteria are presented to represent cogent conceptualizations of the research data on instructional strategies that have research-supported effectiveness. The criteria are listed below.

Research-Based Effective Instructional Strategies

1. Defining instructional expectations
2. Taking student readiness into account
3. Providing effective instructional evaluation
4. Providing corrective instruction
5. Providing contiguity
6. Utilizing repetition effectively
7. Clarifying communication
8. Providing subject matter unifiers
9. Keeping students on task
10. Providing ample teaching time
11. Providing ample learning time

12. Utilizing reminders

13. Providing transfer of learning instruction

14. Providing decision-making instruction

15. Facilitating teamwork

Source: Friedman & Fisher, 1998.

Cautions and Comments

In *Ensuring Student Success: A Handbook of Evidence-Based Strategies* (2000), Friedman elaborates on the instructional strategies by providing an orientation to the strategies, instructional tactics, illustrations of applications, and references. Teaching evaluation can be developed using any number of the evaluation techniques provided earlier to assess teacher performance.

It is important when developing such an evaluation that the developers consider the amount of time that a peer or administrator will need to spend in a classroom to ensure that the strategies are being implemented. The evidence of these strategies in instruction is particularly important when assessing the performance and development of beginning teachers.

Urban Schools

Derivation of Criteria

In the latter part of the 1900s, urban students were increasingly identified as members of language or ethnic minorities and, often, of low-income families. The decrease in rural schools (from 67% of the schools in 1988 to 30% in 2000) saw a rise in urban schools, with a total of 24% of schools in 2000 being in cities. Much of the national research has focused on urban schools during this time. Specific issues addressed relate to differences in cognition, achievement motivation, lack of sense of community, and social control (Gordon & Armour-Thomas, 1992).

Criteria

While the standards and criteria addressed in other sections of Part VI may well involve urban students, it appears important to consider specific criteria that need to be addressed among these students and their schools. In cognition, a number of studies address the importance of knowledge structures (Minsky, 1974) and cognition that is particular to a given social milieu (Bronfenbrenner, 1979). Achievement motivation is evidenced by a student's perceptions of whether his/her intelligence is fixed or malleable. Students who perceive it as fixed identify performance goals that will gain them approval, whereas students who view intelligence as malleable set learning goals. This difference appears to have positive achievement implications for those who set learning goals (Gordon & Armour-Thomas, 1992). A third criterion that is worthy of consideration when evaluating urban schools and the students served by them is the apparent *lack* of community and social control.

Cautions and Comments

The research on issues of cognition and achievement motivation is extensive, and someone designing a program evaluation to determine the impact of these factors on student achievement should be thoroughly familiar with this evidence. However, the issue for evaluators is in determining those aspects of programs and structures that contribute positively to student achievement. The importance of the criteria under urban schools is to consider that these factors may disproportionately influence student achievement and may be difficult to ferret out. Issues of social control and lack of sense of community may contribute to isolated incidents of violence—for example, that generalize to all urban schools because of the magnitude of the real (e.g., 10 students killed) or perceived (e.g., urban schools are all dangerous) problems. While any given behavior may be more apparent (or, in fact, more intense) in an urban school, the purpose of evaluating programs and schools is to determine those things that most highly contribute to student achievement.

14

Standards as Criteria

This chapter provides current national standards in education particular to personnel evaluation and selection, as well as program evaluation. The areas related to personnel are preceded by standards that have been established for the development of personnel evaluations, and likewise the program standards are preceded by standards that have been established for program evaluation. Each area provides information on the derivation of the criteria, the specific standards, cautions and comments, and the known information about the publisher of the standards.

STANDARDS FOR PERSONNEL EVALUATION AND SELECTION

Standards for Personnel Evaluation

Derivation of Criteria

The Joint Committee on Standards for Educational Evaluation (JCSEE), which began in 1975, developed specific criteria to assess systems that are designed to evaluate educators. These criteria continue to be used in 2003 and are continuously evaluated by the JCSEE. The JCSEE has been sponsored by most of the major professional organizations in education and is made up of 16 representatives of those organizations, as well as university and school district personnel knowledgeable in evaluation issues. National and international review panels critiqued the standards, and a Validation Panel evaluated and monitored the overall project. The information is available in the book *The Personnel Evaluation Standards: How to Assess Systems for Evaluating Educators.*

Criteria

The four standards to be considered in assessing systems that evaluate educators are propriety, utility, feasibility, and accuracy. Each of the standards is described and divided into related principles to be considered when conducting an assessment of the evaluation system. The principles related to each standard are as presented in the following figure.

Standards and Principles for Personnel Evaluation

Propriety	*Utility*	*Feasibility*	*Accuracy*
Requires standards to be conducted legally, ethically, and with regard for welfare of evaluatees and clients of the evaluation.	Guides evaluations so they are informative, timely, and influential.	Calls for evaluation systems that are easy to implement, efficient in use of time and resources, adequately funded, and viable.	Requires that obtained information be technically accurate and conclusions linked logically to the data.

Principles for Each of the Standards

Service orientation	Constructive orientation	Practical procedures	Defined role
Formal evaluation guidelines	Defined uses	Political viability	Work environment
Conflict of interest	Evaluator credibility	Fiscal viability	Documentation of procedures
Access to personnel evaluation reports	Functional reporting		Valid measurement
Interactions with evaluatees	Follow-up and impact		Reliable measurement
			Systematic data control
			Bias control
			Monitoring evaluation systems

Source: Stufflebeam, 1988.

Cautions and Comments

While it is unlikely that personnel at an individual school would undertake to assess an evaluation system for educational personnel, understanding the standards of the JCSEE can certainly be important at both the school or district level. Often district personnel develop evaluation systems without the benefit of a professional specifically trained in evaluation. These standards should be considered as part of the overall development of an evaluation system or when assessing the appropriateness of existing evaluation instruments.

The published document provided by the JCSEE is in a readable format. It provides specific principles upon which the standards are based, provides a rationale for the guidelines, and identifies common errors related to the principles and standards.

Publisher

The personnel evaluation standards: How to assess systems for evaluating educators. Corwin Press, 2455 Teller Road, Thousand Oaks, CA 91320-2218; Phone: 805-499-9734; Fax: 800-4-1-SCHOOL; Web site: http://www.corwinpress.com.

Standards for Evaluating Principals and Superintendents

Derivation of Criteria

Interstate School Leaders Licensure Consortium: Standards for School Leadership (ISLLC). These criteria were developed in 1998 by the Council of Chief State Schools Officers (CCSSO), which is the national association for state-level superintendents. The members of the development team included personnel from 24 state education agencies and representatives from various professional associations. The standards were designed to address new criteria in the National Council for the Accreditation of Teacher Education (NCATE) guidelines for school administrators and to encourage discussion about the quality of education leadership.

Criteria

ISLLC Standards

Standard	A school administrator is an educational leader who promotes the success of all students by
1	facilitating the development, articulation, implementation, and stewardship of a vision of learning that is shared and supported by the school community
2	advocating, nurturing, and sustaining a school culture and instructional program conducive to student learning and staff professional growth
3	ensuring management of the organization, operations, and resources for a safe, efficient, and effective learning environment
4	collaborating with families and community members, responding to diverse community interests and needs, and mobilizing community resources
5	acting with integrity, fairness, and in an ethical manner
6	understanding, responding to, and influencing the larger political, social, economic, legal, and cultural context

Source: CCSSO, 1996.

Cautions and Comments

State departments of education and school districts are using these standards to develop evaluation criteria for principals. Using the knowledge, dispositions, and performances (CCSSO, 1996) identified for each of the standards, evaluation instruments are typically designed using some type of rating scale, as identified in the beginning of Part VI. These ratings may be part of a formative, summative, or self-appraisal evaluation.

Caution should be taken when developing rating scales from standards, as presented earlier in Part VI. Of particular note in an administrative rating scale is the concern for limited information, since the one who generally evaluates school administrators (e.g., an assistant superintendent) has limited opportunity to observe the performance of the administrator in his/her natural setting (e.g., a school). One technique that can be used to address some of the limitations of a rating scale is the Delphi Technique. Additionally, while there are some studies available that address the ISLLC standards, there is currently no evidence that any attempts have been made to standardize or critically analyze the criteria for evaluation purposes.

Publisher

Council of Chief State School Officers, One Massachusetts Avenue NW, Suite 700, Washington, DC 20001-1431; Phone: 202-336-7016; Fax: 202-408-8072; Web site: http://www.ccsso.org.

Standards for Selecting Principals

Derivation of Criteria

The Gallup Organization first developed several educator selection instruments in 1989 as part of its Selection Research Instrument. The Principal Perceiver is a research-based instrument designed to aid in the selection of candidates for the position of principal. The instrument was developed through clinical and statistical analysis of responses and field tested several times for reliability and content validity. The publisher provides reliability and validity data. Gallup has developed additional processes aimed at attracting and retaining top candidates. In order to administer the Principal Perceiver, an individual seeking certification on the instrument must consistently demonstrate an 85% item-by-item scoring agreement with Gallup analysts. Annual relicensing is required for continued use of the instrument.

Criteria

The instrument is comprised of predictive and discriminatory items across seven themes. The predictive and discriminatory items are available as part of the training required by the company to administer their selection instrument.

Descriptions of the themes are as follows:

Theme	*Description*
Commitment	Capacity for complete dedication to a career or mission.
Ego drive	Define themselves as significant persons and claim their role as leader.
Achiever	Inner drive that continuously propels one to make things happen and get things done.
Developer	Derive satisfaction from facilitating growth of teachers with whom one works.

Theme	Description
Individualized perception	Attuned to individual differences of teachers.
Relator	Care and concern for teachers by getting to know them.
Stimulator	Exhibits positivity, excitement, and good feelings for the teaching environment with instinct for knowing how to make other people feel good.

Source: The Gallup Organization, The Principal Perceiver.

Cautions and Comments

The purpose of the Principal Perceiver is to provide predictive value in the selection of principal candidates. Information is provided through rigorous training to explain each of the themes and includes cautions that address expected behaviors when a theme is weak. Training through the publisher is required, and ongoing reevaluation of trained personnel is mandatory to continue using the instrument. The publisher makes no claim to perfect match when using the instrument, but addresses the importance of being consistent in assessing needed competencies for a given school and the selection of the person to fill that position.

Publisher

The Gallup Organization, Education Division; Phone: 800-288-8592; Web site: http://education.gallup.com.

Standards for Evaluating Teachers (1)

Derivation of Criteria

Since 1987, the National Board for Professional Teaching Standards (NBPTS) has sought to identify accomplished teaching through standards that have been developed by committees of teachers. As of 2001, 27 of the 31 content areas had standards developed. The standards are developed by these teacher committees and other professional experts and undergo extensive review by the NBPTS and through public comment. Several professional organizations, including the American Association of School Administrators (AASA) and the Council of Chief State School Officers (CCSSO), have encouraged and supported the work of the NBPTS.

Criteria

The NBPTS standards are based on five core propositions that are outlined and explained in the figure on the following page.

Cautions and Comments

Currently the NBPTS publishes standards in subject areas, and through a process of documentation of the core propositions in the subject area teachers can seek certification by the NBPTS. Currently there is no evidence to suggest that students of

Five Core Propositions from the NBPTS (with Explanations) for Accomplished Teachers

Proposition	Teachers are committed to students and their learning.	Teachers know the subjects they teach and how to teach those subjects to students.	Teachers are responsible for managing and monitoring student learning.	Teachers think systematically about their practice and learn from experience.	Teachers are members of learning communities.
Knowledge and Commitment	They make knowledge accessible to all students; act on belief that all students can learn and treat students equitably, recognizing individual differences.	They have rich understanding of the subject(s) they teach and how knowledge is created, organized, linked to other disciplines, and applied to real-world settings.	They have knowledge of how to create, enrich, maintain, and alter instructional settings to capture and sustain students' interest.	They model virtues of an educated person, including curiosity, tolerance, honesty, fairness, respect for diversity, and appreciation of cultural differences, along with the ability to reason.	They work collaboratively with other professionals, are knowledgeable about school and community resources, and are skilled at employing such resources.
Practice	They adjust practice based on observation and knowledge of students' interests, abilities, skills, knowledge, family circumstances, and peer relationships.	They create multiple paths to the subjects they teach and are adept at teaching students how to pose and solve their own problems.	They engage students to ensure a disciplined learning environment.	They strive to strengthen their teaching, critically examine their practice, expand their repertoire, deepen their knowledge, sharpen their judgment, and adapt their teaching to new findings, ideas, and theories.	They work collaboratively and creatively with parents, engaging them productively in the work of the school.

Source: Available from the policy position for NBPTS, Inc.

teachers who are board certified perform any differently on measures of achievement than students of teachers who are not. The standards are currently only used for the purpose of certification by the NBPTS but are under discussion in some states as a replacement for more traditional teacher evaluation systems.

Publisher

The National Board for Professional Teaching Standards, 1525 Wilson Boulevard, Suite 500, Arlington, VA 22209; Phone: 703-465-2700; Fax: 703-465-2715; Web site: http://www.nbpts.org.

Standards for Evaluating Teachers (2)

Derivation of Criteria

The SouthEastern Regional Vision for Education (SERVE) provides summary research on five models of teacher evaluation (1998). They suggest that there is no "right way" to do formative evaluation and provide support for the models based on observation and review of districts which are participating in their initiative to create formative teacher evaluation systems and which support teacher ownership of their professional growth.

Criteria

The five models presented and described are:

1. *Goal-setting*

   Teacher establishes goals with principal.

   Teacher and principal meet throughout the year to discuss progress.

2. *Menu of options*

   Teacher has choice of evaluation sources and methods for personally developed goals.

   Sources include self, peer, parent/student.

   Methods include how source is accessed (e.g., survey, video).

3. *Goal-setting/menu of options*

   Combines setting goals with principal and evaluating through menu of options.

4. *Panel review*

   Teacher participates in a study group and documents progress of students through portfolio.

   Panel of peers from school system reviews work.

5. *Peer coaching*

   Teacher selects colleagues to provide feedback.

Cautions and Comments

The models presented in this formative evaluation process are assessed through a qualitative analysis based on observation and review of the districts participating. Criteria and components of each of the models is provided and discussed. Different strategies were used in each of the districts evaluated.

Because of the influence of SERVE in one region of the country, many school administrators will rely on this evidence in the design of teacher evaluation for their districts. It is important to note that this is a formative evaluation system and is intended for use with experienced and continuing teachers for professional growth. The models are not intended to lead to a summative instrument for contract evaluation or termination.

Publisher

The SouthEastern Regional Vision for Education (SERVE), P.O. Box 5367, Greensboro, NC 27435; Phone: 336-315-7400 or 800-755-3277; Fax: 336-315-7457; Web site: http://www.serve.org.

Standards for Selecting Teachers

Derivation of Criteria

The Gallup Organization first developed several educator selection instruments in the 1980s as part of its Selection Research Instrument. The Teacher Perceiver and the Urban Teacher Perceiver are instruments, based on over 30 years of research, designed to aid in the selection of candidates for the role of teacher. The instruments were developed through clinical and statistical analysis of responses and field tested several times for reliability and content validity. The Teacher Perceiver identifies the top 12 behavioral qualities found in high-performing teachers, and the Urban Teacher Perceiver identifies qualities specific to teachers in urban schools. The publisher provides reliability and validity data. Gallup has developed additional processes aimed at attracting, developing, and retaining top candidates.

Criteria

The Teacher Perceiver and the Urban Teacher Perceiver themes are identified and defined in the following figures.

The Teacher Perceiver

Theme	Description
Mission	Teacher has a belief that students can grow and attain self-actualization and has a goal to make a significant contribution to others.
Empathy	Phenomenon within the teacher that provides feedback about the student's thoughts and feelings.

Rapport drive	Teacher's ability to have approving and mutually favorable relationship with each student.
Individualized perception	Teacher spontaneously thinks about the interests and needs of each student and personalizes program.
Listening	Teacher spontaneously listens with responsiveness and acceptance.
Investment	Teacher receives satisfaction from student growth.
Input Drive	Teacher continuously searches for ideas, materials, and experiences to use in helping other people.
Activation	Teacher stimulates students to think, to respond, and to feel in order to learn.
Innovation	Teacher tries new ideas and techniques.
Gestalt	Teacher has drive toward completeness.
Objectivity	Teacher responds to total situation.
Focus	Teacher has models and goals and is moving in a planned direction.

The Urban Teacher Perceiver

Theme	*Description*
Commitment	Teacher has made conscious decision to contribute to people and work where there is the greatest need.
Dedication	Teacher finds satisfaction from each step of progress in a student's life.
Individualized perception	Teacher has a sense of the differences present in each student and expresses regard for individuality.
Caring	Teacher shows warmth and affection to the students and to relationship development.
Involver	Teacher is a partner to students, to parents, and to other teachers.
Empathy	Teacher shows sensitivity and anticipation.
Positivity	Teacher exhibits a hopeful attitude toward students.
Initiator	Teacher is advocate for students.
Stimulator	Teacher is personally dramatic and receptive to the ideas and opinions of students.
Input	Teacher is intrigued with ideas and seeks those which are applicable to the classroom.
Concept	Teacher has philosophy about what is best for students and is guided by positive learning concepts.

Source: The Gallup Organization.

Cautions and Comments

Both the Teacher Perceiver and the Urban Teacher Perceiver are structured interviews developed through research to aid in the selection of teacher candidates by evaluating the "talent fit" for each environment. In order to administer the Teacher Perceiver, an individual seeking certification on the instrument must consistently demonstrate an 85% item-by-item scoring agreement with Gallup analysts. Annual relicensing is required for continued use of the instrument. Definitions of the themes are provided, and an extensive training program for certification to administer is used to maintain reliability.

Publisher

The Gallup Organization, Education Division; Phone: 800-288-8592; Web site: http://education.gallup.com.

Standards for Evaluating Support Personnel

Derivation of Criteria

Criteria for the evaluation of support personnel, including pupil personnel services, instructional support services, and academic/program development services, are presented in *Evaluating Support Personnel in Education* (Stronge & Helm, 1991), a text written to fill an identified void in the evaluation of school district personnel. These criteria were developed from researching the literature on evaluation and based on what the authors refer to as "an integration of existing evaluation theory placed within the context of a model designed specifically for educational specialists" (p. 37). Each of the steps provides specific frameworks developed from the literature.

Criteria

The steps identified for the evaluation process are as follows: "(a) identify system needs; (b) relate program expectations to job responsibility; (c) select performance indicators; (d) set standards for job performance; (e) document job performance; and (f) evaluate performance" (Stronge & Helm, 1991, p. xii). Examples of evaluation instruments developed using these steps are provided. One example includes a framework for identifying performance indicators (product or process), standards for satisfactory performance, methods documentation, and documented performance.

Cautions and Comments

In many districts around the country, professional support personnel are evaluated using teacher or administrator evaluation instruments and/or systems which do not specifically apply to the work expected of these personnel. The work done by a school psychologist, for example, is neither teaching nor administrative in nature. Therefore, to try and evaluate performance using an instrument designed to do one or the other will likely not provide a substantive or useful evaluation of the performance of the professional support staff.

It is important to remember that while the framework provided identifies steps for the development of an evaluation system for professional support personnel, the quality and usefulness of the evaluation is only as good as the time and effort put into the identification of specific standards of job performance and the assessment process to measure them.

Publisher

Corwin Press, 2455 Teller Road, Thousand Oaks, CA 91320-2218; Phone: 805-499-9734; Fax: 800-4-1-SCHOOL; Web site: http://www.corwinpress.com.

Standards for Selecting Support Personnel

Derivation of Criteria

The Gallup Organization first developed several educator selection instruments in the 1980s as part of its Selection Research Instrument. The Support Services Perceiver is an instrument, based on over 30 years of research, which is designed to aid in the selection of candidates for roles in support positions. The instrument was developed through clinical and statistical analysis of responses and field tested several times for reliability and content validity. The publisher provides reliability and validity data. Gallup has developed additional processes aimed at attracting, developing, and retaining top candidates.

Criteria

The Support Personnel Perceiver themes are identified as follows:

Support Personnel Perceiver Themes and Descriptions

Theme	Description
Belief	Evidence of a value system related to family, work, and rightness, and a desire to be of service to others.
Pride	Importance resulting from certain achievements.
Responsibility	Psychological ownership for work and behavior.
Team	Ability to build mutually supportive relationships with co-workers.
Empathy	Ability to accurately perceive the thoughts and feelings of others.
Gestalt	Tendency toward completeness with an emphasis on organization, accuracy, and work performance.
Kinesthetic	Tendency to be physically active.
Mastery	Competency and knowledge in the job.
Assertiveness	Ability to be straightforward and direct.
Woo	Desire to win the approval of other people.

Source: The Gallup Organization.

Cautions and Comments

The Support Personnel Perceiver is a structured interview developed through research to aid in the selection of candidates by evaluating the "talent fit" for each environment. In order to administer the Support Personnel Perceiver, an individual seeking certification on the instrument must consistently demonstrate an 85% item-by-item scoring agreement with Gallup analysts. Annual relicensing is required for continued use of the instrument. Definitions of the themes are provided, and an extensive training program for certification to administer is used to maintain reliability.

Publisher

The Gallup Organization, Education Division; Phone: 800-288-8592; Web site: http://education.gallup.com.

STANDARDS FOR PROGRAM EVALUATION

Program Evaluation Standards

Derivation of Criteria

In 1981, the Joint Committee on Standards for Educational Evaluation (JCSEE) published specific criteria to assess educational programs. These criteria continue to be used in 2003 and are continuously evaluated by the JCSEE. The JCSEE has been sponsored by most of the major professional organizations in education and is made up of 16 representatives of those organizations, as well as university and school district personnel knowledgeable in evaluation issues. National and international review panels critiqued the standards, and a Validation Panel evaluated and monitored the overall project. The information is available in the book *Standards for Evaluations of Educational Programs, Projects, and Materials.*

Criteria

The four standards to be considered in assessing systems that evaluate educational evaluations and related principles are presented in the figure on the following page.

Cautions and Comments

Nationally, the accountability movement is likely to produce a greater number of school- and district-level personnel interested in evaluating the effectiveness of programs, particularly as they relate to accountability measures. The background provided by the JCSEE should assist administrators in developing or contracting for program evaluations for specific purposes.

The published document provided by the JCSEE is in a readable format and includes descriptions of each of the specific principles upon which the standards are based. The evaluation of programs should be done for a specific purpose and to determine strengths and weaknesses of a program, curriculum, or material. These standards are developed to address the process of evaluation, not the outcome.

Publisher

The program evaluation standards: How to assess evaluations of educational programs. Corwin Press, 2455 Teller Road, Thousand Oaks, CA 91320-2218; Phone: 805-499-9734; Fax: 800-4-1-SCHOOL; Web site: http://www.corwinpress.com.

Standards and Principles for Program Evaluation

Utility	*Feasibility*	*Propriety*	*Accuracy*
Intended to ensure that an evaluation will serve the information needs of intended users.	Intended to ensure that an evaluation will be realistic, prudent, diplomatic, and frugal.	Intended to ensure that an evaluation will be conducted legally, ethically, and with due regard for those conducting and affected by the evaluation.	Intended to ensure that an evaluation will reveal and convey technically adequate information about the features that determine worth or merit of the program evaluated.

Principles for Each of the Standards

Stakeholder identification	Practical procedures	Service orientation	Program documentation
Evaluator credibility	Political viability	Formal agreements	Context analysis
Information scope and selection	Cost effectiveness	Rights of human subjects	Described purposes and procedures
Values identification		Human interactions	Defensible information sources
Report clarity		Complete and fair assessment	Valid information
Report timeliness and dissemination		Disclosure of findings	Reliable information
Evaluation impact		Conflict of interest	Systematic information
		Fiscal responsibility	Analysis of quantitative information
			Analysis of qualitative information
			Justified conclusions
			Impartial reporting
			Metaevaluation

Source: http://www.wmich.edu/evalctr/jc/.

Distance Education Standards

Derivation of Criteria

The Accrediting Commission of the Distance Education and Training Council (DETC) is a duly constituted accrediting body which establishes educational, ethical, and business standards and examines and evaluates distance education institutions using those standards. They report that the procedures and standards have been continuously refined and improved over the last 50 years.

Criteria

The standards established by the DETC have been developed to provide guidelines for institutions seeking accreditation from them. Following are the standards provided by DETC:

An institution must:

- have a clearly defined and stated mission and objectives;
- have reasonably attainable and clearly stated educational objectives and educationally sound, up-to-date courses/programs;
- provide satisfactory educational services;
- offer adequate student services;
- have demonstrated ample student success and satisfaction;
- have a competent faculty;
- have fair admission policies and adequate enrollment agreements;
- advertise its courses/programs truthfully;
- be financially able to deliver high-quality educational services;
- have fair and equitable tuition and refund policies;
- have adequate facility, equipment and record protection; and
- conduct continuous research and self-improvement studies.

Source: http://www.detc.org.

Cautions and Comments

Historically, institutions of higher education and adult learning have been the primary delivery sources for distance education. This includes correspondence courses and televised and recorded courses as well as synchronous and asynchronous computer courses. Much of the research conducted has been on student learning through distance education in higher education. Evaluation of these programs has generally taken the form of accreditation through on-site visits and review of accumulated data and artifacts related to the standards.

There is some research developing on the success rate of distance education learners compared to face-to-face learners. However, to date, it is primarily descriptive data reporting that fewer students complete courses when taken by distance education than face-to-face students. Gooler (1979) identified a number of criteria for evaluating distance education programs, but they are not significantly different than those proposed by the JCSEE for program evaluation in general. Moore (2002) stated that as we "understand better what is known about distance education via the Web, it will become more clear how much is not known, and that, by linking the questions about the application of this new technology to the theories and knowledge acquired through research in earlier technologies, the general quality of research and practice in this field will be advanced."

Understanding that the development of ever more distance education through the Web is likely to expand, even public schools will be more concerned with providing and evaluating distance education. With the teacher shortage, particularly in mathematics and various science areas, public schools (K–12) are beginning to seek distance education as a way to provide courses to students. For example, many states now have specialized schools for science and mathematics (e.g., The Governor's School for Math and Science in South Carolina) which provide distance education delivery to rural schools for Advanced Placement courses. There are a number of program evaluation issues that will arise both for the district taking advantage of the distance education courses and the school or district providing them. Some of these include student knowledge acquisition, course completion, supervision of the students, cost effectiveness, and impact of providing courses that could not otherwise be provided.

In choosing a distance education program, one will want to determine if the program is accredited. In evaluating programs it is important to use the standards previously listed. Given the evolving research in this area and the lack of criteria specifically related to distance education learners, this would be a good place to use the Delphi Technique (previously discussed) to determine criteria from administrators, teachers, learners, and program completers.

Publisher

Distance Education and Training Council (DETC), 1601 18th Street NW, Washington, DC 20009; Phone: 202-234-5100; Fax: 202-332-1386; Web site: http://www.detc.org.

Curriculum Standards for English Language Arts

Derivation of Criteria

The National Council of Teachers of English and the International Reading Association, through an intensive four-year project published in 1996, developed the standards for English language arts. Thousands of educators were involved in writing, reviewing, and revising the many drafts of the document, along with researchers, parents, policymakers, and others across the country who jointly developed the criteria for the standards. The English Language Arts Standards Project was a field-based process that was open and inclusive.

Criteria

The 12 standards for English language arts should be viewed as interrelated and considered as a whole. The standards assume that literacy begins before children start school, and these standards should be used to encourage the development of instruction and curricula that make use of the literacy abilities children bring to school. The standards as defined in the following figure.

English Language Arts Standards

Standard and Explanation

1. Students read a wide range of print and non-print texts to build an understanding of texts, of themselves, and of the cultures of the United States and the world; to acquire new information; to respond to the needs and demands of society and the workplace; and for personal fulfillment. Among these texts are fiction and nonfiction, classic and contemporary works.

2. Students read a wide range of literature from many periods in many genres to build an understanding of the many dimensions (e.g., philosophical, ethical, aesthetic) of human experience.

3. Students apply a wide range of strategies to comprehend, interpret, evaluate, and appreciate texts. They draw on their prior experience, their interactions with other readers and writers, their knowledge of word meaning and of other texts, their word identification strategies, and their understanding of textual features (e.g., sound-letter correspondence, sentence structure, context, graphics).

4. Students adjust their use of spoken, written, and visual language (e.g., conventions, style, vocabulary) to communicate effectively with a variety of audiences and for different purposes.

5. Students employ a wide range of strategies as they write and use different writing process elements appropriately to communicate with different audiences for a variety of purposes.

6. Students apply knowledge of language structure, language conventions (e.g., spelling and punctuation), media techniques, figurative language, and genre to create, critique, and discuss print and non-print texts.

7. Students conduct research on issues and interests by generating ideas and questions and by posing problems. They gather, evaluate, and synthesize data from a variety of sources (e.g., print and non-print texts, artifacts, people) to communicate their discoveries in ways that suit their purpose and audience.

8. Students use a variety of technological and information resources (e.g., libraries, databases, computer networks, video) to gather and synthesize information and to create and communicate knowledge.

9. Students develop an understanding of and respect for diversity in language use, patterns, and dialects across cultures, ethnic groups, geographic regions, and social roles.

10. Students whose first language is not English make use of their first language to develop competency in the English language arts and to develop understanding of content across the curriculum.

11. Students participate as knowledgeable, reflective, creative, and critical members of a variety of literacy communities.

12. Students use spoken, written, and visual language to accomplish their own purposes (e.g., for learning, enjoyment, persuasion, and the exchange of information).

Sources: http://www.ncte.org/standards/standards.shtml or http://www.ira.org/advocacy/elastandards/.

Cautions and Comments

The standards, while extensive, are broad in their descriptions and may complicate the ability to assess student performance and program success. Prior to conducting the evaluation, it will be incumbent upon the evaluator to clarify the purpose of the evaluation and the aspect(s) of any or all standards to be evaluated. Given the developers' caution that the standards are not intended to be distinct and separable, the ability to create any program evaluation in English language arts will require great care and discussion. Techniques that may be used by the evaluator(s) are highlighted in the introduction to Part VI.

Publishers

The National Council of Teachers of English, 1111 West Kenyon Road, Urbana, IL 61801-1096; Phone: 800-369-6283; Fax: 217-328-9645; Web site: http://www.ncte.org.

The International Reading Association, 800 Barksdale Road, P.O. Box 8139, Newark, DE 19714-8139; Phone: 802-731-1600; Fax: 302-731-1057; Web site: http://www. ira.org.

Curriculum Standards for English as a Second Language

Derivation of Criteria

Several groups have contributed to the development of standards for English as a Second Language (ESL) programs, including Teachers of English to Speakers of Other Languages (TESOL), teachers representing individual states, and members of the National Association for Bilingual Education (NABE). Content area standards were examined as part of the process. The standards were released for review and comment in 1996 from educators with experience in linguistically and culturally diverse student learning. TESOL published the final standards in 1997.

Criteria

The ESL standards were written for English Language Learners (ELL) with three goals and three standards within each goal. The standards are as follows:

National Standards for ESL

Goal	*Standards*
To use English to communicate in social settings.	Students will use English to participate in social interactions.
	Students will interact in, through, and with spoken and written English for personal expression and enjoyment.
	Students will use learning strategies to extend their communicative competence.
To use English to achieve academically in all content areas.	Students will use English to interact in the classroom.
	Students will use English to obtain, process, construct, and provide subject matter information in spoken and written form.

Goal	*Standards*
	Students will use appropriate learning strategies to construct and apply academic knowledge.
To use English in socially and culturally appropriate ways.	Students will use appropriate language variety, register, and genre according to audience, purpose, and setting.
	Students will use nonverbal communication appropriate to audience, purpose, and setting.
	Students will use appropriate learning strategies to extend their sociolinguistic and sociocultural competence.

Source: http://www.cal.org/ericcll/digest/0013eslstandards.html.

Cautions and Comments

The standards for ESL learning are intended to state what students should know and be able to do as a result of ESL instruction. Any evaluation of ESL programs will have to ensure attention to the time frame in which students have had to learn English as well as the quality of the instruction received. Acquisition of a second language can be influenced by many factors including age at introduction, opportunities for successful practice, and cultural factors related to acquiring a new language. The evaluator will want to include considerations for these and, possibly, other factors in program evaluation. Some forms of evaluation may be difficult (e.g., surveys) unless they are administered in the individual's native language. This may be particularly true when surveying parents.

Publisher

Teachers of English as a Second Language, 700 South Washington Street, Suite 200, Alexandria, VA 22314; Phone: 703-836-0774; Fax 703-836-7864; Web site: http://www.tesol.org.

Curriculum Standards for Information Literacy

Derivation of Criteria

The American Association of School Libraries (AASL), a division of the American Library Association (ALA), published standards in 1998 that provide information literacy standards for student learning.

Criteria

The nine standards for information literacy are divided into three areas. The standards are presented in the following figure.

National Information Literacy Standards

Information Literacy	*Independent Learning*	*Social Responsibility*
The student who is information literate:	The student who is an independent learner is information literate and:	The student who contributes positively to the learning community and to society is information literate and:
accesses information efficiently and effectively.	pursues information related to personal interests.	recognizes the importance of information to a democratic society.
evaluates information critically and competently.	appreciates literature and other creative expressions of information.	practices ethical behavior in regard to information and information technology.
uses information accurately and creatively.	strives for excellence in information seeking and knowledge generation.	participates effectively in groups to pursue and generate information.

Source: http://www.ala.org/aasl/.

Cautions and Comments

The information literacy standards of the AASL provide a framework for the development of library media programs, which can be developed in a school or for a district. The standards are broad and do not provide specific criteria for addressing them. However, the AASL provides support through its web site, conferences, and publications to assist library media specialists in the development and evaluation of programs. Evaluators will need to consider specific curriculum goals that have been established at the local or state level, in addition to the national standards, in evaluating the effectiveness of a given program in meeting these standards.

Publisher

AASL/YALSA, 50 East Huron, Chicago, IL 60611; Phone: 800-545-2433; AASL direct dial: 312-280-4386; Fax: 312-664-7459; Web site: http://www.ala.org/aasl/.

Curriculum Standards for Mathematics

Derivation of Criteria

The National Council of Teachers of Mathematics (NCTM) has released four major works related to standards in mathematics. In 1989, *Curriculum and Evaluation Standards for School Mathematics* was released, followed by *Professional Teaching Standards for School Mathematics* in 1991 and *Assessment Standards for School Mathematics* in 1995. The most recent publication, *Principles and Standards for School Mathematics* (2000), was designed to offer common language, examples, and recommendations to engage productive dialogue about mathematics education. These standards and principles were developed by groups of teachers and university faculty who are members of the NCTM and were revised based on an extensive open review process by others in the field.

Criteria

The principles and standards serve two different purposes. The principles address issues that influence the development of curriculum frameworks and materials and the planning of lessons, the design of assessment, the assignment of teachers and students to classes, instructional decisions, and staff development.

The standards provide an update to the standards from 1989 to meet students' and society's needs in the twenty-first century. They are created to cover the range of education from pre-kindergarten through twelfth grade. The NCTM provides extensive resources to address the standards on its web site. The principles and standards are presented in the following figures.

NCTM Principles for School Mathematics

Principle	Explanation
Equity	Equity is a core element which demands that reasonable and appropriate accommodations are made to promote access and attainment for all students.
Curriculum	Mathematical ideas are linked to and build on one another so that students' understanding and knowledge deepens and their ability to apply mathematics expands.
Teaching	Effective teaching in mathematics requires understanding what students know and need to learn, and then challenging and supporting them to learn it well.
Learning	Learning requires the alliance of factual knowledge, procedural proficiency, and conceptual understanding.
Assessment	Assessment should enhance students' learning.
Technology	Technology allows students to focus on decision-making, reflection, reasoning, and problem solving.

NCTM Standards for Mathematics

Standard	Explanation
Number and operations	The mathematics program should enable all students to understand numbers, understand meanings of operations, and compute fluently.
Algebra	The mathematics program should enable all students to understand patterns, represent and analyze mathematical situations and structures using algebraic symbols, use mathematical models to represent and understand quantitative relationships, and analyze change in various contexts.
Geometry	The mathematics program should enable all students to learn about geometric shapes and structures and to analyze their characteristics and relationships.
Measurement	The mathematics program should enable all students to understand measur-

Standard	Explanation
	able attributes and apply appropriate techniques, tools, and formulas to determine measurements.
Data analysis and probability	The mathematics program should enable all students to formulate questions, select and use appropriate statistical methods, develop and evaluate inferences and predictions based on data, and understand and apply basic concepts of probability.
Problem solving	The mathematics program should enable all students to build new mathematical knowledge, solve problems, apply and adapt a variety of appropriate strategies, and monitor and reflect on the process of problem solving.
Reasoning and proof	The mathematics program should enable all students to recognize reasoning and proof as fundamental aspects of mathematics, make and investigate mathematical conjectures, develop and evaluate mathematical arguments and proofs, and select and use various types of reasoning and methods of proofs.
Communication	The mathematics program should enable all students to organize and consolidate mathematical thinking through communication, communicate their mathematical thinking coherently and clearly, analyze and evaluate the mathematical thinking and strategies of others, and use the language of mathematics to express mathematical ideas precisely.
Connections	The mathematics program should enable all students to recognize and use connections among mathematical ideas, understand how mathematical ideas interconnect, and recognize and apply mathematics in contexts outside mathematics.
Representation	The mathematics program should enable all students to create and use representations to organize, record, and communicate mathematical ideas; select, apply, and translate among mathematical representations; and use representations to model and interpret physical, social, and mathematical phenomena.

Source: http://www.nctm.org.

Cautions and Comments

There are two aspects of the NCTM *Principles and Standards for School Mathematics* which have implications for program evaluation. First, the six principles serve to address the concern of the members of the organization that mathematics is more than any specific curriculum and that there is recognition that different districts and states may have different reasons for developing specific curricula. These principles can provide a framework for assessing the mathematics program in general in a given school or district. Second, the 10 standards provide a common foundation of mathematics to be learned by all students with consideration for the six principles.

Evaluation procedures used will depend on the purpose of the evaluation and the information desired. For example, a committee of teachers, administrators, and parents might be used to determine if the district curriculum and instructional program in mathematics adheres to the six principles set forth by the NCTM. A note of caution requires that consideration be given to the objectivity needed to critically analyze one's own program. Another example might be a more quantitative analysis of student test scores on standardized tests to evaluate current student achievement toward the standards. Yet another example might be a curriculum matching task conducted by teachers and administrators to ensure that lesson plans and instruction are aligned with the district curriculum and state and national standards as set forth by the NCTM. Different types of evaluation and concerns are set forth in the introduction to Part VI.

Publisher

National Council of Teachers of Mathematics (NCTM), 1906 Association Drive, Reston, VA 20191-1502; Phone: 703-620-9840; Fax: 703-476-2970; Web site: http:// www.nctm.org.

National Accreditation Standards for Educational Institutions (Schools, Colleges, Universities)

Derivation of Criteria

There are five regional associations that are accrediting agencies for public and private schools, colleges, and universities in the United States. They are the Southern Association of Colleges and Schools (SACS), the Western Association of Schools and Colleges (WASC), the Middle States Association of Schools and Colleges (MSASC), the North Central Association (NCA), and the Northwest Association of Schools and Colleges (NASC). This form of accreditation stemmed from a desire to establish standards of quality in schools and colleges nationwide over 100 years ago. This accreditation means that an institution meets established criteria or standards and is meeting its own stated objectives. The criteria are broad in nature relative to the process for accreditation but can also involve various standards of professional groups (e.g., the National Council of Teachers of Mathematics). The process of accreditation is a lengthy self-study carried out by the institution. The self-study is followed by a visit from an external review team made up of professionals trained in the process and not affiliated in any way with the institution seeking accreditation. Additionally, there are more than 80 professional organizations that provide an accrediting process in specialized programs, departments, or schools (e.g., the National Association of Schools of Art).

Criteria

The WASC provides an example of how accreditation is granted. Institutions must provide, through their self-study, compelling evidence that the institution is:

- Substantially accomplishing its own stated purposes;
- Meeting the criteria for planning, organization, curriculum, assessment, and student support;

- Providing ongoing and stable financial, human, and physical resources adequate for delivery of the school's programs;

- Successfully promoting student learning in terms of explicit, adopted academic standards (http://www.acswasc.org/background.html).

Specific criteria exist for different levels of education and by accrediting agencies. Following is an example for the Southern Association for Colleges and Schools (SACS):

Example of Accreditation Criteria

Area	*Standards*
Organization	1. Continuous School Improvement
	2. Beliefs and Mission
	3. Governance and Finance
	4. Leadership
	5. Human Resources
	6. Support Services for Student Learning
	7. Library/Media Services
	8. Facilities
	9. Communication and Community Relationships
Instruction	10. Instructional Design
	11. Curriculum
	12. Citizenship and Conduct
	13. Assessment

Source: http://www.sacs.org/elem/standards/erlychld.pdf.

Cautions and Comments

Accreditation, for the most part, provides some assurances to the consumer (e.g., students, parents, community, potential employers) that the school, college, university, or even program has been reviewed by outsiders and evaluated relative to some set of standards. There are many accrediting organizations, and a caution is provided that accreditation does not mean that every institution is appropriate for every individual. Accreditation should be only one part of any determination that a program, school, or college is appropriate for any given individual or purpose. For students matriculating to college or university, parents should consider the accreditation status of a program, school, or college/university relative to the ability for a graduate of that institution to get into further studies (e.g., from high school to college, graduate school, law school).

Some organizations exist that purport to provide accreditation but are generally not well recognized or accepted. It is always wise to check, not only with the institution in which one is interested, to determine the accreditation status of that institution and to find out which agency is providing the accreditation. If the accreditation is not provided by one of the five regional accrediting agencies, a thorough check of the accreditation process used would be wise. Information regarding the ability of students to get into colleges/universities from high schools, or from colleges/universities to graduate or professional schools, and even regarding the placement success of graduates of the program or college/university, is valuable in making a decision to place a student.

Accreditation provides a vehicle for programs, schools, colleges, and universities to seek independent evaluation and assurances that they are meeting their stated goals against some specific standards.

Publishers

Middle States Association of Schools and Colleges (MSASC), 3624 Market Street, Philadelphia, PA 19104-2680; Web site: http://www.msa.org.

North Central Association (NCA), Arizona State University, P.O. Box 873011, Tempe, AZ 85287-3011; Web site: http://www.ncacasi.org.

Northwest Association of Schools and Colleges (NASC), 1910 University Drive, Boise ID 83725-1060; Web site: http://www2.boisestate.edu/nasc.

Southern Association of Colleges and Schools (SACS), 1866 Southern Lane, Decatur, GA 30033; Web site: http://www.sacs.org.

Western Association of Schools and Colleges (WASC), 985 Atlantic Avenue, Suite 100, Alameda CA 94501; Web site: http://www.wascweb.org/.

National Accreditation Standards for Teacher Education

Derivation of Criteria

The National Council for Accreditation of Teacher Education (NCATE) revises its unit accreditation standards every five years through the Standards Committee of its Unit Accreditation Board. The last revision process began in 1997 and included reviewing literature on research on teaching and learning, on effective teacher preparation programs, and on regional accreditation. The Standards Committee also reviewed standards of accrediting bodies, including the Interstate New Teacher Assessment and Support Consortium (INTASC), the National Board for Professional Teaching Standards (NBPTS), and the NCATE's existing state partnership framework. Feedback was solicited through presentations at professional conferences and through the NCATE's web site.

Criteria

Each college and university that is NCATE accredited must demonstrate effectiveness according to the profession's expectations for high-quality teacher preparation. The standards serve as the basis for assessment of the unit by a Board of Examiners team. There are two sections for the six standards, with each standard containing three components. Those components are: (1) the language of the standard itself; (2) rubrics that delineate the elements of each standard and describe three proficiency levels at which each element is being addressed; and (3) a descriptive explanation of the standard. The standards are as follows:

NCATE Standards for Teacher Education

Candidate Performance	*Unit Capacity*
Candidate Knowledge, Skills, and Dispositions	Field experiences and clinical practice
Assessment System and Unit Evaluation	Diversity
	Faculty Qualifications, Performance, and Development
	Unit Governance and Resources

Source: http://www.ncate.org.

Cautions and Comments

These standards are designed solely for the purpose of evaluating teacher-training programs in the United States for accreditation purposes. In addition to the NCATE standards that serve as a framework for the evaluation process, the NCATE approves standards for the profession in each of 17 professional categories. Those standards are the basis for program evaluation within the framework of the NCATE's standards. The importance of being familiar with these standards for school district personnel lies in the value of hiring teachers from NCATE-approved programs and in understanding the importance of collaborative efforts with colleges and universities in the district's area in order to ensure quality teacher development.

Publisher

National Council for Accreditation of Teacher Education, 2010 Massachusetts Avenue NW, Suite 500, Washington, DC 20036; Phone: 202-466-7496; Fax: 202-296-6620; Web site: http://www.ncate.org.

Curriculum Standards for Physical Education

Derivation of Criteria

In 1995, the National Association for Sport and Physical Education (NASPE) developed standards for physical education following the development (in 1986) of five major focus areas that define what a physically educated person can do. The standards are supported by sample performance benchmarks to describe developmentally appropriate behaviors.

Criteria

The standards are based on five major focus areas defined to specify that a physically educated person (1) has learned skills necessary to perform a variety of physical activities, (2) is physically fit, (3) participates regularly in physical activity, (4) knows the implications of and the benefits from involvement in physical activities, and (5) values physical activity and its contribution to a healthful lifestyle. The content standards are as follows:

National Physical Education Standards

* Demonstrates competency in many movement forms and proficiency in a few movement forms.
* Applies involvement concepts and principles to the learning and development of motor skills.
* Exhibits a physically active lifestyle.
* Achieves and maintains a health-enhancing level of physical fitness.
* Demonstrates responsible personal and social behavior in physical activity settings.
* Demonstrates understanding and respect for differences among people in physical activity settings.
* Understands that physical activity provides opportunities for enjoyment, challenge, self-expression, and social interaction.

Source: http://www.ed.gov/databases/eric_digests/ed406361.html.

Cautions and Comments

The physical education standards provide a framework for the development of curriculum. The NASPE provides curricular recommendations and sample benchmarks for the implementation of developmentally appropriate activities. Evaluation of programs in physical education will likely be highly performance based, and curricula should be measured against the framework provided in the standards.

Publisher

The American Alliance for Health, Physical Education, Recreation & Dance, 1900 Association Drive, Reston, VA 20192-1598; Phone: 800-213-7193; Web site: http://www.aahperd.org/naspe/template.cfm.

Curriculum Standards for Adapted Physical Education

Derivation of Criteria

The first definitive national standards in adapted physical education define what any professional needs to know to teach students with disabilities. The standards were developed through a committee process where a professional in the field headed each standard. The standards were developed through the National Consortium for Physical Education and Recreation for Individuals with Disabilities (NCPERID).

Criteria

National Adapted Physical Education Standards

1. Human Development
2. Motor Behavior
3. Exercise Science
4. Measurement and Evaluation
5. History and Philosophy
6. Unique Attributes of Learners
7. Curriculum Theory and Development
8. Assessment
9. Instructional Design and Planning
10. Teaching
11. Consultation and Staff Development
12. Student and Program Evaluation
13. Continuing Education
14. Ethics
15. Communication

Source: http://www.twu.edu/o/apens/natstnd.html.

Cautions and Comments

The adapted physical education standards provide a framework for the development of curriculum for teaching individuals with disabilities. The NCPERID provides information on major components of the standard, subcomponents, adapted physical education content, and application of content knowledge for assessing individuals with disabilities in adapted physical education. Evaluation of programs in adapted physical education will likely be highly performance based, and curricula should be measured against the framework provided in the standards.

Publisher

The National Consortium for Physical Education and Recreation for Individuals with Disabilities (NCPERID); Phone: 813-974-3443; Fax: 813-974-4979; Web site: http://www.twu.edu/o/apens/ncperid.htm.

Standards for School Counseling

Derivation of Criteria

The American School Counselor Association (ASCA) developed the standards for school counselors in 1997. There are nine standards in three domains that are based on a national survey of practicing school counselors and reviewed by 50 leaders in school counseling. The standards serve as a framework to allow local development to meet needs and improve program quality for students.

Criteria

The domains and standards for school counseling are intended to provide an organizational tool to identify and prioritize an effective school counseling program. The domains and standards are as follows:

National Standards for School Counseling

Domain	*Standards*
Academic Development	A. Students will acquire the attitudes, knowledge, and skills contributing to effective learning in school and across the life span.
	B. Students will complete school with the academic preparation essential to choose from a wide range of substantial postsecondary options, including college.
	C. Students will understand the relationship of academics to the world of work and to life at home and in the community.
Career Development	A. Students will acquire the skills to investigate the world of work in relation to knowledge of self and to make informed career decisions.
	B. Students will employ strategies to achieve future career success and satisfaction.
	C. Students will understand the relationship between personal qualities, education, and training and the world of work.
Personal/Social Development	A. Students will acquire the attitudes, knowledge, and interpersonal skills to help them understand and respect self and others.
	B. Students will make decisions, set goals, and take necessary action to achieve goals.
	C. Students will understand safety and survival skills.

Source: http://www.schoolcounselor.org.

Cautions and Comments

The standards are broad and provide a framework for the development of counselor training programs as well as curricula for grades K–12. The extent to which these standards are addressed in a school or district may well depend on the availability of qualified personnel to design and implement such a program. It is important for the evaluator to assess the purpose of the school-counseling program in its design, as well as to assess it against the national standards. Given that most schools offer specific courses related to counseling, it will be important that the type of evaluation plan to be used includes opportunities for evaluation of data as well as qualitative strategies, as addressed in the introduction to Part VI.

Publisher

American School Counselor Association, 801 North Fairfax Street, #310, Alexandria, VA 22314; Phone: 703-683-2722; Web site: http://www.schoolcounselor.org.

Curriculum Standards for Science

Derivation of Criteria

The Governing Board of the National Research Council (NRC) approved the National Science Education Standards in 1996. The NRC members are drawn from the councils of the National Academy of Sciences, the National Academy of Engineering, and the Institute of Medicine. The NRC reports that the committee responsible for the report of the standards was chosen for their specific competences and with regard for balance. The National Science Teachers Association (NSTA) supports the use of the standards to guide a vision of science education in schools and suggests that the standards provide a framework to make decisions about how well an educational system supports and is progressing toward a scientifically literate society.

Criteria

The standards for science teaching are grounded in five assumptions: (1) changes are needed throughout the entire system, (2) teaching greatly influences what students learn, (3) teachers' perceptions of science as an enterprise and a subject to be taught and learned affects their actions, (4) individual and social processes actively contribute to constructing student understanding, and (5) teachers' actions deeply influence their understanding and relationships with students. The standards focus on qualities most associated with science teaching and the vision of science education described in the following:

The National Science Education Standards

Science Teaching Standards: Define what teachers of science should know and be able to do.

Professional Development Standards: Present a vision for the development of professional knowledge and skills among teachers.

Assessment Standards: Provide criteria against which to judge the quality of assessment practices.

Science Content Standards: Outline what students should know, understand, and be able to do in the natural sciences over the course of K–12 education.

Science Education Program Standards: Describe the conditions necessary for quality school programs.

Science Education System Standards: Provide criteria for judging the performance of the overall science education system.

Source: http://www.nsta.org/159&id=24.

Cautions and Comments

The standards are organized in six general areas and cover the range of teaching, content, assessment, professional development, and program standards. Each of the areas is extensively described and supporting documentation provided. The NSTA is working through various groups to ensure the implementation of the standards and encourages evaluation of them. Depending on the purpose of the evaluation, the specific criteria and descriptions would have to be examined and decisions made regarding which aspects should be included in the evaluation.

Publisher

The National Academies, 2101 Constitution Avenue NW, Washington, DC 20418; Phone: 202-334-2000; Web site: http://www.nationalacademies.org/nrc/governing.html.

Curriculum Standards for Social Studies

Derivation of Criteria

The Curriculum Standards for Social Studies were developed by a Task Force of the National Council for the Social Studies (NCSS) and approved by the NCSS Board of Directors in April 1994.

Criteria

According to the NCSS, the social studies standards provide an irreducible minimum of what is essential in social studies. The standards are established as 10 thematic curriculum standards, and the NCSS provides student performance expectations and instructional guidelines. The standards (presented below) were intended to provide criteria for making decisions about why to teach social studies, what to teach, how to teach well to all students, and how to assess what students can apply of what they have learned. The 10 thematic curriculum standards and accompanying sets of student performance expectations constitute an irreducible minimum of what is essential in social studies.

NCSS Social Studies Standards

Culture: Social studies programs should include experiences that provide for the study of culture and cultural diversity.

Time, continuity, and change: Social studies programs should include experiences that provide for the study of the ways human beings view themselves in and over time.

People, places, and environments: Social studies programs should include experiences that provide for the study of people, places, and environments.

Individual development and identity: Social studies programs should include experiences that provide for the study of individual development and identity.

Individuals, groups, and institutions: Social studies programs should include experiences that provide for the study of interactions among individuals, groups, and institutions.

Power, authority, and governance: Social studies programs should include experiences that provide for the study of how people create and change structures of power, authority, and governance.

Production, distribution, and consumption: Social studies programs should include experiences that provide for the study of how people organize for the production, distribution, and consumption of goods and services.

Science, technology, and society: Social studies programs should include experiences that provide for the study of relationships among science, technology, and society.

Global connections: Social studies programs should include experiences that provide for the study of global connections and interdependence.

Civic ideals and practices: Social studies programs should include experiences that provide for the study of the ideals, principles, and practices of citizenship in a democratic republic.

Source: http://www.ncss.org/standards.

Cautions and Comments

The Curriculum Standards for Social Studies provide a broad framework from which curriculum developers can create specific curricula for schools, districts, and states. While they can be used to assess programs in social studies, the evaluation would need to include the curriculum which has been designed based on the standards. Types of evaluation that could be used are identified in the first part of Part VI.

Publisher

National Council for the Social Studies, 8555 Sixteenth Street, Suite 500, Silver Spring, MD 20910; Phone: 301-588-1800; Fax: 301-588-2049; Web site: http://www.ncss.org.

Content Standards for Special Education

Derivation of Criteria

The Council for Exceptional Children (CEC) has identified 10 standards that are designed to be used across all programs that train teachers for serving students with disabilities. These standards have been approved by the National Council for Accreditation of Teacher Education and were used in 2002 for program approval.

Criteria

The three areas for evaluation of special education programs are Field Experience and Clinical Practice Standards, Assessment System Standards, and Special Education Content Standards. The standards are presented in the figure on the following page. Extensive narrative is provided with each of the standards through the CEC.

National Standards for Special Education Program Evaluation

Field Experiences and Clinical Practice Standard	*Assessment System Standards*	*Content Standards*
	Assessments address components of each content standard	Foundations
	Assessments are relevant and consistent with each content standard	Development characteristics of learners
	Assessments are planned, refined, and implemented by key stakeholders	Individual learning differences
	Multiple measures (both internal and external) are used and are systematic and ongoing across components of the program	Instructional strategies
	The assessment system is clearly delineated and communicated to candidates	Learning environments and social interactions
	Assessments are credible and rigorous	Language
	The assessment system includes critical decision points	Instructional planning
	The assessment data are regularly and systematically compiled, analyzed, and summarized	Assessment
	The assessment data are used for program improvement	Professional and ethical practice
		Collaboration

Source: http://www.cec.sped.org.

Cautions and Comments

The purpose of these standards is to address the preparation of teachers for positions in special education. The unique nature of this field of education requires that there be attention to the specific needs that are evidenced by the disability being addressed. These are addressed in the narrative provided by the CEC. While the standards are, for the most part, used by faculty in college and university teacher preparation programs, they serve to inform school administrators of expectations established for the preparation that future employees in this field should demonstrate.

Publisher

Council for Exceptional Children, 1110 North Glebe Road, Suite 300, Arlington, VA 22201; Voice phone: 703-620-3660; TTY: 703-264-9446; Fax: 703-264-9494; Web site: http://www.cecsped.org.

Standards for Staff Development

Derivation of Criteria

The National Staff Development Council (NSDC) has published standards for professional educators' staff development programs. The original standards, which were written in 1995, have been revised from 27 standards to 12. It is the intention of the NSDC that these standards be used to stimulate discussion and analysis to greater staff development effectiveness.

Criteria

The criteria for staff development are based on three main standards that are elaborated by 12 principles. These are provided in the figure below.

National Standards for Staff Development

Context Standards	*Process Standards*	*Content Standards*
Staff development that improves the learning of all students:		
Organizes adults into learning communities whose goals are aligned with those of the school and district. (Learning Communities)	Uses disaggregated student data to determine adult learning priorities, monitor progress, and help sustain continuous improvement. (Data-Driven)	Prepares educators to understand and appreciate all students, create safe, orderly and supportive learning environments, and hold high expectations for their academic achievement. (Equity)
Requires skillful school and district leaders who guide continuous instructional improvement. (Leadership)	Uses multiple sources of information to guide improvement and demonstrate its impact. (Evaluation)	Deepens educators' content knowledge, provides them with research-based instructional strategies to assist students in meeting rigorous academic standards, and prepares them to use various types of classroom assessments appropriately. (Quality Teaching)
Requires resources to support adult learning and collaboration. (Resources)	Prepares educators to apply research to decision-making. (Research-based)	Provides educators with the knowledge and skills to involve families and other stakeholders appropriately. (Family involvement)
	Uses learning strategies appropriate to the intended goal. (Design)	

Context Standards	*Process Standards*	*Content Standards*
	Applies knowledge about human learning and change. (Learning)	
	Provides educators with the knowledge and skills to collaborate. (Collaboration)	

Source: http://www.nsdc.org.

Cautions and Comments

The standards provide a framework from which to evaluate or develop a staff development plan in a district. It should be noted that the standards and their descriptions are broad, and any plan or evaluation will require specificity at the school or district level in order to ensure that the plan is measurable and/or to know what the evaluation is to assess.

Publisher

National Staff Development Council, P.O. Box 240, Oxford, OH 45056; Phone: 513-523-6029; Web site: http://www.nsdc.org.

Curriculum Standards for Technology

Derivation of Criteria

The International Society for Technology in Education (ISTE) released standards and profiles in 1997 as the first part of a major standards project that will include revised materials and a scope and sequence of educational technology performance indicators. The National Education Technology Standards (NETS) Project is an initiative of the ISTE's Accreditation and Professional Standards Committee.

Criteria

The six broad categories of the technology foundation standards for students provide a framework for planning technology-based activities to address the standards that are to be introduced, reinforced, and mastered by students. The standards are presented within their broad categories in the figure on the following page.

Cautions and Comments

The ever-increasing need to maintain a competitive edge in the technology-literate world requires program standards in order for school personnel to develop and evaluate the effectiveness of technology in their schools. Since 1990, large sums of money have been spent to provide technology in many forms in schools across the country, and the standards provide the framework for evaluating the instructional aspects of that investment. It is important to note that the standards do not limit technology

National Technology Standards for All Students

Category	*Standards*
Basic operations and concepts	Students demonstrate a sound understanding of the nature and operation of technology systems.
	Students are proficient in the use of technology.
Social, ethical, and human issues	Students understand the ethical, cultural, and societal issues related to technology.
	Students practice responsible use of technology systems, information, and software.
	Students develop positive attitudes toward technology uses that support lifelong learning, collaboration, personal pursuits, and productivity.
Technology productivity tools	Students use technology tools to enhance learning, increase productivity, and promote creativity.
	Students use productivity tools to collaborate in constructing technology-enhanced models, preparing publications, and producing other creative works.
Technology communication tools	Students use telecommunications to collaborate, publish, and interact with peers, experts, and other audiences.
	Students use a variety of media and formats to communicate information and ideas effectively to multiple audiences.
Technology research tools	Students use technology to locate, evaluate, and collect information from a variety of sources.
	Students use technology tools to process data and report results.
	Students evaluate and select new information resources and technological innovations based on the appropriateness to specific tasks.
Technology problem-solving and decision-making tools	Students use technology resources for solving problems and making informed decisions.
	Students employ technology in the development of strategies for solving problems in the real world.

Source: http://www.iste.org/standards/index.html.

education to specific classes in technology, but in fact address the broad impact of technology on the student as learner.

Implications for the evaluator in assessing technology from these standards are multiple. First, these standards are designed for instructional considerations, so the evaluator must consider the impact on instructional programs. Second, these standards address learning across the curriculum, so it will be necessary to assess the use and impact across the curriculum. Third, these standards do not address the costs of acquiring, maintaining, and supporting the use of technology, so the evaluator will need to determine these factors through facilities and equipment standards.

Publisher

International Society for Technology in Education, 480 Charnelton Street, Eugene,

OR 97401-2626; Phone: 800-336-5191; Fax: 541-302-3778; Web site: http://www. iste.org.

Standards for Vocational Education

Derivation of Criteria

Criteria for performance standards for vocational education are outcome-based performance indicators intended to provide a basis for each state to evaluate the quality of its vocational technical education programs. The U.S. Office of Vocational and Adult Education (OVAE) developed these standards as required in the Carl D. Perkins Vocational and Applied Technology Education Act (1990). State criteria may exceed these standards, but must include them.

Criteria

Current criteria are provided under the Perkins Act (1990).

- Measures of learning and competency gains, including student progress in the achievement of basic and academic skills;
- One or more measures of performance, such as competency attainment, job or work skill attainment, retention in school/secondary school completion, and placement (in school, job, military);
- Incentives and adjustments designed to encourage service to targeted groups and special population students; and
- Procedures for using existing resources and methods in use by other programs receiving federal assistance, such as the Job Training Partnership Act Program and the Job Opportunities and Basic Skills Training Program (http://www. ed.gov/offices/ovae/standard.html).

Cautions and Comments

These criteria will lead to primarily data-driven (e.g., school completion numbers) or descriptive artifacts (e.g., description of incentives employed to encourage service to special populations). In evaluating vocational programs, it will be necessary to determine individual state and/or district criteria that may have been developed. Clear definitions of terms, such as "competency attainment," will contribute to the quality of the evaluation.

Publisher

Office of Vocational and Adult Education, U.S. Department of Education, 400 Maryland Avenue SW, Washington, DC 20202; Phone: 800-USA-LEARN; Fax: 202-401-0689; Web site: http://www.ed.gov/offices/ovae/standard.html.

Standards for School Facilities Evaluation

Derivation of Criteria

The National School Boards Association (NSBA) provides minimum standards for facility planning. These are designed to enable school districts to define the programmatic, functional, spatial, and environmental requirements of the educational facility.

Criteria

Philosophy Statement. A philosophy statement covers the building as a whole and *each* instructional program.

Program Goals. The educational goals of each instructional program are clearly defined. This includes learning objectives and the psychological and emotional concerns of students, when appropriate (as in the guidance suite and exceptional education rooms).

Program Activities. Well-defined program activities determine functional need and ultimately the design of a successful learning environment. Remember the saying, "form follows function." Program activities, whether in the classroom, media center, or administrative area, determine the "function" of the learning environment.

Student Population. The projected enrollment of the entire building and the maximum capacity needed for each space is important in defining spatial requirements.

Space Summary. Itemizing each functional space and determining square footage allocations is essential in determining total building square footage and establishing a realistic construction budget.

Instructional Technology. New applications of instructional technology planned for the near future and considered for the distant future should be described program by program and in terms of building-wide plans.

Functional Relationship. Each program space should be described in terms of its functional relationship to other activities. Functional relationships should also be established between departments, such as math and science, English and the media center, and administration and guidance.

General Conditions. In addition to the general program requirements identified above, many educational specifications describe internal building requirements in detail, including but not limited to heating and air conditioning, windows, floor coverings, water, lighting, acoustics, access for people and vehicles, and security (http://www.nsba.org/sbot/toolkit/facplan.html).

Cautions and Comments

The development of new school facilities or the renovation of existing facilities is a specialized aspect of school evaluation that requires knowledgeable staff working with specialists in many areas, particularly architecture. The criteria provided by the NSBA provides a basis for interested school and district personnel, as well as parents and other interested community members, to ask relevant questions in a process that frequently engages much of a school board's time. It is important to consider the impact on the educational programs of the facility, since the adage "form follows function" is certainly true for a school building. Some states provide specific criteria for school facilities, and those should be considered as well in any evaluation or development of school facilities' plans.

Publisher

National School Boards Association, 1680 Duke Street, Alexandria, VA 22314; Phone: 703-838-6722; Fax: 703-683-7590; Web site: http://www.nsba.org.

REFERENCES

Baker, A.J.L., & Soden, L. M. (1998). *The challenges of parent involvement research*. ERIC Clearinghouse on Urban Education, Institute for Urban and Minority Education, Teachers College, Columbia University. (ERIC Document Reproduction Service No. ED 419 030)

Becker, H. J., & Epstein, J. L. (1982). *Influences on teachers' use of parent involvement at home* (Report #324). Baltimore, MD: Johns Hopkins University, Center for Social Organization of Schools. (ERIC Document Reproduction Service No. ED 219 364)

Blumberg, A. (1987, November). *A discussion on the effects of local, state, and federal mandates on supervisory practices*. Paper presented at the annual conference of the Council of Professors of Instructional Supervision, Philadelphia.

Bronfenbrenner, U. (1979). *The ecology of human development*. Cambridge, MA: Harvard University Press.

Brown, A. L., & Ferrara, R. A. (1985). Diagnosing zones of proximal development: An alternative to standardized testing? In J. Wertsch (Ed.), *Culture, communication and cognition: Vygotskian perspectives* (pp. 273–305). New York: Cambridge University Press.

Campione, J. C., & Brown, A. L. (1984). Learning ability and transfer propensity as sources of individual differences in intelligence. In P. H. Brooks, R. Sperber, & C. McCauley (Eds.), *Learning and cognition in the mentally retarded* (pp. 137–150). Baltimore, MD: University Park Press.

Carlson, D. L. (1989). Managing the urban school crisis: Recent trends in curricular reform. *Journal of Education 171*(3), 89–108.

Carlson, J. S., & Wiedl, K. H. (1978). The use of testing-the-limits procedures in the assessment of intellectual capabilities in children with learning difficulties. *American Journal of Mental Deficiency 82*, 559–564.

Character Education Partnership. (2002). *Character education*. Available online at http://www.character.org.

Cooper, H. (1989). *Homework* (Research on Teaching monograph series). New York: Longman.

Council of Chief State School Officers (CCSSO). (1996). *Interstate school leaders licensure consortium: Standards for school leaders*. Washington, DC: CCSSO.

Council of Professors of Instructional Supervision. (1988, November). *Resolution on effective teaching*. Annual meeting, San Antonio, TX.

Dembo, M. H., Sweitzer, J., & Lauritzen, P. (1985). An evaluation of group parent education: Behavioral, PET, and Adlerian programs. *Review of Educational Research 55*, 155–200.

Edmonds, R. (1979). Effective schools for the urban poor. *Educational Leadership 37*(1), 15–24.

Epstein, J. L. (1983). *Homework practices, achievements, and behaviors of elementary school students.* (ERIC Document Reproduction Service No. ED 250 351)

Fox, R. B., & Peck, R. F. (1978). *Personal characteristics of teachers that affect student learning.* Paper presented at the annual meeting of the American Educational Research Association, Toronto.

Friedman, M. I. (2000). *Ensuring student success: A handbook of evidence-based strategies.* Columbia, SC: The Institute for Evidence-Based Decision-Making in Education.

Friedman, M. I., & Fisher, S. P. (1998). *Handbook on effective instructional strategies: Evidence for decision-making.* Columbia, SC: The Institute for Evidence-Based Decision-Making in Education.

Glickman, C. D., Gordon, S. P., & Ross-Gordon, J. M. (2001). *Supervision and instructional leadership: A developmental approach.* Boston: Allyn and Bacon.

Good, T., & Brophy, J. (1985). Schools effects. In M. C. Wittrock (Ed.), *Handbook of research on teaching* (3rd ed., pp. 570–602). New York: Macmillan.

Goodson, B. D., & Hess, R. D. (1976). *The effects of parent training programs on child performance and parent behavior.* Stanford, CA: Stanford University. (ERIC Document Reproduction Service No. ED 136 912)

Gooler, D. D. (1979). Evaluating distance education programs. *Canadian Journal of University Continuing Education 6*(1), 43–55.

Gordon, E. W., & Armour-Thomas, E. (1992). Urban education. In M. C. Alkin (Ed.), *Encyclopedia of educational research* (6th ed.). New York: Macmillan.

Gottfredson, D. C. (1987). An evaluation of an organization development approach to reducing school disorder. *Evaluation Review 11*, 739–763.

Hallinan, M. T., & Tuma, N. B. (1978). Classroom effects on changes in children's friendships. *Sociology of Education 51*(4), 270–282.

Hart, A., & Ogawa, R. (1987). The influence of superintendents on the academic achievement of school districts. *The Journal of Educational Administration 25*, 72–84.

Joyce, B., Showers, B., & Rolheiser-Bennett, C. (1987). Staff development and student learning: A synthesis of research on models of teaching. *Educational Leadership 45*(2), 11–23.

Lempesis, C. W. (1984). *A study to identify the competencies that experts agree are important for effective department leaders in secondary schools.* Unpublished dissertation, University of South Carolina, Columbia.

MacCormick, A. H. (1976). *The education of adult prisoners: A survey and a program.* New York: AMS Press. (Original work published in 1931.)

Minsky, M. (1974). A framework for representing knowledge. In P. Winston (Ed.), *The psychology of computer vision* (pp. 94–104). New York: McGraw-Hill.

Moore, D. M. (Ed.). (2002). *Technology and learning: Putting the research to work.* Hot Topics Series. (ERIC Document Reproduction Service No. ED 462 067)

Moore, M. A., & Cozine, G. T. (2000). Readings in Distance Education Number 7: Web-based communications, the Internet, and distance education. Available online at http://www.ed.psu.edu/acsde/readings/annread7.asp.

Palinscar, A. S., & Brown, A. L. (1989). Classroom dialogues to promote self-regulated comprehension. In J. Brophy (Ed.), *Teaching for understanding and self-regulated learning* (Vol. 1). Greenwich, CT: JAI Press.

Palincsar, A. S., & Winn, J. (1992). Dynamic assessment. In M. C. Alkin (Ed.), *Encyclopedia of educational research* (6th ed.). New York: Macmillan.

Reynolds, A., & Wheatley, G. H. (1996). Elementary students' construction and coordination of units in an area setting. *Journal for Research in Mathematics Education 27*(5), 564–581.

Rhodes, J. E., & Jason, L. A. (1988). The retrospective pretest: An alternative approach in evaluating drug prevention programs. *Journal of Drug Education 17*(4), 345–356.

Shakeshaft, C., Campbell, P. B., & Karp, K. S. (1992). Sexism and racism in educational research. In M. C. Alkin (Ed.), *Encyclopedia of educational research* (6th ed). New York: Macmillan.

Shiffrin, R. M., & Atkinson, R. C. (1969). Storage and retrieval processes in long-term memory. *Psychological Review 76*, 179–183.

Slavin, R. E., & Madden, N. A. (1999) *Success for All/Roots and Wings.* Available online at http://www.csos.jhu.edu.

SouthEastern Vision for Education (SERVE). (1998). *Teacher evaluation: The road to excellence.* Greensboro, NC: SERVE.

Stronge, J. H., & Helm, V. M. (1991). *Evaluating professional support personnel in education.* Newbury Park, CA: Sage Publications.

Tyler, R. W. (1950). The organization of learning experiences. In V. Herrick & R. Tyler (Eds.), *Toward improved curriculum.* Chicago: University of Chicago Press.

U.S. Department of Education. (2001). Overview of public elementary and secondary schools and districts: School year 1999–2000. NCES Statistical Analysis Report. Available online at http://nces.ed.gov/pubs2001/overview/table08.asp.

Van Patten, J., Chao, C., & Reigeluth, C. M. (1986). The effects of format and structure of a synthesizer on procedural-decision learning. IDD&E Working Paper No. 22. (ERIC Document Reproduction Service No. ED 289 469)

Wiles, J., & Bondi, J. (2000). *Supervision: A guide to practice* (5th ed.) Upper Saddle River, NJ: Merrill-Prentice Hall.

Wittrock, M. C. (1992). Knowledge acquisition and comprehension. In M. C. Alkin (Ed.), *Encyclopedia of educational research* (6th ed.). New York: Macmillan.

Wixson, K. K., & Lipson, M. Y. (1986). Reading (dis)abilities: An interactionist perspective. In T. E. Raphael (Ed.), *Contexts of school-based literacy* (pp. 131–148). New York: Random House.

Ziegler, S. (1987). *The effects of parental involvement on children's achievement: The significance of home/school links* (Research section report #185). Toronto: Toronto Board of Education. (ERIC Document Reproduction Service No. ED 304 234)

RECOMMENDED READINGS IN EVALUATION

Eisner, E. W. (2002). *The educational imagination: On the design and evaluation of school programs* (3rd ed.). Upper Saddle River, NJ: Merrill-Prentice Hall.

Joint Committee on Standards for Educational Evaluation. (1988). *The personnel evaluation standards: How to assess systems for evaluating educators.* Newbury Park, CA: Sage Publications.

Joint Committee on Standards for Educational Evaluation. (1994). *The program evaluation standards* (2nd ed.). Thousand Oaks, CA: Sage Publications.

Shinkfield, A. J., & Stufflebeam, D. (1995). *Teacher evaluation: Guide to effective practice.* Boston: Kluwer Academic Publishers.

Glossary

Absolute scores: Absolute scores measure each variable across the whole continuum of that variable without regard to age or grade.

Accountability testing: Testing done to determine whether educators, students, and educational institutions are meeting established standards of desirable performance.

Achievement certification tests: Tests used to certify students' achievement of learning objectives.

Admissions tests: Tests used to decide the extent to which individuals are qualified to enter a school or profession.

Age-equivalent score: A score that indicates the age level for which a particular performance is typical.

Aggregation procedures: Procedures used to weigh and summarize scores assigned to specimens of a student's achievement.

Aptitude test: An instrument used to predict individuals' performance in a particular future situation.

Assessment: The process of collecting and analyzing data for the purpose of making decisions about educational variables, including instruction, learning, students, and factors that affect them.

Ceiling criteria: Criteria specified by test authors establishing the highest level of student performance on a test. When the ceiling is reached, students stop taking the test.

Correlation coefficient: A decimal number between .00 and +/−1 that indicates the degree to which quantitative variables are related.

Criterion-referenced instrument: An instrument that enables an individual's performance to be compared to a criterion of desirable performance.

Demographics: Characteristics of a sample or population (e.g., age, education, ethnicity).

Derived score: A score that indicates a person's performance relative to members of a comparison group.

Educator evaluation instruments: Instruments used to compare the performance of educators to criteria of desirable performance.

Ethnographic observations: Observations made to describe behavior and events in naturalistic settings, usually over an extended period of time.

Grade-equivalent score: A score that indicates the grade level for which a particular performance is typical.

Instructional prescription tests: Tests used to determine the lessons to be prescribed for students in order to maximize their opportunity to achieve learning objectives.

Instrument: Any procedure or device used to collect data.

Interview: A method of obtaining data by orally questioning subjects.

Likert scale: A self-reporting instrument that indicates the extent to which respondents agree with statements. It is used to indicate respondents' attitude or belief.

Norm group or **norm sample:** A group with known demographic characteristics, such as age, sex, grade in school, or socioeconomic status, to whom an examinee's test performance may be compared.

Normal-curve equivalents: Standard scores with a mean of 100 and a standard deviation of 21.06.

Norm-referenced instrument: An instrument that enables comparison of an individual's performance to the performance of a group of individuals on the same instrument.

Objective-referenced instrument: An instrument that enables students' achievement to be compared to a learning objective being pursued.

Objectivity (of a test): A test is objective to the extent that different interpreters of the same test results are consistent in their interpretations.

Percentile rank (percentiles): Derived scores that indicate the percentage of people whose scores are at or below a given raw score.

Placement tests: Tests used to determine the programs or classes to which students are to be assigned based on their readiness capabilities.

Population: A group with defined or specified characteristics.

Portfolio: A collection of a student's products used to assess student achievement.

Projective instrument: An instrument that causes respondents to impose their feelings in reacting to neutral, ambiguous stimuli.

Qualitative data: Categorical data usually described using words. Qualitative data vary in type but not degree.

Qualitative observations: Observations made to obtain categorical descriptions of events.

Quantitative data: Data that have been given numerical value.

Questionnaire: A paper-and-pencil instrument that elicits respondents' answers to questions.

Rating scale: An instrument used by judges to rate the performance or products of individuals or groups.

Raw scores: The basic scores derived by following test directions for scoring a test.

Readiness: The ability to perform a task.

Referral: A request for help from a specialist.

Referral tests: Tests used to initially detect underlying causes of students' failure to learn as a basis for seeking the help of an appropriate specialist.

Reliability (of a test): A test is reliable to the extent that there is consistency in the results of repeated administrations of the test to the same individuals or population.

Reliability coefficient: A correlation coefficient that indicates the degree to which results of different administrations of the same test are consistent.

Sample: A representative subgroup of a population.

School evaluation instruments: Instruments used to compare the attributes of schools to criteria of desirable attributes.

Screening: The process of initially searching for evidence of problems.

Standard deviation: A measure of the variability in an array of scores.

Standard score: A derived score that indicates how far a given raw score is from the mean in terms of standard deviation units.

Standardized test: A test in which the administration, scoring, and interpretation adhere to specified procedures.

Stanines: Standard-score bands that divide a distribution into nine parts; the fifth stanine is centered on the mean.

Starting point criteria: Criteria specified by test authors establishing the lower level at which students begin taking a test.

Test: A systematic procedure conceived to observe responses to stimuli for a particular purpose.

Testing: Observing responses to stimuli for a particular purpose.

Validity (of a test): A test is valid to the extent that it facilitates the description of the characteristics in the population it was constructed to describe.

Vocational interest inventories: Instruments used to identify individuals' interest in occupations, vocations, and careers.

Index of Test Titles

Each test reviewed in this handbook is listed below. The tests are alphabetized by test title. The acronym for each test is also specified. Page numbers indicate where tests are reviewed or cited.

Index of Test Acronyms

Most of the tests reviewed in this handbook are commonly referred to with an acronym. Following is an alphabetical index of the acronyms with the test name and the pages on which that test review can be found.

Characteristics Index

Each of the test reviews in this handbook contains a section entitled "Characteristics Described." The following index lists the characteristics included in each of the sections of each test review and gives the pages on which they can be found. Thus, the user can look in the index for the characteristics for which she/he wishes to test and find the review of the test or tests which cover those characteristics.

Test Classification Index

Each test reviewed in this handbook has been assigned a classification indicating a primary purpose of the test. The reader should find this Test Classification Index convenient for locating tests of a particular type. The classifications are in alphabetical order and the tests are alphabetized under the classification label.

Achievement

Adaptive Behavior

College Readiness and Admission

Language

Mathematics

Motor Coordination

Problem Behavior

Reading

Index of Test Authors

This index includes the names of the authors of each test reviewed in the handbook and the page numbers of each test review. In addition, acronyms of each test are given. Where there is no acronym for the test, the complete name of the test is given.

Index of Reference Authors

The names of all of the authors cited in the handbook are included in this index. In addition, the page numbers of their citations are given.

Directory of Educational Test Publishers

This directory provides names, addresses, phone numbers, fax numbers, and web sites for companies that publish most tests used in educational institutions. Publishers are a valuable source of information on test revisions, price changes, specimen sets, and test descriptions. Their catalogs and most web sites are especially rich in information.

Ablin Press Distributors
700 John Ringling Boulevard, #1603, Sarasota, FL 34236-1504; Phone: 941-361-7521; Fax: 941-361-7521

Academic Therapy Publications
20 Commercial Boulevard, Novato, CA 94949-6191; Phone: 800-422-7249; Fax: 888-287-9925; Web site: www.academictherapy.com

Thomas M. Achenbach, Ph.D.
Child Behavior Checklist, University Medical Education Associates, 1 South Prospect Street, Room 6434, Burlington, VT 05401-3456; Phone: 802-656-8313; Fax: 802-656-2602; Web site: checklist.uvm.edu

ADE Incorporated
P.O. Box 660, Clarkston, MI 48347

Advantage Learning Systems, Inc.
P.O. Box 8036, Wisconsin Rapids, WI 54495-8036; Phone: 800-338-4204; Fax: 715-424-4242; e-mail: answers@advlearn.com; Web site: www.advlearn.com

AJA Associates
c/o Marchman Psychology, 720 South Dubuque, Iowa City, IA 52240

American College Testing
2201 North Dodge Street, P.O. Box 168, Iowa City, IA 52243-0168; Phone: 319-337-1000; Fax: 319-339-3021; Web site: www.act.org

American Guidance Service, Inc.
4201 Woodland Road, Circle Pines, MN 55014-1796; Phone: 800-328-2560; Fax: 800-471-8457; Web site: www.agsnet.com

Assessment Systems Corporation
2233 University Avenue, Suite 200, St. Paul, MN 55114-1629; Phone: 651-647-9220; Fax: 651-647-0412; Web site: www.assess.com

Association of American Colleges and Universities
1818 R Street NW, Washington, DC 20009; Phone: 202-387-3760; Fax: 202-265-9532; Web site: www.aacu-edu.org

Australian Council for Educational Research, Ltd.
19 Prospect Hill Road, Private Bag 55, Camberwell, Victoria 3124, Australia

Ballard & Tighe Publishers
48 Atlas Street, Brea, CA 92821

Behavior Data Systems, Ltd.
P.O. Box 44256, Phoenix, AZ 85064-4256

Behavior Science Systems, Inc.
P.O. Box 580274, Minneapolis, MN 55458; Phone: 612-929-6220; Fax: 612-920-4925

Behavioral-Developmental Initiatives
14636 North 55th Street, Scottsdale, AZ 85254; Phone: 800-405-2313; Fax: 602-494-2688; Web site: www.b-di.com

Millard J. Bienvenu, Ph.D.
Northwest Publications, 710 Watson Drive, Natchitoches, LA 71457; Phone: 318-352-5313

Bigby, Havis, & Associates, Inc.
12750 Merit Drive, Suite 660, Dallas, TX 75251; Phone: 972-233-6055; Fax: 972-233-3154; Web site: www.bigby.com

Brain Train
727 Twin Ridge Lane, Richmond, VA 23235; Phone: 804-320-0105; Fax: 804-320-0242

Brookes Publishing Co., Inc.
P.O. Box 10624, Baltimore, MD 21285-0624

Brunner/Mazel, Inc.
1900 Frost Road, Suite 101, Bristol, PA 19007-1598

California Counseling Centers
22797 Barton Road, Suite 200, Grand Terrace, CA 92324

The Cambridge Stratford Study Skills Institute
8560 Main Street, Williamsville, NY 14221

Cambridge University Press
110 Midland Avenue, Port Chester, NY 10573-4930; Phone: 800-872-7423; Fax: 914-937-4712

Canadian Test Centre
Educational Assessment Services, 85 Citizen Court, Suites 7 & 8, Markham, Ontario L6G 1A8, Canada

The CATI Corporation
10 East Costilla, Colorado Springs, CO 80903

Center for Applied Linguistics
1118 22nd Street NW, Washington, DC 20037

Center for the Study of Higher Education
The University of Memphis, Memphis, TN 38152

Centreville School
6201 Kennett Pike, Wilmington, DE 19807; Phone: 302-571-0230; Fax: 302-571-0270

Vicentita M. Cervera, Ed.D.
13 Miller Street, San Francisco Del Monte, Quezon City 1105, Philippines; Phone: 63-411-2673; Fax: 63-371-6490

Checkmate Plus, Ltd.
P.O. Box 696, Stony Brook, NY 11790-0696; Phone: 800-779-4292; Fax: 516-360-3432; Web site: www.checkmateplus.com

Child Welfare League of America, Inc.
Publications Department, 440 First Street NW, Suite #310, Washington, DC 20001-2085; Phone: 202-638-2952; Fax: 202-638-4004; Web site: www.cwla.org

The Clark Wilson Group, Inc.
4900 Nautilus Court North, Suite 220, Boulder, CO 80301-3242

CogniSyst, Inc.
3937 Nottaway Road, Durham, NC 27707

Cogscreen LLC
5021 Seminary Road, Suite 110, Alexandria, VA 22311

The College Board, PSAT/NMSQT Program
P.O. Box 6720, Princeton, NJ 08541-6720; Phone: 609-771-7070; 888-477-PSAT (Counselor Hot-line); e-mail: psat@info.collegeboard.com; Web site: www.collegeboard.org

Communication Skill Builders, A Division of the Psychological Corporation
19500 Bulverde Road, San Antonio, TX 78259; Phone: 800-872-1726; Fax: 800-232-1223; Web site: www.psychcorp.com

Consulting Psychologists Press
3803 East Bayshore Road, Palo Alto, CA 94303; Phone: 800-624-1765; Fax: 650-969-8608; Web site: www.cpp-db.com

CORE Corporation
Pleasant Hill Executive Park, 391 Taylor Boulevard, Suite 110, Pleasant Hill, CA 94523-2275

CTB/McGraw-Hill
20 Ryan Ranch Road, Monterey, CA 93940-5703; Phone: 800-538-9547; Fax: 800-282-0266; Web site: www.ctb.com

Curriculum Associates, Inc.
153 Rangeway Road, P.O. Box 2001, North Billerica, MA 01862-0901; Phone: 800-225-0248; Fax: 800-366-1158; Web site: www.curriculumassociates.com

Denver Developmental Materials, Inc.
P.O. Box 371075, Denver, CO 80237-5075; Phone: 800-419-4729; Fax: 303-344-5622

Department of Research Assessment and Training
1051 Riverside Drive, Unit 123, New York, NY 10032; Phone: 212-543-5536; Fax: 212-543-5386

Development Associates, Inc.
1730 North Lynn Street, Arlington, VA 22209-2023; Phone: 703-276-0677; Fax: 703-276-0432; Web site: www.devassoc1.com

Developmental Therapy Institute, Inc.
P.O. Box 5153, Athens, GA 30604-5153; Phone: 706-369-5689; Fax: 706-369-5690; Web site: www.uga.edu/dttp

Diagnostic Counseling Services, Inc.
P.O. Box 6178, Kokomo, IN 46904-6178

Diagnostic Specialists, Inc.
1170 North 660 West, Orem, UT 84057; Phone: 801-225-7698

Docutrac, Inc.
1330 North King Street, Wilmington, DE 19801

Ed & Psych Associates
2071 South Atherton Street, Suite 900, State College, PA 16801; Phone: 814-235-9115; Fax: 814-235-9115

EdITS/Educational and Industrial Testing Service
P.O. Box 7234, San Diego, CA 92167; Phone: 800-416-1666 or 619-222-1666; Fax: 619-226-1666; Web site: www.edits.net

Educational Activities, Inc.
Attn: Rose Falco, 1937 Grand Avenue, Baldwin, NY 11510; Phone: 800-645-3739; Fax: 516-379-7429; Web site: www.edact.com

Educational Testing Service
Publication Order Services, P.O. Box 6736, Princeton, NJ 08541-6736; Phone: 609-921-9000; Fax: 609-734-5410; Web site: www.ets.org

Educators Publishing Service, Inc.
31 Smith Place, Cambridge, MA 02138-1089; Phone: 800-225-5750; Fax: 617-547-0412; Web site: www.epsbooks.com

Ellsworth & Vandermeer Press, Ltd.
4405 Scenic Drive, Nashville, TN 37204; Phone: 615-386-0061; Fax: 615-386-0346; Web site: edge.net/~evpress

English Language Institute
University of Michigan, TCF Building, 401 East Liberty Street, Suite 350, Ann Arbor, MI 48104-2298; Phone: 734-764-2413; Fax: 734-763-0369; Web site: www.lsa.umich.edu/eli/testing.html

Enhanced Performance Systems, Inc.
1010 University Avenue, Suite 265, San Diego, CA 92103; Phone: 619-497-0156; Fax: 619-497-0820; Web site: www.enhanced-performance.com

Enrichment Press
5441 SW Macadam Avenue, #206, Portland, OR 97201

General Education Development Testing Service
One Dupont Circle NW, Washington, DC 20036-1163; Phone: 202-939-9490; Fax: 202-775-8578; Web site: http://www.acenet.edu

Golden Educational Center
857 Lake Boulevard, Redding, CA 96003

GRM Educational Consultancy
P.O. Box 154, Beecroft, New South Wales 2119, Australia; Phone: 61-2-9484-1598; Fax: 61-2-9875-3638

H & H Publishing Co., Inc.
1231 Kapp Drive, Clearwater, FL 33765; Phone: 800-366-4079; Fax: 727-442-2195; Web site: www.hhpublishing.com

Harcourt Educational Measurement
19500 Bulverde Road, San Antonio, TX 78259-3701; Phone: 800-211-8378; Fax: 877-576-1816; Web site: www.hemweb.com

Hawthorne Educational Services
800 Gray Oak Drive, Columbia, MO 65201; Phone: 800-542-1673; Fax: 800-442-9509

Hay/McBer
Training Resources Group, 116 Huntington Avenue, Boston, MA 02116; Phone: 800-729-8074; Fax: 617-927-5060; Web site: trgmcber.haygroup.com

Hester Evaluation Systems, Inc.
2410 SW Granthurst Avenue, Topeka, KS 66611-1274; Phone: 800-832-3825; Fax: 785-357-4041

High/Scope Press
600 North River Street, Ypsilanti, MI 48198-1898; Phone: 800-40-PRESS; Fax: 800-442-4FAX; Web site: info@highscope.org

Hodder & Stoughton Educational
Hodder Headline PLC, 338 Euston Road, London NW1 3BH, England; Phone: 44-0170-8736000; Fax: 44-0171-8736024

Hogan Assessment Systems, Inc.
P.O. Box 521176, Tulsa, OK 74152; Phone: 918-749-0632; Fax: 918-749-0635; Web site: www.hoganassessments.com

Hogrefe & Huber Publishers
P.O. Box 2487, Kirkland, WA 98083; Phone: 800-228-3749; Fax: 425-823-8324; Web site: www.hhpub.com

Houghton Mifflin Company
222 Berkeley Street, Boston, MA 02116-3764

Human Resource Development Press
22 Amherst Road, Amherst, MA 01002-9709; Phone: 800-822-2801; Fax: 413-253-3490; Web site: www.hrdpress.com

Humanics Learning
P.O. Box 7400, Atlanta, GA 30357-0400; Phone: 404-874-2176; Fax: 404-874-1976

IDEA Center
Kansas State University, 1615 Anderson Avenue, Manhattan, KS 66502-4073; Phone: 785-532-5970; Fax: 785-532-5637; Web site: www.idea.ksu.edu

Imaginart International, Inc.
307 Arizona Street, Bisbee, AZ 85603; Phone: 520-432-5134; Fax: 520-432-5134

Insight Institute, Inc.
7205 NW Waukomis Drive, Kansas City, MO 64151; Phone: 800-861-4769; Fax: 816-587-7198

Institute for Somat Awareness
Michael Bernet, Ph.D., 1270 North Avenue, Suite 1-P, New Rochelle, NY 10804; Phone: 914-633-1789; Fax: 914-633-3152

International Assessment Network
7600 France Avenue South, Suite #550, Minneapolis, MN 55435-5939

International Learningworks
1130 Main Avenue, P.O. Box 1310, Durango, CO 81302; Phone: 800-344-0451; Fax: 970-385-7804; Web site: intllearningworks.com

Inernational Society for General Semantics
P.O. Box 728, Concord, CA 94522; Phone: 925-798-0311; Fax: 925-798-0312; Web site: generalsemantics.com

International Training Consultants, Inc.
P.O. Box 35613, Richmond, VA 23235-0613

JIST Works, Inc.
720 North Park Avenue, Indianapolis, IN 46202-3431; Phone: 800-648-5478; Fax: 800-547-8329; Web site: www.jist@aol.com

Jossey-Bass/Pfeiffer
350 Sansome, 5th Floor, San Francisco, CA 94104

Kendall/Hunt Publishing Company
4050 Westmark Drive, P.O. Box 1840, Dubuque, IA 52004-1840; Phone: 800-228-0810; Fax: 800-772-9165; Web site: www.kendallhunt.com

Kolbe Corporation
3421 North 44th Street, Phoenix, AZ 85018; Phone: 602-840-9770; Fax: 602-952-2706; Web site: www.kolbe.com

LIMRA International
P.O. Box 208, Hartford, CT 06141-0208

Literacy Volunteers of America
635 James Street, Syracuse, NY 13203; Phone: 315-472-0001; Fax: 315-472-0002; Web site: www.literacyvolunteers.org

MetriTech, Inc.
4106 Fieldstone Road, Champaign, IL 61821; Phone: 800-747-4868; Fax: 217-398-5798; Web site: www.metritech.com

Miller & Tyler Limited
Psychological Assessment and Counselling, 96 Greenway, London N20 8EJ, England; Phone: 44-181-445-7463; Fax: 44-181-445-0143

Mind Garden, Inc.
1690 Woodside Road, Suite #202, Redwood City, CA 94061; Phone: 650-261-3500; Fax: 650-261-3505

Modern Curriculum Press
299 Jefferson Road, P.O. Box 480, Parsippany, NJ 07054-0480; Phone: 800-321-3106; Fax: 800-393-3156; Web site: www.pearsonlearning.com.

Monaco & Associates
4125 Gage Center Drive, Suite 204, Topeka, KS 66604

Moving Boundaries
1375 SW Blaine Court, Gresham, OR 97080; Phone: 888-661-4433; Fax: 503-661-5304

Multiple Intelligences Research and Consulting, Inc.
1316 South Lincoln Street, Kent, OH 44240; Phone: 330-673-8024; Fax: 330-673-8810; Web site: www.angelfine.com/oh/themidas

National Association of Secondary School Principals
P.O. Box 3250, 1904 Association Drive, Reston, VA 22091-1598; Phone: 800-253-7746 and 703-860-0200; Fax: 703-476-5432; Web site: www.nassp.org

National Clearinghouse of Rehabilitation Training Materials
5202 North Richmond Hill Drive, Oklahoma State University, Stillwater, OK 74078-4080

National Communication Association
5101 Backlick Road, Building E, Annandale, VA 22003; Phone: 703-750-0533; Web site: www.natcom.org

National Reading Styles Institute, Inc.
P.O. Box 737, Syosset, NY 11791-0737

NCS (Minnetonka)
Sales Department, 5605 Green Circle Drive, Minnetonka, MN 55343

New Standards, Inc.
8441 Wayzata Boulevard, Suite 105, Minneapolis, MN 55426-1349; Phone: 800-755-6299; Fax: 612-797-9993

New Zealand Council for Educational Research
Education House West, 178–182 Willis Street, Box 3237, Wellington 6000, New Zealand

NFER-Nelson Publishing Co., Ltd.
Darville House, 2 Oxford Road East, Windsor, Berkshire SL4 1DF, England

Occupational Research Centre
"Highlands" Gravel Path, Berkhamsted, Hertfordshire HP4 2PQ, United Kingdom

P.D.P. Press, Inc.
12015 North July Avenue, Hugo, MN 55038; Phone: 651-439-1638; Fax: 651-351-7361; Web site: members.aol.com/prodeupryl

Personal Strengths Publishing
P.O. Box 2605, Carlsbad, CA 92018-2605; Phone: 800-624-7347; Fax: 760-730-7368; Web site: www.personalstrengths.com

Pinkerton Services Group
6100 Fairview Road, Suite 900, Charlotte, NC 28210-3277; Phone: 800-528-5745; Fax: 704-554-1806; Web site: www.pinkertons.com

Preschool Skills Test
c/o Carol Lepera, P.O. Box 1246, Greenwood, IN 46142; Phone: 317-881-7606

PRO-ED
8700 Shoal Creek Boulevard, Austin, TX 78757-6897; Phone: 800-897-3202; Fax: 800-397-7633; Web site: http://www.proedinc.com

Program Development Associates
P.O. Box 2038, Syracuse, NY 13220-2038; Phone: 800-543-2119; Fax: 315-452-0710; Web site: www.pdassoc.com

Psychological and Educational Publications, Inc.
P.O. Box 520, Hydesville, CA 95547-0520; Phone: 800-523-5775; Fax: 800-447-0907

Psychological Assessment Resources, Inc.
P.O. Box 998, Odessa, FL 33556-9908; Phone: 800-331-8378; Fax: 800-727-9329; Web site: www.parinc.com

The Psychological Corporation
19500 Bulverde Road, San Antonio, TX 78259; Phone: 800-228-0752; Fax: 210-339-5873; Web site: www.psychcorp.com

Psychological Growth Associates
Products Division, 3813 Tiffany Drive, Lawrence, KS 66049; Phone: 785-841-1141; Fax: 785-749-2190

Psychological Publications, Inc.
P.O. Box 3577, Thousand Oaks, CA 91359-0577; Phone: 800-345-8378; Fax: 805-373-1753; Web site: www.psionline.com

Rebus, Inc.
P.O. Box 4479, Ann Arbor, MI 48106-4479; Phone: 800-435-3085; Fax: 734-665-4728; Web site: www.rebusinc.com

Renaissance Learning, Inc.
P.O. Box 8036, Wisconsin Rapids, WI 54495-8036; Phone: 800-338-4204; Fax: 715-424-4242; Web site: www.renlearn.com

Research for Better Schools, Inc.
444 North Third Street, Philadelphia, PA 19123-4107; Phone: 215-574-0133; Fax: 215-574-0133; Web site: www.rbs.org

Riverside Publishing Company
425 Spring Lake Drive, Itasca, IL 60143-2079; Phone: 800-323-9540; Fax: 630-467-7192; Web site: www.riverpub.com

Scholastic Testing Service, Inc.
480 Meyer Road, Bensenville, IL 60106-1617

Search Institute
700 South 3rd Street, Suite 210, Minneapolis, MN 55415-1138; Phone: 800-888-7828; Fax: 612-376-8956; Web site: www.search-institute.org

Selby MillSmith, Ltd.
30 Circus Mews, Bath BA1 2PW, United Kingdom; Phone: 44-1225-446655; Fax: 44-1225-446643; Web site: www.selbymillsmith.com

The Sidran Foundation
2328 West Joppa Road, Suite 15, Lutherville, MD 21093; Phone: 410-825-8888; Fax: 410-337-0747; Web site: www.sidran.org

Sigma Assessment Systems, Inc.
511 Fort Street, Suite 435, P.O. Box 610984, Port Huron, MI 48061-0984; Phone: 800-265-1285; Fax: 800-361-9411; Web site: www.sigmaassessmentsystems.com

Slosson Educational Publications, Inc.
P.O. Box 280, East Aurora, NY 14052-0280; Phone: 888-756-7766; Fax: 800-655-3840; Web site: www.slosson.com

Sopris West
4093 Specialty Place, Longmont, CO 80504; Phone: 800-547-6747; Fax: 888-819-7767; Web site: www.sopriswest.com

Stoelting Company
620 Wheat Lane, Wood Dale, IL 60191; Phone: 630-860-9700; Fax: 630-860-9775; Web site: www.stoeltingco.com/tests

Swets Test Publishers
P.O. Box 820, 2160 SzLisse, The Netherlands; Phone: +31 252 435375; Fax: +31 252 435671; Web site: www.swets.nl/

Teachers College Press
Teachers College, Columbia University, 525 West 120th Street, Box 303, New York, NY 10027; Phone: 212-678-3929; Fax: 212-678-4149; Web site: www.tc.columbia.edu

Thames Valley Test Company, Ltd.
7–9 The Green, Felmpton, Bury St. Edmunds, Suffolk IP28 6EL, England; Phone: 44-1284-728608; Fax: 44-1284-728166; Web site: www.tvtc.com

Therapy Skill Builders—A Division of The Psychological Corporation
19500 Bulverde Road, San Antonio, TX 78259-3701; Phone: 800-872-1726; Fax: 800-232-1223; Web site: www.psychcorp.com

Touchstone Applied Science Associates (TASA), Inc.
4 Hardscrabble Heights, P.O. Box 382, Brewster, NY 10509-0382; Web site: www.tasa.com

Training House, Inc.
22 Amherst Road, Pelham, MA 01002-9745; Phone: 609-452-1505; Fax: 609-452-2790; Web site: www.traininghouse.com

Trust Tutoring
912 Thayer Avenue, Suite #205, Silver Spring, MD 20910; Phone: 301-589-0733 or 800-301-3131; Fax: 301-589-0733; Web site: www.wdn.com/trust

Universal Attention Disorders, Inc.
4281 Katella Avenue, #215, Los Alamitos, CA 90720; Phone: 800-729-2886; Fax: 714-229-8782; Web site: www.tovatest.com

University of Maryland
University Counseling Center, Shoemaker Hall, College Park, MD 20742

University of Minnesota Press
Test Division, Mill Place, Suite 290, 111 Third Avenue South, Minneapolis, MN 55401-2520; Phone: 612-627-1963; Fax: 612-627-1980; Web site: www.upress.umn.edu/tests

Vollage Publishing
73 Valley Drive, Furlong, PA 18925

Vine Publishing, Ltd.
10 Elgin Road, Bournemouth BH4 9NL, United Kingdom; Phone: 44-1202-761766; Fax: 44-1202-761766

Virtual Knowledge
200 Highland Avenue, Needham, MA 02194

Western Psychological Services
12031 Wilshire Boulevard, Los Angeles, CA 90025-1251; Phone: 310-478-2061; Fax: 310-478-7838; Web site: http://www.wpspublish.com

Wide Range, Inc.
P.O. Box 3410, 15 Ashley Place, Suite 1A, Wilmington, DE 19804; Phone: 800-221-9728; Fax: 302-652-1644; Web site: www.widerange.com

Wintergreen/Orchard House, Inc.
425 Spring Lake Drive, Itasca, IL 60143-2076

Wonderlic, Inc.
1795 North Butterfield Road, Libertyville, IL 60048-1238; Phone: 800-323-3742; Fax: 847-680-9492; Web site: www.wonderlic.com

About the Authors of the Handbook

MYLES I. FRIEDMAN, Ph.D. is Distinguished Professor Emeritus of Education at the University of South Carolina. A renowned educator and author, his books include *Rational Behavior, Teaching Reading and Thinking Skills, Improving Teacher Education, Teaching Higher Order Thinking Skills to Gifted Students, Taking Control: Vitalizing Education, Ensuring Student Success, Improving the Quality of Life*, and, with Steven P. Fisher, *Handbook on Effective Instructional Strategies*. He has spent more than 30 years conducting and applying research to improve education. Dr. Friedman's master's and Ph.D. degrees in Educational Psychology were earned at the University of Chicago.

CHARLES W. HATCH, Ph.D. is President of CWH Consulting Company, Newberry, South Carolina. He earned a Master of Arts in Teaching at Johns Hopkins University and a doctorate in Educational Research and Measurement at the University of South Carolina. He has taught college courses in tests and measurement, statistics, and test preparation. Dr. Hatch has published an "Introductory Handbook of Measurement," "An Introductory Handbook for Statistical Package Programming," and on the subject of predicting freshman retention. He has served as a consultant on test preparation, college retention, and microcomputers and software.

JACQUELINE E. JACOBS, Ph.D. is Associate Professor in the Department of Educational Leadership and Policies at the University of South Carolina. She earned a bachelor's degree in Special Education and Elementary Education, a master's degree in Curriculum and Supervision, and a doctorate in Special Education and Higher Education Administration. She served as a teacher and principal and won an Outstanding Principal Award. She teaches courses in evaluation and measurement in special education. Her publications include articles on the role of the principal, reading recovery, and kids killing kids in school.

AILEEN C. LAU-DICKINSON, Ed.D. has earned a doctorate in Special Education Administration, a master's degree in Speech Science, and a bachelor's degree in Speech Education. She is certified in the fields of speech correction, mental retardation, visually handicapped, speech and drama, and as a school psychologist. She has taught numerous courses in assessment. She is currently in private practice assessing and teaching students with speech and language disorders and learning disabilities. She is a Fellow of the American Speech-Language-Hearing Association and received the Frank R. Kleffner Clinical Career Award, presented by the South Carolina Speech-Language-Hearing Association. Dr. Dickinson is the author of a number of publications and presentations on developmental assessment and instruction.

AMANDA B. NICKERSON, Ph.D. is an Assistant Professor of School Psychology in the Department of Educational and Counseling Psychology at the University of Albany, State University of New York. She has taught classes on emotion, motivation, personality development, and psychopathology and has worked at the Devereaux Day School in Downington, Pennsylvania. She also received a doctoral Leadership Fellowship from the U.S. Department of Education, Office of Special Education and Rehabilitation Services. Dr. Nickerson has published on the subjects of essential skills for direct care professionals, parent and peer relationships, crisis intervention, and violence prevention, and has received a research grant to study intimacy and prosocial behavior in early adolescents.

KATHERINE C. SCHNEPEL, Ph.D. is a self-employed research and measurement consultant. She has earned a master's degree and a doctorate in Educational Research and Measurement and a bachelor's degree in Psychology. She has served as an adjunct professor in the departments of Educational Psychology and Educational Leadership and Policy at the University of South Carolina. She has made presentations on testing and measurement and mastery learning and has been employed as a research and measurement specialist at Richland School District One, Columbia, South Carolina. Subjects she has taught include test item writing, interpreting test scores, measuring student achievement, and program evaluation.